Financial Management
IN THE SPORT INDUSTRY

Matthew T. Brown
UNIVERSITY OF SOUTH CAROLINA

Daniel A. Rascher
UNIVERSITY OF SAN FRANCISCO

Mark S. Nagel
UNIVERSITY OF SOUTH CAROLINA

Chad D. McEvoy
ILLINOIS STATE UNIVERSITY

Holcomb Hathaway, Publishers
Scottsdale, Arizona 85250

Library of Congress Cataloging-in-Publication Data

Financial management in the sport industry / Matthew T. Brown ... [et al.].
    p. cm.
  Includes bibliographical references and index.
  ISBN 978-1-934432-04-4
    1. Sports—Finance.   2. Sports administration.   3. Sports—Economic aspects.
I. Brown, Matthew T.
  GV716.F555 2010
  796.0691—dc22

                                                                    2010012979

Please note: The author and publisher have made every effort to provide current website addresses in this book. However, because web addresses change constantly, it is inevitable that some of the URLs listed here will change following publication of this book.

Consulting Editor: Packianathan Chelladurai

Holcomb Hathaway, Publishers, Inc.
8700 E. Via de Ventura Blvd., Suite 265
Scottsdale, Arizona 85258
480-991-7881
www.hh-pub.com

10 9 8 7 6 5

ISBN PRINT: 978-1-934432-04-4
ISBN EBOOK: 978-1-934432-34-1

Printed in the United States of America.

Brief Contents

Contents

TIME VALUE OF MONEY   87

PART II
Financial Management   105

INTRODUCTION TO FINANCIAL MANAGEMENT   107

BUDGETING   133

7 DEBT AND EQUITY FINANCING   163

8 CAPITAL BUDGETING   185

PART III

Application of Financial Management in Sport   207

9 FACILITY FINANCING   209

10 VALUATION 245

11 FEASIBILITY STUDIES 279

12 ECONOMIC IMPACT ANALYSIS 301

PART IV
Financial Attributes of Select Sport Industry Segments 327

13 PARK AND RECREATION AGENCIES 329

COLLEGE ATHLETICS   353

PROFESSIONAL SPORT   399

Preface

I had been teaching sport finance for several years when the need for this text became apparent. During my time at Ohio University, the graduate and undergraduate Sports Administration and Facility Management programs evolved, and as students became grounded in introductory accounting, economics, and finance courses, it became apparent that there was a need for a text that truly explored financial management in the sport industry. At the time, most sport finance texts focused on revenue generation in sport, with little focus on financial management. Feedback from students and their quest for new knowledge moved us to write *Financial Management in the Sport Industry*.

In today's financial climate, there is a need for readers to understand finance and the importance of sound financial management. Over the past two decades, through periods of financial growth and turmoil, the sport industry has grown tremendously—the estimate of its growth and current value vary depending on the source, but we all agree it is large and growing. As the industry and the discipline of sport management have grown, the need to better prepare students to assume managerial roles in sport organizations has also grown. This need is underscored by the movement of several renowned sport management programs into business schools and the creation of specialized sport management MBAs. As mentioned above, we believe that change is also needed in books devoted to sport finance, which need to focus not only on revenue acquisition but also address basic financial management concepts in sport. In this book, we go even further to discuss how finance works in the sport industry.

Part I, Finance Basics, introduces sport finance and basic financial concepts and explains the tools and techniques of financial quantification using industry examples. Topics covered in this section include the analysis of financial statements and ratios, risk, and time value of money. In Chapter 2 we use the financial statements of Under Armour as a basis for discussing balance sheets, income statements, and statements of cash flow, and we revisit these financial statements when discussing and calculating financial ratios. Chapter 3 relates risk to the revenue sharing model used by the National Football League. In Chapter 4, the time value of money is explored using examples such as deferred salary issues related to the Arizona Diamondbacks and Pittsburgh Penguins.

Part II covers the foundations of financial management—the decisions within sport organizations to ensure wealth maximization. Budgeting, debt and equity financing, and capital budgeting are addressed, using examples from the sport industry such as the Milwaukee Brewers receipt of $3.85 million from the local government to operate Miller Park. This part segues between traditional texts on the fundamentals of financial management and a text on these fundamentals as applied to the sport industry. Here we go beyond just providing examples in a sport context to discussing how finance actually works in the sport industry. For example, we address how a team uses debt and equity financing and why one method over the other may be selected. We also explain the importance of capital budgeting when planning for a new facility.

Part III of this book applies financial management concepts to the industry through the examination of facility financing, valuation, feasibility studies, and economic impact. Much of this section is written based on our past consulting experiences with industry partners, including several professional teams, various sports leagues, and several municipalities. Finally, Part IV examines financial management in three sectors of the industry: parks and recreation, collegiate athletics, and professional sport. We provide an in-depth analysis of the mechanics of financial management within each of these sport sectors.

This book is designed so that it can be used in either an upper level undergraduate or graduate course in a sport management program. Students do not need a previous background in finance to grasp the material. Part I, Finance Basics, provides the needed introduction to financial concepts. After reading the chapters in Part I, students will be prepared for material in the remaining sections.

The text can also be used by students in business schools in an upper-level finance course or students in an MBA/Sport Management program. Chapters 1 and 5 through 15 can be used for an in-depth study of sport finance. Part II, Financial Management, contains material that would be covered in a Principles of Financial Management course at either the undergraduate or first-year MBA level. However, the topics in these chapters are addressed from the sport industry's perspective, addressing what works and what doesn't work. Part III, Application of Financial Management in Sport, and Part IV, Financial Attributes of Select Sport Industry Segments, should be completely new material for most readers, providing a detailed view of financial management in those segments.

Special Features

In an effort to make this text useful and to facilitate understanding of financial management topics, the following features have been included:

Case Studies. When teaching sport finance, we have found that the case-based method is one of the best means to help students learn the material. Each chapter contains a current case on a relevant topic, and, at the end of the cases, questions are provided to help students understand how financial management concepts have been or should have been applied in the given situation. These cases invite in-depth analysis and discussion of selected topics.

Sidebars. Throughout the text, sidebars are used to provide additional context. Often explaining a financial management concept is not quite enough for readers unfamiliar with finance to grasp a new concept. To reinforce the understanding and the application of concepts to the sport industry, sidebars offer additional examples, with topics ranging from the financial turnaround of an NCAA Division I athletic program to the financial practices of selected international sport organizations to the development of various professional women's leagues over the past twenty years.

Concept Checks and Practice Problems. The concept check questions and financial problems found at the end of the chapters emphasize key concepts and aid in the review of chapter material. Further, the practice problem section reinforces the use of numerous financial management tools and formulae in the sport industry including the creation of financial statements, the calculation of a capital budget for an addition of a fixed asset to a team's portfolio, and the application of time value of money principles when developing endowed programs at colleges and universities.

Glossary of Key Concepts. Key concepts are defined when they first appear in the text. They also appear in a glossary at the end of the text. Since financial concepts discussed in one chapter often apply to several chapters and topics in the text, the glossary will be helpful when readers need to review a concept presented earlier.

Acknowledgments

All of us wish to thank those who reviewed this book in various stages and offered suggestions for its improvement. Their input helped us to make this a better book. These individuals are: Jan Bell, St. Thomas University; Steve Dittmore, University of Arkansas; Joris Drayer, University of Memphis; Dianna Gray, University of Northern Colorado; Daniel F. Mahoney, Kent State University; Joel Maxey, The University of Georgia; J. Christopher McGrath, Georgetown University; John Miller, Texas Tech University; Michael Mondello, The Florida State University; Stephen Shapiro, Old Dominion University; Robert Taylor, California University of Pennsylvania; Nathan Tomasini, Virginia Commonwealth University; Galen Trail, Seattle University; Sharianne Walker, Western New England College; and Jason Winfree, University of Michigan.

I first wish to thank those students who pushed me to develop a better finance course and develop better materials, particularly the Ohio graduate and undergraduate classes of 1999 through 2005. I especially want to thank those 2:05 students for their enthusiasm and encouragement while I was at Ohio.

Next, this project would not have been possible without my coauthors, Dan, Mark, and Chad. It has been great writing with you over the years. I appreciate the quality of your work and most importantly your friendship. Completing this project has taken longer than anticipated to complete with job changes and additions to our families. Thanks for sticking with the project and seeing it through to completion.

I also must thank Tom Regan. Tom was one of the first to teach a sport finance course and much of what I teach today is based on his early work. Tom is a leading authority on financial accounting and budgeting and wrote the budgeting chapter for this book (Chapter 6). He also was the chair of the Department of Sport and Entertainment Management at the University of South Carolina and was responsible for bringing me to USC. As chair, he gave me time to further develop my teaching ideas, refine course delivery methods, and dive deeper into research. Under his leadership, my research productivity and scholarship improved and developed. This text is better as a result.

To my friends and colleagues at Ohio and South Carolina, thank you for your friendship and support. Both Andy Kreutzer and Doc Higgins are great mentors, and they have helped shape and influence the sport industry. Frank Roach provided a teaching schedule that enabled me to focus on research and complete this work.

To my wife, Becky, and sons Jake and Luke, thanks for letting me sneak away to complete this manuscript. Your support at home is truly appreciated.

Finally, Colette Kelly at Holcomb Hathaway, Publishers has been extremely patient with us. Her edits, comments, and work on early drafts have been insightful and made significant improvements to the text. Colette, Gay Pauley, Sally Scott, and the rest of the Holcomb Hathaway staff have been great to work with and we appreciate all they have done to make the project a reality. I am glad that my friendship with Chella and his relationship with Holcomb Hathaway made this all possible.

MTB

Many people were involved, either directly or indirectly, in helping develop this book and its content. The reason for writing this book is, of course, because of the enthusiastic students who want to understand all there is to know about mana-ging sport organizations. I must thank those students who read earlier versions of the chapters and asked questions that led to clarifications. I also learned a great deal more during this process than I thought I would, by forcing myself to be clear about various ideas and concepts, and also reviewing my co-authors' chapters.

I want to thank my wife and partner, Heather, for helping with the gathering, organizing, check-ing, and cleaning data for some of the chapters, but more importantly for her patience and encourage-ment. Along the way, she produced two beautiful boys, Aidan and Lucas, which of course added to the amount of patience she needed in supporting me in the book's final stages. I hope Aidan and Lucas enjoy sport as much as I have, both on and off the field.

Len Perna and Mitch Zeitz both indirectly pro-vided ideas and examples for a few of my chapters. I thank them for that and their leadership in their respective fields within the business of sports. I must thank Dick Irwin and Bill Sutton for getting me started studying economic impact. Additionally, my work with Dick over the past decade has helped develop my thoughts on that subject.

Colette Kelly at Holcomb Hathaway has been very supportive and pushed us along in a kind but effective manner. She also found very helpful reviewers who provided important insights. Thank you for all of this Colette. I want to thank my colleagues at USF, especially Stan Fasci and Peggy O'Leary, for supporting me and running a tight ship so I could have the time to write.

The most satisfying part of this has been my work with my coauthors, Matt, Mark, and Chad. I want to thank them for having me be a part of this team. Matt, especially, carried the burden of moving us along. My friendships with each of them will be the most important and long-lasting outcome of this book. Thank you all for your excellent work.

DAR

I would first like to thank my family and close friends, who have provided continual support for this project. There would have been no way to complete a book of this magnitude without my loved ones providing the time needed to focus on writing and editing. My wife Leslie has been espe-cially patient as this book moved from rough idea to finished manuscript and through production. I was extremely fortunate to work with esteemed coauthors on this book and other projects. Matt, Dan, and Chad consistently challenge me to think and inspire me to see what can be accomplished. My colleagues in the Sport and Entertainment Management Department at the University of South Carolina have also provided consistent support. It is a blessing to be able to come to work with people who are not only dedicated professionals but also wonderful friends. The students I have had the privilege to teach throughout my career have provided an outlet for my (sometimes) crazy ideas. I hope that I have been able to teach them as much as they have taught me. Colette Kelly and the staff at Holcomb Hathaway remained patient throughout our endeavors and for that I will be forever grateful.

MSN

I would like to thank all those involved in pub-lishing this book. Colette Kelly and the staff at Holcomb Hathaway were excellent to work with. Thanks as well to the many reviewers who provid-ed excellent advice on how to improve the text.

Thank you to all of my students and col-leagues at Illinois State University. Because of you, coming to work each morning is a pleasure. Helping our students grow, learn, and chase after their dreams of working in the sport industry is incredibly rewarding.

Thanks also to my wonderful family—to my wife Kerry for being so supportive and for being such a terrific partner and mother, and to our boys, Andy and Luke, who bring a smile to my face each and every day. I look forward to sharing my love of sport with you in the years to come.

Finally, thank you to Matt, Dan, and Mark for including me in this project. I appreciate both your collaboration and your friendship very much.

CDM

About the Authors

Matthew T. (Matt) Brown is the graduate director and an associate professor in the Department of Sport and Entertainment Management at the University of South Carolina. He teaches graduate and undergraduate sport finance courses and researches in the areas of sport finance and sport business. His current research focus is on the changing business practices of Asian professional sport leagues. Brown's research has led to publications in the *Journal of Sport Management, Sport Marketing Quarterly, Entertainment and Sport Law Journal, International Journal of Sport Finance,* and *Sport Management Review.* In addition, he has made more than 50 national and international research presentations.

Brown has been a consultant for a variety of organizations in the sport and tourism industries. His clients have included the Center for Exhibition Industry Research, the International Association of Assembly Managers, minor league hockey teams, minor league baseball teams, the Ohio Golf Course Owners Association, and the State of South Carolina. He currently serves as a consultant for the Columbia Blowfish, a wood bat baseball team in the Coastal Plain League. In addition to his work with the Columbia Blowfish, Brown has served as the chief financial officer of the Southern Ohio Copperheads and treasurer of the Board of Directors of the Southern Ohio Collegiate Baseball Club. He also has served as the treasurer of the North American Society for Sport Management. In 2003, Brown was named the Jefferson College Alumnus of the Year.

Brown received his doctorate in sports administration from the University of Northern Colorado. Prior to joining the faculty at the University of South Carolina, he was a faculty member in the Sports Administration and Facility Management program at Ohio University. His primary teaching responsibilities were in the dual-degree MBA/MSA graduate program, where he taught sport finance and research methods courses to first and second-year MBA students.

Daniel Rascher teaches and publishes research on sports business topics, and consults to the sports industry. He specializes in economics and finance and more specifically in industrial organization, antitrust, valuation, economic impact, market readiness, feasibility research, marketing research, damage analysis, strategy, and labor issues in the sport industry. Rascher founded SportsEconomics to enable sports enterprises to capitalize on the sport industry's transition from hobby status to multibillion dollar industry. As founder and president of SportsEconomics, LLC, managing partner at OSKR, LLC, and former principal at LECG, LLC, his clients have included organizations involved in the NBA, NFL, MLB, NHL, NASCAR, MLS, PGA, NCAA, minor league baseball, NHRA, AHL, Formula One racing, Champ Car racing, Premier League Football (soccer), professional cycling, media, IHRSA, as well as sports commissions, local and state government, convention and visitors bureaus, entrepreneurs, and business-to-business enterprises.

Rascher received his Ph.D. in Economics from the University of California at Berkeley. He is director of academic programs and associate professor for the Sport Management Program at the University of San Francisco (USF), where he also teaches courses in sports economics and finance and sports business research methods. Prior to joining USF, Rascher was an assistant professor at the University of Massachusetts, Amherst. He has authored articles for academic and professional journals, book chapters, and a textbook in the sport management and economics fields, and has been interviewed hundreds of times by the media regarding various aspects of the business of sports. Rascher has served on the editorial boards of the *Journal of Sport Management, Sport Management Review, International Journal of Sport Finance,* and the *Journal of the Quantitative Analysis of Sports.* He has been named Research Fellow of the North American Society for Sport Management. Rascher is also certified as a valuation analyst (AVA) by the National Association of Certified Valuation Analysts. He has testified as an expert witness in federal and state courts and in arbitration proceedings, and has provided public testimony numerous times to state and local governments.

Mark S. Nagel, Ed.D., became a faculty member in the Department of Sport and Entertainment Management at the University of South Carolina in 2006. Prior to joining USC, he was the director of the graduate sport management program at Georgia State University. At Georgia State he was responsible for all aspects of the sport management program including recruiting and advising students, developing and scheduling courses, identifying and supervising adjunct faculty, and maintaining alumni and sport business relationships. Nagel has also previously worked in sport management programs at the University of West Georgia and San Jose State University. He currently serves as an adjunct faculty member at the University of San Francisco and St. Mary's College, where he teaches summer courses in sport administration. Before pursuing a career in academia, Nagel worked in different areas of sport management—primarily in athletic coaching and administration as well as campus recreation. During his years as an assistant coach of the women's basketball team at the University of San Francisco, he helped lead the team to three NCAA Tournament appearances and a spot in the 1996 Sweet 16.

Nagel has authored or co-authored numerous articles in refereed journals such as the *Journal of Sport Management, Sport Marketing Quarterly, Entertainment and Sport Law Journal, International Journal of Sport Finance,* and *Sport Management Review.* In addition, he has published extensively in professional journals, written numerous academic book chapters, and given dozens of research presentations. Nagel also served as treasurer for the North American Society for Sport Management and the Sport and Recreation Law Association.

Chad D. McEvoy is an associate professor at Illinois State University, where he is the coordinator of the sport management graduate program. Prior to pursuing a career in academia, McEvoy worked in marketing and fundraising in intercollegiate athletics at Iowa State University and Western Michigan University. He has conducted research projects for clients at various levels of sport, including professional sport, intercollegiate athletics, Olympic sport, and sports agency organizations.

McEvoy holds a doctoral degree from the University of Northern Colorado, a master's degree from the University of Massachusetts, and a bachelor's degree from Iowa State University, each in sport management/administration. His research interests focus on revenue generation and ticket pricing in commercialized spectator sport settings. McEvoy has published articles in journals including the *Journal of Sport Management, Sport Management Review, Sport Marketing Quarterly,* and the *International Journal of Sport Management and Marketing.* His research has been featured in numerous media stories and interviews including *The Wall Street Journal, Sports Illustrated.com, ESPN.com, Chicago Tribune, Philadelphia Inquirer, Atlanta Journal-Constitution, Portland Oregonian,* and *Kansas City Star.* McEvoy appeared as a panelist before the prestigious Knight Commission on Intercollegiate Athletics in 2008 and he served as the co-editor of the *Journal of Issues in Intercollegiate Athletics.*

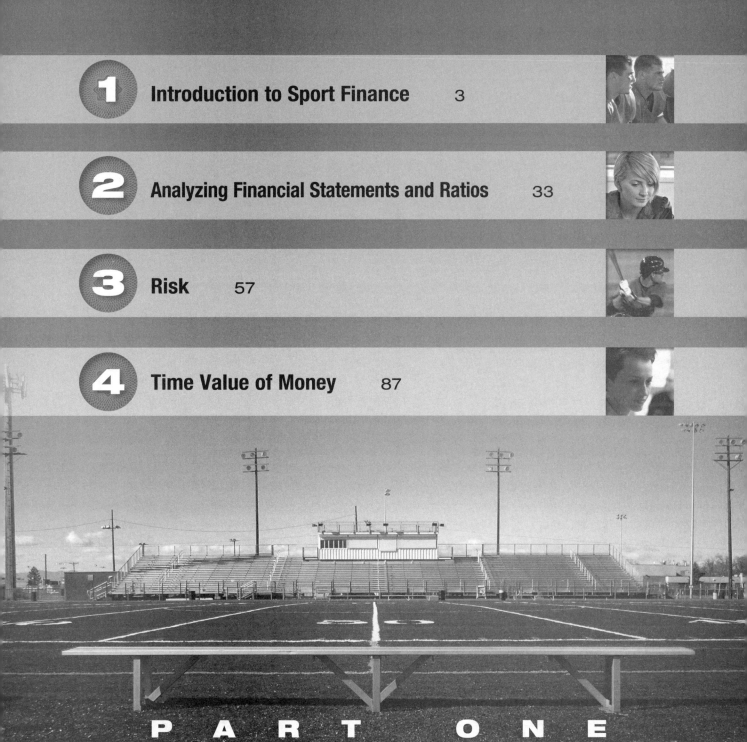

PART ONE

Finance Basics

1

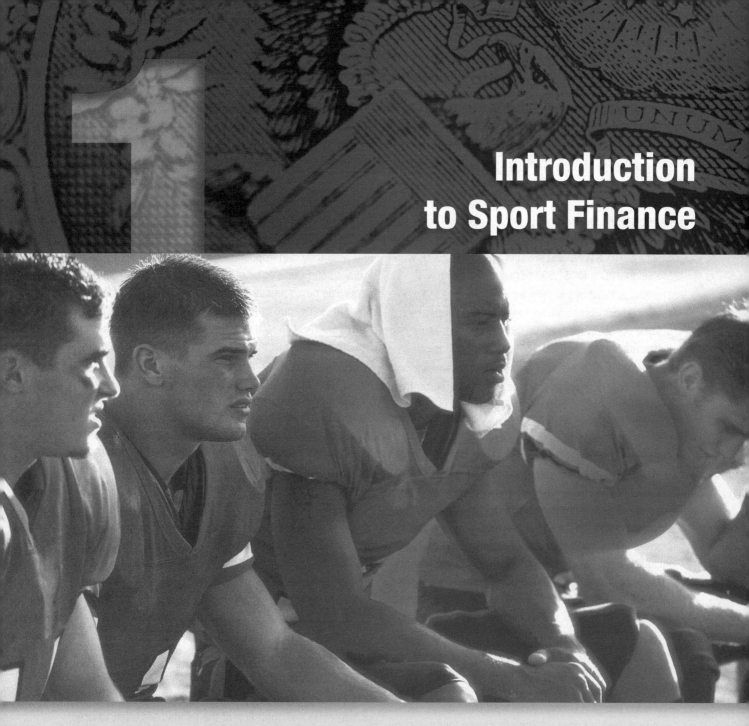

Introduction to Sport Finance

capital markets

debt financing

distributed club ownership model

equity financing

finance

financial management

gift financing

government financing

gross domestic product (GDP)

gross domestic sports product (GDSP)

investments

money markets

multiple owners/private investment syndicate model

multiple owners/publicly traded corporation model

North American Industry Classification System (NAICS)

retained earnings

Sherman Antitrust Act

single-entity structure

single owner/private investor model

sustainability

wealth maximization

KEY CONCEPTS

Introduction

Why is an understanding of financial management important? Consider the example of the construction of a new stadium or arena. This area of sport finance is often in the news because a new stadium or arena directly impacts local residents, businesses, and government. Here are a few examples:

- In 2008, the New York Yankees replaced old Yankee Stadium, built for $2.5 million in 1923, with new Yankee Stadium. The $1.3 billion stadium opened in 2009, with top seats selling for $2,500 per seat, per game.

- The Dallas Cowboys are levying a one-time $150,000 personal seat license fee on fans who wish to purchase season tickets in the stadium's best locations. Luxury suites are selling for up to $500,000 per season.

- For the Minnesota Twins, a new stadium means access to previously unavailable revenue. The Twins currently share the Hubert H. Humphrey Metrodome with the Minnesota Vikings. The facility is poorly designed, not only for watching a baseball game but also for generating baseball revenue. The Twins receive almost nothing from luxury suite rentals; rather, the money from luxury suite sales goes to the Vikings. The city keeps a portion of revenue generated from parking, concessions, and in-stadium advertising. In the new facility, scheduled to open in 2010, the Twins will keep almost all revenue, including naming rights (sold to Target), premium seats, and luxury suites. The average ticket price for a premium seat will be approximately $52 per game. A membership fee of $1,000 to $2,000 will also be charged to premium seat ticket holders for access to the exclusive club areas within the stadium (Roberts & Murr, 2008).

- Lucas Oil Stadium, the home of the Indianapolis Colts of the National Football League (NFL), opened in 2008, replacing the RCA Dome, which had been built in 1984. The best seat at Lucas Oil Stadium can be found in one of its Super Suites. These suites sell for $235,000 per season, with all of the revenue from their sale going to the Colts (Roberts & Murr).

These examples represent the revenue side of constructing new venues—the large price tags of which put them in the news. But what about other financial management issues related to a facility's construction, for example, how the revenue is shared and how ongoing operating expenses will be met? To consider these issues and how they can impact a community, let's return to the Indianapolis Colts example. Although Lucas Oil Stadium generates new revenue for the Colts, none of the stadium-generated revenue goes to the Capital Improvement Board (CIB) yet. The CIB is the governmental entity operating the stadium and managing its debt service—the cash required over a specific time period for repaying the principle and interest on the debt ("Indy Wrestles," 2009).

The $675 million stadium was paid for through a municipal bond issue backed primarily by a 1% tax increase on prepared food in nine of the ten counties surrounding Indianapolis. However, the revenue increases generated through the increased tax cover only the facility's debt service. No funds were made available for the operation of the facility. With the tax revenue allotted for debt service and stadium revenue going to the Colts, the CIB has been operating the stadium at a $20 million annual deficit ("Indy Wrestles"). As a result of poor financial management—specifically plans and forecasts relating to the operating costs of the new stadium—state officials had to act. The citizens of the metropolitan area likely will be required to pay for the stadium's operating costs through some form of tax increase.

As the above examples show, the revenue generated in these new venues attract a large amount of media attention. However, financial management issues related to the construction and operation of the venues are often ignored, overlooked, or perhaps not understood. When this happens, as in the case of Indianapolis, the importance of understanding financial management becomes clear.

In this chapter, we will introduce you to key concepts in finance, many of which will be discussed in greater depth in later chapters. You may encounter terms with which you are unfamiliar. To gain a working knowledge of these terms, refer to the Glossary at the end of the book.

WHAT IS FINANCE?

Finance, the science of fund management, includes application of concepts from accounting, economics, and statistics. Within finance, there are three interrelated sectors: (1) money and capital markets, (2) investments, and (3) financial management (Brigham & Houston, 2001). **Money markets** are markets for highly liquid, short-term securities; **capital markets** are markets for intermediate or long-term debt, as well as corporate stock. Hence, the money and capital markets sector includes securities markets such as the New York Stock Exchange and the Chicago Mercantile Exchange. Investment banking falls within this sector as well, as do insurance and mutual fund management.

As opposed to this first sector, the focus of the **investments** sector is on security choices made by individual and institutional investors as they build portfolios. Merrill Lynch and Edward Jones are companies operating within this sector.

The **financial management** sector involves decisions within firms regarding the acquisitions or use of funds, usually with the goal or outcome of **wealth maximization,** or maximizing the overall value of the firm. To achieve wealth maximization, the finance department forecasts future revenues and plans future expenses. In sport, this may include calculating cash flow increases resulting from a move to a new facility (as shown in the chapter introduction) and determining how much the organization can increase player payroll as a result of the forecast. The finance department also performs a portion of the control function of management. Through coordination with other departments in an organization, the finance department pursues efficiency of operation and resource utilization. The finance department makes investment and financing decisions, working with financial markets and investment firms when necessary. The type of debt financing to be used when constructing a new stadium is but one example of these decisions.

Although a firm in the sport industry may be structured as a for-profit, not-for-profit, or governmental entity, for-profit sport enterprises have many commonalities with other types of for-profit business. As such, the financial management of a sport organization is often quite similar to the financial management of organizations in other industries. These commonalities include value creation, or increasing the value of a firm over time, and revenue growth. However, there are areas of difference. One major difference is the diverse objectives of firm owners within sport (Foster, Greyser, & Walsh, 2005). Although sport organizations usually compete for wealth maximization, an owner in professional sport might not be interested in this goal. Rather, the owner may be more interested in winning championships or in seeking celebrity status by being one of a select few professional sport franchise owners. Another goal of the owner may be to protect a community asset. The differing objectives of owners can harm the competitive balance in a league, particularly in terms of winning championships. For example, an extremely wealthy owner with a willingness to incur losses over several seasons can create an imbalance in competition. As a result, at the beginning of a season, only a few teams may have a realistic chance of winning a championship. Leagues have reacted by implementing salary constraints, revenue sharing, and other similar mechanisms that create both competition between franchises on the field and cooperation regarding financial management off the field.

FIVE WAYS TO FINANCE THE OPERATION OF A SPORT ORGANIZATION

hether an owner's objective is wealth maximization or winning and whether the sport organization is for-profit, not-for-profit, or governmental, a manager in the sport industry will encounter five methods used to finance the organization (see Exhibit 1.1). These include three methods typically used by for-profit companies to finance their operations: debt, equity, and reinvestment of prior earnings. In sport, however, two additional financing methods are often available: government funding and gifts. Examples of each will be seen throughout this text. A brief introduction to each is presented here.

Debt

When an organization borrows money that must be repaid over a period of time, usually with interest, **debt financing** is being used. Typically in sport, teams issue bonds or borrow from lending institutions (or in some instances their league) to finance operations through debt. The New York Yankees financed the new Yankee Stadium in this way. The team borrowed $105 million from a group of banks, including Goldman Sachs, to pay for cost overruns. The team also borrowed more than $1.2 billion through the tax-exempt and taxable bond markets (Kaplan, 2009). Debt financing may be either short-term or long-term; short-term debt obligations are those repaid in less than one year, and long-term obligations are those repaid in more than one year. A key point of financing operations with debt is that the lender does not gain an ownership interest in the organization. The sport organization's obligation is limited to the repayment of the debt.

---

exhibit **1.1** Methods used to finance sport organizations.

METHOD	DEFINITION	EXAMPLE
Debt	Borrowing money that must be repaid over time, usually with interest	Construction of the new Yankee Stadium
Equity	Exchanging a share or portion of ownership of the organization for money	Green Bay Packers' renovation of Lambeau Field
Retained earnings	Reinvestment of prior earnings	Packers Franchise Preservation Fund
Government	Funding provided by federal, state, or municipal sources, including land use, tax abatements, direct stadium financing, state and municipal appropriations, and infrastructure improvements	Tax-backed bonds issued by the New Jersey Sports & Exposition Authority to support Giants Stadium
Gift	Charitable donations, either cash or in-kind	Donations of $13 million per year to Duke University for athletic scholarships

Equity

In contrast to debt financing, in **equity financing,** the owners exchange a share or portion of their ownership for money. The organization therefore obtains funds for operations without incurring debt and without having to repay a specific amount of money at a given time. A drawback is that ownership interest will be diluted and the original owners may lose control as additional investors are added. Stephen M. Ross used equity financing to raise capital after purchasing the Miami Dolphins in 2009. He sold minority interests in the team to several partners, including singers Marc Anthony and Gloria Estefan (Talalay, 2009). Few sport organizations issue stock, a common form of equity financing outside the sport industry. One of the few, the Green Bay Packers, used $20.6 million of stock proceeds to help finance the renovation of Lambeau Field ("Lambeau Field," 2003).

Two reasons account for the fact that professional team sport organizations do not typically issue stock to raise equity capital. One reason is that little can remain hidden when a company is publicly traded. To comply with Securities and Exchange Commission (SEC) regulations, publicly traded organizations must file annual reports detailing the accounting activities of the organization. A team that claims financial hardship in seeking public funding for a new stadium may have difficulty convincing the municipality of the need if financial reports reveal significant positive cash flow. A second reason is that teams that issue stock must answer to their shareholders. Stockholder demands for profitability might run counter to the goal of winning on the field (for example, the team might be unable to acquire a player at the trading deadline because of the near-term financial loss that would result from the acquisition). Concern over public ownership is so great that the NFL does not allow its teams to be publicly owned. The league instituted a ban on public ownership in 1960 (Kaplan, 1999).

As noted above, the Green Bay Packers are an exception to the norm and the NFL rule. To keep the franchise from leaving Green Bay, Wisconsin, the team went public in 1923, and today the Packers continue to be exempt from the NFL's prohibition on issuing shares. However, unlike those of a typical publicly traded company, the Packers' shares do not appreciate in value and are not traded on a stock exchange.

Despite sport organizations' reluctance to use equity financing, teams in leagues other than the NFL have raised significant amounts of capital by doing so. The Cleveland Indians raised $60 million through the team's initial public offering (IPO) in 1998. The Florida Panthers, Boston Celtics, Vancouver Canucks, and Colorado Avalanche all have used equity financing. Today, however, these teams are privately held (Kaplan, 1999).

Retained Earnings

In addition to financing through debt and equity, organizations can finance operations or the acquisition of assets through the reinvestment of prior earnings. The portion of earnings that a firm saves in order to fund operations or acquire assets is termed **retained earnings.** The reinvestment of retained earnings is generally considered a type of equity financing, as this financing method is often used by publicly traded companies, when they choose to reinvest earnings rather than pay them to shareholders as dividends. However, in sport, financing through the reinvestment of retained earnings should be considered separately from equity financing, because organizations in the industry—with the exception of sporting goods manufacturers and retail stores—are typically privately held. Although earnings may be distributed to team owners, in sport they are often used to finance the acquisition of players, improve operations, or make other investments.

The Green Bay Packers reinvest retained earnings to maintain a competitive and successful football operation and to preserve the franchise and its traditions ("President's Annual Report," 2005). However, because the franchise is owned by its shareholders and not a single, wealthy individual, the organization is at a disadvantage when reacting to business challenges. A wealthy owner is able to use personal funds to infuse cash into a sports organization. To overcome this disadvantage, the Packers have created the Packers Franchise Preservation Fund. By providing liquidity, the fund is intended to improve the sustainability of the corporation and franchise. Between 2004 and 2005, $13.3 million in retained earnings was allocated to the fund, which had grown to $127.5 million by June 2009.

Government Funding

In the sport industry, it is common for private organizations, such as professional sports teams, to receive funding from governmental sources. In addition, public high schools and universities typically receive a portion of their financing through direct or indirect government funding, and this funding may support sport programs at these schools. For all sport organizations, **government financing** may be provided by federal, state, or municipal sources and may include land use, tax abatements, direct stadium financing, state and municipal appropriations, and infrastructure improvements. Exhibit 1.2 provides examples of direct stadium financing from government sources.

exhibit 1.2 Select tax-backed stadium/arena bond issues.

STADIUM/ARENA	ISSUER	SECURITY
Giants Stadium	New Jersey Sports & Exposition Authority	State appropriation
Camden Yards	Maryland Stadium Authority	State appropriation
Soldier Field	Illinois Sports Facility Authority	State appropriation
Comerica Park	Detroit/Wayne County Stadium Authority	Limited property and county tourism tax
Great American Ballpark	Hamilton County, Ohio	Subordinate sales tax
FedEx Forum	Memphis & Shelby County Sports Authority	Car rental, hotel/motel taxes, water utility payments
Edward Jones Dome	Regional Convention & Sports Complex Authority	State, county, city appropriations
Raymond James Stadium	Tampa Sports Authority	Sales tax, sales tax rebates
American Airlines Arena	City of Dallas, Texas	Hotel occupancy, car rental taxes
RBC Center	Centennial Authority	Hotel occupancy tax
Target Center	City of Minneapolis, Minnesota	General obligation pledge

Source: Fitch Ratings, 2010. Reprinted by permission of Fitch, Inc.

Gifts

Gift financing includes charitable donations, either cash or in-kind, made to an organization. Gift financing is a primary source of operating and investing income for major collegiate sports programs. It is also a supplemental source for minor college programs and non-profit sport organizations. According to Wolverton's 2009 report on fundraising in college athletics, National Collegiate Athletic Association (NCAA) Division I–Football Bowl Subdivision (FBS) schools received over $1.1 billion in cash gifts during 2008. See Exhibit 1.3 for athletic donations to the universities in the Southeastern Conference.

College athletic programs use revenue from gifts to offset the rising costs of collegiate sport, build or renovate facilities, and increase endowments; Duke University, for example, raises approximately $13 million each year for athletic scholarships. Other institutions use gift financing to offset losses in institutional (government) financing resulting from cuts in state government funds to colleges and universities. Most institutions are also seeking to increase their athletic department endowments (see Exhibit 1.4). Duke hopes to increase its endowment to $350 million. At one time, Stanford University's athletic endowment was over $500 million and generated $25 million annually for scholarships and additional program needs.

OVERVIEW OF THE INDUSTRY

 he sport industry is large and diverse. This makes classifying the industry and measuring its size and scope difficult. Federal agencies use the **North American Industry Classification System (NAICS)**, developed by the U.S.

2007–2008 Southeastern Conference athletic department donations.   exhibit   **1.3**

SCHOOL	TOTAL	NCAA RANK BY TOTAL	GIFTS FOR PRIORITY SEATING	GIFTS FOR LUXURY SUITES	GIFTS FOR FACILITIES	GIFTS FOR ENDOWMENTS
Alabama	$27,900,000	15	$6,800,000	$8,200,000	$8,800,000	$1,200,000
Arkansas	$11,610,987	46	$0	$150,000	$200,000	$50,000
Florida	$45,600,000	2	$23,400,000	$11,600,000	$10,300,000	$100,000
Georgia	$36,068,068	5	$29,925,000	$3,260,000	$1,182,500	$4,494,206
Kentucky	$16,600,000	37	$10,900,000	$1,800,000	$4,800,000	$41,200
Louisiana State	$30,435,296	10	$4,502,325	$11,854,265	$7,324,430	$2,170,736
Mississippi	$13,462,889	42	NA	NA	NA	NA
Mississippi State	$14,029,862	40	$7,504,946	$3,463,810	$2,556,388	$496,700
South Carolina	$18,189,350	34	$1,827,425	$1,697,301	$1,974,011	$100,925
Tennessee	$38,385,450	3	$13,381,302	$6,030,168	$14,580,616	$2,478,959
Vanderbilt	$8,200,000	48	$2,870,000	NA	$1,700,000	$2,700,000

Note: Auburn did not respond.   *Source:* Wolverton, 2009. Copyright © 2009, *The Chronicle of Higher Education.* Reprinted with permission.

exhibit   1.4   Top athletic department endowments (2008).

INSTITUTION	ENDOWMENT
North Carolina–Chapel Hill	$212,000,000
Duke	$150,717,426
Boston College	$100,000,000
Georgia Tech	$80,058,950
Virginia	$61,873,981
Washington	$56,000,000
Georgia	$51,000,000
Penn State	$49,390,069
Connecticut	$48,051,366
Ohio State	$46,139,682

Source: Wolverton, 2009. Copyright © 2009, *The Chronicle of Higher Education.* Reprinted with permission.

Census Bureau, to measure and track the business economy in the United States. Each business is classified as part of a larger industry. However, the sport industry is not classified as an industry in the NAICS. Instead, the sport industry as it is commonly conceived is scattered across at least 12 different industries in the NAICS (see Exhibit 1.5). The largest grouping of sport businesses is within the Arts, Entertainment, and Recreation segment (NAICS 71).

The Arts, Entertainment, and Recreation segment is described as follows by the U.S. Department of Labor's Bureau of Labor Statistics (BLS). First, this segment employs a large number of seasonal and part-time workers. Those employed in the industry tend to be younger than employees in other industries, and wages are relatively low. As of 2008, the BLS forecast for the industry as a whole was promising. Barring ongoing recessionary trends, rising incomes and increasing leisure time over the next ten years should lead to an increase in demand in this sector ("The 2008–09 Career Guide," 2008). Almost all leisure-time activities, other than watching movies, are included in this industry sector.

The BLS classifies this sector into three large subsectors: live performances or events; historical, cultural, or educational exhibits; and recreation or leisure activities ("The 2008–09 Career Guide"). The live performances or events subsector includes professional sports, commercial sport clubs, sport promotion companies and agencies, and dog and horse racing facilities. Privately owned museums, such as the National Baseball Hall of Fame and Museum, are found in the subsection for historical, cultural, or educational exhibits. The recreation and leisure activities subsector includes golf courses, fitness facilities, bowling centers, and health clubs. The BLS further divides the subsectors of the Arts, Entertainment, and Recreation segment, assigning NAICS codes to smaller divisions. Exhibit 1.6 lists the codes for spectator and recreational sport divisions. These subsectors range from sport teams and clubs to bowling centers and marinas.

NAICS codes for sport businesses.   exhibit   1.5

CODE	INDUSTRY	SUBINDUSTRY	SPORT BUSINESS TYPES
237	Construction	Heavy and Civil Engineering Construction	Field Construction
315	Manufacturing	Apparel Knitting Mills	Sport Apparel
335	Manufacturing	Electrical Equipment, Appliance, and Component Manufacturing	Stadium Lighting
339	Manufacturing	Miscellaneous Manufacturing	Sporting Goods Manufacturing
423	Wholesale Trade	Merchant Wholesalers, Durable Goods	Sporting Goods Wholesale
424	Wholesale Trade	Merchant Wholesalers, Nondurable Goods	Sportswear
451	Retail Trade	Sporting Goods, Hobby, Book, and Music Stores	Sporting Goods
453	Retail Trade	Miscellaneous Store Retailers	Used Sporting Goods
515	Information	Broadcasting (except Internet)	Sports Television
516	Information	Internet	Sport Internet Sites
532	Real Estate and Rental Leasing	Rental and Leasing Services	Sports Equipment Rental
561	Administrative and Support and Waste Management and Remediation Services	Administrative and Support Services	Ticketing
611	Educational Services	Educational Services	Sport and Recreation Instruction
621	Health Care and Social Assistance	Ambulatory Health Care Services	Sports Physical Therapists
711	Arts, Entertainment, and Recreation	Performing Arts, Spectator Sports, and Related Industries	Spectator Sports
712	Arts, Entertainment, and Recreation	Museums, Historical Sites, and Similar Institutions	Halls of Fame
713	Arts, Entertainment, and Recreation	Amusement, Gambling, and Recreation Industries	Recreation and Club Sports
722	Accommodation and Food Services	Food Services and Drinking Places	Concessions
811	Other Services (except Public Administration)	Repair and Maintenance	Sport Equipment Repair
813	Other Services (except Public Administration)	Religious, Grantmaking, Civic, Professional, and Similar Organizations	Leagues and Governing Bodies

Source: www.census.gov/cgi-bin/sssd/naics/naicsrch?chart=2007

NAICS CODE	DEFINITION
711211	Sports Teams and Clubs
711212	Racetracks
711219	Other Spectator Sports
711310	Promoters of Performing Arts, Sports, and Similar Events with Facilities
711320	Promoters of Performing Arts, Sports, and Similar Events without Facilities
711410	Agents and Managers for Artists, Athletes, Entertainers, and Other Public Figures
712110	Museums
713910	Golf Courses and Country Clubs
713920	Skiing Facilities
713930	Marinas
713940	Fitness and Recreational Sports Centers
713950	Bowling Centers
713990	All Other Amusement and Recreation Industries

Source: www.census.gov/cgi-bin/sssd/naics/naicsrch?chart_code=71&search=2007%20NAICS%20Search

FINANCIAL SIZE OF THE SPORT INDUSTRY

Academicians and sport industry professionals frequently discuss, quote, and cite the size of the sport industry in the United States. According to Rascher (2001), the size of the United States sport industry grew from $47 billion in 1986 to $152 billion in 1995, a real annual growth rate of 8.8%. King (2002) stated that the industry grew to $195 billion in 2001 (an annual growth rate of 4.24% since 1995). However, an examination of these raw numbers can be misleading due to methodological differences in calculating the size of the industry.

The size of any industry can be determined by calculating its gross product. The overall size of an economy is measured by its **gross domestic product (GDP)**. GDP is the market value of the goods and services produced within the borders of a county, state, country, or other region in a given year. To determine the size of the sport industry, we calculate the **gross domestic sports product (GDSP)**. GDSP is defined as the market value of a nation's output of sport-related goods and services in a given year. This includes the value added to the economy by the sport industry, as well as the gross product originating from the sport industry.

Efforts to measure GDSP must avoid a double count (one of the guidelines for calculating GDP), that is, the duplication of dollars that could be accounted for in two or more ways. Double counting often results in errors in estimates measuring the sport industry, when secondary spending is included as part of the calculation. For example, player salaries should not be counted when determining GDSP, because this amount is already included in ticket prices. (When organizations set ticket prices, they account for the salary of professional athletes—essentially a production cost or cost of goods sold; see Chapter 2—in the final price of the ticket.) As an intermediary cost of production, salary should not be counted separately from ticket revenue in calculations of industry size. To count it separately is to count it twice.

In the first major study on the size of the United States sport industry, *Sports Inc.* magazine calculated the industry's size at $47 billion (Sandomir, 1988). However, the study did not follow U.S. Department of Commerce rules for computing GDP and made no effort to determine the economic impact of the industry on the United States (Meek, 1997). Meek performed a study that did avoid double counting and resulted in the figure of $152.2 billion for the size of the sport industry. Street and Smith's *SportsBusiness Journal* determined that $194.64 billion was spent in sports during 2001 (King, 2002). In a subsequent description of the report's methodology, Broughton (2002) noted that the amount reported was not a measure of the size of the industry but only a measure of sport-related spending. The author stated that when traditional economic standards were applied (i.e., avoidance of double counting), the size of the industry was measured to be $31.76 billion.

As Exhibit 1.7 shows, Meek's study and the study conducted by *SportsBusiness Journal* show remarkable differences at first glance in the size of the sport industry, although both studies applied traditional economic standards for measuring

Comparison of the size of the sport industry under two definitions. **exhibit** **1.7**

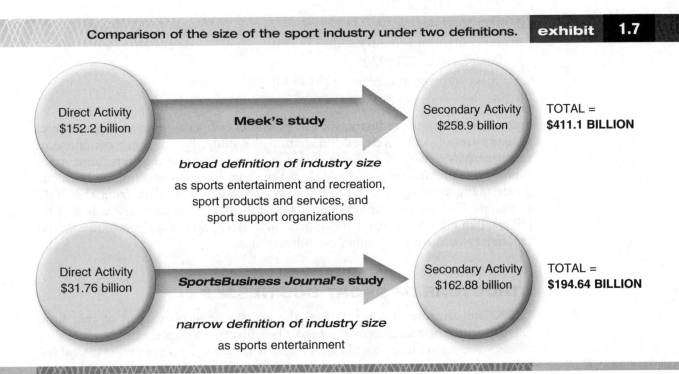

Sources: Meek (1997); King (2002).

an industry. However, the two studies define the sport industry differently. In Meek's study, the sport industry was defined as having three components: (1) sports entertainment and recreation, (2) sport products and services, and (3) sport support organizations, e.g., the United States Olympic Committee (USOC), the NCAA, and USA Swimming. Meek, therefore, used a broad definition of sport that included both amateur and recreational sport in addition to spectator sport (sports entertainment). The *SportsBusiness Journal* study measured only organized sport (sports entertainment), a narrower segment of the sport industry. Additionally, the *SportsBusiness Journal*'s total of $194.64 billion is actually the *supported* economic activity of organized sport in the United States, or the economic impact of organized sport in the United States. Meek's calculation of the supported economic activity of the industry was $411 billion. Again, the differences in these numbers are primarily due to different definitions of the industry itself.

In 2008, Humphreys and Ruseski conducted yet another study on the size of the sport industry. In this study, the authors defined the sport industry differently than both Meek and the *SportsBusiness Journal*. Here, the industry had three parts: (1) individual participation in sport, (2) attendance at spectator sporting events, and (3) following sporting events through some form of media. This definition of sport is broader than *SportsBusiness Journal*'s definition, as it includes participatory sport, but it is narrower than the definition in Meek's study. For example, it does not include sport support organizations. Within NAICS 71 (the Arts, Entertainment, and Recreation industry), the authors specifically examined:

- spectator sport teams and clubs (NAICS 711211)
- racetracks (711212)
- other spectator sports (711219)
- golf courses and country clubs (713910)
- skiing facilities (713920)
- fitness and recreation centers (713940)
- bowling centers (713950)

Subsectors within the industry, such as promoters of performing arts, sports, and similar events (7113), were excluded from the study, because they contain economic activity outside the sport industry (e.g., promotion of the performing arts). From the manufacturing sector (33), the authors included sporting and athletic goods manufacturing (33992). Based on their analysis of data from the 2002 Economic Census, the authors stated that the size of the industry was $81.85 billion. Exhibit 1.8 compares the *Sports Inc.*, Meek, *SportsBusiness Journal*, and Humphreys and Ruseski studies on industry size.

STRUCTURE OF SPORT BUSINESSES

The structure of a firm affects the tax and legal obligations of that firm. Different structures offer different benefits. For example, a firm's options for raising funds are based on its business structure, as is the personal legal liability of its managers and employees. As we will discuss in Chapter 5, several different structures are available to business entities. These structures include governmental,

exhibit   1.8

Comparison of studies on the size of the sport industry in the United States (figures in billions).

INDUSTRY SIZE	ADJUSTED SIZE (2002 DOLLARS)	DEFINITION OF INDUSTRY	YEAR OF ESTIMATE	STUDY
$47.0	$77.15	None	1986	*Sports Inc.* (Sandomir, 1988)
$152.2	$179.43	Sports entertainment and recreation, sport products and services, sport support organizations	1995	Meek, 1997
$31.76	$32.51	Organized sports	2001	*SportsBusiness Journal* (Broughton, 2002)
$81.85	$81.85	Individual participation in sport, attendance at spectator sporting events, mediated sport revenues	2002	Humphreys & Ruseski, 2008

non-profit, sole proprietorship, partnership, limited liability corporation (LLC), Subchapter S corporation, and C corporation. Each structure has unique advantages and disadvantages that affect the financial management of the organization.

Collegiate athletic departments are classified as governmental or non-profit businesses, depending on whether the department is a part of a state college or university, such as University of North Carolina–Chapel Hill, or is a part of a private university, such as Duke University.

In professional sports, most franchises are operated as for-profit businesses. They are structured under various ownership models. After describing these ownership models we will discuss the structures of sport leagues, conferences, and associations.

Franchise Ownership Models

Most franchises are formed under one of three ownership models (Foster, Greyser, & Walsh): single owner/private investor model, multiple owners/private investment syndicate model, or multiple owners/publicly traded corporation model.

Single owner/Private investor model

In the **single owner/private investor model,** one individual, often an independently wealthy person, owns the firm. The owner may play an active role in the operation of the franchise, or, after selecting key managers, the owner may be hands off. For example, the Dallas Mavericks are owned by technology entrepreneur Mark Cuban. Cuban plays an active role in both business and basketball operations.

Multiple owners/Private investment syndicate model

The most common model for team ownership is the **multiple owners/private investment syndicate model.** It is the most common for two reasons. First, the value of franchises has risen so high that it is difficult for one individual to be able to afford to purchase a franchise on his or her own. Second, as discussed previously, the publicly traded corporation model has many disadvantages versus the private investment model—and one league, the NFL, even forbids it.

When individuals pool their resources to purchase a franchise and incorporate as a partnership, LLC, or the like, they are forming an ownership group under the multiple owners/private investment syndicate model. For example, in 1995 a group of long-time friends and fans including Fred Hanser, William DeWitt, Jr., and Andrew Baur purchased the St. Louis Cardinals. Each ownership group is governed by an investment syndicate document, which outlines the decision rights of the owners, including who will represent them in league meetings. Sometimes the ownership group has a dominant individual who appears to be a single owner, as was the case for many years when an ownership group purchased the New York Yankees, and George Steinbrenner was viewed as the sole owner of the team. Any disputes that arise among the owners may be resolved through arbitration or legal action (see Sidebar 1.A).

Multiple owners/publicly traded corporation model

The third model of ownership is the **multiple owners/publicly traded corporation model**. With the exception of the Green Bay Packers, this model is not used in the United States. Typically, it is employed by European professional soccer franchises such as Manchester United, whose shares have traded on the London Stock Exchange. Under this model, a franchise is governed by a board of directors who are elected by shareholder vote. The board of directors appoints the team's senior management. In the case of the Packers, the NFL restricts the franchise's shareholders, as shares cannot be traded on the open market and anti-takeover provisions prevent any one individual from amassing a majority of the team's shares and thereby becoming the team's majority owner.

Although only one U.S. sport franchise is publicly owned by stockholders, some franchises are owned by publicly traded corporations such as Comcast and Cablevision. Comcast owns the Philadelphia Flyers and 76ers, while Cablevision owns the New York Knicks and Rangers. Corporations such as Time Warner, Disney, News Corp., and Anheuser-Busch have also owned U.S. sport franchises in the past.

League Structures

The structure of a team's league affects the financial management of a sport organization as well. Leagues operate to ensure the viability of the league. Decisions made at the league level include admissions criteria, the structure of competition, revenue sharing, and player relations. These criteria affect the financial management of a team (see Chapters 14 and 15), and the structure of the league also affects the team's financial management.

A league may be structured either as a single entity or with distributed club ownership (Foster, Greyser, & Walsh).

Single-entity ownership model

With a **single-entity structure,** a single group or an individual owns the league and all of the teams that compete within that league. This structure is frequently used with new or start-up leagues. For example, the American Basketball League (ABL)

In 2003, Time Warner was in the process of selling the Atlanta Hawks (National Basketball Association [NBA]), Atlanta Thrashers (National Hockey League [NHL]), and Phillips Arena to a single buyer, David McDavid. However, questions were raised about McDavid's ability to finance the purchase. At about the same time, Michael Gearon, Jr., and Rutherford Seydel spoke with Time Warner about the possibility of purchasing the assets. The response from Time Warner was that they could make the purchase if outside financing was not used and if the agreement could be completed within a week. Gearon and Seydel approached sports investment banker John Moag to help find additional partners. Bruce Levenson, Ed Peskowitz, and Steve Belkin were soon added to the investment group. With four additional minority partners, the Atlanta Spirit LLC was born. Nine men in total were members of the partnership, with five—Belkin, Levenson, Peskowitz, Gearon, and Seydel—holding majority interest. From the time Gearon and Seydel first met with Time Warner to discuss the purchase of the assets, only eight days elapsed until the partnership was formed (King & Lombardo, 2005).

The partnership agreement called for management by consensus, with the majority partners sharing three controlling votes: one for Belkin, one for Levenson and Peskowitz, and one for Gearon and Seydel. Belkin was to represent the group with the NBA, and Levenson was to represent the group with the NHL. The two would, according to the partnership agreement, be bound to act according to consensus (King & Lombardo).

An early sign of disagreement among the partners caused Belkin to have a "put" option placed into the ownership agreement, whereby he could sell his shares of the partnership for 85% of their fair market value beginning in June 2006. Disagreements over minor issues then arose, relating to the initial financing of the LLC, ticket allotment for the NBA All-Star Game, titles of partners in media guides and other publications, and player payroll budgets. Finally, the authority to trade players caused a split among the three voting groups of majority owners. The lack of a defined managing partner became a major issue (King & Lombardo).

When NBA Commissioner David Stern became aware of the issues between the partners, he asked the NBA's executive vice president of legal and business affairs, Joel Litvin, to intervene. Stern was concerned that the disagreements among the majority owners could harm the team's basketball operations and therefore harm the NBA. When Litvin could not resolve the conflict, Stern met with the owners face to face and ordered the group to resolve their issues. Belkin, the Spirit's representative to the NBA, then vetoed a trade that the other partners favored. The trade was to bring Joe Johnson to the Hawks for two future first-round draft picks. Belkin cited his role as the NBA team governor as his reason for acting counter to the remaining partners' preferences. He wrote,

> Both the NBA and NHL require that a single individual be designated by each team "to manage the business and affairs of the team and to act for and bind the team." I served in that role as NBA Governor of the Hawks. I was fine with a "3-vote system" on all matters that did not conflict with league requirements and I abided by that system. (King & Lombardo, para. 48)

The board of managers voted 2–0 to trade Joe Johnson and informed Belkin that they would remove him as NBA governor if he interfered with the trade. After his veto, the managing board removed Belkin as NBA governor, and on August 8, 2005, Belkin countered with a temporary restraining order. By August 19, Levenson, Peskowitz, Gearon, and Seydel agreed to buy out Belkin's share and pay him more than the 85% premium to have him leave.

Three and a half years later, the buyout amount still had not been determined, because the contract outlining the buyout process was vague and the group could not agree on a process or a price. When Belkin agreed to the buyout in 2005, the price was to be determined by up to three appraisals (see Chapter 10). The first appraiser was to be hired by Belkin and the second by either party objecting to the findings of the first appraisal. However, both sides objected to the first appraisal, and the contract did not state what process should be followed if both objected. Both wanted to select the second appraiser. The parties had agreed to litigate contract disputes in Maryland, so a state circuit court judge heard the facts. The judge ruled that Belkin had the right to select the second appraiser. The judge also ruled that since Levenson, Peskowitz, Gearon, and Seydel had missed the deadline to pay the price set by the second appraisal, Belkin could buy them out at cost. This decision was overturned at the appellate level. A new trial began February 2009, and resolution has not yet been reached. At trial, the judge may decide that the remaining partners can choose the second appraiser, that Belkin can select the second appraiser, or that the buyout contract cannot be used at all. This would cause the partners to revert to the original 2004 partnership agreement, which outlines a different buyout process entirely (Swartz, 2009).

was owned by a group of investors, the Women's National Basketball Association (WNBA) was owned by the NBA, Major League Soccer (MLS) by a group of investors, and the XFL by World Wrestling Entertainment (WWE) and the NBC television network.

An advantage to the single-entity structure is that antitrust law does not apply, as it does to leagues using the distributed club ownership model. Collusion, agreements that eliminate competition, and other violations of antitrust law are not possible when one entity owns a league and all of its teams. Therefore, single-entity leagues can place franchises in preferred cities and assign a player to a specific team in a specific city. For example, the WNBA, in an effort to build a loyal following, assigned Lisa Leslie to the LA Sparks franchise. Leslie was a well-known collegiate player in southern California, as she had competed at USC. The league also assigned Sheryl Swoops, a standout basketball star at Texas Tech, to the Houston Comets. The assignment of players to teams also allows a league to promote competitive balance within the league so that no one team dominates competition.

A financial advantage for single-entity leagues is that player salary costs are constrained. Players sign contracts with the league, so there is no bidding for players on an open market. In 2008, the average MLS salary was $129,395. David Beckham was the league's top earner at $6.5 million guaranteed, and 46 players earned the league minimum, $33,000. The league's salary philosophy is to pay for impact players while constraining costs on defenders and goalkeepers (Bell, 2008). The Arena Football League (AFL) was considering reorganizing as a single-entity league in the hope of reducing costs. The AFL had a $25 million operating loss prior to suspending its operations (Lombardo, 2008).

A drawback to single-entity status is that it provides little economic incentive at the club level (Foster, Greyser, & Walsh). For the franchises, there is no benefit to operating well, as the benefits are completely shared with the other franchises in the league. This is one of the reasons why the WNBA and NBA Development League began to move away from the single-entity structure and toward the distributed club ownership model (Lombardo).

In addition, single-entity leagues have been challenged in court under the **Sherman Antitrust Act** (1890). The Act forbids contracts and other actions among businesses in restraint of trade. In *Fraser v. MLS* (1998), players were seeking to end the practice of league-negotiated contracts. They felt that negotiating with the league eliminated competition for player services among teams and thereby reduced their earnings potential. In *Fraser,* the courts reaffirmed that, for leagues structured as a single entity, the Sherman Act does not apply. The court affirmed that the league and its investors (team operators) functioned as a single entity and, therefore, were a single economic unit.

Distributed club ownership model

The **distributed club ownership model** is used by Major League Baseball (MLB), the NBA, the NHL, and the NFL. Under this league structure, each individual franchise has its own ownership group. League-wide revenues, such as those from national television contracts, are collected at the league level and distributed to each team to cover net costs. Leagues usually are structured as non-profit organizations governed by representatives from each team. The team representatives select a commissioner to run the daily operations of the league. Leagues may own affiliated for-profit entities. For example, the NFL owns and operates NFL Enterprises, which includes NFL.com and Sunday Ticket, and NFL Properties, the licensing arm of the league.

Within this structure, conflicts related to the financial management of the league can arise. Large-market franchises and small-market franchises tend to have differing philosophies on revenue sharing, for example. League and club conflicts often arise over territorial rights. A player and a league may come into conflict as well. Disputes often end up in court, and the resulting court decisions affect the structure of the distributed club ownership model.

Many of these disputes fall under antitrust law. In contrast to court decisions involving single-ownership leagues, courts have consistently ruled that leagues structured under the distributed club ownership model are subject to antitrust law. The only exception is MLB, which was granted an exemption from antitrust law in *Federal Baseball v. National League* (1922), which was reaffirmed in *Flood v. Kuhn* (1972). Courts have stated that a degree of cooperation at the league level is warranted in order for the league to create its product, but they also have noted that teams conduct activities separate from the league, such as entering into local radio and television contracts. Hence, the teams and leagues are separate legal entities and subject to the Sherman Act. In *NFL v. NASL* (1982), the court ruled that the NFL was subject to U.S. antitrust law. The court reaffirmed this in *McNeil v. NFL* (1992) and *Sullivan v. NFL* (1994). In *McNeil,* the court found that the league's "Plan B" free agency was more restrictive than reasonably necessary to maintain competitive balance within the league. Further, "Plan B" free agency caused economic harm to the players. This decision led to unrestricted free agency in the NFL. An earlier case, *Mackey v. NFL* (1976), led to the end of the league's reserve system, which essentially bound a player to one team over his career.

As for the NBA, the courts ruled in 1971 that the league was subject to antitrust law. Prior to *Haywood v. NBA* (1971), the NBA required graduating high school players to wait four years before becoming eligible to play in the league. The court's decision in *Haywood* allowed high school graduates and those attending some colleges to declare themselves eligible for the NBA draft.

FINANCIAL AND ECONOMIC FACTORS AFFECTING SPORT

The sport industry relies on the discretionary income of spectators and participants, and is sensitive to changes in the economy. From 1999 to 2009, the United States has experienced two recessions. The first began after the September 11, 2001, terrorist attacks and lasted for less than one year. The second some would say began as early as December 2007, with the economy showing indications of recovery beginning late 2009. (Because recessions can be determined only in hindsight, the beginning and end dates cannot be established until about 18 months later.) The impact of these recessions can be seen in statistics for employment in the arts, entertainment, and recreation industry, of which sport is

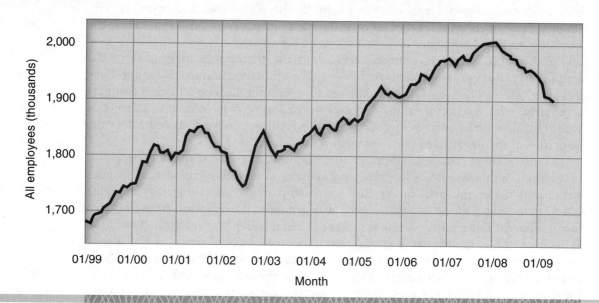

Source: http://www.bls.gov/data/.

a major part (see Exhibit 1.9). As the economy entered a recession and spending slowed in 2001, many jobs within the industry were shed. From September 2001 to September 2002, approximately 60,000 jobs were lost. In March 2008, the industry reached a historic high in employment numbers—2.0 million. When the economy slowed throughout 2008, jobs again were shed. Since its peak, as of July 2009, the industry had lost 106,900 jobs.

Not only has a slowdown in spending by spectators and participants affected jobs within the industry, but reductions in advertising spending, particularly by the automotive industry, and hospitality spending have also had major impacts on sport. Some segments of the industry have been affected more than others, and within industry segments some organizations have been affected more than others. Many factors affect the economics of sport, but five must be watched closely in the upcoming years: (1) the impact of the current economic cycle on sport, (2) the effect of television revenues, (3) the relationship between sport teams and real estate holdings, (4) a push for sustainability in sport, and (5) populism's impact on the governance of sport.

Economic Cycle

As the economy cycles through periods of growth and contraction, the sport industry is affected. During periods of growth, the sport industry has benefited greatly, as during the 1990s. Most leagues, both major and minor, added teams. New leagues, such as the WNBA and ABL, were formed, and teams and athletic departments across the country spent billions constructing new stadia and arenas.

As the economy contracts, the sport industry is also affected, as during the economic downturns of 2001 and 2008/2009. Leagues ceased operation (e.g., the AFL), teams declared bankruptcy (e.g., the Phoenix Coyotes) or ceased operation (e.g., the Columbia Inferno), construction slowed or stopped altogether, and sponsorship revenue declined. *SportsBusiness Daily* noted the following impacts of the 2008 economic downturn:

- The Dallas Cowboys failed to have a naming rights deal signed by the completion of their new stadium.
- MLB teams cut ticket prices for 2009, hoping to keep fans coming to ballparks despite unemployment approaching 10% nationwide.
- Automotive advertising spending was down $100 million by the end of 2008 ("Economy Could Affect," 2008).

In the following sections, we will discuss several sport industry segments that are especially sensitive to changes in economic conditions.

USOC

A slowing economy, especially when coupled with a financial crisis, affects the renewal of sport sponsorships (Last, 2009)—and sport has become more reliant than ever on corporate revenue from these sponsorships. For the United States Olympic Committee, this is especially true. The USOC receives no direct government funding, unlike other national Olympic committees across the globe. Therefore, the USOC relies heavily on corporate support, and sponsorship revenue accounts for 45% of its $150 million average annual budget. Unfortunately, in 2008, as the recession was deepening, most USOC sponsorship agreements expired following the Summer Olympic Games. Several corporations ended their sponsorship. Home Depot and Bank of America did not renew their 16-year sponsorships, and General Motors, a sponsor since 1984, did not renew. Kodak, which had been associated with the Olympic Games since 1896, ended its sponsorship, too. John Hancock also decided not to renew its sponsorship, although the company had been an Olympic sponsor since 1994. Each sponsorship agreement was worth between $4 million and $5 million on average per year. Considering the sponsorship losses from these companies alone, the USOC had to replace more than $16 million and as much as $20 million in annual revenue. Additional losses in revenue may come, too. Anheuser-Busch agreed to return as a sponsor, but it lowered the level of its commitment (Macur, 2009; Pells, 2009). As the economy began to recover, the USOC added BP, Proctor & Gamble, and Deloitte as sponsors prior to the 2010 Vancouver Olympics, thereby offsetting some of the losses (Mickle, 2010).

Collegiate athletics

College athletics are also significantly affected by changing economic conditions. For example, as the economy expanded during the late 1980s and through the 1990s, Stanford University built its athletic department endowment to over $500 million. In 2008, when the financial markets collapsed, Stanford saw the size of the endowment shrink 20% to 30%. As a result, the university eliminated 21 athletic department staff positions and reduced the department's budget by $7 million.

Stanford was not alone in cutting sports. Prior to the 2009/2010 academic year, 30 NCAA schools did so as well. The University of Washington eliminated men's and women's swimming, and the Massachusetts Institute of Technology cut eight teams. Although the University of Cincinnati did not drop programs, it eliminated scholarship funding for three men's sports teams.

Coaching salaries may also be affected during an economic downturn. In 2009, for example, coaches from Arizona State University, the University of Arizona, Clemson University, and the University of Wisconsin took unpaid furloughs (Schlabach, 2009).

Some fear that economic slowdowns will further increase the disparity between the larger NCAA Division I – FBS schools and the smaller ones (Schlabach). This seemed to be the case in 2009, when not all athletic departments were affected by the downturn. Although most schools experienced a decrease in ticket revenue for 2009, larger programs were able to offset those losses. The University of Georgia expected ticket revenue for football to be down $2.5 million to $3.0 million in 2009. The university, however, had just signed an eight-year, $92.8 million marketing and media rights contract. Further, as a member of the Southeastern Conference (SEC), the school received $11 million from the conference in 2009 and expected to receive an additional $6.2 million in 2010 due to the conference's new television contract with CBS and ESPN. Other examples of larger schools not experiencing significant impact from economic downturns include the University of Michigan's athletic department, which had a $9 million surplus at the end of fiscal year 2008. In 2008, the University of Florida was able to increase its athletic budget by $5.9 million, and the University of Texas' football program generated $73 million in revenue during the 2008 football season (Schlabach).

Women's professional sports

Women's professional sports are extremely sensitive to changes in the economy (Kreidler, 2009). For example, after the 2008 season ended, the Houston Comets of the WNBA folded. The Comets were one of the league's most successful franchises and one of six teams not owned by NBA-affiliated parties (see *Case Analysis: The Growth of a League* at the end of the chapter). The team's demise created fear within the league and among its followers that NBA owners—who owned eight of the 13 teams in the league—would shut down teams not making money (or even possibly the league itself) in efforts to cut costs, as several NBA franchises were having financial difficulties.

The Ladies Professional Golf Association (LPGA) also struggled. By mid-2009, only 14 of 29 events had secured sponsors for 2010. Tour stops were dropped in 2009 due to loss of sponsorship. The financial situation became so bad that tour players removed LPGA commissioner Carolyn Bivens from her position.

As is the case with intercollegiate athletic departments, not all women's professional sports are affected equally by difficult economic conditions. For example, the Women's Tennis Association (WTA) was not greatly affected by the slowing economy in 2008 and 2009, and in 2007 a new women's professional soccer league was launched. Women's Professional Soccer (WPS) replaced the Woman's United Soccer Association (WUSA), which began play in April 2001—just prior to the start of the decade's first recession. WUSA lasted only three seasons and incurred $100 million in losses. It is too early to tell how WPS will fare in its first years (Kreidler).

NASCAR

Perhaps surprisingly because of its rapid growth in popularity, NASCAR has also proved vulnerable to changing economic conditions. Of the major North American sports leagues, NASCAR appears to have been affected the most by the latest recession, because of sponsorship losses and the impact of higher gasoline prices.

To run a top program in NASCAR, a team must generate between $20 million and $25 million in revenues per year, of which $15 million to $20 million must come from the team's primary sponsors. With a slowing economy, sponsors became hard to find (Newton, 2008). Further, exclusive sponsorship rights agreements between Sprint and NASCAR have forced some long-time sponsors out of the league, including AT&T and Alltel. Sprint now holds the naming rights to NASCAR's premiere series.

As a result of diminishing sponsorship opportunities, toward the end of 2007 Petty Enterprises, one of the best known and most historic NASCAR teams, began exploring the idea of merging their team with another team or selling to another team (Caraviello, 2007). The team had won 268 races between 1949 and 1999 but could no longer afford to compete.

In another example, Chip Ganassi Racing shut down operation of its number 40 car during the 2008 season. The team could not find a sponsor for the car and decided to focus its efforts on its two remaining cars.

Higher gasoline costs affect NASCAR more than other leagues (Klayman, 2008). Many NASCAR fans travel long distances to see races, often traveling in recreational vehicles. High gasoline costs affect the ability of some fans to drive to the races. In 2008, the average percentage drop in ticket sales at NASCAR Sprint Cup races was in the mid–single digit range as gas prices reached $4 a gallon.

Television Revenue

Another important factor in sport finance is television revenue. It is a guaranteed form of revenue, with long-term contracts in place between leagues, conferences, teams, and networks. Fortunately for sport teams and leagues, television revenues somewhat insulate the industry from short-term slowdowns in the economy. The NFL's television contracts extend through the 2011 season, while MLB's run through 2013 and the NBA's goes through 2016 (Last, 2009). The annual values of these contracts are $1.9 billion, $696 million, and $930 million, respectively. These figures do not include revenues from international broadcast rights, the Internet, or satellite/cable league packages. For example, through 2014 the NFL will receive $1 billion per year from DirecTV for exclusive rights to NFL Sunday Ticket, a package of out-of-market Sunday games. MLB, tapping a new revenue stream, received approximately $1 million in 2009 in revenues from the sale of its iPhone app, which streams live video of games.

At the collegiate level, the SEC's new television contracts with ESPN and CBS have a term of 15 years. The league will earn over $200 million per year from these television rights (Barnhart, 2008).

Television revenues also provide NASCAR with some insulation. Although the recent economic slowdown affected attendance at events and revenue from sponsorships, the league has a $4.48 billion, eight-year television contract with ESPN, Fox, and TBS/TNT, running through 2014 (Klayman).

Finally, the USOC expects to receive $255 million in television revenues from the 2010 Winter Olympics and the 2012 Summer Games, somewhat offsetting the impact of recent sponsorship losses (Macur, 2009).

Real Estate

The development of real estate surrounding stadium and arena venues has become a popular means to generate additional revenue. As teams in some communities have found it more difficult to fund stadia and arenas with public tax dollars, teams have turned to real estate development to help offset the debt service of privately financed facilities. The most successful example is L.A. Live. This development, which encompasses 27 acres surrounding the Staples Center in Los Angeles, features complementary entertainment venues, including broadcast studios, restaurants, movie theaters, music clubs, and the Grammy Museum. The Anschutz Entertainment Group owns both the development and the Staples Center, as well as the Los Angeles Kings of the NHL and a portion of the Los Angeles Lakers. Both the Kings and Lakers play home games in the Staples Center. L.A. Live has long-term leases with ESPN, Ritz Carlton, Regal Theaters, and the Grammy Museum, to name a few (Van Riper, 2009).

In contrast to L.A. Live, many team-owned real estate developments struggled with the strained credit market caused by the collapse in the housing market in 2008. The Tampa Bay Lightning's ownership group was to develop 5.5 acres around the arena after purchasing the franchise in 2008. During 2009, however, the team lost money after debt service and was unable to break ground on the development. Both the Dallas Cowboys and Texas Rangers, which shared land in Arlington, Texas, were to develop Glorypark—a 1.2-million-acre parcel of housing, hotels, automobile dealerships, stores, and restaurants. During 2008, the development was put on hold, with no deadline for breaking ground. (It must be noted that the Lightning and the Rangers are both highly leveraged, with the Rangers having a debt to franchise value ratio of 66%—see Chapter 2.) As a result of the delays on Glorypark, the Cowboys carry $623 million of debt on the team's new stadium (Van Riper).

Sustainability

When sustainability or sustainable development is discussed today, it is typically in relation to the "green" movement. However, sustainability and venue construction and usage have been topics of discussion in the sport industry for many years. The 1987 Brundtland Report defined **sustainability** as meeting today's needs without compromising future generations' ability to meet their own needs. In sport, the glut of sport arenas built for mega-sporting events such as the Olympics or World Cup and even the overbuilding of publicly financed arenas in metropolitan areas have been questioned.

The New York City metropolitan area will soon boast five sporting arenas. Two of the existing four are already losing money: Prudential Center and Nassau Coliseum. In New Jersey, the Devils left the Izod Center for the new, publicly subsidized Prudential Center. Now the team has asked the state to demolish the Izod Center in order to eliminate competition for events from the older arena. The Izod Center is run by the New Jersey Sports and Exposition Authority, and the Nets currently play there. The Devils have attempted to convince the Nets to move to the Prudential Center, in hopes that the newer arena will host more events and become profitable. However, the Nets are planning for the new Barclays Center in Brooklyn. Meanwhile, Madison Square Garden is undergoing a $500 million renovation, and the New York Islanders are threatening to leave the Nassau Coliseum unless local officials approve the team owner's plans to rebuild the arena. When all five arenas are in operation, there will be 100,000 seats to fill on a nightly basis within a 30-mile radius—not including the remaining stadia, and the performing arts complexes and theaters operating in the area (Bagli, 2009). Madison Square Garden has three anchor tenants, but the other four arenas would each have only one anchor. With an estimated 200 event dates needed per year to produce a profit, these four arenas are expected to struggle financially.

Many other cities have similar problems with sustainable development, though on a much smaller scale than New York. Glendale, Arizona's Jobing.com Arena is losing money and must compete for events with Phoenix's US Airways Center and Arizona State's on-campus arena. Glendale's arena may soon face the additional challenge of replacing its anchor tenant, as the Phoenix Coyotes filed for bankruptcy in 2009. In Minnesota, the Target Center, owned by the City of Minneapolis, competes directly with the Xcel Energy Center in St. Paul, a publicly subsidized facility. Both facilities are losing money. Finally, in Columbus, Ohio, the NHL's Blue Jackets are negotiating with Franklin County to sell the money-losing Nationwide Arena. Nationwide Arena competes for events with Ohio State's Schottenstein Center (Bagli).

Questions regarding the sustainable development of venues have been raised in connection with Olympic sport. The Chinese government spent $43 billion on the 2008 Summer Olympic Games; however, many of the venues constructed for the games proved to be too big and too expensive for the ongoing hosting of events. The National Stadium (Bird's Nest) had only one event scheduled for 2009, while annual maintenance costs amounted to $9 million. The facility's owners have stated that they intend to turn the venue into a shopping mall. A baseball stadium that opened in spring 2008 has already been scheduled for demolition. Only the National Aquatics Center (Water Cube) is used regularly. Sound-and-light shows with dancing fountains are produced at the venue (Demick, 2009).

According to Matheson (2008), the Olympics became an economic disaster for the Chinese, as sport-related infrastructure projects led to little long-term economic growth. Improvements to airports, highways, and transit systems that were needed to host the Games will provide long-term benefits, but the sports infrastructure cannot easily be converted to other uses.

Beijing is not alone in experiencing losses from unused facilities constructed for hosting specific international events and their attendees. Of the ten new stadia built in South Korea to host the 2002 World Cup, most are unused today. Montreal finished paying for its Olympic Stadium 30 years after hosting the 1976 Games. The facility was largely unused when debt obligations were finally met. Full-service hotels in Lillehammer, Norway, built to handle the influx of visitors for the games, struggled after the 1994 Winter Olympics. Forty percent had gone bankrupt a few years after the games ended.

Politics

Since *Federal Baseball* (1922), the case in which the Supreme Court held that MLB is not subject to the Sherman Antitrust Act, sport and government have been intertwined. Change in the nation's political climate can have a significant impact on the industry. NASCAR, for example, benefited from its relationship with several members of Congress after Congress passed the financial services bailout bill in 2008. The bill included language that classified motorsports facilities as "amusement parks and other entertainment complexes." Hence, track owners could depreciate the cost of new fixed assets over a seven-year period rather than a 15-year period, and taxes paid by track owners would be reduced in the years immediately following the capital expenditures ("Bailout Bill Includes," 2008).

Changes to the depreciation schedule positively affected NASCAR, but several proposed changes to laws could have a devastating impact on the sport industry. Important examples are legislation relating to corporate sponsorships and to regulation of the cable industry.

Proposed legislation affecting corporate sponsorships

Senator John Kerry proposed the TARP Taxpayer Protection and Corporate Responsibility Act early in 2009 after celebrity website TMZ posted a story questioning the use of taxpayer funds at the Northern Trust Open (Newport, 2009). The Act would prevent any Troubled Asset Relief Program (TARP) recipient from hosting, sponsoring, or paying for entertainment events unless the company receives a waiver from the Treasury Secretary ("Secretary of Golf," 2009). The TMZ story stated that Northern Trust, recipient of $1.6 billion from TARP, held lavish parties, fancy dinners, and concerts with famous singers. Soon after publication of this story, Representative Barney Frank sent a letter to Northern Trust, co-signed by 17 additional representatives, demanding that the company return the $1.6 billion. Columnists across the political spectrum, including Maureen Dowd and Bill O'Reilly, joined in the criticism (Newport). Ignored in the storm of criticism were the business benefits that the sponsorship brought to Northern Trust, such as providing access to decision makers in business, reaching potential new customers, and increasing the firm's visibility.

Soon after the TMZ publication, Morgan Stanley, recipient of $10 billion in TARP funds, and Wells Fargo, recipient of $25 billion, announced changes to their golf sponsorships. Morgan Stanley decided to remain a sponsor of the Memorial Golf Tournament, but company executives did not entertain clients at the event. Wells Fargo, owner of Wachovia, reduced its presence at the Wachovia Championships held outside Charlotte, North Carolina (Newport).

In 2008, the banking industry spent $900 million on sports sponsorship rights fees and $122.3 million on sports advertising. Although Congress has yet to pass legislation restricting sponsorship spending, the impact of the outcry in Congress has already been damaging. Similar complaints relating to "extravagant" spending by TARP recipients have decimated the Las Vegas economy. Shortly after Barney Frank criticized Northern Trust, Wells Fargo, Citigroup, and US Bancorp canceled events, including employee events, in Las Vegas to avoid drawing attention from Congress. Even though studies have shown that there are benefits to employee reward programs, banks have backed off the programs and either canceled them or moved events from destination locations such as Las Vegas to lower-profile cities, like Cleveland or St. Louis (Nicklaus, 2009).

While legislation to restrict sponsorship spending was being proposed and financial institutions were being criticized about their "extravagant" sponsorship spending, the sport industry did little to support its partners (Lefton & Mickle, 2009). Unless the sport industry provides better support to its corporate backers, it may face major losses of revenue. This happened to the hospitality industry in Las Vegas. There, the impact resulting from Congress' actions has been staggering. During the first 90 days of 2009, 340 events were cancelled, costing the local economy $131.6 million in non-gambling spending. Adding to the pullout from Las Vegas was a statement by President Obama that companies should not go to Las Vegas on the taxpayer dime (Spillman, 2009). Although sponsorship revenue is somewhat protected by the long-term nature of many sponsorship contracts, Lefton and Mickle argue that the sport industry must be proactive to protect the $900 million per year in sponsorship rights fee revenue that teams and leagues currently receive.

Proposed legislation related to the cable television industry

Legislation restricting sponsorship would certainly affect the industry negatively, but changes to the regulation of the cable television industry could be even more profound. In 2004, Congressman Nathan Deal introduced the Video Programming Choice and Decency Act of 2004. This Act's purpose was the reregulation of the cable television industry. Under Deal's proposal, consumers would be guaranteed the choice of purchasing individual cable channels rather than being forced to purchase a bundled package of channels. Supporting Deal and calling for change were the Concerned Women for America, Parents Television Council, the Consumers Union, and the Consumer Federation of America (Weiner, 2009).

Since the 1984 Cable TV Act, cable companies have determined which channels are included in a bundle of packages (Weiner). The cable companies pay the cable channels based on the number of subscribers to a bundled package. Rates are set in negotiations between the channel and cable company. As demand for a channel increases, the owner can charge the cable company more. For example, in 2009 ESPN charged cable and satellite operators an average of $3.65 per month per subscriber. Given that approximately 98 million households receive ESPN, ESPN generates $4.3 billion in subscriber revenue alone (Sandomir, 2008). ESPN then uses revenue from subscribers to outbid leading sport programming competitors for the best sport properties. Terrestrial networks (as opposed to satellite or cable) CBS, Fox, and NBC rely solely on revenues from advertisers. ESPN was able to outbid Fox by $100 million for the rights to carry the Bowl Championship Series (BCS) from 2011 to 2014 (Sandomir, 2008).

If Congress reregulates cable and allows consumers to choose channels on an individual basis, the impact on ESPN's business model is unknown. Of the current 98 million subscribers, who receive the channel as part of a basic cable package, how many would be willing to pay for the channel if given the choice? If only half pay for the channel, how much would ESPN have to raise the subscription price to offset the loss in subscribers? Then, if the rate increases, how many additional consumers would decide not to pay the higher monthly rate for ESPN?

Television, ticketing, and sponsorships are the main revenue sources for many sport organizations. A legislative change to the business model of cable television may have a profound impact on the television revenue of all these organizations. Consider that ESPN currently owns the rights to Monday Night Football, various collegiate properties, MLB, portions of the four tennis majors, and golf's British Open, and as more properties move exclusively to cable, ESPN has begun to consider acquiring Olympic rights and the World Series (Sandomir, 2008). If ESPN's business model changes, the impact on rights fees is unknown— but if ESPN loses revenue and the ability to outbid competitors, the impact could be significant.

CONCLUSION

The sport industry is large and diverse, with many factors that affect financial management within the industry. Financial managers strive to maximize wealth by forecasting revenues, planning for expenses, arranging financing, and making investment decisions. A team owner's objective might not be to maximize wealth. Goals other than wealth maximization have resulted in salary constraints, revenue sharing, and other control mechanisms under which financial managers in the industry must function.

In addition to debt and equity financing, sport organizations rely on retained earnings, government financing, and gift financing. These forms of financing will be used to varying degrees depending on the subsector of the industry. The ownership structure of a team and the structure of the league will also affect financing decisions.

Growth in the sport industry is linked to the performance of the economy as a whole. Newer leagues are more likely to be affected by sudden changes in the economy, as are organizations without long-term guaranteed forms of revenue. Teams often attempt to bolster revenues through initiatives such as real estate development. Such initiatives, however, may further increase teams' exposure to changes in the economy. Financial managers in sport must be aware of factors that may affect the operation of their organization and must be proactive to protect valuable revenue sources.

CONCEPT check

1. What are the five forms of financing, and how is each used within sport?
2. What is financial management? How does financial management differ in the sport industry as compared to other industries?
3. Why does the definition of the sport industry affect the calculation of its size? How should the industry be defined?
4. Which has the greater impact on financial management: the structure of a league or the structure of a team?
5. Many factors affect the economics of sport. What are some not discussed in the chapter? How do they affect financial management within the industry?
6. Why is sustainability in the sport industry linked to the green movement?
7. What legislative actions currently being considered in Congress may affect the financial management of sport?

CASE analysis   *The Growth of a League*

For many years, women's professional basketball struggled for consistency in the United States. Since 1978, when the Women's Professional Basketball League (WBL) was formed, leagues have had difficulty surviving beyond a few seasons. The WBL lasted for only three seasons, and it was ten years before a second professional league, the Liberty Basketball Association (LBA), was launched. The LBA folded after only one exhibition game. A year later, another league was created: the Women's World Basketball Association. Although this league was more successful than the LBA, it too folded shortly into its first season. Finally, 1996 saw the launch of the American Basketball League, and the Women's National Basketball Association launched a year later. The ABL lasted for two and a half seasons (Jenkins, 2009). The WNBA entered its 13th season in 2009.

The WNBA began as a single-entity league in 1996, with its first season starting in June 1997. It was formed by the NBA Board of Governors and owned by the league. Since its founding, the number of franchises and the franchise locations have fluctuated. The league's first 16 players were dispersed to the inaugural eight teams, and the rest were selected by the teams via a draft ("History of the WNBA," 2009). The Women's National Basketball Players Association (WNBPA) was formed soon thereafter, negotiating its first collective bargaining agreement (CBA) with the WNBA in 1999. This was the first CBA in women's professional sports. Under this CBA, rookie minimum salary increased by 75%, and veteran minimum salary doubled. Year-round health coverage and a retirement plan

were provided. Contracts became guaranteed, and players earned a collective share of league licensing income ("About the WNBPA," 2009).

The WNBA introduced a draft lottery in 2001, and by 2003 the league and the WNBPA signed a new CBA. This CBA created the first free agency system in women's sports ("About the WNBPA"). The most significant change during this timeframe, however, was the NBA Board of Governors' vote to allow individual team ownership, moving the league from a single-entity model to a distributed club ownership model. Further, teams could be owned by non-NBA owners and could be located in non-NBA markets. On January 28, 2002, the Mohegan Tribe, located in Connecticut became the first non-NBA owner in league history when it was awarded the Orlando Miracle franchise ("WNBA's Greatest Moments," 2009).

In 2005, the Chicago Sky became the second WNBA franchise to be owned and run by a non-NBA entity (the team's first season was 2006), and the Washington Mystics were transferred from Wizards owner Abe Pollin to Lincoln Holdings, LLC ("WNBA's Greatest Moments"). The Los Angeles Sparks became independently owned in 2006, as did the Houston Comets in 2007, although the Comets folded prior to the 2009 season. The sixth independently owned team was the expansion Atlanta Dream, which began play in 2008 ("WNBA Expands," 2007).

The league also began to move toward profitability. Its first television agreement under which it would receive a rights fee was an eight-year agreement (2009–2016) signed with ABC,

ESPN, and ESPN2. Teams including the Phoenix Mercury and Los Angeles Sparks sold sponsorship rights to their uniforms, with LifeLock appearing on Phoenix's uniform and Farmers Insurance on the Sparks' uniform. David Stern, commissioner of the NBA, stated that the WNBA was budgeted to break even in 2009 ("NBA Getting Through," 2009).

As the league moved away from single-entity status and toward profitability, the third CBA was signed. This six-year agreement, which began in 2008, sets the WNBA salary cap at $803,000 per team in 2009 and increases it to $900,000 by 2013. For players with three-plus years of WNBA experience, the minimum salary is $51,000. The maximum salary for a player with six or more years is $99,500. Rookies are to receive a minimum of $35,190 (*Women's National*, 2008). Thirteen teams began play in 2009, with five owned by entities outside the NBA. To contain costs, rosters were reduced from 13 players to 11.

The league's viability, however, is a subject of concern, especially since the demise of the Houston Comets. Attendance has been averaging 8,000 over the past few seasons and shows no signs of growth. Rebecca Lobo, one of the league's first stars, expressed her concern about the league's future in her comment, "If NBA owners are having financial difficulties, what is the first thing they're going to look to shed?" (Kreidler, para. 18).

CASE QUESTIONS

1. Why was the WNBA structured as a single-entity league when it was founded? What advantages or disadvantages did the structure provide to the league?

2. What impact did the first CBA have on the WNBA, and how did each of the CBAs affect the league's profitability?

3. What factors have caused the WNBA to move away from the single-entity structure?

4. For new leagues, why is the single-entity structure appealing? At some point, do start-up leagues have to move away from this structure? Why or why not?

references

About the WNBPA. (2009). Retrieved July 20, 2009, from http://www.wnbpa.com/about_wnbpa.php.

Bagli, C.V. (2009, June 29). As arenas sprout, a scramble to keep them filled. *The New York Times*. Retrieved June 30, 2009, from http://www.nytimes.com/2009/06/29/nyregion/29arenas.html.

Bailout bill includes tax breaks for NASCAR tracks, facilities. (2008, October 6). *SportsBusiness Daily*. Retrieved October 6, 2008, from www.sportsbusinessdaily.com/article/124459.

Barnhart, T. (2008, August 26). SEC rakes in billions with ESPN deal. *The State*. Retrieved August 26, 2008, from http://www.thestate.com/gogamecocks/v-print/story/502259.html.

Bell, J. (2008, April 9). MLS salary structure is a matter of rich man, poor man. *New York Times*. Retrieved April 10, 2008, from http://www.nytimes.com/2008/04/09/sports/soccer/09soccer.html.

Brigham, E.F., & Houston, J.F. (2001). *Fundamentals of financial management* (9th ed.). Orlando, FL: Harcourt College Publishers.

Broughton, D. (2002, March 11–17). Methodology. *SportsBusiness Journal, 4*(47), 25–26.

Brundtland, G.H. (1987, March). *Our common future: Report of the world commission on environment and development*. New York: Oxford University Press.

Caraviello, D. (2007, September 17). Economic reality forces Pettys to explore change. *NASCAR.com*. Retrieved July 24, 2009, from http://about.nascar.com/2007/news/headlines/cup/09/17/kpetty.blabonte.petty.partnership.

Demick, B. (2009, February 22). Beijing's Olympic building boom becomes a bust. *Los Angeles Times*. Retrieved February 23, 2009, from http://articles.latimes.com/2009/feb/22/world/fg-beijing-bust22.

Economy could affect Cowboys' stadium naming-rights search. (2008, October 20). *SportsBusiness Daily*. Retrieved October 20, 2008, from http://www.sportsbusinessdaily.com/article/124822.

Federal Baseball Club v. National League, 259 U.S. 200 (1922).

Fitch Ratings. (2002, September 16). *Economics of professional sports: Rating sports transactions*. New York: Author.

Flood v. Kuhn, 407 U.S. 258 (1972).

Foster, G., Greyser, S.A., & Walsh, B. (2005). *The business of sports*. New York: South-Western College Publishers.

Fraser v. Major League Soccer, LLC, 180 F.R.D. 178 (D. Mass. 1998).

Haywood v. National Basketball Association, 401 U.S. 1204 (1971).

History of the WNBA. (2009). Retrieved July 20, 2009, from http://www.wnba.com/about_us/historyof_wnba.html.

Humphreys, B.R., & Ruseski, J.E. (2008). The scope of the sports industry in the United States. In B.R. Humphreys & D.R. Howard (Eds.), *The business of sports: Vol. 1. Perspectives on the sports industry* (pp. 1–31). Westport, CT: Praeger Publishers.

Indianapolis expects teams to add cash. (2009, May 7). *MediaVentures.* Retrieved August 6, 2009, from http://football.ballparks.com/NFL/IndianapolisColts/newindex.htm.

Indy wrestles with venue deficits. (2009, March 18). *VTPulse, 8*(9), 2–5.

Jenkins, S. (2009). History of women's basketball. Retrieved July 20, 2009, from http://www.wnba.com/about_us/jenkins_feature.html.

Kaplan, D. (1999, June 7). Going public makes company an open book. *SportsBusiness Journal.* Retrieved September 14, 2005, from http://www.sportsbusiness journal.com/article/16928.

Kaplan, D. (2009, March 16). Yanks get new loan for ballpark. *SportsBusiness Journal.* Retrieved March 17, 2009, from http://www.sportsbusinessjournal.com/article/61849.

King, B. (2002, March 11–17). Passion that can't be counted puts billions of dollars in play. *SportsBusiness Journal, 4*(47), 25–26.

King, B., & Lombardo, J. (2005, September 19). Atlanta partnership, formed in 8 days, dissolved in sea of squabbles. *SportsBusiness Journal.* Retrieved June 20, 2009, from http://www.sportsbusinessjournal.com/article/46968.

Klayman, B. (2008, June 30). High gasoline prices pinch NASCAR fans. *USA Today.* Retrieved June 30, 2008, from http://www.usatoday.com/money/industries/energy/2008-06-30-nascar-gas_N.htm.

Kreidler, M. (2009, July 24). State of uncertainty for women's sports. *ESPN.com.* Retrieved July 24, 2009, from http://sports.espn.go.com/espn/pring?id=4352885&type=story.

Lambeau Field. (2003, September 15). *SportsBusiness Journal.* Retrieved February 19, 2009, from http://www.sportsbusinessjournal.com/article/33243.

Last, J.V. (2009, January 30). Are pro sports too big to fail? *The Wall Street Journal,* p. W11.

Lefton, T., & Mickle, T. (2009, March 2). Beaten-up banks. *SportsBusiness Journal.* Retrieved March 2, 2009, from http://www.sportsbusinessjournal.com/article/61682.

Lombardo, J. (2008, February 25). A new play for the AFL? *SportsBusiness Journal.* Retrieved July 20, 2009, from http://www.sportsbusinessjournal.com/article/58179.

Mackey v. National Football League, 543 F2d 606 (1976).

Macur, J. (2009, January 12). For U.S.O.C., sponsorships become a challenge. *New York Times.* Retrieved January 20, 2009, from http://www.nytimes.com/2009/01/12/sports/olympics/12olympics.html.

Matheson, V. (2008, August 22). Caught under a mountain of Olympic debt. *The Boston Globe.* Retrieved August 22, 2008, from http://www.boston.com/bostonglobe/editorial_opinion/oped/articles/2008/08/22/caught_under_a_mountain_of_olympic_debt/.

McNeil v. National Football League, 790 F. Supp. (D. Minn. 1992).

Meek, A. (1997). An estimate of the size and supported economic activity of the sports industry in the United States. *Sport Marketing Quarterly, 6*(4), 15–22.

Mickle, T. (2010, February 15). USOC adding BP as sponsor. *SportsBusiness Journal.* Retrieved March 20, 2010, from http://www.sportsbusinessjournal.com/article/64822.

National Football League v. North American Soccer League, 459 U.S. 1074 (1982).

NBA getting through tough times. (2009, March 12). Retrieved July 20, 2009, from http://tvnz.co.nz/basketball-news/nba-getting-through-tough-times-2539976.

Newport, J.P. (2009, February 28). No entertaining, please—it's golf. *The Wall Street Journal,* p. W4.

Newton, D. (2008, July 1). With Ganassi pulling the plug on a team, question remains: Will it get worse? *ESPN.com.* Retrieved July 2, 2008, from http://sports.espn.go.com/espn/pring?id=3470082&type=story.

Nicklaus, D. (2009, March 1). Maritz, lodging industry in crossfire as politicians attack "junkets." *St. Louis Post-Dispatch.* Retrieved March 3, 2009, from http://www.stltoday.com/stltoday/emaf.nsf/Popup?ReadForm&db=stltoday%5Cbusiness%5Ccolumnists.nsf&docid=0CA1378A9DB432FE8625756B000A2631.

Pells, E. (2009, June 3). Bank of America wants more out of USOC sponsorship. *The Seattle Times.* Retrieved August 6, 2009, from http://seattletimes.nwsource.com/html/sports/2009264103_apolyusocsponsor.html.

President's annual report: 2004–2005. (2005). Green Bay, WI: Green Bay Packers, Inc.

Rascher, D. (2001, August 1). What is the size of the sports industry? *Sports Economics Perspectives, 1*(1). Retrieved from http://www.sportseconomics.com.

Roberts, J.L., & Murr, A. (2008, October 20). If you build it, will they pay? *Newsweek,* E6–E8.

Sandomir, R. (1988, November 14). The $50-billion sports industry. *Sports Inc.,* 14–23.

Sandomir, R. (2008, November 25). Assets and subscriber revenue give ESPN an edge in rights bidding. *The New York Times.* Retrieved November 17, 2008, from http://www.nytimes.com/2008/11/25/sports/ncaafootball/25sandomir.html.

Schlabach, M. (2009, July 14). Programs struggle to balance budget. *ESPN.com.* Retrieved July 24, 2009, from http://sports.espn.go.com/print?id=4314195&type=story.

Secretary of golf. (2009, February 25). *The Wall Street Journal,* p. A14.

Spillman, B. (2009, March 11). Local economy down as event cancellations pile up. *Las Vegas Review-Journal.* Retrieved March 11, 2009, from http://www.lvrj.com/news/41078067.html.

Sullivan v. National Football League, 34 F3d 1091 (1994).

Swartz, K.E. (2009, January 24). Atlanta Spirit circus resumes. *The Atlanta Journal-Constitution.* Retrieved July 20, 2009, from http://www.ajc.com/services/content/printedition/2009/01/24/spirit0124.html.

Talalay, S. (2009, July 21). Marc Anthony buys stake in Miami Dolphins. *South Florida Sun-Sentinel.* Retrieved July 21, 2009, from http://www.sun-sentinel.com/sports/miami-dolphins/sfl-marc-anthony-dolphins-s072009,0,3720783.story.

The 2008–09 career guide to industries. (2008). *Bureau of Labor Statistics.* Retrieved February 27, 2008, from http://www.bls.gov/oco/cg/print/cgs031.htm.

Van Riper, T. (2009, July 14). Where real estate is whacking sports. *Forbes.* Retrieved July 24, 2009, from http://www.forbes.com/2009/07/14/real-estate-pro-sports-business-sports-real-estate.html.

Weiner, E. (2009, July 23). United States Congress needs to change cable tv law. *MCNSports.com.* Retrieved July 23, 2009, from http://www.mcnsports.com/en/node/7469.

WNBA expands to Atlanta. (2007, October 17). Retrieved July 20, 2009, from http://www.wnba.com/dream/expansionrelease_071012.html.

WNBA's greatest moments. (2009). Retrieved July 20, 2009, from http://www.wnba.com/about_us/greatest_moments_020508.html.

Women's National Basketball Association collective bargaining agreement. (2008, January 24). Retrieved July 20, 2009, from http://www.wnbpa.com/documents/2008WNBACBA_003.pdf.

Wolverton, B. (2009, January 23). For athletics, a billion dollar goal line. *The Chronicle of Higher Education,* A1, A12–A13, A16.

Analyzing Financial Statements and Ratios

Introduction

The 2003 publication of *Moneyball: The Art of Winning an Unfair Game* popularized the use of objective, evidence-based decision making in the sport industry. Michael Lewis' book details the inner workings of the front office of the Oakland Athletics baseball club and how Athletics General Manager Billy Beane and his staff utilized objective data and statistical analysis to gain a competitive advantage over other Major League Baseball teams, most of which could afford to dramatically outspend the Athletics for talent.

For the sport industry, as in other industries, the use of quantitative data and objective decision making in financial analysis is vital. Just as baseball general managers use analytical tools such as on-base plus slugging percentage (OPS) and value over replacement player (VORP) to objectively scrutinize players' production and value, financial analysts use accounting data, summarized in documents such as balance sheets and income statements, to compute metrics that allow them to examine the financial strength and performance of an organization. The results of this type of financial analysis provide insights to a variety of the organization's stakeholders, including its management, customers, current and potential investors, lenders, and suppliers. Each of these stakeholders may be concerned with the past, present, and likely future financial performance and status of the organization. Just as a baseball executive is disadvantaged by not fully understanding objective statistical analysis (as described in *Moneyball*), so too is a manager in the sport industry who does not grasp the tools of financial analysis. This chapter will provide the foundation for understanding financial analysis. It focuses first on financial statements, such as the balance sheet, that use accounting data to provide a summary of financial performance. The latter portion of the chapter focuses on the computation of financial ratios that provide objective interpretations of the data provided by key financial statements.

FINANCIAL STATEMENTS

Just as the general manager or coach/manager reviews statistical records in order to evaluate the performance of a sports team, the manager of a business organization examines data to evaluate the organization's financial health and performance. The primary source of this type of data is the company's financial statements. Financial statements are the equivalent of box scores or statistics sheets, allowing managers to assess the organization's financial status.

The three basic financial statements are the balance sheet, the income statement, and the statement of cash flows. Each of these is examined in this chapter. These financial statements are constructed from the organization's accounting records. Their preparation typically follows generally accepted accounting principles (GAAP), which are a standard set of guidelines and procedures for financial reporting. Individuals who wish to better understand the financial operations of an organization would benefit by obtaining some accounting background. (A detailed examination of accounting principles is beyond the scope of this text.)

Publicly traded companies—those whose stock is traded on one of the many stock exchanges that exist in the United States, such as the New York Stock

Exchange (NYSE) and National Association of Securities Dealers Automated Quotations (NASDAQ), and internationally, such as the London and Tokyo stock exchanges—are required to release their financial statements to the public regularly. Private firms, including the vast majority of North American professional sport organizations, are generally not required to disclose financial statements or other related information to the public.

To illustrate concepts relating to financial statements, as well as other concepts in this chapter, we will examine financial statements from two sport industry organizations throughout the next sections. Exhibits 2.1, 2.3, and 2.5 present financial statements for Under Armour, a Baltimore-based apparel company perhaps best known for its performance sportswear. Under Armour is a publicly held corporation whose stock is traded on the New York Stock Exchange. As such, Under Armour is required to release its financial data to the public on both a quarterly and an annual basis. The financial statements included in this chapter are from Under Armour's 2008 annual report. Exhibits 2.2 and 2.4 display financial statements for the Green Bay Packers of

SIDEBAR

Publicly Traded Companies in the Sport Industry   2.A

Stock in dozens of sport industry organizations is available for trade on various stock exchanges, including both well-known exchanges such as the NYSE and NASDAQ and smaller ones such as the American Stock Exchange (AMEX). Examples of publicly traded sport organizations include sports apparel and sporting goods companies such as Nike, Reebok, and Callaway Golf; media companies, including Walt Disney (which owns ESPN) and Comcast; and motorsports companies such as International Speedway Corp. and Speedway Motorsports, each of which owns and operates NASCAR racetracks. Not represented among publicly traded companies are professional sports franchises. Currently, no major North American professional team is a publicly traded corporation, although some teams, such as the New York Knicks and Rangers, owned by Cablevision, are subsidiaries, or parts, of publicly traded corporations. In the 1980s and '90s, franchises such as the Boston Celtics, Florida Panthers, and Cleveland Indians sold stock through major exchanges; however, each of those teams has since privatized its ownership.

the National Football League. As discussed in the previous chapter, the Packers are unique among NFL teams in being owned publicly by stockholders, whereas all other NFL teams are privately owned by individuals. As privately owned businesses rather than publicly held corporations, the other NFL teams are not required to share their financial data with the public. The Packers, being publicly held, release the team's financial statements during its annual shareholder meeting each summer.

The Balance Sheet

The **balance sheet** is a picture or snapshot of the financial condition of an organization at a specific point in time. The balance sheet is unique among the financial statements in that it represents the organization's financial condition *on the date on which it is prepared* (thus the reference to the snapshot or picture), whereas the other two financial statements reflect the organization's financial performance over a period of time. The balance sheet is organized in three primary sections: assets, liabilities, and owners' equity. A company's **assets** are what it owns, including items such as cash, inventory, and **accounts receivable,** or the money a company is owed by customers. **Liabilities,** conversely, are the organization's financial obligations or debts owed to others. **Owners' equity,** which is also referred to as shareholders' equity or stockholders' equity, is an estimated measure of the ownership value of the company. On the balance sheet, owners' equity is equal to the company's assets minus its liabilities. Stated differently, the balance sheet is always truly "in balance," as the assets—the first half of the statement—must equal the total of the liabilities and owners' equity—the second half of the balance sheet. This balance is assured through the use under GAAP of **double-entry bookkeeping,** where each transaction made by an organization is entered or recorded twice, once on the debit side of the accounting records and once on the credit side. The result of this accounting system is a balanced sheet, where the sum of the organization's assets is equal to the combined sum of its liabilities and owners' equity. Exhibits 2.1 and 2.2 display balance sheets for Under Armour and the Green Bay Packers, respectively. Note on Exhibit 2.1 that Under Armour's assets at the end of 2008 were equal to the total of its liabilities and shareholders' equity, as follows:

$$\text{assets} = \text{liabilities} + \text{shareholders' equity}$$
$$\$487.555 \text{ million} = \$156.458 \text{ million} + \$331.097 \text{ million}$$

Assets on a balance sheet are listed in order of **liquidity,** or how quickly the asset can be converted into cash, with the most liquid assets listed first. Hence, cash will almost always be the first asset listed, at the top of the balance sheet. Further, assets are typically divided into the categories of *current assets* and *long-term assets*. Current assets are those that are likely to be converted into cash within one year's time. Liabilities are similarly listed according to their maturity, or when the liability or debt is due to be paid by the organization. Liabilities with the earliest maturity dates are listed first. Liabilities due within one year are labeled **current liabilities,** and those due after one year are labeled **long-term liabilities.** Common examples of current liabilities include employee salaries and accounts payable, or purchases from suppliers on credit, whereas long-term liabilities include mortgage loans for facility construction or renovation and employee pension obligations.

As stated previously, owners' equity, or assets minus liabilities, represents an estimate of the value or ownership stake of the company. It should be noted that this figure is often a very rough and inaccurate estimate, for several reasons (Shapiro & Balbirer, 2000). First, asset and liability figures represent the items' value at the time of purchase, not necessarily their present value. Land bought decades ago would be listed as an asset on the balance sheet at the cost that was paid for the land at that time, even if that land has increased in value many times since then. Second, the assets listed on the balance sheet do not include intangible assets such as branding, management expertise, or product positioning. Nike's balance sheet, for example, does not account for the value of its brand and the "swoosh" mark developed through countless marketing campaigns over the past three decades. Third, the balance sheet does not include **contingent liabilities,** debts that may or may not occur, such as the result of ongoing litigation against the company. Contingent liabilities are frequently disclosed in a notes or footnotes section associated with the balance sheet and other financial statements.

An examination of the balance sheets in Exhibits 2.1 and 2.2 reveals considerable differences in terminology. GAAP establishes standard procedures for accounting and the reporting of information on financial statements, but it allows considerable flexibility for companies to report their financial data in a manner that is appropriate for their particular business enterprise. If you find terminology in the balance sheet or other financial statements unfamiliar or confusing, note that many of these terms and concepts will be explained throughout this chapter.

exhibit   2.1

Under Armour, Inc. and subsidiaries consolidated balance sheets (in thousands, except share data).

	DECEMBER 31, 2008	DECEMBER 31, 2007
Assets		
Current assets		
Cash and cash equivalents	$102,042	$40,588
Accounts receivable, net	81,302	93,515
Inventories	182,232	166,082
Prepaid expenses and other current assets	18,023	11,642
Deferred income taxes	12,824	10,418
Total current assets	$396,423	$322,245
Property and equipment, net	73,548	52,332
Intangible assets, net	5,470	6,470
Deferred income taxes	8,687	8,173
Other non-current assets	3,427	1,393
TOTAL ASSETS	$487,555	$390,613
Liabilities and Stockholders' Equity		
Current liabilities		
Revolving credit facility	$25,000	—
Accounts payable	72,435	$55,012
Accrued expenses	25,905	36,111
Current maturities of long-term debt	7,072	4,111
Current maturities of capital lease obligations	361	465
Other current liabilities	2,337	—
Total current liabilities	$133,110	$95,699
Long-term debt, net of current maturities	13,061	9,298
Capital lease obligations, net of current maturities	97	458
Other long-term liabilities	10,190	4,673
TOTAL LIABILITIES	$156,458	$110,128
Stockholders' equity		
Class A Common Stock, $.0003 1/3 par value (100,000,000 shares authorized as of December 31, 2008 and 2007; 36,808,750 shares issued and outstanding as of December 31, 2008, and 36,189,564 shares issued and outstanding as of December 31, 2007)	$ 12	$ 12
Class B Convertible Common Stock, $.0003 1/3 par value (12,500,000 shares authorized, issued and outstanding as of December 31, 2008 and 2007)	4	4
Additional paid-in capital	174,725	162,362
Retained earnings	156,011	117,782
Unearned compensation	(60)	(182)
Accumulated other comprehensive income	405	507
Total stockholders' equity	$331,097	$280,485
TOTAL LIABILITIES AND STOCKHOLDERS' EQUITY	$487,555	$390,613

exhibit   2.2   Green Bay Packers balance sheets.

FISCAL YEAR ENDED MARCH 31,	2009	2008
Assets		
Current assets		
Cash	$3,632,166	$0
Inventories	4,164,838	1,666,631
Unamortized signing bonuses	14,943,628	15,530,776
Accounts receivable	9,710,475	7,191,971
Deferred income taxes	7,425,157	7,449,867
Other current assets	3,974,229	2,055,972
Total current assets	$43,850,493	$33,895,217
Investments	$166,035,479	$216,324,253
Property & equipment, net	50,731,444	48,871,670
Other assets		
Unamortized signing bonuses	15,266,649	27,613,660
Deferred income taxes	0	0
Other non-current assets	22,447,772	10,912,760
Total other assets	$37,714,421	$38,526,420
TOTAL ASSETS	$298,331,837	$337,617,560
Liabilities and Stockholders' Equity		
Current liabilities		
Cash overdraft		
Current maturities of long-term liabilities (deferred compensation)	$4,948,206	$4,240,425
Notes payable	1,001,169	13,768,155
Accounts payable	2,784,481	3,609,180
Accrued expenses	12,317,625	24,114,093
Accrued income taxes	0	0
Deferred revenues	10,099,549	3,137,558
Total current liabilities	$31,151,030	$48,869,411
Long-term liabilities		
Note payable	$8,466,997	$8,100,000
Deferred compensation	11,346,314	13,133,884
Litigation settlement	0	0
Deferred income taxes	0	0
Other	14,243,022	12,947,511
TOTAL LONG-TERM LIABILITIES	$34,056,333	$34,181,395
Stockholders' equity		
Common stock and additional paid-in capital	$22,335,711	$22,335,711
Retained earnings	232,418,674	228,396,734
Unrealized gain on investments, net		
Accumulated other comprehensive income	(21,629,911)	3,834,309
Total stockholders' equity	$233,124,474	$254,566,754
TOTAL LIABILITIES AND STOCKHOLDERS' EQUITY	$298,331,837	$337,617,560

The Income Statement

The **income statement,** also referred to as the statement of earnings or the profit and loss statement, shows the organization's income over a specified period of time and is typically issued on an annual or quarterly basis. For the specified time period, the income statement lists the organization's **revenues,** or income generated from business activities, such as the sale of goods or services, and the organization's **expenses,** or funds flowing out of the organization as costs of doing business. Exhibits 2.3 and 2.4 provide examples for Under Armour and the Green Bay Packers. When expenses are subtracted from revenues, the resulting figure is the organization's net income (or net loss, if expenses were greater than revenues over the period of time). Net income is frequently referred to as profits or earnings.

An organization's books may be kept on a cash basis or an accrual basis, and it is important to note the differences between these two methods and the resulting impact on the income statement. *Cash basis accounting* recognizes transactions when money is either received or paid out. *Accrual basis accounting,* on the other

Under Armour, Inc. and subsidiaries consolidated income statements (in thousands, except per share amounts).   exhibit 2.3

	YEAR ENDED DECEMBER 31,		
	2008	2007	2006
Net revenues	$725,244	$606,561	$430,689
Cost of goods sold	370,296	301,517	215,089
Gross profit	$354,948	$305,044	$215,600
Operating expenses			
Selling, general, and administrative expenses	278,023	218,779	158,682
Income from operations	$76,925	$86,265	$56,918
Interest income (expense), net	(850)	749	1,457
Other income (expense), net	(6,175)	2,029	712
Income before income taxes	$69,900	$89,043	$59,087
Provision for income taxes	31,671	36,485	20,108
Net income	$38,229	$52,558	$38,979
Net income available per common share			
Basic	$0.79	$1.09	$0.83
Diluted	$0.77	$1.05	$0.79
Weighted average common shares outstanding			
Basic	48,569	48,021	46,983
Diluted	49,890	49,959	49,587

exhibit   2.4   Green Bay Packers income statements.

FISCAL YEAR ENDED MARCH 31,	2009	2008
Operating Income		
Ticket & media income		
Home games, net	$31,097,266	$30,889,618
Road games	16,175,953	15,138,643
Television and radio	94,484,631	87,584,700
Total ticket and media income	$141,757,850	$133,612,961
Other operating income		
Private box income	$12,827,613	$12,059,952
NFL properties income (other NFL revenue)	36,458,755	32,853,116
Expansion\revenue sharing income		
Marketing\pro shop, net	43,717,750	50,256,737
Atrium revenue (added 2004)		
Other: local media, concessions, and parking (net)	13,167,973	12,552,566
Total other operating income	$106,172,091	$107,722,371
Total operating income	$247,929,941	$241,335,332
Operating Expenses		
Player costs	$138,697,272	$124,651,348
Game expenses (operations/maintenance, net)	7,700,551	7,567,872
General and administrative	31,693,990	35,227,539
Team expenses	26,394,103	26,459,884
Sales and marketing expenses	23,334,394	26,008,492
Pro shop expenses		
Atrium expenses		
Lambeau redevelopment costs		
Total operating expenses	$227,820,310	$219,915,135
Profit (loss) from operations	$20,109,631	$21,420,197
Other income (Expense)		
Interest expense		
Interest and dividend income		
Gain on sale of investments and other assets, net		
Other income (expense)	$(11,187,691)	$14,369,619
Income before expansion revenue and provision for income taxes	8,921,940	35,789,816
Provision for income taxes	4,900,000	12,425,000
Net income before expansion revenue	$4,021,940	$23,364,816

hand, accounts for income when it is earned and expenses when they are incurred, rather than when the money is exchanged. For example, if Under Armour makes a major sale in fiscal year (FY) 1 but does not actually receive payment until FY 2, under accrual basis accounting, the sale is included as revenue on Under Armour's FY 1 income statement. (A **fiscal year** is a 12-month period over which a company budgets its money; it may or may not begin in January, and so the term *fiscal year* distinguishes it from the calendar year.) Under cash basis accounting, the money would be included as revenue only when it is received in FY 2. Some sole proprietorships and other businesses utilize cash basis accounting, but most corporations and partnerships are required by GAAP to follow accrual basis accounting. The limitation of cash basis accounting, as it pertains to the income statement, is that sales made during a particular time period cannot be recognized on the income statement if payment has not yet been received, even if payment is forthcoming. Under accrual basis accounting, the lag time between when a transaction is made and when payment is exchanged is acknowledged through another financial statement, the statement of cash flows, to be discussed later in this chapter.

> ### The Birth and Growth of Under Armour　2.B
>
> The corporate history of Under Armour (UA) is not a long one, as UA started in 1996, but it is one of tremendous growth. UA founder and CEO Kevin Plank was a football player at the University of Maryland in the 1990s. Like many athletes, Plank tired of sweating through cotton t-shirts each practice and workout, and wearing those heavy, wet shirts as a result. In 1995, as a senior, he found a fabric similar to the skin-tight compression shorts players wore and had some shirts made from that fabric. Plank refined the shirts through trial and error, testing his product on fellow University of Maryland athletes. Plank graduated in 1996 and launched UA. The company sold 500 shirts that first year, resulting in $17,000 in sales. UA has grown quickly since, with sales of $25 million in 2001, $430 million in 2006, and $725 million in 2008. While it may be unlikely that UA will continue to grow at this same rapid rate, the company is posed to be a formidable competitor in the sports apparel industry for the foreseeable future.

Experts disagree about whether income statements truly reflect actual earnings or profit (Higgins, 2009; Shapiro & Balbirer, 2000). For example, when firms account for depreciation (the reduction in value of an asset due to age or use), a number of options are available, and the approach chosen can greatly influence expenses, and thus net income or loss, on the income statement. A related issue is taxation. Accounting decisions—particularly in regard to depreciation and inventory—are frequently made in an effort to minimize taxes. This can result in financial statements, especially income statements, that lack objectivity. Another issue is how the company accounts for expenditures in the areas of research and development (R&D) and advertising. These two areas represent investments in the future revenues of the company, yet they are typically accounted as expenditures when spent rather than in the future, when their benefits are reaped. If a company makes cuts in these areas in difficult times, the result may be an increased net income (or decreased net loss) in the short term. Such action could, however, be harmful to the long-term future of the company.

The Statement of Cash Flows

For any company to be successful in the long term, it must generate more cash than it spends, known as a positive cash flow. Negative cash flows may be sustainable in the short term, but few companies can survive long periods of spending more than they generate. The income statement and balance sheet, however, do not provide insight into this simple fact.

Whereas the income statement provides information about the revenues and expenses flowing into and out from an organization, the **statement of cash flows** tracks cash in and cash out. The ability to track cash coming into and going out of the business is of particular importance to an organization that uses accrual basis accounting. The cash flows statement provides data as to whether the company has sufficient cash on hand to meet its debts and obligations, which is not provided by the balance sheet or the income statement of firms utilizing accrual basis accounting. In addition to revealing differences between accrual basis accounting and cash transactions, the statement of cash flows is free from the influence of noncash expenses, such as depreciation—unlike the income statement. On the income statement, the depreciation of an asset such as a stadium or an office building is listed as an expense, yet depreciation does not reflect any true monetary expenditure. The statement of cash flows provides a simpler examination of cash generated and spent. Exhibit 2.5 is Under Armour's statement of cash flows from its 2008 annual report.

Whereas the balance sheet states the status of the company's assets, liabilities, and equity at a single point in time, without showing trends over time, the statement of cash flows examines cash transactions over a period of time and so can provide additional context for the information in a balance sheet.

exhibit 2.5 Under Armour, Inc. and subsidiaries consolidated cash flow statements (in thousands).

YEAR ENDED DECEMBER 31,	2008	2007	2006
Cash flows from operating activities			
Net income	$38,229	$52,558	$38,979
Adjustments to reconcile net income to net cash provided by (used in) operating activities			
Depreciation and amortization	21,347	14,622	9,824
Unrealized foreign currency exchange rate (gains) losses	5,459	(2,567)	161
Loss on disposal of property and equipment	15	—	115
Stock-based compensation	8,466	4,182	1,982
Deferred income taxes	(2,818)	(4,909)	(6,721)
Changes in reserves for doubtful accounts, returns, discounts, and inventories	8,711	4,551	3,832
Changes in operating assets and liabilities:			
Accounts receivable	2,634	(24,222)	(20,828)
Inventories	(19,497)	(83,966)	(26,504)
Prepaid expenses and other assets	(7,187)	(2,067)	(3,997)
Accounts payable	16,957	11,873	8,203
Accrued expenses and other liabilities	(5,316)	11,825	10,681
Income taxes payable and receivable	2,516	3,492	(5,026)
Net cash provided by (used in) operating activities	$69,516	$(14,628)	$10,701

	2008	2007	2006
Cash flows from investing activities			
Purchase of property and equipment	$(38,594)	$(33,959)	$(15,115)
Purchase of intangible assets	(600)	(125)	—
Purchase of trust-owned life insurance policies	(2,893)	—	—
Proceeds from sales of property and equipment	21	—	—
Purchases of short-term investments	—	(62,860)	(89,650)
Proceeds from sales of short-term investments	—	62,860	89,650
Net cash used in investing activities	$(42,066)	$(34,084)	$(15,115)
Cash flows from financing activities			
Proceeds from revolving credit facility	$40,000	$14,000	—
Payments on revolving credit facility	(15,000)	(14,000)	—
Proceeds from long-term debt	13,214	11,841	$ 2,119
Payments on long-term debt	(6,490)	(2,973)	(2,413)
Payments on capital lease obligations	(464)	(794)	(1,840)
Excess tax benefits from stock-based compensation arrangements	2,131	6,892	11,260
Proceeds from exercise of stock options and other stock issuances	1,990	3,182	3,544
Payments of debt financing costs	—	—	(260)
Payments received on notes from stockholders	—	—	169
Net cash provided by financing activities	35,381	18,148	12,579
Effect of exchange rate changes on cash and cash equivalents	(1,377)	497	(487)
Net increase (decrease) in cash and cash equivalents	$61,454	$(30,067)	$ 7,678
Cash and cash equivalents			
Beginning of year	$40,588	$70,655	$62,977
End of year	102,042	40,588	70,655
Non-cash financing and investing activities			
Fair market value of shares withheld in consideration of employee tax obligations relative to stock-based compensation	—	—	$734
Purchase of property and equipment through certain obligations	$2,486	$1,110	2,700
Issuance of warrants in partial consideration for intangible asset	—	—	8,500
Settlement of outstanding accounts receivable with property and equipment	—	—	350
Reversal of unearned compensation and additional paid-in capital due to adoption of SFAS 123R	—	—	715
Other supplemental information			
Cash paid for income taxes	$29,561	$30,502	$20,522
Cash paid for interest	1,444	525	531

Cash flow statements are typically organized in three sections: operations, investing, and financing. *Operations* refers to the organization's cash flows from normal business operations, such as cash flowing in from the sale of products or services, or cash flowing out to pay employees' salaries. *Investing* activities include the buying and selling of fixed assets, such as the purchase of property. *Financing* refers to the company's debt and equity financing, such as the sale of stock or repayment of a loan. For an example, see Under Armour's statement of cash flows in Exhibit 2.5.

FINANCIAL RATIOS

Just as the general manager of a baseball team can take a sheet of statistics and compute various figures, such as batting average, slugging percentage, and earned run average, in order to evaluate teams and players, a business manager can utilize accounting data provided in the financial statements discussed above in order make similar types of analyses. For example, instead of dividing at bats by hits to find batting average, the business manager may divide net income by shareholders'/owners' equity to calculate a metric called return on equity. The remainder of this chapter focuses on the computation and analysis of similar measures, known as financial ratios. Financial ratios provide key information about the condition and performance of a company and are, therefore, vital for managers to understand. This chapter will focus on many of the most important and commonly used ratios. These ratios are organized into five sections based on their type: liquidity, asset management, financial leverage, profitability, and market value. Exhibit 2.6 summarizes these ratios.

Liquidity Ratios

Recall that liquidity refers to the ability to convert an asset into cash quickly. Liquidity ratios measure an organization's ability to pay its short-term liabilities or debts with its short-term assets. A company that lacks sufficient short-term assets, such as cash, inventory, and accounts receivable, to pay off debts that are coming due in the near future may be forced to refinance its debts or borrow additional money in order to meet its financial obligations.

Current ratio

The most commonly used liquidity measure is the current ratio. The **current ratio** measures the organization's ability to meet its current liabilities (those due within a year) with its current assets. The following formula is used to calculate the current ratio:

$$\text{current ratio} = \frac{\text{current assets}}{\text{current liabilities}}$$

Both current assets and current liabilities are found on the balance sheet. Using data from Exhibit 2.1, Under Armour's current ratio for December 31, 2008, is calculated as follows:

$$\text{current ratio} = \frac{\$396,423,000}{\$133,110,000} = 2.98$$

Summary of key financial ratios. exhibit 2.6

RATIO	DESCRIPTION	FORMULA
Liquidity Ratios		
current ratio	The organization's ability to meet its current liabilities (those due within a year) with its current assets	$\dfrac{\text{current assets}}{\text{current liabilities}}$
quick ratio	The organization's ability to meet its current liabilities with current assets other than inventory	$\dfrac{\text{current assets} - \text{inventory}}{\text{current liabilities}}$
Asset Management Ratios		
total asset turnover ratio	How efficiently the organization is utilizing its assets to make money	$\dfrac{\text{net sales}}{\text{average total assets}}$
inventory turnover ratio	How often the organization sells and replaces its inventory over a specified period of time	$\dfrac{\text{cost of goods sold}}{\text{average inventory}}$
Leverage Ratios		
debt ratio	How the organization finances its operation with debt and equity	$\dfrac{\text{total liabilities}}{\text{total assets}}$
interest coverage ratio	The organization's ability to pay the interest on its debt owed	$\dfrac{\text{earnings before interest and taxes (EBIT)}}{\text{interest expense}}$
Profitability Ratios		
net profit margin	The percentage of the organization's total sales or revenues that was net profit or income	$\dfrac{\text{net income}}{\text{sales or revenues}}$
return on equity	The return rate that the organization's owners or shareholders are receiving on their investment	$\dfrac{\text{net income}}{\text{shareholders' or owners' equity}}$
Market Value Ratios		
market value	An estimate of the organization's worth according to the stock market	price per share of common stock x number of outstanding shares
price-to-earnings ratio	An estimate of how much money investors will pay for each dollar of the organization's earnings	$\dfrac{\text{price per share of common stock}}{\text{earnings per share}}$

(We add three zeroes to each of the values from the balance sheet because the figures in Exhibit 2.1, except for stock share information, are abbreviated and rounded to the nearest thousand.) The current ratio suggests that Under Armour has the ability to cover its short-term liabilities nearly three times over with current assets. Likewise, the Green Bay Packers' current ratio for March 31, 2009, can be calculated from data from their balance sheet (see Exhibit 2.2):

$$\text{current ratio} = \frac{\$43,850,493}{\$31,151,030} = 1.41$$

In general, a higher current ratio figure is preferable, as it represents a healthy ability to cover debts with assets such as cash and accounts receivable. A company with a high current ratio is less likely to need to convert longer-term assets into cash or borrow money to cover liabilities. It is possible, however, for a current ratio to be too high. This may represent inefficient company management that is not maximizing the use of its cash balance or that is carrying excessive inventory (Helfert, 2002; Shapiro & Balbirer). A current ratio near 2:1 is commonly viewed as a good target for many companies (Helfert). Using this standard, Under Armour's current ratio of 2.98 may be seen as overly high.

It should be noted, however, that current ratio values—as well as most other financial ratios—must be evaluated in context, especially when we are using them as comparative tools. The first context in which financial ratios should be viewed is against other firms within the same industry. Before making a judgment as to whether Under Armour's current ratio is excessive, we should compare it to that of rival companies, such as Nike. Another important context for comparison is the company's own history. Financial ratios should be examined relative to their values in previous time periods to evaluate trends in the company's financial position.

Quick/Acid-test ratio

Another frequently used measure of liquidity is the **quick ratio,** also known as the **acid-test ratio.** Like the current ratio, the quick ratio provides information about the organization's ability to meet its current liabilities with current assets. The quick ratio, however, does not include inventory among current assets. If a company faces a financial emergency and needs to convert assets into cash in order to meet pending obligations, inventory is likely to be difficult to convert into cash as quickly as other assets. It may take months for a company to sell its inventory at full value, or the company may have to discount the inventory deeply to sell it rapidly. According to Higgins (2009), sellers may receive 40% or less of inventory's book value through a liquidation sale. Because inventory is viewed as being the least liquid of a company's current assets, the quick ratio is often useful as a more conservative alternative to the current ratio.

The quick ratio is simply a modified version of the current ratio. It is calculated as follows:

$$\text{quick ratio} = \frac{\text{current assets} - \text{inventory}}{\text{current liabilities}}$$

The inventory value may be found on the balance sheet. Under Armour's quick ratio for December 31, 2008, is calculated as follows:

$$\text{quick ratio} = \frac{\$396,423,000 - \$182,232,000}{\$133,110,000} = 1.61$$

Under Armour can cover its short-term liabilities 1.61 times over with its current assets other than inventory. For an apparel company with significant inventory, this signifies that Under Armour is not overly encumbered with short-term debt and has sufficient assets to cover that debt if necessary. The Green Bay Packers' quick ratio for March 31, 2009, can also be calculated from data from the balance sheet:

$$\text{quick ratio} = \frac{\$43,850,493 - \$4,164,838}{\$31,151,030} = 1.27$$

As a professional sport franchise, the Packers do not possess significant inventory. Hence, it should not be surprising that the current ratio and quick ratio have similar values. The Packers' inventory may consist of apparel and merchandise in team souvenir shops, for example, but it is relatively small when compared to the inventory of a sports apparel corporation such as Under Armour. Recall that financial ratios should be compared against those of industry competitors. In the case of the Packers, we would examine other professional sport franchises.

Asset Management Ratios

How effectively a company utilizes its assets and resources to generate sales is important information for business managers. All companies have a limited amount of resources. Those that are most efficient in using those limited resources to produce sales are likely to be successful. Several ratios measure companies' asset management. Two of the most common are the total asset turnover ratio and the inventory turnover ratio.

Total asset turnover ratio

One measure of how efficiently an organization is utilizing its assets to make money is the **total asset turnover ratio.** This ratio requires information from both the company's balance sheet and its income statement, in the following formula:

$$\text{total asset turnover ratio} = \frac{\text{net sales}}{\text{average total assets}}$$

The net sales value, sometimes labeled as net revenues, is found on the income statement (see the Under Armour example in Exhibit 2.3). Total assets, which includes both current assets and long-term assets, is listed on the balance sheet. To find average total assets, we average the company's total assets at the beginning and at the end of the period of interest, often the fiscal year. For Under Armour, these asset values are given in Exhibit 2.1. Total assets at the end of 2008 were $487,555,000. The beginning-of-period total assets are assumed to be identical to total assets at the end of the previous period—in this case, December 31, 2007—which were $390,613,000. We average these two figures to find the average total assets value. The entire calculation proceeds as follows:

$$\text{total asset turnover ratio} = \frac{\$725,244,000}{(\$487,555,000 + \$390,613,000) / 2}$$

$$= \frac{\$725,244,000}{\$439,084,000}$$

$$= 1.65$$

In FY 2008 Under Armour's revenues exceeded assets by a considerable amount, suggesting that the company is using its assets efficiently.

Data from Exhibits 2.2 and 2.4 allow us to calculate the Green Bay Packers' total asset turnover ratio for FY 2009. On the Packers' income statement, net sales is represented by total operating income. The calculation is as follows:

$$\text{total asset turnover ratio} = \frac{\$247,929,941}{(\$298,331,837 + \$337,617,560) / 2}$$

$$= \frac{\$247,929,941}{\$317,974,699}$$

$$= 0.78$$

The Green Bay Packers' revenues were 78% of their assets at the end of the 2009 fiscal year. As with other ratios, these values should be compared to the organization's own historical values as well as to industry competitors for analysis.

Inventory turnover ratio

Another ratio that is useful in evaluating asset management is the **inventory turnover ratio,** which measures how often a company sells and replaces its inventory over a specified period of time, typically a year. For some firms, particularly those in manufacturing and retail, this is an especially important ratio, as inventory is often a large asset for these companies. A manufacturer—like Under Armour—that must sell a high volume of relatively low priced products in order to be profitable must turn over its existing inventory frequently. If the inventory is sitting in warehouses and on shelves rather than being sold in a timely manner, it will be difficult for the company to be financially successful.

Inventory turnover ratio is calculated with the following formula:

$$\text{inventory turnover ratio} = \frac{\text{cost of goods sold}}{\text{average inventory}}$$

Cost of goods sold (COGS) includes those costs that are directly attributable to the production of goods or products to be sold, including raw materials and labor costs. Cost of goods sold, sometimes labeled *cost of sales,* is typically listed immediately after net sales (or net revenues), near the top of the income statement. Recall that inventory is found on the balance sheet, and we calculate average inventory by finding the average of the inventory values at the beginning and the end of the time period of interest.

Using data from Exhibits 2.1 and 2.3, we calculate Under Armour's inventory turnover ratio for 2008 as follows:

$$\text{inventory turnover ratio} = \frac{\$370,296,000}{(\$182,232,000 + \$166,082,000) / 2}$$

$$= \frac{\$370,296,000}{\$174,157,000}$$

$$= 2.13$$

To interpret this figure, we may say that Under Armour turned over, or sold and replenished, its inventory 2.13 times during 2008. Of course, in general, a higher value is preferred. Once again, note that this value is difficult to interpret without comparisons to industry competitors and the company's own history. This particular ratio is especially industry-specific. Industries that sell very low cost items, such as a grocery store, are likely to turn over inventory much more rapidly than industries selling luxury items, such as jewelry or yachts. Inventory turnover ratio values should reflect these differences. While the inventory turnover ratio is a vital metric for manufacturers (like Under Armour) and retail companies, it is not an important indicator for a sport franchise such as the Green Bay Packers. Because the Packers do not produce goods in the same way that Under Armour does, the Packers do not report a cost of goods sold or cost of sales value on their income statement (see Exhibit 2.4). Accordingly, the inventory turnover ratio for the Packers is not presented here.

Leverage Ratios

Leverage refers to how a company chooses to finance its operation with debt versus equity. A company that relies extensively on borrowing money to operate is considered to be heavily leveraged. Such a company faces greater risk of financial problems than one not so reliant on debt.

Debt ratio

A useful financial leverage ratio is the **debt ratio,** sometimes referred to as the debt-to-assets ratio. The debt ratio is a quite simple, yet telling measure of an organization's leverage. It is calculated with the formula:

$$\text{debt ratio} = \frac{\text{total liabilities}}{\text{total assets}}$$

Both total liabilities and total assets are found on the balance sheet. (Total assets is equal to current plus short-term assets, and total liabilities is equal to current plus long-term liabilities.) A lower debt ratio is generally preferable, as a higher value signifies heavier borrowing and increased financial risk. This ratio is unique among those presented in this chapter; with all other ratios, a higher value is preferred to a lower one. From data in Exhibit 2.1, we calculate Under Armour's debt ratio for December 31, 2008, as follows:

$$\text{debt ratio} = \frac{\$156,458,000}{\$487,555,000} = 0.32$$

Under Armour's debt was approximately one-third of the value of its assets. Note that the debt ratio is often reported in percentage form, in this case 32%. Money borrowed from creditors makes up 32% of the value of Under Armour's assets.

The Green Bay Packers' debt ratio for March 31, 2009, may also be calculated from data in their balance sheet (see Exhibit 2.2):

$$\text{debt ratio} = \frac{\$31,151,030 + \$34,056,333}{\$298,331,837} = 0.22$$

Because the Packers' balance sheet does not list a total liabilities figure, we must add their total current liabilities and total long-term liabilities to find this value ($31,151,030 + $34,056,333). Recall that companies structure their financial statements with slight differences and nuances to fit their own particular operations.

Interest coverage ratio

Another tool for understanding a company's financial leverage is the **interest coverage ratio,** sometimes called the times interest earned ratio. As the name of this ratio implies, the interest coverage ratio measures a firm's ability to pay the interest on its debt. Consider this on an individual level: persons who carry a debt balance on a credit card—as millions do—know that while they may not be able to pay the full balance by the next payment due date, they must at least pay a minimum amount, which is often approximately equivalent to the interest on the balance. This concept applies at the organizational level as well. Many companies may not be able to pay the full amount of debt owed in the short term, but a company that cannot at least pay the interest on its debt is at risk for significant financial problems. The interest coverage ratio measures a company's ability to pay interest on debt out of income or earnings. It is calculated with the following formula:

$$\text{interest coverage ratio} = \frac{\text{earnings before interest and taxes (EBIT)}}{\text{interest expense}}$$

The interest coverage ratio formula involves a term that is common in financial analysis and accounting: **earnings before interest and taxes (EBIT).** EBIT, found on the income statement, is defined as

$$\text{EBIT} = \text{operating revenue} - \text{operating expenses} + \text{non-operating income}$$

The interest expense value is found on the income statement. When a company reports no non-operating income, EBIT is often used synonymously with the terms *operating income* or *operating profit.* Using data from Under Armour's income statement (Exhibit 2.3), we calculate the company's interest coverage ratio for FY 2008 as follows:

$$\text{interest coverage ratio} = \frac{\$76,925,000}{\$850,000} = 90.50$$

Note that Under Armour's income statement labels EBIT as income from operations. The interest coverage ratio value of 90.50 suggests that Under Armour can cover its interest expense more than 90 times over with its earnings or operating income.

The Green Bay Packers' income statement shows that the Packers had no interest expense in the 2009 fiscal year. In this case, the interest coverage ratio for the Packers cannot be calculated and is immaterial.

Profitability Ratios

A primary purpose of a for-profit business is, of course, to generate a profit. A number of financial ratios measure the profitability of a company. We will discuss two of the most useful profitability ratios: net profit margin and return on equity. These ratios evaluate the performance of the company and its management in controlling expenses and generating profit.

Net profit margin ratio

A widely used profitability ratio is net profit margin. The **net profit margin ratio,** the percentage of total sales or revenues that was net profit or income, measures the effectiveness and efficiency of the organization's operations. A higher value represents a company that is efficient in its production and operations. A low net profit margin may reflect inefficient operations and poor management, as well as a company that would be at risk financially if sales were to decline. Net profit margin is calculated as follows:

$$\text{net profit margin} = \frac{\text{net income}}{\text{sales or revenues}}$$

Both net income and sales or revenues may be found on the income statement. Recall that net income is essentially the "bottom line" of the income statement itself and is traditionally listed near or at the end of the income statement. Conversely, the sales or revenues value is commonly listed at the beginning of the income statement. From data in Exhibit 2.3, we calculate Under Armour's net profit margin for FY 2008 as follows:

$$\text{net profit margin} = \frac{\$38,229,000}{\$725,244,000} = 5.27\%$$

Net profit margin is reported in percentage form, as it represents the percentage of sales that returned to the company's ownership in the form of profits on their capital. Under Armour's net profit margin for FY 2008 was a little over 5%. In other words, Under Armour spent nearly 95% of the money generated by sales in 2008 on everything from manufacturing to employee pay to advertising, while approximately 5% was returned to ownership as profit. Again, we must compare this value to the company's own history and to industry competitors in order to draw valid conclusions.

The Green Bay Packers' net profit margin in FY 2009 may be calculated from data from the income statement in Exhibit 2.4, as follows:

$$\text{net profit margin} = \frac{\$4,021,940}{\$247,929,941} = 1.62\%$$

The Packers realized just a 1.62% return on their sales as profit in their 2009 fiscal year. In other words, for every dollar in revenue generated, the Packers returned to ownership less than two cents (1.62 cents, to be precise) in profit. Note, however, that as a community-owned professional sports team, the Packers likely do not have the same incentive or motivation to generate large profits as does a more traditional for-profit corporation, such as Under Armour.

Return on equity ratio

Another important measure of profitability is the **return on equity ratio,** which measures the rate of return a company's owners or shareholders are receiving on their investment. Like net profit margin, return on equity bases a measure of efficiency on net income. The return on equity ratio, however, compares net income to shareholders' or owners' equity instead of revenues. The formula is:

$$\text{return on equity} = \frac{\text{net income}}{\text{shareholders' or owners' equity}}$$

Net income is typically found near the end of the income statement. Shareholders' or owners' equity is found on the balance sheet. Under Armour's return on equity for FY 2008 is calculated as follows, from data in Exhibits 2.1 and 2.3:

$$\text{return on equity} = \frac{\$38,229,000}{\$331,097,000} = 11.55\%$$

Like net profit margin, return on equity is reported in percentage form, as it represents the percentage of ownership stake or equity that the company's owner-ship realized as profit during a period of time. Under Armour's return on equity for 2008 was more than 11%. From data in Exhibits 2.2 and 2.4, we calculate the Green Bay Packers' return on equity for FY 2009 as follows:

$$\text{return on equity} = \frac{\$4,021,940}{\$233,124,474} = 1.73\%$$

The Packers earned less than a 2% return on their ownership or equity as profit in the 2009 fiscal year. While this may seem low, note that the Packers are a community-owned, non-profit organization. This is unique among major profes-sional sport franchises.

Market Value Ratios

The final set of financial ratios is helpful in estimating the book value of a com-pany. The two ratios discussed in this section, market value and price-to-earnings ratio, are quick methods to estimate the value of a company. Valuation is discussed further in Chapter 10.

Market value ratio

Perhaps the quickest method of estimating the value of a company is by finding its **market value** according to the stock market. A company's market value may be computed with the following formula:

$$\text{market value} = \begin{array}{c} \text{price per} \\ \text{share of} \\ \text{common stock} \end{array} \times \begin{array}{c} \text{number of} \\ \text{outstanding} \\ \text{shares} \end{array}$$

While this method for estimating a company's worth is convenient and easy, it is not necessarily the most precise method. One notable problem is that stock prices often reflect investors' speculation about the future potential of a company rather than its present performance (see Chapter 7).

To estimate the value of Under Armour, we can refer to stock information found on the company's balance sheet (Exhibit 2.1) in the stockholders' equity section. Under Armour had 36,808,750 shares of stock outstanding at the end of 2008. (Be careful not to add zeroes to the figures for share information. All val-ues on Under Armour's balance sheet are given "in thousands, except per share amounts"—referring to stock share information.)

Stock price is not available on any of Under Armour's financial statements. Fortunately, numerous sites on the Internet, including Under Armour's own web-site, provide historical stock price data. Under Armour's stock closed at $23.84

at the end of trading on December 31, 2008, on the New York Stock Exchange. Therefore, the market value of Under Armour on that date was:

market value = 36,808,750 shares × $23.84 = $877,520,600

According to the stock market, Under Armour was worth more than $877 million as of the end of 2008.

Because the Green Bay Packers' stock is not traded publicly on a stock exchange, a stock price is not available, and it is not possible to calculate the Packers' market value using this method.

Price-to-earnings ratio

The **price-to-earnings ratio,** or **P/E ratio,** is a widely used measure of corporate performance and value, particularly among stock market investors. The P/E ratio estimates how much investors will pay for each dollar of a company's earnings (Harrington, 2003). One of the strengths of the P/E ratio is that its scaled nature allows comparisons of the market values of companies of all sizes. The P/E ratio is calculated with the following formula:

$$\text{price-to-earnings ratio} = \frac{\text{price per share of common stock}}{\text{earnings per share}}$$

To calculate the P/E ratio, we must first determine earnings per share, by using the following formula:

$$\text{earnings per share} = \frac{\text{net income}}{\text{number of outstanding shares of common stock}}$$

Recall that net income is found on the income statement, and stock share information is found on the balance sheet. Once we have found earnings per share, we divide the stock price by earnings per share to find the P/E ratio. Using data from Exhibits 2.1 and 2.3, along with the December 31, 2008, stock price, we determine Under Armour's P/E ratio as follows:

$$\text{price-to-earnings ratio} = \frac{\$23.84}{\$38,229,000 \,/\, 36,808,750}$$

$$= \frac{\$23.84}{\$\ 1.04}$$

$$= 22.95$$

Under Armour's stock price at the end of 2008 was nearly 23 times the company's earnings.

When calculating the P/E ratio, be careful in your use of the data. In this example, we multiplied the net income figure by 1,000, because the income statement gives net income in thousands. The stock share data, however, should not be multiplied by 1,000. Doing so would result in a wildly inaccurate P/E ratio value.

In general, a higher P/E ratio is preferred, but not always. A high P/E ratio can signify subpar earnings or net income, which, of course, is not desirable. Because stock price is a component of the P/E ratio formula, P/E ratio values are heavily influenced by investors' speculation about a company's potential for growth and success in the future, reflected in the stock price. Companies with high P/E ratio values are often perceived to have high growth potential. In this regard, a P/E ratio says as much about investors' beliefs about the future of a company as it does about present performance (Higgins, 2009).

CONCLUSION

The ability to examine, understand, and calculate financial statements and financial ratios is vital for a financial manager in the sport industry—or any industry, for that matter. Financial statements are comparable to box scores or statistical data that the manager/coach or general manager must be able to read and comprehend in order to understand the performance of players and the team. Financial ratios are analytical tools that help managers evaluate statistical data, just as a calculation tool such as earned run average or slugging percentage helps a baseball executive, or a quarterback's passer rating would help a football executive. This chapter discussed several categories of financial ratios and provided two important examples for each category. Remember that these represent just a few important and commonly used financial ratios, and many more are available to help you analyze companies' performance. Bear in mind that financial ratios should not be examined in isolation, but rather must be compared to the company's own historical data and to competitors' ratios. These provide the context necessary for understanding a company's performance and condition.

CONCEPT *check*

1. What are the three major sections of the balance sheet? Provide at least one example of items that would be found in each of those sections.
2. What is the primary difference between an income statement and a statement of cash flows?
3. What is the purpose of computing financial ratios?
4. If an organization's current ratio value is below 1.00, what might that suggest about the organization?
5. What information do leverage ratios provide?
6. Why is the price-to-earnings ratio so widely used among investors?
7. This chapter repeatedly states that financial ratios are most valuable when viewed in comparison to the organization's historical ratio values and competitors' values. Why is this context valuable when examining financial ratio values?

PRACTICE *problem*

Exhibits 2.7 and 2.8 show a Nike balance sheet and income statement. For the purposes of this problem and the case analysis that follows, use the data for 2009 to compute the ten financial ratios discussed in this chapter for Nike. For the financial ratios using stock data, use Nike's Class B common stock and a price per share of $57.05.

MAY 31,	2009 (IN MILLIONS)	2008 (IN MILLIONS)
ASSETS		
Current assets		
Cash and equivalents	$ 2,291.1	$ 2,133.9
Short-term investments	1,164.0	642.2
Accounts receivable, net	2,883.9	2,795.3
Inventories	2,357.0	2,438.4
Deferred income taxes	272.4	227.2
Prepaid expenses and other current assets	765.6	602.3
Total current assets	$ 9,734.0	$ 8,839.3
Property, plant, and equipment, net	$ 1,957.7	$ 1,891.1
Identifiable intangible assets, net	467.4	743.1
Goodwill	193.5	448.8
Deferred income taxes and other assets	897.0	520.4
Total assets	$13,249.6	$12,442.7
LIABILITIES AND SHAREHOLDERS' EQUITY		
Current liabilities		
Current portion of long-term debt	$32.0	$6.3
Notes payable	342.9	177.7
Accounts payable	1,031.9	1,287.6
Accrued liabilities	1,783.9	1,761.9
Income taxes payable	86.3	88.0
Total current liabilities	$ 3,277.0	$ 3,321.5
Long-term debt	$ 437.2	$ 441.1
Deferred income taxes and other liabilities	842.0	854.5
Commitments and contingencies	—	—
Redeemable Preferred Stock	0.3	0.3
Shareholders' equity		
Common stock at stated value		
Class A convertible—95.3 and 96.8 shares outstanding	0.1	0.1
Class B—390.2 and 394.3 shares outstanding	2.7	2.7
Capital in excess of stated value	2,871.4	2,497.8
Accumulated other comprehensive income	367.5	251.4
Retained earnings	5,451.4	5,073.3
Total shareholders' equity	$ 8,693.1	$ 7,825.3
Total liabilities and shareholders' equity	$13,249.6	$12,442.7

| exhibit | 2.8 | Nike, Inc. consolidated income statements. |

YEAR ENDED MAY 31,	(IN MILLIONS, EXCEPT PER SHARE DATA)		
	2009	2008	2007
Revenues	$19,176.1	$18,627.0	$16,325.9
Cost of sales	10,571.7	10,239.6	9,165.4
Gross margin	$ 8,604.4	8,387.4	7,160.5
Selling and administrative expense	6,149.6	5,953.7	5,028.7
Restructuring charges	195.0	—	—
Goodwill impairment	199.3	—	—
Intangible and other asset impairment	202.0	—	—
Interest income, net	(9.5)	(77.1)	(67.2)
Other (income) expense, net	(88.5)	7.9	(0.9)
Income before income taxes	$ 1,956.5	$ 2,502.9	$ 2,199.9
Income taxes	469.8	619.5	708.4
Net income	$ 1,486.7	$ 1,883.4	$ 1,491.5
Basic earnings per common share	3.1	3.8	3.0
Diluted earnings per common share	3.0	3.7	2.9
Dividends declared per common share	1.0	0.9	0.7

CASE analysis   *A Financial Analysis Comparison of Nike and Under Armour*

According to the Sporting Goods Manufacturers Association (2009), sporting goods in the United States was a $66 billion industry in 2008. Within the industry, sports apparel was the largest subcategory, generating $29 billion in 2008. Under Armour is an emerging competitor in the sports apparel category, in which Nike has long been recognized as the leader. Using the financial ratios for Nike that you computed in the Practice Problem and the financial ratios for Under Armour provided throughout this chapter, compare the financial health of Nike and Under Armour by answering the questions below.

CASE QUESTIONS

1. In what ratio areas is Nike stronger than Under Armour?
2. In what ratio areas is Under Armour stronger than Nike?
3. If you were an investor considering purchasing stock in either Nike or Under Armour, which company would you choose? Explain and support your answer.

references

Green Bay Packers financial data. (n.d.) Retrieved from http://www.joe.bowman.net.

Harrington, D.R. (2003). *Corporate financial analysis in a global environment* (7th ed.). Cincinnati: South-Western College Publishing.

Helfert, E.A. (2002). *Techniques of financial analysis: A guide to value creation* (11th ed.). New York: McGraw-Hill/Irwin.

Higgins, R.C. (2009). *Analysis for financial management* (9th ed.). New York: McGraw-Hill/Irwin.

Shapiro, A.C., & Balbirer, S.D. (2000). *Modern corporate finance: A multidisciplinary approach to value creation.* Upper Saddle River, NJ: Prentice-Hall.

Sporting Goods Manufacturers Association. (2009, April 2). Sporting goods down 3.2% in 2008, but industry outperforms national consumer durable goods GDP [Press Release]. Retrieved from www.sgma.com.

Under Armour financial data. (n.d.) Retrieved from http://www.uabiz.com.

Risk

3

Introduction

Risk is often overlooked in sport management. It affects many areas of finance, including the rate of interest, bond rates, estimates of cash flows, the cost of capital, and capital structure. A good understanding of risk will greatly assist with financial analysis, as well. **Risk** is a measure of the uncertainty of returns or uncertainty about future conditions that may affect the value of money. As this definition suggests, there is a relationship between risk and return. As Groppelli and Nikbakht (2000) note, the return on one's money or investment should be proportional to the risk involved with the investment. The measurement of risk is, therefore, paramount for prudent financial management.

Unfortunately, little has been written about financial risk in sport. Perhaps this is due to the general feeling that the business of sport, especially professional sport, is recession proof. In a *Wall Street Journal* article, Last (2009) asked, "Are pro sports too big to fail?" (p. W11). As the U.S. economy slowed in 2008, some in sport declared that the industry was indeed recession proof. In general, the belief was that during periods of economic uncertainty people turn to sport to escape the economic realities of life. Last probed this idea in his *Wall Street Journal* article. He noted that the pro-sports bubble might be about to burst and that the industry's 90-year boom could be over.

Beginning with the idea that the weak in a struggling economy go out of business first, Last noted that minor professional sports have shown signs that the economic slowdown is having a significant impact. The Arena Football League, in existence since 1987, canceled its 2009 season. The LPGA tour eliminated three tour events and cut $5 million in prize money, and the WNBA saw the Houston Comets, its premier franchise, cease operations. However, major professional sport leagues show some signs of strength. Television ratings for NFL regular season games were strong in 2008. During the 2009 off-season, the top three free agents in professional baseball signed for a combined $423 million. This was a 7.1% increase from 2008. Professional baseball attendance in 2008 was only slightly below its all-time high of 79.5 million in 2007. Although teams and leagues laid off employees in 2008 and 2009, and some NFL teams struggled to sell out playoff games in January 2009, teams continue to build new stadia and fans continue to pay more for parking, concessions, and tickets.

So, what is the risk? Has professional sport grown so large that its bubble, like the dot com bubble and the housing bubble, will soon burst? Or is sport affected by recession as any other industry would be affected? How does risk affect the financial management of sport teams, leagues, and properties? This chapter discusses risk and how concepts related to risk apply in sport.

RELATIONSHIP BETWEEN RATE OF RETURN AND RISK

 hen a sport organization makes an investment, it expects that the money invested today will earn more in the future. The gain or loss of an investment over a period of time is the **rate of return.** Measuring return allows the organization to know the financial performance of its investment. We can measure the return on any type of investment—from an investment in a new player to the investment in a stadium renovation. The easiest way to measure the return of an investment is in dollar terms. **Dollar return** is simply the result of subtracting the amount invested from the amount received:

dollar return = amount received − amount invested

However, this method of measuring return is problematic. First, the size or scale of the investment is important. Without knowing the size of the investment, we cannot meaningfully evaluate the sufficiency of the return. Second, the timing of the return is important (see the discussion of time value of money in Chapter 4). Hence, the preferred method is to calculate a measure called the *rate of return,* or *percentage return,* rather than dollar return. Rate of return corrects for differences in the scale of investments, and, when calculated on an annual basis, it also solves the timing problem. Rate of return is calculated as follows:

$$\text{rate of return} = \frac{\text{amount received} - \text{amount invested}}{\text{amount invested}}$$

This formula standardizes the investment's return by measuring the return per investment unit.

In a more technical definition, risk measures the volatility of rates of return (Groppelli & Nikbakht). When investing in a new facility, for example, the organization should forecast the expected cash flows, or return, of the new project and how those cash flows will impact the organization's overall finances. Obviously, those forecasts could turn out to be wrong, because investments do not always return what we expect. The less certain we are that an investment will return what we expect, the higher the rate of return we demand will be, in order to compensate for the risk. As risk increases for the stadium project, the rate of return required to invest in that project also increases. Exhibit 3.1 illustrates this relationship.

Relationship between risk and return.   **exhibit**   **3.1**

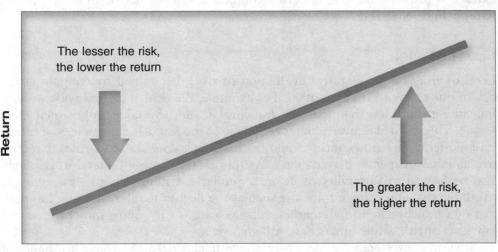

Volatility is the amount of fluctuation that occurs in a series of similar investment returns and the degree to which those returns deviate from the average. More volatility translates into greater risk.

Time is a factor in risk. Cash today is worth more to an investor than the same cash in the future, because the future is uncertain (see Sidebar 3.A). When money is invested, there is always uncertainty as to whether the investment will be repaid. Similarly, when a bank lends money, it takes the risk that the loan may not be repaid. The investor or lender must be compensated for risking today's cash, or it will lack incentive to make the investment or loan. For example, if a friend asks you to lend him money to help finance the purchase of a minor league baseball franchise, you might decide to lend him $1 million in cash. You are giving up the safety of having that $1 million in cash today in exchange for an uncertain future return. For example, the franchise might lose money and your friend might not be able to repay your investment. As a result, you might ask that the $1 million be paid back one year from now, along with an additional $70,000 return for your $1 million investment. The rate of return would be 7%, which is the $70,000 additional return divided by the initial investment amount of $1 million. To convince you to give up the safety of your $1 million cash, your friend will have to pay an additional $70,000, due to the risk associated with the future return of your money. The financial principle underlying the request for an additional $70,000 is that there is more risk in the future than the present. There is also more risk in larger investments, all else being equal. If you were asked to invest $2 million, your risk increases and you likely would ask for a return greater than 7%. The rate of return required increases as risk increases.

MEASURING RISK

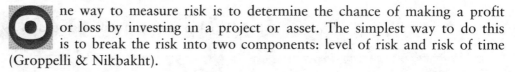ne way to measure risk is to determine the chance of making a profit or loss by investing in a project or asset. The simplest way to do this is to break the risk into two components: level of risk and risk of time (Groppelli & Nikbakht).

Level of Risk

Level of risk is a comparative evaluation of risk, determined by comparing the risk of one asset or firm to another. For example, the risk associated with an NFL franchise is much less than that of a franchise in another major professional sport league. This is true because a high percentage of the league's income is guaranteed via long-term television contracts and because the league has strict rules that control its largest expense, player salary. As this example suggests, level of risk may also be viewed as variability of income. Similarly, within a league, for example MLB, the risk of owning a franchise such as the Boston Red Sox is much less than that of a franchise in a small market, such as Kansas City. Some franchises have a low level of risk, while others have a high level.

Risk-free investments are short-term investments deemed to have no chance of loss. For example, U.S. treasury bills have a 90-day maturity and are backed by the federal government's guarantee to pay. The **risk-free rate** is the interest paid on

Risk and Deferred Compensation

SIDEBAR

T oday's dollar is worth more than tomorrow's. In professional sport, risk affects players as they negotiate salary, especially when deferred compensation is part of the negotiation. *Deferred compensation,* or deferred salary, is salary whose payment is delayed under contractual terms. In the National Football League, teams structure contracts with deferred compensation due to strict salary cap rules that limit the amount a team can spend on player payroll in a given season. In other leagues, teams sometimes take a buy now, pay later approach and use deferred salaries to do so. One of these teams, the Arizona Diamondbacks, nearly went bankrupt as a result. According to Birger (2009), the Diamondbacks almost became the first team to win a major sports championship one year and declare bankruptcy the next. Financial problems arose because the team overspent on free agents. Over its first seven years of operation, the Diamondbacks lost $353 million. Due to resulting cash flow shortages, the team's management convinced free agents to accept contracts with large, backloaded deferred salary payments. In 2009, the team still owed $58 million to players who were no longer with the organization. Agent David Falk has referred to deferred salary as "funny money" (Conrad, 2006). The deferred portion of a player's contract is not always guaranteed (especially in the NFL).

Even if deferred salary is guaranteed, if a team declares bankruptcy a player may never be paid in full. Mario Lemieux, a player for the NHL's Pittsburgh Penguins, knows this well.

3.A

On October 13, 1998, the Pittsburgh Penguins filed Chapter 11 bankruptcy. As a result, 200 individuals and businesses became unsecured creditors (Anderson, 2005).

At the time the Penguins declared bankruptcy, they owed $114.3 million. Of that amount, $55.2 million was secured debt (e.g., money owed to banks) and $1.4 million was priority debt (e.g., money owed to the IRS). The unsecured debt was $57.7 million, and the three largest unsecured creditors were Lemieux, Fox Sports Net, and SMG (Anderson). Under U.S. bankruptcy law, unsecured creditors are paid last, and they often receive less than 50% of what is owed. As a major creditor (Lemieux held over half of team's unsecured debt), Lemieux had a large incentive to find a way to salvage the $32.5 million in deferred compensation owed to him (Sandomir, 1999). Four plans were presented to the bankruptcy judge. The unsecured creditors committee backed Lemieux's plan, under which Lemieux offered to forgive $7.5 million of debt owed to him and transfer another $20 million of debt into equity, so that only $5 million of his claim remained. The court approved Lemieux's plan on June 24, 1999 (Anderson). Although Lemieux received only $5 million of the deferred salary owed to him (15.4% of the original amount owed), he also received controlling interest in the Penguins. Lemieux became one of only a few former players to own a major league team (Sandomir). Ten other players were unsecured creditors at the time of the bankruptcy filing, as well. Combined, they were owed $7.4 million (Anderson).

risk-free investments that provide a guaranteed return. (**Interest** is the cost of borrowing money.) As the level of risk increases above zero, the risk-free rate increases by a **risk premium,** the difference between rate of return for the risky investment and the risk-free rate. Therefore, total risk includes the risk-free rate plus a risk premium, or

total risk = risk-free rate + risk premium

Exhibit 3.2 lists differences in rates of return for bonds based on their level of risk. (For a discussion of bonds, see Chapter 7.) As all the bonds in this example are 30-year bonds, the difference in interest rates is due to the bonds' level of risk. The 30-year U.S. Treasury bond yields less than the 30-year AAA rated-corporate bond because less risk is associated with investing in U.S. Treasury bonds. Investors will seek a risk premium, here 1.307%, for AAA-rated corporate bonds because they carry a greater risk than do U.S. Treasury bonds.

| **exhibit** | **3.2** | Risk premiums and level of risk. |

TYPE	RISK-FREE RATE	TIME RISK PREMIUM	LEVEL OF RISK PREMIUM	INTEREST RATE
30-year U.S. Treasury bonds	0.180%	4.123%	0.000%	4.303%
30-year municipal bonds (AAA insured)	0.180%	4.123%	0.547%	4.850%
30-year municipal bonds (AA)	0.180%	4.123%	1.047%	5.350%
30-year corporate bonds (AAA)	0.180%	4.123%	1.307%	5.610%

Note: Rates as of June/July 2009.

The risk associated with owning a sport franchise affects the franchise's cost of borrowing money. Those with lower risk have a lower discount rate or required rate of return; that is, they pay lower rates to borrow money. Therefore, the return for the low-risk franchise will receive a better valuation in the marketplace than the same return generated by a high-risk franchise. In essence, the market rate reflects the chance that the investors will receive their money back. An investment in a large-market Major League Baseball team is more likely to be paid back than an investment in a small-market team, so the large-market team equates to a lower return. Investments in NFL franchises are less risky than investments in franchises in other major sporting leagues. Hence, NFL franchises find it easier and less expensive to borrow money.

The impact of a franchise's level of risk on its ability to borrow was clear during the recent credit market meltdown. From September 2008 through May 2009, only teams in large markets or with strong brands were able to execute debt deals. Franchises able to acquire or extend debt included the Pittsburgh Steelers, New York Yankees, and Dallas Cowboys. In May 2009, the Orlando Magic became the first mid-tier team to receive a loan in nine months, a $100 million loan from Goldman Sachs. The team, however, is paying a high rate for the loan—450 interest points over LIBOR. (**LIBOR**, the **London Interbank Offered Rate,** is a benchmark interest rate based on the rate that banks in the London interbank market pay to borrow unsecured funds from each other.) Prior to the credit market freeze in 2008, the Magic likely would have had to pay only 200 interest points over LIBOR (Kaplan & Lombardo, 2009).

Risk of Time

The second component of risk is the **risk of time,** the fact that risk increases as the length of time funds are invested increases (Groppelli & Nikbakht). Exhibit 3.3 illustrates the impact of time on risk. In this table, the risk-free rate is 0.18%, which was the auction rate of 90-day Treasury bills on July 13, 2009. As all of the securities in the table are issued by the federal government, the differences in interest rate, which reflects total risk, are attributable to the risk of time. As the length of time between issue date and maturity date increases, the risk premium increases. This increase reflects the risk of time.

| The impact of time on risk. | **exhibit** | **3.3** |

TYPE	RISK-FREE RATE	RISK PREMIUM	INTEREST RATE
90-day Treasury bills	0.180%	0.000%	0.180%
52-week Treasury bills	0.180%	0.365%	0.545%
2-year government notes	0.180%	0.971%	1.151%
5-year government notes	0.180%	2.520%	2.700%
10-year government notes	0.180%	3.185%	3.365%
30-year government bonds	0.180%	4.123%	4.303%

Note: Rates as of June/July 2009.

DETERMINANTS OF INTEREST RATES

The interest rate on a given debt security, called the **nominal interest rate,** consists of the real risk-free rate of interest plus multiple risk premiums. These include risk premiums based on the risk of time and the level of risk, which reflect the riskiness of the security itself, and premiums reflecting **inflation** (the devaluation of money over time) and liquidity (the marketability of the security—how quickly it can be turned into cash). (These premiums are defined and discussed below.) The nominal interest rate, or quoted interest rate, on a marketable security is expressed as:

nominal interest rate = $k = k^* + \text{IP} + \text{DRP} + \text{LP} + \text{MRP}$

where k^* = real risk-free rate of interest,
   IP = inflation premium,
  DRP = default risk premium,
   LP = liquidity premium, and
  MRP = maturity risk premium.

The **real risk-free rate** of interest, k^*, is the rate of interest on a riskless security if inflation were not expected. It can also be viewed as the rate of interest on a short-term U.S. Treasury bill in an inflation-free environment. In Exhibit 3.3, the real risk-free rate is 0.18%. The **nominal,** or quoted, **risk-free rate** of interest, k_{RF}, on a security such as a U.S. Treasury bill is the real-risk free rate (k^*) plus an inflation premium (IP). Therefore,

nominal risk-free rate = $k_{\text{RF}} = k^* + \text{IP}$

The **inflation premium (IP)** is the portion of an investment's return that compensates the investor for loss of purchasing power over time. We calculate it by determining the expected average inflation rate over the life of the security. (See Chapter 4.)

To account for the risk that a borrower might default, a **default risk premium (DRP)** is added to the nominal interest rate. If the borrower defaults, the investor will receive less than the promised return. The default risk of U.S. Treasuries is zero, so Treasuries have no default risk premium. As the riskiness of the borrower increases, the default risk increases. The greater the default risk, the higher the default risk premium and the higher the interest rate. (This concept is similar to the level of risk discussed earlier and illustrated in Exhibit 3.2.)

The terms of a bond contract and the financial strength of the entity issuing the bonds are factors in default risk. Moody's Investor Service, Fitch Ratings, and Standard and Poor's Corporation (S&P) all assign quality ratings to bond issues. These ratings measure the likelihood that the bond will go into default. The highest ratings are Aaa (Moody's) and AAA (Fitch and S&P). These bonds are very safe, with little default risk. Exhibit 3.4 provides an overview of the bond ratings used by the three agencies.

Another premium included in the nominal interest rate is the **liquidity premium (LP)**, also referred to as the marketability premium. It is added for securities that are not liquid. A security is considered liquid if it can be sold in a short amount of time at a reasonable price.

Because an increase or decrease in interest rates affects the value of outstanding securities, the **maturity risk premium (MRP)** accounts for the risk of a change in the value of a security due to changes in interest rates. **Interest rate risk** is the risk that interest rates will increase, causing a decline in the value of the security. Increases in interest rates affect long-term securities more than short-term securities, so interest rate risk is higher for long-term securities. Hence, the maturity risk premium increases as the security's yield to maturity increases.

Declining interest rates also pose a risk, called **reinvestment rate risk.** This primarily affects short-term bills, increasing as the maturity of the bill decreases.

---

exhibit   3.4   **Guide to bond ratings.**

| | AGENCY | | |
FITCH	S&P	MOODY'S	RISK
AAA	AAA	Aaa	Highest credit quality, with smallest degree of risk
AA	AA	Aa	Very high credit quality and very low credit risk
A	A	A	High credit quality and low credit risk; economic situation can impact risk
BBB	BBB	Baa	Good credit quality, with moderate credit risk
BB	BB	Ba	Speculative, with questionable credit quality
B	B	B	Highly speculative, with high credit risk
CCC	CCC	Caa	Substantial credit risk, with poor credit quality
CC	CC	Ca	Very high level of credit risk, usually in default on deposit obligations
C	C	C	Exceptionally high level of credit risk, typically in default, with low potential recovery values

This risk reflects the fact that the investor may lose income if at the time the funds are reinvested the interest rate on the bonds has gone down.

If the real risk-free rate of interest and the risk premiums are known, we can calculate the nominal interest rate. As previously discussed, the nominal interest rate on a marketable security is:

nominal interest rate = $k = k^* + IP + DRP + LP + MRP$

To calculate the nominal interest rate (k) for a five-year U.S. Treasury bond, we add the real risk-free rate of interest (k^*), inflation premium (IP), default risk premium (DRP), liquidity premium (LP), and maturity risk premium (MRP). Treasury securities have essentially no default or liquidity risk, so DRP = 0 and LP = 0. Hence, for a Treasury bond with $k^* = 0.5\%$, IP = 3.4%, and MRP = 0.2%,

$$k = k^* + IP + DRP + LP + MRP$$
$$= 0.5\% + 3.4\% + 0 + 0 + 0.2\%$$
$$= 4.1\%$$

The nominal interest rate for this five-year U.S. Treasury bond is 4.1%.

RISK AND INVESTMENT RETURNS

Investment risk measures the likelihood of low or negative future returns. As the chance for a low or negative investment return increases, the riskiness of the investment increases. Typically, investment risk focuses on the future performance of a company's stock, so this concept applies directly to publicly traded companies. In North America, the Green Bay Packers are the only publicly traded major league team. Collegiate sport teams are subsets of larger governmental or non-profit educational entities and, therefore, are not publicly traded. In major professional sports, International Speedway Corporation (ISCA) and Speedway Motorsports Inc. (TRK), both affiliated with NASCAR and its major tracks, are publicly traded. In addition, the major sporting goods manufacturers are publicly traded. However, the concept of investment risk can be applied beyond publicly traded companies, especially in consideration of stand-alone risk.

Stand-Alone Return and Risk

One approach to analyzing investment return and risk is to consider the investor's risk as if only one asset were held. This is **stand-alone risk.** When analyzing the investment, we examine the stand-alone expected rate of return and stand-alone risk in isolation from other investments.

Calculating stand-alone expected rate of return

A potential investor who is considering buying a professional sports franchise, for example, should not invest unless the expected rate of return is high enough to compensate for the perceived risk of the investment. According to data from *Forbes*, the average value of an NFL franchise increased 8.6% in 2008, 6.9% in 2007, and 9.6% in 2006. The three-year average increase was 8.4%. During this time, the St. Louis Rams were rumored to be for sale after the death of long-time owner Georgia Frontiere. The three-year average increase in the Rams' value from 2006 to 2008 was 7.0%. Since the expected rate of return was 1.4% less than the league's average increase, a potential investor might be hesitant to purchase the franchise. The potential investor might attempt to purchase the franchise at a discount as compared to the average price of an NFL franchise. Because investment risk, or the uncertainty of future cash flows, is a component of value, a lower team value may reflect greater risk.

This example provided a simple analysis of expected rate of return. A more thorough analysis involves evaluating probabilities. A **probability distribution** is a list of all possible outcomes (projected returns) of an investment, with a probability assigned to each outcome. The sum of all probabilities must equal 1.0. Exhibit 3.5 lists the probabilities of investment returns in two NFL franchises. The **expected rate of return** for an investment is the sum of each possible outcome multiplied by its probability. For Franchise X, the expected rate of return of $142.8 million is the sum of the three probable returns. Each *probable return* is the product of the projected return and the probability of that outcome occurring. The expected rate of return for Franchise Y, $139.5 million, was calculated in the same way. Mathematically, the expected rate of return ($\hat{k}$) is expressed as

$$\text{expected rate of return} = \hat{k} = \sum_{i=1}^{n} P_i k_i$$

where i is a specific occurrence,*

n is the number of occurrences,*

P_i is the probability of occurrence, and

k_i is the possible outcome.

* i and n, as part of summation, will not be defined in subsequent formuli.

For NFL Franchise X, the investor estimates a 35% chance of a low return of $134.5 million, a 50% chance of an average return of $142.4 million, and a 15%

---

exhibit   3.5   Projected returns and probabilities for two franchise investments (millions).

PROBABLE OUTCOME	PROJECTED RETURN *(k)*	WEIGHT OR PROBABILITY *(P)*	PROBABLE RETURN *(P × k)*
NFL Franchise X			
Low	$134.5	0.35	$47.08
Average	$142.4	0.50	$71.20
High	$163.5	0.15	$24.53
Expected rate of return			$142.80
NFL Franchise Y			
Low	$119.0	0.20	$23.80
Average	$134.5	0.40	$53.80
High	$154.7	0.40	$61.87
Expected rate of return			$139.47

chance of a high return of $163.5 million (see Exhibit 3.5). The expected rate of return for Franchise X is calculated as follows:

$$\hat{k}_{\text{Franchise X}} = \sum_{i=1}^{n} P_i k_i$$
$$= .35(\$134.5) + .5(\$142.4) + .15(\$163.5)$$
$$= \$142.8 \text{ million}$$

Note that the return that is actually earned during a given period of time is the *realized rate of return* ($\bar{k}$). The realized rate of return usually differs from the expected rate of return.

When the number of possible outcomes is practically unlimited, we use a continuous probability distribution to calculate the expected rate of return. The **standard deviation (SD,** denoted by σ) is a measure of variability in a distribution of numbers and, in the case of an investment, indicates the riskiness of the investment. A lower-risk investment will take the form of a tighter, or more peaked, distribution. Investments with probability distributions that have wider dispersion from the expected value are riskier. In Exhibit 3.6, the distribution with the tallest peak is the one with the lowest standard deviation (σ = 0.3) and the lowest risk.

The standard deviation of a probability distribution is calculated as follows:

$$\text{standard deviation} = \sigma = \sqrt{\sum_{i=1}^{n} (k_i - \hat{k})^2 P_i}$$

where k_i is the outcome of a specific occurrence,
$\hat{k}$ is the expected return, and
P_i is the probability of the return.

Continuous probability distributions. **exhibit** **3.6**

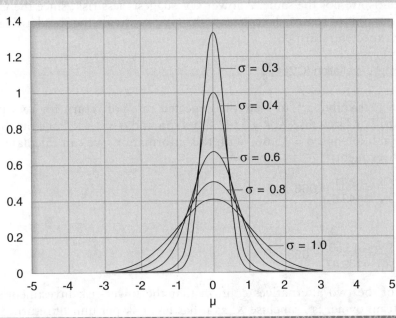

σ = standard deviation
μ = mean

We calculate the standard deviation of the investment in Franchise X as follows:

1. Find the expected rate of return ($\hat{k}$) from the previous calculation:

   $\hat{k}_{\text{Franchise X}}$ = \$142.8 million

2. Subtract the expected rate of return ($\hat{k}_{\text{Franchise X}}$) from each possible outcome (k_i) to obtain a list of deviations (see Exhibit 3.5 for each possible outcome for Franchise X):

   Deviation$_i$ = $k_i - \hat{k}_{\text{Franchise X}}$
   Deviation$_1$ = $(134.5 - 142.8) = -8.3$
   Deviation$_2$ = $(142.4 - 142.8) = -0.4$
   Deviation$_3$ = $(163.5 - 142.8) = 20.7$

3. Calculate the variance (σ^2) of the probability distribution. To do this, sum the squares of each deviation multiplied by the probability of its corresponding outcome:

   $$\sigma^2 = .35(-8.3)^2 + .5(-0.4)^2 + .15(20.7)^2$$
   $$= 24.11 + 0.08 + 64.27$$
   $$= 88.46$$

4. Take the square root of the variance:

   $$\sigma = \sqrt{88.46} = 9.41$$

Calculating stand-alone risk

The **coefficient of variation (CV)** measures the stand-alone risk of an investment. It is useful when we are comparing the expected returns on two alternative projects whose returns are not the same. A lower CV suggests less risk, since the CV indicates risk per unit of return. To calculate the CV, we divide the standard deviation (σ) by the expected return ($\hat{k}$):

$$\text{coefficient of variation (CV)} = \frac{\sigma}{\hat{k}}$$

Return to Exhibit 3.5 to view the expected rates of return for two possible investments. For Franchise X, $\hat{k}$ = \$142.8 million and σ = 9.41. For Franchise Y, $\hat{k}$ = \$139.47 million and σ = 13.66. With this information, we can calculate the CV for each investment:

$$CV_X = \frac{\sigma_X}{\hat{k}_X} = \frac{9.41}{142.8} = .066$$

and

$$CV_Y = \frac{\sigma_Y}{\hat{k}_Y} = \frac{13.66}{139.47} = .098$$

The CVs of the two alternatives confirm that the lower-risk investment for the potential team owner is Franchise X, as it has less risk per unit of return.

When presented with two alternatives for investment that have the same expected rate of return, most investors will select the investment with the lower risk. Investors tend to be **risk averse:** when presented with two investment alternatives with the same expected rate of return, most investors will select the alternative with the lower risk. Hence, most investors will seek a higher rate of return for riskier investments and require a risk premium.

Portfolio Return and Risk

By holding more than one asset, an investor can eliminate some of the risk inherent in the individual assets. Hence, most financial assets are held in **portfolios**—combinations of assets held by individual investors—and investors are concerned with portfolio return and portfolio risk.

An investor chooses assets with the goal of maximizing the return of the overall portfolio while minimizing overall risk. To do so, the investor examines both the expected rate of return and risk of each individual asset and the degree to which each asset affects the rate of return and risk for the entire portfolio.

Calculating portfolio expected rate of return

To calculate the **expected return on a portfolio** $(\hat{k}_p)$, we sum the weighted average of the expected returns of each asset:

$$\text{expected return on a portfolio} = \hat{k}_p = \sum_{i=1}^{n} w_i \hat{k}_i$$

where w_i is the weight (percentage) of the total portfolio invested in an individual asset, and

$\hat{k}_i$ is the expected rate of return of the asset.

For example, suppose Portfolio 1 is valued at $1 million, with $200,000 invested in each of five companies. The following returns can be expected for the stocks held in Portfolio 1:

STOCK	$\hat{k}$
Company A	10.0%
Company B	9.5%
Company C	11.5%
Company D	3.5%
Company E	6.0%

To calculate the expected return on Portfolio 1, we proceed as follows:

$$\text{expected return on a portfolio} = \hat{k}_p = \sum_{i=1}^{n} w_i \hat{k}_i$$
$$= w_1 \hat{k}_1 + w_2 \hat{k}_2 + \ldots + w_n \hat{k}_n$$
$$= 0.2(10.0\%) + 0.2(9.5\%) + 0.2(11.5\%) + 0.2(3.5\%) + 0.2(6.0\%)$$
$$= 8.1\%$$

If the owner of Portfolio 1 decided to invest in the Rams, with an average annual return of 7.0%, the expected return of the portfolio would decrease. Suppose the portfolio's owner purchased $1,000,000 of the Rams. The portfolio now would be as follows:

PORTFOLIO A:

STOCK	$\hat{k}$
Company A	10.0%
Company B	9.5%
Company C	11.5%
Company D	3.5%
Company E	6.0%
Rams	7.0%

The total value of the portfolio would now be $2 million, with $200,000 invested in each of companies A through E and $1 million invested in the Rams. Each of assets A through E makes up 10% of Portfolio 1 and has a weight of 0.1. The investment in the Rams has a weight of 0.5. Now,

$$\hat{k}_p = w_1\hat{k}_1 + w_2\hat{k}_2 + \ldots + w_n\hat{k}_n$$
$$= 0.1(10.0\%) + 0.1(9.5\%) + 0.1(11.5\%) + 0.1(3.5\%) + 0.1(6.0\%) + 0.5(7.0\%)$$
$$= 7.55\%$$

Calculating portfolio risk

Calculating a portfolio's risk (σ_p) is not as simple as computing the weighted average of the individual assets' standard deviations. The portfolio risk is actually smaller than the weighted average of the individual assets' standard deviations—this is why portfolios are so attractive to investors. A portfolio's risk depends not just on the standard deviations of the individual assets' risks but also on the correlation (degree of relationship) between those risks. If securities are added to a portfolio that have low standard deviations but that have the same patterns of movement and dispersion around the expected rate of return as the assets already held in the portfolio, the risk of the portfolio will remain unchanged.

The **correlation coefficient** (r) measures the degree of the relationship between two variables. In portfolio analysis, the correlation coefficient measures how closely the returns of an asset move relative to the returns of the other assets held in the portfolio. The measure ranges from +1.0, where the two variables move in the exact same way, to −1.0, where the two variables move exactly opposite to each other. When there is no correlation between the variables, r = 0.0. Typically, the correlation between assets in a portfolio is positive but less than +1.0.

Correlations reflect the degree to which *two* assets change together. A correlation cannot be calculated for an entire portfolio. We can, however, calculate multiple correlations between various combinations held within a portfolio. More usually, when we analyze a portfolio, we select one individual asset to be represented by one variable, with the rest of the portfolio represented by the second variable.

A general rule on diversification states that as an investor adds assets to a portfolio, the riskiness of the portfolio decreases, as long as the assets are not perfectly positively correlated. If the assets already in the portfolio are highly correlated, diversifying the portfolio does little to reduce its risk if the new asset is perfectly positively correlated with the existing portfolio. By adding assets that are not perfectly correlated to the existing portfolio mix, the investor can eliminate some but not all risk. A truly riskless portfolio does not exist.

The correlation coefficient of two assets is calculated as follows:

$$\text{correlation coefficient of two assets} = r_{x,y} = \frac{\sum\limits_{i=1}^{n} \dfrac{\left(\overline{k}_{x,i} - \hat{k}_{x,i}\right)\left(\overline{k}_{y,i} - \hat{k}_{y,i}\right)}{n}}{\sigma_x \sigma_y}$$

where $\hat{k}$ is the actual rate of return,

$\overline{k}$ is the expected rate of return, and

σ is the standard deviation.

The volatility $(\overline{k} - \hat{k})$ of the two assets (x,y) relative to each other is measured in the numerator. In the denominator, the product of the two assets' standard deviations standardizes the **covariance**—the degree to which the two variables change together—between the assets (Groppelli & Nikbakht). Because the covariance is standardized, the correlation coefficient helps find the assets that move differently than those already held in a portfolio. Groppelli and Nikbakht add that the equation can also be expressed as

$$\text{correlation coefficient of two assets} = r_{x,y} = \frac{\text{covariance } (x,y)}{\sigma_x \sigma_y}$$

Exhibit 3.7 illustrates the concept of covariance. The chart depicts the rates of return for Stocks X and Y over a five-year period. The two stocks represent a

The rates of return for Stocks X and Y over a five-year period. **exhibit** **3.7**

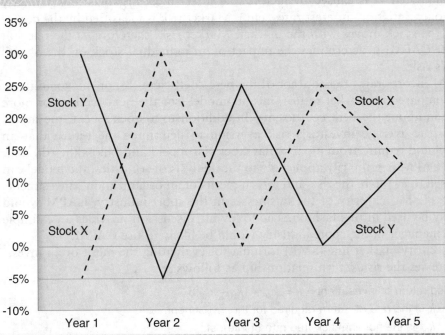

perfectly negative correlation ($r = -1.0$). When the rate of return rises for Stock X, Stock Y's return falls. When Stock Y's return rises, Stock X's return falls.

The key to building a portfolio that reduces overall risk is that it must not contain assets that are all highly positively correlated. Holding a well-diversified portfolio is less risky than holding a stock as a solitary asset, and holding two highly *negatively* correlated assets is less risky than holding a stock as a solitary asset. Brigham and Houston (2001) add that almost half of the riskiness of an individual stock can be eliminated if that stock is held in a well-diversified portfolio (one containing 40 or more stocks). Note, however, that a completely diversified portfolio will lose money if the whole market is in decline, as a diversified portfolio will move as the market moves.

Analyzing the relation between portfolio rate of return and portfolio risk

Capital asset pricing model. The **capital asset pricing model (CAPM)** provides a means to analyze the relationship between risk and rate of return. A stock or bond's **required rate of return** is the profit that an investor would require in order to consider the investment worth purchasing, given its riskiness. The CAPM is built on the notion that this required rate of return is equal to the risk-free rate of return plus a risk premium, with the risk reflecting the portfolio's diversification. Under this model, the **relevant risk** of a stock is its contribution to the riskiness of a diversified portfolio.

CAPM divides risk into two components: diversifiable risk and market risk. **Diversifiable risk** is the portion of a stock's risk that can be removed through a well-diversified portfolio. This type of risk is caused by events that are unique to the company issuing the stock. **Market risk** is the portion of a stock's risk that cannot be eliminated. It is caused by factors that affect most organizations similarly (the economy, inflation, interest rates, etc.). Market risk is measured by the degree to which the stock moves with the market. Market risk, therefore, is the relevant risk under CAPM. It determines the impact of an individual stock on the overall portfolio's risk.

CAPM incorporates the concept of the **beta coefficient** (ß), or the volatility of a stock compared to market return, into its model (see the next section for more information about the beta coefficient). In addition to a stock's beta, the model factors in the average investor's risk aversion to determine the return that an investor would require from a particular stock. Groppelli and Nikbakht add that, although CAPM is primarily applicable to the analysis of securities, the model can also be used to evaluate the risk and return merits of an organization's investments and assets. For a majority of the businesses in the sport industry, CAPM would most likely be used in this fashion. The following discussion provides an example of how a manager in the sport industry would be likely to use CAPM.

The **security market line (SML)** formula for evaluating the merit of an investment expresses the risk/return relationship as follows:

required return of investment = $k_i = k_{RF} + (k_M - k_{RF})ß$

where k_i is the rate of return required for the investment,

k_{RF} is the nominal risk-free rate of interest,

k_M is the expected average stock market return, and

ß is the beta of the firm's investments.

For example, to evaluate an investment in a new arena, the organization would first estimate the nominal risk-free rate (k_{RF}) based on U.S. Treasury securities. For an arena with a 30-year useful life, the nominal risk-free rate (k_{RF}), based on the interest rate of a 30-year U.S. Treasury bond, is currently 4.3% (see Exhibit 3.2). Next, it is necessary to calculate the beta (ß) of the organization's portfolio of assets. We will assume that this value is 1.3. Finally, the organization will estimate the market's expected rate of return (k_M). We will assume a value of 8.0%. This is the forecaster's best guess at how the market will perform, on average, over the next year, based on past performance. For example, the S&P 500 was 7% from 1950 through 2008. Using the SML equation, the required return on the investment in the facility is:

$$\text{required return on investment} = k_i = k_{RF} + (k_M - k_{RF})\text{ß}$$
$$= 4.3\% + (8.0\% - 4.3\%)1.3$$
$$= 4.3\% + 4.81\%$$
$$= 9.11\%$$

If the franchise can earn 9.11% on the equity capital—the money the firm is reinvesting in itself by investing in the arena—the owners of the team should be willing to invest in the new facility, based on its risk and return merits as evaluated under CAPM. Earnings would likely come from increased revenues generated by the new arena, especially from luxury suites, club seats, naming rights, and personal seating licenses.

Beta coefficient. As discussed above, CAPM incorporates the concept of beta (β). Beta reflects the degree to which a stock increases or decreases with the increase or decrease of the overall market. An average-risk stock is a stock that tends to move with the market. Such a stock has a beta of 1.0. A stock that is twice as volatile as the market will have beta of 2.0, and a stock that is half as volatile will have a beta of 0.5. As volatility increases, risk increases. Therefore, stocks with betas greater than 1.0 are riskier than the market, and those with betas less than 1.0 are less risky than the market. Beta is the most relevant measure of any stock's risk.

Betas for securities are available from sources such as Bloomberg. Exhibit 3.8 lists the beta coefficients for the stock of 18 companies in the sport industry. The table reveals that the stock of most sport-related organizations has risk greater than the market (β > 1.0). This is especially true in motorsports and sporting goods retail. All listed motorsports-related stocks have betas greater than 1.0, and all but Foot Locker in the retail sector have betas greater than 1.0. Among the companies listed in the table, those in the sport and entertainment sector have the lowest risk, with betas well below 1.0.

The beta of a portfolio is the weighted average of the individual securitys' betas:

$$\text{Beta of portfolio} = \beta_p = \sum_{i=1}^{n} w_i \beta_i$$

where w_i is the weight of the ith security, and

β_i is the beta of the ith security.

exhibit	3.8	Beta coefficients for sport-related companies (July 2009).

	SYMBOL	BETA
Motorsports		
International Speedway Corp.	ISCA	1.16
Speedway Motorsports Inc.	TRK	1.28
Dover Motorsports Inc.	DVD	1.28
Sporting goods retail		
Dick's Sporting Goods	DKS	1.40
Hibbett Sports Inc.	HIBB	1.21
Foot Locker Inc.	FL	0.97
Finish Line Inc.	FINL	1.16
Zumiez Inc.	ZUMZ	1.22
Sporting goods manufacturers		
Nike Inc.	NKE	0.96
Under Armour Inc.	UA	1.17
K Swiss Inc.	KSWS	1.11
Callaway Golf Co.	DEL	1.13
Crocs Inc.	CROX	1.28
Columbia Sportswear Co.	COLM	0.91
Heelys Inc.	HLYS	0.69
Sport and entertainment organizations		
United States Basketball League Inc.	USBL.OB	0.55
International Fight League Inc.	IFLI	0.80
World Wrestling Entertainment Inc.	WWE	0.86

Source: Yahoo! Finance (http://finance.yahoo.com/).

For example, suppose an investor has a portfolio of three sport-related stocks:

COMPANY	BETA	WEIGHT
Speedway Motorsports	1.28	40%
Foot Locker	0.97	30%
Under Armour	1.17	30%

For this portfolio,

$$\beta_p = \sum_{i=1}^{n} w_i \beta_i$$
$$= w_1\beta_1 + w_2\beta_2 + w_3\beta_3$$
$$= .4(1.28) + .3(0.97) + .3(1.17)$$
$$= 1.154$$

The beta for this portfolio indicates that it has an above-average risk.

SOURCES OF RISK

Groppelli and Nikbakht (2000) discuss sources of risk that may affect an organization's returns. They divide risk into three categories: external business activity, industry and company risk, and global risk. Risk related to external business activity arises from current economic conditions, political developments, and inflation. Examples of industry and company risk include risks common to a particular industry, technological changes, and environmental and social concerns. Finally, the global sources of risk include changes to regulations regarding import and export activities, expropriation, and changes in exchange rates.

This section discusses how some of these risks, including current economic conditions, political developments, and global issues, affect sport.

Current Economic Conditions

One source of risk related to external business activity is current economic conditions. Although the sport industry was once considered recession proof, the recession that began in late 2007 did affect teams and leagues, as likely will future downturns. An economic slowdown, especially when coupled with troubles in the credit market, can have a major impact on financial management in sport.

Capital finance

As lending standards tighten in a credit crisis, the economy's impact on the bond market affects teams' and cities' capital financing endeavors. In 2008, for example, debt became more expensive as a result of the economic and banking crisis. During this time, the Arlington, Texas, city council sought to refinance a portion of the municipal bonds that it had used to finance part of the new Dallas Cowboys Stadium. The municipal bonds were initially issued in 2005 as **synthetic fixed-rate bonds,** bonds that have elements of both a fixed-rate bond and a variable-rate bond. Their interest rate ranged from 3% to 4%. The tightening credit market caused an increase in the interest rate during the spring of 2008, to 7%. Three months later, the rate climbed to 8%, and the rate peaked at 9% during the summer of 2008, resulting in a $500,000 monthly interest rate increase (Schrock, 2008). The city then sought to refinance the bonds at a fixed rate of approximately 6% ("Cowboys, City Council," 2008). In total, the city was seeking to refinance $164 million of the synthetic fixed-rate bonds.

After encountering difficulty refinancing, the city decided to attempt to refinance only a portion of the bonds. Arlington converted $104 million of the $164 million to a fixed rate of approximately 6%. The city also financed $10 million in closing costs, which included bond insurance and fees required to terminate the previous financing agreement. The remaining $60 million was left on the fluctuating rate. Due to the changes in the bond market, the debt service costs to the city increased by $44 million over the life of the issue (Ahles & Schrock, 2008).

At about the same time, Jerry Jones, the Dallas Cowboys' owner, announced that the team had refinanced $435 million worth of debt for the new Cowboys Stadium. The variable rates from the initial offering had fluctuated dramatically during the year, increasing the required bond payments and the cost of the overall project. This led the Cowboys to refinance at a fixed rate of 5% ("Cowboys Refinance $435M," 2008).

Both the city of Arlington and the team were affected by the risk associated with variable-rate bonds. The tightening credit market led to an increase in rates, raising the total cost to finance the project and affecting the operating budgets of the team and the city.

Auction-rate bonds, a common method of financing facility construction, can also be greatly negatively impacted by changes in the bond market. An **auction-rate bond** is a form of long-term debt that acts like short-term debt, in which interest rates are reset through auctions held no more than 35 days apart (Schnitzler, 2008). In 2007, the New York Giants sold seven series of bonds totaling $650 million. The March 24, 2008, auction failed to attract enough bidders. When there are not enough bidders for this type of bond, a penalty interest rate is calculated based on the terms of offer. The team was obliged to pay 22% interest on $53 million in bonds. Additionally, the team began paying 11.5% on the $70.85 million in bonds that were successfully auctioned that day. The Giants chose to redeem $100 million of the bonds ("NFL Giants Redeeming," 2008).

The State of Indiana financed the entire $700 million Lucas Oil Stadium with auction-rate bonds. As a result, like the Giants, the state was exposed to the risk of drastic changes in interest. Unlike the Giants, however, the maximum interest rate the state must pay is 15% (Schnitzler).

Operating budgets

In addition to affecting capital finance, an economic slowdown can also have an effect on operating budgets. In 2009, for example, MLB attendance was down 5% during the first six weeks of the season (Fisher, 2009). During this period, to keep fans coming to games, sport organizations resorted to discounting tickets and providing ticket promotions. These included two-for-one tickets, family nights, gas card deals, e-savers, dollar nights, college nights, and economic stimulus plans for fans (Fisher, 2008). With the combination of fewer fans coming to games and the fact that those who were attending were taking advantage of discounts and promotions, revenues from ticket sales were down for most clubs in 2009. Short-term advertising and sponsorship revenues also decreased. However, for professional teams and major college programs, long-term contracts with sponsors and media rights partners softened the full impact of the slowing economy.

Sport organization risk is reduced when revenues are guaranteed. Teams with a greater percentage of guaranteed income have less risk than those with lower percentages of guaranteed income. For many sport organizations, their most significant revenue comes from sources protected by long-term contracts ("Struggling Economy Likely," 2008). In 2009 the Southeastern Conference signed a long-term media rights deal with CBS and ESPN that significantly increased member school revenues, despite the slowdown in the economy and the struggle to sell season tickets that some schools faced. Similarly, the NBA had just completed the first year of an eight-year, $7.5 billion deal with ESPN, ABC, and Turner (Kaplan & Lombardo).

However, the timing of the expiration of long-term contracts does affect leagues. For example, in 2009, the PGA Tour lost five automotive title sponsors and was threatened with losing more. Thirteen of its events were sponsored by banks, investment firms, and credit card companies. As long as financial markets remain in turmoil, the PGA Tour and other sport organizations are vulnerable to losing sponsors. In the case of the PGA Tour, each sponsorship agreement was worth approximately $32 million over four years ("Struggling Economy Likely").

League loan pools

League loan pools are also affected by economic conditions. Because the risk of an individual franchise is greater than the risk of an entire league (this is similar to the risk of an individual asset being greater than the risk of a portfolio), leagues borrow to create **loan pools** that provide lower-cost capital to affiliated franchises. The NBA, for example, created its loan pool in 2003 and renewed the $1.96 billion debt in May 2009. Seventeen NBA teams can borrow from the fund. Due to the condition of the credit markets in 2009, the cost rose from 75 points over LIBOR to approximately 175 points over LIBOR (i.e., by 1%). The NBA is fortunate, however. When the credit markets froze after the collapse of Lehman Brothers in September 2008, the NFL and MLB were unable to renew their loan pools. As their loans "termed out," the leagues had to begin to pay accelerated principal payments, and teams that borrowed from league funds have had to begin to repay the league (Kaplan & Lombardo). The NHL also renewed its loan pool during May 2009. The NHL's loan pool now totals $200 million; the loan pools of the NBA, NFL, and MLB each total approximately $2 billion (Kaplan, 2009).

Political Developments

Change in the political environment can also affect financial risk in sport. Policy decisions at the local, state, and national levels directly impact the business of sport. For example, at the local and state levels, policy is set regarding the public funding of venues, income tax rates for athletes, and amusement tax rates on ticket revenues. Federal policy on sport often includes antitrust regulations and labor relations laws. Over time, policy may shift as the attitudes and beliefs of the electorate change and as the values of society shift. Financial managers must be aware how changes in the political environment may affect the sport industry.

In 2008, with government bailouts of the financial sector and the automobile industry, members of Congress asked whether sponsorship spending by firms receiving taxpayer support is a prudent use of public money ("Struggling Economy Likely"). As of 2009, companies in the financial sector had $2.47 billion in obligated payments for naming rights to U.S. and Canadian sports venues (Lefton & Mickle, 2009).

In 2008, banking was the fourth largest category in sport sponsorship spending, at $900 million. Additionally, banks spent $122.3 million on advertising in sport (Lefton & Mickle). Exhibits 3.9 and 3.10 list the amounts banks have spent on sport-related advertising and on naming rights. However, after financial services firms received bailout money from the Troubled Asset Relief Program, the political landscape changed and revenue to sport from the financial services sector was put at risk. Citigroup's naming rights deal for the new Mets ballpark in particular drew fire and attracted attention to banks' expenditures on sport sponsorship. The total value of Citigroup's deal with the Mets was $400 million, or $20 million per year for 20 years. As New York City struggled to deal with the credit crisis in 2008, the bank received $45 billion in federal TARP funding. This led U.S. Representative Barney Frank to state, when questioning the Citigroup naming rights agreement, "I don't think anybody has ever opened a bank account or decided to buy a CD because a bank's name is on the stadium" (para. 14).

Although banks had stated that TARP funds were not used and would not be used for sponsorship spending, Congress continued to focus on the "wasteful" use of taxpayer resources. Dennis Kucinich, a congressional representative from Ohio, led the charge. He stated,

> People in my district are struggling to survive, they're losing jobs, they're losing their homes, whole industries are at risk, and someone's getting a bailout and they can spend huge amounts of money to put their name on the stadium. It's just not right. It shows a lack of appreciation for the climate we're in. . . . Once you start getting funds from the United States taxpayers, it's not a private matter any more. You're now playing in the federal league. (Lefton & Mickle, paragraphs 43–44)

exhibit   3.9   Banks' advertising spending in sport.

COMPANY	2008
Bank of America Corp.	$43,858,273
Royal Bank of Scotland	$11,272,773
Charles Schwab Corp.	$8,165,118
JPMorgan Chase & Co.	$8,086,165
Wells Fargo & Co.	$7,873,821
PNC Financial Services Group	$5,919,632
Northern Trust Corp.	$5,323,988
U.S. Bankcorp	$5,030,469
Citigroup Inc.	$3,420,986
ING Groep NV	$3,175,739

Source: Lefton & Mickle (2009), as appeared in *Street & Smith's SportsBusiness Journal*, with permission.

exhibit   3.10   Banks and naming rights.

VENUE	TOTAL VALUE	YEARS	AVERAGE/YEAR
Barclays Center	$400 million	20	$20 million
Citi Field	$400 million	20	$20 million
Bank of America Stadium	$140 million	20	$7 million
Lincoln Financial Field	$139.6 million	20	$7 million
Invesco Field at Mile High	$120 million	20	$6 million
TD Banknorth Garden	$119.1 million	20	$6 million
Prudential Center	$105.3 million	20	$5.3 million
Citizens Bank Park	$95 million	25	$3.8 million
RBC Center	$80 million	20	$4 million
M&T Bank Field	$75 million	15	$5 million

Source: Lefton & Mickle (2009), as appeared in *Street & Smith's SportsBusiness Journal*, with permission.

A changing political environment may affect both the sport and venues industries through the outcome of certain court cases, such as the bankruptcy proceedings of the Phoenix Coyotes. According to Muret (2009), the Coyotes, an NHL team, were the first major professional sports team to declare bankruptcy while party to a long-term lease. The outcome of the bankruptcy proceedings may make it more difficult for publicly financed venues to secure financing, as the loss of a major tenant could cause a shortage in the revenues needed to retire municipal bond debt. As a result, cities may decide the risk of entering into a partnership with a franchise is too great.

Global Issues

As business has become more global, financial managers face new issues. In North America, the league most affected by global issues on a consistent basis is the National Hockey League. This league has the highest percentage of Canadian franchises. Most of the Canadian franchise revenue is earned in Canadian dollars, whereas the NHL's collective bargaining agreement (CBA) requires that all player contracts be paid in U.S. dollars. As a result, most of the expenses of these franchises are in U.S. dollars. As the Canadian dollar strengthens, a Canadian team's revenue increases while its expenses decrease (see Exhibit 3.11 for historical exchange rate data). As a result, Canadian teams are more profitable. Fluctuation in the exchange rate between the Canadian dollar and U.S. dollar affects the profitability not only of the Canadian teams but also of the U.S. teams and the league as a whole.

For the 2008/2009 season, the NHL salary cap rose to $56.7 million ("NHL Salary Cap," 2008), increasing for the fourth straight year. As the salary cap is tied directly to overall league revenues, the increase in the cap is attributable to record attendance (ticket revenues are the source of a majority of team and league revenues) and the strength of the Canadian dollar. While the Canadian dollar remains strong, the cap can continue to rise (Burnside, 2008). The collective bargaining

Historical conversion averages: U.S. dollar to Canadian dollar.   **exhibit   3.11**

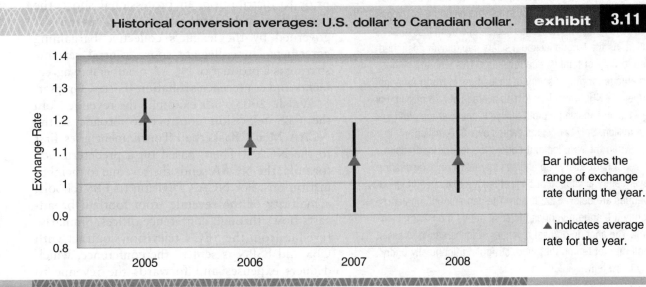

Bar indicates the range of exchange rate during the year.

▲ indicates average rate for the year.

agreement with the players includes not only a salary cap but also a salary floor. The salary floor, the minimum amount a team can spend on player payroll, grew to $40.7 million for the 2008/2009 season. Some teams in smaller, nontraditional U.S. markets complained that they could no longer turn a profit, even with revenue sharing. These teams included the aforementioned Phoenix Coyotes (who were in bankruptcy at the time), the Atlanta Thrashers, the Nashville Predators, the Florida Panthers, and the Columbus Blue Jackets ("NHL Owners Growing," 2008).

REVENUE SHARING AND RISK

Each individual franchise or athletic department operates within its own financial environment, facing risk that sometimes is unique to that franchise or department. However, franchises and athletic departments also cooperate in several ways even while their teams are competing on the field, and one of the ways is in financial management. In both college athletics and professional sport, leagues use **revenue sharing** to support weaker franchises and increase the competitive balance within the league. A byproduct of revenue sharing is that each individual organization's risk is lessened. Revenues are shared through pools under several models.

Revenue Pools

Each league has two basic pools of revenue that may or may not be shared by teams within the league: central and local. **Central revenues** are revenues paid directly to the league. These revenues are then distributed to member organizations. Typically, net costs of operating the league, association, or conference are deducted prior to distribution. In professional sport, the degree to which teams share central revenues is governed by the league's collective bargaining agreement. In collegiate sport, central revenue sharing is a product of NCAA membership agreements and conference affiliation (Foster, Greyser, & Walsh, 2005). For example, the revenue from the CBS television contract to broadcast the NCAA Men's Basketball Tournament goes first to the NCAA. Then, based on a predetermined formula, the NCAA sends the revenue to member institutions. For NCAA Division I – FBS schools, a majority of the revenue from football broadcasts flows through conference offices. Similarly, revenue from the SEC's television contract with CBS and ESPN is sent to the conference, which deducts expenses and forwards the revenue to member institutions.

SIDEBAR

Reducing Risk at the Franchise Level

3.B

Over the past ten years, some leagues have moved to reduce risk at the franchise level. MLB increased the sharing of local revenues, and the NFL began modestly sharing local revenues. The league that changed its revenue sharing model most drastically, however, was the National Hockey League. Prior to locking out the players in 2004, the owners of franchises and league management decided that the financial structure of the league needed modification. During the 2002/2003 NHL season, with total revenues of $1.996 billion and total expenses of $2.269 billion, the league had an operating loss of $273 million. As the league lacked a salary cap, player costs had risen to 75% of total league revenues. This was the highest percentage for player salary of all leagues in North America. Further, 19 NHL franchises lost an average of $18 million. For the 11 teams making a profit that year, the average profit was $6.4 million. Only two teams earned over $10 million.

When the NHL lockout ended, the league had implemented a hard salary cap and had increased revenue sharing. Player salary is capped at 54% of league revenues, if league revenues are below $2.2 billion. The cap amount increases slightly if league revenues increase above the $2.2 billion mark. The sharing of local revenues was increased to assist small market teams that were struggling financially under the old system.

Local revenues, such as those from teams' home ticket sales, local television and radio, advertising, and sponsorship, are also shared. The specific revenues that are shared and the degree to which they are shared varies by league. For example, in the NFL, teams contribute 40% of all home ticket sales revenue to a central fund each week. At the end of the season, the fund is divided among all 32 teams. Further, under the NFL's new CBA, approximately $150 million of additional local revenue filters from the top 15 financial franchises to the bottom 15. MLB shares many different forms of local revenues after deducting stadium expenses. The local revenues to be shared are placed in a single pool. Each year, $326 million is sent from the highest to the lowest revenue franchises.

Revenue Sharing Models

Each league uses one of three models for sharing revenue (Foster, Greyser, & Walsh). Under the first, the league provides higher revenue allocations to teams with low local revenues. MLB has used this model, as has the NFL since signing its most recent CBA.

Under the second model, the league provides equal allocations to all teams in the league. Under the NFL's old CBA, players received only a portion (65.5%) of the league's central revenues, and the league's central revenues were shared equally among clubs. Under the new CBA, players receive 59.9% of *all* league revenues, both central and local, including previously unshared revenues generated by franchises at the local level. Because of the great disparity in revenues generated locally within the NFL, the owners modified the league's revenue sharing formula to support teams with smaller local revenue pools. The NFL now uses the first model described.

By examining two NFL franchise revenues, Team X and Team Y, we can see why a group of owners sought to change the revenue sharing model. Team X is located in a medium/large market with a newly renovated stadium, and Team Y is located in a small market with an older facility. Revenues for each team are shown in Exhibit 3.12.

The salary cap under the new CBA, which is set at a percentage of total revenues, now affects Team Y more than Team X, because Team Y earns less in local revenue. With a $105 million cap, Team X's ratio of player salary to total revenue is 0.53 ($105,000,000/$200,000,000). For Team Y, the ratio is 0.66 ($105,000,000/$160,000,000).

At the college level, the SEC uses an equal allocation formula for distributing conference media revenues to member institutions. Most college conferences distribute revenues in a similar fashion.

Comparison of revenues of two NFL teams.   **exhibit   3.12**

REVENUE TYPE	TEAM X	TEAM Y
Local	$89,000,000	$49,000,000
Central	$111,000,000	$111,000,000
Total	$200,000,000	$160,000,000

The third revenue sharing model favors teams that generate higher revenue. The Premier League, the elite football (soccer) league in England, uses this model. Franchises are rewarded for the effective financial management of their clubs.

CONCLUSION

Risk affects the financial management of all sport organizations. Interest rates, bond rates, estimates of cash flow, and the cost of capital are all affected by changes in risk, as are rates of return. Because cash today is worth more to an investor than the same cash in the future, risk premiums compensate investors for risking today's cash. These premiums include an inflation premium, default risk premium, liquidity premium, and maturity risk premium.

An investment may be evaluated as a stand-alone investment or as a part of a larger portfolio of investments. For a stand-alone investment, the expected rate of return must be higher than the perceived risk. For an investment to be added to a portfolio, the investor will examine how the new asset affects the risk and return of the portfolio. The goal is to maximize the return of the portfolio while minimizing risk. Diversification is an important approach to reducing the risk of a portfolio. Financial managers use the Capital Asset Pricing Model to analyze the relationship between risk and rate of return for securities. CAPM allows the manager to analyze diversifiable and market risk by incorporating the beta coefficient of a security or a portfolio of securities, using the Security Market Line (formula). CAPM is typically used to analyze securities; however, it can also be used to evaluate the risk and return merits of an organization's investments and assets.

Managers in sport organizations must be aware of risks that may affect the organization's finances. Leagues have been proactive in reducing the risks that member clubs face—but there is no risk-free investment. Managers must strive to analyze risk carefully to protect their organization's financial assets.

CONCEPT *check*

1. How does risk affect the financial management of sport organizations?
2. Describe the process of determining a nominal interest rate.
3. Of MLB, the NBA, and the NHL, which league has the most risk, and which has the least? Why?
4. What must players and agents understand about risk? How should an agent structure a player's contract if it contains deferred compensation?
5. What risk factors should a team consider when deciding whether to build and fund a new venue? How are the risk factors different if a municipality is funding the construction?
6. If you were advising an investor interested in purchasing a sport franchise, what advice would you give?
7. Among NCAA men's basketball teams, which team would you expect to have the highest value? Why? How do you think conference affiliation affects value among these teams?

PRACTICE *problems*

1. You have the opportunity to purchase NFL Franchise A. The probability distribution of expected returns for the franchise is as follows:

PROBABILITY	RATE OF RETURN
0.1	−20%
0.2	0%
0.4	7%
0.2	15%
0.1	25%

   What is the expected rate of return for an investment in Franchise A? What is the standard deviation?

2. An owner of several sport assets holds the following portfolio:

ASSET	INVESTMENT	BETA
Team A	$100,000,000	0.5
Team B	$100,000,000	1.0
Facility A	$100,000,000	1.5
Total	$300,000,000	

   What is the beta of this portfolio?

3. Boggs Sports Holdings has a total investment of $500 million in five companies:

	INVESTMENT (IN MILLIONS)	BETA
Company A	$130	0.3
Company B	$160	1.5
Company C	$70	3.2
Company D	$90	2.0
Company E	$50	1.0
Total	$500	

   What is the beta of this portfolio?

4. For the portfolio described in Problem 3, if the risk-free rate is 10% and the market risk premium is 5%, what is Boggs' required rate of return?

5. You have been hired as the manager of a portfolio of ten sport assets that are held in equal dollar amounts. The current beta of the portfolio is 1.9, and the beta of Asset A is 2.1. If Asset A is sold and the proceeds are used to purchase a replacement asset, what beta would the replacement asset have to have in order to lower the portfolio beta to 1.6?

6. The Sports Investment Fund has a total investment of $5 million in the following portfolio:

	INVESTMENT	BETA
Asset A	$900,000	1.2
Asset B	$1,100,000	−0.4
Asset C	$1,000,000	1.5
Asset D	$2,000,000	0.9
Total	$5,000,000	

The market's expected rate of return is 10%, and the risk-free rate is 4%. What is the required rate of return?

7. Following is a distribution of returns:

PROBABILITY	RETURN
0.4	$35
0.5	$24
0.1	−$15

What is the coefficient of variation of the expected dollar return?

CASE analysis   *Risk and Team Values*

Risk directly affects the values of professional teams. Groppelli and Nikbakht state that to maximize the value of a firm, managers must focus on increasing the growth rate of cash flows and reducing the risk or uncertainty of those cash flows. One measure of an organization's risk is its credit rating. According to Fitch Ratings (2002), factors affecting the risk of cash flows, and, therefore, the credit rating of leagues and teams, include player salary restraints, national television contracts, revenue sharing among member clubs, league influence on team financial matters, debt limits, and the relationship with the players' union.

Exhibit 3.13 compares the average franchise value for the NFL and MLB from 2004 through 2008. The fact that the average value of a NFL franchise is more than twice that of the average MLB franchise is due in part to differing levels of risk.

Fitch Ratings discussed the factors that led to its conclusion that the NFL has the highest credit rating of all leagues. Primarily, the NFL is best able to withstand economic slowdowns that affect sponsorships, naming rights agreements, and the disposable income of fans. Its risk is reduced by lucrative long-term contracts with its media partners, strong relations with the NFL Players Association (NFLPA), and the willingness of team owners to be proactive in working together for the betterment of the league. The teams cooperate on merchandising and licensing revenues

and have agreed to the creation of a league-funded loan pool, the G-3 Fund, to help individual franchises build new stadia that will increase local revenues. Further, the league is the most competitively balanced from top to bottom, thanks to its hard salary cap. The hard cap controls the largest team expense, reducing the risk of team financial losses and improving the league's creditworthiness. The NFL also limits the debt that a franchise can incur, reducing risk for both the league and its teams.

Fitch Ratings rates the creditworthiness of MLB lower than that of the NFL because the MLB is exposed to greater risk. Although revenue sharing has increased under the latest MLB CBA, teams share only a small percentage of overall television revenue. Each team is able to negotiate and keep most (or, for some teams, all) of its local television revenues. The league does not have a hard salary cap, and although labor relations have improved greatly, MLB and the players association have a history of poor relations. Fitch Ratings notes that as MLB moves its economic model closer to that of the NFL, its risk will decrease and its rating will improve.

The importance of acquiring and securing revenue sources and the impact of doing so on risk and value is evident in an examination of collegiate football teams (see Exhibit 3.14). *Forbes* calculates the value of NCAA Division I – FBS teams in its reporting on the revenues of athletic programs. Exhibit 3.14 lists the 20

exhibit   3.13   **Average value of NFL and MLB franchises, 2004–2008 (in millions).**

	2004	2005	2006	2007	2008
NFL	$733	$819	$898	$957	$1,040
MLB	$295	$332	$376	$431	$472

Source: Forbes.com. Reprinted by permission of Forbes Media LLC ©2010.

| | Valuations of college football teams, 2007 (in millions). | exhibit 3.14 |

UNIVERSITY	CONFERENCE	VALUE
Notre Dame	Independent	$ 101
Texas	Big XII	$ 92
Georgia	SEC	$ 90
Michigan	Big 10	$ 85
Florida	SEC	$ 84
LSU	SEC	$ 76
Tennessee	SEC	$ 74
Auburn	SEC	$ 73
Alabama	SEC	$ 72
Ohio State	Big 10	$ 71
Oklahoma	Big XII	$ 70
South Carolina	SEC	$ 69
Penn State	Big 10	$ 69
USC	Pac 10	$ 53
Arkansas	SEC	$ 53
Texas A&M	Big XII	$ 50
Washington	Pac 10	$ 50
Nebraska	Big XII	$ 49
Michigan State	Big 10	$ 44
Wisconsin	Big 10	$ 43

Source: Forbes.com. Reprinted by permission of Forbes Media LLC ©2010.

most valuable football teams in 2007. The average value of these teams was $68 million. The list clearly indicates that teams in conferences with higher cash flows and lower risk or uncertainly of those cash flows are more highly valued than teams in conferences without lucrative long-term media contracts. (In Notre Dame's case, the team itself has secured these contracts.) For example, the SEC has eight of the 20 most valuable teams, according to *Forbes*. The league has a lucrative contract to broadcast football games nationally, and revenue from that contract flows back to its member schools. Notre Dame's contract with NBC provides similar revenues. The Big 10, with five teams listed, has created its own television network to generate revenues for member institutions.

A recent history of winning has little impact on a team's value. Notre Dame has struggled for several years but is ranked as the most valuable program. The history of the University of South Carolina in football is mediocre at best, but the team benefits from its membership in the SEC. The value of the South Carolina football team is $16 million greater than that of the University of Southern California team—which is the highest valued Pac 10 team and has a winning program on the field.

CASE QUESTIONS

1. What current economic conditions might affect the credit rating of a team or league?

2. Which teams' credit ratings might be most negatively affected during a recession?

3. What must the NFL do to maintain its high credit rating?

4. What can MLB do to improve its credit rating?

references

Ahles, A., & Schrock, S. (2008, December 3). Arlington refinances much of its debt for Cowboys stadium. *Star-Telegram*. Retrieved December 4, 2008, from http://www.star-telegram.com/330/v-print/story/1071095.html.

Anderson, S. (2005, August 20). Penguins pay off nearly all creditors. *Pittsburgh Post-Gazette*. Retrieved July 14, 2009, from http://www.post-gazette.com/pg/05232/557229.stm.

Birger, J. (2009, February 19). Baseball battles the slump. *CNNMoney.com*. Retrieved July 14, 2009, from http://money.cnn.com/2009/02/18/magazines/fortune/birger_baseball.fortune/index.htm.

Brigham, E.F., & Houston, J.F. (2001). *Fundamentals of financial management* (9th ed.). Orlando, FL: Harcourt College Publishers.

Burnside, S. (2008, July 6). Memo to owners: The cap is what you wanted; make it work. *ESPN.com*. Retrieved on July 7, 2008, from http://m.espn.go.com/nhl/story?storyId=3475686.

Conrad, M. (2006). *The business of sports: A primer for journalists*. Mahwah, NJ: Lawrence Erlbaum Associates.

Cowboys, city council having issues with stadium-financed bonds. (2008, September 3). *SportsBusiness Daily*. Retrieved September 3, 2008, from https://www.sportsbusinessdaily.com/article/123692.

Cowboys refinance $435m worth of debt for new $1.1b stadium. (2008, December 5). *SportsBusiness Daily*. Retrieved December 5, 2008, from http://www.sportsbusinessdaily.com/article/126048.

Fisher, E. (2008, July 7). Cheap seats. *SportsBusiness Journal*. Retrieved August 1, 2008, from http://www.sportsbusinessjournal.com/article/59474.

Fisher, E. (2009, May 18). All eyes focus on MLB attendance. *SportsBusiness Journal*. Retrieved May 18, 2009, from http://www.sportsbusinessjournal.com/article/62485.

Fitch Ratings. (2002, September 16). *Economics of professional sports: Rating sports transactions*. New York: Author.

Foster, G., Greyser, S.A., & Walsh, B. (2005). *The business of sports*. New York: South-Western College Publishers.

Groppelli, A.A., & Nikbakht, E. (2000). *Finance* (4th ed.). Hauppauge, NY: Barron's Educational Series, Inc.

Kaplan, D. (2009, May 18). NHL is latest to get a credit deal done. *SportsBusiness Journal*. Retrieved July 15, 2009, from http://www.sportsbusinessjournal.com/article/62478.

Kaplan, D., & Lombardo, J. (2009, May 11–17). $100M loan for arena is pure magic. *SportsBusiness Journal*, 12(4), 1, 27.

Last, J.V. (2009, January 30). Are pro sports too big to fail? *The Wall Street Journal*, p. W11.

Lefton, T., & Mickle, T. (2009, March 2). Beaten-up banks. *SportsBusiness Journal*. Retrieved March 2, 2009, from http://www.sportsbusinessjournal.com/article/61682.

Muret, D. (2009, March 11). Coyotes' lease issues called a bad precedent for public facility financing elsewhere. *SportsBusiness Journal*. Retrieved May 11, 2009, from http://www.sportsbusinessjournal.com/article/62462.

NFL giants redeeming $100m in auction-rate bonds for stadium. (2008, April 16). *SportsBusiness Daily*. Retrieved April 16, 2008, from http://www.sportsbusinessdaily.com/article/120079.

NHL owners growing wary of league's revenue-sharing system. (2008, October 13). *SportsBusiness Daily*. Retrieved December 28, 2009, from http://www.sportsbusinessdaily.com/article/124637.

NHL salary cap ceiling rises to $56.7m for 08–09 season. (2008, June 27). *The SportsBusiness Daily*. Retrieved June 28, 2008, from http://www.sportsbusinessdaily.com/article/121958.

Sandomir, R. (1999, September 2). Hockey: Lemieux is finally the emperor of the Penguins. *The New York Times*. Retrieved July 14, 2009, from http://www.nytimes.com/1999/09/02/sports/hockey-lemieux-is-finally-the-emperor-of-the-penguins.html.

Schnitzler, P. (2008, February 25). State debt tactics backfire. *Indianapolis Business Journal*. Retrieved September 16, 2008, from http://www.ibj.com/html/detail_page.asp?content=11607.

Schrock, S. (2008, November 11). New game plan for refinancing. *Star-Telegram*. Retrieved November 11, 2008, from http://www.star-telegram.com/stadium/story/1041607.html.

Struggling economy likely to pose problems for sports. (2008, October 6). *SportsBusiness Daily*. Retrieved October 6, 2008, from http://www.sportsbusinessdaily.com/article/124438.

4

Time Value of Money

annuity

compound interest

Consumer Price Index (CPI)

default

discount rate

future value (FV)

nominal value

perpetuity

present value (PV)

real value

simple interest

time value of money

KEY CONCEPTS

Introduction

"Money makes money. And the money that money makes makes more money."

BENJAMIN FRANKLIN

Imagine a sports agent asking her client if he would rather have a $100,000, $102,000, $110,000, or $120,000 payment. The obvious choice is to take the $120,000. But if the agent were to ask the athlete if he wanted $100,000 immediately, $102,000 to be paid one year from now, $108,000 in 18 months, or $120,000 in three years, what should the athlete choose? The choice can properly be made only with an understanding of the yearly, monthly, or even daily changes in the purchasing power of money—known as the *time value of money.* A variety of financial and economic concepts—including inflation, risk, future value of money and annuities, liquidity, present value of money and annuities, and interim compounding—must be understood before the time value of money can be applied to real-world sport management problems. Each of these concepts impacts the answers to questions such as the one presented at the beginning of this paragraph.

INFLATION

If someone were to travel back in time to 1955, she would experience instant sticker shock. Prices for nearly all items would be lower—just ask someone 30 years older than you about what it used to cost to buy things. A single dollar could purchase more goods or services in 1960 than in 2010. This loss of purchasing power, or **real value,** is the result of inflation. Prices tend to increase over time and the value of money tends to decrease, even though the **nominal value,** or face value, of money remains the same.

Inflation Rate

The inflation rate affects all financial decisions, particularly those related to long-term investments. Hence, financial managers are wise to understand and monitor the inflation rate. Organizations that invest their money for future purchases must ensure that they are receiving interest that at least matches the rate of inflation, or the real value of their investment will decrease. Although the nominal value of a dollar has remained the same over the past 25 years, the real value of that dollar has dramatically decreased; in other words, the products or services that that dollar can purchase have diminished.

To understand the effect of inflation, consider a recreation center that places $10,000 into a checking account and receives no interest. The rate of inflation will gradually erode the value of the money. For instance, if the annual rate of inflation is 2%, the real value of the $10,000 will decrease by 2% over the year, even though the account has experienced no loss in nominal value (the account balance remains the same). Conversely, if a recreation center saves $10,000 in a bank account for one year and receives 3% interest, and the rate of inflation is 2%, the realized change in purchasing power will be:

$10,000 × .03 = $300 (interest received)

$10,000 × .02 = $200 (purchasing power lost)

real change in value = interest received − purchasing power lost

= $300 − 200

= $100

Although the organization now has $10,300 in the account, the ability to purchase products has increased by only $100. The recreation center may wish to explore investments that receive higher returns relative to inflation.

Consumer Price Index

Economists compute the inflation rate by studying changes in the **Consumer Price Index (CPI).** The CPI is the result of a calculation based on the prices of goods and services in more than 200 categories reflecting the current lifestyle of the typical American consumer to determine the overall change in real prices during a period (Bureau of Labor Statistics, n.d.). The Bureau of Labor Statistics, which is the government agency responsible for calculating the CPI, allocates the 200 smaller categories into nine larger categories and estimates the percentage of spending for each category for a typical U.S. household (Exhibit 4.1). The CPI helps consumers understand the difference between the real value and nominal value of money and how the purchasing power of their money is changing. The nominal amount of money needed to purchase products or services typically increases over time, but economists and financial managers are interested in the real value of dollars—the purchasing power those dollars retain.

The Bureau of Labor Statistics tracks the CPI and provides monthly charts for various products and services, as well as information for various cities and regions throughout the country (http://www.bls.gov/cpi/home.htm#tables). (The BLS website also provides a "CPI Inflation Calculator" that determines the change in the value of money over a specified period. For instance, using the calculator, one can quickly determine that $100 in 1989 had the same buying power as $173.01 in 2009.) In March 2009, in the midst of a significant economic slowdown, the CPI *decreased* over a 12-month period, for the first time since 1955 (Zigler, 2009).

It is imperative that financial managers understand that individual items or services may experience inflation-related changes that deviate from the overall rate. Financial managers must understand the forces working within their industries,

Consumer Price Index. **exhibit** **4.1**

The calculation of the Consumer Price Index is based on the prices of a "basket" of goods and services that is intended to be representative of a typical consumer's purchases. The "basket" currently includes goods and services from the following categories in the percentages noted:

Food and beverages	16%	Recreation	6%
Housing	41%	Education	3%
Clothing	4%	Communication	3%
Transportation	17%	Other	4%
Medical care	6%		

Source: http://www.econedlink.org/lessons/index.cfm?lesson=EM323.

Are prices always higher in the present than in the past? In other words, does purchasing power always decrease over time? Let's take a look at one item likely to be of concern to a student. What has happened to the price of gasoline? Certainly, gasoline is more expensive in nominal terms now than it was in the past. However, we must consider the rate of inflation to determine whether the purchasing power for gas has increased, decreased, or remained relatively unchanged for consumers.

Changes in gasoline prices typically result in extensive media attention and complaints from consumers. Exhibit 4.2

4.A

shows four periods in U.S. history when gasoline prices were extremely high. During World War I and World War II gasoline was expensive due to shortages, as most of the country's gasoline supply was used for military purposes. During the late 1970s, unrest in the Middle East and economic conditions in the United States resulted in a large increase in prices. And during 2008, gasoline reached its highest nominal price in U.S. history. However, the inflation-adjusted price was not considerably higher than at other times in U.S. history.

because even if the overall inflation rate remains relatively stable, an increase in prices for certain items—for example, travel or sporting equipment—could have a major negative impact on their organization.

Despite tremendous growth in the popularity of Major League Baseball from 1950 to 1990, ticket prices actually decreased in price in real terms. Andrew Zimbalist (1992) noted that if 1950 MLB ticket prices were adjusted for inflation, they would average $8.74, whereas the average cost of an MLB ticket in 1990 was $7.95. However, from 1991 to 2001, the average ticket price increased by 120%, while the CPI increased only 30% (Corwin, 2001). MLB tickets have continued to increase in price since 2001, which has caused some to question whether teams may be pricing out many of their core customers, as well as future generations of fans (Herbert, 2009).

RISK

Like inflation, risk, or uncertainty about the future and future returns, may also affect the value of money. Risk often leads to financial losses. It is much harder to predict what will happen in the sport industry in five years than in five days. For this reason, most sport managers are reluctant to invest cash for a long period of time unless the expected payoff from the investment is significant. Typically, financial managers contemplate the risk versus the reward of an investment before making any financial decision, but they are especially particular in making investments that will extend far into the future.

Deferred Salaries: Team and Player Risk

With deferred salaries, players and teams try to optimize the value of their money over time. A team may contemplate deferring players' salaries when it needs additional cash in the short term to sign new players, attract or retain coaching or administrative personnel, make capital improvements, or enhance some other facet of the operation. When the team defers a portion of a player's contract, it hopes that retaining the

Gasoline prices, adjusted for inflation, 1918–2009.   exhibit   4.2

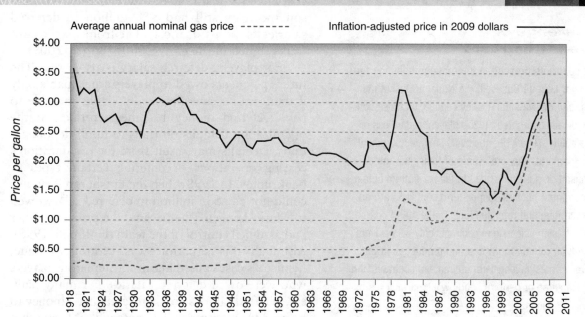

Note: Prices are average annual prices, *not* peak prices, so peaks are smoothed out considerably.

Source of data: U.S. Energy Information Administration CPI-U Inflation index, www.bls.gov.

Source: Adapted from www.InflationData.com and Timothy McMahon.

money for other expenditures will result in enhanced revenues, and that those revenues will exceed future expenditures when the deferred salaries must be paid.

The Arizona Diamondbacks made a run at the 2001 World Series by assuming long-term financial risks through the deferral of player salaries. Prominent players—Randy Johnson, Steve Finley, Curt Schilling, and others—were signed to lucrative contracts for the 2001 season that deferred over $16 million to future years (on top of $37 million that the team had previously deferred for the 1998 through 2000 seasons) (Rovell, 2001). In the short term, deferring salaries helped the Diamondbacks field a team that won the 2001 World Series. Unfortunately, anticipated revenue increases from the highly successful season did not materialize. During the years following the 2001 season, the Diamondbacks were not able to retain many players from their championship team because the commitments to deferred salaries drained the team's cash reserves. The team was forced to borrow money to pay the deferred salaries coming due, and veteran players who left the team via free agency or for retirement were often replaced with rookies and other less experienced and, often, less skilled players. Though the new players did not cost the team nearly as much money to employ, the team's fortunes on the field dramatically decreased. By 2004, the team had fallen to a Major League worst 51–111. It was not until 2007 that the Diamondbacks recovered sufficiently to achieve a winning record. Although the Diamondbacks have dramatically reduced

SIDEBAR

The Challenge of Multi-year Contracts   4.B

Multi-year contracts present an interesting challenge for teams in Major League Baseball, the National Basketball Association, and the National Hockey League, as those contracts are typically guaranteed to the players regardless of their future ability. (The NHL, however, provides a special method for teams to "buy out" some of their guaranteed contracts based on a player's age.) In teams' fight to obtain or retain prominent players, longer-term contracts are an important recruiting and retention tool. The team, of course, must attempt to sign longer-term contracts only with players who are likely to remain motivated and productive in the future. Players who sign long-term guaranteed contracts and then become injured or perform poorly will limit their teams' future financial options.

The purchasing power of future compensation is difficult to calculate when contracts extend for long periods of time. The team must predict not only the player's future performance ability but also the appropriate compensation. For players and their agents, future compensation must account not only for performance but also for inflation. For example, MLB All-Star outfielder Johnny Damon's compensation for each of the 2006 through 2009 seasons was $13 million, meaning that even with minimal inflation during that time, Damon saw a yearly decrease in the purchasing power of his salary ("USA Today Salaries Databases," 2009).

When the Cleveland Browns drafted wide receiver Braylon Edwards in 2005, he signed a contract that included a $6.5 million signing bonus. Lamont Smith, Edwards' agent, remarked, "It was a priority for us . . . because we believe in the time value of money. When you wait for your money, you are providing the team with an interest-free loan" (Mullen, 2005, para. 24). For star NFL players, the signing bonus not only ensures that much of their contract money is guaranteed but also assures them that inflation will not erode the purchasing power of their compensation. The majority of NFL players must play each week with the risk that injury or poor performance may lead to termination of their (non-guaranteed) contracts.

their payroll since 2001 and have built a more cost-effective team, at the start of the 2009 season the team still had $58 million in deferred salaries to be paid, most of it from player contracts signed in the early 2000s (Birger, 2009).

For players, deferred salary is also a risk. The future payments owed to players are valuable only if the team remains financially viable and able to pay. Deferred money becomes worthless if the organization **defaults** on (fails to fulfill) its obligations. Defaults may result from the organization's ceasing operations or entering certain types of bankruptcy. In 1998 when the Pittsburgh Penguins could not pay $35 million in deferred salary owed to Mario Lemieux, he became the primary owner and assumed control of the team (Hoffman, 1998). Although this situation was certainly unique, Lemieux's case caused alarm for numerous players who were owed deferred salaries. For many players, deferred salaries are their safety net—money to be used for retirement. The potential of losing that money is a risk that the player and his or her agent must consider when negotiating deferred compensation. When the NHL's Phoenix Coyotes declared bankruptcy in 2009, some were concerned that deferred salaries might not be paid once the bankruptcy case was concluded ("Q&A Part 2," 2009). Fortunately, the league was able to arrange a sale, and the franchise continued its normal financial operations. In professional leagues, if the financial survival of the league is in serious doubt, players should exercise great caution in accepting deferred salary payments.

Policies on Deferred Salaries

The deferral of salaries is certainly not a new phenomenon in sport finance. During the early 1970s, teams in the American Basketball Association (ABA) and the NBA battled to acquire the services of players. To attract and retain players, the ABA instituted the "Dolgoff Plan" (Pluto, 1990): Teams in the ABA would offer multimillion-dollar contracts to potential players but would defer a large portion of the contract. To help the potential player and the player's agent feel secure that the future payments would be made, the team often invested money for the player's deferred salary in an annuity with a prominent corporation. Although the NBA criticized the ABA's plan, teams in the ABA were able to attract enough quality players that *all* professional basketball players' salaries dramatically increased, and eventually, in 1976, the leagues merged (Pluto). Although some of the deferred money was never paid out, in some cases former ABA players received money long after the ABA had merged with the NBA. Examples include current NBA agent and commentator Len Elmore, whose deferred compensation included $80,000 each year for 1981 to 1984 plus $105,000 for 1985. Former ABA player and NBA coach Dan Issel received semimonthly deferred payments beginning in 1974 and continuing until 1983; he received an additional $12,000 per year from 1989 to 1999 (Pluto).

Some of the major North American professional sport leagues have attempted to address the risks of deferred salaries.

- MLB: Teams must show that money deferred can be paid off in the next four years, even if the money is contractually deferred beyond four years.
- NFL: The team must place deferred payments in a league fund for administration and future disbursement.
- NBA: Only 30% of a total contract value may be deferred, and it must be paid within two years of the contract's completion.
- The NHL does not restrict teams regarding deferred payments. (Rovell, 2001)

FUTURE VALUE

To determine the costs and benefits of financial decisions such as deferring salaries, financial managers must understand and be able to compute the **future value** (FV) of a payment—the value of that payment at a certain date in the future determined by calculating the change in value of money when an interest rate is applied over the intervening period of time. Initial computations of future values provide a nominal value of money; financial managers must then assess the expected rate of inflation and potentially provide an estimate for risk to determine the real value of money after time. The question posed at the opening of this chapter dealt with a $100,000, $102,000, $110,000, or $120,000 payment. A financial manager or agent can appropriately advise a client which payment to take only by understanding the present and future value of a dollar.

Suppose a sport organization invests $100 in a savings bond that pays 5% interest annually for five years. To determine what the value of the investment will be after one year, we perform a simple calculation:

original investment + interest = future value
$100 + (5%)($100) = $105

To determine the value beyond one year, we must distinguish between simple and compound interest. **Simple interest** is calculated only on principal. After year one, under simple interest the investment of $100 would continue to grow at a rate of $5 per year, for a total value of $125 after five years. **Compound interest,** on the other hand, is calculated on principal and on the interest generated by that principal. Thus, determining the value of the investment under compound interest requires the following formula:

$$FV = PV(1 + i)^n$$

where FV = future value

PV = the present value of the initial investment (principal)

i = rate of interest per period

n = number of periods

As an example, again consider the sport organization that invests in a savings bond:

$$FV = 100 \times (1.05)^5$$
$$= 100 \times (1.05 \times 1.05 \times 1.05 \times 1.05 \times 1.05)$$
$$= 100 \times 1.2763$$
$$= 127.63$$

Fortunately, it is not necessary to memorize this formula; with a table we can look up values rather than calculate them (see Table A.1 in the Appendix). The future value table gives a future value interest factor (FVIF). To find the FVIF, determine the number of periods (in this example it is expressed in years) of the investment. Find this row in the table and then move across to the column for the interest rate. This is the FVIF. Now, simply multiply the FVIF by the initial investment.

For an investment at 5% interest for five years, the FVIF is 1.2763. Multiplying this factor by $100 (the initial investment) yields $127.63. Notice that this value is higher than the $125 received under simple interest. To see a dramatic difference in simple versus compound interest, change the time period from five to 20 years and the amount invested to $100,000. With simple interest, the future value is $100,000 + (20 [years] x 5,000 [simple interest]) = $200,000. With compound interest, the future value is $100,000 x 2.6533 = $265,330. This problem illustrates why financial managers prefer to receive compound interest on their investments and why Albert Einstein is believed to have remarked that the most powerful force in the universe is compound interest.

ANNUITIES AND PERPETUITIES

Often, the value of an investment is paid out or received not in one lump sum but over time in multiple payments or receipts. Any series of equal payments or receipts made at regular intervals is termed an **annuity**. Annuity payments may occur annually, quarterly, monthly, or at any other regular interval. Examples of annuities include regularly scheduled mortgage payments, individual retirement account (IRA) contributions, loan payments, and pension payments. An annuity has a scheduled end point. If the payments or receipts were to continue forever, this would be considered a **perpetuity**. Perpetuities are rarely established, for obvious reasons. Forever is certainly a long time.

FUTURE VALUE OF AN ANNUITY

 sport manager may wish to determine the future value of an investment that is funded on a regularly scheduled basis (an annuity). For instance, a sport team may need to determine how much money it would have after investing $1,000 per year for five years at 5% interest. The financial manager would use the following formula:

$$FVA = PMT\left(\frac{(1+i)^n - 1}{i}\right)$$

where FVA = future value of an annuity,
PMT = payment,
i = rate of interest per period, and
n = number of periods

For the example given above, the calculation would proceed as follows:

$$FV = 1,000\left(\frac{(1.05)^5 - 1}{0.05}\right)$$

$$= 1,000\left(\frac{(1.05 \times 1.05 \times 1.05 \times 1.05 \times 1.05) - 1}{0.05}\right)$$

$$= 1,000\left(\frac{1.2763 - 1}{0.05}\right)$$

$$= 1,000\left(\frac{0.2763}{0.05}\right)$$

$$= 1,000\,(5.5256)$$

$$= \$5,525.60$$

Fortunately, we can use a table (see Table A.2 in the Appendix) to simplify the above equation to $FV_a = PMT \times FVIFA$, where FVIFA is the future value interest factor of an annuity, from the table.

To find the FVIFA, determine the number of periods of the investment. Find this row in the table and then move across to the column for the interest rate. This is the FVIFA. Simply multiply the FVIFA by the investment amount per period. For $1,000 invested per year at 5% interest for five years, the FVIFA is 5.5256, yielding a future value of $1,000 x 5.5256 = $5,525.60.

The following examples demonstrating the use of the FVIFA show the importance of time and persistence in the creation of wealth. First, suppose two sport managers open retirement accounts and commit to invest $3,000 each year, earning 7% interest, until they retire. The first sport manager starts investing at age 25 and continues until age 65. The second investor starts at age 35 and invests until age 65. When the investors reach age 65, the first will have accumulated over 40 years of time. Her investment will have a FVIFA of 199.64. Multiplied by $3,000, this yields an FV of $598,920. The second investor will have accumulated over 30 years of time, for an FVIFA of 94.461. His FV will be $283,383. The total difference from the additional ten years of investment, with only $30,000 in cash paid in, is $315,537. Any IRA holder can use

SIDEBAR

The Greatest Deal in Sports?

4.C

The idea of guaranteeing anyone money forever would cause most sport organizations to cringe. But the NBA has paid and will continue to pay three people who have no connection to the league tens of millions of dollars in compensation—simply because of a deal struck many years ago. When the NBA and ABA were discussing a merger in 1976, the NBA agreed to absorb four teams: the New York [now New Jersey] Nets, Denver Nuggets, San Antonio Spurs, and Indiana Pacers. In addition, the owner of the Kentucky Colonels was paid $3 million to fold the team, leaving the St. Louis Spirits as the remaining ABA team. Although the owners of the Spirits, Ozzie and Danny Silna, and their lawyer, Don Schupak, initially desired to enter the NBA, when it became apparent the NBA did not want to merge their team, they negotiated one of the greatest (for them) sport finance deals in history (Pluto, 1990; Rovell, 2002). The Spirits' owners received $2.2 million in cash plus 1/7 of a share of national television money from each of the four merged ABA teams—in perpetuity. Essentially, the Spirits' owners are guaranteed to receive 4/7 of the annual television share for an NBA team, *forever.* At the time, the value of the television contracts was minimal, but during the 1980s the Spirits' owners received roughly $8 million in television revenue. From 1990 through 1998 they received just under $41 million, and from 1998 through 2002 they received $50 million (Rovell, 2002). Despite protests, lawsuits, and buyout attempts, the Spirits' owners (who currently run an embroidery business) have retained their share of television money. In total, the Spirits' owners have collected over $100 million, and at no time have they had to pay for rising salaries of players or other expenses incurred through ownership.

the Future Value of an Annuity Table to determine how much money he or she will have upon retirement (in nominal terms), given an expected rate of return and yearly investment.

In addition to the impact of time, interest rate changes (even small ones) can have a dramatic effect on the yield of an investment. In the preceding example, the first person invested for 40 years at 7% interest, yielding $598,920. If the interest rate increased from 7% to 8%, the FVIFA would be 259.06, and the yield would be $3,000 x 259.06 = $777,180—an increase of $178,260. If the interest rate increased to 9% per year, the overall yield would be $3,000 x 337.88 = $1,013,640. The change in an interest rate may appear small, but it can result in tremendous changes in the final yield. Readers should note the importance of investigating the effect that a minor change in interest rate can have on the yield of an investment. If the interest rate increases from 7% to 8%, this is a 14% increase [(8 − 7)/7 = 14%]. An interest rate change from 7% to 10% is a percentage increase of 43% [(10 − 7)/7 = 43%]. As discussed in Chapter 2, when the Federal Reserve changes interest rates, dramatic changes in loans, investments, and other financial activities may result. Sport managers are wise to anticipate interest rate changes and plan financial activities with future rates in mind.

Once the future value of a single payment or of an annuity is determined, the financial manager can compare this value with the expected rate of inflation to determine the real change in value. In addition to inflation, risk levels associated with different potential interest rates may affect the decision to invest in certain projects, as discussed in Chapter 3. For some financial decisions, a lower potential return may be acceptable for an investment with lower risk. In all cases, the organization or individual is working to maximize the real value of money.

LIQUIDITY

An understanding of inflation, a tolerance for risk, and the computation of future value are all critical to short- and long-range financial decisions. In addition, the sport manager must understand the significance of liquidity before investing capital in any project. As discussed in Chapter 2, an asset's liquidity is the readiness with which it can be converted to cash. Often, organizations own assets (such as real estate) that cannot easily be sold to raise cash to pay short-term obligations. Before committing resources to long-term investments, individuals and organizations must understand the importance of maintaining liquidity. Those who cannot effectively meet their cash obligations (payroll, facility overhead, etc.) may be forced to alter short- and long-term financial commitments, sell assets (often at a discount) for immediate cash, or file for bankruptcy. For this reason, sport managers typically expect greater returns from investments that require a longer period until maturity or that cannot be redeemed for cash without substantial penalty. In addition, after an initial investment is made, subsequent investments of similar risk will often be considered only if higher returns can be realized.

For example, suppose a recreation center that has $20,000 in cash commits $9,000 of that amount to a capital improvement project, such as an additional basketball court, that will generate increased participation fees. However, revenue from the new court will not be realized for one year. During that time, the facility is less likely to use an additional $9,000 for another project with a similar expected return, as that would leave only $2,000 in reserve for short-term obligations or emergencies. Most likely, the financial manager would require any second project not only to offer a higher return on investment but also to return cash within one or two months.

PRESENT VALUE

 etermining the future value of investments is only part of understanding the time value of money. Sport managers must also understand the concept of **present value** (PV). Present value is today's value of a future cash flow—the current value of a payment that will be received or paid in the future. We calculate present value by applying a discount rate to the future cash flow. The **discount rate,** or capitalization rate, is a measure of risk or uncertainty. It is determined by the person performing the calculation, e.g., a financial manager, based on his or her estimate of future inflation rates, interest rates, and business activity.

If we revisit the problem from the opening of the chapter, one option for the player's agent is to accept $120,000 for her client, payable in three years. To determine how valuable (in today's dollars) that future $120,000 is, the agent would apply a discount rate—say 6% for the purpose of this example. The present value could be compared with the $100,000 that the athlete could receive immediately. If the present value of $120,000 is greater than $100,000 (and assuming the athlete does not need the cash immediately), the better choice is to defer the salary. If the present value of $120,000 in three years is less than $100,000, then the athlete should take the $100,000 now.

To compute the present value, we use the following formula:

$$PV = FV\left(\frac{1}{(1+i)^n}\right)$$

where PV = present value
     FV = future value
      i = discount rate per period
     n = number of periods

For $120,000 payable in three years with a 6% discount rate,

$$PV = \$120,000\left(\frac{1}{(1+0.06)^3}\right)$$
$$= \$120,000\left(\frac{1}{(1.06 \times 1.06 \times 1.06)}\right)$$
$$= \$120,000\left(\frac{1}{1.19106}\right)$$
$$= \$120,000(0.8396)$$
$$= \$100,752$$

Notice that the present value formula is the inverse of the future value formula.

Just as we can easily compute the future value of a dollar by using a table, we can use the table Present Value of $1 (Table A.3 in the Appendix) to compute the present value of a dollar with the Present Value Interest Factor (PVIF). To find the PVIF, determine the number of periods until the income is realized and move across that column to the appropriate discount rate. For example, suppose a minor league baseball team anticipates sponsorship revenue of $15,000 to be realized in four years. What is the present value of that future payment if the discount rate is 9%? We can find the PVIF by examining Appendix Table A.3. For four periods and a 9% discount rate, the PVIF is 0.7084. Hence, the present value is 0.7084 x $15,000 = $10,626.

Often, the financial manager cannot accurately predict the future. For this reason, when financial managers estimate present values of future cash flows, they utilize multiple discount rates to calculate a variety of potential results. At all times, sport managers must remember that projections can change, especially over longer periods of time. During the late 1970s, the inflation rate often exceeded 15%. Creditors collecting fixed long-term payments saw the purchasing power of their receipts diminish dramatically. Although inflation rates are not likely to return to such high rates in the United States, they do fluctuate from year to year. When forecasting for the future, it is advisable to utilize at least three different discount rates and to consider the *worst*-case scenario the most likely outcome. This will result in any financial surprises being positive rather than negative.

To help in understanding the present value of future money, we can look at Appendix Table A.3 to see how changing the discount rate to adjust for risk affects the present value of a future expected payment. As the discount rate increases, the present value of a future income decreases (see Exhibit 4.3).

The present value also allows us to compare different investment opportunities to determine which is the best alternative. Suppose a minor league baseball team received two sponsorship offers, one for $15,000 and one for $17,000, both to be paid in four years. Although the second payment would be higher, suppose the risk of default with this company is higher, so a discount rate of 12% as opposed to 9% is applied. Which is the better investment opportunity?

Option 1: PV = 0.7084 × $15,000 = $10,626

Option 2: PV = 0.6355 × $17,000 = $10,803

Option 2 yields a higher present value and should be selected given the information provided.

It is important for sport financial managers to remember that many financial decisions are made in spite of the numbers. This is not always advisable, but in some cases decision makers may give up the higher present value of a certain project in favor of a less risky investment. In other cases, owners may be

exhibit 4.3	Inverse relationship between present value and risk.		
FUTURE INCOME	**DISCOUNT RATE**	**PVIF, 5 YEARS**	**PV OF FUTURE INCOME**
$10,000	12% (higher risk)	0.5674	$5,674
$10,000	6% (average risk)	0.7473	$7,473
$10,000	3% (lower risk)	0.8626	$8,626

tempted to choose certain investment options for political or public-relations reasons, against financial advice. In these cases, the financial manager must ensure that decision makers have a complete understanding of the options and the financial ramifications of each choice. Unfortunately, too often decisions are made without a thorough investigation or understanding of available financial material.

PRESENT VALUE OF AN ANNUITY

A sport manager may wish to determine the present value of a series of future cash flows (an annuity). Suppose an agent negotiated a long-term sponsorship deal that called for yearly payments to an athlete of $10,000 for five years, and the agent felt that a discount rate of 10% was appropriate. We could determine the present value for each individual year and then total those amounts to determine the present value of the future cash flows. It is far easier to calculate the present value of an annuity. Note that these calculations assume the cash flows in each period are equal.

We can compute the present value of an annuity with the following formula:

$$PVA = PMT\left(\frac{1 - \frac{1}{(1+i)^n}}{i}\right)$$

where PVA = present value of an annuity
PMT = payment per period
i = discount rate
n = number of periods

$$PVA = \$10,000\left(\frac{1 - \frac{1}{(1+0.10)^5}}{0.10}\right)$$

$$= \$10,000\left(\frac{1 - \frac{1}{1.10 \times 1.10 \times 1.10 \times 1.10 \times 1.10}}{0.10}\right)$$

$$= \$10,000\left(\frac{1 - \frac{1}{1.61051}}{0.10}\right)$$

$$= \$10,000\left(\frac{1 - .62092}{0.10}\right)$$

$$= \$10,000\left(\frac{.37908}{0.10}\right)$$

$$= \$10,000(3.7908)$$

$$= \$37,908$$

By using the Present Value Interest Factor of an Annuity (PVIFA) from Table A.4 in the Appendix, we can reduce the above equation to PVA = Payment x PVIFA. To determine the PVIFA, simply find the period of the annuity on the

Present Value of an Annuity Table and read across to the discount rate. For the calculation above,

PVA = $10,000 (3.7908) = $37,908

Consider a sport agent who has two potential sponsors for her client. Sponsor A is willing to pay the athlete $10,000 each year for five years, with a discount rate of 5%. Sponsor B is ready to pay the athlete $12,000 each year for five years, with a discount rate of 10%. Which is the better option?

Sponsor A: PV = $10,000 × 4.3295 = $43,295.00
Sponsor B: PV = $12,000 × 3.7908 = $45,489.60

Sponsor B is the better financial choice, given the information provided.

Often, the better choice between two payment options is the one that is lower in nominal terms, because, as the result of a lower discount rate, it has greater real value after discounting. Suppose Sponsor A is willing to pay $10,000 a year for five years, discounted at 4%, while Sponsor B is ready to pay the athlete $12,000 a year for five years, discounted at 12%. In this case, the better option is Sponsor A:

Sponsor A: PV = $10,000 × 4.4518 = $44,518.00
Sponsor B: PV = $12,000 × 3.6048 = $43,257.60

Many state lotteries offer winners a choice in how they receive their winnings: either the winner can receive the prize in equal payments over a predetermined number of years (often 20 or 30), or the winner can elect to receive a *portion* of the prize amount in a lump sum payment. To make a wise choice, the winner must understand the time value of money. Each winner will have different short-term financial obligations, long-term goals, tolerance for risk, and preferences for liquidity. Unfortunately, unscrupulous firms often attempt to purchase the right to future payments from winners who are unaware of the financial ramifications of their disbursement choices. Decisions regarding state lottery winnings have such importance that states have developed websites to educate winners about the financial implications of their decisions.

INTERIM YEAR COMPOUNDING

For all previous examples involving interest, we have assumed that the interest is compounded (calculated and added to principal) once per year. However, in many financial arrangements, interest is compounded each quarter, month, week, or, in some cases, day. To adjust for compounding on a basis other than annual is simple. Depending on whether you are computing the present or future value of a dollar, or of an annuity, one merely determines the number of periods and uses the appropriate table to find the factor needed for the calculation.

Suppose, for example, that a sport organization wishes to determine the future value of $1,000 invested for two years receiving 12% interest, compounded quarterly. To determine the future value, we would first find the interest rate for the compounding period. Since there are four quarters in a year, we divide the annual interest rate of 12% and find that the interest per quarter is 3%. Since the investment period is two years, the number of compounding periods is eight. From the future value table we find that the FVIF for eight periods at 3% interest is 1.2668, yielding a future value of $1,000 x 1.2668 = $1,266.80. Note that if the 12% interest were compounded yearly, the future value would be $1,000 x 1.2544 = $1,254.40, a difference of $12.40.

Financial institutions often advertise that they compute interest payments to customers on a quarterly, monthly, weekly, or even daily basis. Before placing funds in any institution, the consumer should calculate the interest that she will receive on deposits. In some cases, daily compounding of interest may not exceed the interest computed monthly or even yearly. By understanding the concept of compounding and utilizing the time value of money tables, investors can make informed evaluations.

CONCLUSION

Let's return to the question that introduced this chapter. Which option should the athlete choose among his four potential payments? As discussed in this chapter, in order to make an informed decision, the athlete must understand or estimate his current and future need for liquidity, the potential investments available to him and the risks associated with each investment, and the current and future rates of inflation. An athlete who needs immediate cash would be compelled to take the $100,000 now, without even investigating other options. An athlete without liquidity concerns or with immediate access to a loan should investigate each potential investment's yield and the associated risks before making a decision.

It is critical not only that sport managers be able to calculate the present and future value of money, but also that they understand the immediate needs of the firm and how the time value of money, inflation, the organization's risk tolerance, and its need for liquidity impact short- and long-term strategies. Proper financial analysis can lead to long-term financial success, but a failure to understand the time value of money and to implement sound financial strategies may yield financial disaster.

SIDEBAR

William Andrews Wants His Money Now   4.D

During the early 1980s William Andrews was one of the top halfbacks in the NFL. While playing for the Atlanta Falcons from 1979 through 1983, Andrews rushed for more than 5,000 yards and accumulated more than 2,500 yards receiving. As part of one of his contract negotiations, Andrews agreed to a deferred compensation plan that would pay him $200,000 per year for 25 years ($5 million) after his playing career was complete. In 2001, Andrews negotiated a deal where he would give up his deferred compensation in exchange for an immediate $2 million from Hanleigh Co. (Kaplan, 2001). Although the money he received was only 40% of the total due him from the Falcons, Andrews determined that he could invest the money and receive a greater return than what the Falcons had agreed to pay him.

For Hanleigh Co., the risk of the Atlanta Falcons' defaulting on their financial obligation must have seemed minimal, as NFL teams have been stable for many years and the prospect is strong that they will remain financially solvent. Hanleigh Co. does assume risks, however, from time, inflation, and lack of liquidity. Over the length of the contract, numerous factors could diminish the value of the annual $200,000 payments. For one, inflationary pressure could diminish purchasing power. In addition, immediate payment of $2 million to Andrews meant an immediate loss of capital to Hanleigh, which could be critical if Hanleigh Co. were to need money to meet short-term financial obligations. The financial analysts at Hanleigh Co. likely investigated the investment options available to them, their level of liquidity, and their tolerance for risk, and determined that it was better to receive $200,000 per year for the remaining years of the contract rather than investing their $2 million in other financial opportunities.

For William Andrews, the desire to receive immediate money was more important than the longer-term security of a regular payment. He may have needed immediate liquidity to pay off some obligation. More likely, Andrews computed the return available from potential investments and determined it was more profitable for him to take the immediate cash. Andrews, of course, assumes the risks associated with his investment decisions. If with the $2 million he generates more than $200,000 per year, his investment decision will have been sound. However, if his returns do not exceed his contracted payments, the decision to take immediate cash was in error.

CONCEPT *check*

1. Explain the concept of inflation. How does inflation affect saving and investing?

2. How does a preference for liquidity influence an individual or organization's financial decisions?

3. Explain the difference between simple and compound interest.

4. What aspects of the time value of money must professional sport organizations and athletes consider when negotiating contracts?

5. What mistake did the NBA make in its dealings with the owners of the St. Louis Spirits?

6. What are some advantages and disadvantages of deferring salaries (both from the player's and the team's perspectives)?

7. What concerns should a sport organization contemplate when negotiating future payments from sponsorships or other long-term agreements?

PRACTICE *problems*

1. What is the real increase in value if $1,500 is invested for one year at 5% interest and the rate of inflation during that time is 1.79%.

2. A sport organization has a commitment from a sponsor for a $17,000 payment in three years. What is the present value of that money if it is discounted at (a) 3%, (b) 5%, and (c) 9%?

3. You are the financial manager for a recreation center that has signed an option to purchase new elliptical machines for $22,000 in two years. If you have an investment opportunity that guarantees 7% interest, how much must you invest to have the necessary funds to purchase the elliptical machines?

4. An athlete signs a five-year endorsement deal with a prominent sponsor. Under this deal the athlete will receive $5,000 each year for the first three years and $6,500 each year for the final two years. What is the present value of the total deal if the payments are discounted 6%?

5. What is the future value of $12,000 invested at 8% interest, compounded yearly for ten years?

6. If an investor commits $4,500 to an IRA each year for 30 years and receives 6% interest, what will her total investment be worth at the end of the 30 years?

7. A bank offers customers the option of receiving interest compounded quarterly, semi-annually, or annually. If the rate of interest is the same, which is the best option for the customer?

8. What is the difference between $10,000 invested for ten years at 3% interest, compounded yearly, and at 8% interest, compounded semi-annually?

CASE analysis

Time Value of a Sponsorship

The director of marketing of your organization asks for your advice regarding sponsorship deals she is contemplating. She has to choose between the following: a 15-year sponsorship paying $100,000 per year; a 15-year sponsorship initially paying $75,000 per year and increasing 5% each year; and a 15-year sponsorship initially paying $45,000 per year but increasing 12% each year.

CASE QUESTIONS

1. Determine the present value of each year for each proposal, as well as the total present value of each proposal.

Compute two different outcomes, one with a discount rate of 5% and one with a discount rate of 10%.

2. Which proposal should the marketing director choose?

3. What questions about her firm and about the potential sponsors should she contemplate?

4. How do these questions affect the decision? Fully explain your answer.

references

Birger, J. (2009, February 19). Baseball battles the slump. *Fortune.* Retrieved December 30, 2009, from http://money.cnn.com/2009/02/18/magazines/fortune/birger_baseball.fortune/index.htm.

Bureau of Labor Statistics. (n.d.). Frequently asked questions. Retrieved December 27, 2009, from http://www.bls.gov/cpi/cpifaq.htm.

Corwin, M. (2001, April 4). MLB's ticket prices risk alienating fans. Retrieved October 24, 2004, from http://www.yaledailynews.com/article.asp?AID=15265.

Herbert, B. (2009, October 16). Pricing the kids out. *The New York Times.* Retrieved December 30, 2009, from http://www.nytimes.com/2009/10/17/opinion/17herbert.html?_r=1&em.

Hoffman, D. (1998, November). Penguins file for bankruptcy protection. *Stadium and Arena Financing News, 2*(21), 1.

Kaplan, D. (2001, March 12–18). Securitization era opens for athletes. *SportsBusiness Journal, 3*(1), 43.

Mullen, L. (2005, August 22). The NFL's vanishing bonus. *SportsBusiness Journal.* Retrieved December 17, 2005, from http://www.sportsbusinessjournal.com/index.cfm?fuseaction=search.show_article&articleId=46518&keyword=NFL's,%20vanishing,%20bonus.

Pluto, T (1990). *Loose balls.* New York: Simon & Schuster.

Q&A Part 2: Revisiting the Phoenix Coyotes bankruptcy. (2009, June 1). *SportsJudge Blog.* Retrieved December 30, 2009, from http://sportsjudge.blogspot.com/2009/06/q-part-2-revisiting-phoenix-coyotes.html.

Rovell, D. (2001, May 9). Creative financing 101: Deferred salaries. Retrieved May 10, 2001, from http://espn.go.com/mlb/s/2001/0509/1193881.html.

Rovell, D. (2002, January 22). Spirit of ABA deal lives on for Silna brothers. Retrieved December 30, 2009, from http://sports.espn.go.com/espn/print?id=1295194&type=story.

USA Today. Salaries Databases. (2009). Retrieved October 24, 2009, from http://content.usatoday.com/sports/baseball/salaries/default.aspx.

Zigler, B. (2009, April 15). Yearly CPI falls; first time in over five decades. Retrieved December 30, 2009, from http://www.hardassetsinvestor.com/component/content/article/3/1519-yearly-cpi-falls-first-time-in-over-five-decades.html?year=2009&month=04&Itemid=39.

Zimbalist, A. (1992). *Baseball and billions.* New York: Basic Books.

P A R T   T W O

Financial Management

Introduction to Financial Management

Introduction

Financial management is a component of operating any business and, more important, is a necessary and critical aspect of anyone's personal life. Balancing a checkbook, determining a monthly budget, and investing for retirement are financial management activities familiar to many. The work of chief financial officers (CFOs), comptrollers, and other staff members in finance departments is certainly more complex and detailed than what most individuals undertake for their personal finances, but the idea of finance—the application of a series of principles to maximize wealth—applies to both individuals and businesses.

In any sizable organization the finance department will handle most of the long-term financial management issues, but it is vital that *every* member of the organization have some comprehension of finance. Understanding the basics of finance enables a manager to interact more effectively with the financial analysts whose job it is to decipher the numbers. Financial acumen is critical for promotion in most organizations. The leaders of any department, at the least, will be involved in budgeting and forecasting decisions. The financial "Golden Rule" always applies: "He who has the gold makes the rules."

ECONOMIC PRINCIPLES

Although this book focuses on advanced financial principles, we will briefly review some fundamental economic principles, likely familiar to everyone, that form the basis of finance. **Economics** has been defined by Walter Wessel as "the study of how people choose to allocate their scarce resources" (2000, p. 2). Key economic principles outlined in this section include: (1) demand, scarcity, and price; (2) microeconomics versus macroeconomics; and (3) wealth maximization/profits.

Demand, Scarcity, and Price

The choices individuals and organizations make will be influenced by the interdependent factors of demand, scarcity, and price. **Demand** is the quantity of a product or service desired by consumers; **scarcity** describes the situation when the availability of a resource does not meet current demand; and **price** is defined as what one party (the buyer) must give to obtain what is offered by another party (the seller). For instance, economic principles are at work when the Professional Bowlers Association (PBA) Tour announces a new event on its schedule. For the chosen bowling alley, a variety of factors influence its ability to set prices. The number of available tournament passes to be sold (scarcity and lack of it) and the anticipated customer demand determine the price that the alley can charge. However, even if there is high demand, if the PBA decides to schedule an additional tournament close to a current one, more tickets to PBA events become readily available for customers in this marketplace (i.e., the scarcity of tickets changes), and this may reduce the potential ticket price.

North American professional sport franchises and leagues employ the economic concept of scarcity in a variety of ways. The most prominent way is that leagues create scarcity by *not* expanding into every metropolitan area that could potentially support a franchise. With viable alternative cities available, teams often can demand financial concessions from their current metropolitan areas in exchange for their remaining in the current location. Although Charlotte and Portland are larger than some cities that currently have MLB franchises, the league has not rushed to expand into those areas and others similar to them. Current teams seeking new facilities, such as the Tampa Bay Rays, have utilized these non-MLB cities as bargaining chips (Rogers, 2007; "Will Charlotte," 2006). Despite being the second largest metropolitan area in the United States, Los Angeles has not had an NFL team since the Los Angeles Raiders and Los Angeles Rams left the area for Oakland and St. Louis, respectively, in 1995. Representatives of a variety of NFL teams, including the Arizona Cardinals, Jacksonville Jaguars, and Indianapolis Colts, have at least mentioned, and in some cases actually used, the threat of moving to Los Angeles as a bargaining chip during negotiations with their home markets for a new facility (Joyner, 2006; "Lucas Oil," 2006).

Leagues have established internal rules to restrict franchise movement in an effort to maintain scarcity. Most North American professional sport leagues have territorial rules restricting franchise movement within the proximity of a current team. This provides the established franchise with greater bargaining power when negotiating contracts with sponsors and media partners. For instance, even though more than 3 million people live in San Bernardino County (an area just east of Los Angeles, California), MLB prohibits any MLB team from moving into that area, since it is considered part of the "home market" of the Los Angeles Dodgers and the Los Angeles Angels of Anaheim (Nagel, Brown, McEvoy, & Rascher, 2007). When the Montreal Expos moved to Washington D.C. to become the Washington Nationals in 2005, Baltimore Orioles owner Peter Angelos was given control of the Nationals' regional cable television rights and a guaranteed sale price of $365 million if he were to sell the Orioles, as compensation for the infringement on his territory (Nagel et al.). By protecting team territories, leagues help ensure individual franchises will have every opportunity to exploit their scarcity power to maximize their financial position.

Microeconomics versus Macroeconomics

The field of economics is typically divided into microeconomics and macroeconomics. An understanding of each is critical to financial decision making. **Microeconomics** refers to the study of issues that occur at the firm level, such as supply, demand, and pricing. Many of the decisions that financial managers make are determined by microeconomic factors. Such decisions might include setting prices for athletic club memberships or tickets for an upcoming event, or deciding whether to offer a new product line or to pay for training for current employees to learn new job processes. To make these decisions, the financial manager must evaluate the microeconomic forces at work in the business.

In addition to microeconomic forces at the firm level, macroeconomic forces effect every individual and business throughout the world. **Macroeconomics** refers to the study of forces that affect numerous or even all sectors of the overall economy, such as income, unemployment, and inflation at the community, national, regional, or global level. It is critical that financial managers track economic conditions and make their best attempt to predict how macroeconomic forces will affect their operations. Certainly, no one can be certain what will occur in the future, but research and planning can assist the decision-making process. If the national or state economic outlook is poor, for example, it may not be an ideal time to expand production, because customers may not be able to purchase the additional inventory. However, if economic conditions are poor but research indicates that the economy will improve soon, the business may want to expand before their competitors do, to capture the increased demand that will develop once the economic environment has changed. Since interest rates are often lower during an economic downturn, it is typically more favorable to take out loans when the overall economy is sluggish rather than when the economy is performing well. This issue will be discussed in greater detail later in this chapter.

At various levels—cities, counties, states, regions, and countries—economic conditions and outlooks differ from place to place. However, although differences certainly exist in every area, regions around the world are now much more interwoven than in the past. As Thomas Friedman has discussed extensively (2000; 2005), we now have a "worldwide economy." Incidents that disrupt markets in one country can have a tremendous impact on countries on other continents. For example, in 1997, the Asian currency crisis caused economic problems in North America and Europe (Friedman, 2000). More recently, the problems in the United States housing market have affected investors in other countries, because many brokerage houses around the world purchased mortgage notes sold by U.S. lending institutions. An unexpectedly high number of these mortgages have entered foreclosure, and investors around the world have been left with little or no return on their investments. Given the **globalization** of finance—the integration of economies into one "world economy"—no longer can financial managers view macroeconomic conditions solely at the national level. The economic world will continue to shrink as technology continues to enable jobs, capital, and information to move swiftly around the world, often with merely the click of a mouse.

Financial managers usually do not compartmentalize microeconomic and macroeconomic factors in their decision-making processes. Every economic factor must be contemplated, whether it is specific to the firm or applicable to the overall economy. With proper decisions arrived at after evaluation of the appropriate economic environments, firms and individuals can achieve consistent profits and long-term wealth maximization.

Wealth Maximization/Profits

Financial managers must conduct accurate appraisals of potential and realized profits. A distinction must be made between accounting profit and economic profit. An **accounting profit** is earned when revenues exceed costs and expenses over a particular period of time (see Chapter 2). **Economic profit** is determined after including the **opportunity costs** (costs in terms of foregone alternatives) associated with the financial decision. Accounting profit does not necessarily accurately reflect the results of the individual's or organization's financial decisions. For example, if an individual starts a sport promotion business and has $20,000 net income over the first year, an accounting profit of $20,000 has been realized. However, a calculation of economic profits must include the opportunity costs of not working for someone else. If the individual quit a job that paid $40,000 a year, the economic profit would not be $20,000; instead, it would be $20,000 (gained through the business activities) less $40,000 (lost by not working), for a net of *negative* $20,000.

This example is typical of new businesses. Starting a business is a risky venture, and even when the business is turning an accounting profit, the economic profit may be negative when opportunity costs are factored into the analysis. What may be more important is what will happen in the second, third, and subsequent years of the life of the business. Typically, **entrepreneurs,** people who establish a business venture and assume the financial risk for it, understand that a short-term economic loss will be overcome if and when the business becomes successful. Working for someone else may be advantageous in the short term, but most wealthy individuals at some point took risks and endured temporary losses to establish a business.

In addition to understanding the importance of generating profits and creating long-term wealth, entrepreneurs—and anyone responsible for the operation and success of a business—should be aware that the way a business is structured can have a tremendous impact on its financial performance and on the individual risk of the owners.

BUSINESS TYPES

Most businesses start when an individual or a small group has an idea to create a new product or service or to improve a product or service that already exists. When the initial idea is born, the entrepreneurs do not necessarily think about the importance of forming the new business in a manner that will maximize their short- and long-term financial position. Usually, the primary focus is on developing the idea and determining whether it is viable in the marketplace. However, every business owner, even someone who is earning part-time income from a "hobby," should understand the ramifications of the organizational structures in his or her industry. In the sport industry, these structures include government-operated organizations, non-profits, sole proprietorships, partnerships, subchapter S corporations, limited liability corporations or limited liability partnerships, and C corporations.

Government-Operated Organizations

It is important to remember that governments can operate businesses. In the sport industry, high school and collegiate athletic departments at public schools are ultimately operated by the government. Since the athletic department is a component of the public school, and the public school is operated by the city or county school district or the state, the government entity has ultimate authority over and responsibility for the athletic department's actions and financial performance. Chapter 14 details some of the important and unique financial considerations of intercollegiate athletic departments, and Chapter 13 discusses recreational programs, which are often subsidiaries of a government agency.

Most private businesses want minimal government involvement in their affairs. When San Diego Padres owner Joan Kroc offered to donate all or a portion of the Padres to the city of San Diego, MLB immediately voiced its displeasure (Swank, 2004). Major League Baseball owners also rejected the suggestion of Carl Pohlad, former owner of the Minnesota Twins, that a portion of his team be sold to the state of Minnesota. If a sizable portion of the Padres or the Twins were to be owned by the government, citizens would have greater access to information about the financial operation of an MLB team, because information about how government agencies spend their money is available to citizens through **Freedom of Information requests** (sometimes referred to as "sunshine laws"). Fortunately for MLB, it retains an **antitrust exemption** that permits it to restrict the sale of franchises and ultimately determine who is eligible to become an owner.

Non-profits

Non-profit organizations—those that are not conducted for the profit of owners—operate under a variety of specific rules that make them distinct from for-profit enterprises. One of the main rules governing non-profits is that shareholders never receive dividends; most non-profit organizations that generate more revenues than expenses and costs will spend that money to further the organization's business interests, whereas a for-profit business's net income would likely be distributed to the shareholders as dividends. A variety of sporting events are operated by non-profit organizations. For instance, the Professional Golfers Association (PGA) Tour is a non-profit company, and it requires that all PGA Tour events be operated on a non-profit basis.

Sole Proprietorships

The vast majority of for-profit businesses in the United States operate as sole proprietorships. A **sole proprietorship** is a business that is legally owned and operated by a single individual. No formal paperwork is required to establish the business, and the paperwork necessary to sustain the business is minimal (compared to other business types). Extensive meetings to determine strategy and company direction are not necessary, as the owner can simply make decisions unilaterally. Sole proprietorships are typically easier to sell than other business types. The business exists as long as the owner is operating it, and all profits belong to the owner.

However, the simplicity of the sole proprietorship presents some drawbacks. It can be more difficult for a sole proprietorship to raise capital than for other business types. More important, the owner is personally liable for the business's activities. A successful lawsuit against the business can result in the owner being required to sell personal assets to pay the judgment. Most owners of sole proprietorships purchase liability insurance to guard against the financial ramifications of potential lawsuits. Because sport and recreation activities tend to have a higher likelihood of physical injury than activities provided in many other industries, owners of sole proprietorships in sport and recreation often require additional insurance or choose to convert to an alternative business structure. Some of the business structures discussed below can provide a **corporate veil** separating the business from the owner. This protection from personal liability is an important reason why owners often choose one of these alternative structures.

Partnerships

A **general partnership** is simply the joining of two or more individuals with the intent to own and operate a business. The partnership agreement may divide ownership equally or unequally. Most attorneys will advise against operating a business as a 50/50 partnership, even if the owners are family members, because a 50/50 partnership can result in a stalemate. Neither partner in such a partnership can institute policy without the permission of the other, since business decisions must be approved by a majority (50.1%) of the owners. However, disproportionate ownership positions may place the **minority partner** or partners at a disadvantage. If a two-person partnership is owned with a 60/40 split, the minority partner is entitled to only 40% of the profits and only 40% of the influence in company decisions. That partner can be outvoted on any organizational issue. Typically, investors in partnerships who take minority positions are not likely to invest as much money as they would if they were receiving control.

A general partnership may be established either formally or informally. An **express partnership** can be created by a contract between the parties. An **implied partnership** may exist if individuals merely act as partners, such as by sharing a company checking account or by jointly signing for a business loan. Owners must understand the consequences of their actions when operating a business, as a court will examine the activities of the owners when determining liabilities.

A partnership presents the same disadvantages as a sole proprietorship. The partners have personal liability for company losses or judgments. In some cases, minority partners may be personally liable for a greater share of the company's liabilities than their percentage of ownership. If a partner who owns 60% of a business goes bankrupt, a judgment against the business may result in the minority partner being required to cover financial obligations of the insolvent general partner, even though the minority partner owns only 40% of the company. For this reason, some partnerships involve **limited partners**—partners who are liable only for their direct financial contribution and do not perform any formal managerial role

SIDEBAR

Al Davis Becomes Raiders' General Partner   5.A

Perhaps the most intriguing partnership agreement in professional sport involves the NFL's Oakland Raiders. Al Davis had been the head coach and general manager of the Oakland Raiders in the American Football League (AFL) from 1963 through 1966. After achieving on- and off-field success, he became commissioner of the AFL in 1966. At the time, the AFL and the NFL were competing to sign players and attract fans. Davis, never one to compromise easily, sought to gain an advantage over the NFL by signing the majority of the latter's star quarterbacks and instituting an aggressive marketing plan (Harris, 1986).

Almost immediately after Davis became commissioner, however, three AFL owners secretly negotiated with the NFL to merge the leagues. When the leagues merged without Davis' input, Davis was upset, as he felt the AFL could have succeeded against the NFL. Davis felt his work made him the likely choice to become NFL Commissioner after the merger. However, the NFL retained Commissioner Pete Rozelle.

After the AFL–NFL merger, Al Davis signed a ten-year contract to return to Oakland as general manager and part owner of the Raiders. He was offered a 10% stake in the team—a stake valued at approximately $1 million—for only $18,500 (Harris). More important, Davis was named managing general partner. Ed McGah and Wayne Valley were the other general partners.

After continued success on the field and in the front office, Davis utilized language in the partnership agreement to his advantage. When other teams contacted him about becoming their general manager, Davis convinced McGah that he needed to sign over complete ownership control of the Raiders to him. McGah, in one of the most amazing incidents in sports business history, signed a contract he did not even bother to read. The contract essentially named Al Davis the Raiders' "controlling" owner (Harris). The partnership agreement that governed the franchise stipulated that if any two of the general partners agreed to a contract, the other had no recourse. Even though Valley owned the largest percentage of the team, Davis controlled the franchise and would represent the organization on all matters. Valley eventually sold his shares in the partnership after his litigation to regain control of the franchise failed.

What Type of Owner Do Fans Want?   SIDEBAR

In North American professional sports, the owners of most teams are individuals or groups of individuals. Typically, sports teams are not held as C corporations. In fact, the NFL bars publicly traded companies and non-profit organizations from owning franchises. The current public ownership status of the Green Bay Packers is permitted because the team was organized as a non-profit organization before the current NFL ownership rules were established (Eichelberger, 1998; "Stock and financial history," n.d.). The NFL requires that one individual own at least 30% of the franchise and that the owner does not control a majority interest in a team from Major League Baseball, the National Basketball Association, or the National Hockey League (Chass, 2003; Eichelberger). The NFL wants an individual owner to be ultimately responsible for each team's operation. In addition, it wants each franchise to have one decision maker at league meetings. These rules also ensure that individual teams are less likely to change their "organizational philosophy," since the ownership is retained by one individual rather than a group of shareholders (Tucker, 2003).

There have been cases of large Fortune 500 companies holding a professional sport franchise in their portfolio. New York Yankees owner George Steinbrenner purchased the franchise from the Columbia Broadcasting System (CBS) in 1973. The Atlanta Braves of MLB were owned by media mogul Ted Turner for many years. The flamboyant Turner was often seen at games and on television discussing his hope for the teams' on-field success (Conlin, 2008). Although Turner certainly wanted to generate a profit, he was primarily concerned with attempting to win the National League Pennant and the World Series. When Turner sold the team to AOL-Time Warner, many fans noticed a change: AOL-Time Warner operated the team much as they operated their numerous other corporate holdings (Conlin). The team was required to set a strict yearly budget. Whereas Turner was often willing to trade for talented but expensive players in the middle of the season, fans perceived AOL-Time Warner as being solely interested in achieving a specific return on investment rather than fielding the best possible team to compete for championships (Tucker).

The Disney Corporation owned the Los Angeles Angels of Anaheim from 1996 to 2003. Although Disney initially thought it could conduct extensive cross-promotions of the team with its theme parks, movies, and other entertainment offerings, it discovered that the benefits of MLB ownership mainly pertain to the "ego gratification" of the team's owner. (An owner of a professional sport franchise will be known throughout the team's metropolitan area and potentially throughout the United States and parts of the rest of the world.) Despite the Angels' 2002 World Series win, Disney soon realized that the team could not generate the same return on investment as its other holdings and sold the team to Artie Moreno in 2003 (King, 2003). Moreno has since inspired many Angels fans, who feel that he has done more to acquire players and provide a winning environment for the team ("Moreno keeps promise," 2008).

in the operation of the business. Limited partners must remember that the general partner or partners do have personal liability and that a judgment or other financial loss could bankrupt the general partners and, hence, the overall company. It is important to note that limited partners may hold more than 50% of the ownership in a company. A limited partner who owns 60% of an organization does not have any formal role in the company's operation but is entitled to 60% of the profits.

A partnership ends when a partner dies or goes bankrupt or when the partnership engages in any illegal activity. A partnership may also be discontinued by the courts if one of the partners is adjudicated insane. A difficulty sometimes arises when terminating partnerships if the business is not making money. Ultimately, if the business cannot make money, the partnership will be dissolved. In some cases, however, the partners may have differing opinions about the future financial viability of the company. If the partners cannot agree on whether to continue the business, a resolution may require court intervention. The court may dissolve the partnership or may determine how, and at what compensation, one or more partners may exit.

Subchapter S Corporations

The main financial advantage of a **subchapter S corporation** (often called an S corp) is that profits flow through the business to the shareholders and are taxed only once, as ordinary income to the shareholders. A second advantage is that the shareholders are shielded from personal liability (beyond their investment) by the corporate veil. A subchapter S corporation can own subsidiaries that operate independently (from a legal standpoint), which enables the S corp to be shielded from liability, as well.

Subchapter S corporations do have some significant drawbacks, particularly if the owners seek to grow the business and involve a wide variety of investors. Subchapter S corporations must be based in the United States, and all of the investors—who may number no more than 100—must be from the United States. An S corp can issue only one form of **stock** (a security that represents an ownership percentage of a company), meaning every share must have the same voting rights and dividend allotments. Many businesses that do not anticipate having a large, diversified ownership structure and do not intend to operate outside the United States choose to be incorporated as subchapter S corporations. Numerous sports businesses in the United States are S corps.

Limited Liability Corporations or Limited Liability Partnerships

Forming and operating a subchapter S corporation requires extensive paperwork and attention to detail. For this reason, many business owners choose to operate as a **limited liability corporation (LLC)** or a **limited liability partnership (LLP)**. An LLC or LLP operates in many ways like a subchapter S corporation. Profits flow through to the investors and are taxed as ordinary income. The LLC and LLP structures also provide a corporate veil against personal liability. However, LLCs and LLPs are typically easier to establish than S corps, through simple paperwork filed in the state where the LLC or LLP will initially operate. Tax forms are also much easier to fill out and file than those for a subchapter S corporation. However, because LLCs and LLPs are fairly new business entities, national standards regarding their operation do not yet exist. Individual states govern LLCs and LLPs in a variety of ways. In some states, rules for LLCs and LLPs have been determined through legislative or judicial action, but in other states ground rules have not been firmly established. States also differ in their laws regarding taxation of LLC and LLP owners. Investors should seek financial and legal advice regarding the formation and operation of LLCs and LLPs.

C Corporations

When most people think of corporations, they think of Fortune 500 companies such as Disney or General Motors. Disney and General Motors are indeed corporations, but specifically they are classified as **C corporations** (often called C corps). Many, but not all, of the 500 largest companies in the world operate as C corporations, for the primary reason that C corporations may seek investors and conduct business activities around the world. To become a C corporation, a company must file extensive paperwork in its home state. Because of its favorable state laws, Delaware is home to many of the largest C corps, despite the fact that these companies typically do not do much, if any, business in Delaware. Once established, the corporation must hold annual meetings, elect a board of directors, and provide specific annual paperwork to the government and to shareholders.

The C corporation provides the corporate veil that protects investors from personal liability. However, unlike a subchapter S corporation, a C corporation is taxed as a separate legal entity before any profits that remain may be provided to shareholders. Since the shareholders must then pay taxes on their dividends, C corporations are said to be subject to "double taxation." For example, if a subchapter S corporation profited $200,000, that money would flow through to the owners' personal taxes. If the individual tax rate was 35%, then the owners would pay a total tax of $70,000. However, a company operated as a C corporation would first pay corporate taxes on the $200,000 profit. With a corporate tax rate of 35%, the corporation pays $70,000 in tax, leaving $130,000. If the company were to issue a dividend to the owners for the entire $130,000, the owners would pay 35% tax on the $130,000.

Companies organized as C corporations are not limited in the number of shareholders. In addition, the company can issue different classifications of stock and can sell stock to foreign nationals and institutional investors. A profitable company operated as a partnership, LLC, or subchapter S corporation may elect to change its structure to a C corporation, called "going public." By "going public" the owner or owners potentially can generate a tremendous amount of money, and other investors also can take a significant stake in the operation of the company. Decisions regarding the direction of the company are made by the majority of shareholders. If one person or group of people holds 50.1% of the stock, then that person or group has the power to set policies. In most cases, when a company goes public, no one owner retains more than 50.1% of the stock. Factions of stockholders must vote together to establish or alter company policies. In some cases, prominent founders of companies have been "forced out" of their management positions by other shareholders working in concert.

Exhibit 5.1 summarizes the advantages and disadvantages of the various business structures.

exhibit   5.1   Advantages and disadvantages of various business structures.

TYPE	ADVANTAGES	DISADVANTAGES
Sole proprietorship	Easily created and managed Flow-through taxation	Personal liability Raising capital
Partnership	Easily created Flow-through taxation	Potential management disputes Personal liability (except limited partners)
S corp	Flow-through taxation Limited liability	Limited number of potential investors Costs of formation and operation Single classification of stock can be issued
LLC/LLP	Flow-through taxation Limited liability	Undefined and inconsistent state operating standards
C corp	Limited liability Unlimited number of investors Different classifications of stock can be issued	Costs of formation and operation Double taxation

STOCK MARKETS

Every company uses stock as a vehicle of ownership. Every company has stock, but not every company is publicly traded. The vast majority of companies are privately held, meaning new investors, whether individuals or institutions, must be invited to purchase stock. The stock of companies that do go public will be listed for sale on a **stock market** or **stock exchange.** Stock exchanges exist around the world; the most prominent in the United States are the New York Stock Exchange (NYSE) and the National Association of Securities Dealers Automated Quotations (NASDAQ). Each exchange lists the stocks of companies that are available to purchase or sell. To be listed on the exchange, the company must meet a variety of requirements, most of them relating to company capitalization, revenues, and number of outstanding shares. The stock exchange acts as the clearinghouse for brokers to buy and sell listed companies.

The New York Stock Exchange, sometimes known as the "Big Board," is the largest exchange in the world when measured by market capitalization. However, it ranks only third in the world by number of listings, behind the Bombay Stock Exchange in Mumbai, India, and NASDAQ—the world's first electronic stock market, which typically attracts emerging and technology companies. Most of the industrialized nations of the world have at least one stock exchange. The Internet has enabled investors to buy and sell stocks directly in each of these markets.

Many non–North American professional sport franchises are listed on stock markets around the world. One of the more notable stock offerings was for Manchester United in 1991 (Kaplan, 2001). For many years Manchester United has been one of the most powerful brand names in sport, and when it went public its stock was quickly purchased by fans around the world. North American professional sport franchises are currently not traded on a stock market, but some teams have been listed in the past. The New England Patriots of the NFL, the Cleveland Cavaliers and Milwaukee Bucks of the NBA, and the Baltimore Orioles of MLB were all taken public in the 1960s or 1970s. Each of them has since returned to private ownership. More recently, shares of the Boston Celtics were offered to

SIDEBAR

What Is the Dow Jones?   **5.C**

The performance of the overall stock market is a matter of interest to many people, not only investors. One way to examine the market's overall performance is to track a specific stock market to see how all of its stocks have performed. Since each market lists hundreds or even thousands of stocks, the overall stock market may need to be dissected further into stock market indexes to examine the overall market's performance or the performance of market subsectors. The Dow Jones Industrial Average (the "Dow") is the most famous stock market index. In 1884—long before computers were available to crunch massive quantities of numbers—Charles Henry Dow created the index to attempt to track the overall market by following the stock price fluctuations of a few selected stocks. Dow's original index included 11 stocks. It increased to 12 stocks in 1896, 20 stocks in 1916, and then finally 30 in 1928. As the overall economy has changed, the companies representing the Dow have also been changed. The Dow lists only well-known and widely held *large-cap* companies, those with a *market capitalization*—the market price of a company, computed by multiplying the number of outstanding shares by the price per share—greater than $5 billion. General Electric is the only company that remains from Henry Dow's original list. The Dow is computed by using a scaled average that accounts for stock splits.

Since the Dow contains only large-cap stocks, some investors turn to other indexes for a broader picture of the stock market's performance. The Standard and Poor's 500 (S&P 500) represents 70% of all U.S. publicly traded companies. Note that the S&P 500 does not list the 500 largest companies, but rather 500 companies that, together, are believed to provide an accurate indication of the overall performance of the stock market. Other popular indexes include the Russell 2000, which tracks the performance of *small-cap stocks* (stocks of companies with a market capitalization between $250 million and $1 billion) and the Wilshire 5000, which tracks the performance of all publicly traded companies in the United States. These indexes tend to move in similar directions over an extended period of time, but short-term market conditions may affect the indexes differently.

the public in 1986, and shares of the Cleveland Indians were offered in 1998. These stocks attracted some interest, but they were initially priced too high for most investors to achieve expected financial returns (Much & Phillips, 1999). The Celtics were taken private in 2002, and the Indians were taken private in 2000.

GOVERNMENT INFLUENCE ON THE BUSINESS ENVIRONMENT

The U.S. government has a vested interest in the financial success of individuals and corporations. A prolonged poor economy hurts citizens, and since citizens may vote for many government positions, the government must at least tacitly acknowledge the state of the economy and appear to be addressing economic concerns. Although the United States operates under a **capitalist** economic system, in which the majority of capital is privately owned, over the past 100 years it has moved away from 19th-century **laissez-faire** economics—where the government meddled little in the business environment beyond setting and enforcing rudimentary laws—toward a more **socialistic** system, where the government is more actively involved in owning and administering means of production.

Two important events in the 20th century spurred the U.S. government into taking a more active role in the business community. During the Great Depression, President Franklin D. Roosevelt enacted extensive expensive government programs to provide food for the poor and work for the unemployed. After the economic downturn was over, many of these programs were not repealed. Then, during President Lyndon B. Johnson's administration in the 1960s, Congress passed expensive **Great Society** initiatives to combat poverty. Much of the legislation passed during Johnson's tenure, such as Medicare and Medicaid, is still active.

The long-term economic results of Roosevelt's and Johnson's policies have been mixed. Massive amounts of spending did help to spur some economic activity, but many economists believe the government's large financial commitments could have been better utilized in the private sector. The programs have clearly created an expectation among the majority of the country's citizens that the government will be actively involved in their individual and business affairs. Currently, the government's overall role in the economy encompasses a variety of areas of influence. Our discussion in this chapter will center on two important governmental functions: monetary policy and fiscal policy.

Monetary Policy and the Federal Reserve

Monetary policy is policy the government sets to control the supply, availability, and cost of money. In most cases, when monetary policy decisions are made, the vast majority of American citizens pay little attention. The **Federal Reserve**, or "Fed," is the primary organizing body that attempts to maintain the overall economic health of the United States. Established in 1913, the Federal Reserve acts as the "nation's bank," controlling the nation's currency and lending money to the government, among other functions. The Federal Reserve's main goal is to manage the economy so it grows steadily. Its secondary goal is to control inflation—the devaluation of the currency. Inflation is not unusual (see Chapter 4), but a high

The Unique Ownership of the Green Bay Packers   SIDEBAR

5.D

Although the NFL requires its teams to be controlled by a primary individual owner, it has allowed the Green Bay Packers to maintain its ownership structure despite violating NFL rules. The Packers have a unique history and ownership structure. The Green Bay franchise, formed in 1919, was initially owned by the Indian Packing Company—hence the nickname "Packers" ("Birth of a team," n.d.). During its first few years the team was not financially successful, and it was on the verge of folding in 1923. However, A. B. Turnbull, publisher of the *Green Bay Press–Gazette,* and four other men worked to save the team for the community ("Stock & financial history"). In August 1923 the Packers were re-formed as a non-profit organization called the Green Bay Packers Corporation, and stock certificates for 1,000 shares of stock were sold at $5 apiece ("Stock & financial history"). Because the team was established as a non-profit organization, owners of the team would not be financially rewarded. However, the initial stock sale ensured that the team would remain financially viable and that it would stay in Green Bay.

When the team encountered additional financial difficulty in 1935, the franchise was reorganized as Green Bay Packers, Inc., and more shares were sold. The franchise also sold stock in 1950 at $25 per share. Unlike the earlier purchasers, who primarily lived in Green Bay, for the 1950 sale of stock, citizens across Wisconsin and former Green Bay residents living in other states came forward to purchase shares. The team no longer "belonged" to Green Bay but had become "Wisconsin's team," as over $50,000 was raised in an 11-day period ("Stock & financial history"). The team experienced tremendous on-field success in the 1960s under legendary coach Vince Lombardi, and as its NFL television exposure increased, the Packers began to attract fans from around the country. Many admired the rich history of the Packers and venerable Lambeau Field.

Despite the Packers' on-field success, by the 1990s the economics of the NFL had dramatically changed. The team was financially successful, but Lambeau Field was in need of considerable upgrades. Other NFL teams played in newer facilities that offered luxury suites and club seating. The Packers could continue to draw sellout crowds, but in order to maximize stadium revenues Lambeau Field needed significant remodeling. Since the team was owned by the community, raising funds would require an additional sale of stock. The NFL supported the Packers' plan to amend the articles of the corporation to offer additional shares to the general public. In November 1997 the Packers offered 400,000 shares to the general public ("Stock & financial history"). The response was overwhelming, and the team was able to raise millions of dollars to pay for the Lambeau Field renovations. Citizens in every state and in some foreign countries purchased shares. Many of the shares were exchanged as Christmas gifts (Wolfley, 1997).

Owners of stock in the Packers are motivated by sentiment rather than the expectation of financial gain. Shareholders may attend an annual meeting and vote on franchise issues, but they will never receive a dividend. In addition, shares may only be sold back to the team, at a significant discount from their initial price ("Stock & financial history"). However, shares can be given or bequeathed to others. The team's unique financial structure has enabled it to remain in Green Bay while the rest of the teams in the NFL play in much larger metropolitan markets.

rate of inflation, like those encountered in the late 1970s, causes significant damage to the economy.

The Federal Reserve system includes 12 district Federal Reserve Banks and numerous member banks across the United States. Seven governors serve 14-year terms on the Federal Reserve Board, with staggered terms to ensure continuity. Each of the governors is appointed by the President of the United States and approved by Congress. The length of time each governor serves is longer than the terms served by the President and members of Congress, to diminish political interference and enable the Federal Reserve to serve the short- and long-term financial interests of the country rather than the whims of elected politicians. Typically, the governors meet approximately every six weeks, with additional meetings scheduled if needed.

The Federal Reserve acts to

- regulate the nation's currency supply,
- serve as banker for many government agencies,
- lend to banks,
- audit banks,
- control the currency,
- guard more than 10,000 tons of gold held in the New York Federal Reserve Bank, and
- administrate the transfer of funds via checks.

In most cases, the Federal Reserve does not need to act often or dramatically to maintain the economy. Typically, the overall economy shifts gradually, and the Fed can take subtle action to attempt to nudge it in a positive direction. However, during times of concern, the Federal Reserve may need to act often. If the economy is rapidly slowing or expanding, the Fed may meet more than once every six weeks to set interest rates. Natural disasters, such as Hurricane Katrina, or terrorist acts, such as those that occurred on September 11, 2001, can cause dramatic shifts in the overall economic climate. The Federal Reserve will meet and act, sometimes multiple times in a month, if needed.

Although the Federal Reserve performs many functions, it focuses primarily on two main areas: setting interest rates and monitoring the money supply. The Fed studies a variety of evaluation measures before making changes in interest rates or the money supply. These measures include changes in unemployment claims, durable goods orders, housing starts, new factory orders, and overall consumer confidence.

Setting interest rates

The first primary responsibility of the Federal Reserve is to set interest rates. The Fed does not mandate the rates individual lending institutions charge customers for loans for cars, homes, higher education, and so forth, but it does establish lending policies, and it sets two important interest rates. The **discount rate** is the rate at which banks may borrow money from the Federal Reserve. This rate is used primarily as a baseline for setting other rates—the vast majority of banks do not ever borrow money from the Federal Reserve, as it is seen as a sign of financial trouble for the bank and is typically a last resort. However, banks do borrow money from other banks on a daily basis. The rate a bank charges another bank when it loans excess money through the Federal Reserve is the **federal funds rate.**

The reason banks borrow money from each other is that the Federal Reserve requires every bank to have a reserve available in case customers wish to withdraw their deposits. This reserve is essentially 10% of total deposits, although the stipulations are complex (Morris & Morris, 1999). One factor that led to the Great Depression of the 1930s was that a large number of customers visited their local branches to withdraw funds, and some of the banks did not have sufficient money available to give to them. A financial panic ensued as more and more customers became concerned that money was not available. This caused banks to fail. The U.S. government has established the Federal Deposit Insurance

Corporation (FDIC) (not a part of the Federal Reserve) to assure citizens that their money is safe in banks. Typically, savings accounts and some (though not all) other accounts are insured by the federal government up to $250,000 in the event a bank fails.

Each day, banks determine how much money they have on deposit and how much money they have loaned to customers. Since banks earn profits by loaning money and charging interest, they benefit from loaning as much money as possible. To adhere to the Fed's reserve requirement, banks that do not have enough money on hand on a given day must borrow from other banks (or the Federal Reserve, in dire situations) to increase their reserve. Banks that are in good financial standing can typically find other banks willing to loan them money. Each day, hundreds of banks borrow from and lend to one another to maintain their reserve requirement and maximize financial returns. It is not uncommon for a bank to borrow money from another bank one day and then loan money back to that other bank a few days later, as each bank's overall deposits fluctuate through customers' making deposits, taking out loans, and so forth. Computers enable the timely and orderly computation and transfer of money.

The Federal Reserve monitors the overall economic health of the United States (and to a lesser extent the rest of the world) and attempts to

SIDEBAR

What Is the Impact of an Interest Rate Change?   5.E

The Federal Reserve typically changes the discount and federal funds rates by only a quarter of a percent. If the Fed feels the economy needs a more dramatic change, it may increase or decrease the rates by a half percent or more. A hundredth of a percent is called a *basis point*. If the Federal Reserve cuts rates by one quarter of one percent, then it has cut rates by 25 basis points. Note that a 25 basis point increase or decrease is not the same *percentage change* for different established rates. If a 10% rate is cut by 25 basis points, the change in the rate is 2.5%, but if a 5% rate is cut by 25 basis points, then the change in the rate is 5%. Most people pay no attention to the Fed's changes in interest rates, until they start shopping for a loan. Even a small increase of 25 basis points can dramatically alter the monthly or yearly interest payment, particularly when the loan has a large principal or a long term.

For instance, a person who wishes to purchase a $250,000 house and can make a down payment of $50,000 would need a mortgage loan for the remaining $200,000. Most home mortgages have a term of 10, 15, 20, or 30 years, although some mortgages have a term of 40 or even 50 years. Exhibit 5.2 shows the effect of a small increase or decrease in rates on a monthly mortgage payment.

Monthly payment (principal and interest) for a $200,000 loan.   **exhibit   5.2**

| RATE | TERM | | | | |
	10 YEARS	15 YEARS	20 YEARS	30 YEARS	40 YEARS
6.00%	$2,220.41	$1,687.71	$1,432.86	$1,199.10	$1,100.43
6.25%	$2,245.60	$1,714.85	$1,461.86	$1,231.43	$1,135.48
6.50%	$2,270.96	$1,742.21	$1,491.15	$1,264.14	$1,170.91
6.75%	$2,296.48	$1,769.82	$1,520.73	$1,297.20	$1,206.71
7.00%	$2,322.17	$1,797.66	$1,550.60	$1,330.60	$1,242.86
8.00%	$2,426.55	$1,911.30	$1,672.88	$1,467.53	$1,390.62

set the discount and federal funds rates at a level that will maintain the overall economic health of the nation. If the Federal Reserve believes the economy is slowing down, it may lower the interest rates in an effort to cause more money to "flow" through the economy. Lower interest rates encourage citizens and businesses to borrow money, and when a business borrows money, it will often expand its production, hire new workers, and so forth. The Federal Reserve seeks to avoid a national **recession**—two consecutive quarters of negative growth in the nation's gross domestic product—as that can result in a dramatic increase in unemployment.

When the Fed reduces the interest rates at which banks borrow money from each other, other interest rates typically fall in consequence. For instance, some banks set their **prime rate**—the rate they charge their "best" customers—a few percentage points higher than the federal funds rate. If the federal funds rate goes down, the prime rate likely will decrease. Banks are likely to change some but not all of their rates as soon as the Federal Reserve sets its rates. Credit card rates are not changed as often as the federal funds rate, because credit card debts are **unsecured claims,** debts issued without any collateral. (**Collateral** is an asset(s) pledged to a lender to be used as repayment of a loan in the event of default.)

During times when the economy is performing well, the Federal Reserve may elect not to change the rates, but if the Fed feels the economy is performing *too* well, it may raise interest rates. An overheated economy can lead to inflation, as businesses will be expanding rapidly. When businesses increase output, they tend to require new workers, and if there are not sufficient workers available, the businesses will begin to offer much higher wages to entice workers away from other businesses. This is obviously a good environment in which to work, but only to a point. If wages increase too rapidly, inflation can become rampant. By raising interest rates, the Federal Reserve slows the rate of increase in the overall economy. It becomes more expensive for individuals and businesses to borrow money, resulting in fewer purchases and lower overall production.

The difference between a 30-year mortgage at 6.0% interest and a 30-year mortgage at 6.25% interest, for example, is $32.33 per month. When multiplied by 360 (the number of payments to be made over the 30-year period), the monthly difference results in a total of $11,638.80. The difference between 6.0% and 7.0% is even more dramatic: the monthly difference of $131.50 results in a total difference of $47,340. Any individual or company that is anticipating taking out a loan would be wise to observe the Federal Reserve's actions on interest rates.

Monitoring the money supply

In addition to setting interest rates, the Federal Reserve attempts to control the overall amount of money in the economy. The public money supply is measured in three ways:

- **M1** measures liquid assets in the form of cash and checking accounts.
- **M2** includes all of the money in M1 plus all money in savings accounts and **certificates of deposit (CDs)**—FDIC-insured debt instruments issued by banks and savings and loans with a fixed term and a specific interest rate. This money is not likely to be spent as readily as M1 money.

- **M3** includes all of the money in M1 and M2 plus the assets and liabilities, including long-term deposits, of financial institutions. In 2006, the Federal Reserve announced that it would no longer publish M3 statistics, but other entities continue to estimate and publish this information.

These measures and other information help the Federal Reserve determine the likelihood that money will be spent in the near future. The M1 and M2 tables are available at www.federalreserve.gov/releases/h6/Current/.

Increasing the money supply. If the Federal Reserve believes the economy needs more money to maintain or increase its overall health, it will increase the overall money supply by creating new money with which it buys securities from banks and other financial institutions. The financial institutions in turn spend, loan, or invest the new money. The Fed must be careful that it does not create too much money. Simply "printing" more money to pay off current financial obligations is a recipe for hyperinflation. After World War I, the German government printed too many marks (German currency at the time), and their value decreased to such an extent that people were burning their paper money, since that was more efficient than gathering wheelbarrows full of money to use to buy firewood.

Decreasing the money supply. The Federal Reserve can also remove money from the economy by issuing government securities. Financial institutions usually will be interested in purchasing the newly issued securities, because they are backed by the United States government and typically provide a solid rate of return. As financial institutions purchase the securities, money is removed from the economy—until the securities are due to be repaid, with interest. The overall supply of money in the economy is ever changing. It is not uncommon for the Federal Reserve to issue securities one day and then buy them the next.

Fiscal Policy

Another function of the government in relation to the economy is setting **fiscal policy**—governmental decisions to collect and spend money in order to influence the economy. With more than 300 million people in the United States, there are more than 300 million opinions regarding exactly how much money the government needs and where the government should spend its money. Politicians have different views regarding spending priorities, but it seems none of them ever complain about having too much money to spend. The legislative and the executive branches of the government have direct influence on the United States' fiscal policy. Congress passes a federal budget, and then the President signs it into law. Each individual state, county, and city also has a fiscal policy, which is managed by governors, mayors, city council members, and so forth. Debates regarding the collection and spending of money, at every level of government, can become contentious. Often, compromises must be made to avoid a government shutdown when the debate runs past a fiscal deadline. The fiscal policies of governments, such as decisions about taxes and depreciation, influence sport entities as well as other businesses. In some cases laws are enacted that specifically affect the sport industry, such as "jock tax" legislation (discussed later in this chapter).

Taxes

Governments need revenues to defray the cost of providing services. These revenues are typically raised by charging a variety of different taxes. Every citizen who owes the government money must pay her or his taxes on time or incur penalties and late fees. In addition, delinquent taxes can result in criminal charges against the offending party. Notorious mobster Al Capone, a mob boss during the Prohibition era, used intimidation, physical violence, extortion, and, in some cases, murder to sustain his criminal enterprises. Despite these well-known violations of the law, it was his failure to pay federal income taxes that led to Capone's eventual imprisonment in 1931.

Every business must spend considerable time and money ensuring that it adheres to the various applicable tax codes. It is beyond the scope of this book to detail how various federal, state, and local taxes affect sport business operations. However, a sport business or an individual who understands the overall tax code and its unique aspects can save hundreds of thousands or even millions of dollars. For instance, under the Federal Insurance Contributions Act, every employee pays 2.9% of wages (technically half is paid by the employer and half is paid by the employee) for Medicare (King, 2005). Signing bonuses, however, were exempt from the 2.9% tax until December 2004, when the Internal Revenue Service (IRS) changed its interpretation of the tax regulations for signing bonuses for MLB players. Major League Baseball had long argued that signing bonuses should not be taxed as wages. Signing bonuses and wages are treated the same for federal income tax purposes, but until the 2004 ruling they were taxed differently for Medicare. When the IRS altered its rules, some players and teams realized they had been paying taxes on signing bonuses that they did not owe. Baseball agent Scott Boras understood both the previous rules and the ramifications of the new interpretation. After negotiating Carlos Beltran's $119 million contract with the New York Mets, he insisted that Beltran sign the contract prior to January 12, 2005—the date the new IRS ruling would take effect. Signing the contract prior to the deadline saved Beltran $319,000 in Medicare taxes on his $11 million signing bonus (King, 2005).

Depreciation

Depreciation, the allocation of an item's loss of value over a period of time, is an important factor in the determination of a business's tax debt. Items such as machinery, buildings (but not land), computers, and desks purchased in the operating of a business have a useful life, and once their useful life is completed, they typically must be replaced. The tax code permits businesses to deduct the loss of value of business assets from their tax obligations. For instance, if a fitness club purchases a computer, each year the computer will lose some of its initial value. At the end of its useful life, the business will need to replace the computer with a new one.

The IRS recognizes a variety of methods to determine the yearly loss of value of a particular item. For simplicity, this discussion will describe four of the main methods.

Straight-line. Estimating straight-line depreciation is straightforward. The total cost of the item minus its estimated salvage value is divided by its useful life to determine its yearly depreciation allowance. For a computer with a cost of $1,000, a useful life of five years, and no salvage value, the depreciation would be ($1000

– $0)/5 = $200 per year. The $200 is recorded as a deduction against yearly revenue. If the business had operating income of $100,000, its tax obligation would be calculated on $99,800. During each of the next four years, the business will be able to deduct $200 from its tax obligation.

Sum-of-years-digits. Straight-line depreciation is simple and easy to calculate, but it is not necessarily accurate in assessing the loss of value an item experiences during its useful life. In some cases items depreciate quickly, and in others the item retains a greater portion of its value until the completion of its useful life. The **sum-of-years-digits** method attempts to take the non-linear loss of value into account. As in the straight-line method, we must estimate the useful life of the item. We then add the number of years of the item's life as follows: for a life of two years, the result is 1 + 2 = 3. For the computer that will be depreciated over five years, the sum is 1 + 2 + 3 + 4 + 5 = 15. This figure serves as the denominator for every year's calculation. The year number, counted in reverse, serves as the numerator. We count in reverse because most items depreciate quickly after purchase (sometimes known as decelerating depreciation), so the largest amount of depreciation is taken first. See the depreciation schedule in Exhibit 5.3.

If the item will depreciate slowly in the beginning (known as accelerating depreciation), the schedule would be reversed, with the largest amount depreciated in the last year. In most cases, regardless of an item's "actual" useful life, individuals and companies will seek to take the largest depreciation possible as soon as possible, due to the time value of money (see Chapter 4). Deferring taxes is typically an excellent way to boost short-term profits and long-term wealth. In the event an item that initially was estimated to have no salvage value proves to have value at the end of its life, the government requires **depreciation recapture** taxes be paid.

Double-declining balance. This depreciation method is the most aggressive in allocating loss of useful life to the early years of an asset's use. In this method, we estimate the total years of useful life and calculate the straight-line depreciation percentage. However, for double-declining balance depreciation, we double the estimated depreciation percentage. Then, the percentage used in the calculation is

Five-year sum-of-years-digits depreciation schedule for a $1,000 computer with no salvage value.   **exhibit 5.3**

YEAR	PROPORTION DEPRECIATED	AMOUNT DEPRECIATED	REMAINING AMOUNT TO BE DEPRECIATED
Year 1	5/15	$333.33	$670.00
Year 2	4/15	$266.67	$403.33
Year 3	3/15	$200.00	$203.33
Year 4	2/15	$133.33	$70.00
Year 5	1/15	$66.67	$0

exhibit	5.4	Five-year double-declining balance depreciation schedule for a $1,000 computer with a useful life of five years.

YEAR	STRAIGHT-LINE PERCENTAGE	DOUBLE-DECLINING BALANCE PERCENTAGE	AMOUNT DEPRECIATED	REMAINING AMOUNT TO BE DEPRECIATED
1	20%	40%	$400.00	$600.00
2	20%	40%	$240.00	$360.00
3	20%	40%	$144.00	$216.00
4	20%	40%	$86.40	$129.60
5	20%	40%	$51.84	$77.76

multiplied by the remaining amount of money to be depreciated. After the depreciation calculations have been performed, a certain amount of money will remain to be depreciated. This amount is the theoretical salvage value. If the actual salvage value is higher, then depreciation recapture must be paid; if the actual salvage value is lower, then additional depreciation can be taken during the last year of the item's useful life. Exhibit 5.4 shows how double-declining balance depreciation works.

Units of production. Perhaps the most accurate method for depreciation is the **units of production** method. For this method, we must estimate the total number of items that will be produced by the asset during its useful life. The depreciation schedule is calculated simply by dividing the total number of items produced during a given year by the total number of items the asset will produce during its useful life. The resulting percentage is multiplied by the original purchase price to determine the yearly depreciation. Exhibit 5.5 shows the use of units-of-production depreciation for a copier costing $2,000 that is expected to produce 10,000 copies and to have zero salvage value at the end of its useful life.

exhibit	5.5	Units-of-production depreciation schedule for a copier costing $2,000 that is expected to produce 10,000 copies and to have zero salvage value.

YEAR	# OF COPIES PRODUCED	DEPRECIATION PERCENTAGE	COPIES REMAINING	AMOUNT DEPRECIATED
1	3,000	30%	7,000	$600
2	2,000	20%	5,000	$400
3	1,500	15%	3,500	$300
4	1,500	15%	2,000	$300
5	1,200	12%	800	$240
6	800	8%	0	$160

Bill Veeck Tax Interpretation Changes Sport Finance SIDEBAR

5.F

Bill Veeck, owner of numerous Major League Baseball franchises from 1941 to 1980, was known primarily for his marketing activities. Veeck dramatically changed the way the game of baseball was promoted and presented. Though they are commonplace now, his ideas, such as providing non-baseball entertainment like fireworks, exploding scoreboards, and on-field parades, were revolutionary when he first introduced them. His marketing acumen led to Veeck's election to the Baseball Hall of Fame in 1991.

Although Bill Veeck was known primarily for his marketing activities, perhaps his greatest contribution to the business of sports was his understanding of the U.S. tax code and the application of depreciation. In 1959 Veeck successfully argued that the government should utilize his interpretation of the depreciation laws. His financial plan was soon copied by most of the other owners in the league (Zimbalist, 1992).

The essential elements of Veeck's plan involved the depreciation of contracts for players currently on a team's roster at the time of the owner's purchase of the franchise. Traditionally, when a player was purchased from another team (which happened far more often in Veeck's time then now, because most of the minor league teams were then not affiliated with a Major League club), that expense was charged off taxable income, like any other operating expense. However, when an owner bought an entire team, all assets were simply transferred to the new owner.

Veeck wished to write off the existing player contracts from his taxes. To do this, he needed to control 80% of a franchise when he (and his investors) initially purchased the team. Prior to the purchase, Veeck would establish a new organization, and the team would then sell the players to the new organization for at least 90% (and usually higher) of the agreed-upon purchase price *prior* to selling the rest of the team (name, logos, merchandise, media contracts, and so forth). Since the players had been purchased rather than transferred with the other team assets, they could be depreciated on the new organization's taxes. Veeck, and most owners who mimicked his plan, depreciated the cost of the players over three to ten years (Veeck, 1996), which considerably lowered the owners' taxable income.

Once accepted by the IRS, the effect of this plan was dramatic. Purchasing professional sport franchises became a valuable tax shelter, which attracted new owners who had made fortunes in other industries and dramatically increased franchise values (Zimbalist). Veeck's initial tax plan has since been altered by the Omnibus Tax Act of 2004, which permits a new owner to deduct 100% of the team's purchase price over a 15-year period (Fort et al., 2008).

The units-of-production depreciation schedule is ideal for items that are clearly related to some sort of tangible production. For items that lose value simply due to time, the units-of-production schedule may not be optimal. As with the other depreciation schedules, if the item retains value beyond its anticipated useful life, then adjustments to taxable income may be required.

Choice of depreciation method. The choice of depreciation method is determined by a variety of factors. In some cases the federal government mandates that certain types of items be depreciated in a specific manner. In other cases the government permits individuals and businesses to utilize the depreciation schedule they feel is appropriate—with IRS permission, of course. For specific information about which depreciation method to use, see www.irs.gov/publications/p946/ch01.html#en_US_publink1000107337.

Jock taxes

Professional athletes are subject to a variety of special taxes. Since professional sport attracts much media and fan attention, it is easy to know where and when professional athletes "work" in a particular location. California has had laws since the early 1980s requiring out-of-state residents to pay taxes on income earned while in the state. California was certainly able to collect taxes from full-time, part-time, and seasonal employees who received a W-2 from a business located in the state, but it was not until 1991 that the state realized it could track professional athletes "working" in California. After the Chicago Bulls defeated the Los Angeles Lakers in the NBA Championship, the state of California sent the Bulls' players and coaches a tax bill for the time they spent "earning" salaries in the state (Smith, 2007; Williams, 2003). In response, Illinois assessed its own state taxes against professional athletes. Eventually, individual cities and counties realized they could also enact and enforce **jock taxes** on highly paid, visible professional athletes.

Jock taxes are based on the athlete's time spent "working" within a particular jurisdiction. The state or local government would prefer to tax an athlete based on time spent in the state divided by the number of games played in a season, but jock taxes typically count the "duty days," from the first day of training camp to the last day of the team's season, to determine how much tax is owed. For example, if a professional baseball player has 225 duty days from the start of spring training in March until the conclusion of the season in early October, and he spends 25 days playing games in California, he will receive an income tax bill based on the 11% (25 days/225 days) of his yearly salary he earned in the state. Most states issue a tax credit for income taxes paid in other states, but California does not, resulting in potential double taxation (Smith).

Although jock taxes have been assessed since 1991, litigation continues regarding how much individual athletes actually owe. Scott Radinsky of the Chicago White Sox sued the state of Illinois for the manner in which it administered its jock tax against him (Rovell, 2003). Other athletes have complained that jock taxes are often assessed even when the athlete does not visit a city as part of the team's travel party. Many players on injured reserve do not travel with their team while they rehabilitate, and in those cases the player may be able to argue that he or she did not earn any salary in the state even though the team played there.

Jock taxes are not limited to the United States. Alberta, Canada, home to the Edmonton Oilers and the Calgary Flames of the National Hockey League, began to assess jock taxes in 2003 (Schechter, 2002). When the Montreal Expos played games in Puerto Rico, players were assessed a jock tax. The special tax was passed just days before the first games. Although the players were required to pay, Major League Baseball, the participating teams, and the promoter of the games were granted a waiver absolving them of tax liability on their profits (Rovell).

The complex nature of jock taxes has resulted in many teams' hiring additional staff for their payroll departments to monitor the tax bill players and coaches may owe in various jurisdictions (Smith). Players have also had to retain accountants to ensure they adhere to the various laws. Ray Suplee, an accountant who works for a variety of professional athletes, noted, "My clients' returns are typically 12 to 15 inches thick" (Williams, p. 25). Some players consider the potential state and local taxes in their decision to sign with particular teams. The old adage, "It is not what you make, but what you keep," certainly applies to a well-paid professional athlete. Paying 10.3% in state income taxes in California versus no state income taxes in Florida could mean a difference of hundreds of thousands or even millions of dollars in taxes over the life of a multimillion-dollar contract. For some professional

The "Fair Tax": A New Way to Collect Taxes?   SIDEBAR

5.G

As long as there are organized societies there will be debates about taxes. Certainly, taxes are necessary to fund government activities, but every citizen probably has different ideas about who should pay taxes, how much each person should pay, and the proper method of collecting government revenue. Each of the states in the union has different methods of collecting taxes. While many states, such as Georgia, California, and New York, charge individuals income tax, other states, such as Florida, Texas, and Washington, have no state income tax, generating revenue from other forms of taxation, such as taxes on property, sales, and tourism. The state of Nevada has long utilized taxes on tourism and gambling activities (among others) rather than income taxes to generate revenue. Other states have recently realized that gambling activities can be a lucrative source of state revenue (McCredie, 2008). Forty-two states now have established some form of a state lottery that produces revenue (McCredie).

The United States federal government collects a variety of taxes from individuals and businesses. These include income taxes, capital gains taxes, social security taxes, Medicare taxes, and estate taxes, among many others. The current United States tax code is 67,204 pages long, whereas The Holy Bible is 1,291 pages and War and Peace is 1,444 pages ("67,204-page code," 2007). The 67,204 pages cover thousands of tax credits and deductions, and leave as many tax loopholes. In the sport industry, as in others, businesses often argue with the IRS about what the tax code requires. For instance, the Tampa Bay Rays successfully argued in court that money they received for advance ticket sales prior to their franchise having played any games should be taxed in the year the games were played (Moskel, 2002). The tax code did not clearly state exactly how to handle that situation. The current system is so complicated and opaque that even Internal Revenue Service Commissioner Mark Everson had an accountant compute his taxes since he was not sure if he could understand the code. Everson noted, "I don't want to get a letter from the IRS saying I made a mistake" ("67,204-page code," para 5).

Adhering to the cumbersome federal tax laws costs a tremendous amount of time and money. It is estimated that American citizens and businesses spend over 6 billion hours and $225 billion each year in the effort to adhere to the code (Boortz & Linder, 2008). This time and money could certainly be spent more effectively in other pursuits—such as working to streamline businesses operations, designing better products,

and providing improved services. For individuals, a simpler tax code would afford them more time and money for investing, retirement planning, and spending leisure time with family and friends. The overall inefficiency and costs of adhering to the current tax code have concerned a variety of groups and caused many to plead for a simpler tax code (Edwards, 2006).

One of the more popular tax reform proposals in recent years is the *flat tax.* The United States currently assesses income taxes on citizens based on their yearly income, with different Americans paying different income tax rates. Under a flat tax, every American would pay the same tax rate, and the myriad deductions and tax loopholes would be eliminated. Steve Forbes advocated a 17% flat tax rate when he sought the Republican Presidential nomination in 1996 and 2000. Forbes did not win the nomination, but his flat tax idea attracted media attention and some support. Forbes continues to promote in articles, books, and speeches the merits of the flat tax as a necessary reform.

A more recent tax reform idea is the **"fair tax."** Georgia Congressman John Linder has repeatedly introduced legislation in the U.S. House of Representatives that would repeal the entire current tax code and replace it with a consumption tax. Many European countries use a similar tax called a *value-added tax (VAT).* European countries employing the VAT also assess a variety of other taxes, but Linder's plan would eliminate all other forms of taxation except for a 23% national sales tax. If the fair tax were implemented, Americans would no longer need to keep receipts, hire accountants, and worry about specific deductions. They would be taxed only when they purchased retail products and services (Boortz & Linder). The more a person consumed, the higher the taxes that person would pay. The poor would pay no taxes, since the fair tax plan mandates a monthly "pre-bate" for every American to cover the tax obligation for the basic necessities of life (Boortz & Linder). The fair tax is designed to be revenue neutral, meaning the federal government would receive the same amount of revenues that it would under the current system.

The main obstacle for the flat and fair tax plans is that members of Congress support the current system. Under a complex tax code, government officials can solicit financial support from lobbyists for specific deductions and loopholes. Members of Congress, regardless of party affiliation, have little reason to seek radical reform to a system that provides them considerable financial support and political power.

athletes, such as tennis players, it is easier (for tax adherence purposes) and much less expensive to live in a country, such as Monaco, where there is no income tax rather than deal with the unwieldy United States tax laws (Sweet, 2002).

CONCLUSION

Understanding microeconomic and macroeconomic concepts and trends is critical to the success of any sport entity. In addition, the government's monetary and fiscal policies will impact financial decision making. Successful financial managers will work within the established tax codes to minimize tax obligations legally. As governments continue to seek revenue sources, it is likely that new tax laws—some which may be specifically targeted to sport businesses—will be passed. Successful financial managers will be able to adapt their operations quickly to remain profitable when tax changes occur.

CONCEPT *check*

1. Define microeconomics and macroeconomics. What are the main differences between the two?
2. How do professional sports leagues utilize the concept of scarcity when locating franchises?
3. Define and discuss monetary policy. What specific actions can the Federal Reserve take to achieve its goals?
4. List actions that a government can take for establishing its fiscal policy. What are some fiscal policies specifically targeted to the sport industry?
5. What is a basis point? How does a change in a few basis points affect a loan?
6. Define inflation and explain how it may affect sport business operations.
7. What is a market index? What is an index designed to accomplish?
8. Explain the important differences between general and limited partners.
9. What are the differences between a C corp and an S corp?
10. What is an LLC and an LLP? Why have they become more popular business entities over the last ten years? What concerns should an investor investigate before forming an LLC or LLP?
11. How has globalization affected sport finance in the last ten years? How might it affect sport financial management in the future?

PRACTICE *problems*

1. If an interest rate is currently 6% and a lending institution announces a 25 basis point increase, what percentage of increase does this represent?
2. Calculate the straight-line and sum-of-years-digits depreciation schedules for a $450 video camera that will have a salvage value of $50 after five years of use.

3. Calculate the double-declining balance depreciation schedule for a $1,000 item that will last four years. What is the estimated salvage value?

4. For a fitness center purchasing a $3,000 photocopier expected to produce 30,000 copies, calculate the units of production depreciation schedule if the following number of copies are expected to be made each year: Year 1, 12,000; Year 2, 8,000; Year 3, 6,000; Year 4, 3,000; Year 5, 1,000.

CASE analysis   Schedule Changes at Darlington Raceway

Darlington Raceway is one of the most important tracks in the history of NASCAR. Opened in 1950, Darlington Raceway became a model for many tracks that would be built later in the 1950s and 1960s. For many years, NASCAR held two Sprint Cup Series races at the track—one in the spring and one on Labor Day weekend. In 2003, because of decreased demand for the spring Darlington race and NASCAR's desire to expand its presence to other areas of the United States, the Labor Day date was given to another track, and the Darlington Labor Day weekend event was rescheduled for November. In 2005, Darlington's two Sprint Cup Series weekends were merged into one held on Mother's Day weekend. The other date was rescheduled for another track.

1. How might NASCAR's decision to reduce Darlington's races from two to one be received by regular attendees at both events?

2. How might NASCAR's decision affect ticket pricing for the one remaining Darlington race? Explain your answer, referring to the economic and financial principles discussed in this chapter.

3. What would you guess has happened to Darlington's attendance at its one Sprint Cup Race?

4. Did NASCAR make the correct decision in this situation? Explain and justify your answer.

references

67,204-page code confounds taxpayers, yet Congress sits by. (2007, April 4). *USA Today.* Retrieved July 29, 2008, from http://blogs.usatoday.com/oped/2007/04/post_7.html.

Birth of a team and a legend. (n.d.). Retrieved July 19, 2008, from http://www.packers.com/history/birth_of_a_team_and_a_legend/.

Boortz, N., & Linder, J. (2008). *FairTax: The truth. Answering the critics.* New York: HarperCollins.

Chass, M. (2003, May 16). Baseball: With quick approval, Moreno buys Angels from Disney. *The New York Times.* Retrieved July 27, 2008, from http://query.nytimes.com/gst/fullpage.html?res=9903E2DA173EF935A25756C0A9659C8B63&sec=&spon=.

Conlin, B. (2008, July 30). Braves not the same without Turner. *Philadelphia Daily News.* Retrieved August 2, 2008, from http://www.philly.com/philly/sports/phillies/20080730_Bill_Conlin__Braves_not_the_same_without_Ted_Turner.html.

Edwards, C. (2006, April). Income tax rife with complexity and inefficiency. Retrieved August 10, 2008, from http://www.cato.org/pubs/tbb/tbb-0604-33.pdf.

Eichelberger, C. (1998, September 1). NFL may drop ownership rules. *The Journal Record.* Retrieved July 27, 2008, from http://findarticles.com/p/articles/mi_qn4182/is_19980901/ai_n10120517/pg_1.

Fort, R., Gerrard, B., Lockett, A., Humphreys, B., Soebbing, B., Tainsky, S., Winfree, J., & Coulson, E. (2008). Bill Veeck, the IRS, and the Omnibus Tax Act of 2004. *Proceedings of the North American Society for Sport Management Conference,* Toronto, Ontario, Canada.

Friedman, T.L. (2000). *The Lexus and the olive tree.* New York: Anchor Books.

Friedman, T.L. (2005). *The world is flat.* New York: Farrar, Straus and Giroux.

Harris, D. (1986). *The rise and decline of the NFL.* New York: Bantam.

Joyner, J. (2006, May 24). NFL to move existing team to Los Angeles—eventually. *OTB Sports.* Retrieved July 28, 2008, from http://sports.outsidethebeltway.com/2006/05/nfl-to-move-existing-team-to-los-angeles/.

Kaplan, D. (2001, August 6–12). Club's financial rise dates to market debut. *SportsBusiness Journal, 4*(16), 30.

King, B. (2003, April 21–27). Angels' reduced price raises questions. *SportsBusiness Journal, 5*(52), 5.

King, B. (2005, January 31–February 6). Tax change cuts into baseball bonuses. *SportsBusiness Journal, 7*(38), 10.

Lucas Oil to sponsor Colts stadium. (2006, February 28). Retrieved July 27, 2008, from http://www.bizjournals.com/losangeles/stories/2006/02/27/daily12.html.

McCredie, S. (2008, March 27). The best and worst states for taxes. Retrieved August 3, 2008, from http://articles.moneycentral.msn.com/Taxes/Advice/TheBestAndWorstStatesForTaxes.aspx.

Moreno keeps promise to Angels fans. (2008, July 29). Retrieved August 4, 2008, from http://mlb.mlb.com/news/article_perspectives.jsp?ymd=20080729&content_id=3220123&vkey=perspectives&fext=.jsp.

Morris, K.M., & Morris, V.B. (1999). *The Wall Street Journal guide to understanding money and investing.* New York: Lightbulb Press.

Moskal, J. (2002, October 21–27). Devil Rays get win vs. IRS. *SportsBusiness Journal, 5*(26), 16.

Much, P.J., & Phillips, J.S. (1999). *Inside the ownership of professional sports.* Chicago: Team Marketing Report.

Nagel, M.S., Brown, M.T., McEvoy, C.D., & Rascher, D.A. (2007). Major League Baseball anti-trust immunity: Examining the legal and financial implications of relocation rules. *Entertainment and Sport Law Journal, 4*(3). Available: http://www2.warwick.ac.uk/fac/soc/law/elj/eslj/issues/volume4/number3/nagel/.

Rogers, P. (2007, January 12). Relocating a team to Portland makes sense. Retrieved July 18, 2008, from http://sports.espn.go.com/mlb/hotstove06/columns/story?columnist=rogers_phil&id=2727901.

Rovell, D. (2003, April 7). Baseball, not players, receive tax break from Puerto Rico. Retrieved July 27, 2008, from http://espn.go.com/mlb/s/2003/0407/1535207.html.

Schecter, B. (2002, March 25–31). 12.5% tax hits NHL players. *SportsBusiness Journal, 4*(49), 8.

Smith, M.C. (2007, April 17). "Jock taxes" mean athletes well fleeced. *OC Register.* Retrieved July 24, 2008, from http://www.ocregister.com/ocregister/sports/columns/article_1654569.php.

Stock and financial history. (n.d.). Retrieved July 19, 2008, from http://www.packers.com/history/fast_facts/stock_history/.

Swank, B. (2004). *Baseball in San Diego: From the Padres to Petco.* Charleston, SC: Arcadia Publishing.

Sweet, D. (2002, June 3–9). Monte Carlo beckons tax-weary European pros. *SportsBusiness Journal, 4*(6), 19.

Tucker, T. (2003, February 16). Chairman or the board? *Atlanta Journal Constitution.* D1, D3.

Veeck, B. (1996). *The hustler's handbook.* Durham, NC: Baseball America.

Wessel, W. (2000). *Economics* (3rd ed.). Hauppauge, NY: Barron's.

Will Charlotte house an MLB team? (2006, January 19). Retrieved July 18, 2008, from http://journals.aol.com/sportzassassin/SPORTZASSASSINSSPORTSJOURNAL/entries/2006/01/19/will-charlotte-house-an-mlb-team/1375.

Williams, P. (2003, March 17–23). Pay as you go: States make the road taxing for athletes and accountants. *SportsBusiness Journal, 5*(47), 25.

Wolfley, B. (1997, November 29). Packers stock purchasers are buying for others. *Milwaukee Journal Sentinel.* Retrieved July 19, 2008, from http://www2.jsonline.com/sports/sday/sday112997.stm.

Zimbalist, A. (1992). *Baseball and billions.* New York: Basic Books.

6

Budgeting

This chapter is contributed by Tom Regan.

base budget

budget

budget time horizon

business planning horizon

capital expenditure
  budget

cash budget

decision package

decision unit

expense budget

fixed cost

forecast

going concern

incremental budget

line-item budgeting

mixed cost

modified zero-based
  budgeting (MZBB)

output budgeting

periodic expense

planning

program budget

program planning
  budgeting system
  (PPBS)

reduced-level budget

revenue budget

sensitivity analysis

step cost

strategic planning horizon

variable cost

zero-based budgeting
  (ZBB)

KEY CONCEPTS

Introduction

Budgeting is an indispensable tool of management and corporate governance. A budget aids management in financial coordination, and because the annual budget of a corporation requires board approval, it also helps ensure the fulfillment of the board's wishes.

Beyond these facts, the definition and functions of budgeting vary widely among organizations. In the United States, sport organizations regard budgeting mostly as a tool for financial planning. A **budget** is considered to be a set of financial statements based on projections resulting from a particular scenario—generally, the most likely or hoped-for scenario. A budget, therefore, reflects management's opinions about future financial circumstances. Budgets and financial plans are often developed and used similarly, emphasizing the comparison of income and outlay entries—a practice adopted from public corporate bodies. In addition to providing a comparison of income and expenses, a budget can also serve several other functions: to motivate, coordinate, and communicate.

The budget as a means of motivation. Because budgets aid in performance measurement, performance evaluation, and the determination of pay, a carefully considered budget directs managers toward the company's goals. When personal benefits are coupled with business objectives (often expressed in financial form) and when subordinates participate in the planning process, a budget can supply incentive for the work force to act on behalf of the organization.

The budget as a means of coordination. Because the development of a budget provides an opportunity to consider and plan for the future, the process helps management understand and overcome challenges in earning a profit. Certain budgeting techniques enable managers to uncover production bottlenecks and other problems and to correct any errors in forecasting.

The budget as a means of communication. For management to be effective, subordinates need enough information about organizational goals to be able to act appropriately. Superiors need up-to-date information about progress and results. Budgeting can serve these functions in a formal business setting.

WHAT IS A BUDGET?

A budget quantifies planned revenues and expenses for a period of time. It also includes planned changes to assets, liabilities, and cash flows (Smith, 2007). A budget facilitates the control process and helps with the coordination of an organization's financial activities. Budgets are prepared in advance of the period of time they cover. They are based on the objectives of the business and are intended to show how policies are to be pursued in order to achieve objectives.

A budget is a financial plan that sets out a business's financial targets, expressed in monetary terms. It is an agreed-upon plan of action for a given period of time that reflects the policy to be pursued and the anticipated outcomes related to that policy, and it is set out in numerical or financial terms.

RELATION OF PLANNING AND FORECASTING TO BUDGETING

A clear distinction must be made between a plan, a forecast, and a budget.

Planning

Planning is usually a first step, prior to forecasting and budgeting. **Planning** is the establishment of objectives and the formulation, evaluation, and selection of the policies, strategies, tactics, and actions required to achieve those objectives. The planning process produces a *plan* that, along with information about the environment, provides information for the forecasting process.

Forecasting

A **forecast** is a prediction of future events and their quantification for the purpose of budgeting. The difference between a forecast and a plan is that a forecast is simply a prediction, whereas a plan defines what we are going to do. (A budget is technically a plan, because it concerns actions to be taken.) A forecast relates to events in the environment, relevant to the implementation of the plan, over which the business has either no control or only very limited control. The environment considered may be internal, external, or personal—all have effects on decision making. A forecast is a prediction of the future as it relates to the organization's plan. The terms *forecast, prediction, projection,* and *prognosis* are typically used interchangeably.

The field of forecasting is concerned with approaches to determining what the future holds and with the proper presentation and use of forecasts. It includes the application of judgment as well as quantitative (statistical) methods. Research on forecasting has produced many changes in recommended practice, especially since the 1960s. Many assumptions about the best way to generate forecasts have been found to be wrong. For example, the practice of basing forecasts on regression models that fit historical time-series data has been found to be inaccurate. Sometimes the research findings have been upsetting to academics—such as the discovery that in many situations relatively simple models are more accurate than complex ones (Makridakis & Wheelwright, 1982; Ord, Hibon, & Makridakis, 2000).

Forecasts may be conditional. That is, if policy A is adopted, then X is most likely to occur, but if B is adopted, then Y is most likely. Forecasts of future values are often for a time-series, such as the number of tickets that will be sold in a year or the likely demand for season tickets. A forecast may also predict a one-off event, such as the outcome of free agency or the performance of a new recruit. A forecast may project a distribution, such as the locations of potential security risks or the sales of merchandise among different age cohorts.

The individuals who complete a budget will determine the forecasting tasks to be done. For example, a budget may require estimates of future tickets sales, merchandise sales, concessions, donations, gifts, and licensing fees. This is part of the planning stage of budgeting.

The forecasting task itself may be complex. In order to estimate sales, for example, a prudent manager will look at past sales histories and various factors that influence sales. Marketing research may reveal that sales are expected to stabilize, because the organization cannot produce enough to sustain growth in sales or because a general economic slowdown is anticipated to result in falling sales. In such a case the budget team will need input from administration, managers, and other parties in related cost centers. This is just a sample of the process of developing forecasts.

Forecasting is concerned with what the future *will* look like, while budgeting is concerned with what it *should* look like, from management's point of view. If the sport organization does not like the forecasts, it can generate other plans until a plan is found that leads to acceptable outcomes. Of course, many organizations take a shortcut and merely change the forecasts. This is analogous to a family deciding to change the weather forecast so they can go to a baseball game.

Guidelines for forecasting

The approaches to forecasting described below should be helpful in the budgeting process.

1. Forecasting relies on past relationships and making predictions from historical information. However, if these relationships change, forecasts become inaccurate. For example, if a team's star player retires or signs with another team in the offseason, forecasts of attendance for the next season will likely be inaccurate. Hence, we must both extend past trends and make adjustments for known changes.

2. Consider developing several forecasts under different potential scenarios. Assign a probability to each scenario and calculate a weighted average to arrive at an acceptable forecast. This is often called **sensitivity analysis.**

3. Longer planning periods tend to produce less accurate forecasts. To increase accuracy, consider shortening the planning period. The appropriate length of a planning period will also depend on how often plans must be evaluated, which in turn will depend on sales stability, business risk, financial conditions, and the organization's budgeting approach.

4. Forecasts of large interrelated items are more accurate than forecasts of specific itemized amounts. For example, a forecast for the entire athletic department for one academic year will be more accurate than a forecast for one specific game. The variations in single games will tend to cancel each other out within a group of games. An overall economic forecast will be more accurate than an industry-specific forecast.

We now turn to budgeting, the process of determining what your organization and its activities *should* look like in financial terms.

BUDGET PREPARATION

In a typical organization, each department submits an annual budget recommendation, which, once approved, is incorporated into the organization's annual operating budget. This budget becomes the basis of authority for the financial operation of each department during the fiscal year. The organization should set a general budgeting policy to guide resource allocation on the basis of program justifications.

The budget formulation process should:

1. Define financial objectives, which determine the direction and thrust of each department's operations;

2. Establish goals for achieving these objectives within the budgeted timeframe;

3. Identify the activities and quantify the elements needed to achieve established goals; and

4. Describe the factors and situations that may affect planned activities.

Each year, the budget formulation process is initiated by the organization's business manager, chief financial officer (CFO), or comptroller. Employees with budgetary responsibilities should obtain copies of the previous year's budget, review it carefully, and use it as the basis for budget recommendations for the coming year. Requests for capital expenditures, equipment, and administrative expenditures should be carefully itemized and fully described. Requests for new positions and other increases in the budget may also be made at this time. These recommendations will be reviewed by the appropriate business manager, the CFO, or the comptroller.

The business office typically initiates the planning cycle on or around the end of the second financial quarter of each fiscal year; team coaches and department administrators begin soon after. The schedule and approach to the budgeting process will vary depending on the size of the organization.

Timing and Budgets

Individuals involved in budgeting should consider three distinct time periods: the *budget time horizon,* the *business planning horizon,* and the *strategic planning horizon.* The **budget time horizon** is the immediate future, which can be predicted with a reasonable degree of certainty on the basis of past business decisions and commitments. The budget time horizon is generally considered to be the next 12 months. The **business planning horizon** is the period over which forecasts can be made with a reasonable degree of confidence—generally, three to five years. Individuals who are developing budgets usually gather data to produce short-term and long-term budgets for these two time periods. They might inquire, for example, how ticket sales have changed over the past year, two years, three years, and five years and use the pattern to make forecasts and produce short- and long-term budgets. Finally, the **strategic planning horizon** extends far into the future; planning for this time period focuses on the long-term aspirations of the sport organization and management.

Keys to Successful Budgeting

Successful budgeting depends on the involvement of the entire organization in both the planning and the implementation phases. Hence, two keys to successful budgeting are (1) input from the entire organization and (2) a means of sharing the budget across the organization.

Input from each cost center, department, or management unit is vital to drawing up a budget that realistically reflects revenue and expenses from each unit, department, or sport. A budget arrived at in a "top down" fashion—that is, with input only from the head office or higher administration—is not likely to be accurate or effective.

To share the budget across the organization, user-friendly software, such as Microsoft Excel, is indispensable. If an organization wants grassroots involvement, managers must have tools they feel comfortable using, and every task must be simplified through software and technology. Online data capture and transparency of data will help coaches, managers, and assistants become involved in the budgeting process, which in turn will result in a process that is far more efficient.

Furthermore, a budget must be sustainable. Budgets do not go away, and they must be adapted to changes as readily as possible. The first step toward sustainability is gaining "buy-in" from the administration and department heads. With everyone pulling in the same direction, the organization moves forward together. Involving each department, coach, and employee in developing and maintaining the budget helps assure buy-in, congruence, and efficiency.

Best Practices in Budgeting

Budgeting should be a value-added activity. These best practices can transform budgeting into a value-added activity:

1. Link budgeting to strategic planning, since strategic decisions usually have financial implications.
2. Make budgeting procedures part of strategic planning. Strategic assessments should include identification of historical trends, competitive analysis, and other activities that might otherwise take place within the budgeting process.
3. During the budgeting process, spend less time collecting and gathering data and more time generating information for strategic decision making.
4. Get agreement on summary budgets before you spend time preparing detail budgets.
5. Automate the collection and consolidation of budgets across the organization. For easy updating, all users should have access to budgeting software.
6. Set up the budget so that it will accept changes quickly and easily. Budgeting should be a continuous process and one that encourages alternative thinking.
7. Design a budget that will give lower-level managers some form of fiscal control over their own areas of responsibility.
8. Leverage your financial systems by establishing a data warehouse that can be used for both reporting and budgeting.

Not all of the best practices can be implemented in every sport organization. Time and resources vary among athletic departments and sport enterprises. Effective budgeting requires understanding the resources available and the skills and limitations of the personnel working on the budgeting process.

APPROACHES TO BUDGETING

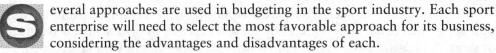everal approaches are used in budgeting in the sport industry. Each sport enterprise will need to select the most favorable approach for its business, considering the advantages and disadvantages of each.

Regardless of the approach, budgeting is an easy process when revenues are increasing. In past decades, sport enterprises have enjoyed increasing revenue forecasts, the result of ticket price increases, significant media revenues, luxury and box seating expansion, and lucrative naming rights deals. Budgeting becomes more difficult in an environment where revenues are decreasing and expenses must be cut. During periods of recession or flat revenue streams, the budget becomes a tool for motivation, communication, and, in some cases, job security.

Individuals in all sport job titles are affected by the budgeting process, and all departments—including marketing, operations, tickets, sponsorship, sport information, and administration—must be involved in it. Budgetary decisions should be in accord with management's priorities and revenue growth to attain the goals of the organization.

For example, suppose the goal of an athletic department is to finish first or second in the Southeastern Conference in every sport. It would behoove every coach, staff member, and administrator to become involved in the budgeting process. If the women's basketball recruiting budget was being reduced—and you were the women's basketball coach—would you still be able to reach the top ten percent? A coach who is not involved in the budgeting process might not be aware of an impending reduction. Yet that coach will be evaluated at the end of the year on his team's performance, just the same. If your team needs to be in the top 10 percent of the conference, you would benefit by becoming involved in the budgeting process to ensure that resources are allocated so that you can meet that goal.

This section discusses in detail the following four approaches to budgeting:

1. Incremental budgeting
2. Program planning budgeting system (PPBS)
3. Zero-based budgeting (ZBB)
4. Modified zero-based budgeting (MZBB)

Regardless of the budgeting approach, there are also budgets within budgets. These include revenue budgets, expense budgets, cash budgets, and capital expenditure budgets. Each is briefly summarized at the end of this section.

Incremental Budgeting

A form of line-item budgeting often called the object-of-expenditure budget was the earliest type of budget format used in private, public, and non-profit entities. It was considered an innovative development by financial reformers in the early 1900s and remains a popular form of budgeting even today. The line-item budget achieved prominence with the establishment of the executive budget, which assigned responsibility and accountability for spending to the organization's chief executive. This gave the chief executive a powerful instrument for controlling departmental and agency demands for money.

Line-item budgeting is a technique in which *line items* (also known as objects of expenditure) are the main focus of analysis, authorization, and control. Typical line items include supplies, personnel, travel, and operational expenditures. See chapter Appendix 6.A for a list of typical expenditures in an athletic department. An **incremental budget** is a form of line-item budgeting in which next year's budget is arrived at by either decreasing or increasing last year's budget for each line item by the same percentage (as opposed to a zero-based budget, discussed later in this chapter, which clears the deck and starts all over again). An incremental budget is based on projected changes in operations and conditions. This approach to budgeting tends to lead to budgetary increases over time.

In Appendix 6.A, the revenues for each line item were increased by 1% and the expenses for each line item were increased by 2% for the 2009–2010 budget.

Incremental budgeting is often called the "fair share" approach. It has this name because no one sport program or department is increased or cut at a different level than the others. With a computer spreadsheet, preparing an incremental budget is very quick. This form of budgeting is usually associated with top-down management style, and it has two important characteristics. First, funds are allocated to departments or organizational units, and the managers of these units then allocate funds to activities as they see fit. Second, as mentioned previously, an incremental budget develops out of the previous year's budget, and only the incremental change in the budget request is reviewed.

Each of these characteristics creates problems. Incremental budgeting is particularly troublesome when top management seeks to identify inefficiencies and waste. In fact, inefficiencies tend to grow in an organization that uses incremental budgeting, because inefficiencies are easily hidden. In a typical budget of this type, nothing ever gets cut. Because top management looks only at the requests for incremental changes, money may be provided for an activity long after the need is gone.

The incremental budgeting approach is not recommended, as it fails to take into account changing circumstances. Moreover, it encourages managers to "spend up to the budget" to ensure a comparable allocation in the next period. This is a "spend it or lose it" mentality, by which managers are sure to spend all that is allocated to them in fear that if a surplus remains, their requests for an incremental increase will be denied. See Exhibit 6.1 for a summary of the advantages and disadvantages of incremental budgeting.

Program Planning Budgeting System

The **program planning budgeting system (PPBS)** is an approach to developing a **program budget,** one in which expenditures are based primarily on programs of work and secondarily on the character and object of the work. It is a transitional type of budget between the line-item budget and the performance budget (where the relationship between program inputs and outputs is measured). Program budgets group the traditional categories of expenditure used in line-item budgets under agencies or programs. For example, under the heading of the marketing department we would find personnel, office supplies, and advertising. The purpose of program budgeting, as the name suggests, is to highlight the units of activity that the line items support.

In this approach, the organization's policy decisions lead to a specific budget and specific multi-year plans. In this way PPBS contributes to the organization's planning process. The goal of PPBS is to link planning with budgeting systematically in the service of clearly identified goals.

PPBS is associated with **output budgeting,** in which specific goals and objectives form the framework for a strategic process. Output budgeting was introduced to the United States in the mid-1960s by Charles J. Hitch, meeting some resistance from administrators. The technique has since been introduced into other countries. The U.S. Department of Defense has used PPBS for many of its strategic projects.

Advantages and disadvantages of incremental budgeting. **exhibit** **6.1**

ADVANTAGES

- The budget is stable and change is gradual.

- Managers can operate their departments on a consistent basis.

- The budget is relatively simple to prepare and easy to understand.

- Conflicts may be avoided if departments are seen to be treated similarly.

- Coordination between budgets is easier to achieve.

- The impact of changes can be seen quickly, because the budget is relatively easy to prepare and modify.

DISADVANTAGES

- Activities and methods of working are assumed to continue in the same way as before.

- The budget process provides no incentive for developing new ideas.

- The process provides managers no incentives to reduce costs.

- This approach encourages managers to spend up to the budget to ensure that the budget is maintained next year.

- The budget may become out of date and no longer relate to the level of activity or type of work being carried out.

- Changes in the priority for resources may not be reflected in the budget.

- Budgetary slack may be built into the budget, which is never reviewed. Managers may have overestimated their requirements in the past in order to obtain a larger budget allocation, and this situation is never reviewed or remedied.

PPBS integrates into the planning and budgeting process a number of techniques for

- identifying, costing, and assigning a complexity of resources,
- establishing priorities and strategies in a major program, and
- forecasting costs, expenditures, and achievements in the immediate financial year or over a longer period.

Planning is the essence of program budgeting, and if a budget is not connected to a plan, it is not a true budget. Many agencies organize the budget into functional categories or sets of activities, but unless a plan gives purpose to these functional categories and activities, it is difficult to identify the purposes the line item categories are intended to serve. Program expenditures should be related to a set of objectives, which in turn are connected to goals, for a true program budget to exist. The development of goals and objectives for an organization or program unit is fundamental to management planning and PPBS. Together, the goals and objectives plus budgeted resources provide an overall plan. Once a set of long-range goals or general directions has been established, a series of directly related, measurable short-range objectives can be developed. The short-range objectives are the projected or planned achievements for the agency or program during the planning period. Whether these objectives will actually be achieved depends on the resources made available and the ability of management.

As stated above, a PPBS budget includes performance objectives, measurement criteria, a productivity measure, and effectiveness measures, unlike the line-item budget presented earlier. In addition, and like the line-item budget, it includes revenue and expenditure information. Consider as an example a summer community tennis camp (see chapter Appendix 6.B). The emphasis of this budget is on outcomes: meeting the performance objectives set for the camp. The three performance objectives are matched to the demand, workload, productivity, and effectiveness outcomes to ensure the program is meeting the objectives set for it.

As another example, suppose a collegiate athletic department has a goal of being in the top 10% of programs within its conference. To achieve this goal, administrative officials and coaches set this objective: build a new state-of-the-art facility in order to recruit the best players. By recruiting the best players, the teams using the new facility and its amenities (e.g., locker rooms, weight rooms, and training room) will improve their chances of moving into the top 10%. If this athletic department uses PPBS for major capital expenditures, it will need to incorporate the planning, programming and budgeting concepts during the facility's construction phase. In professional sports, an organization's goal might be to increase revenue streams so that the franchise can better compete with larger market teams. This goal may lead to the objective of a new facility, which should enhance the revenue streams from the sale of luxury and box seats.

Program budgeting has several advantages. By connecting the budget to a plan, it enables an organization to allocate its scarce resources purposefully. This clarity of purpose in turn enables managers to understand how the work of their particular unit contributes to the work of the organization as a whole. Other advantages pertain to staff involvement in the initial stages of the project. The personnel involved often have significant input, and their needs form the basis of the final budget. For the larger, government-funded sport entity, program budgeting provides a visible and concrete expression to the citizens of how their tax dollars are being spent. Many college athletic departments are state funded, and, as a consequence, have a public non-profit mentality. Yet the department must exist in a competitive environment.

The advantages that come from rationally and systematically connecting means to ends and dollars to program come with disadvantages. One serious disadvantage for managers is that PPBS limits their flexibility in shifting dollars from one program to another. Over time programs build up strong constituency support, which means that any program cuts may attract strong external opposition. Program budgeting has been likened to buying all perfectly matching suits of clothes—it is difficult to treat the parts as interchangeable. In addition to limiting flexibility and increasing the potential for conflict, true program budgeting is quite time consuming. Staff must be involved and their input and buy-in are required. The more employees involved in budgeting, the more the timeline expands. Another disadvantage is that the evaluation process is often weak. The length of the budgeting process seems to limit the evaluation process, especially after completion. Finally, a budgeting system like PPBS sometimes allows athletic departments to support irrational objectives, such as moving into NCAA Division I–Football Bowl Subdivision from a lower division (see Chapter 14) and increasing from 20 to 28 sports when the department and its institution do not have the resources to support these changes.

Exhibit 6.2 lists the advantages and disadvantages of PPBS budgeting.

Zero-Based Budgeting

Zero-based budgeting (ZBB) is a budgeting approach and a financial management strategy intended to help decision makers achieve more cost-effective delivery of goods and services. It is well suited to the service industry—of which the sport business is part—and has been a common approach to budgeting in the service industry for over 50 years. ZBB originated with Peter Pyhrr at Texas Instruments in the late 1960s. Pyhrr's book on the subject remains the most definitive and comprehensive study of this approach to budgeting (1973). His goal was to create a decision-making mechanism that would force an organization to remain competitive in a rapidly changing set of market conditions. He believed this could best be achieved by putting managers in the position of constantly asking why they are doing what they are doing and whether they should be using their resources to do something else.

Advantages and disadvantages of PPBS. **exhibit** **6.2**

ADVANTAGES

- Enables an organization to allocate its resources purposefully.
- Shows managers how their departments' work relates to the whole organization.
- Provides evidence to citizens of how a department is spending tax dollars.
- Gets staff involved at an early stage and allows them significant input.

DISADVANTAGES

- Limits flexibility to shift dollars between programs.
- Increases the potential for conflict if programs with strong support receive cuts.
- Is time consuming due to staff involvement and need for staff buy-in.
- Results in a weak evaluation process due to program length.
- May allow support for irrational objectives.

One of the best ways of putting this question at the center of attention is for managers to begin each budget year with no assumption that they will have what they received last year. What if managers had to start over from scratch each year and justify everything they were doing from the ground up? In short, why not create a level playing field for all managers, and assume that they could stop what they have been doing and use the resources to do something else instead? Wouldn't this generate more innovation and new product lines, thus ensuring the company constant market preeminence? Pyhrr thought so, and he created ZBB to achieve this goal.

ZBB requires building a budget from a "zero base." That is, the budget is not based on the previous year's budget, but rather starts all over again from a clean slate. This is the opposite of incremental budgeting, and it is designed to attack the major drawback of incremental budgets—the fact that resource allocation tends to become routine and inefficient. Sport is a fast-changing environment, and ZBB has become a staple budgeting approach for administrators who want to control costs and achieve operational efficiency in this kind of environment. Zero-based budgeting helps to prevent budgets from creeping up each year with inflation, and ZBB also shifts the "burden of proof" to the manager, who must justify why his or her department or sport should receive any budget at all.

ZBB has four requirements:

1. Each budget period starts fresh—budgets are not based on past budgets.

2. Budgets are zero unless managers make the case for resources. The relevant manager must justify the whole of the budget allocation.

3. Every activity is questioned as if it were new, before any resources are allocated to it.

4. Each plan of action has to be justified in terms of total expected cost and benefit, with no reference to past activities.

The philosophy of always questioning why we should continue doing what we have been doing is the heart and soul of zero-based budgeting. This philosophy and the system that Pyhrr created have been adopted by profit and non-profit organizations and used in government and athletic departments across the country. Through ZBB, budgeting can become a driving force to shape departmental and business policy and force more systematic planning.

Key elements of the ZBB system are decision units, base budgets, reduced-level budgets (RLB), and decision packages that are priority ranked. Each part of the organization where budget decisions are made is referred to as a **decision unit.** The **base budget** is defined as the expenditure level necessary to maintain last year's service level at next year's prices. In short, it increases the existing budget by the rate of inflation. The **reduced-level budget** defines a percentage that the budget must be reduced; for example, by 2 percent. The reduced-level budget includes services considered critical or essential, and it may include new or existing programs. **Decision packages** are discrete additions to the reduced-level budget, ranked in priority order, to maintain existing programs, serve increased workloads, or add new programs. Decision units may be asked to create decision packages beginning with a base budget or reduced-level budget. As the ZBB process begins, managers frequently use cost worksheets like the one given in chapter Appendix 6.C.

Ranking the decision packages

An important characteristic of zero-based budgeting is that it forces prioritization. Within the organization, each department and its related activities are ranked. When revenue may be insufficient to meet demand for spending, it is useful for the organization to have a ranking of sports, programs, and activities based on their effectiveness, as well as potential alternatives to expensive or ineffective programs. Despite its virtues, in good revenue years ZBB can accommodate poor decisions, but in years of financial exigency, tough decisions must be made. ZBB requires all managers involved in the budget process to agree to the priority and ranking of their departments and activities. This requirement creates accountability.

In the ZBB process, decision packages are evaluated and ranked in order of importance. On the example cost worksheet (chapter Appendix 6.C), the decision packages are ranked as Object 01, 02, and so forth. Note that subgroups are also ranked (e.g., under Position Salaries, we find Object 01: 1. Coaches, 2. Administrative Secretary, and 3. Secretary). Establishing the ranking performance measurement tools, including cost/benefit analyses, is clearly very important, but the application of subjective judgment is also appropriate. This is because few activities can be reduced to a manageable number of measures, and some measures may not be practical because of difficulties in real-world application or the expense of data collection. For example, a manager may believe that there would be a "feel-good" factor in taking a particular course of action, such as not cutting a team that has been a historical power even though it makes business sense to do so. This could never be accurately quantified and is subjective, but may be valid.

Usually the highest rankings in the decision package for an athletic department are salaries and benefits for the administration, coaches, and staff, as seen in chapter Appendix 6.C. For example:

1. Football coach
2. Basketball coach

The athletic director should consider which coach and which sport are most important to the department, and how the sport matches the department's goals and objectives (e.g., to compete on a national level in football and to compete for conference championships in all other sports). The matching of budget priorities with goals is essential for the success of any athletic department, particularly major BCS athletic departments. If football generates 80% of an athletic department's revenue, how does this factor into the allocation of resources in the overall athletic department budget? The football program will likely receive most of the department's resources. But suppose you are the softball coach or the equestrian team coach—what would you say about the hefty allocation of resources to the football program? The reality of the situation is that the department would have no softball or equestrian budget without football, so these coaches cannot effectively question the allocation of resources to football. This brings us to the next section.

Allocating resources

The ranking list results in a priority order for the allocation of resources. The most important items are funded, whether they are existing or new, and in lean years, funding for the lower-ranking items can be reduced. Returning to the ZBB cost worksheet (chapter Appendix 6.C), note that the Coaches and Administrative Secretary positions are fully funded, but funding for the Secretary position has been reduced by half. The final budget will be made up of the decision packages that have been approved for funding, allocated in the appropriate operational units.

Under ZBB, previous decisions are not supposed to influence the new budget. Previous outlays for coaches and facilities should, in theory, not be considered. Reality, however, is not theory, and previous budget outlays, especially for coaches and facilities, do matter in preparing the new budget.

Advantages and disadvantages

The zero-based budgeting process of setting priorities provides significant account-ability to the administrators, coaches, and staff who developed the criteria. In cases where revenues are flat or decreasing, the lowest-ranked priorities may be eliminat-ed, and conflicts and resistance should be less than under other budgeting systems.

ZBB is no panacea, however. Like incremental budgeting, it has its own set of drawbacks. It increases paperwork and requires time to prepare, managers tend to inflate the benefits of activities that they want funded, and the eventual outcome may not differ much from what would occur with an incremental budget. Exhibit 6.3 summarizes the advantages and disadvantages of ZBB.

---

exhibit   6.3   Advantages and disadvantages of ZBB.

ADVANTAGES

- Forces budget setters to examine every item.
- Allocates resources based on results and needs.
- Fosters a questioning attitude.
- Eliminates waste and budget slack.
- Prevents creeping budgets (using the previous year's figures with an additional percentage).
- Encourages managers to look for alternatives.
- Has a strong evaluation component.

DISADVANTAGES

- Is a complex, time-consuming process.
- May result in an emphasis on short-term benefits to the detriment of long-term planning.
- Does not officially consider previous money outlays.
- May be unrealistic (it is impossible to eliminate some programs, e.g., sports, although the budget indicates they should be).
- Is affected by internal politics and can lead to annual conflicts over budget allocation.

Modified Zero-Based Budgeting

As service-level budgeting entities, sport organizations are positioned to use a **modified zero-based budgeting (MZBB)** approach. In this approach, spending levels are matched with services to be performed. Under zero-based budgeting, a great deal of effort can be devoted to documenting personnel and expense requirements that are readily accepted as necessary, such as travel expenses for required road games, utility expenses for home games, and staff expenses for home games. MZBB reduces this effort by starting at a base that is higher than zero. An appropriate starting point for a department or program might be 80% or 85% of current spending levels. High-priority requests above this level may be identified in order to restore part or all of the current year's service levels.

Elements of MZBB

MZBB has the following characteristics:

- Uses cost identification and behavior techniques
- Begins with a floor of expenses
- Includes decision or add packages
- Requires managers to reduce their budgets by a predetermined percentage
- Puts existing programs in competition with new ones

The use of cost identification and cost behavior techniques (recognizing how costs react to changes in volume) enhance this budgeting approach. Costs are identified as fixed, variable, mixed, or step costs. **Fixed costs** do not vary with volume, whereas **variable costs** change with volume (see Exhibit 6.4). For example, an

Comparison of the movement of variable costs (in the same direction at the same rate as their associated activity) to that of step costs (constant within a range of use but different between ranges of use).

exhibit   6.4

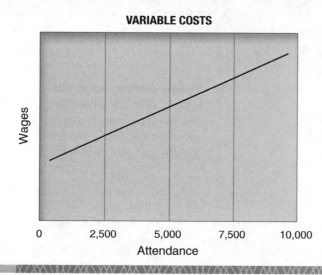

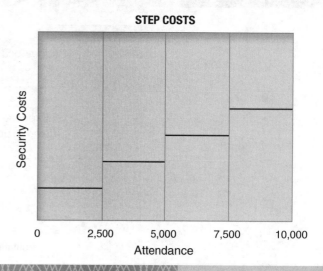

arena has certain expenses necessary to open the doors for fans for a sport event, regardless of the number of fans. This base is the same for 5,000 or 30,000 fans. These costs include administrative salaries and benefits, property insurance, property taxes, payroll taxes, and depreciation. Other fixed expenses are discretionary and might reflect organizational policies in the form of periodic appropriation for training and development, special promotions, and opponent guarantees, to name a few. Variable expenses for an arena will include cost of goods sold, wages (part time), and the opponent's share of the gate receipts. **Mixed costs** contain both fixed and variable elements. An example is utilities, which include a flat rate plus a cost for each unit used. For a sport arena, mixed costs would include repairs and maintenance, as well as utilities. Finally, **step costs** are constant within a range of use but differ between ranges of use. For example, the cost for security might be fixed under contract, with one rate for event attendance of zero to 2,500 patrons, a higher rate for attendance between 2,501 and 5,000, and a still higher rate for attendance from 5,001 to 7,500.

MZBB focuses on variable expenses, and this is why it is a practical approach to budgeting.

Exhibit 6.5 provides an overview of the MZBB focus. The expense floor represents the fixed costs of operations. These costs are the organization's minimal costs needed to stay in business and represent approximately 70% of total expenses. The top level (approximately 30%) represents mixed and variable expenses. This section is the focus of MZBB.

Zero-based budgeting focuses time and effort on all expenditures. Modified zero-based budgeting is more efficient in focusing time and effort on variable expenses and accepting fixed expenses as necessary. All departments and programs will have a base need for expenditures—the minimum necessary for the department or program to operate. MZBB focuses time, energy, and management decision making on the area above this budgetary starting point. Underlying the

---

exhibit   6.5   MZBB starting point.

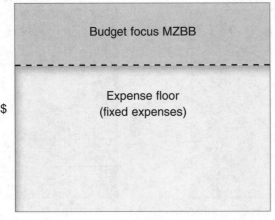

Budget focus MZBB

Expense floor
(fixed expenses)

$

Activities

Budget starting point: This is the cost of doing business. The going concern incurs the expenses below this line just to operate and provide services.

MZBB process is the concept of the **going concern**—the assumption that the entity will operate indefinitely. A sport entity whose status isn't in question would be prudent to budget for the variable costs, those above the starting point. This will focus effort on areas that pertain to the goals and objectives of the organization and increase the efficiency of the budgeting process.

In general, MZBB asks managers to reduce their budgets to a predetermined level (a percentage of the previous year) and then add back requests for funding. Although this process places some existing programs in competition with new programs, it saves managers the strain of justifying all costs for all programs from the ground up.

In practice, athletic departments and public sector organizations that use MZBB require managers to submit "decision" or "add packages" for discrete activities or programs that need funding above a predetermined reduced level. In the submission stage of the budget process, managers are forced to reduce their appropriation requests to 80% to 90% of the base budget. A manager may then reconfigure existing activities into new decision packages that may bring the total budget request up to 110% to 115% of the previous year's budget.

By this means, new programs may be considered for funding. For example, an athletic department might be presented with the choice of reducing some current operations in favor of adopting a new program, funding the new program out of the savings gained by reducing the existing program. "Service-level budgeting" may be a better description of this budgeting approach, which begins with the minimum costs of providing a given service.

MZBB provides an occasion for managers to try something new and puts them on notice that they cannot assume the status quo. This can be unsettling to employees and managers, who may find their programs part of a "cut" package. Even if their activity is never cut, the employees and managers may feel unappreciated. Because of this potential for demoralization and the extensive time often required for the preparation of decision packages, zero-based budgeting processes, including MZBB, may not be appropriate for use in the public sector, especially where many activities are legally mandated.

Steps in MZBB

Step 1. The first step in MZBB is to identify expenses. Mark each expense type as fixed, mixed, or variable. Simply write F, M, or V next to the category (or in another column in a spreadsheet).

Step 2. Next, allocate fixed and mixed expenses. Fixed expenses will probably include the largest expenses, such as debt service and management salaries. Most fixed expenses are probably not negotiable without dramatic business changes or disruptions, so they provide a "hard landscape" around which you will fill in (and prioritize) the variable expenses. By identifying fixed and mixed expenses first you are able to focus on the smaller, more negotiable amounts that remain.

Some expenses are **periodic expenses.** These are expenses for which we set aside money each month, in order to have sufficient funds when the expense is incurred. Examples are new vehicles, retirement bonuses, certain one-time events, purchases of computer software and equipment, and some insurance payments.

Some organizations simply divide these expenses by 12 and set aside that amount each month. However, this approach will not work if the expense is less than a year away. Instead, for each expense, count how many months away it is, and divide the total expense amount by the number of months. For example, if the company plans to purchase a new car in four months with a down payment of $15,000, you would divide $15,000 by 4 and budget that amount, $3,750, each month. If an additional car will be purchased in the next fiscal year, and the purchase is at least a year away, you would divide the expense by 12 and set aside that amount each month.

This approach may cause strain on the budget at first, but as short-term expenses are paid, the monthly allocations for those expenses will decrease, freeing up cash.

Step 3. Once you have allocated the fixed and mixed expenses, circle back to identify any fixed expenses that could be eliminated. What remains will be the floor of expenses. You will concentrate on the expenses above the starting point line.

Step 4. Next, average the mixed expenses to determine the average amount spent per month over the last 6 to 9 months (some organizations may want to look at a fiscal year of expenses). Convert the average monthly mixed expense to annual expenses. For example, if the average monthly utility expense was $26,500, the annual expense is $318,000. Consider the economic reality that your organization will face during the next budget period. For example, how will the global demand for fuel impact utility rates over the next year? Exact estimates are not necessary; you will make adjustments as the process continues.

Step 5. Next, address and prioritize the variable expenses. The prioritizing of variable expenses is essential to MZBB, and it is the difference between MZBB and ZBB.

Step 6. The above expenses must be offset against anticipated revenues. Subtract total expenses from total revenues to arrive at the starting point for anticipated profit or loss from operations. Note that the goal of budgeting is not to break even (to make income equal expenses). Although you should conduct breakeven analyses to ensure that a net operating loss will not occur, you should budget for a profit or a positive residual, depending on the profit/non-profit status of your organization. By making trade-offs between one category and another, adjust the expense and revenue figures until income equals or exceeds expenses. In this process conflict often arises between sports, departments, coaches, and administration, because it exposes their conflicting *values*. If the conflict becomes too heated, it may be necessary for the parties to take a break and continue later.

Remember that you will refine the budget as you go. It is a process: Prepare, Compare, Repair.

Budgeting takes time, and it does not end when departments or programs submit their revenue and expense estimates. Many meetings and individual sessions will be necessary to discuss the numbers and the reasoning behind these numbers. Each meeting or session should focus on the goals and objectives of the department and the organization.

Advantages and disadvantages of MZBB. **exhibit** **6.6**

ADVANTAGES

- Focuses budget setters on variable costs.

- Allocates resources based on results and variable needs.

- Fosters a questioning attitude.

- Encourages managers to look for alternatives.

- Has a strong evaluation component.

- Is less time consuming than ZBB.

DISADVANTAGES

- May result in an emphasis on short-term benefits to the detriment of long-term planning.

- Does not consider previous money outlays.

- May be unrealistic, because some programs (e.g., sports) cannot be eliminated.

- Is affected by internal politics and can lead to annual conflicts over budget allocation.

The ZBB cost worksheet found in chapter Appendix 6.C may be used for MZBB as well. Whereas under ZBB each program, function, or activity must justified and placed in a decision packet, MZBB allows a starting point of 80% to 85% of the previous year's budget. Managers use decision or add packages to justify an increase in their unit's allocations above the starting point.

For example, in chapter Appendix 6.C, Professional Part-time salaries are ranked more important than Supporting Service Part-time salaries. Under ZBB, this package would start at zero, and changes to the budget would be based on the priority of the cost-decision package. Under MZBB, however, the package may start at 80% of last year's funds ($3,710.40). To request funds for new activities above the 80%, the manager would submit an add package. The add package would include $5,862 for the new Supporting Service Part-time request.

Advantages and disadvantages

MZBB focuses on the portion of the budget that has flexibility rather than the entire budget. Fixed and mixed costs cannot be eliminated if a service is to be offered, but variable expenses can be often eliminated or reduced—or increased, when warranted. MZBB combines the best advantages of ZBB with the simplification of focusing on the variable costs above the budget starting point. See Exhibit 6.6 summarizing the advantages and disadvantages of MZBB.

Budgets within Budgets

Within each budget type are additional budgets. These budgets track an organization's revenue, expenses, cash, and capital expenditures, and they are some of the most important planning tools an organization can use. They show the impact that the budget will have on future organizational revenues, expenses, cash flows, and capital expenditures.

Revenue budget

The **revenue budget** is a forecast of revenues based on projections of the organization's sales. For example, to set appropriate ticket prices, athletic directors, general managers, and administrators must consider the strength of their schedule, their conference affiliation, the competition, the advertising budget, their sales force effectiveness, and other relevant factors, and they must estimate sales volume. Then, based on estimates of demand at various prices, they select the appropriate prices. The result of sales estimates is the revenue budget.

Expense budget

The expense budget is found in all units within a firm and in not-for-profit and profit-making organizations alike. The **expense budget** for each unit lists its primary activities and allocates a dollar amount to each. Sport managers give particular attention to so-called fixed and semi-fixed expenses—those that remain relatively unchanged regardless of volume. As attendance drops or increases, variable expenses tend to control themselves because they change with volume.

Cash budget

The **cash budget** forecasts how much cash the organization will have on hand and how much it will need to meet expenses. This budget can reveal potential shortages or the availability of surplus cash for short-term investments.

Capital expenditure budgets

Investments in real estate, stadia, arenas, buildings, and major equipment are called capital expenditures. These are typically substantial expenditures, in terms of both magnitude and duration. Their magnitude and duration can justify the development of separate budgets for each of these expenditures. **Capital expenditure budgets** allow management to forecast future capital requirements, to keep on top of important capital projects, and to ensure that adequate cash will be available to meet expenses as they become due. Capital budgeting is discussed in detail in Chapter 8.

CONCLUSION

Planning is a controlling activity of decision makers. The "mechanical" (the actual budget on paper) is only part of the planning approach, which involves managerial and motivational elements. Decisions about the future of an athletic department, professional sport organization, or non-profit entity are often made in budgeting meetings. The budgeting process will indicate where next year's growth will focus and what areas will benefit from additional funds. It behooves every manager to take an interest in the budgeting process—and not only because bonuses depend partly on meeting budgetary objectives. Get involved: budgeting affects every department and every individual in the organization.

CONCEPT *check*

1. Why is the budgeting process important to the success of a sport organization?
2. How do budgeting and forecasting differ?
3. How does incremental budgeting differ from program planning budgeting? How does it differ from zero-based budgeting?
4. What are the strengths and weaknesses of incremental budgeting?
5. How does program planning budgeting differ from zero-based budgeting?
6. What are the strengths and weaknesses of program planning budgeting?
7. What are the strengths and weaknesses of zero-based budgeting?
8. How does modified zero-based budgeting differ from zero-based budgeting?
9. What are the advantages and disadvantages of modified zero-based budgeting?
10. In team sport (professional or college), which form of budgeting should be used?

PRACTICE *problems*

1. The Columbia Arena Company formed in 2010 and uses the accrual basis of accounting. Using the company's 2010 budget provided on the next page, develop a pro forma operating budget for 2011 based on the following revenue and expense estimates:

   a. It is forecasted that costs and expenditures will change in 2011 as follows:

      - Merchandise COGS, G&A, Event Costs, and Maintenance will increase by 4.7%.
      - Concessions COGS will increase by 7.5%.
      - Utilities will increase by 8.0%.
      - Personnel will increase by 1.5%.
      - Insurance, Contract Services, Marketing, Management Fee, and Reserve are forecasted to remain the same.

   b. The Arena is expected to generate cash receipts in 2011 as follows:

      - All rent will increase by 4.7%.
      - Concessions Gross will increase by 5.0%.
      - Merchandise Gross, Suite Revenue, Club Seating Revenue, Advertising Revenue, and Naming Rights are forecasted to remain the same.
      - Box Office, Parking, and Ticket Fee revenues will decrease by 2.7%.

COLUMBIA ARENA COMPANY
2010 OPERATING BUDGET

Revenues	
Rent from Sports Teams	$ 425,934.00
Rent from Events	$ 668,636.00
Equipment Rent	$ 25,292.00
Concessions (Gross)	$2,304,703.00
Merchandise (Gross)	$ 224,393.00
Advertising and Sponsorships	$ 532,500.00
Naming Rights	$ 300,000.00
Box Office	$ 138,120.00
Suite Revenue	$ 717,185.00
Club Seat Revenue	$ 504,000.00
Ticket Fees	$ 600,000.00
Parking	$ 442,212.00
Total Revenues	$6,882,975.00
Less COGS:	
Concessions COGS	$1,382,822.00
Merchandise COGS	$ 112,196.00
Total COGS	$1,495,018.00
Gross Profit	$5,387,957.00
Operating Expenses	
Personnel	$ 900,000.00
G&A	$ 200,000.00
Non-reimbursed Event Costs	$ 150,000.00
Utilities	$ 450,000.00
Insurance	$ 250,000.00
Maintenance	$ 339,267.00
Contract Services	$ 110,000.00
Marketing and Promotion	$ 200,000.00
Management Fee	$ 100,000.00
Reserve	$ 150,000.00
Total Operating Expenses	$2,849,267.00
Operating Income (Loss)	$2,538,690.00

2. After you have calculated the 2011 budget, suppose your boss asks you to revise it so that overall revenues increase by 4% and operating expenses decrease by 1.5%.

   a. Based on current trends in facility management, what revenues do you anticipate can be increased? What expenses can be decreased?

   b. Use the 2011 budget that you created in Problem 1 and create a new 2011 budget based on the revenue increases and expense decreases outlined in Problem 2 and your work on Problem 2a.

CASE analysis
Southern Ohio State University

The intercollegiate athletics department at Southern Ohio State University (SOSU) has major budgeting issues. For the 2010 fiscal year, the university's Board of Trustees has approved an $18.7 million budget for the department. The budget projects a $1.3 million shortfall. After SOSU's president shifted $1.3 million to athletics to cover the shortfall, groups across campus complained loudly about the role of intercollegiate athletics on SOSU's campus.

The SOSU athletic program competes as an NCAA Division I – FBS team. The school is a member of a mid-major conference and has 16 varsity teams, the minimum number required by the NCAA for competition at the Division I level. The athletic department's budget is relatively small compared to other Division I – FBS teams. The team's football budget was in the bottom half of conference budgets in fiscal year 2008. For the 2009 fiscal year, the budget was cut by 5%. The athletic department employs relatively few staff members, but in 2009 ten positions were cut, saving the department $700,000. In fiscal year 2009, the department spent $18.7 million while generating $4.1 million in revenues. After the athletic department's portion of student fees was transferred to the department, it had a $1.8 million deficit. The department has overspent by a total of approximately $7.5 million over the past few fiscal years.

Beyond its athletics department, the university as a whole faces serious budgeting challenges. Due to the recession and declining state support, SOSU will have to cut between $10 million and $21 million in fiscal year 2011. For fiscal year 2012, the cuts may grow higher, to as high as $36.5 million. As the university acts to balance its budget, many are questioning the athletic department's deficit spending. One member of SOSU's faculty senate stated, "The athletics department drains resources at a time when academics are being threatened by overall cuts at the university." Other faculty members are asking whether operating the athletic department is worth the expense.

CASE QUESTIONS

1. If you were advising the athletic director at SOSU, what budgeting advice would you provide?

2. What budgeting approach should the athletic department use if it intends to balance its budget in the 2011 fiscal year?

3. For an average athletic department, which budgeting method would most likely keep the program from running a deficit? Why?

APPENDIX *chapter 6*

6.A   Athletic budget, incremental budgeting.

THE PROGRAM UNIVERSITY
DEPARTMENT OF INTERCOLLEGIATE ATHLETICS
PROJECTION 2009–2010

	2007–2008 BUDGET	2008–2009 BUDGET	INCREMENTAL BUDGET 2009–2010
INCOME			
I. Admissions & Guarantees			
A. Men's basketball	$1,000,000	$1,008,000	$1,018,080
B. Football	7,044,000	7,874,560	7,953,306
C. Baseball	50,000	50,000	50,500
D. Women's basketball	12,002	10,000	10,100
E. Soccer	15,000	10,000	10,100
F. Other	5,000	5,000	5,050
TOTAL	$8,126,002	$8,957,560	$9,047,136
II. Athletic Fees			
A. Matriculation fees	$475,000	$475,000	$479,750
B. Debt service	610,000	610,000	616,100
TOTAL	$1,085,000	$1,085,000	$1,095,850
III. Program Club Revenues			
A. Contributions	$5,800,000	$5,800,000	$5,858,000
B. Investment income	120,020	150,000	151,500
C. Endowment income	125,000	125,000	126,250
D. Non-cash gifts in kind	160,000	150,000	151,500
E. Royalties	50,000	50,000	50,500
F. Jr. program club	10,000	10,000	10,100
G. Parking	4,000	5,000	5,050
H. Credit card revenue	5,000	10,000	10,100
I. Miscellaneous	5,000	5,000	5,050
TOTAL	$6,279,020	$6,305,000	$6,368,050
IV. Other Revenues			
A. Radio & television			
1. Basketball	$31,250	$31,250	$31,562
2. Football	218,750	218,750	220,938
3. Talent reimbursement	20,020	20,020	20,220
4. Miscellaneous	5,000	5,000	5,050
TOTAL RADIO & TV	$ 275,020	$ 275,020	$ 277,770

	2007–2008 BUDGET	2008–2009 BUDGET	INCREMENTAL BUDGET 2009–2010
B. Corporate sponsorships	$600,000	$600,000	$606,000
C. Mailing & handling fees	45,000	45,000	45,450
D. Investment income	220,020	300,000	304,900
E. Concessions	435,000	500,000	505,000
F. Souvenirs	15,000	20,020	20,220
G. Programs	75,000	80,000	80,800
H. Conference revenue sharing	1,900,000	1,900,000	1,919,000
I. Stadium rental	0	25,000	25,250
J. Miscellaneous	5,000	5,000	5,050
K. NCAA distribution	190,000	190,000	190,000
TOTAL	$3,485,020	$3,665,020	$3,701,670
V. Subsidy from non-restricted reserve for debt service	$125,000	$125,000	$125,000
TOTAL PROJECTED REVENUE	$19,375,062	$20,412,600	$20,615,476

EXPENSES

	2007–2008 BUDGET	2008–2009 BUDGET	INCREMENTAL BUDGET 2009–2010
I. Revenue Sports			
1. Men's basketball	$1,283,873	$1,078,823	$1,100,399
2. Football	4,468,639	6,033,300	6,153,966
TOTAL	$5,752,512	$7,112,123	$7,254,365
II. Men's Olympic Sports			
1. Baseball	$441,725	$335,575	$342,287
2. Golf	169,010	146,708	149,642
3. Soccer	293,860	248,871	253,848
4. Swimming & diving	289,427	214,291	218,577
5. Tennis	207,867	173,751	177,226
6. Track indoor/outdoor & CC	273,643	260,555	265,766
TOTAL	$1,675,532	$1,379,751	$1,407,346
III. Women's Olympic Sports			
1. Basketball	$461,671	$421,049	$429,470
2. Softball	243,285	175,760	179,275
3. Volleyball	275,587	210,307	214,513
4. Swimming & diving	294,496	198,512	202,482
5. Tennis	215,081	147,661	150,615
6. Golf	147,469	117,612	119,964
7. Track indoor/outdoor & CC	273,643	86,567	88,298
TOTAL	$1,911,232	$1,357,468	$1,384,617
IV. Cheerleaders			
TOTAL	$94,017	$87,893	$89,651

	2007–2008 BUDGET	2008–2009 BUDGET	INCREMENTAL BUDGET 2009–2010
V. Support Services			
1. Sports information	$447,805	$449,114	$458,096
2. Medical/training	626,036	608,565	620,736
3. Booster club	1,352,586	1,325,929	1,352,448
4. Administration	1,573,484	2,222,982	2,267,442
5. Facilities/grounds/projects	1,105,053	1,024,196	1,044,680
6. Business office	227,895	251,791	256,827
7. Ticket office	377,642	324,354	330,841
8. Academic support	365,089	355,637	362,750
9. Strength/conditioning	159,665	148,256	151,221
10. Recruiting	209,264	203,779	207,855
11. Compliance	54,446	57,645	58,798
12. Olympic sports administration	349,668	345,277	352,183
13. Jr. Booster club	15,700	13,700	13,974
14. Wellness program	126,840	130,820	133,436
15. Concessions	74,100	74,100	75,582
16. Programs football/basketball	52,002	52,002	53,042
17. Video support	191,324	139,588	142,380
18. Marketing, development	564,057	385,947	393,666
19. Student support services	105,347	103,678	105,752
20. Stadium	183,772	172,388	175,836
TOTAL	$8,161,775	$8,389,748	$8,557,543
VI. Capital Improvement/Maintenance and Debt Service	$2,011,300	$2,011,300	$1,900,000
TOTAL PROJECTED EXPENDITURES	$19,606,368	$20,338,283	$20,593,522
TOTAL PROJECTED REVENUE	$19,375,062	$20,412,600	$20,615,476
PROJECTED INCOME OVER EXPENDITURES	($231,306)	$74,317	$21,953

| 6.B | Summer junior tennis camp budget, program planning budgeting system. |

Description
Designed to introduce tennis and provide recreational opportunities and competitive opportunities

Performance Objectives
1. Provide junior tennis opportunities for the community.
2. Increase the number of programs by 20% over the previous year.
3. Achieve at least a 90% positive satisfaction rating from participants.

MEASUREMENT	PROGRAM	OBJECTIVE	2008 ACTUAL	2009 APPROVED	2009 REVISED	2010 PROJECTED
Demand		1	12	16	14	16
Estimated Participants	Lil Bits	1	17	20	19	20
	Stars	1	19	20	18	20
	Novice	1	18	20	25	30
Estimated Programs	Tournament Play	2	5	5	5	6
Workload						
Actual Registrations	Lil Bits	1	12		14	
	Stars	1	17		19	
	Novice	1	19		18	
	Tournament Play	1	18		25	
Actual Participants		1	66		76	
Actual Programs		2	5		5	
Productivity						
Average Cost per Participant		1	$173		$180	
Effectiveness						
Program participation increase (decrease) over previous year		1	7%	15%	15%	13%
Program offerings increase (decrease) over previous year		2	0%	0%	0%	20%
Percentage positive ratings from participants		3	85%	90%	89%	90%

FISCAL RESOURCES			2008 ACTUAL	2009 APPROVED	2009 REVISED	2010 PROJECTED
Revenue	Fees		$11,400	$12,880	$13,670	$15,680
Expenses	Personnel		$6,000	$6,000	$6,000	$7,500
	Maintenance/Operations		$2,000	$2,000	$2,000	$2,150
	Tennis Balls		$625	$650	$700	$850
	Marketing		$1,500	$1,500	$1,500	$1,500
Profit (Loss)			$1,275	$2,730	$3,470	$3,680

Adapted from Brayley & McLean (1999).

6.C   Zero-based budgeting cost worksheet.

PROGRAM, FUNCTION,
OR ACTIVITY   ATHLETIC DIRECTOR OR AND COACHES

Position Salaries (Object 01) Position Title	Current FTE	Current $	Grade	Position Code	Request FTE	Request $	Change $	Change FTE	Justification/Purpose	Account Number
Coaches	35.0	$3,055,667	AD	1008	35.0	$3,055,667	—	—	Provide support to underperforming coaches	3-614-1-21
Admin. Sec. I	1.0	48,673	14	4130	1.0	48,673	—	—	Clerical support for the project	2-614-1-40
Secretary	2.0	85,097	12	4120	1.0	42,549	$(42,549)	(1.0)	Realign 1.0 position to provide more flexible clerical part-time salaries and consultant services	2-614-1-40
Subtotal	*38.0*	*$3,189,437*			*37.0*	*$3,146,889*	*$(42,549)*	*(1.0)*		

Other/Non-position Salaries (Object 01)	Current $	# Hrs.	# Days	Rate	# of Persons	Request $	Change $	Justification/Purpose	Account Number
Professional Part-time	3,500	100		$35.00	1.0	3,500	0		2-614-1-82
Supporting Service PT	1,138	67		$16.98	1.0	7,000	5,862	Flexible part-time assistance needed for peak summer/ fall season	2-614-1-90
Subtotal	*4,638*					*$10,500*	*$5,862*		

Consultants/Other Contractual Svcs. (Object 02)	Current $	# Hrs.	# Days	Dates of Service	Rate	Request $	Change $	Justification/Purpose	Account Number
Consultants/camps	0	40		Nov–Jan		$53,238	$53,238	Help train trainers/ coaches	5-614-2-01
Subtotal	*0*					*$53,238*	*$53,238*		

6.C   **Zero-based budgeting cost worksheet,** continued.

PROGRAM, FUNCTION, OR ACTIVITY   **ATHLETIC DIRECTOR AND COACHES**

Supplies and Materials (Object 03)	Current $	Request $	Change $	Justification/Purpose	Account Number
Athletic/program supplies	$41,500	41,500	0	Materials for staff to support training activities	4-614-3-33
Subtotal	*$41,500*	*$41,500*	*0*		

Other/Including Benefits for Supp. Projects (Object 04)	Current $	Request $	Change $	Justification/Purpose	Account Number
Local travel	$114,700	$114,700	0	Travel from office to schools and out of town games	
Subtotal	*$114,700*	*$114,700*	*0*		
GRAND TOTAL	38.0 $3,350,275	$3,366,827	$16,552		

Employee Benefits from Realignment (Amount to Dept. of Financial Services)	Salary from above	Prof. @ 20% (.20)	Supp Svc @ 40% (.40)	Part-time @ 8% (.08)	Request $
Reduce for 1.0 coach	$(42,549)	—	$(17,021)	—	$(17,021)
Add for Support Svcs Part-time	5,862	—	—	$469	$469
Total Benefits	$(36,687)	0	$(17,021)	$469	$(16,552)

references

Brayley, R.E., & McLean, D.D. (1999). *Managing financial resources in sport and leisure service organizations.* Champaign, IL: Sagamore.

Makridakis, S., & Wheelwright, S.C. (1982). *The handbook of forecasting: A manager's guide.* Hoboken, NJ: Wiley.

Ord, K., Hibon, M., & Makridakis, S. (2000, October). The M3-competition. *International Journal of Forecasting, 16*(4), 433–436.

Pyhrr, P. (1973). *Zero-base budgeting.* New York: Wiley.

Smith, J.A. (2007). *Handbook of management accounting* (4th ed.). London: CIMA.

Debt and Equity Financing

Introduction

Individual people, families, and businesses often have money available that is not being used in their day-to-day lives or businesses. Instead of just keeping this money under the proverbial mattress, they have the opportunity to invest. At the same time, businesses are in need of money or financing in order to expand their operation, buy new equipment, launch new products, and so forth. In other words, there are suppliers of financial capital and purchasers of this capital. The financial markets and intermediaries help these two sides find each other.

A sport organization in need of financing may decide to raise capital by allowing investors to own part of the company in exchange for the funding or financing (equity financing), or they may decide to borrow money (debt financing). The choice of one or the other (or some of both) depends on the overall cost of each and the related risks. In essence, a financing decision is based upon the risk (and creditability) of the company. Typically, companies with lower risk and steady cash flows choose to issue debt. Companies that have higher risk in their cash flows (i.e., they cannot guarantee an interest payment) usually issue equity.

How does a company go about completing a financial transaction to raise capital? The company will probably select one of three methods for completing these financial transactions. The first is a direct transfer, whereby the business sells its stocks or bonds directly to investors (savers) without using any type of financial institution. When corporate bonds are floated or stock is offered through a secondary stock offering, this is done directly to the market. A second method is to use an investment bank as an intermediary. The business sells its bonds or stocks to the investment bank, which resells them to the market. A third method is that savers invest their money with a financial intermediary, such as a bank, which then issues its own securities. When a person puts money into a bank, the bank then lends that money out to another person or entity. The saver has no direct connection to the borrower. The bank makes money by paying a lower interest rate to savers than it receives from borrowers. Mutual funds, insurance companies, and pension funds may also act as financial intermediaries.

This chapter discusses equity financing through the sale of shares of stock and its debt counterpart, the sale of corporate bonds and loans, but first we will discuss required rate of return, which affects both equity and debt financing.

REQUIRED RATE OF RETURN

 he required rate of return is the annual return that an investor would require from a particular investment, whether in stocks or bonds, to account for the riskiness of the investment.

Factors Influencing the Required Rate of Return

An investor purchasing stock (equity) in a company will require a return of at least a certain amount. The amount will depend on (1) production opportunities, (2) time preferences for consumption, (3) risk, and (4) inflation.

Production opportunities. The quality or nature of the **production opportunities** of the investment—that is, the reason the company needs the money in the first place—matters to the **return on equity capital**—the combination of dividend payments and capital gains. In other words, the quality of the new product offering or geographic expansion (two examples of production opportunities) will affect the financial return from the project. If the company believes that it can create large returns from the project once it receives the equity capital, it may be willing to pay higher returns on that capital. However, competition to invest in a projected high-return business opportunity helps to keep the cost of equity capital down. A competitive market will dampen the production opportunities effect, because multiple equity investors desiring to invest in the project will outbid each other, reducing the expected return on equity capital. As in any market, the final expected return on equity capital is the result of a balance between the supply of possible investments and the demand to invest in these projects.

Time preferences for consumption. Consumers or businesses considering an investment will base their decision partially on their time preferences for consumption. As discussed in Chapter 4, those with a high preference for consuming now will require a higher return on equity capital than those with a low preference for consuming now.

Risk. A potential investor will also consider the risk involved in the investment in terms of the size of the dividend payments (and when they will be paid) and the expected stock appreciation. With a higher perceived risk, the required rate of return on equity capital will also have to be higher, to entice investors to provide capital for the project.

Inflation. Inflation affects all financial investments, in that gains from the sale of securities will be undercut by the increased cost of goods and services. Gains must be high enough to outpace inflation and to reward the investors. If expectations for future inflation rise, then the required rate of return will also rise, reflecting the expected future inflation.

Calculating the Required Rate of Return

The required rate of return will be higher if the investor sees a substantial probability of the investment becoming worthless or worth less than expected. An investor could buy a short-term U.S. Treasury bill (T-bill) and earn its rate without fear of default. Hence, the required rate of return begins at the risk-free or T-bill rate. Then, the investor will add percentage points reflecting default risk, inflation risk, liquidity risk, and maturity risk.

You will note that this adding of percentage points is similar to the calculation of the nominal interest rate, as discussed in Chapter 3. See that chapter for definitions of these risk premiums. The formula for the required rate of return (k) as it applies to different types of securities is shown in Exhibit 7.1.

From this exhibit, one can see that short-term T-bills will have lower required rates of return (based only on k^* and IP), because they are less risky, whereas long-term corporate bonds (and other corporate securities) will have higher required rates of return, because of various additional risk premiums.

| exhibit | 7.1 | Formula for the required rate of return. |

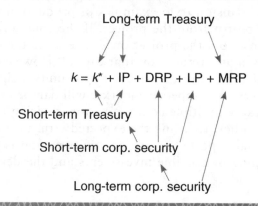

$$k = k^* + IP + DRP + LP + MRP$$

By graphing interest rates against the time to maturity for bonds with equal credit quality, including government bonds, one can create the **yield curve** (or term structure of interest rates). The most frequently reported yield curve is one that plots three-month, two-year, five-year, and 30-year U.S. Treasury debt. Exhibit 7.2 shows a curve for 11 maturities, as of December 1, 2008. Typically, the yield curve slopes upward, with a diminishing slope as maturity increases. Longer maturities generally entail greater risk than short maturities because there is more uncertainty in the far

| exhibit | 7.2 | Yield curve for U.S. Treasury bills as of December 1, 2008. |

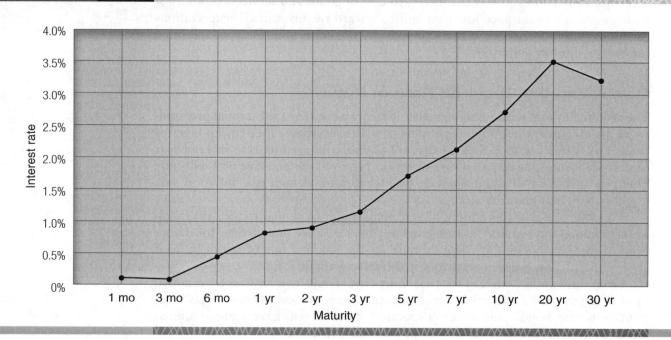

future than in the near future. However, the yield curve may be humped or downward sloping. A downward sloping yield curve is rare and is known as an *inverted yield curve*. It is caused by a market expectation of lower interest rates in the future that outweigh the maturity risk premium. When yield curves are inverted, a recession typically follows.

The **liquidity spread** is the difference between a long-term interest rate (e.g., 30 years) and a short-term interest rate (e.g., three months). This spread will be greater if the risk in the distant future of adverse events is high relative to the risks of the near-term future.

EQUITY

 s discussed above, equity financing involves the exchange of capital (money) for an ownership stake in the company. This section discusses the various forms of equity financing and stocks (equity ownership).

Types of Equity Financing

Although equity financing is typically considered simply the infusion of equity into a firm in exchange for company shares, this type of financing actually includes

The yield curve for U.S. Treasury bills as of March 2, 2007.   **exhibit   7.3**

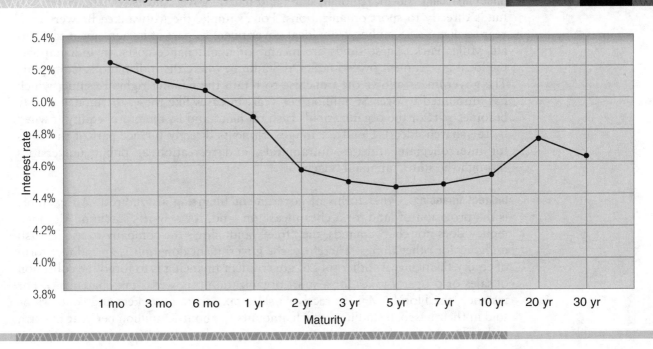

three additional funding sources: retained earnings, government funding, and gifts or donations.

Shares

One way to finance a large project is to issue shares of the company in exchange for money. The buyers of those shares will own stock (typically common stock) in the company, meaning they will own some percentage of the company and will be entitled to a portion of any dividends the company may pay out. **Dividends** are periodic payments made to shareholders of a company as a way of distributing profits to the shareholders. Through the sale of stock, the company obtains financing for a large project (such as a new product line, new geographic market, or the acquisition of a complementary company).

Retained earnings

In another form of equity financing, the firm simply uses cash on hand, or retained earnings, to finance a large project. Technically, the shareholders own the cash on hand—it is their equity. Depending on the board of directors' decision, it could be given to the shareholders in the form of a dividend or it could be reinvested in the company (or some of each).

Government funding

A third form of equity financing is the use of government funding. Chapter 9, "Facility Financing," discusses ways the government has traditionally helped finance sport stadia and arenas. This section describes those methods in brief.

Direct financing. Local, regional, state, and federal governments sometimes provide funds directly to sport organizations. For example, the Milwaukee Brewers each year receive $3.85 million from local government as part of its agreement to operate Miller Park. These funds are meant for maintenance costs. In Indianapolis, the local government owns Lucas Oil Stadium, where the Indianapolis Colts play. The government allows the franchise to retain the naming rights revenue, which has amounted to over $6 million per year. In cases like these, the money simply becomes part of the organization's cash on hand and is, therefore, equity (owned by the shareholders). Finally, state governments directly finance part of the costs for intercollegiate athletics, intramurals, and recreation at public universities through the states' annual budgets.

Indirect financing. Other forms of government financing are indirect. An example is the provision of land, or a cheap lease on land, for a sports stadium. Although money does not change hands, the "free" land allows the company to use its cash on hand for other things. Therefore, the government donation is an indirect form of equity financing. Another tool of government financing is to forgo the collection of sales or property taxes for a sport organization (known as **tax abatement**). For instance, the Florida Marlins receive a sales tax rebate on tickets and concessions sold in their baseball stadium, which amounts to about $2 million per year in extra cash. The organization adds this amount to its cash on hand (and owners' equity).

Gifts

Finally, some sport organizations solicit and receive tax-free donations or gifts. Any non-profit organization set up as a 501(c)(3) can receive donations and provide the donor with a receipt allowing the donor to take a tax deduction. Some intercollegiate athletic departments generate 10% or more of their annual budget through donations. In 2008, The Ohio State University generated over 20% of its athletics budget from donations to the university. These donations add to the cash on hand. Although non-profit organizations and universities do not have equity holders, they do have equity or net assets that management may use in operating the organization.

Stocks

All for-profit businesses have equity ownership—someone owns the business, even if it is one person who owns 100% of the equity (or stock) in the business and even if the equity is not traded on a stock market. Sport teams, for instance, are owned either by a single person (such as Ralph Wilson, owner of the Buffalo Bills), by multiple owners privately (such as the St. Louis Cardinals), or by multiple owners, with the equity or stock traded on public markets (formerly the case for the Cleveland Indians and Boston Celtics). The latter ownership type is now more common in the English Premier League. As mentioned previously, the NFL prohibits the publicly traded ownership model, with the exception of the Green Bay Packers.

Common stock is held by the owners of a company. State and federal laws govern the specific rights and privileges of ownership, but ownership always implies control of the business. Usually, this means that shareholders (also called stockholders—those owning "shares" of stock) elect a **board of directors** (BoD) whose job is to select the executives and management and to supervise the overall direction of the company. Those executives hire the remaining employees. Thus, shareholders exercise and maintain their control through the BoD, not by directly running the day-to-day operations of the company. Typically, board members own shares or are granted options to buy shares, in order to align their interests with those of the stockholders.

Price of equity

Just like other goods, financial goods have prices. The price of borrowing money is the interest rate, meaning that the borrower must pay the lender interest, corresponding to the interest rate, in order to borrow the money. Typically, the borrower also pays a transaction fee. The price of obtaining capital by issuing stock takes the form of dividend payments and loss of equity by the company's owners. Any capital gain, or appreciation in the stock price, is now shared with the equity holders who provided the capital.

Calculating stock values

As discussed in Chapters 4 and 10, the value of a share of stock is equal to the present value of its expected dividend stream. See Chapter 4 for the calculations of the present value of a future cash flow and Chapter 10 for valuation of a company. As shown in Exhibit 7.4, the present value of a share of NewFangled Sports Products, Inc. (NFSP) is worth about $14.86, based on the present value of the expected

exhibit   7.4   Valuation of stock.

VALUE OF NEWFANGLED SPORTS PRODUCTS, INC. STOCK BASED ON DIVIDEND PAYMENTS

		PROJECTED				
	FYE CURRENT YEAR	FYE CY+1	FYE CY+2	FYE CY+3	FYE CY+4	TERMINAL YEAR
① Expected Dividend Payment Per Share	$1.00	$1.10	$1.15	$1.20	$1.30	$1.40
② Discount Period in Years	0.00	1.00	2.00	3.00	4.00	
ⓐ Discount Factor	1.000	0.8890	0.7904	0.7027	0.6247	0.6247
ⓑ Discount Rate	12.5%					
ⓒ Perpetual Growth Rate	4.0%					
ⓓ Terminal Value						$16.51
③ Present Value–Cash Flow/Terminal Value	$1.00	$0.98	$0.91	$0.84	$0.81	$10.31
④ **Net Present Value**	**$14.86**					

Notes:

ⓐ Reflects end-of-year discounting convention.

ⓑ Based upon the Weighted Average Cost of Capital as reported in Ibbotson's *Cost of Capital Yearbook* (data through June 2006) for SIC 3949.

ⓒ Based upon estimated long-term cash flow growth rate of the economy in general.

ⓓ Terminal Value = (Terminal Year Cash Flow / (Discount Rate – Perpetual Growth Rate))

future dividend stream. The first row ① shows the expected dividend payments. This forecast may be based on what an equity analyst who covers this company (analyzes it for his or her investment bank employer) feels the dividend payments are going to be, or it may be based on guidance from the CEO of NFSP.

The discount period ② simply reflects how far into the future from the current year the payment is expected to be made. Here the assumption is one dividend payment per year. As discussed in Chapter 4, the discount factor ⓐ is

$$\frac{1}{(1 + i)^n}$$

where *i* is the discount rate and *n* is the number of periods

In other words, the $1.10 dividend is worth only $1.10 × 0.8890 = $0.98 today, because the shareholder will not receive it until one year from today. The discount rate ⓑ is based on the required rate of return, as discussed above and in Chapters 3 and 4. It reflects the riskiness of the expected dividend payments. The **perpetual growth rate** ⓒ is an expected annual growth rate in the dividend payment beyond the four years forecasted, in perpetuity (forever). This rate is projected by the equity analyst and is usually tied to the average U.S. gross domestic product growth rate. The calculation of the terminal value ⓓ is explained in Chapter 10.

Essentially, this is the total value of the stock at the end of Year 4. This value is reflected as a $10.31 present value ③. The net present value ④ of a share of NFSP with the expected dividends shown is the sum of each year's value in the present value row (i.e., summing $1.00, .98 . . .), equalling $14.86.

The concepts of discount rate and present value are fundamental tools of finance. We can use them in many different situations where a cash flow exists over multiple time periods.

Changes in stock prices

In casual conversation, people often talk about a stock being valuable because the price of the stock has risen since they purchased it or because the price is expected to rise. Thus, the person could sell the shares for a **capital gain** (the increase in a stock's price since purchase). Why would the stock price go up? The simple reason is that another person thinks the stock is more valuable than what the owner paid. Why would that person think the stock is more valuable? This line of reasoning will lead eventually to the conclusion that the point of owning a share of stock (or ownership in the company) is to share in any profit that is made. Profits are disbursed to stockholders through the mechanism of dividends. As discussed previously, dividends are payments made to shareholders, usually on a quarterly or annual basis. In other words, shareholders own the company, and they share in the profits of the company.

Many companies pay a consistent dividend each year instead of varying it according to actual profits. This reduces the financial risk of stock ownership in that company. A company may choose to return $1 per share of stock in dividends as a way of giving the owners what is due them. Other companies base the dividends somewhat on the company's profits. For instance, Nike paid 25 cents per share each quarter during FY 2009, 23 cents per share each quarter for FY 2008, and 19 cents per share each quarter for FY 2007. Nike has paid a dividend since 1984. Still other companies, including many on the NASDAQ, do not pay dividends but instead invest the money back into the company rather than obtaining financing through debt or some other means. For example, Under Armour has not paid any dividends, because it is a young company that is reinvesting its net profits in the growth of the company, with the hopes of creating even larger profits. The presumption is that

SIDEBAR

Apple Offers No Bytes

7.B

Apple Inc. grew quickly in the early 1980s and helped build the personal computer industry. It has been profitable for most of the years of its existence. In fact, sales of the iPod and iPhone have boosted Apple's income to over $5 per share (on total income of approximately $5 billion in 2008). Apple has over $11 billion in cash on hand, with another $22 billion in current assets. Since 2003, its revenues have grown by 500% and its income went from nearly zero to the aforementioned $5 billion. It finances its R&D with annual expenditures and does not have a lot of capitalized investment in equipment, plants, and so forth, because it outsources manufacturing. Yet, it pays no dividends and historically paid them for only eight years during the late 1980s and early 1990s, when it had much lower profits and less cash on hand. Why does Apple not distribute dividends? It is not using this cash to buy back shares of Apple stock.

Idle cash does not earn high returns for Apple (and its shareholders), so why hold that much for so long? This is the big question, and some surmise that Apple is reserving the cash to buy up other companies. What does Apple have in mind—who will it scoop up? Google and Cisco also do not pay dividends. Is Apple simply preparing itself for battle against these titans as they enter the consumer electronics product market? In the long run, investors expect Apple to pay dividends. Note that Warren Buffett, perhaps the most prescient investor over the past few decades, also does not pay a dividend from his Berkshire Hathaway fund. His role is to buy companies, so he needs the funds to do so.

Under Armour will pay dividends in the future. Dividends are the fundamental reason for owning stock.

If a company were to state credibly that it was *never* going to distribute a dividend, why would someone want to buy a share of that stock? A person might hope that someone else would be willing to pay more for the share in the future (the greater fool theory). One would ask why *that* person would be interested in buying a share of stock that would never provide dividend payments. Logically, no future purchaser would be interested, and the stock's value should be zero. In other words, to extract any money out of owning a share of stock, the owner must receive a dividend payment. For this reason, the value of a stock is based only on expected future dividend payments, not on any capital gain anticipated from selling the stock—because that capital gain itself is based on expected future dividend payments.

Yet stocks do change hands, and that is because different people have different expectations for how big or small future dividends are going to be, among other reasons, such as the seller needing immediate funds or differences in calculated required rates of return. Also, investors may sell shares of a company because they believe other companies provide better investment opportunities, with higher expected dividend payments and relatively lower stock prices. Proof of this point is in what happens each quarter when a company announces its earnings. If it misses earnings by a few cents per share, its stock price usually drops to reflect the expected drop in the future dividend stream. This is because dividends are, in the long run, tied to earnings. Companies do not necessarily set the exact dividend amount each year based on that year's earnings, but over time earnings will determine how much money is available to be distributed as dividends.

DEBT

N ow that we have discussed the sources of equity financing and its pricing, let's consider debt financing. The two major sources of debt financing are corporate bonds and loans. Companies issue corporate bonds to raise capital. The investors or buyers of the bonds may range from large institutions to individual people. For reasons discussed below, some investors prefer to own both stocks and bonds. **Loans,** on the other hand, are usually provided by financial intermediaries, such as banks or insurance companies. Loans operate similarly to bonds, except that loans are not originated through a publicly traded market, as bonds are. After discussing bonds and loans in more detail, we will look at what happens when a firm cannot repay or restructure its debt.

Bonds

As mentioned above, bonds are a financial mechanism that organizations use to raise capital through debt (as opposed to equity). A **bond** is a promise to pay back borrowed money plus interest to the investor who has purchased the bond. The par value or face value of a bond is the amount of principal that the bond will be worth at maturity. The face may represent a single investor's total investment (say $75,000), or the investor may purchase bonds with smaller par values (say, 75 bonds worth $1,000 each). The owner of a bond may sell it to someone else at any time, and the new owner will collect the principal repayment at maturity. The sale price may be higher or lower than the par value, depending on various types of risk. A bond's **coupon rate** is the rate that the organization is paying for use of the money, the equivalent of an interest rate. A bond's maturity is the number of years from issuance until the principal (or par value) will be paid back. Typically, corporate bonds have maturities of six to ten years.

A bond does not provide the investor any ownership privileges, as stock does. The bond holder will receive a fixed payment stream over time. This arrangement has a lower risk than ownership shares of stock, which will rise and fall daily and provide varying dividend payments. An equity (stock) owner, however, has a say in how the company is managed (usually through a vote on the membership of the BoD), whereas a bond holder is not entitled to vote on the management of the company. Bond holders, however, are usually first in line to receive some payment from liquidated assets if the company should go bankrupt. Essentially, stocks and bonds present a trade-off between risk and reward: the bond holder has less risk but usually receives lower expected total returns from ownership (at least historically) compared to equity owners.

Call provisions and premiums

Sometimes a borrower will obtain sufficient funds and decide to pay off the bonds before the maturity date. Each bond issue usually includes a **call provision,** which allows the borrower to pay the bond off early. Often, a minimum period, called the call protection period, guarantees the lender some interest payments, which should compensate her or him for the costs of the purchase transaction. After the call protection period, the borrower can pay off the bonds by repaying the principal plus a **call premium** (a fee assessed when the borrower pays off the principal prior to the maturity date). Often, the call premium is equal to one year's interest payments, if the call occurs during the first year, and it declines each year thereafter. The typical formula is

$$\text{call premium} = \frac{N-t}{N}\,\text{INT}$$

where N is the full number of years of maturity (e.g., for a 30-year bond, $N = 30$),

t is the number of years since the issue date, and

INT is the interest payment.

For example, suppose a 30-year bond for $10 million has an interest rate of 8%. The annual interest payment is, therefore,

$$0.08 \times \$10,000,000 = \$800,000$$

If the borrower wishes to pay off the bond in Year 10, then the call premium would be

$$\left(\frac{(30-10)}{30}\right)\$800,000 = \$533,333$$

The borrower would owe $10 million plus $533,333 at the end of Year 10.

Note that the call premium usually declines as time moves forward and maturity approaches. This is not always the case, however. For instance, in January 2009, the

Dallas City Council approved the full payment of over $61 million in city government bonds that were initially issued in 1998 as part of the financing of American Airlines Center. The call premium was 1% flat, or about $610,000, so the total payment consisted of $61 million in principal plus $610,000 for the call premium. The city decided to cash in the bonds and reissue new ones, because calculations showed that it would save over $10 million in present value as a result of lower interest rates in 2009 versus 1998. This is similar to refinancing one's home mortgage because interest rates have dropped, and having to pay an early payoff penalty of 1%. The ability to call a bond and pay it off early provides flexibility to the issuing company. Typically, borrowers pay a higher interest rate for bonds with a call provision.

Rating a bond

Rating a bond is similar to "scoring" a loan applicant. The rating is intended to convey the likelihood that payments will be made in full and that the borrower will not default. **Default risk** is the risk that a borrower will not pay back the principal of a debt plus interest. Analysts arrive at ratings by studying the financial performance of the corporation issuing the bonds, using indicators such as some of the ratios described in Chapter 2. The company's earnings stability, the regulatory environment, potential product liability, and similar issues affect the **bond rating**.

Rating agencies such as Moody's and Fitch rate bonds as a service to investors. Ratings range from a high of AAA to a low of D. If a bond has a high risk of default, the borrower will have to raise the interest rate in order to interest investors. **Junk bonds** have a bond rating below BBB, such as BB, B, C, or D. These bonds have a significant chance of default and thus offer much higher coupon rates.

Returns

Investors can make money from a bond in two ways. First, they may receive an annual or periodic payment, called the **annual coupon interest payment**. This is a periodic return from owning the bond and is analogous to a dividend payment. Second, the investor may earn a capital gain upon selling the bond, if it is sold prior to maturity. This one-time gain from the sale of the asset is similar to the capital gain from selling a share of stock.

The **current yield** is the amount that the investor earns annually from the interest payment, compared to the price of the bond. Current yield is expressed as a percentage return and is defined as

$$\text{current yield} = \frac{\text{annual coupon interest payment}}{\text{current price of the bond}}$$

In other words, the annual interest payment received from a bond is fixed (the coupon rate), but the price of the bond may vary with changes in interest rates, inflation, required rates of return, and so forth. A bond paying 10% with a par value of $1,000, 10-year maturity, and a price of $1,000 will have a current yield of 10%. If the price were $887 (see the example below), the current yield would be 11.27%:

$$\frac{0.10 \times \$1,000}{\$887} = 11.27\%$$

The **capital gains yield** of a bond is the annualized percentage change in the price of the bond relative to its current price. Mathematically, it is

$$\text{capital gains yield} = \frac{\text{expected change in bond's price}}{\text{beginning-of-year price}}$$

If the bond was sold for \$887, and its sale price a year later was \$950, then the capital gains yield is 7.1%:

$$\frac{(950 - 887)}{887} = \frac{63}{887} = 7.1\%$$

The sale price of a bond might rise because of a decrease in the discount rate due to lowered inflation expectations. See below for a discussion of bond valuation.

When we combine the two ways to make money from a bond, we have the **total expected return** from owning the bond. For the bond described above, the total expected return would be

$$\text{total expected return} = \text{current yield} + \text{capital gains yield} = 11.27\% + 7.1\% = 18.36\%$$

The difference is due to rounding. This is quite a substantial annual return. The term **yield to maturity (YTM)** is often used to denote the total annualized return from owning a specific bond. It is the same as the total expected return.

Calculating the value of a bond

Once an investor has purchased a bond, she or he can either hold it and receive the interest payments plus the principal upon maturity or sell the bond at some time and receive its price at that time. As discussed in Chapters 4 and 10, the value of any asset is equal to the present value of the future payment streams, discounted at some discount rate. Recall that the discount rate is based on the required rate of return. Thus, the riskiness of the investment plays a role in determining its discount rate. (An example of calculating a discount rate is provided in Chapter 10.)

If interest rates rise after an investor has purchased a bond, then higher-yielding bonds (those with higher payments because of higher interest rates) will be available to potential buyers, thus driving down the price of the investor's bond. In mathematical terms, higher interest rates cause higher discount rates, which lead to lower valuations for streams of payments. The risk that the price of a bond will go up or down is known as interest rate risk.

The present value of a bond is the price that a buyer would pay for it prior to maturity. On the day of maturity, of course, a buyer would pay the principal amount, because that is what the bond holder will collect on that day. The following formula provides the present value of a bond:

$$PV = \frac{IP}{(1+d)^1} + \frac{IP}{(1+d)^2} + \ldots + \frac{IP}{(1+d)^N} + \frac{M}{(1+d)^N}$$

where IP = interest payment,
d = discount rate or required rate of return,
N = number of annual payments, and
M = value at maturity.

In other words, the present value equals the sum of the present values of the interest payments, plus the present value of the principal payment (M), which is due at maturity N years in the future.

Consider the present value on the issue date of a 10-year bond, with par value $1,000, coupon rate 10%, and a discount rate of 8%. For each of ten years, a $100 interest payment will be made, and at the end of ten years the principal will be paid back. In nominal terms, $2,000 will be paid out over the ten years. However, the present value on the bond's issue date of that payment stream is

$$PV = \frac{\$100}{(1+0.08)^1} + \frac{\$100}{(1+0.08)^2} + \ldots + \frac{\$100}{(1+0.08)^{10}} + \frac{\$1,000}{(1+0.08)^{10}} = \$1,134.20$$

Therefore, one could sell the bond for $1,134 on its issue date. After five years, the bond would be worth less, because only five years of payments would remain. If the discount rate were higher (12%)—perhaps because of higher expected inflation or default risk or interest rate risk—the present value of the bond would decrease to $887. If the coupon rate were 8% and the discount rate were also 8%, the bond's present value might be surprising:

$$PV = \frac{\$80}{(1+0.08)^1} + \frac{\$80}{(1+0.08)^2} + \ldots + \frac{\$80}{(1+0.08)^{10}} + \frac{\$1,000}{(1+0.08)^{10}} = \$1,000$$

As this example shows, when the discount rate of a bond is the same as the interest rate, the present value is equal to the par value. The explanation illustrates the nature of the discount rate. If an investor is looking for an 8% rate of return on a $1,000 bond, and the bond is paying 8% interest, the investor is getting exactly what he or she is looking for in terms of return. For a ten-year bond, the nominal payments would total $1,800. If the maturity were 20 years, the nominal payments would total $2,600—but the present value would still equal the par value, $1,000, because the annual required rate of return is being met by the interest payments. However, for a bond paying 10% interest, the present value to an investor with a required rate of return of 8% would be greater than the par value.

Loans

The key aspects of a loan include its maturity, its interest rate, and any pre-payment provisions. The economics of a loan are similar to those of a bond, and the two have become even more similar in recent decades as lenders have begun to put loans into packages or pools (which may include thousands of loans) and buy them from and sell

When Can Debt Transform into Equity?   7.C

A **convertible bond** offers some of the features of both equity and debt. The investor has the option to convert the bond into a fixed number of shares of stock in the company, at a stock price agreed upon at the issuance of the bond—usually 25% to 35% higher than the current stock price at the time of issuance. If the stock price rises, the bond holder sees an increase in the value of the bond, because it can be converted into stock and sold if the stock price is above the conversion price. Effectively, the bond buyer is purchasing a **stock option**, a contract that allows the bond holder to purchase a specified number of shares of stock for a certain price.

If the stock price drops, the investor still receives interest payments from the bond itself. Because of the increased upside of convertible bonds, their coupon rates are lower than those of traditional bonds. For the company offering the bonds, convertible bonds offer savings, at least in the short run, because the debt payments will be lower. If the share price rises, the flood of bonds being converted to equity will dilute the equity of existing shareholders—thus keeping the stock price from rising very high.

them to other financial companies. This practice enables lenders to diversify their holdings by selling off some loans and purchasing others.

An example of a loan in the sport industry is the NFL's $1.5 billion secured loan. Even during the economic downturn of 2008, Fitch gave the loan an "A" rating (Nov. 18, 2008). This rating was based on large long-term television contracts and a hard salary cap (although the league was trying to change the cap in its 2009 collective bargaining agreement negotiations). Fitch projects that the NFL will maintain solid financial ratios. The mechanics of the secured loan account allow the lenders to access the television money prior to any distributions to teams or other outflows. The primary risk comes from the uncertain outcomes of collective bargaining.

Trade Credit

Short-term financing often takes the form of trade credit rather than a loan. **Trade credit,** for example, is credit granted by a manufacturer to a retailer. By agreement, after the manufacturer ships its product to the retailer for sale, the retailer may delay payment for a period of time depending on the terms (typically 30, 60, or 90 days). In essence, the manufacturer is providing the retailer short-term financing for the retailer's purchases from the manufacturer. It is in the best interest of manufacturers to help their downstream retailers remain solvent. In the United States, the size of trade credit (as a percentage of total business financing) is only a few percentage points less than the amount that commercial banks lend to businesses. This type of financing cannot be used for any substantial changes to the business, such as expansion, simply because the term is too short.

Nike provides a good example of trade credit. At the end of 2008, the company had nearly $2.8 billion in accounts receivable (A/R), meaning that customers (e.g., downstream retailers such as Foot Locker) owed the company $2.8 billion. Nike also had less than $1.3 billion in accounts payable (A/P), meaning that it owed suppliers that amount (for instance, for raw materials for the production of Nike products). Because the money Nike expects to receive from customers is more than double the money it expects to pay out to vendors, it is not surprising that Nike is willing to ship its product downstream to retailers and allow those retailers to pay in the future. On the other hand, Foot Locker had net receivables of $53 million and $187 million in A/P. This is also not surprising, because Foot Locker is being allowed to take its time in paying Nike (and other product suppliers), while collecting directly from customers, who pay in cash or with a credit card, so that Foot Locker receives the income immediately.

Bankruptcy

If a company is unable to pay its debts and restructure its debt, it is insolvent. When this happens, the company must enter **bankruptcy,** the process of liquidation or reorganization of an insolvent firm. A bankruptcy court either will order **liquidation** of the company—the sale of its assets piece by piece, effectively removing the company from existence—or will allow the company to reorganize in a way that makes it more valuable than if it were liquidated. The court will choose the method that is likely to provide the highest value to the company's creditors.

Note that the selected method will not necessarily provide the highest value to the equity holders—they took on the risk of bankruptcy when they bought into the company. If the company is to be reorganized, the court usually appoints a committee of unsecured creditors to undertake this task. They may decide to restructure the firm's debt by reducing the interest rate on the debt, extending the date to maturity, or exchanging some of the debt for equity. The goal is to reduce the debt payments sufficiently that the company's cash flow can cover them. If this is not possible, liquidation is the best alternative.

When a company is liquidated, its assets are generally divided according to the priority of claims as shown in Exhibit 7.5. Secured claims take first priority. A **secured claim** is a debt for which the borrower provided collateral—an asset that the creditor has the right to seize if the debt is not paid. For instance, in a home mortgage, the lender (usually a bank) has the right to take ownership of the house and sell it if mortgage payments are not made. This is a secured loan, and the house is collateral. Recall that an unsecured claim is a debt in which the creditor has no right to seize any assets from the company or person who borrowed the money. Credit card debt is an example: the card issuer has no right to seize any products you purchased with the card, even if you do not repay the debt. Consistent with the concepts of risk and interest, secured debt will have a lower interest rate than unsecured debt, because the risk for unsecured debt lenders is higher.

Note that, in general, any debt that is termed *senior* or *subordinated* has higher or lower priority, respectively, than other debt obligations of the company.

One can see why the court-appointed committee that undertakes reorganization of a bankrupt business consists of unsecured creditors—they are so far down the priority list that they will be motivated to make the best decisions, in order to have a chance of getting paid. If the committee were made up of secured creditors,

---

exhibit   7.5   The priority of claims on the assets of a company in liquidation.

1. Secured claims

2. Trustee's costs

3. Expenses incurred after bankruptcy was filed

4. Wages due workers (up to a limit, sometimes $2,000 per worker)

5. Claims for unpaid contributions to employee benefit plans

6. Unsecured claims for customer deposits up to some limit (applicable to banks)

7. Federal, state, and local taxes

8. Unfunded pension plan liabilities

9. General unsecured creditors

10. Preferred stockholders, up to the par value of their stock

11. Common stockholders—if anything is left

they would have little incentive to ensure payments to parties farther down the priority list. Shareholders would not be the best choice, either: they may prefer to reorganize, in hopes that their shares will become worth something, even if the best move is to liquidate.

TRADE-OFFS OF EQUITY FINANCING

In Europe, especially Britain, dozens of professional soccer teams are publicly traded. One of the main reasons for selling equity has been to raise capital in order to improve the teams' stadiums. Securing funds by selling shares to the public has also allowed some British soccer teams to pursue other ventures, such as running a chain of pubs, selling apparel and other leisure products, and building hotel and restaurant facilities. Of course, the teams have also used much of the money to acquire better players. This has had the effect of substantially raising soccer players' salaries in recent decades.

In the United States, in October 1996, the Florida Panthers of the NHL sold shares to the public and were listed on the NASDAQ exchange (and later on the NYSE). For less than half ownership of the team, the public paid $67 million. Independent valuation analysts had pegged the value of the entire team at $45 million only a few months earlier. At first, the Panthers were the primary asset of the company, and fans were targeted to buy shares. However, after only a month of being publicly traded, the entity began to purchase other leisure assets, such as resorts and a golf course. Within two years, the hockey team accounted for only about 10% of the company's assets.

As discussed earlier, many North American sport leagues either strictly prohibit publicly traded franchises or have rules requiring all owners to approve any transfer of ownership. Outside of spectator sports, the sport industry includes many publicly traded companies, such as Nike (ticker symbol NKE), Callaway Golf (ELY), and Dick's Sporting Goods (DKS). The remainder of this section will discuss the pros and cons of equity versus debt financing and specifically of publicly traded equity financing.

> ## SIDEBAR
>
> ### Fanchester United 7.D
>
> Would you pay $50 to $60 per year to be able to vote to trade a player or fire a coach of your favorite team? MyFootballClub, a British company, started in 2007 with the idea of allowing fans to own a soccer team and run it the way they want to. The founder set up a website (myfootballclub.co.uk) to raise capital by selling memberships at £35 per year. Once the company had sufficient funds, seven months after launching, it purchased EbbsFleet United (located in Kent, England) for £600,000. The club now boasts more than 32,000 members from 80 different countries, including thousands of members in the United States. Each member can vote on issues related to the roster, who will start, the marks and logos of the team, and so forth. The team is building a new stadium and is relying on the membership for key decisions and some funding. The club does not intend to pay dividends, but will reinvest net profits back into the club.

Advantages of Publicly Traded Equity Financing

Taking a company public provides many advantages to the owners. First, it provides access to capital or financing that does not require interest payments or even repayment of the principal. However, investors do expect that dividends will be paid once the capital has been used to increase the company's profitability.

Second, once a company becomes a publicly traded entity, it is much easier to issue another round of stock or issue corporate bonds. This is because the financials are now open to the public and in compliance with Securities and Exchange Commission requirements.

A third advantage of going public is that it makes it easier for the owners to carry out an exit strategy. A privately held business does not have a readily available price for its shares. A publicly traded company allows an owner to exit the business with relative ease. If the owner's name is tied to the brand of the business, then selling the shares all at once might impact the overall value of the business (and the price at which the owner can sell the shares). Think of how Steve Jobs is tied to Apple's success, or Phil Knight to Nike's success. For this reason an owner may not be able to sell his or her shares all at once, but would exit gradually by selling a few shares at a time.

In the **initial public offering (IPO)**, the company for the first time offers shares to the public in order to generate cash for the business. When a publically traded company offers shares for sale to the public, this is called a secondary offering. A secondary offering does not generate cash for the business if it consists solely of an owner's shares, because the cash goes to the stock owner, not the business.

For example, in November 2005, Under Armour offered shares to the public in an IPO. The apparel company had seen quick growth in its short lifespan, increasing sales from $5 million in 2000 to over $240 million by 2005. The offer of 9.5 million shares owned by the company and 2.5 million owned by private investors yielded over $100 million in capital for the company. Shares were offered at $13 and quickly closed over $25. Founder Kevin Plank was able to sell $13 million in shares, piggybacking on the IPO, but then was under a "lockout" period in which he could not legally sell any shares for 180 days. In May 2006, once the lockout was over, he sold about $50 million worth of stock. Lockouts are common after IPOs; they are intended to show the investing public that the "insiders" aren't cashing out and leaving the company but instead are maintaining their leadership roles and navigating the company forward.

The owner of a sports team who wishes to exit will probably find a ready market of billionaires interested in buying the franchise. Given the limited number of teams and the fact that a would-be owner can't just create a new team, there is always demand for franchises. Thus, an IPO is not a necessary exit strategy.

A fourth reason a company benefits from becoming publicly traded is the free publicity generated by the initial public offering process and subsequent coverage of the company's financials. Unfortunately, the publicity can also be bad if the stock price plummets or the company is perceived as weak. When the Arena Football League's Orlando Predators went public, articles in *BusinessWeek* and *Slate* were not very upbeat about the team's financial future.

The ability to attract and retain key employees, a fifth rationale, is enhanced for a publicly traded company, because the company can offer stock options (an option for an employee to buy stock at a set price in the future, provided the person is still with the company). Stock options can provide incentive for the employee to help make the company more profitable and to stay with the company. Stock options can allow employees at all levels to participate in the growth of the company. Even suppliers and customers of the company may be offered stock options (sometimes at a "friends and family" discount). This helps to align the entire value chain producing the product or service and getting it to market.

A sixth motivation for going public is that it increases the equity in the company, allowing it to issue debt, if the need arises. With increased equity, the interest rate on debt will be lower than it would otherwise be. This is because, as discussed in Chapter 2, offering equity as collateral shows the lender or investor that the company already possesses funds and that owners have an interest in the company's success.

Finally, mergers and acquisitions are more easily arranged for a publicly traded company, because its value is readily determined.

A privately held company may also offer stock options and benefit from some of the advantages discussed above. However, the value of the stock options for these companies is unknown, because the stock is not publicly traded (it has no market price). Offering stock options does not help these companies in the merger and acquisition processes.

Disadvantages of Publicly Traded Equity Financing

The above reasons for going public may give the impression that it is always a good idea, but there are disadvantages. First, the cost of issuing stock is very substantial, often up to 10% or 20% of the value of the company (depending on its size). The fees for lawyers and underwriters (bankers who arrange, finance, and execute a stock offering) may amount to a large portion of the proceeds. When the Cleveland Indians went public in 1998, they paid just above 10% of their proceeds to the lawyers and underwriters (about $6.2 million). Of course, issuing debt is also costly, but usually less so than issuing stock.

Second, the time required for preparations to go public can be a burden on the operations of a company. Key executives usually travel on a "road show" to inform potential institutional buyers about the IPO.

Third, if the time is not ripe to go public, the IPO may be postponed or stopped altogether. All of the expense and time involved in the process might go for naught. This could happen if the stock market or the economy takes a turn for the worse during the many months between inception of the process to the actual IPO (up to a year).

Fourth, a very important reason that many sport teams and leagues are not publicly traded is the lack of operating confidentiality. The team's prices, margins, salaries, and future plans would be available to competitors, employees, customers, suppliers, and the general public (including fans), because the SEC requires financial disclosure and annual reports. This is a primary factor that sport team owners mention when asked why they don't go public. In fact, it is typically in a sport franchise's interest to appear that it is struggling financially, for the reasons listed below.

- In negotiating with a players association, a league wants to be able to claim that revenues are low, so money is not available to share with players.
- In bargaining with a city to get a new stadium, a sport franchise benefits from an appearance that it cannot pay for a large portion of the stadium.
- From a publicity perspective, a franchise might want fans to think that it is struggling to break even (or losing money), so that it can justify raising ticket prices.

■ To avoid antitrust scrutiny, sport leagues prefer their franchises to appear that they are breaking even at best. This was the case when MLB's Commissioner Selig was called into Congress to testify (see case study in Chapter 10).

It would be difficult for some teams and leagues to show financial hardship and make the above claims if their financials were open to the public. The SEC's disclosure rules require public announcements of changes to a company that might "materially" affect the stock, *prior* to those changes being made. This requirement can play havoc with team management and the timing of decisions. For example, a team would have to disclose in advance that it is going to make a trade, sign a player to a free agent contract, or fire its head coach. This could create a bargaining and public relations fiasco.

Fifth, for most publicly traded companies, the original owners do not own 50% or more of the business. This means that founders of a company could be voted out of management (this happened to Steve Jobs, one of the founders of Apple, in 1985) or even, through a takeover where their shares are purchased, lose their ownership completely. The North American major sport leagues all have provisions in their bylaws allowing existing team owners to block the sale or purchase of a franchise if they do not approve the new owner. If a team were publicly traded, this kind of provision could not be legally enforced.

Sixth, public ownership reduces an organization's strategic flexibility. For publicly traded companies, the BoD must approve all major decisions, and each quarter "Wall Street" expects income growth. In contrast, firms with more debt financing typically have greater flexibility to maneuver in changing markets. A company that is debt financed can make a strategic investment that may cause losses for a number of years but that will pay off handsomely down the road. Furthermore, investors may desire annual dividends, even if the company would be better off reinvesting that money. In sports, some owners of a franchise want to maximize profits and other owners want to maximize the chance to win championships. A publicly traded sport team would likely have many owners of both types, resulting in tension over the direction of the business. The Canucks, Celtics, and Panthers each have experienced litigation against the majority shareholders, with the "outside" shareholders claiming that the "insiders" were operating the team to their sole benefit. Traditional publicly traded businesses will almost all be run to maximize profits, so a team with a goal of winning championships may find public ownership counter to its aims.

Seventh, conforming to the SEC's accounting and tax requirements is expensive, certainly more so than the requirements of a private company. In addition, a publicly traded company must set up an investor relations group or pay to outsource this function. When the Boston Celtics went public in 1986, sending annual reports to the many shareholders who owned one share of stock proved very expensive. The costs of printing exceeded the value that the team obtained from the shareholder's purchase of the stock. Sport franchises learned from the Celtics' difficulties and subsequently have required higher minimum purchases of stock. The Florida Panthers required a $1,000 minimum stock purchase.

Finally, an eighth reason for a company to avoid going public involves the financial strategy of IPOs. To ensure an initial upward movement, and the positive publicity and momentum that can come with it, the underwriters usually set the price artificially below what they believe the market is willing to pay. This artificially low price means that the company is essentially selling part of itself for less than it is worth—buyers are getting the stock for less than the value of the owners' shares.

Often, companies with lower risk to their future cash flow are more easily able to issue debt for their financing needs. A firm with risky future cash flows might be forced to issue equity and share the risk with other investors.

CONCLUSION

This chapter discussed the uses of and methods for debt and equity financing. The ability of firms to raise capital efficiently has allowed developed nations to sustain high economic growth for many decades. The financial industry creates efficiency by bringing together those with excess capital (investors) and those in need of capital. It allocates capital resources according to expected gains, accounting for risks. The sport industry is no different in its capital needs. In spectator sports, however, the desire to sell equity shares to the public is dampened, compared to most other industries, because of resistance to the transparency of financials.

The economic recession that began in December 2007 has brought changes to the structure and regulatory oversight of the financial industry. As of this writing, the changes have not yet been completed and their impacts are not fully understood. However, the fundamental nature of providing investors with investments and businesses with financing has not changed.

CONCEPT *check*

1. Does higher expected inflation increase, decrease, or have no effect on the required rate of return?
2. What methods can a company use to raise capital?
3. Does a company share its risk by issuing equity or debt?
4. What are some of the advantages of equity financing?
5. What are some of the disadvantages of equity financing, specifically for sport teams?
6. Is the yield curve typically upward or downward sloping? Why?
7. How are the features of a convertible bond similar to both debt and equity?

PRACTICE *problems*

1. Using the information in Exhibit 7.4 for NewFangled Sports Products, Inc., calculate the new NPV of a share of stock if the perpetual growth rate doubled from 4% to 8%. Additionally, if the terminal year dividend payment increased from $1.40 to $2.80, what is the new share price?
2. A share of NewFangled Sports stock is expected to provide a $1 per year dividend payment the first year, growing at 8% thereafter. Using a discount rate of 12%, what is the share worth with a 15-year horizon? What is it worth valued into infinity? Compare these results.

3. A minor league professional hockey team embarks on an aggressive facility expansion that requires additional capital. Management decides to finance the expansion by borrowing $40 million and by halting dividend payments to increase retained earnings. The projected free cash flows are $5 million for the current year, $10 million for the following year, and $20 million for the third year. After the third year, free cash flow is projected to grow at a constant 6%. The overall cost of capital is 10%. What is the total value? If the company has 10 million shares of stock and $40 million total debt, what is the price per share?

CASE analysis   *Debt Decisions*

Owners of sport franchises face tough decisions related to capital structure when they decide a new facility is needed. The St. Louis Cardinals were faced with these decisions when they decided to privately finance much of their new stadium.

The Cardinals' owners decided that a stadium was needed to replace Busch Stadium II, the team's home from 1966 to 2005. As the plans for the new stadium (Busch Stadium III) were announced, the owners stated that the new facility was needed to generate additional revenues for the franchise. With increased revenues, the franchise would better be able to compete for top players. However, since the facility opened in 2006, the team's debt has limited spending on payroll.

In a presentation to business students at Webster University, Cardinals chairman Bill DeWitt outlined the expenses of the club. Player salaries made up 50% of the team's expenses. Team operations (i.e., travel and coaching salaries) were another 10%, as were player development costs and facility operations expenses. Five to seven percent of expenses were for business operations. The remaining portion of expenses was interest on the team's debt (Strauss, 2009).

The Cardinals are in the 21st largest media market based on households. Thanks to a loyal fan base and high attendance, the team had the eighth highest revenues in MLB in 2008, gen-erating over $200 million. However, player payroll, which began at $92.5 million at the beginning of the season, ended at $100.8 million. This was the 12th highest in the league. The team plans to maintain a player payroll of approximately $100 million as long as attendance does not decline.

The owners borrowed approximately $300 million to build Busch Stadium III. The team pays more than $20 million per year in principal and interest on the two instruments that were used to finance the club's portion of the new stadium. The club operates on tight margins and is well managed financially. Further, with attendance in 2009 at 3 million plus and very high local television ratings, revenues are close to maximized. Without cutting expenses elsewhere, the team has limited flexibility and cannot increase payroll without losing money.

CASE QUESTIONS

1. Has the Cardinals' decision to use debt financing hurt the on-field performance of the organization? If so, how?

2. What form of debt financing did the team most likely use to raise its $300 million portion of the stadium construction costs?

3. What equity financing options could the club have considered to raise some of the capital to build the new stadium?

references

Cheffins, B.R. (1999). Playing the stock market: "Going public" and professional team sports. *Journal of Corporation Law 24*(3), 641–680.

Strauss, J. (2009, December 6). Cardinals say debt limits spending. *St. Louis Post-Dispatch*. Retrieved December 14, 2009, from http://www.stltoday.com/stltoday/sports/stories.nsf/cardinals/story/E904AD414CCE5946 8625768400064FFF?OpenDocument.

8

Capital Budgeting

capital budgeting

capital expenditure

current expenditure

discount rate

discounted payback period

incremental cash flow

initial cost

internal rate of return

modified internal rate of return

net present value

payback period

terminal value

KEY CONCEPTS

Introduction

In 2000, after 24 years, the Seattle Kingdome was imploded. The former home of the Seattle Seahawks and Mariners, the Kingdome hosted Pele in its debut and was the venue for events as diverse as the Billy Graham Crusade and Evel Knievel's jump over 18 buses. In all, more than 3,000 events were held at the Kingdome, and 73 million people attended them (Lynch, 2000a). At $67 million, its cost was half that of other stadia built during the same era (Lynch, 2000b). But when its ceiling tiles fell in 1994, $70 million in repairs were required, and the Kingdome's future was uncertain. As the stadium also lacked luxury boxes, club seating, and other amenities expected of modern stadia, local politicians began to consider replacing the facility (Lynch, 2000a).

The Seattle Mariners were first to quit using the facility, when they moved to the $550 million Safeco Field in 2000. When the State of Washington's Referendum 48 passed, creating financing for a new football stadium complex, the Kingdome's fate was sealed (Rodgers, 1997). Three years later, it took 21 miles of detonation cord, 6,000 holes drilled into the concrete structure and packed with dynamite, $9 million, and 17.6 seconds to bring down the 110,000 tons of concrete (Lynch, 2000a, 2000b). In its former footprint now stands Qwest Field, a $430 million structure that is the new home of the Seattle Seahawks (Cameron, 2002).

The story of the Kingdome provides a good illustration of why capital budgeting is important. When it was imploded, the taxpayers of King County, Washington, still owed $26 million on the facility (Cameron). In tangible terms, the facility may be considered to have been a bad investment for the citizens, as debt was owed at the time of its demise. A capital budget can help ensure that the new taxpayer-funded facility will be paid off before the end of its useful life.* As you will learn in this chapter, a capital budget can also help you evaluate, compare, and select projects to achieve the best long-term financial return on capital investments.

*The public paid $300 million of the costs for Qwest Field. The Seahawks were responsible for the remaining amount, including any cost overruns (Marois, 2000).

DEFINING CAPITAL BUDGETING

Capital budgeting focuses on capital expenditures and specifically the analysis of capital expenditures to decide which expenditures should be made. More precisely, **capital budgeting** is the process of evaluating, comparing, and selecting capital projects to achieve the best return on investment over time. Groppelli & Nikbakht define it as investment decision making that justifies capital expenditures. This process is an important factor in the success or failure of an organization since investments in fixed assets affect the financial health of the organization for many years.

A **capital expenditure** is the use of funds to acquire operational assets that will help the organization earn future revenues or reduce future costs. These are long-term expenditures amortized over a period of time (Groppelli & Nikbakht, 2000). Examples of capital expenditures in sport include the purchase of a new artificial turf field for a football stadium, the purchase of a new Zamboni machine for a hockey rink, and the construction of a stadium or arena. These expenditures involve a large amount of cash, debt, and other resources that will be committed over long periods of time.

It is important to differentiate between a capital expenditure and a current expenditure. Whereas a capital expenditure is long term and amortized over time, a **current expenditure** is short term and is completely written off during the same year as the expense is incurred. Because capital expenses utilize resources over time, they are investments that require a commitment of resources today with the expectation of receiving benefits in the future. For a major Division I institution, this may mean an investment in a new basketball facility with luxury and club seating. A university will decide to invest in the facility with the hope that the facility will return new and additional revenue to the athletic department.

As stated previously, capital budgeting focuses on capital expenditures. Capital budgeting offers several benefits. First, a capital budget helps management plan the amount and timing of resources that will be needed. For example, a capital budget developed for a stadium renovation might include the timing and amounts of payments for a new $850,000 installation of FieldTurf. A team might put down a large amount at the beginning of the project and pay the rest off through smaller payments over time. A capital budget is also helpful in evaluating alternative capital expenditures. Should FieldTurf, AstroPlay, or a natural grass field be installed? The development of a capital budget will include an evaluation of these alternatives to determine which best utilizes the organization's resources.

A capital budget also focuses management's attention on cash flows. The capital budget allows the manager to identify new cash that will arise from a project and compare that new cash flow to the expenditures the project demands. This information, combined with knowledge of the timing and amount of resources needed, helps management coordinate responsibility centers within the organization to ensure that all financial obligations are met.

THE PROCESS OF CAPITAL BUDGETING

 o complete the capital budgeting process, financial managers use a method comprising four distinct parts:

1. Determine the initial cost of the project or projects.
2. Determine the incremental cash flow of a project.
3. Select the capital budgeting method.
4. Conduct a post-audit analysis.

Most of the methods for completing a capital budget include the evaluation of cash flow risk (based on inflation, interest rates, and project length) and then the determination of an appropriate discount rate for use in analysis of the project. In the case of a capital budget, the **discount rate** is the required rate of return to justify an investment. After the discount rate is calculated, the asset's value to the organization is estimated on a present value basis, and the present value of expected cash inflows is compared to the cost of the project. If the present value of the project exceeds its cost, the project should be accepted and included in the organization's capital budget. Given a choice between two or more projects, managers should select the project that contributes most to the organization's net income.

These steps are outlined in detail below.

Determine the Initial Cost of the Project

The **initial cost** of a project is the actual cost of starting the project, adjusted for any installation, delivery, or packing costs; discounts to the initial price; the sale of existing equipment or machinery; and taxes. For an example of determining the initial cost of a project, let's look at the cost of replacing a natural grass football field with FieldTurf.

The first step in calculating the initial cost of the FieldTurf installation is to record the invoice price of the investment. The cost to replace the grass field with FieldTurf is $719,500, based on the amount quoted to the university for field materials and installation.

Next, we calculate additional expenses. As the invoice price includes packing, delivery, and installation, we need not adjust for these costs. However, due to problems with the university's current grass field, which was installed in the previous year, the university will receive a rebate (discount from the initial cost) of $250,000 if it chooses to replace the grass field with an artificial surface. Hence, the initial cost of the investment must be reduced by the $250,000 rebate. Therefore, the initial cost of the investment is $469,500.

Often, another adjustment is necessary for the sale of existing machinery or equipment and the tax consequences of that sale. However, in this example, the FieldTurf is replacing the damaged sod in the stadium, and nothing will be sold, so no adjustment is necessary. We use the following formulae to calculate the initial cost of a project:

$$IC = IP + ATP - DTP - EQP + TOE$$

$$IC = IP + ATP - DTP - EQP - TCE$$

where IC = initial cost of the project

   IP = invoice price of the new investment

   ATP = adjustments to price, such as installation costs, delivery, and packing

   DTP = any discounts to the initial price (IP)

   EQP = revenue from the sale of existing equipment

   TOE = taxes paid on the sale of equipment above book value

   TCE = tax credit on the sale of equipment below book value

For the purchase of FieldTurf, recall that the invoice price of $719,500 includes the price of the new investment and the price for delivery and installation. The university received a \$250,000 rebate on the installation. In this case, EQP = \$0 and TOE = \$0. (Note that there is also no tax liability or tax credit when equipment is sold at book value.) Hence,

IC = \$719,500 − \$250,000 − \$0 + \$0 = \$469,500

Determine the Incremental Cash Flow of a Project

After calculating the initial cost of a project, we compute the project's incremental cash flow. **Incremental cash flow** is the cash flow created through the implementation of a new project. It consists of any cash flow from the project that is greater than the cash flow that currently exists. The steps to determine incremental cash flow are:

1. Calculate additional net earnings (ANE) from the new project:

   ANE = ENEPI − ENEWP

   where ENEWP = estimated net earnings without the new project and
         ENEPI = estimated net earnings if the new project were included

2. Calculate the additional tax benefit of the depreciation (ADT) on the new fixed asset:

   ADT = TAX × DEP

   where TAX = tax rate and
         DEP = additional depreciation of the new fixed asset

3. Calculate the incremental cash flow (ICF), using the results of steps 1 and 2:

   ICF = ANE + ADT

   where ANE = additional net earnings from the new project and
         ADT = additional tax benefit on the new fixed asset

Using these formulae, we can calculate the incremental cash flow of the FieldTurf project. For Step 1, we must first determine the estimated net earnings without the new project (ENEWP) and the estimated net earnings with the new project (ENEPI). If the university were to keep its current natural grass field, it is estimated that the annual net earnings would be \$3,300,000. With the change to FieldTurf, it is estimated that earnings would rise to \$3,500,000, as additional revenue would be generated from hosting state high school playoff football games.* This additional revenue would come from facility rental fees and additional parking and concessions revenue and amounts to \$200,000 after expenses for operations are removed. Therefore, to calculate Step 1:

ANE = \$3,500,000 − \$3,300,000 = \$200,000

As a university is a not-for-profit entity, there are no tax ramifications due to additional depreciation. Hence, for Step 2:

ADT = \$0

---

*Due to the durability of the artificial surface, more playoff games can be scheduled in a short period of time. An artificial turf field also allows high school playoff games to be played Friday night and college games to be played on Saturday.

Thus, the calculation for the incremental cash flow (Step 3) for this project is

ICF = $200,000 + $0 = $200,000

If, rather than a university, the organization in this example were a professional football team, Step 3 would become important. Suppose estimated net earnings without the new project (ENEWP) for Team X are $34.5 million. The team's chief financial officer (CFO) determines that by installing field turf, the team could host three college games and three state championship football games in addition to the current ten home NFL pre-season and regular season games. This additional revenue would lead to increased estimated earnings (ENEPI) of $40.5 million. For Step 1:

ANE = $40,500,000 − $34,500,000 = $6,000,000

As Team X is a for-profit business, the tax benefit of depreciation must be calculated. Using straight-line depreciation, the additional depreciation (DEP) is $71,950. (The cost for the FieldTurf is $719,500, and it has an estimated useful life of ten years.) At a corporate tax rate (TAX) of 35%, the calculation for Step 2 is

ADT = .35 x $71,950 = $25,182.50

For this project, incremental cash flow (Step 3) is

ICF = $6,000,000 + $25,182.50 = $6,025,182.50

Select the Capital Budgeting Method

Once the initial cost of the project and the project's incremental cash flows are calculated, we can complete the capital budgeting process using any of several methods, including average rate of return, payback period, discounted payback period, net present value, profitability index, internal rate of return, and modified internal rate of return. Each method has advantages and disadvantages; net present value is the method most managers prefer. This chapter focuses on net present value and the two methods that are the foundation of net present value analysis, payback period and discounted payback period. We will also examine internal rate of return and modified internal rate of return.

Payback period

The number of years required to recover a capital investment is called the **payback period.** Calculating the payback period of a project is a very basic capital budgeting tool. For any project to be accepted in a capital budget, the project's payback period must be less than the maximum acceptable payback period set by the organization. When a choice must be made between two or more alternative projects, the one with the shortest payback period should be selected.

Single-project payback period calculation. Suppose a project has an initial cost of $52,700. Incremental cash flows are estimated to be $22,000 in Year 1 and $18,600, $19,250, and $23,000 in subsequent years. Your firm's maximum acceptable payback period is three years. As the finance manager in charge of this project, should you accept it into your department's capital budget?

To determine the answer, it is necessary to calculate the payback period. First, we list the expected cash flows:

YEAR	ICF
0	($52,700)
1	$22,000
2	$18,600
3	$19,250
4	$23,000

By adding the yearly incremental cash flow to the initial cost of the project, we can determine the approximate time needed to recover the project's costs.

YEAR	ICF	CUMULATIVE CASH FLOW
0	($52,700)	($52,700)
1	$22,000	($30,700)
2	$18,600	($12,100)
3	$19,250	$7,150
4	$23,000	$30,150

This analysis shows that the project's costs are recovered between years 2 and 3. As the payback period is less than the three years set by your firm, the project should be accepted as part of the division's capital budget. To determine a more exact payback date, notice that between years 2 and 3 the cumulative return moves from −$12,100 to $7,150. During Year 3, incremental cash flow is $19,250. We know that by Year 3 the project has reached its payback date. To determine exactly when in Year 2 the payback date is reached, we divide the amount of the last negative cumulative return by the incremental cash flow of the year the cumulative return is positive:

−$12,100 ÷ $19,250 = −0.628

Hence, the payback period is reached 0.628 years past Year 2, or in 2.628 years. (We disregard the fact that the value is negative.) To convert the fraction of the year to weeks, we multiply 0.628 by 52 weeks:

0.628 x 52 weeks = 32.7 weeks

The payoff period for this project is two years and 33 weeks.

Two-project payback period calculation. When choosing between two projects, we must compare the cash flows of the two projects.

YEAR	PROJECT S ICF	CUMULATIVE CASH FLOW	PROJECT L ICF	CUMULATIVE CASH FLOW
0	($1,000)	($1,000)	($1,000)	($1,000)
1	$500	($500)	$100	($900)
2	$400	($100)	$300	($600)
3	$300	$200	$400	($200)
4	$100	$300	$600	$400

As always, any project must meet the maximum payback period. For this organization, the maximum is three years. If both projects meet the three-year minimum, the project with the shorter payback period is preferred.

A quick analysis of each project's cumulative cash flow reveals that Project S reaches payback faster than Project L, in 2.33 years versus 3.33 years. Project S also meets the payback period maximum. Project S should be accepted into the firm's capital budget.

Advantages and disadvantages of the payback period method. Of all the methods, the payback period method is the easiest to use. Few calculations are required to determine how long it will take to recover the initial investment. The payback period method is also the easiest to understand. Most important, the method provides information on how long a firm's funds will be tied up in a project. All else being equal, projects with shorter payback periods provide more liquidity than ones with longer payback periods.

This method also has two major flaws. First, it ignores time value of money concepts (see Chapter 4), as it fails to take into account the cost of capital. It does not recognize the difference between the value of a $1,000 incremental cash flow in the first year and a $1,000 incremental cash flow in the fourth year. Second, this method ignores cash flows produced beyond the payback period. Project A may reach its payback period faster, but over the useful life of the project, Project B may increase the firm's cash flow more.

Discounted payback period

To improve upon the payback period methodology, we may use the **discounted payback period** method. This method is similar to the payback period with one major exception: it factors time value of money concepts into the calculation by discounting the expected cash flows at the project's initial cost of capital. Recall that the discount rate is the rate of return a company must reach in order to justify its investment. We use this method to determine the number of years necessary to recover the initial cost of a project using discounted cash flows (DCFs).

Single-project discounted payback period calculation. Suppose a project has an initial cost of $52,700. Incremental cash flows are estimated to be $22,000 in Year 1 and $18,600, $19,250, and $23,000 in subsequent years. The cost of capital is 10%. Your firm's maximum acceptable discounted payback period is three years. What is the discounted payback period for this project? How does it compare to the payback period? Should the project be accepted?

To determine the answers, we begin by examining the cash flows on a present value basis. By looking at the expected present value of the future cash flows, we can compare the cost of the initial outlay with those future cash flows, in today's dollars. We use the present value interest factor (PVIF; see Table A.3 in the Appendix) to discount the cash flows. In Year 0, the initial cost of $52,700 is not discounted, as the value of $52,700 today is $52,700. For Year 1, we apply the discount rate of 10% to the $22,000 cash flow for that year. From Table A.3, we find that PVIF for one year at 10% is 0.909. The discount rate is also applied to the cash flows for years 2 through 4. By adding the discounted cash flows to the initial cost of the project, we can determine the approximate time needed to recover the project's costs.

YEAR	ICF	PVIF	DCF	CUMULATIVE CASH FLOW
0	($52,700)	—	($52,700)	($52,700)
1	$22,000	0.909	$19,998	($32,702)
2	$18,600	0.826	$15,364	($17,338)
3	$19,250	0.751	$14,457	($2,881)
4	$23,000	0.683	$15,709	$12,828

Analysis of the discounted cash flows shows that the project's initial costs are recovered between years 3 and 4. Additional calculations would find that the exact payback period is in 3.18 years, or three years and nine weeks. As the discounted payback period is greater than the firm's maximum payback period, the project would not be included in the capital budget.

By comparing the discounted payback period of this project to the non-discounted payback period, we can see the effect of the value of money over time. Recall that the payback period for this project is two years and 33 weeks when we do not consider this effect; it is 28 weeks later when we do.

Two-project discounted payback period calculation. When choosing between two projects, we compare the cash flows of the two projects. The following projects both have a discount rate of 10%.

PROJECT S

YEAR	ICF	PVIF	DCF	CUMULATIVE CASH FLOW
0	($1,000)	—	($1,000)	($1,000)
1	$500	0.909	$455	($545)
2	$400	0.826	$331	($241)
3	$300	0.751	$225	$11
4	$100	0.683	$68	$79

PROJECT L

YEAR	ICF	PVIF	DCF	CUMULATIVE CASH FLOW
0	($1,000)	—	($1,000)	($1,000)
1	$100	0.909	$91	($909)
2	$300	0.826	$248	($661)
3	$400	0.751	$301	($360)
4	$600	0.683	$410	$50

The project with the shorter discounted payback period should be selected for inclusion in the company's capital budget. Examining the cumulative returns, we see that Project S reaches discounted payback between years 2 and 3 (in 2.95 years, to be exact). Project L reaches discounted payback between years 3 and 4 (3.88). As Project S has a quicker discounted payback, it should be selected for inclusion in the capital budget over Project L.

Advantages and disadvantages of the discounted payback period method. As the discounted payback period method incorporates the time value of money into its calculation, it is a great improvement over the payback period method. It also provides information on the length of time funds will be committed to the project. However, this method, like the payback period method, does not consider the cash flows beyond the discounted payback period.

Net present value

As previously stated, net present value is the capital budgeting method managers generally prefer for evaluating a single project or comparing two or more projects. **Net present value** (NPV) is a discounted cash flow method in which the present value of a project's future cash flows are compared to the project's initial cost. Projects are accepted if NPV is positive. Mathematically,

NPV = present value of future cash flow − initial cost

$$NPV = \sum_{t=0}^{n} \frac{CF_t}{(1+k)^t} - \text{initial cost}$$

where CF_t is the expected net cash flow in period t,

k is the project's cost of capital, and

n is the number of periods.

Using this formula, we calculate the present value (PV) of cash flows for each year and sum the present values to find the net present value. Cash outflows are denoted by negative cash flows, and cash inflows are denoted by positive flows. If the NPV is positive (i.e., the present value of the project's future cash flows is greater than the initial cost), the project should be accepted. If the present value is less than the initial cost (the NPV is negative), the project should be rejected. In this case, money would be lost if the project were accepted.

Two-project NPV calculation. To calculate a project's NPV, we find the present value of each cash flow, discounted at the project's cost of capital. Both the cash inflows and outflows of the project must be included. Up to this point, this process is the same as that for calculating a discounted payback period. Next, we sum the discounted cash flows to obtain the project's NPV. For Project S and Project L above, the NPV of each project is the sum of the discounted cash flows. This will be the same as the final cumulative cash flow figure. The NPV of Project S is $79 and of Project L $50. If we must choose one, we would select the project with the higher NPV, Project S, for inclusion in the capital budget. If both projects have a negative NPV, neither project would be accepted.

Single-project NPV calculation. Often, NPV analysis focuses on a single project, and the criterion for acceptance in the capital budget is that the NPV must be equal to or greater than zero.

Project T has an initial cost of $9,000 and a cost of capital of 10%. The expected useful life is four years. In years 1 through 4, the anticipated cash flows are $6,000, $4,000, $3,000, and $2,000. Should this project be recommended?

First, we calculate the discounted cash flows by using the PVIF from Appendix Table A.3:

YEAR	ICF	PVIF	DCF	CUMULATIVE CASH FLOW
0	($9,000)	—	($9,000)	($9,000)
1	$6,000	0.909	$5,454	($3,546)
2	$4,000	0.826	$3,304	($242)
3	$3,000	0.751	$2,253	$2,011
4	$2,000	0.683	$1,366	$3,377

After determining the discounted cash flow for each year, we calculate the sum of the discounted cash flows or look at the final cumulative cash flow figure. As the sum of the discounted cash flows is $3,377, Project T would be accepted into the firm's capital budget.

Project Z would require an initial investment of $40,000. The cost of capital is 8%. The expected cash flows and discounted cash flows are as follows:

YEAR	ICF	PVIF	DCF	CUMULATIVE CASH FLOW
0	($40,000)	—	($40,000)	($40,000)
1	$16,000	0.926	$14,816	($25,184)
2	$12,000	0.857	$10,284	($14,900)
3	$9,000	0.794	$7,146	($7,754)
4	$7,000	0.735	$5,145	($2,609)

Because the present value of the cash inflows, $37,391, is less than the present value of the cash outflows, $40,000, the NPV for Project Z is negative. Hence, the project is not recommended for inclusion in the organization's capital budget.

If a project has a positive NPV, it will generate cash above its debt service. Therefore, it provides the required return to shareholders, and the excess cash accrues to the shareholders. Because Project Z has a negative NPV, it would remove cash from the firm to service the project's debt. If wealth maximization is the goal, only projects that improve the firm's cash flows should be accepted.

Advantages and disadvantages of NPV. Most managers prefer to use NPV for capital budgeting. The method analyzes cash flows rather than net earnings, consistent with modern finance theory. Furthermore, it considers time value of money concepts, discounting cash flows by the project's cost of capital. Most important, it identifies projects with a positive NPV, which will increase the firm's value. Thereby, the owners of the firm will gain wealth.

The NPV method does have some disadvantages. One major disadvantage is that the method requires a detailed prediction of the project's future cash flows. For the hypothetical examples in this section, the useful life of the project is four years. In sport, however, the useful life is often much longer. For example, computing the NPV of a new stadium would require forecasting cash flows for the entire useful life of the stadium. Usually, this period is assumed to be 30 years. Calculating the NPV for new Busch Stadium requires forecasting cash flows from 2006 until 2036. Given that stadium revenue streams have experienced massive changes during the past 15 years (primarily driven by the addition of luxury suites, club seating, and personal seat licenses; Brown, Nagel, & Rascher, 2003), forecasting these revenues is extremely difficult. A second disadvantage of the NPV method is that it assumes that the discount rate will remain the same over the useful life of the project. In many instances, the cost of capital, and therefore the discount rate, changes as firms refinance debt.

Internal rate of return

Internal rate of return (IRR) is the term for the discount rate at which the present value of estimated cash flows is equal to the initial cost of the investment. In other words, IRR is the discount rate at which the NPV is equal to zero. NPV is a more advantageous capital budgeting method than internal rate of return. However,

Using Technology to Calculate NPV

The use of either a spreadsheet or a financial calculator can make the calculation of NPV easy. Consider the following example:

As athletic director of a mid-major university in Ohio, you are overseeing the renovation of the football stadium. The stadium has seating for 25,500. Several prominent boosters have approached you to request the installation of an artificial turf field. They argue that by putting artificial turf in the stadium, the school could attract better recruits and thereby improve its performance on the field. Additionally, the boosters state that several early round high school playoff games could be played in the stadium, increasing community goodwill, generating additional revenues for the program, and creating an economic impact for the community from out-of-town spectator spending. After listening to these arguments, you decide to analyze the facts.

Based on your research on synthetic athletic fields, you decide either to install FieldTurf or to leave the natural grass field in place. FieldTurf incorporates the latest innovations in synthetic playing surfaces and has been installed by Michigan, Boston College, and Nebraska. If it makes financial sense for the department, you are leaning toward installing the synthetic field, especially since there are problems with the current natural grass field that was installed last year. Because of these problems, the university will receive a rebate of $250,000 if it chooses to replace the grass field with an artificial surface.

Installing FieldTurf would cost $719,500. The initial cost of the investment would be only $469,500, however, as the $250,000 rebate would be applied to the invoice cost of the field. You estimate that with this field, you can host three high school playoff dates per year. The games would generate $200,000 in incremental cash flow from parking, rental fees, and concession revenues, after expenses. The department would have to make payments on the field at an annual rate of 7%. The life of the field is estimated to be ten years.

You are now ready to decide whether to install FieldTurf or keep the stadium's current natural grass field. You will use a spreadsheet to examine the cash flows over the life of the project (see Exhibit 8.1).*

From your spreadsheet analysis, you see that the NPV is positive, so you decide to move forward with the project. The discounted payback period is two years and 34 weeks. In the middle of the third year, the project will begin to create additional cash inflows that can benefit the athletic department's operations.

Finding the NPV of this project with a financial calculator is also easy, and it is easier to use a spreadsheet if a present value interest factor table is not available. We simply enter the cash flows into the cash flow register, along with the value of the discount rate, and press the NPV key. A financial calculator would give an NPV of $935,216.30. The difference between this value and the one given by the spreadsheet is due to PVIF rounding differences.

*Usually, financial managers use a spreadsheet to conduct capital budgeting analyses. Once a spreadsheet with formulas has been set up, values can easily be changed to see how variations would affect the project's NPV.

IRR is widely used in business, and therefore it is important for financial managers to understand how to calculate it (Brigham & Houston, 1999). We calculate IRR as follows:

$$\sum_{t=0}^{n} \frac{CF_t}{(1 + IRR)^t} = 0$$

where CF_t is the expected net cash flow in period t,
 n is the number of periods, and
 IRR is the internal rate of return.

The only unknown in this equation is IRR. We simply solve for the value of IRR to find the internal rate of return.

IRR is a measure of a project's rate of profitability. A project with an IRR greater than its cost of capital is advantageous to the organization and should be accepted into the capital budget. When the IRR exceeds the cost of capital, a sur-

	A	B	C	D	E	F
				FieldTurf Analysis.xlsx [Last saved by user] - Microsoft		
	Home Insert Page Layout Formulas Data Review View Add-Ins					
	H21		f_x			
1			Analysis of FieldTurf			
2						
3	Time	ICF	PVIF @ 7%	DCF	Sum	
4	0	$ (469,500.00)		$ (469,500.00)	$ (469,500.00)	
5	1	200,000.00	0.935	187,000.00	(282,500.00)	
6	2	200,000.00	0.873	174,600.00	(107,900.00)	
7	3	200,000.00	0.816	163,200.00	55,300.00	
8	4	200,000.00	0.763	152,600.00	207,900.00	
9	5	200,000.00	0.713	142,600.00	350,500.00	
10	6	200,000.00	0.666	133,200.00	483,700.00	
11	7	200,000.00	0.623	124,600.00	608,300.00	
12	8	200,000.00	0.582	116,400.00	724,700.00	
13	9	200,000.00	0.544	108,800.00	833,500.00	
14	10	200,000.00	0.508	101,600.00 ◄	935,100.00 ◄	=E13+D14
15						
16	NPV =	$ 935,100.00 ◄ =E14		=B14*C14		
17						

plus accrues to the firm's stockholders. By accepting a project whose IRR is greater than the cost of capital, the financial manager increases shareholder wealth.

To calculate IRR with a financial calculator, enter the expected cash flows into the cash flow register, then press the IRR key.

Calculating IRR with constant cash flows. If cash flows are constant over the useful life of a project, we can calculate IRR without a financial calculator or a spreadsheet. Dividing the initial cost of a project by its annual cash flow gives the present value interest factor of an annuity (PVIFA). We can look up the value in a PVIFA table (see Appendix Table A.4) to discover an approximation of IRR.

For example, suppose Project D has an expected useful life of six years and anticipated annual cash flows of $5,000. The initial cost is $20,555. If the cost of capital is 10%, should the project be accepted into the firm's capital budget?

We divide the initial cost of the project by the annual cash flow to find the PVIFA.

PVIFA = 20,555 ÷ 5,000 = 4.111

In the PVIFA table (Appendix Table A.4), we find that for a term of six years a PVIFA of 4.111 results from a rate of 12%; therefore, the project's IRR is 12%. As this value is greater than Project D's cost of capital (10%), the project should be accepted.

Ballpark Villages and Arena Districts SIDEBAR

I n the National Football League, it is widely accepted that a new stadium, featuring all of the latest revenue-producing amenities, is an important factor in the financial success of a team (Brown, Nagel, & Rascher, 2003). Revenue accruing from these capital projects provides an important competitive edge for franchises in a league where about 70% of all revenue is shared. In other leagues, the situation is different.

Major League Baseball's St. Louis Cardinals provide an example of the difference between the use of new revenues generated from non-NFL stadia and NFL stadia. The Cardinals opened Busch Stadium III in April 2006. The stadium was built for $388 million, with the team owners paying approximately 77% of the costs. Fans paid $40 million of construction costs through the purchase of seat licenses, and public money was used as well. The public funds included a $30 million tax abatement (Miklasz, 2005b).

The Cardinals moved into their new stadium at a time when it appeared the club was awash in new revenues. In their last year at Busch II, the club drew 3.5 million fans. When these fans went to games in the new stadium, they paid higher ticket prices, and many sat in a greatly expanded section of premium seats. Additionally, the team had just left longtime radio broadcast partner KMOX for a more lucrative radio arrangement with KTRS. Finally, the Cardinals reportedly expected to receive $23 million from MLB due to the success of MLB.com, the XM Radio league rights fee, and the sale of the Washington Nationals. Despite these new revenues, the club kept its 2006 team payroll at the same level as 2005 (Miklasz, 2005a).

Team officials had claimed that a new stadium was needed to generate the revenues necessary to field a competitive team. They claimed that the revenues from the new luxury and club seating areas would increase significantly and that they would be in a position to raise payroll significantly (Miklasz, 2005b). In fact, it was reported in *SportsBusiness Journal* that local revenue would rise between 15% and 20%, to approximately $150 million, during the 2006 season (Fisher, 2005). What was not mentioned was that a large portion of this new revenue—$15 million annually for the next 22 years—would be used to retire the debt on the stadium (Miklasz, 2005b). In all, the new stadium has generated only an additional $5 million to $10 million for the club, after bond payments.

Why would a team like the Cardinals finance a large portion of a new stadium themselves, if it would not lead to a significant improvement in the financial performance of the club? For the owners of the Cardinals and teams in similar situations, the new revenues from a stadium might not alone justify the construction. However, the financial picture changes if the land around the site presents an opportunity for commercial development.

The Cardinals are one of several teams currently building or planning to build a ballpark village or arena district to generate additional revenues. The Cardinals and the Cordish Company are partnering to develop eight acres next to Busch III (on the site formerly occupied by Busch II). Ground will not be broken for that project until after the new stadium construction is completed. The $450 million ballpark village will include between 500 and 1,000 residential units that will support the area's new restaurants in the off-season. An additional 20,000 to 150,000 square feet of office space will also be built, depending on demand for space (Brown, 2005; Fisher). Only when this project is completed will the Cardinals have additional revenue to spend on team payroll.

In New York City, three new sport facilities are planned. The public share of funding for each of these facilities is below 25% (Zimbalist, 2005). The $800 million Atlantic Yards in Brooklyn is part of a $3.5 billion residential and commercial development that will be home to the New York Nets. San Diego's Petco Park is also part of a large development project. Public funding paid approximately 67% of the $474 million cost of the stadium; however, the city received a binding $150 million residential real estate commitment for development around the stadium. The San Diego Padres' owner has spent $550 million for development of residential, hotel, and retail space around the stadium (Fish, 2005).

As the costs of new facilities continue to increase, and as teams are obliged to pay a greater share of funds for facility construction, the trend of packaging stadia and arenas as a part of larger redevelopment projects will continue. The team with the most profitable redevelopment—not the most profitable stadium or arena—will gain an advantage within the league. The Cardinals or another MLB team that is paying the majority of stadium development costs will need to use the facility as an anchor for a greater development. In the NFL, teams like the Indianapolis Colts can still find success with profitable stadiums alone.

Now, suppose Project F has an initial cost of $42,560, an anticipated useful life of eight years, cost of capital 18%, and expected cash flows of $9,800 per year. Should Project F be accepted into the company's capital budget?

The PVIFA for this project is

PVIFA = 42,560 ÷ 9,800 = 4.343

In the PVIFA table, we find that a PVIFA of 4.343 with a term of eight years implies a rate of 16%. Project D's IRR is 16%. As this is less than the project's cost of capital, the project should not be accepted.

Calculating IRR with irregular cash flows. When cash flows are not constant, we can find IRR by trial and error using the formula given on p. 196. A financial calculator or spreadsheet software that provides financial analysis formulae is very valuable for this type of calculation.

Comparing IRR to NPV. Recall the details of the analysis involving installation of FieldTurf. The initial cost of the project was $469,500, with annual incremental cash flows of $200,000 over the ten-year useful life of the field. The project's cost of capital was 7%. What is the IRR? Does the IRR lead to a different decision than the NPV method?

Using the data entered in Exhibit 8.1, we can quickly calculate the project's IRR by using the software's IRR function (see Exhibit 8.2).

The IRR, 41%, is significantly higher than the project's cost of capital, and both the IRR and NPV methods indicate that the project should be undertaken. When a project is being considered on its own merits, the NPV and IRR methods will give the same accept or reject decision. However, when we are analyzing two or more projects in order to select one, the results may conflict—even if both projects have positive NPVs and IRRs greater than their costs of capital. For mutually exclusive projects, NPV may indicate Project A should be accepted, while IRR may indicate Project B should be accepted. This may occur in two circumstances:

1. The projects differ greatly in financial size.
2. The projects differ greatly in the timing of cash flows.

It is generally accepted that when these conflicts arise, NPV is the method of evaluation that should be used (Brigham & Houston).

Modified internal rate of return

When a project involves a large cash outflow sometime during or at the end of its useful life, in addition to the cash outflow at the beginning, it is said to have non-normal cash flows. For a project with non-normal cash flows, IRR may not be usable as a capital budgeting method, because multiple IRRs may exist. Stadia and arenas often have non-normal cash flows when they are renovated or improved. From 1995 to 1999, in the NFL alone, eight franchises, or 27%, played in stadia that underwent at least $20 million in renovations during that time frame (Brown, Nagel, & Rascher).

exhibit   8.2   Calculating IRR with a spreadsheet.

	A	B	C	D	E	
1			Analysis of FieldTurf			
2						
3	Time	ICF	PVIF @ 7%	DCF	Sum	
4	0	$ (469,500.00)		$ (469,500.00)	$ (469,500.00)	
5	1	200,000.00	0.935	187,000.00	(282,500.00)	=E4+D5
6	2	200,000.00	0.873	174,600.00	(107,900.00)	
7	3	200,000.00	0.816	163,200.00	55,300.00	
8	4	200,000.00	0.763	152,600.00	207,900.00	
9	5	200,000.00	0.713	142,600.00	350,500.00	
10	6	200,000.00	0.666	133,200.00	483,700.00	
11	7	200,000.00	0.623	124,600.00	608,300.00	
12	8	200,000.00	0.582	116,400.00	724,700.00	
13	9	200,000.00	0.544	108,800.00	833,500.00	
14	10	200,000.00	0.508	101,600.00	935,100.00	
15						
16	NPV =	$ 935,100.00	=E14		=B5*C5	
17	IRR =	41%	=IRR(B4:B14,0.4)			

For projects with non-normal cash flows, we recommend the modified internal rate of return (MIRR) for finding a project's rate of return. MIRR is the discount rate where the present value of the project's costs is to equal the present value of the project's terminal value (Brighton & Houston). Here, **terminal value** is the future value of the cash inflows compounded at the project's cost of capital. When the present value of the costs equals the present value of the terminal value, we have

$$PV_{costs} = \sum_{t=0}^{n} \frac{COF_t}{(1+k)^t} = \frac{TV}{(1+MIRR)^n}$$

where COF_t is the cash outflow in period t,
   k is the project's cost of capital,
   n is the number of periods,
   MIRR is the modified internal rate of return,
   PV_{costs} is the present value costs, and
   TV is the terminal value.

In this equation, the first and second terms give the present value of the cash outflows when discounted at the cost of capital. In the rightmost term, the numerator

---

*For projects with non-normal cash flows, NPV can be applied and will lead to correct capital budgeting decisions. MIRR is a method for finding a project's rate of return in these situations.

is the compounded value of the inflows (terminal value), with the assumption that the cash inflows are reinvested at the cost of capital.

If the investment costs are all incurred during Year 0, and the first operating cash inflows occur in Year 1, then we can use the following MIRR equation:

$$PV_{costs} = \frac{TV}{(1+MIRR)^n} + \frac{\sum_{t=1}^{n} CIF(1+k)^{n-t}}{(1+MIRR)^n}$$

Spreadsheet software provides a convenient method for calculating MIRR. Exhibit 8.3 shows such a calculation.

We calculate the terminal value by compounding the cash inflows at the cost of capital (7%). In a spreadsheet, we enter the formulas as shown in Exhibit 8.3. In the spreadsheet, the present value of the project's cost is $469,500. The terminal value of the project is calculated by summing future value of the expected cash inflows. The RATE function in Excel is then used to calculate MIRR. Here the present value and terminal value of the project, along with the number of periods (10), are entered into Excel to calculate the rate of growth, or MIRR. Or, we may use a financial calculator and enter the following data: N = 10, PV = –469,500, PMT = 0, FV = 2,736,400. Press the I key, and the MIRR for the project, 19.39%, will be displayed.

Calculating MIRR with the equation for MIRR and a spreadsheet.   **exhibit**   **8.3**

	A	B	C	D	E
				FieldTurf Analysis.xlsx [Last saved by user]	
	Home	Insert	Page Layout	Formulas	Data	Review	View	Add-Ins
124		f_x			
1		Analysis of FieldTurf			
2					
3	Time	ICF	FVIF @ 7%	Terminal Value	
4	0 $	(469,500.00)			
5	1	200,000.00	1.838 $	367,600.00 ⟵ =B5*C5	
6	2	200,000.00	1.718	343,600.00	
7	3	200,000.00	1.606	321,200.00	
8	4	200,000.00	1.501	300,200.00	
9	5	200,000.00	1.403	280,600.00	
10	6	200,000.00	1.311	262,200.00	
11	7	200,000.00	1.225	245,000.00	
12	8	200,000.00	1.145	229,000.00	
13	9	200,000.00	1.07	214,000.00	
14	10	200,000.00		200,000.00	
15			Terminal Value = $	2,763,400.00 ⟵ =SUM(D5:D14)	
16					
17		PV of TV = $	469,500.00 ⟵ =(B4)*–1		
18		NPV =	$0.00		
19					
20		MIRR =	19.39% ⟵ =RATE(A14,0,–C17,D15)		

Rather than calculating MIRR by applying the equation in a spreadsheet or using a financial calculator, we can use a spreadsheet's MIRR financial function to calculate MIRR conveniently (see Exhibit 8.4).

The fact that MIRR assumes that cash inflows are reinvested at the cost of capital rather than at the project's IRR makes MIRR a better predictor of profitability. It provides a better estimate of a project's rate of return, and it overcomes multiple problems that arise with the IRR method when cash flows are non-normal. MIRR will lead to the same project selection decision as NPV and IRR when we are considering two mutually exclusive projects of equal size and with the same expected useful life.

Conduct a Post-Audit Analysis

The final step in the capital budgeting process is to conduct a post-audit analysis when the project has been completed. This step is often a forgotten element in the capital budgeting process. In the post-audit, we compare the project's actual

exhibit   8.4   Calculating MIRR with a spreadsheet's MIRR function.

◢	A	B	C	D	E	F
1			Analysis of FieldTurf			
2						
3	Time	ICF	PVIF	DCF	Sum	
4	0	$ (469,500.00)		$ (469,500.00)	$ (469,500.00)	
5	1	200,000.00	0.935	187,000.00 ←	(282,500.00) ← =E4+D5	
6	2	200,000.00	0.873	174,600.00	(107,900.00)	
7	3	200,000.00	0.816	163,200.00	55,300.00	
8	4	200,000.00	0.763	152,600.00	207,900.00	
9	5	200,000.00	0.713	142,600.00	350,500.00	
10	6	200,000.00	0.666	133,200.00	483,700.00	
11	7	200,000.00	0.623	124,600.00	608,300.00	
12	8	200,000.00	0.582	116,400.00	724,700.00	
13	9	200,000.00	0.544	108,800.00	833,500.00	
14	10	200,000.00	0.508	101,600.00	935,100.00	
15					=B5*C5	
16	NPV =	$ 935,100.00 ← =E14				
17	IRR =	41% ← =IRR(B4:B14,0.4)				
18	MIRR =	19% ← =MIRR(B4:B14,0.07,0.07)				

results with the predicted results and attempt to explain any differences. Post-audit analyses allow managers to make improvements to the firm's forecasting techniques. Generally, the most successful organizations are ones that place great emphasis on post-audits.

Brigham and Houston indicate that several complications can arise in the post-audit analysis. First, because of uncertainty in the forecasting of cash flows, a percentage of projects undertaken will not meet the firm's expectations. Also, projects often fail to meet expectations for reasons beyond the firm's control. See the accompanying sidebar for an example of a stadium project that had unexpected results. At times, these reasons for failure are ones that no one could realistically anticipate, such as Hurricane Katrina's effect on the sport industry along the entire Gulf Coast. It is also difficult to separate the operating results of one investment, such as a new grass or artificial field, from those of a larger system, such as a stadium. Finally, if disappointments arose because of employees' capital budgeting deficiencies, discovering this fact will not be helpful if those responsible for entering into a project are no longer with the firm.

CONCLUSION

Capital budgeting is a process for analyzing the capital expenditures of an organization. The process involves identifying the initial cost of the capital project, determining the incremental cash flows resulting from the project's implementation, analyzing the project with one of five capital budgeting methods, and performing a post-audit analysis. All five of the capital budgeting methods discussed in this chapter provide relevant information that will be useful when a manager is selecting a project for inclusion in a firm's capital budget.

The risk and liquidity of a project are indicated by both the payback and the discounted payback method. We found in the FieldTurf case that the project reached its discounted payback period in two years and 24 weeks. As the project had an expected useful life of ten years, the athletic director is taking a relatively small risk by entering into this fairly liquid project.

NPV, which indicates the present value of the dollar benefit of a project to the company, provides the best measure of a project's profitability. In the FieldTurf

SIDEBAR

Montreal's Olympic Stadium
8.C

Olympic Stadium, part of Quebec's $2.6 billion 1976 Summer Olympic construction, was paid off in 2006. Originally, the facilities for the Olympics were to cost $250 million. Many factors led to the increase in costs, including a five-month strike that halted construction in 1975, corrupt contractors, and the government's diversion of tobacco tax dollars from the event to other governmental projects.

Surprisingly, the Montreal Olympic Games ran an operating surplus, but cost overruns at Olympic Stadium left a $1 billion debt from the stadium alone. After hosting the track and field events as well as the opening and closing ceremonies of the 1976 Olympics, Olympic Stadium was home to the Montreal Expos from 1977 to 2004. Other events held in the venue included trade shows, monster truck rallies, concerts, and Canadian Football League games.

Over its 30-year life, the stadium needed many costly repairs. A retractable roof, called for in the original plans, never worked properly and was replaced by a permanent structure. In 1999, a part of this structure collapsed while a car show was being set up, and it was discovered that the structure could no longer withstand Montreal snowfalls. Therefore, no events could be held in the stadium from December to March. In 1991, a 55-ton concrete beam fell off the side of the stadium, leading to costly repairs and forcing the Expos to play the final month of the season on the road. Engineers have determined that the stadium cannot be imploded due to its unique concrete structure. The cost to dismantle the structure would be $500 million, about half of the cost of its construction. The government is faced with the problem of generating revenue from the stadium despite its lack of a major tenant and its closure for four months of the year.

case, the present value benefit to the athletic department of installing the artificial turf is $935,100. IRR also measures profitability but expresses it as a percentage of return, which some decision makers prefer. Stating that the installation of FieldTurf will return at 41% is a convincing argument that the athletic director can present to the university's administration.

MIRR offers the same benefits as IRR but improves on the IRR's reinvestment assumption while avoiding the problems that IRR presents with non-normal cash flows. When cash flows are non-normal, MIRR is the best indicator of a project's rate of return. Using MIRR, the athletic director will find that the FieldTurf installation would provide a 19% rate of return, rather than the inflated 41% return indicated by the IRR. MIRR is preferred in analyses of stadia and arenas, as these facilities often have non-normal cash flows.

CONCEPT *check*

1. What is capital budgeting?
2. What major information (data) do you need for capital budgeting when you want to compare projects?
3. What relevant information is provided in each capital budgeting method?
4. What is the problem with multiple IRRs, and when in sport would they occur?
5. In sport, which method of capital budgeting is superior? Why?
6. What is the purpose of the post-audit in the capital budgeting process?

PRACTICE *problems*

1. Project M has a cost of $65,125, expected net cash inflows of $13,000 per year for ten years, and a cost of capital of 11%. What is the project's payback period (to the closest year)?
2. What is the project's NPV?
3. What is the project's IRR?
4. What is the project's discounted payback period?
5. What is the project's MIRR?
6. Based on the answers to questions 1–5, should the project be accepted? Why or why not?
7. Your division is considering two facility investment projects, each of which requires an upfront expenditure of $15 million. You estimate that the investments will produce the following net cash flows:

YEAR	PROJECT A	PROJECT B
1	$5,000,000	$20,000,000
2	$10,000,000	$10,000,000
3	$20,000,000	$6,000,000

What are the project's net present values, assuming the cost of capital is 10%? 5%? 15%? What does this analysis tell you about the projects?

Currently, the residents of the Athens Parks and Recreation District suffer from a significant deficiency in swimming opportunities. The Parks and Recreation District serves just over 63,187 people in the center of rural southeast Ohio. The original "city pool," which served the community for 30 years, was recently declared obsolete.

The Parks and Recreation District staff recommended that instead of building another traditional pool, a recreation pool should be constructed. Their reasons were as follows. First, they believed that such a pool offered a superior recreational experience compared to a traditional six- to eight-lane pool. This rationale was explained by a parks and recreation staff member in the following interview, which appeared in the *Athens News* on August 16, 2004:

> The current city pool was built in 1972 and is a lap-pool, though not many people actually swim laps in it, Schwartzhoff said. The city is considering changing it to a recreational pool, he added. The Nelsonville swimming pool, which has a water slide and fountains, is a recreational pool, and Schwartzhoff said the recreation department will look at ideas such as what Nelsonville built. He added that the city also may look at a "0 depth" pool, meaning it's one that you can walk into instead of having to climb or jump in.

The second reason for suggesting a recreation pool was economic. Experience with leisure pools in other parts of the country suggested it was probable that revenues from such a facility would at least equal operational costs and probably exceed them. Thus, instead of losing $40,000 a year (as is currently happening), the new pool is likely to produce a surplus.

To determine the cost and attendance projections, the Athens Park and Recreation District hired a consulting firm that specializes in recreational pool facilities. Their preliminary feasibility study determined that the total development cost of the pool project would be $3.7 million and that the facility would have a 30-year useful life. The consultants estimated initial annual operation and maintenance costs to be $212,000, rising at 3.2% annually. The uniqueness of the facility led the consultants to project substantial local and regional (50-mile radius) demand, with annual attendance ranging from a conservative estimate of 80,000 to the most optimistic of 250,000 users each year, of which half would be children. They suggested an admission price of $5 for adults and $3.50 for children, with increases of 25% every ten years. The study implied that the pool would be profitable but did not provide a detailed pro forma analysis.

The wave pool was a major story in the local paper. As a result, the Parks and Recreation District surveyed 200 residents to gauge their opinions on the pool. The following was reported in the March 7, 2005, *Athens News:*

> At least 200 Athens residents will be surveyed beginning this week to see if . . . they would be willing to pay increased taxes in order to build such a facility.

> The City Recreation Department has been discussing the possibility of building a new outdoor pool to replace the current pool, renovating the current pool, or possibly building an addition to the Athens Community Center and putting an indoor pool and locker-room area in the addition. . . .

> City officials will use the survey information to gauge interest in a new pool facility, and whether they should move forward with looking at the feasibility of such a project, Schwartzhoff said.

> The survey asks around 15 questions, including the following:

> "Would you be willing to support a 0.05 percent ongoing income-tax increase (50 cents for every $1,000 of income) to help with operations of an indoor (or) outdoor aquatic facility?"

> "Would you be willing to support a 0.1 percent income tax increase ($1 for every $1,000 of income) for 20 years to build an indoor (or) outdoor aquatic facility?"

Based on the results of the survey, the Athens Parks Board has decided to go forward with the project. They voted unanimously to set aside a five-acre tract of land in one of the most accessible parks for development of the new facility. The major issue now facing the board is how to finance both the construction and the operation of the proposed aquatic facility.

The survey results indicated that few residents (35%) were willing to pay more income tax to support the pool, but more were in favor of an increase in income tax as compared to an increase in property tax (18% in favor). The taxable value of real property in the Athens Parks and Recreation District is $514 million. This is 35% of the estimated market value of real property in the district. The most recent census data can be found at the U.S. Census Bureau's website (http://factfinder.census.gov/home/saff/main.html?_lang=en). The district has $1,536,014 of outstanding debt, with a 2% debt ceiling capacity (i.e., the district can borrow up to 2% of the taxable value of real property within the district). Revenue bonds are unlikely to be salable unless they can be redeemed within a 20-year period. The present rate of interest for 20-year revenue bonds is 7%. The rate for a 30-year general obligation bond is 5%.

MTB, Inc., a South Carolina–based sport consulting firm, has been hired to research and report on the following questions:

CASE QUESTIONS

1. What are the feasible financing strategies for this project? Each of the funding alternatives identified must be sufficient to cover both construction and operating costs.

2. For each of the financing alternatives identified, provide a brief description, evidence to support its economic feasibility, and a discussion of its relative pros and cons from both a financial and a political perspective.

3. Which alternative is the best strategy for the district? Why?

references

Brigham, E.F., & Houston, J.F. (1999). *Fundamentals of financial management* (9th ed.). New York: Harcourt College Publishers.

Brown, L. (2005, July 18). Cards move forward on Ballpark Village. *SportsBusiness Journal*. Retrieved November 11, 2005, from http://www.sportsbusiness-journal.com.

Brown, M., Nagel, M., & Rascher, D. (2003, May). *The impact of stadia on wealth maximization in the national football league: To build or renovate?* Paper presented at the meeting of the North American Society for Sport Management, Ithaca, NY.

Cameron, S. (2002, August 19). Seahawks stadium and exhibition center. *SportsBusiness Journal*. Retrieved January 7, 2005, from http://www.sportsbusiness journal.com.

Fish, M. (2005, June 20). Tight public money forces teams to get creative with stadium finance plans. *Sports-Business Journal*. Retrieved November 21, 2005, from http://www.sportsbusinessjournal.com.

Fisher, E. (2005, October 3). Making success a tradition. *SportsBusiness Journal*. Retrieved November 21, 2005, from http://www.sportsbusinessjournal.com.

Groppelli, A.A., & Nikbakht, E. (2000). *Finance* (4th ed.). Hauppauge, NY: Barron's Educational Services, Inc.

Lynch, J. (2000a, March 23). City is ready to put dome behind it. *The Oregonian*, p. A12.

Lynch, J. (2000b, March 23). Landmark's rise and fall. *The Oregonian*, pp. A1, A12.

Madden, T.D. (1998). *Public assembly facility law: A guide for managers of arenas, auditoriums, convention centers, performing arts centers, race tracks and stadiums*. Irving, TX: International Association of Assembly Managers.

Marois, M.B. (2000, March 20). Demolition of Seattle Kingdome will clear way for new construction debt. *The Bond Buyer, 331*(30852), 3.

Miklasz, B. (2005a, December 7). Owners cash in, make Jocketty pinch pennies. *St. Louis Post-Dispatch*. Retrieved December 14, 2005, from http://stltoday.com.

Miklasz, B. (2005b, December 10). Cards owners use new park as an excuse to scrimp. *St. Louis Post-Dispatch*. Retrieved December 14, 2005, from http://stltoday.com.

Rodgers, A. (1997, September 27). The yes vote: A case study in voter persuasion. *The Bond Buyer, 321*(30235), 16A–17A.

Zimbalist, A. (2005, June 27). Big apple can take a shine to the new threesome of sports facilities. *Sports Business Journal*. Retrieved November 21, 2005, from http://www.sportsbusinessjournal.com.

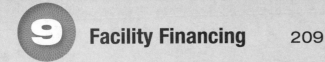

PART THREE

Application of Financial Management in Sport

Facility Financing

Introduction

This chapter discusses why sports facilities are built with public and/or private money, how much it costs to build them, the different sources for financing them, public/private partnerships, and the role of public policy in their construction.

REASONS FOR BUILDING NEW SPORT FACILITIES

 ho benefits from a new stadium? Sport teams and team owners, leagues, fans, and even businesses and the residents of a city or region may benefit from a new sport facility.

Teams and Owners

A team and its owner may benefit from a new stadium in numerous ways. A new facility can generate substantially higher revenues from tickets, concessions, sponsorship, merchandise, personal seat licenses (PSLs), luxury suites, and other premium seating, because customers demand, and are willing to pay for, better seating and atmosphere, food, restrooms, amenities, and access. When NFL teams move into a new stadium, they witness an increase of about 85% in local revenues that are not shared with other teams and see an increase in franchise values of 35% (Brown, Nagel, McEvoy, & Rascher, 2004). Another advantage is that a new facility can reduce the impact of winning on franchise revenues. Fans attend games because of the facility and not solely because of the team's performance. This can smooth out overall revenues and budget for years, lowering financial risk (and borrowing rates).

At the same time, a franchise that moves into a new facility also generally has an incentive to improve its on-the-field performance, because doing so will help it leverage the full value of the facility. Each new fan the team attracts to the facility will spend more money in a new stadium than in an old stadium on concessions, merchandise, and so forth. Thus, the return on an investment in better players is higher, so the franchise has an incentive to increase its investment in talented players. Empirically, of the 14 MLB teams that have opened new ballparks from 1991 through 2001, 11 of them increased their team payrolls in the years immediately following the move into the new stadium (Baade, 2003). Of course, the cause-and-effect may also be that the new stadium provides the financing to increase payrolls (under the assumption that the owners could not finance player payrolls from other sources).

Finally, NFL rules have given owners motivation to build new stadia for reasons other than those listed above. According to the rules, the league shares most of the revenue that individual teams generate (specifically, national media and licensing revenues and ticket revenues). Certain revenue streams, however, that increase substantially in new stadia belong to the owner, such as naming rights, sponsorships, concessions, parking, and luxury suite or premium seating revenues. Additionally, the NFL has a large fund, most recently known as the G-3 fund, that provides low-interest loans to help teams build new stadia.

A franchise's incentive to build a new stadium is further enhanced if it can obtain partial financing from local, regional, or state government. A city can improve its justification for investing public money if other political jurisdictions also invest (surrounding counties, the state, the federal government, or other cities), thereby lowering the direct cost to the city. In Milwaukee, Miller Park was financed through several different sources, including the City of Milwaukee, which gave $18 million toward construction and loaned another $15 million. This is less than 5% of the nearly $400 million in total construction costs, including infrastructure costs (see Exhibit 9.1). The $30 million in naming rights that Miller Brewing Co. paid could be considered local public financing (discussed later), because the stadium is majority owned by the city's special baseball district. However, if the Brewers were not playing in the stadium, the value of the naming rights would be significantly less, so most of the naming rights funds invested in the stadium should be attributed to the team and not the city.

When cities and other political entities invest, the team will receive most, if not all, of the additional revenue generated within the stadium but will have to pay only part of the cost. The cost of adding $30 million in new players, however, is fully borne by the team and not shared with local government.

Stadium funding sources.   **exhibit**   **9.1**

MILLER PARK (2000) PROJECTED FUNDING SOURCES

Naming rights and upfront concessionaire payments	$30,000,000	(1)
Milwaukee business community loans	14,000,000	
City of Milwaukee loan	15,000,000	
Bradley Foundation loan	20,000,000	
WPBD tax-exempt bonds	160,000,000	(2)
City of Milwaukee	18,000,000	
Milwaukee County	18,000,000	
State of Wisconsin	36,000,000	
MLB letter of credit	10,000,000	
Certificates of participation	45,000,000	(3)
Helfaer Foundation loan	1,000,000	
Total funding sources	$367,000,000	

Note: This is a projection. Actual costs were substantially higher. The team receives all revenue and is responsible for operating expenses. The team pays $1.1 million in annual rent but receives $3.85 million per year for maintenance and repairs.

(1) Naming rights revenue from Miller Brewing Co.

(2) The Wisconsin Professional Baseball District owns 64% of the stadium and issued tax-exempt bonds backed by a 1/10 of a cent increase in the sales tax and a 1% increase in the room tax for Milwaukee County and the four surrounding counties.

(3) As explained later in the chapter, COPs were used to purchase a scoreboard and other amenities and were paid back via a sales tax.

Leagues

Leagues, and not just their individual teams, desire new construction, because all members benefit through revenue sharing of increased ticket sales.

Fans

Sport fans gain from new stadia with enhanced offerings, better amenities, restrooms, food, and so forth. Although ticket prices typically increase in new stadia, more fans attend games in these stadia, providing evidence that fans consider themselves better off.

Cities and Geographic Regions

Cities and their businesses and residents may or may not be better off with a new stadium, depending on the cost to the city. Reasons commonly cited for investing public money in new sport facilities are that they will

- provide economic impact to the community (see Chapter 12),
- increase national and international awareness of the city and enhance its image, thereby increasing future tourism (and possibly firms and families relocating to the city),
- provide a cornerstone for economic development in a blighted or underutilized area,
- generate civic pride among residents, or give the city "major league" status,
- provide quality of life services similar to public parks and museums,
- provide positive externalities, including **psychic impact** (the emotional impact of having a local sports team),* discussed below, and
- generate political capital for local politicians.

Positive externalities

Generally, businesses pay for their own offices and manufacturing facilities, without government intervention or subsidies. For very large projects, however, such as an automobile manufacturing plant or a sports facility, a company may create competition between political jurisdictions (e.g., cities or states), which may result in government intervention or subsidy. This was the case with the $754 million DaimlerChrysler facility in Georgia. State and local subsidies totaled approximately $320 million after DaimlerChrysler chose Georgia over South Carolina. States engaged in a bidding war for the facility because of the potential increase in jobs, local earnings, and taxes. Georgia officials felt that the plant not only would generate quality jobs but also would cause growth in other automotive businesses (such as auto suppliers and parts manufacturers) in the area, creating a net positive economic gain to the region.

These overflow effects, or positive externalities, can help governments justify public investment in private industry. **Positive externalities** are benefits produced by an event that are not captured by the event owners or sports facility. In sport,

---

*Psychic impact is also termed *psychic income* or *public consumption benefit* in the academic literature.

it is clear that some local businesses, such as restaurants, bars, retail stores, and hotels, benefit from having sporting events in town. Local radio stations and newspapers also benefit from local sports, often dedicating an entire segment or section to them. Even newscasts commit a daily segment to sports. If sports were not important to listeners, viewers, and readers, these media outlets would focus on something else. These are clearly positive externalities from sports, for which the local team does not collect payments. (Negative externalities, such as traffic congestion caused by sporting events, also occur.)

The fact that the team cannot charge local restaurants for increased customer traffic means that this aspect of a sporting event is a **public good,** a good that is **non-rival** and **non-excludable**—meaning that its consumption by one customer does not prevent another customer from consuming it, and the team cannot prevent someone from enjoying the good (via television, the Internet, the newspaper, discussions with friends, and so forth). As Allan Sanderson (1999) suggests:

> Sports represent a socially-consumed commodity. Water-cooler conversations and office greetings frequently turn on casual greetings such as, "How 'bout them Redskins?" Even if ardent fans are not present in the stands, they can watch games on television and radio, follow their favorite team or athlete through newspaper accounts, and exchange numbers and notions with friends, neighbors, and colleagues. (p. 189)

As a result of positive externalities, the local team may underinvest in a stadium, or a sports league may decide not to launch a new franchise, because it is not financially worth it to the team or league. However, it may be worth it to the city and its residents. The issue is that the private business (the team) cannot charge for the full value of its business to the community. As a result, the quality of the stadium or the number of teams in the league will be less than what the public wants—not socially optimal. A public subsidy might be justified on these grounds. Public subsidies for stadium development can help push a league over the threshold to offer more expansion franchises. Baade and Matheson (2006) show that stadium subsidies have evoked expansions in major professional sports in the United States, moving the number of teams closer to the socially optimal level.

Psychic impact

Similarly, Sanderson discusses the fact that psychic impact, which is an externality, may justify public subsidies. The team is not able to charge residents for being happy about the local team (although it tries, through the sale of novelties, merchandise, and apparel carrying the team's name and logo). Sanderson notes:

> Studies suggest that, on average, recycling is an economic loser because the total collection costs exceed the value of the materials to be recycled. But people, even armed with that information, and knowing that recycling is implicitly taking away from other worthwhile foregone alternatives, such as more police, parks, and street repairs, or even a tax rebate, may still vote to continue recycling their newspapers, cans and bottles because the "feel-good" factor is sufficiently large. The corresponding question here is how large the feel-good factor of a professional franchise or a new stadium is, in terms of civic pride or even some "existence value." (p. 189)

The loss of a local team, if it moves to another city, may be so devastating in terms of psychic impact that a public investment is justified. A key task for politicians is to find a way for those who benefit to pay for it, and for those who do not care about or benefit from sports to pay nothing.

Controversy regarding benefits to political jurisdictions

Controversy often arises because those who gain the most from the construction of a new sport facility are not always those who pay for the facility's construction and upkeep, and because many of the benefits discussed above may not materialize sufficiently to justify the expense. In fact, most academic studies measuring the economic impact of sport facilities (not teams or sporting events) fail to find enough net gain to a community to justify the often large public outlays (Siegfried & Zimbalist, 2000). However, non-economic reasons, such as psychic impact, may in fact justify public investment. As Owen notes, "the focus on economic impact misses the true source of value teams have for cities as public goods" (2006). Owen finds that for the states of Michigan and Minnesota, psychic impact values of $100 million per major professional sport team (i.e., NFL, MLB, NHL, and NBA) are reasonable estimates, with some going much higher than that. As will be discussed later in this chapter, the average public subsidy for a sport facility since 1990 is about $125 million, with adjustments for land acquisition, forgone taxes, and other effects raising that figure to $195 million (Owen). Therefore, the psychic impact value does not typically cover the full cost of a public subsidy, but when combined with the economic impact effect it could justify some public facility investments.

So why do sport teams receive large amounts of public funding? Economic and psychic impact values exist for other businesses as well, such as an open air mall, but those businesses often do not receive public funding. The fact that a sport league has control over the number of franchises means it can prevent a city from hosting a team even if the city wants one. The threat of relocation to another city, known as **franchise free agency,** often motivates a city to help build a facility for a local team. If the team can not realistically move, it may not be able to obtain a significant subsidy. Some subsidy may be justified if the quality of the stadium, if it were financed solely by private investment, would be less than what the market demands. Perry (2002) estimates that the Washington Redskins could justify a private investment of only $155 million in a new stadium; however, as discussed below, other estimates suggest that NFL teams could finance nearly the entire cost of a new stadium. The bottom line is that the residents of cities do not want to see their hometown team move to another city, so they are usually willing to foot the bill for most of a facility's construction and maintenance costs. For all of these reasons, we have seen unprecedented growth in the construction of sport facilities.

HISTORICAL PHASES OF FACILITY FINANCING: PUBLIC VERSUS PRIVATE FUNDING

The construction of sport facilities in the United States has come in three major waves over the past century and has seen changes in the degree of **private financing**—financing that does not use public dollars—and **public financing**—the use of public funds to finance a project.

Phase 1

Twenty-seven facilities were built from the late 1880s through the end of the Depression. One of these still stands today—Wrigley Field. During the first half of the first wave, stadia were 100% privately financed. Not until 1923 and the construction of Los Angeles Coliseum was public money used to build a major professional sport stadium. Overall, during the first wave 31% of the costs of construction was financed with public money (Keating, 1999; Baade). Of the 27 facilities built prior to World War II, only five received public funding.

Phase 2

During the second phase, from 1960 to 1979, 57 major sport facilities were built, many in the all-purpose mold—able to house a baseball and football team or a basketball and hockey team. The second wave saw a significant increase in the cost of construction and in the amount the public was willing to pay, as Exhibit 9.2 shows.* On average, public financing covered 83% of the cost of the new stadia during this phase.

*In fact, the public financing trend began immediately after World War II, but not many facilities were built until 1960.

Public subsidies for sport stadium construction. exhibit **9.2**

PERIOD	NUMBER OF STADIA BUILT	NUMBER OF STADIA PUBLICLY FINANCED	COST OF STADIA ($M, 1997 DOLLARS)	PUBLIC SUBSIDIES ($M, 1997 DOLLARS)	PERCENTAGE OF CONSTRUCTION PUBLICLY FINANCED
1887–1923	14	0	129.8	0.0	0
1887–1939	27	5	493.6	155.0	31.4
1923–1939	13	5	363.9	155.0	42.6
1947–1959	8	7	163.2	161.5	98.9
1960–1969	25	21	2,601.4	1,720.7	66.1
1970–1979	32	29	4,279.5	3,989.2	93.2
1980–1986	13	13	822.0	764.0	92.9
1987–1999	55	51	9,488.7	6,220.2	70.6
2000–2002	18	17	4,968.0	3,119.4	62.8
2003–2009	15	14	4,726.3	4,270.0	90.3
Total 1887–2009	193	157	27,542.8	20,400.1	74.1

Source: Keating (1999), recreated from R. A. Baade, "Evaluating studies for professional sports in the U.S. and Europe." *Oxford Review of Economic Policy, 19*(4), 585–597, by permission of Oxford University Press.

Phase 3

Construction was relatively quiet during the early 1980s, but in 1987—with the opening of Dolphin Stadium, quickly renamed Joe Robbie Stadium—a third building spree began. It has continued to this day, netting nearly 90 new facilities over a 20-year period. These buildings are often positioned to look like classic sport stadia of the past, but they usually house only one major tenant, not two. In fact, during this wave, over 80% of the major professional sport facilities in the United States have been replaced or substantially upgraded. The facilities that are currently in use cost a total of approximately $24 billion (in 2003 dollars), with the public paying about $15 billion (Crompton, Howard, & Var, 2003). Exhibit 9.3 shows recent activity in stadium construction.

Returning to Exhibit 9.2, we see that during the current wave, the percentage of the costs of sport facilities that is financed by the public has declined slightly, to about 71%. Overall, since World War II, approximately 10% of stadia built did not receive public funding.

If we drill down deeper into the current trends, as Zimbalist and Long have done, the public share of facility costs fell from the 1970s through the 1990s but has flattened out since 2000 at around 58% (Zimbalist, 2006). Even though the share of funding by the public has decreased, the amount in nominal terms has increased because of the steep increases in stadium construction costs.

exhibit   9.3   Sport facility construction trends, 1997–2010 (nominal dollars).

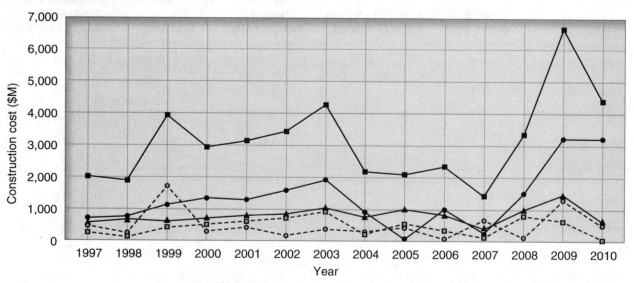

Historical Analysis of Construction Costs

According to the Construction Cost Index (CCI, a measure of inflation in the construction industry), prices in that industry rose by 5.2% annually from 1962 through 2003. In contrast, general inflation (measured by the Consumer Price Index) was 4.5% over the same time period. The difference may seem small, but an item costing $100 in 1962 and rising at the CCI rate would cost $792 in 2003 and only $609 if it were rising at the CPI rate, a 30% difference.

We can use the CCI to adjust stadium construction costs for inflation in order to compare all stadia in real dollars. From 1960 to 1994 the real cost of stadia (data does not include arenas) rose, on average, about 1.76% per year (doubling in price in real terms over nearly 40 years). However, since 1990 the real cost of stadium construction has risen an average of 2.3% per year, 30% higher than the previous growth rate. According to information compiled by Crompton, Howard, and Var, the average cost of a stadium built from 1995 to 2003 is $339 million in 2003 dollars, whereas the cost of stadia built during the 1960s is $179 million (in 2003 dollars). Overall, stadium construction costs have risen significantly faster than inflation in the rest of the economy, and the total dollar amount in real terms (comparable over time) has also risen substantially. (The same can be said for arenas, whose costs have grown at an average annual real rate of 4.35% since 1970, from $87 million to $223 million.)

As shown in Exhibit 9.4, accounting for real costs versus nominal costs has a striking impact on the perception of the rising costs of sport facilities. In nominal terms, the costs of old stadia were a small fraction (about 12%) of the costs of new stadia. However, in terms of the real costs, old stadia were about half as expensive

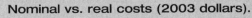

Nominal vs. real costs (2003 dollars).   **exhibit**   **9.4**

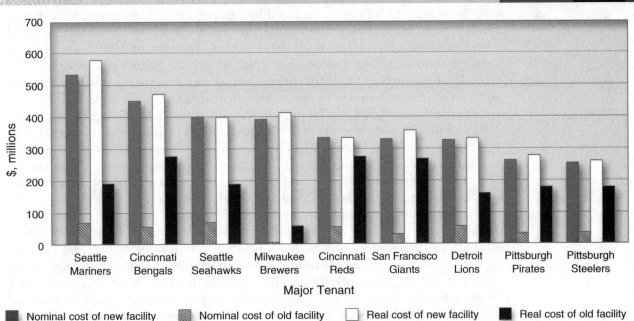

SIDEBAR

Choice of an Inflation Index Matters

9.A

An important aspect of the analysis of construction costs is that the choice of inflation index matters. If we use the more common CPI, the real cost of sport facilities has risen over time (even recently), but if we use the CCI, that is not the case. All construction costs have risen over time more than costs for consumer products in general (evident in the CPI). Therefore, if a community were to build a museum instead of a sport facility, those costs would also be much higher than in previous decades. Complaints about the rising real costs of stadium construction have little merit if the alternative is another construction project with equally high inflation, such as a library or museum. Of course, the debate over whether public money should be used for a stadium versus another building does have merit.

as new ones. It is important to make comparisons over time with real costs, not nominal costs (which, unfortunately, are often the basis of comparisons). Stadia are of much higher quality than they used to be, with many more amenities, so the quality-adjusted cost may actually be lower than in previous eras.

Given that the average percentage of a stadium's cost that the public pays has shrunk, but the total real cost of stadium construction has risen, we must ask whether the real amount of public dollars spent on stadia is rising or falling. The answer depends. From 1962 to 1994, total public funding for sport stadia (not arenas) rose in real terms by about 3.5%, using the CCI as the measure of inflation. During that same period, the public's share of funding remained fairly constant, around 85%. These statistics suggest that the real amount of public dollars spent was rising. However, from 1995 to 2003, total public funding for sport stadia declined in real terms by about 3.5%, when compared to the cost of all construction projects. Similarly, the real cost borne by the public for construction of sport arenas has dropped by about 2.0% per year since 1977, when compared to the cost of all construction projects. During this more recent period, the real amount of public dollars spent seems to have been falling.

Stadia and arenas differ in two major ways in terms of public finance. One is that stadia are much more expensive overall, which is one of the reasons why the percentage that is publicly financed has dropped from only about 85% during 1961–1994 to 62% during 1995–2003. Arenas are much less expensive to build overall, and they can attract many more events (upwards of 200 events per year in a new arena in a large metropolitan area), so private financing is more feasible. From 1961 through 1984, 100% of the cost of arena financing was borne by the public. That figure dropped to about 44% from 1985 through 2003.

Exhibit 9.5 lists NBA and NHL facilities built in the United States during 1998–2002 and the share of the costs borne by the public. Typically, private sources fund the more expensive facilities in larger markets because the economics of the facilities can justify it (e.g., higher luxury suite, premium seating, sponsorship, and naming rights revenue and more events), and the threat of a team leaving for another market is much less serious—would the Lakers really ever leave Los Angeles?

We must make two important points before leaving this analysis of the costs of stadium construction and how much the public bears. First, as Long (2005) notes, calculations of stadium construction costs typically do not include the cost (or opportunity cost) of land acquisition and forgone taxes. As described later, public stadium financing often involves giving away the land or leasing it cheaply, and forgoing various taxes, such as sales tax and property tax, that would normally be collected from the stadium. Long estimates these amounts would add as much as 57% to calculations of construction costs.

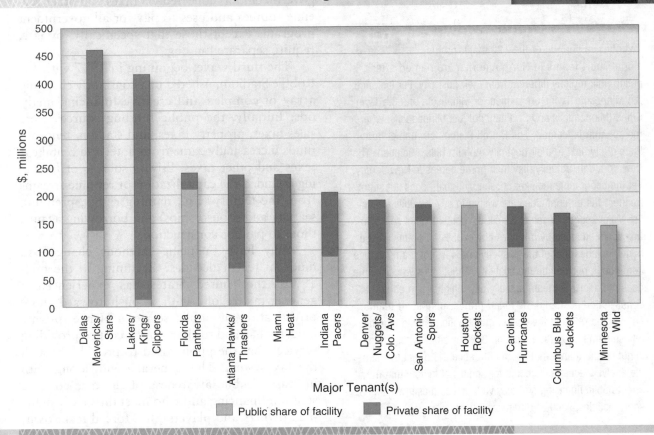

Public and private funding for NBA and NHL arenas.   exhibit   9.5

Major Tenant(s)

☐ Public share of facility   ☐ Private share of facility

Second, lease arrangements with teams have become more beneficial to team owners than they used to be, often allowing the owners to receive all forms of revenue from the stadium (including from non-sport events), with the city collecting a very small annual rent for the stadium's use. For instance, the Baltimore Ravens' football stadium, which opened in 1998, cost approximately $200 million, with the public paying 90% of the costs. The team pays no rent and keeps all revenue streams, while the city authority covers the costs of maintenance and game-day staff. It is not hard to understand why Art Modell moved his team from Cleveland to Baltimore.

Changes in Financing Methods

As noted earlier, the types and methods of financing, not just the amount, have changed over the three waves of construction. During the pre-WWII wave, most facilities were privately financed. After the war, the second wave saw growth in public financing of stadia. Typically, the financing methods were quite simple. These included floating **general obligation bonds (GOBs)**, which last for 20 years or so, with the debt and interest payments paid each year directly out of the general funds of local government(s) coffers. The general fund of a government (city,

SIDEBAR

What's in a Name? Money

Twenty-five percent of the 122 major professional sport teams in North America are named after geographic regions different from their host city. For instance, the Minnesota Twins are named for Minnesota and the Twin Cities (Minneapolis and St. Paul), not just Minneapolis, where the stadium is located. The Detroit Pistons are named after the big city next to their host city, Auburn Hills, Michigan. The New York Jets actually play their home games in New Jersey. Yet the geographic moniker chosen by a team does not seem to affect the amount cities are willing to pay in public finance. For Major League Baseball teams, the percentage of construction costs financed by a team's city is 35% for teams whose name includes that of the host city and 44% for teams whose name does *not* include the host city. Thus, cities whose name does not adorn the team actually pay a higher percentage of construction costs. For all major professional sport teams, on average, 32% of the cost of construction is paid by cities whose name is on the team and 30% by cities whose name is not on the team—not much difference. Note that this simple analysis does not account for additional factors that may affect public financing and may vary across these two sets of sport facilities, such as differences in city size.

county, or state) is the pool of money that the government has collected via taxes and other revenue sources and uses to pay for all government programs except those that specifically, by law, require separate funding.

The third wave, beginning in 1987 with Joe Robbie Stadium, ushered in a constantly changing array of complex and creative financing methods. Initially, the public funding sources were sales taxes, property taxes, and stadium rent, but funds increasingly came from hotel and rental car taxes and other taxes. Private sources of financing included the capitalization of revenue streams from the facility (e.g., naming rights, premium seating, and sponsorships) and borrowing against those to pay for construction.

Why have financing methods changed so much in recent decades? Beginning in the mid-1970s, the United States has experienced a general tax revolt, with a push toward more privatization of public services. Hence, private industry has had to share in the cost of providing services that the public used to provide through the tax system. This general trend, along with increased public awareness of the true costs of stadium financing and who most directly benefits (i.e., owners and players), has forced team owners to increase their private financing of stadia.

The Deficit Reduction Act of 1984 prevented tax-exempt bonds from being sold to finance luxury suites. More generally, the 1986 Tax Reform Act (a significant overhaul of the tax system) prohibited tax-exempt bonds from being used to fund sport facilities where a single organization would be responsible for 10% or more of revenues. In other words, a facility that hosted many different events but did not have a major tenant could use tax-exempt bonds, because the facility would be deemed a public use facility, whereas a facility with a single tenant could not use tax-exempt bonds. These laws caused the interest rates on bonds used to pay for sport facilities to increase (in order to give the same competitive return to investors as tax-exempt bonds). Since these bonds cost more to use, other sources of financing began to develop that were not affected by these recent legal changes, such as sales taxes and hotel and car rental taxes.

General growth in the demand for sports and subsequent revenues enabled owners to justify paying part of stadium costs. City officials, recognizing this growth in demand and revenues, fought harder to convince owners to help pay for construction. In 1987 Joe Robbie discovered new revenues available from leasing luxury suites and used the initial lease payments (and guarantees of future payments) to finance part of construction. Similarly, the Carolina Panthers invented the modern use of personal seat licenses in 1993, generating about $150 million in revenues.

Recent developments by sport leagues, including the G-3 fund in the NFL, have helped team owners find cheaper financing options to help pay for stadia.

As noted earlier, the trend toward more private financing has halted or stabilized in the past few years. As Zimbalist notes, sport leagues and their owners still have leverage in negotiating with cities, especially smaller ones, because they can move to another location if a deal is not to their liking. Also, even though voters are more aware of the true financial costs and benefits of publicly financed sport facilities, they continue to vote in favor of them. The quality-of-life or psychic impact value of sport teams playing in modern stadia may be high enough to justify these expenditures. When disaggregated into per capita costs, a $250 million public financing package costs about $20 million per year in debt payments, which is about $10 per person per year in a region of 2 million people. As voters have learned this, many may have decided that having a sport team is worth the cost of one movie ticket per year.

PUBLIC FINANCING

s we have just discussed, public financing remains a major source of funding for sports facilities. This section will discuss the principles of public financing, sources and techniques of financing, and calculations involved.

Public Financing Principles

Public financing principles determine the financing sources that are appropriate for a given project. Two of these principles are the concepts of equity and efficiency.

Equity principles

Equity is a measure of fairness. It includes three major ideas: vertical equity, horizontal equity, and the benefit or user pays principle (Baade & Matheson). **Vertical equity** is concerned with the taxpayer's ability to pay, typically calling for a tax that does not cause poorer persons to bear a disproportionate share. **Horizontal equity** suggests that individuals with similar incomes should pay similar amounts of a tax. The **benefit principle,** or user pays principle, states that those who benefit from a particular project ought to be the ones taxed. For funding a stadium, a ticket tax on sporting events would satisfy the benefit principle much more than a cigarette tax.

Consider the following examples of how we apply the equity principles to public funding for sport facilities. Hotel, rental car, and **sin taxes** (taxes on alcohol and cigarettes) fail the user pays or benefits principle, because the users of a sport facility are not the ones being taxed, except by coincidence. Sin taxes also fail the horizontal equity principle, because people with the same ability to pay (similar income) will pay different amounts of tax, depending on whether they smoke or consume alcohol. If lower income people smoke more than higher income people, then a sin tax will fail the vertical equity principle as well. However, sin taxes are efficient at generating revenues, because their demand is price inelastic (the demand does not change much as a result of a price change). A related effect of taxing specific products or services is that the tax is shared by the consumer and

SIDEBAR

If the Public Pays More for the Stadium, Will Tickets Be Cheaper? 9.C

Is there a *quid pro quo* between the public paying more money for a professional football stadium and getting lower priced tickets once the stadium is built? In other words, if a franchise is able to save money on construction costs, will it pass some of those savings on to the ticket buyer? Consistent with economic theory, NFL franchises do not appear to set ticket prices based on the amount of public financing they receive for the stadia in which they play. Economic theory suggests that the franchise will simply pocket any savings from building a football stadium and not pass them on to the public. Pricing decisions are based on the demand to see games and on changes in the variable costs of selling tickets and providing seating. Brown, Rascher, and Ward (2006) have shown that ticket prices are also related to general increases in demand over time, team quality, inflation, consumers' ability to pay in the local market, and the presence of a new stadium (although not how it was financed). Overall, an increase in public funding by 10% reduces ticket prices by only 42 cents, all else being equal. Public financing does seem to reduce ticket prices, but not by much.

producer (depending on their relative elasticities). Thus, hoteliers will oppose a hotel tax, because it will cut into their profit and make them less competitive with hotels in other destinations. Even if the hotel tax raises the expected amount of revenue per hotel guest, it may reduce the number of guests. Ticket taxes and personal seat licenses do satisfy the benefits principle, because users of the facility pay them. However, these sources usually cannot fully fund the public's portion of the cost of a stadium. A television tax on sport channels might satisfy the benefits principle and generate substantial funding.

Efficiency principle

The **efficiency principle** calls for a tax to be easy to understand, simple for government to collect, low in compliance costs (meaning that it is not expensive for taxpayers to calculate and pay), and difficult for taxpayers to evade. Moreover, for a tax to be effective in raising tax revenues sufficient to pay for a stadium, it should be applied to products or services with low price elasticity of demand. **Price elasticity of demand** refers to the percentage decrease in the number of units sold compared to the percentage increase in the price of the product. An elasticity of −0.5 means that raising prices by 10% reduces sales by 5%. A product with a high price elasticity of demand would see a substantial decrease in the quantity sold if a tax were imposed, which would offset much of the proposed tax gain.

Public Financing Sources and Techniques

As the costs of facilities have risen, many more sources of financing beyond the general funds of a city, county, or state have been cobbled together to pay for them. Although the use of money from the general fund is on the decline compared to other techniques, it is still popular enough to have helped fund sport facilities for the Milwaukee Brewers (using city, county, and state general fund sources), Philadelphia Phillies, Cincinnati Bengals, Detroit Lions (where Wayne County sold property worth $20 million to raise funds), Houston Texans, and Tampa Bay Lightning, to name a few. This section will examine public sources of financing and how they are implemented. The list in Exhibit 9.6 provides a summary of public financing sources.

General obligation bonds

Historically, general obligation bonds were the most common method of facility financing, besides tapping into the general fund, and they continue to be very common. This is because they spread the cost of the facility over a 20- or 30-year period.

- General obligation bonds
- Certificates of participation
- Revenue bonds
- Tax increment financing and property taxes
- Sales tax
- Tourism and food and beverage taxes
- Sin taxes
- Sale of government assets
- State appropriations
- Ticket tax/surcharge or parking revenues/tax
- Lotteries and gaming revenues
- Player income taxes
- Reallocation of existing budget
- Indirect sources of public financing
  - Land donations
  - Infrastructure improvements
  - Tax abatements

The term "general obligation" refers to the fact that the issuer (usually a city, county, or state) has a commitment to repay the principal plus interest (debt payments) through whatever means are necessary, including tapping into the general fund of the city, county, or state. Because the risks of purchasing GOBs for investment are lower than the risks of other bonds, the interest rates are lower (often up to 2% lower), allowing for smaller debt payments. Further, a debt service reserve fund (a separate, or escrow, account that can be tapped into for unforeseen reasons, funded by annual payments) is usually not required, because of the low risk, so the total dollar amount of the bonds necessary to pay for the stadium or arena is lower. Thus, the total cost of the facility may be less than if higher interest rate instruments are used.

A disadvantage of GOBs is that their use may limit the amount of other bonds that the city, county, or state can use for schools, bridges, and other projects. These political jurisdictions are limited in the total amount of bonds (or debt) that can be outstanding or owed, and debt ceilings vary across jurisdictions. Additionally, any voter approval that is needed can raise the total cost of the financing. It is not surprising that the use of GOBs may require a vote, because the funds to pay off GOBs are public dollars, mostly supplied by residents.

To further explore the advantages and disadvantages of GOBs, let's consider whether they satisfy the three equity principles. To do this, we must examine the

SIDEBAR

Tax-Exempt Auction-Rate Bonds Can Backfire

A number of recently built or refurbished sport facilities have been financed through tax-exempt auction-rate bonds. For auction-rate bonds, the annualized interest rate is set at auctions held every seven to 35 days. Typically, these bonds have lower interest rates than their fixed-rate counterparts because of the risk of the interest rate going up. This is similar to residential housing mortgages, where a borrower can opt for a fixed-rate mortgage at a higher rate than an adjustable rate mortgage (ARM).

Sport facilities in Louisiana, Indiana, New Jersey, Washington D.C., and Cleveland have been financed by auction-rate bonds issued by the respective city or state. Franchise owners have also issued these bonds, including owners of the New York Giants, New England Patriots, and Dallas Cowboys. As the fallout from the sub-prime mortgage crisis has reached full swing, the interest rates (and monthly payments) on these bonds have skyrocketed. For instance, debt payments on $238 million of bonds sold for upgrades to the Louisiana Superdome, about $500,000 during January 2008, more than tripled to $1.8 million in February because the interest rate on the bonds went from about 4% to 12%. The interest rate increased because, for the first time, the auction lacked bidders; investors were worried about the safety of these investments because bond insurers were suffering and the investors feared they risked failure. The bond insurance companies have been stretched as they have been forced to pay out on many of the bonds related to sub-prime mortgages.

The rate on $190 million of bonds sold by the New Jersey Sports and Exhibition Authority in November 2007 rose from 4.3% to more than 15% during one week in February 2008. Similar events occurred for Lucas Oil Stadium (Indianapolis Colts) and Cleveland Browns Stadium.

source of funds used to pay off GOBs. At the state level, sales taxes or income taxes provide the largest source of funds; for local governments, property taxes are usually the largest source of general funds, although in some situations sales taxes generate more revenue.

Obviously, GOBs do not satisfy the benefits principle, because everyone in a given jurisdiction pays for the facility, not just those who benefit. However, to the extent that property taxes pay off the GOBs and the facility helps to increase property values (this point is debatable and specific to each case), GOBs can come closer to satisfying the benefits principle. GOBs do satisfy the efficiency principle, because they are not burdensome or difficult to understand and cannot be easily avoided. They may or may not satisfy the horizontal and vertical equity principles, depending on whether the largest sources of funding for the general fund follow those principles. Property taxes may satisfy the vertical equity principle, assuming that the individuals who earn more income own higher valued property and pay higher taxes.

An advantage of GOBs from the bond buyer's perspective is that they are generally tax exempt, meaning that the buyer does not pay taxes on earnings from these bonds. This allows the interest rate on the bonds to be low compared with taxable bonds. For example, the New York City General Obligation series (2008) offers a yield of 4.02%. On a taxable equivalent basis, that is the same as 6.18% for someone in the 35% tax bracket. (Earning 6.18% but having to pay 35% of it in taxes results in a 4.02% equivalent [$6.18 \times (1 - 0.35)$]). The City of Minneapolis used GOBs to cover 85% of the purchase of the Target Center in 1995. The construction projects to build facilities for the Jacksonville Jaguars, Nashville Predators, Seattle Mariners, and Tampa Bay Rays over the past few decades all used city, county, or state GOBs as a major financing vehicle. The revenues used to pay off these bonds have included hotel taxes, rental car taxes, food and beverage taxes, sales taxes, and others. If these were to fall short, the general fund would be tapped.

Certificates of participation

A **certificate of participation (COP)** is an instrument that a government agency or non-profit corporation set up to build a facility will sell to one or more financial institutions to obtain the initial capital for construction. Then, the agency or non-profit leases the facility either directly to the tenant(s) or to a facility operator and uses the lease payments to pay off the COP.

Because COPs are backed by lease payments, they are riskier than GOBs and therefore have a higher interest rate. However, they do not require a public vote, so they are often used because they circumvent direct decision-making by voters. They also typically do not count against the debt ceiling of the political jurisdiction, depending on applicable law. For instance, Miller Park in Milwaukee issued $78 million in COPs that were paid back, not by the team or facility operator directly, but through sales taxes.* This highlights the flexibility in the source of payments for COPs. The flexibility was needed to circumvent a construction cap on public funding. The COPs did not count against the cap.

Revenue bonds

Revenue bonds are a form of public financing that is paid off solely from specific, well-defined sources, such as hotel taxes, ticket taxes, or other sources of public funding. If the specific source of funding does not meet expectations, the bonds will not be paid off in full. Thus, when compared to GOBs, the interest rates are higher for revenue bonds and a debt service reserve is necessary. Revenue bonds require a debt service coverage payment—an annual payment into an escrow account to cushion against the risk of the revenue sources backing the debt being insufficient. Therefore, the total cost of using revenue bonds is much higher than that of GOBs, because of the added risk. An advantage is that because the funding is from a narrower source than GOBs, revenue bonds can be tailored to satisfy the benefits principle, especially if a ticket tax is used. For sport-related construction, revenue bonds typically have terms of 15 to 30 years, generally do not require voter approval, and do not count against the debt ceiling of the political entity using them.

If the source of funding for the bonds is expected to grow over time (e.g., hotel tax revenues will increase because of increasing hotel rates and tourism), then variable interest bonds may be used, which require lower payments initially and higher payments nearer to the maturity of the bond. A creative method to attempt to achieve the advantages of both GOBs (lower interest rates) and revenue bonds (satisfaction of the benefit or user pays principle) is to arrange that any shortfalls in revenue bonds will be backed by the general fund (thus nearly ensuring their payment). Essentially, this turns the revenue bond into a GOB, but the payments still come from a specific source, such as ticket taxes. Another method of raising the investment grade of revenue bonds is to require an "insurance wrap," whereby the payments are insured. This method can reduce the interest rate of the bonds, but the insurance expense increases the costs.

Examples of the use of revenue bonds in sport facility construction include the following:

- Dolphin Stadium used $30 million in revenue bonds (out of $115 million in total financing) that were paid off by the private sector.

---

*Note that the projected COP funding was for $45 million, but the actual amount needed, due to unexpected major construction delays and costs, was $78 million.

- Cinergy Field, built in 1970 in Cincinnati, was paid for entirely with $44 million in revenue bonds that were backed by stadium revenues (team rent and parking).

- Jacobs Field in Cleveland was built with stadium-backed revenue bonds that financed just over 10% of its cost.

- For the Nashville Predators' home arena, financing included $77.5 million in revenue bonds backed by a sales tax on tickets and merchandise.

Lease revenue bonds are a version of revenue bonds in which the revenue stream backing the payment of the bonds is a lease. For instance, a 20-year naming rights deal (which is a contract or lease) may be the source of funds to pay off lease revenue bonds, as opposed to a tax on ticket sales (which is not a lease, but an expected or forecasted revenue stream). As stadia and arenas have become able to generate more revenues through better amenities, financing through lease revenue bonds has become more common. These bonds are often backed by luxury suite or premium seating revenues, concessions contracts, or sponsorship deals, as well as naming rights deals. Normally, these would be considered private financing sources (discussed later). This is where a partnership between public and private sectors creates synergies—the public entity can float a low interest rate bond, and the private entity can generate funding for the bond's payment because of demand for its sport team.

An example of lease revenue bond financing in recreation comes from Montgomery County, Maryland, which built a swim center with lease revenue bonds that were paid for through a lease between the county and the financing authority established to manage the facility. The county's lease payments cover the principal plus interest on the bonds. The Baltimore Ravens' football stadium was paid for through state lease revenue bonds backed by proceeds of the Maryland state lottery and personal seat licenses.

Tax increment financing and property taxes

Proponents of tax increment financing often claim that the public does not pay for this source of facility funding. The rationale for this claim is that with **tax increment financing (TIF)**, only "incremental" (additional or new) taxes generated from a certain source (traditionally property taxes) finance the facility, and those incremental tax revenues would not exist without the facility. The original uses of the taxes collected at the base value are still funded—only the additional tax revenues are used to pay the facility costs. One might argue that a second-best use of the property would also be able to generate some of those incremental tax revenues, but it is true that existing public revenues are not used for the financing. That is TIF's main objective.

For this type of financing, a base year and tax assessed value is determined. After the facility is built, any increases in tax revenues resulting from the improvement of the area are used to pay off the tax increment bond. This method captures the assessed valuation growth within a certain TIF district (a predefined area that is geographically related to the facility being built). If the area does not witness increased tax revenues, then the TIF bond may fail. That is, essentially, how tax increment financing works. Like revenue bonds, TIF bonds are riskier than GOBs.

Because the surrounding TIF district needs to see increases in property values, tax increment financing was historically used to help revitalize blighted areas within larger urban communities. Mixed-use development around the stadium is expected to increase property values and thereby help pay off the TIF financing. The risk is, of course, that property values might decline. A proposal for a new sport arena and entertainment district in Sacramento offered an option to rely on TIF. The TIF option was to include the incremental property taxes, utility taxes, sales taxes, and hotel taxes collected in the 240-acre entertainment district. Ziets (2002) states,

> The risks with this kind of a development-based financing plan are two-fold: (i) the market may not bear what is required by the developer, in which case the team may struggle to finance the development and the City may not realize sufficient taxes; and/or (ii) absent a specific requirement to develop, the hoped-for development may never materialize thus resulting in a shortfall in tax revenues. As a result, cities typically will secure any bonds backed by the incremental taxes with a general fund pledge or a more secure stream of revenues.

For AT&T Park (originally Pac Bell Park), often cited as being entirely privately financed, financing included $15 million of TIF funded through the Redevelopment Agency in San Francisco, while the rest of the stadium's cost was privately financed. This is an example of stadium construction financed without using existing tax revenues. Because of the substantial property value increases in San Francisco since construction of the stadium began, this TIF project has presented virtually zero risk.

Sales tax

Sales tax revenues are the most common source of public financing for sport facilities. Some facilities use only sales tax revenues for the public portion of financing. These have included facilities built for the Arizona Diamondbacks, Colorado Rockies (see Exhibit 9.7), Phoenix Suns, Tampa Bay Buccaneers, Phoenix Coyotes, and Minnesota Wild. A number of methods are available for using sales taxes to pay for facilities. One is to raise the sales tax rate a small amount and "pay as you go." Maricopa County, in Arizona, increased the county sales tax by 0.25% from April 1995 through November 1997, raising $238 million during the construction period. This covered most of the public financing for Bank One Ballpark (now Chase Field).

Another method is to issue government bonds and pay them off through an increase in the sales tax. In this method, the payment period is longer (and more interest is paid), but the cost each year is lower than the "pay as you go" method. Small increases in sales taxes do not impose a large burden on any one specific person or group, so strong opposition is often less likely—whether or not it is justified. For the baseball stadium built in Arlington, Texas, for the Rangers, the public financing package included $135 million in 15- and 20-year bonds. Sales tax revenues grew more quickly than anticipated, and the bonds were paid off after just ten years. A similar result occurred in Denver, where the 18-year bonds took only six years to pay off (see Exhibit 9.7). In another example, more than half of the cost of renovating Lambeau Field will have been paid for by a one-half cent

exhibit   9.7   **Sales tax funding for facility construction.**

COORS FIELD (COLORADO ROCKIES)

Denver metro area sales tax (0.1% increase)	$72,000,000	(1)
Denver metro area sales tax bond issuance (0.1% increase)	103,000,000	(2)
District investment earnings	15,000,000	(3)
Rockies equity	12,000,000	
Premium seating revenue	16,000,000	
Concessionaire fees	7,000,000	
Equipment lease proceeds	6,000,000	(4)
Total funding sources	$231,000,000	

(1) Collected during the period of construction of the facility; spans six counties.

(2) Set to be paid back over the 18-year period of the bonds. Due to growth in sales taxes collected, this was paid off after six years.

(3) The metropolitan baseball district, which owns the facility, invested $15 million.

(4) Equipment purchased by the district and leased to the team.

sales tax increase in Brown County, Wisconsin, whose proceeds are going to pay off long-term bonds.

Still another method is to fund a facility through sales taxes limited to those collected from the facility itself or from a district in the immediate vicinity. This may include a diversion of current sales taxes related to the immediate region or funding through new sales taxes that will be collected at the facility, with or without an increase in the sales tax rate. For the Seattle Seahawks' football stadium, sales taxes collected at the stadium complex are being used to pay off over $100 million in financing.

Tourism and food and beverage taxes

As voters have become more adamant in opposing large amounts of public support for sport facilities, proponents have been reducing the use of sales taxes and instead have begun to tax non-residents. **Tourism taxes** include taxes on hotel stays and rental cars, and may also include food and beverage taxes in certain districts. Under these plans, visitors to the area, not local residents (to the extent that local residents do not rent cars locally) help finance the stadium. The success at the ballot box for these types of financing mechanisms has been relatively high. However, as Baade and Matheson suggest, residents of one city will be tourists in another city, and they may then face high hotel and car rental taxes. Another drawback is that the number of tourists to a city may decline as the cost of visiting that city increases. Event planners (including those in the sport industry) are especially sensitive to hotel and rental car taxes when they are planning major, heavily attended events.

Nonetheless, these taxes are very popular and have been used to finance facilities for the Houston Astros (2% hotel tax increase and 5% rental car tax increase), Tampa Bay Rays (1% hotel tax increase), St. Louis Rams (3.5% hotel tax increase), Seattle Mariners (2% rental car tax increase), and Indianapolis Colts (3% increase in hotel taxes and 2% increase in car rental taxes), to name a few.

King County (Seattle) sold bonds supported by an increase in the food and beverage (F&B) tax of 0.5%. It was the single largest source of financing, providing $150 million for the stadium. Marion County, containing Indianapolis, raised F&B taxes by 1% and expects to generate $274.5 million to pay off debts on Lucas Oil Stadium (see Exhibit 9.8).

These taxes generally fail the benefits principle, because tourists (as well as hoteliers and car rental operators) are not necessarily the users of sport facilities. Although F&B taxes do not satisfy the benefit principle, they do typically fulfill some sense of vertical equity, in that people with higher incomes spend more on food and beverages outside of the home and, hence, pay a larger share of the taxes than people with lower incomes.

Sin taxes

Sin taxes are another type of financing source that generally receives less opposition, presumably because the items being taxed are considered socially undesirable. These taxes are regressive, because people with low incomes tend to spend a higher proportion of their income on cigarettes and alcohol, relative to those with high incomes. The taxation of cigarettes and alcohol is sometimes claimed to have a side

---

Facility funding through tourism and food and beverage taxes.   **exhibit**   **9.8**

LUCAS OIL STADIUM (INDIANAPOLIS COLTS)

Team	$50,000,000
City for termination of Colts' lease	50,000,000
Marion County F&B tax (up 1%)	274,500,000
County hotel tax (up 3%)	134,200,000
County car rental tax (up 2%)	30,500,000
Sports development tax	85,400,000
Sporting event ticket tax (up 1%)	36,600,000
Restaurant tax (up 1%)	36,600,000
Sale of Colts license plates	6,100,000
Total funding sources	$703,900,000

Note: Team will retain $121.5 million naming rights (20-year agreement).

Team retains all game day revenue and half of revenue from non-Colts events. City pays all operating and maintenance costs.

benefit of reducing smoking and drinking, but this assertion is paradoxical, because if the use of cigarettes and alcohol were to decline significantly, insufficient tax revenues would be generated to make sin taxes a feasible financing mechanism.

For construction of the baseball stadium where the Cleveland Indians play, financing included a 15-year tax on cigarettes and alcohol. Specifically, $3 per gallon was charged on liquor, 16 cents per gallon on beer, and 4.5 cents per pack of cigarettes. Given the success of sin taxes in Cleveland, nearby Akron may use a similar tax to fund a Major League Soccer stadium. These taxes remain less common than tourism taxes.

Sale of government assets

Local, regional, and state governments own a great deal of land, and at times they determine that its best use is in the hands of private industry. Some sport facilities have been partially financed through government sales of land, with the proceeds serving as a direct source of financing. Land may also be an indirect source of financing (as discussed later in the chapter).

The Charlotte Bobcats' arena was financed partially through the local government's sale of land for $50 million, and other assets for $25.8 million. Wayne County, Michigan, generated $20 million from the sale of some of its properties, to be used for the financing of Ford Field, where the Detroit Lions play.

State appropriations

Many sport facilities receive some funding from the state governments. Local residents might be more apt to back a stadium project if they know that some money is coming from the state. For instance, Miller Park received $36 million from the State of Wisconsin, $18 million each from the county and city, and additional funding from other sources (some of which were also public). The St. Louis Rams' stadium received 50% of its public financing from the State of Missouri. Similarly, the Tennessee Titans' facility received $55 million from the State of Tennessee, through general obligation bonds.

Revenues from tickets and parking

To satisfy the benefits principle, many facility financiers are turning to ticket taxes and parking revenues or taxes to help pay for construction and maintenance costs. Typically, these sources do not cover the bulk of financing, but they can make an important contribution. Many political jurisdictions (cities, townships, counties, and states) require a vote to raise taxes, but in some situations a "surcharge" does not require a vote. The economics of a tax versus a surcharge are not much different, yet the law in many cases does not require a vote for a surcharge. Facilities for the Mariners, Phillies, Pacers, Browns, Eagles, and Lightning have been partially financed through ticket taxes at the facility or general admission taxes at all local sporting events. At Reliant Stadium in Houston, fans pay a 10% ticket tax (not to exceed $2 per ticket) and a $1 ticket surcharge. In many cases, local sales taxes also apply to the purchase of tickets. For the Arizona Cardinals' football stadium, a $4.50 ticket surcharge is generating $35 million in stadium financing.

Parking taxes or surcharges function in the same way as ticket taxes. City parking revenues generated over $10 million of the $157 million cost for the St.

Pete Times Forum, home of the Tampa Bay Lightning. Reliant Stadium has a 10% parking tax. At the arena for the Minnesota Wild, game-day parking revenues are helping to pay off its $65 million bond from the City of St. Paul. At Ford Field, the local sport authority (set up to build and manage the local sport facilities) sold the rights to parking revenues to the nearby Detroit Tigers for $20 million, even though Ford Field is home to the NFL's Detroit Lions. The Tigers used the revenue for stadium funding. The Seahawks' stadium is expected to generate $4.4 million in parking tax revenues, to fund about 1% of total stadium costs.

Lotteries and gaming revenues

State-run lotteries and local gaming establishments are creative, non-sport sources of financing. The Baltimore Orioles were one of the first teams to play in a new stadium built during the latest wave of stadium financing. In 1992, the Orioles began play at Camden Yards, for which most of the construction costs were financed through lease revenue bonds and notes backed by special sport-themed state lottery tickets. The Seattle Mariners and Seahawks play in facilities that are funded partially from state lottery revenues. For Safeco Field, home of the Mariners, $50 million in bonds were secured by lottery revenue related to newly created lottery games. Public funding for the Seahawks from sport-related lottery games amounted to nearly $128 million.

The Pittsburgh Penguins flirted with moving to Kansas City but stayed in Pittsburgh because a financing deal was put in place that included approximately $7.5 million per year, for 30 years, in payments from PITG Gaming's casino income. An additional $7.5 million per year comes from the State of Pennsylvania's slot machine economic development fund.

Lottery and gaming sources of funding are generally considered regressive, failing the horizontal equity principle because people with lower incomes play the lottery or engage in gaming activities more often, and spend a higher proportion of their income or wealth in doing so than those with higher incomes. Proponents of the use of lottery and gaming revenue often note that these activities are optional.

Player income taxes

Those in favor of charging athletes of visiting teams an income tax draw a parallel to the use of non-resident taxes, such as tourism taxes, to help fund a sport facility. It seems logical that the athletes who benefit from the facility should help to fund it. Many states and cities tax the income of visiting players, usually charging between 1% and 4% of the salary earned during the athlete's time within the state or city. Most of the revenues go into the political jurisdiction's general fund. However, the City of Pittsburgh uses the revenue directly to pay off the bonds on its baseball and football stadia (PNC Park and Heinz Field). A groundswell of opposition to these taxes argues that no other visiting entertainers are taxed—only athletes in major professional sports. Because minor league athletes and those outside the "Big 4" are not necessarily taxed, this tax raises questions of fairness, although it satisfies the vertical equity principle.

A public financing proposal in 2003 in Washington D.C. included a player income tax that was projected to generate approximately $5 million per year in funding, which was to go directly to paying off the public's portion of stadium debt. The financing plan ultimately chosen did not include this tax.

Utility and business license taxes

Utility taxes are state and local taxes on energy consumed, which are collected along with customers' utility payments. General business taxes include state and local corporate income taxes and sales and use taxes collected from businesses. The Washington Nationals play in a baseball stadium that is funded partially by $14 million per year in general business taxes (collected from businesses with more than $3 million in annual revenue) and $15 million per year in utility tax revenues. For the FedEx Forum, home of the Memphis Grizzlies, financing included $30.4 million in revenues from the city's electric utility. Instead of the utility paying franchise, property, or sales taxes to the City of Memphis, Memphis Light, Gas, and Water (MLGW) provides **payments in lieu of taxes (PILOT)**. Essentially, the City is simply using some of the payments that it receives from MLGW to pay for the stadium. PILOT financing is common when the land used for a stadium does not generate property taxes (because it is owned by the government). In some cases, such as a proposal in New York City, the franchise would make some payments in lieu of property taxes.

Reallocation of existing budget

In a very few cases, cities have funded sport facilities through their existing budgets, either by reallocating budget dollars or by assuming new incremental revenues from a specific source (e.g., hotel taxes). This funding method is uncommon because the public is often not willing to reduce funding for existing government programs in order to build sport facilities. Allegheny County, Pennsylvania, partially funded new stadia for the Pittsburgh Pirates and Steelers through reallocation of its existing Regional Asset District (RAD) budget (which included local revenues from certain sales taxes). Allegheny County was successful in this approach, in part because the RAD was already funding the existing Three Rivers Stadium. The savings achieved by demolishing Three Rivers Stadium were applied to the new buildings. The same concept was used in Philadelphia, when the city funded Veterans Stadium. This approach may be appropriate in any situation where the public sector funds operating costs of the current facility. In other situations, states have simply budgeted for these projects in their general fund. Pennsylvania, Tennessee, and Ohio are examples of states that have assisted local municipalities in funding sport facilities through budget allocations or through debt as part of the state's capital budget.

Indirect sources of public financing

Indirect sources of public financing include non-cash sources (land donations, infrastructure improvements) and exemptions from payments such as property or sales taxes (i.e., tax abatements).

Land donations. The San Francisco 49ers struggled in 2008 to develop a stadium plan for a location in the San Francisco Bay Area. In June 2008, voters in the city approved an advisory measure (a non-binding measure but similar to a survey of residents) to allow a developer to use 720 acres of city-owned land for free to build a football stadium and other structures. A common misperception about arrangements such as this one is that if a city or county provides land for free to build a sport facility (whether it is given outright to the team owner or is leased), the cost is zero, because no dollars change hands. However, the actual cost to the political jurisdiction includes the opportunity cost—the lost opportunity to sell the land to a private entity at a market price. Most stadium financing plans have some form of opportunity cost, although it is rarely mentioned as part of the total cost of the facility.

Perhaps a more important type of "land donation" is the government's use of eminent domain to obtain access to land owned by private citizens. In November 2009, the New York State Court of Appeals ruled that the city could secure the land needed for the New Jersey Nets' new basketball arena in Brooklyn by forcing current residents and businesses to move and paying them a fair market value for their real estate.

Infrastructure improvements. Infrastructure improvements to accommodate new facilities—such as freeway exits, road expansions, parking lot entrances and exits, and sewer and electrical systems—are most often paid for by local and state governments (or sometimes the federal government, through special transportation grants). These costs are rarely included in the overall cost of financing a facility. One could argue that any new use of land would require some form of infrastructure improvements, so these should not be considered when facility construction is compared to other options. That would be true only if the developer would not be paying any of those costs and if the cost of infrastructure improvements would be the same for various alternative uses.

Tax abatements. Tax abatements exempt the beneficiary from paying certain taxes, such as property or sales taxes. Thus, the local government is helping to finance the stadium by *not* charging the franchise taxes that would presumably have been paid by an alternative user of the space. The City of Sandy, Utah, for example, is providing a $10 million property tax rebate to the ownership group that will build an MLS stadium there.

Most sport facilities are publicly owned and leased to the team, which exempts them from paying property taxes altogether. As discussed in Chapter 12, many states are reviewing these situations to determine whether these are actually private businesses operating in public buildings. In Florida, sport teams are now required to pay property taxes (although each county can lower the property tax payments or even reduce the assessed value of the facility). The Columbus Blue Jackets pay property taxes that amount to about half of what would normally be paid based on the county assessor's valuation of Nationwide Arena.

The Houston Texans, an NFL team, play in Reliant Stadium, whose owners receive a sales tax rebate to cover part of the cost of the stadium. The Jaguars received similar financing in Jacksonville, Florida. The Florida Marlins are also receiving a sales tax rebate, on tickets and concessions in their new facility, that is expected to provide $2 million per year that the team can put toward stadium financing.

Chapter Appendix 9.A summarizes some of the more common forms of public financing for stadia and arenas.

Calculating Public Payments for Stadium Financing

To calculate the annual payment for a general obligation bond—for instance, so that public officials and residents will understand the annual cost—we use a payment schedule table like the one for the new Minnesota Twins ballpark shown in Exhibit 9.9. This project has a relatively simple financing mechanism. Hennepin County will pay for 75% of the stadium and related infrastructure through a 0.15% sales tax

exhibit   9.9   Example payment schedule for a new Minnesota Twins ballpark.

NO	PAYMENT DATE	BEGINNING BALANCE	INTEREST	PRINCIPAL	ENDING BALANCE	CUMULATIVE INTEREST	TOTAL PERIODIC PAYMENT	PAYMENT PER RESIDENT
1	12/15/2008	$392,000,000.00	$19,521,600.00	$5,920,455.88	$386,079,544.12	$19,521,600.00	$25,442,055.88	$22.67
2	12/15/2009	386,079,544.12	19,226,761.30	6,215,294.59	379,864,249.53	38,748,361.30	25,442,055.88	22.56
3	12/15/2010	379,864,249.53	18,917,239.63	6,524,816.26	373,339,433.28	57,665,600.92	25,442,055.88	22.45
4	12/15/2011	373,339,433.28	18,592,303.78	6,849,752.11	366,489,681.17	76,257,904.70	25,442,055.88	22.34
5	12/15/2012	366,489,681.17	18,251,186.12	7,190,869.76	359,298,811.41	94,509,090.82	25,442,055.88	22.23
6	12/15/2013	359,298,811.41	17,893,080.81	7,548,975.07	351,749,836.34	112,402,171.63	25,442,055.88	22.12
7	12/15/2014	351,749,836.34	17,517,141.85	7,924,914.03	343,824,922.30	129,919,313.48	25,442,055.88	22.01
8	12/15/2015	343,824,922.30	17,122,481.13	8,319,574.75	335,505,347.55	147,041,794.61	25,442,055.88	21.90
9	12/15/2016	335,505,347.55	16,708,166.31	8,733,889.57	326,771,457.98	163,749,960.92	25,442,055.88	21.79
10	12/15/2017	326,771,457.98	16,273,218.61	9,168,837.28	317,602,620.70	180,023,179.53	25,442,055.88	21.68
11	12/15/2018	317,602,620.70	15,816,610.51	9,625,445.37	307,977,175.33	195,839,790.04	25,442,055.88	21.57
12	12/15/2019	307,977,175.33	15,337,263.33	10,104,792.55	297,872,382.78	211,177,053.37	25,442,055.88	21.46
13	12/15/2020	297,872,382.78	14,834,044.66	10,608,011.22	287,264,371.56	226,011,098.03	25,442,055.88	21.36
14	12/15/2021	287,264,371.56	14,305,765.70	11,136,290.18	276,128,081.38	240,316,863.74	25,442,055.88	21.25
15	12/15/2022	276,128,081.38	13,751,178.45	11,690,877.43	264,437,203.95	254,068,042.19	25,442,055.88	21.14
16	12/15/2023	264,437,203.95	13,168,972.76	12,273,083.13	252,164,120.82	267,237,014.94	25,442,055.88	21.04
17	12/15/2024	252,164,120.82	12,557,773.22	12,884,282.67	239,279,838.16	279,794,788.16	25,442,055.88	20.93
18	12/15/2025	239,279,838.16	11,916,135.94	13,525,919.94	225,753,918.22	291,710,924.10	25,442,055.88	20.83
19	12/15/2026	225,753,918.22	11,242,545.13	14,199,510.76	211,554,407.46	302,953,469.23	25,442,055.88	20.73
20	12/15/2027	211,554,407.46	10,535,409.49	14,906,646.39	196,647,761.07	313,488,878.72	25,442,055.88	20.62
21	12/15/2028	196,647,761.07	9,793,058.50	15,648,997.38	180,998,763.69	323,281,937.22	25,442,055.88	20.52
22	12/15/2029	180,998,763.69	9,013,738.43	16,428,317.45	164,570,446.24	332,295,675.65	25,442,055.88	20.42
23	12/15/2030	164,570,446.24	8,195,608.22	17,246,447.66	147,323,998.58	340,491,283.88	25,442,055.88	20.32
24	12/15/2031	147,323,998.58	7,336,735.13	18,105,320.75	129,218,677.82	347,828,019.01	25,442,055.88	20.22
25	12/15/2032	129,218,677.82	6,435,090.16	19,006,965.73	110,211,712.10	354,263,109.16	25,442,055.88	20.12
26	12/15/2033	110,211,712.10	5,488,543.26	19,953,512.62	90,258,199.48	359,751,652.42	25,442,055.88	20.02
27	12/15/2034	90,258,199.48	4,494,858.33	20,947,197.55	69,311,001.93	364,246,510.76	25,442,055.88	19.92
28	12/15/2035	69,311,001.93	3,451,687.90	21,990,367.99	47,320,633.94	367,698,198.65	25,442,055.88	19.82
29	12/15/2036	47,320,633.94	2,356,567.57	23,085,488.31	24,235,145.63	370,054,766.22	25,442,055.88	19.72
30	12/15/2037	24,235,145.63	1,206,910.25	24,235,145.63	0.00	371,261,676.48	25,442,055.88	19.62
							$763,261,676.48	

Notes: Population assumed to grow at an annual rate of 0.5%.

This table shows a payment schedule for a constant payment. The actual payment plan being pursued combines variable and fixed interest rates expected to average 4.98%. The average annual payment will differ from year to year but will be slightly lower than that shown in the table.

increase. Tax-free county bonds worth a total of $392 million will be sold and paid back over 30 years. The payment schedule in Exhibit 9.9 shows the annual payments on the 30-year bonds, which are paying a 4.98% interest rate. Note that the total payments (given at the bottom of the table) far exceed the original cost, because the interest is being paid over a lengthy period of time. To avoid having to pay $392 million during the construction period, the residents will pay only $25.4 million per year, but will have to do so for 30 years. The annual payments are constant, but the portion of those payments that goes toward paying off principal (as opposed to interest) increases, until the final year, when the entire project is paid off.

To make the payment schedule more meaningful, we can divide the annual payment by the population of the political jurisdiction paying for the venue, to get a sense of what it will cost per person to finance the stadium. Hennepin County has a population of 1,122,093 (estimate as of 2006). Thus, the payment per person begins at over $22 per year and decreases to under $20 per year, assuming a population growth rate of 0.5%. See the far right column in Exhibit 9.9.

PRIVATE FINANCING

A fair question to ask is: why aren't sport facilities 100% privately financed, like the buildings of other industries. As discussed above, one reason is that private investors may not be willing to build spectacular palaces that lure many high-profile events, because much of the revenue will flow to businesses outside the building. For this reason, the public has to contribute to the construction. But what is the private return on new sport facilities?

Private Return on New Facilities

As discussed at the beginning of this chapter, private returns on new sport facilities can be quite substantial. Put in terms of attendance, Coates and Humphreys (2005) show that the impact is largest in Major League Baseball, with a typical franchise selling about 2.5 million incremental tickets over the eight seasons that follow the opening of a new facility. An NFL team sells only about 138,000 additional tickets over a five-year period (the likely reason for the lower number is that most NFL teams sell out even in old stadia). In terms of return on investment, Baade shows that MLB teams earn an ROI of about 20.5% when they build new stadia. For a new football stadium for the Washington Redskins, analysis showed that the maximum private investment that would break even would be only $155 million. Anything beyond that would create a loss for the investor. To get a $500 million stadium built, the public would have to finance 70% of it.

Private Financing Sources and Techniques

The sources of private financing are unlimited, in the sense that an owner can use whatever money he or she possesses, if he or she so chooses. Billionaire owners can tap their private net wealth. However, many choose to tie the financing sources to the franchise itself, rather than to their own finances. For instance, most stadium financing packages include annual rent payments from the team to the owner of the facility. However, annual rents range from zero to a few million dollars (e.g., the Texas Rangers pay $3.5 million per year). Rents, therefore, cannot cover the entire private facility financing obligation.

Contractually obligated income

Contractually obligated income (COI) is a revenue stream that a team receives under multi-year contracts. For example, the San Francisco Giants signed luxury suite holders to five- and seven-year contracts and club seat holders to three- and five-year contracts, thus nearly guaranteeing those revenue streams. Other possibilities for COI are multi-year pouring rights sold to concessionaires, naming rights, and sponsorship. Often, it is important that the team secure these revenue streams upfront (or sign contracts with terms of five to seven years or more). These revenue sources may serve as collateral for loans. For instance, a team can pledge as collateral the revenues from naming rights, sponsorship rights, pouring or concessionaire's rights, premium seating deposits, or ticket surcharges. In 2000, the San Francisco Giants borrowed $170 million from Chase Manhattan Bank with collateral from naming rights, signage, and other COI. The team also collected charter seat license revenue of approximately $70 million.

Asset-backed securities

Instead of borrowing from a bank, a franchise may package guaranteed COI or expected revenue streams together and sell bonds based on these assets, known as **asset-backed securities (ABS)**. This technique, called **securitization,** is most often used with financial instruments that pay interest, instead of COIs or revenue streams. Because COIs provide known and consistent payments, they can be securitized in this way, as can other predictable revenue streams. Staples Center in Los Angeles was financed partially through securitization. The "security" is derived from the naming rights revenue from Staples, ten corporate founding partners' agreements, two concessions agreements, premium seat revenues, a ticket sales contract with TicketMaster, and the revenues from 101 of 160 luxury suites. The naming rights deal alone is reportedly worth $100 million over 20 years. The $315 million in bonds are taxable, pay an interest rate of 7.653%, and mature in 27 years.

PUBLIC/PRIVATE PARTNERSHIPS

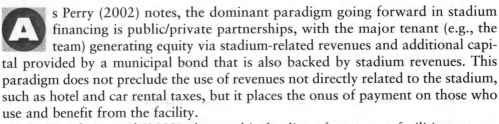s Perry (2002) notes, the dominant paradigm going forward in stadium financing is public/private partnerships, with the major tenant (e.g., the team) generating equity via stadium-related revenues and additional capital provided by a municipal bond that is also backed by stadium revenues. This paradigm does not preclude the use of revenues not directly related to the stadium, such as hotel and car rental taxes, but it places the onus of payment on those who use and benefit from the facility.

As Ziets has noted (2002), the trend in funding of new sport facilities appears to be shifting away from tax increases. Public officials are now looking to alternative sources of capital, including

- taxes generated directly from the facility, the team, players, and other facility users or vendors;

- taxes generated from redevelopment surrounding the facility; and
- special assessments in a uniquely identified sports and entertainment district.

The most compelling justification for a strategy of this type is that, in effect, the users or beneficiaries who frequent the district fund the facility over time through their use of the district. These mega–real estate projects are often developed by partnerships of public and private entities. For instance, the public entity may set up special tax districts to collect revenue to help pay for the district financing and may provide infrastructure for the area (e.g., roads, water, and electricity). The private developer might build the facility and the surrounding district, with the help of many private businesses.

This issue of who pays, along with many others, is a matter of public policy. This section discusses first the sometimes congruent but often conflicting goals of public and private parties and second the public policy issues that affect public/private partnerships related to facility financing.

Goals of Public versus Private Parties

Public and private parties in partnership focus on different goals. Franchises are concerned with league restrictions, site/design control, facility control/management, revenue control, and cash flow. Most leagues restrict the debt ratio that a team may establish. For instance, an NBA team can have at most $175 million in debt, whereas an NHL team can have debt up to half of the franchise's value (Kaplan, 2008).

The financing goals of team owners are to maximize contractually obligated income and minimize debt service payments and coverage requirements. Team owners also desire a strong voice in the design of a facility in order to maximize COI, even if they are paying a minority of the cost of construction. The revenue potential of a sport facility is affected by the number and design of luxury suites, club seats, food venues, and so forth. Often, the owner will advocate a higher total cost, in order to provide better amenities and generate better contracts for luxury seating, than the government counterpart or partner will favor.

In the past, team owners did not manage the publicly owned facilities in which their teams played. In recent decades, team owners have desired complete management of the sport facility. This allows them not only to control scheduling for their teams but also to schedule other events, such as family shows, motorcycle or monster truck events, and professional wrestling. Many leases provide for the team owner to retain most, if not all, of the revenues generated by the facility. Management of the facility and control over revenue are complementary. Team owners have done a much better job of getting the most use out of facilities than have government managers. The management of facilities is currently an issue in Japan, where local government owns and operates most buildings and there is no strong push to maximize net revenues flowing from the building.

The financing goals of government in these partnerships are to maximize the credit quality of pledged revenues, maintain debt service coverage, and maintain a reserve fund. Government agencies tasked with overseeing sport facilities also care about resource allocation, the amount of public financing required, the impact on the government's borrowing credit, the government's share in the upside of a facility (e.g., naming rights, parking, rent), and the possibility that the team may relocate if the facility is not built.

Where Do We Start? The Mayor Knows

9.E

In the early stages of a feasibility study to build a new arena for the Sacramento Kings, the mayor of Sacramento noted that the following issues had to be addressed before any type of public/private financing partnership could be determined.

1. Which sources of financing would require voter approval and which could be passed by the local government without a vote?

2. Of the possible financing sources, who would pay for them—would users of the arena pay, or local residents, or tourists, or local businesses?

3. Would the arena be paid for now or in the distant future with government bonds of 20- or 30-year terms?

4. Who would be responsible for cost overruns or financing shortfalls?

5. Who would pay the costs of selling the various revenue streams at the arena (naming rights, sponsorships, luxury suites, etc.), given that the city would own the arena, but the team would manage and operate it?

6. Between the city and the team, who would keep which revenue streams, such as parking, concessions, and naming rights?

These are some of the essential questions on which public policy analysis of stadia focuses.

The question of resource allocation is always of concern to local and regional governments. Is $200 million of the public's money better spent on a sport facility or on a new library and school? As discussed above, there may or may not be justification for spending millions of dollars from public coffers on a sport facility. Most cities limit how much outstanding debt they will take on. Public financing that is to be paid back from sources other than the general fund, such as sources related to the stadium itself (e.g., ticket taxes and parking revenues), does not typically count against a city's debt limit. Washington D.C. used revenue bonds rather than general obligation bonds to help finance the Washington Nationals' ballpark. One of the reasons for the use of revenue bonds may be that they do not count against the city's debt limit.

When the Cleveland Browns relocated to Baltimore to become the Baltimore Ravens, the City of Cleveland immediately went to the NFL with a request for an expansion team for the city, which it received a few years later. The cost to the public of building a stadium for the expansion team was approximately $200 million (another $100 million was private money). According to people familiar with the situation, to keep the Browns from moving to Baltimore would have cost approximately $190 million, notwithstanding personal issues of the owner wanting to move.

Public Policy Issues and Public/Private Partnerships

Before policy makers determine the type of financing sources to be used in a public/private partnership, they must consider some important issues in regard to financing, such as the following:

- Who will own the facility?
- Should the public financing package be put to a vote?
- What should be the payment terms?
- Who will be responsible for cost overruns?
- Who will pay the costs of and keep the revenue from future revenue streams?
- What sources of public financing can be used?

Ownership

Most likely the first question that policy makers will consider is who will own the facility: the major tenant (or other private organization) or the city, county, state, or a combination thereof? Most facilities are owned by a public entity, often a joint authority of multiple political jurisdictions. For example, the Oracle Arena in Oakland, California is owned by the Oakland–Alameda County Coliseum Authority, a joint authority of the City of Oakland and Alameda County.

Why would a public entity own a facility? The most obvious reason relates to property taxes. Public entities (i.e., cities or stadium authorities) do not pay property taxes, but private businesses do. For a $475 million stadium sitting on $25 million worth of land, a 1% property tax would cost about $5 million per year to the stadium owner. The franchise saves $5 million per year in property taxes when the city owns the stadium and leases it to the major tenant. As discussed in Chapter 12, some states are changing these laws to begin charging the major tenant a property tax. Another reason that a city might own a stadium is that it has paid most of the cost of building it and can use it for additional events. In the end, however, cities often allow the team to manage the entire facility and all of its events. An example is the new Dallas Cowboys stadium in Arlington, Texas.

Voter approval

A second important decision for policy makers is whether the public financing package should be voted upon by local residents or decided upon by politicians without a popular vote. Some sources of financing, such as raising sales taxes or hotel taxes, require voter approval in most jurisdictions, but reallocation of existing sales tax revenues often does not require voter approval. There have been instances when voters turned down a public financing package, but a version was approved outside the voting process. In Milwaukee, for instance, a statewide vote to create a sports lottery to fund a new Brewers stadium failed, so the state legislature passed a bill that raised the sales tax by 0.1% in the counties surrounding the stadium (see Exhibit 9.1). The decision to hold a public vote opens up many sources of financing, but compliance with a requirement for a public vote can be very costly. It also adds risk to the process: all of the work and effort involved in building a financing package might go for naught if the public votes no. However, if this is the will of the people, so be it.

Payment terms

A third policy decision to be made prior to choosing financing sources is whether to pay for the facility now or later. Some facilities have been paid for with a current increase in sales taxes, whose revenues pay off the facility within a few years (as in Denver and San Antonio). Many more facilities are financed through the sale of 20- or 30-year bonds paid for through sales tax revenues; but the actual payments occur over the 20- or 30-year term of the bonds. This is a fundamental decision for all sorts of public financing, not just sport-related financing. It is essentially the same as deciding whether to buy a house with cash or to take out a 30-year mortgage. The total payments will be much higher, but they will occur over a longer period of time, thus pushing most of the cost into the future.

Responsibility for cost overruns

As with many complex construction projects, the final actual cost of a stadium or arena often exceeds the expected cost. A study done in the mid-1990s of 14 facilities showed that cost overruns for stadia averaged about 73% (see Bess, 1995).

Policy makers must determine in advance who will be responsible for cost over-runs—the public entity, the franchise, or some other organization. The Mariners' new stadium cost $517 million, about $100 million over budget. The franchise paid the additional costs, thus protecting the public (see Exhibit 9.10).

Management of future revenue streams

When a new sport facility is created, many revenue streams must be initiated and managed. The sale of **naming rights**—the right to place a firm's name on a facility (a form of sponsorship)—is paramount to getting a new stadium financed and completed. Policy makers must determine who will pay the costs of selling those rights. Similarly, who will pay the costs of selling luxury suites, concessions rights, sponsorship rights, PSLs, and so forth? The overall cost of selling these revenue sources frequently runs into the millions of dollars. Additionally, when it comes time to renegotiate these deals, who will pay *those* costs?

Even more important is the question of who will keep which of the revenue streams. Although the cost of selling those assets is substantial, it is a fraction of the revenue that will flow from them. In the case of naming rights, the purchaser often pledges the payment for them as part of the financing package. As discussed in the section on private sources of financing, naming rights revenue can exceed $100 million (e.g., Philips paid $168 million in a 20-year deal). In some very complicated leases, the public entity shared a little in ticket sales (via an admissions tax) and parking (perhaps the first $500,000 after the first $1 million), or even was able to rent out the facility on some non-game days for certain events in which it would share net revenues.

More recently, cities have opted to exit the stadium management business and allow the team or a third party (such as AEG or SMG) to manage the facility in

---

exhibit 9.10   Cost overruns in stadium construction.

SAFECO FIELD (SEATTLE MARINERS)

Lottery proceeds	$50,000,000	
Team bank loans	25,000,000	
Interest income	5,000,000	
County GO bonds (0.5% F&B tax)	150,000,000	
County GO bonds (2% rental car tax)	71,000,000	
County GO bonds (0.017% state tax credit)	71,000,000	(1)
5% admission tax	25,000,000	
Personal seat licenses	20,000,000	
Team owner (covering cost overruns)	100,000,000	
Total funding sources	$517,000,000	

(1) The state has a 6.5% sales tax, of which 0.017% will be returned to the county.

exchange for a fee. Often the managing entity receives a portion of net revenues from hosting any events in the facilities, plus a minimum management fee. For example, SMG recently signed a deal to manage the Liberty Bowl stadium under which it will receive 20% of any revenues above $1.66 million (Masilak, 2008).

Financing sources

A key general question about the sources of financing, addressed earlier in this chapter, is what sources of public financing can be used and who, ultimately, will pay for those sources. Just about everyone in a community pays a little when the source is a general sales tax. On the other hand, only attendees of events at the facility pay when the source is a ticket tax. This is probably the most important fundamental factor in facility financing.

CONCLUSION

As the nominal and real costs of sport facilities continue to rise, the sources and methods of financing have become very complex and creative. Moreover, partnerships between political jurisdictions and team owners have increased, as has the public's understanding of the benefits and costs of sport facilities. What will the next wave of stadium financing bring?

CONCEPT *check*

1. How can a stadium or arena be built without putting too much financial burden on a local government?
2. How does location affect the costs of a stadium or arena project? What are the pros and cons of locating a stadium downtown versus out near a highway?
3. When the construction ends up costing more than initial projections, should the local government be responsible for paying the additional costs?
4. Of the following list of public financing sources, which ones satisfy the principles of horizontal equity, vertical equity, the benefits principle, and efficiency?

general obligation bonds	certificates of participation
revenue bonds	tax increment financing and property taxes
sales tax	tourism and food and beverage taxes
sin taxes	sale of government assets
state appropriations	ticket and parking revenues
player income taxes	lotteries and gaming revenues
land donations	reallocation of existing budget
infrastructure improvements	tax abatements

PRACTICE *problem*

Calculate the savings in total construction costs from issuing a $100 million revenue bond paying out at 7% rather than a GOB paying out at 5%, both with a 25-year maturity.

CASE analysis

Financing an NBA Arena

Devise a public financing plan for a new NBA arena in the city of Sacramento. The arena will have a total cost of $350 million, and the public will finance 60% of the construction cost. Both the City of Sacramento and Sacramento County will participate in the financing of the arena. Devise a public financing plan that utilizes at least three different sources.

CASE QUESTIONS

1. Determine the total amount that must be financed.
2. Determine which sources will be used and what changes to those sources must be made (e.g., raising hotel taxes 0.5%).
3. Determine the amount of financing that will be generated from each source. These amounts should sum to the total amount that must be financed.
4. Determine the timing: when money will be collected from each source and when it will be paid back. For instance, if a general obligation bond is used and it is paid for with an increase in hotel taxes, what is the annual payment necessary to pay it off?
5. Create a table showing the sources of financing, the total amount financed from each source, the annual payment amounts, and the time period of those payments.

APPENDIX chapter 9

9.A   Sources of financing for stadia and arenas.

League	Team	Sales tax	Hotel tax	Rental car tax	Food & beverage tax	Long-term loan	Entertainment tax	Sin tax	Parking tax	Property tax	Wage tax	Admission tax	Lottery revenues	Sewer & water revenues	Gas tax	General fund
MLB	Astros		✓	✓												
MLB	Brewers	✓	✓													✓
MLB	Cardinals					✓										
MLB	Diamondbacks	✓														
MLB	Giants									✓						
MLB	Indians							✓								
MLB	Mariners	✓		✓	✓							✓	✓			
MLB	Mets									✓						
MLB	Nationals			✓								✓				
MLB	Orioles												✓			
MLB	Padres		✓													
MLB	Phillies			✓								✓				✓
MLB	Pirates		✓						✓		✓					
MLB	Rangers	✓														
MLB	Reds	✓														✓
MLB	Rockies	✓														
MLB	Tigers		✓	✓												✓
MLB	Twins	✓														
MLB	White Sox		✓													✓
MLB	Yankees								✓	✓						
NBA	Bobcats		✓			✓										

League	Team	Sales tax	Hotel tax	Rental car tax	Food & beverage tax	Long-term loan	Entertainment tax	Sin tax	Parking tax	Property tax	Wage tax	Admission tax	Lottery revenues	Sewer & water revenues	Gas tax	General fund
NBA	Cavaliers							✓								
NBA	Grizzlies															✓
NBA	Hawks			✓												
NBA	Heat		✓													
NBA	Magic		✓	✓											✓	
NBA	Mavericks		✓	✓												
NBA	Pacers	✓	✓	✓	✓			✓				✓				
NBA	Rockets		✓	✓												
NBA	Spurs		✓	✓												
NBA	Suns	✓														
NBA	Thunder	✓														
NBA	Timberwolves						✓		✓	✓						
NFL	Bengals	✓														✓
NFL	Broncos	✓														
NFL	Browns			✓					✓			✓				
NFL	Buccaneers	✓														
NFL	Cardinals	✓									✓					
NFL	Colts				✓											
NFL	Cowboys	✓	✓	✓												
NFL	Eagles			✓								✓				
NFL	Falcons		✓													
NFL	Jaguars	✓	✓													
NFL	Lions		✓	✓												✓
NFL	Packers	✓														
NFL	Rams		✓													✓
NFL	Ravens												✓			
NFL	Seahawks	✓	✓	✓									✓			
NFL	Steelers	✓	✓													✓
NFL	Texans		✓	✓												
NFL	Titans													✓		✓
NHL	Coyotes	✓								✓						
NHL	Hurricanes		✓													
NHL	Lightning	✓	✓	✓	✓				✓			✓				✓
NHL	Panthers	✓	✓													
NHL	Predators															✓
NHL	Sabres															✓
NHL	Sharks															✓
NHL	Stars		✓	✓												
NHL	Thrashers			✓												
NHL	Wild	✓														

Source: Goal Group estimates, Mark Nagel.

references

Baade, R.A. (2003). Evaluating subsidies for professional sports in the united states and Europe: A public-sector primer. *Oxford Review of Economic Policy, 19*(4), 585–597.

Baade, R.A., & Matheson, V. (2006). Have public finance principles been shut out in financing new stadiums for the NFL? *Public Finance and Management, 6*(3), 284–320.

Bess, P. (April 2, 1995). Coors Field and the state of the Art. *Denver Post.*

Brown, M., Nagel, M., McEvoy, C., & Rascher, D. (2004). Revenue and wealth maximization in the National Football League: The impact of stadia. *Sport Marketing Quarterly, 13*(4), 227–235.

Brown, M., Rascher, D., & Ward, W. (2006). The use of public funds for private benefit: An examination of the relationship between public stadium funding and ticket prices in the National Football League. *International Journal of Sport Finance, 1*(2), 109–118.

Coates, D., & Humphreys, B.R. (July 2005). Novelty effects of new facilities on attendance at professional sporting events. *Contemporary Economic Policy, 23*(3).

Crompton, J., Howard, D., & Var, T. (2003). Financing major league facilities: Status, evolution, and conflicting forces. *Journal of Sport Management, 17*(2), 156–184.

Kaplan, D. (March 17, 2008). Court filing: NFL carrying $9B of debt. *SportsBusiness Journal, 1.*

Keating, R. (April 5, 1999). Sports pork: The costly relationship between Major League sports and government. *Policy Analysis, 339,* 1–33.

Long, J.G. (May 2005). Full count: The real cost of public funding for major league sports facilities. *Journal of Sports Economics.*

Masilak, J. (June 18, 2008). SMG may run Liberty Bowl: City panel OKs hiring consultant to manage stadium. *Memphis Commercial Appeal.*

Owen, J. (2006). The intangible benefits of sports teams. *Public Finance and Management 6*(3), 321–345.

Perry, C. (May 2002). The cheap seats. *Project Finance.*

Sanderson, A. (1999). In defense of new sports stadiums, ballparks, and arenas. *Marquette Sports Law Journal,* 10.

Siegfried, J., & Zimbalist, A. (2000). The economics of sports facilities and their communities. *The Journal of Economic Perspectives 14*(3).

Ziets, M. (2002). Analysis of a new sports and entertainment district in Sacramento. Goal Group L.L.C., SportsEconomics, and Keyser Marston Associates.

Zimbalist, A. (September 18, 2006). Leagues' power, consumers' attitude fuel resurgence of facility financing. *SportsBusiness Journal.*

10 Valuation

arms' length

asset-based approach

capital structure

capitalization rate

controlling interest

cost approach

discounted cash flow (DCF)

discount factor

fair market value

fiduciary duty

income approach

market approach

marketability

mid-year convention

minority discount

price-to-revenue ratio

related-party transaction

residual value

synergistic premium

transfer pricing

valuation date

KEY CONCEPTS

Introduction

This chapter will discuss the general approaches and specific techniques for valuing an enterprise or asset. An *asset* is any item of economic value. Examples include cash, securities, inventory, equipment, property, and intellectual property. An *enterprise* is generally considered to be a legal entity, association, business, corporation or the like, or a unit of an organization. Enterprises often hold many assets. Determining the value of individual assets or of an enterprise as a whole is the job of an appraiser or valuation analyst.

It is often easier to value an entire business than a portion of a business, such as a brand or the name of a sports team. One reason for this is that a successful organization creates complementarities or synergies among its assets, which increase the value of the business beyond the sum of the values of the individual assets. For instance, a hockey team without a compelling name, logo, and so forth has a certain value. A name and a logo, although they may be very compelling, have very small values separate from a team. Putting the name and logo together with the team increases the value of the combined entity more than the sum of the individual values. Attempting to value the name and logo is very difficult, because revenues that flow from the name and logo are not easy to separate from revenues that flow from the team itself (whose games create fans who purchase logoed products). This obvious example shows that it is easier to value an entire franchise, using its total revenues, than to try to value a portion of the franchise.

The valuation of assets is a common task in sport finance. Consider the following scenarios:

- A person may wish to purchase a sport franchise. How much should he or she pay for the franchise? At what price should the seller be willing to sell?

- A corporation may be interested in sponsoring a sport organization by paying a fee to place its name on a facility or on signage within the facility. How much should the company pay for this form of marketing? What price should the facility owners charge for the naming rights? This type of valuation is known as *sponsorship valuation.* It is a fundamental aspect of sport marketing, especially for corporations—such as Coca-Cola or Anheuser-Busch—that regularly spend in excess of $100 million annually on sport sponsorships.

- A professional golfer may be interested in receiving endorsement income in exchange for wearing clothing or golf shoes, using clubs, or carrying a golf bag that represents a corporation. How much can the golfer charge for the endorsement? Valuation techniques can help her determine a fair endorsement value.

In sport, as in other industries, it is extremely important to understand the context of a valuation. Most financial valuation tasks require a clear description of the industry in which the subject enterprise participates and the future expectations for the industry. For example, let's consider the context of Major League Soccer. An important first step in understanding this context would be to determine where the league is headed. A few years ago, the league's expansion plans included the goal of having 16 teams by 2010 (up from 12 in 2006). Attendance in recent years has been stable. New soccer-specific stadia are being built that will enhance each team's revenues. MLS's sponsorship and media deals have grown recently and are expected to continue to grow. Soccer viewership is up in the United States, and the game is played by more American kids than just about any other sport. Next, knowing how an entity is organized is also an important aspect of its context. MLS is organized as a single entity, meaning that it is a single business or one company. (This structure has been successfully defended in court.) A person who wants to run an MLS team invests in the league as opposed to an individual team, and the league assigns the operation of a team. This method helps control costs, especially player costs. This is just a snippet of what an analyst would consider in order to understand the context of a valuation.

The context is important because valuation is forward looking. Understanding where the business is headed is actually more important than understanding where it came from. However, aside from plans, expectations, and hopes, the information that is available is necessarily historical: we look into the future by looking backward through a rearview mirror.

Valuation is part science and part art. The result is an estimate of the true underlying value. A valuation is always uncertain, with the uncertainty arising both from the asset being valued and from the valuation methodology.

We will begin this chapter by discussing the common standards of value and the adjustments made to valuations for marketability and controlling interest (defined below). Then we will present three important approaches to valuation. When valuing any asset, it is important to consider multiple valuation approaches. If more than one approach can be used, then the multiple findings can be compared to arrive at a final estimate of value.

FAIR MARKET VALUE

 final determination of value depends on the standard of value being used. A widely used standard of valuation is **fair market value**—the net price for an asset that would result in a transaction between a willing buyer and a willing seller, neither of whom is under compulsion to buy or sell, both having reasonable knowledge of the relevant facts, and the two parties being at arms' length. A *willing seller* is one who is not being forced to sell the asset. If a person files for bankruptcy and is forced to sell an ownership interest in a local sporting goods store, this is not a willing seller, but a forced seller. Being at **arms' length** means that the buyer and seller (whether they are individuals, businesses, or estates) are not "related" in any way. This means that

- they have no familial relationship,
- neither party is a subsidiary of the other,
- neither party has an ownership interest in the other, and
- the parties have no financial relationship.

If any of these statements are not true, then the price of the transaction might not be at fair market value. However, they *could* choose to determine the fair market value and use that price for the transaction. Thus, one could show that even though the two entities are not at arms' length, they chose a price as if they were.

ADJUSTMENTS TO VALUE

Once the value of a business has been determined, certain adjustments may be required to arrive at the appropriate value of a specific ownership interest in the business. The two most common adjustments relate to whether the ownership interest effectively controls the business (**controlling interest**) and whether the ownership interest is freely marketable (**marketability** or liquidity).

A third type of adjustment is necessary if the business will be purchased for strategic or synergistic reasons. In this case, the purchaser might pay more for it than would someone purchasing it for stand-alone financial reasons. As an example, suppose that a regional brewery purchased an MLB team. One reason for the purchase might be that the brewery would be able to sell beer at the stadium during games. The brewery might be willing to pay a higher price than another investor would because of this synergistic tie with its core business. The incremental or added price is sometimes called the **synergistic premium**. The adjustments for controlling interest, marketability, and synergy will be discussed below.

Controlling Interest

A controlling interest is an ownership interest that effectively controls the business. The necessary elements of control must be in place. The elements of control include

- choosing management and their compensation and perquisites,
- acquiring or liquidating assets,
- setting dividend policies, and
- controlling company strategy and direction.

To understand the value of control, it is helpful to review the basic principles of corporate governance. The stockholders of a corporation do not directly manage the corporation's affairs; instead, they elect directors who are charged with this responsibility. The majority stockholder controls the corporation by controlling the board of directors. Only if the majority shareholder happens to run the business along with owning a share in it does that shareholder have direct control instead of indirect control. The ability to control the board of directors offers a number of benefits to a majority stockholder. For example, he can cause the corporation to employ himself or family members. Control of the corporation provides a higher degree of job security for the controlling stockholder or family members than is normally available in the employment market.

Thus, an individual who owns a majority of stock normally will control the board of directors and, therefore, control selection of management, dividend distribution policy, and his or her own employment. For a sport team, a controlling interest allows an owner to choose the general manager, coaches, and even players. It also allows the owner to control ticket prices, team colors, the team name, logos, and perhaps even location. An investor without controlling interest would not possess these elements of control.

A **minority discount** is an adjustment to the value of a share because it is not controlling. A non-controlling interest is also termed a minority interest. The key to identifying a controlling versus a minority interest is whether the owner possesses the elements of control listed above. In certain situations, a shareholder may possess these elements of control even though the interest is less than 50% of the voting stock.

As you might expect, a controlling interest in a business is worth more than a non-controlling interest on a per-share basis. In other words, an investor might pay $10 per share to buy into a business without gaining controlling interest. Another investor might be willing to pay $18 per share to buy into that same business if she thereby gained control of the business. If the seller understands this and if there are enough bidders, the fair market value of the controlling interest will be higher than the non-controlling interest.

Prior to performing an appraisal (another common term for valuation), it is necessary to evaluate the facts and circumstances of the situation to determine whether the asset will provide effective control. The conclusion from the analysis must reflect the appropriate standard of value. For example, if the valuation technique that is used gives a conclusion based on a non-controlling interest, then, if the transaction is for a controlling interest, a controlling interest premium (also called a control premium) may be required. If on the other hand, the valuation technique gives a conclusion based on a controlling interest, but the asset being valued is not a controlling interest, then the analyst must make an adjustment downward (a minority discount) to reflect the non-controlling interest.

Estimating a non-controlling interest discount

The minority discount is the difference in the price that one would pay to purchase a non-controlling interest (typically a small ownership stake) versus a controlling interest in a business. The prices of stocks listed on stock exchanges include a minority discount, because these are prices that individuals have paid to purchase shares without acquiring control.

When estimating the appropriate discount for a minority or non-controlling interest, it is important to specify the aspects of control that are not available to the minority block of owners. (If there is nothing different about being a minority shareholder versus a majority shareholder, then control is worth nothing.) The following are a few important general principles:

- Valuation of a minority interest discount is highly dependent on the specific circumstances.

- Fiduciary duties reduce the value of control. Here, **fiduciary duty** means the responsibility of management to act in the best interests of all shareholders. For example, a majority owner has a duty not to keep an unfair portion of cash flow (e.g., through overpaying herself in her role as manager or expensing items to the company that are not directly related to the business), compared to what goes to a minority shareholder. In modern corporations, ownership and control do not necessarily go together, and fiduciary duties ensure that those who do have control act in the interests of the owners.

- If the distribution of cash flows is based on ownership percentages, the valuation of control should be reduced.

- A significant minority interest may possess some aspects of control.

- A minority interest that is expected to become a controlling interest at some point in time has elements of control.

SIDEBAR

Measuring Controlling and Minority Interest Stock Prices   10.A

In 2002, the Boston Celtics were publicly traded (the ticker symbol was BOS), meaning that the team's shares were available to the general public to buy and sell. On September 26, 2002, the closing price was $10.60 for one share of BOS. On the next day, it was announced that Lake Carnegie LLC would purchase a controlling interest in the team. The NYSE halted trading in the stock.* Trading resumed nearly two weeks later (on October 9, 2002) at a price of $28. A few months later (December 31, 2002), the Lake Carnegie transaction was completed, with a final price listed on the stock exchange of $27.50. The non-controlling price (or unaffected price, as it is also known) was $10.60, and the controlling interest price was $27.50. Thus, the controlling interest premium was

$$\frac{\$27.50}{\$10.60} = 159.43\%^\dagger$$

---

*Although it is rare, stock exchanges sometimes prevent trading in certain companies for part of a day or more if there are irregularities with the financials of the company or if significant information about the company is unclear. In addition, stock trading that is automatically done by computers (program trading) can be halted if the market indexes move up or down too much.

†If any shareholders knew or speculated about the acquisition prior to the public announcement, the stock price might have crept up in the days or weeks prior to the announcement. To measure the unaffected price, we must find a price where no knowledge about the announcement was incorporated into the stock price.

Estimating controlling interest premiums

When the valuation approach results in a valuation based on a non-controlling interest, the analyst may need to estimate the value of a controlling interest. The following methods provide information for determining the incremental value of control.

Controlling/non-controlling changes in ownership. Perhaps the most direct evidence for the value of control would be changes in ownership that involve both controlling and minority interests at about the same time. Given the prices of these transactions, the analyst could determine the fair market value of the price of one share for a minority interest and for a controlling interest. The equation for controlling interest premium (CP) is

$$CP = ((\text{price paid for control/price paid for minority interest}) - 1)100\%$$

If the price in the minority interest transaction was $10 per share and in the controlling interest transaction was $18 per share, then the control premium would be 80%.

The minority discount is given by

$$\text{minority discount} = \frac{CP}{100 + CP}$$

Thus, for the example above, the minority discount is

$$\frac{80\%}{100 + 80\%} = 44.4\%$$

If the analyst does not have the necessary information on recent transactions in the subject company, an alternative is to discover similar businesses for which the control premium (or the minority discount) is known. Suppose the analyst needs to know the control premium for a sport team. One source of information is the stock market, where the price per share for minority interests in similar companies is provided on a second by second basis.

Sidebar 10.A provided an example of measuring the minority interest stock price and the controlling interest stock price.

When we compare stock prices on different dates, we must keep in mind the possibility that the stock market in general could change substantially between the two dates and that the difference in the stock prices reflects, at least in part, general changes in the market (and economy) instead of a control premium. For the Boston Celtics purchase, it turns out that the S&P 500 did not change much over the time period, so the net control premium would be about the same as the initial estimate. (Recall that the S&P 500 is simply the aggregation of 500 stocks into an index that S&P deems to be reflective of the stock market in general. We can study the S&P 500 and apply the conclusions to the stock market as a whole.) To account for general movement in the stock market between the unaffected price date and the transaction price date, we discount the premium by the growth in the S&P 500 over the same time period. The final adjusted controlling interest premium is 154.80%. Exhibit 10.1 shows that the announcement of the controlling interest transaction caused a substantial increase in the stock price.

The Cleveland Indians, a publicly traded company in the late 1990s, provide another example. On May 12, 1999, the stock traded at $9.94. The next day,

Effect on a stock price of announcing a controlling interest transaction. **exhibit** **10.1**

Boston Celtics Stock
March 2002–December 2002

12/31/02 Stock delisted: $27.50

10/9/02 Trading resumes: $28.00

9/27/02 Intended sale announced: $11.35 (trading halted)

9/26/02 Day before sale announced: $10.60

Richard Jacobs announced that he intended to sell his controlling interest in the team (although no specific buyer was named at the time). At the end of the day, the stock price had risen to $16.25. On November 4 of that year, Lawrence Dolan announced his intention to purchase the team. The stock price went up to $20.63. The transaction was completed on February 15, 2000, with the stock price at $22.56. Given that the unaffected price is $9.94, the controlling interest premium in the Cleveland Indians purchase was 127.04%. When we adjust for movement in the S&P 500 over the same time period, the controlling interest premium becomes 123.5%. The control premium is confirmed in Exhibit 10.2.

The examples described above are two of the few cases in which we can calculate a controlling interest premium in the sale of a sport business, because these teams were publicly traded rather than privately held corporations. Obviously, among sports apparel and sporting goods companies we can find many examples of publicly traded companies. For instance, in August 2005, adidas-Salomon offered to buy Reebok for $59 per share, a jump of 34% over Reebok's share price just prior to the announcement. The deal closed at the end of January 2006 at the same price of $59 per share. Thus, the control premium was 34%, assuming Reebok's price prior to the announcement did not reflect any knowledge of the possible takeover.

In fact, for the Boston Celtics and Cleveland Indians purchases, the control premium was much higher than is typical for companies in other industries (e.g., Reebok's control premium of 34%). It is not surprising that sport franchises would have high control premiums for reasons discussed next.

Mergerstat/Shannon Pratt's Control Premium Study. To determine control premiums, we can refer to a database of control premium estimates compiled by the com-

exhibit   10.2   Effect on a stock price of announcing a controlling interest transaction.

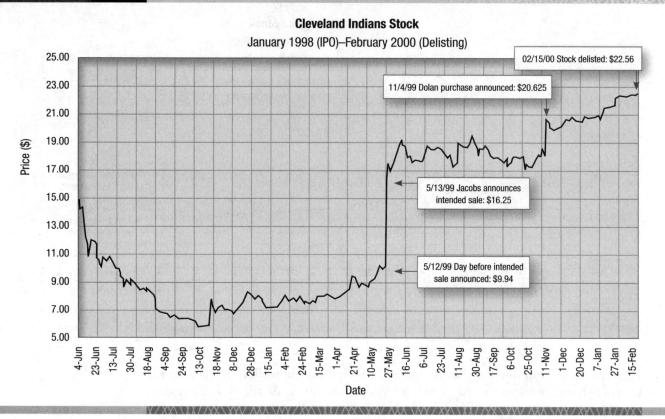

Cleveland Indians Stock
January 1998 (IPO)–February 2000 (Delisting)

02/15/00 Stock delisted: $22.56

11/4/99 Dolan purchase announced: $20.625

5/13/99 Jacobs announces intended sale: $16.25

5/12/99 Day before intended sale announced: $9.94

pany Mergerstat, along with the renowned appraiser Shannon Pratt, aptly named the Mergerstat/Shannon Pratt's Control Premium Study (CPS for short). For the Amusement and Recreation Services industry (SIC 79), the CPS shows a control premium for 2000–2005 of 55.3%, much higher, on average, than for other industries.* For the period 2003–2005, the average control premium across all industries in the study (including international transactions) was 29%. The CPS database includes information for subsets of SIC 79, such as SIC 7941 (Professional Sports Clubs and Promoters). This code contains, for example, a transaction involving the holding company that owns the Florida Panthers hockey franchise.

Bona fide offers. Another source of information on control premiums, or asset valuation in general, is bona fide offers on sport-related businesses. A remarkable and rare example was an offer in 2005 to purchase an entire major professional sport league. On March 2, 2005, Game Plan, LLC and Bain & Company offered $3.5 billion to purchase the entire NHL. This figure later rose to $4.3 billion (Eichelberger, 2006). A few weeks earlier, on February 16, 2005, the NHL season had been cancelled, and

---

*The U.S. government created the SIC coding system to classify businesses in categories assigned numerical codes. Although it is still widely used, recently it has been supplanted by the North American Industry Classification System (NAICS) discussed in Chapter 1.

uncertainty about the future of the NHL was very high. During the time between the cancellation of the season and the Game Plan/Bain offer, the Anaheim Mighty Ducks were sold to Henry Samueli for $70 million, substantially below the $108 million pre-lockout value that *Forbes* placed on the team. It is understandable that in a time of high uncertainty about the future of the league, the price for a franchise would decrease. These pieces of information provide some evidence as to the controlling interest premium of the NHL. We have a transaction for one team and an offer to buy the entire league during the same time period. Information about the future of the league was likely similar across these two situations. We can calculate a discount on the value of the Mighty Ducks due to the lockout and extrapolate that value to all NHL teams. The result is a league value of $3.176 billion. (The lockout discount is simply the transaction price of $70 million divided by *Forbes'* estimate of $108 million.) The Game Plan/Bain offer of $4.3 billion for control of the league, during this time of uncertainty, establishes a controlling interest premium of 35.4% (4.3/3.176 − 1). This is a lower bound, because the NHL owners did not accept that offer. A sale of the NHL would have required an offer higher than $4.3 billion; hence, the actual control premium would have been higher.

In this example, a bona fide offer provided some evidence about the value and control premium of the NHL. This example, however, took place during a period of high uncertainty, so although it provides information about the value of league control, we probably do not have reasonable knowledge of the facts, given that the future of the league was highly uncertain.

Value of the control premium in sport versus other industries. The control premium is higher in sport than in other industries because there are many reasons to own a sport franchise above and beyond annual operating profits. Besides profits, ownership of a sport team can provide

- benefit as a consumption good (meaning that the owner enjoys the role of operating the team),
- associated rights or income streams,
- synergies with the owner's other businesses or assets,
- shelters from federal income tax,
- profit taking from the expense side (e.g., paying oneself an inflated salary or lawfully charging parts of one's personal life on the company's books), and
- league revenue sharing and future expansion fees.

As Randy Vataha has stated, "In non-sports businesses, the control premium is generally a function of operational control and does not include the notoriety factor that can add significant value to the control premium of a professional sports team" (Rascher, 2006). An owner has authority over who coaches the team, who plays on the team, the style of offense and defense, the type of entertainment provided at home games, and so forth. As a result, for many people, control of the management and decision making for a sport team would be far more exciting than, say, controlling an iron-ore extraction company.

Researchers have studied whether "sportsman" owners exist in professional sport. A "sportsman" owner is an owner who purchases and manages a team mostly for its consumption benefits (i.e., the enjoyment of winning games and operating a team) instead of its investment benefits. According to Stefan Késenne, analysis of soccer clubs in Europe shows that some are not managed under a pure profit maximization objective; management includes the desire to win (separate from its effects on profitability) in the decision process (Késenne, 2006). As another example, the major reason the NHL did not accept the Game Plan/Bain offer was that a number of owners did not want to sell at any price. They liked owning a hockey franchise. Economist Rod Fort finds that "the portion of ownership value not associated with annual operations appears to be significant" (Fort, 2006). Explaining why he purchased the Boston Celtics along with Wycliffe Grousbeck, Stephen Pagliuca said, "We both viewed the Celtics as a community asset, a labor of love, really, not as an investment for investors" (Shanahan, 2004).

Another reason to own a sport franchise, beyond direct net cash flow and enjoyment, is that team ownership may bring associated rights or income streams. For example, team owners in most sport leagues have complete or nearly complete operating rights to the facilities in which their teams play. Thus, owning a team might provide income through the facility operation itself. Wayne Huizenga owned the Florida Marlins and the stadium in which the team played. He earned revenues from premium seating, naming rights, parking, signage, and merchandise through the stadium company, not the team—yet without the team, the stadium would not have provided these revenue sources (Zimbalist, 1998). This is a typical example of a **related-party transaction,** a transaction between two businesses that have some form of pre-existing relationship (more generally defined as **transfer pricing,** the pricing of assets transferred within an organization).

Similarly, an owner's other businesses may benefit. For instance, George Steinbrenner, owner of the New York Yankees, created YES, a regional sports network, reportedly worth $850 million. Rupert Murdoch claims that his ownership of the Dodgers prevented Disney from creating a regional sports network in Southern California, and that alone was worth his investment in the team (Zimbalist, 2003). The Atlanta Braves were once owned by Ted Turner, who also owned the Braves' media company, TBS. Reportedly, the media fees paid to the Braves were zero.

Another reason for ownership is that management salaries and payments, an expense item on the franchise's income statement, often go to the owner—who is also an executive of the team. Franchise ownership can also provide shelters from federal taxes through vehicles such as the roster depreciation allowance. The IRS allows the full purchase price of a team to be allocated to player contracts over 15 years. The contracts are considered depreciable assets for tax purposes (Brunner, 2006).

Synergistic Premium

When we calculate a control premium, we must be very careful to account for **synergistic premiums**—amounts that a buyer might pay over the control premium for reasons of strategy or synergy. The concept of control relates to making decisions regarding the business, such as the direction of the firm, marketing, compensation, and so forth. Often, however, buyers acquire companies for strategic or synergistic reasons (such as a regional brewery purchasing a sport team). Synergistic relationships are often revealed in related-party transactions and transfer pricing.

Where synergies exist, the purchase price may include a synergistic premium. A brewery might pay a price that is higher than the current per-share price for a franchise, not just because it wants control of the franchise but because it also desires the synergy of selling and promoting its beer at the games. The 34% premium that adidas paid to Reebok not only gives adidas control of Reebok, but also—as adidas has stated to its shareholders and the public—offers many synergies for adidas. For instance, adidas' ties and distribution network in Europe can help Reebok sell there (as is the case for Reebok's ties in the United States). Reebok is a sales-driven company, while adidas focuses on technology and performance. Combining these two strengths will enhance the offerings of both brands. Further, the combined size of the business will enable both adidas and Reebok to get better terms from retailers. The 34% premium that adidas paid likely includes both a control premium and a synergistic premium. Separating these is very difficult.

On the other hand, there are not likely to be any substantial synergistic reasons for the purchases of the Indians, Celtics, or NHL. In a recent study, Andrew Zimbalist (2003) discusses synergistic ownerships in MLB. He finds these relationships for approximately half of the teams in MLB, but not for the Cleveland Indians. The press coverage regarding the Celtics purchase does not mention any synergistic reasons (although some may exist). The offer for the NHL by consulting and finance companies does not suggest any obvious synergistic benefits. Thus, we can assume that the control premium for these transactions did not have a component for synergies.

Marketability Discount

Sometimes we value an equity interest in a closely held business based on observations of transactions in a publicly traded stock, such as price-to-earnings or other multiples. In these cases we must apply a *marketability discount,* also known as liquidity discount, because the sale of stock in publicly traded companies is easier than that of privately held (closely held) companies. The marketability discount, therefore, is based on the premise that an ownership interest that is readily marketable is worth more than an interest that is not readily marketable. This premise is justified because the owner of an interest in a closely held company cannot sell shares in the public market to achieve liquidity.

If, on the other hand, we estimate the value of a non-marketable asset by reference to appraisals of or transactions in similarly non-marketable assets, no marketability adjustment is necessary. For example, a real estate appraiser could estimate the value of a building by reference to recent sales of similar buildings in similar locations. All of the buildings would have similar relative marketability, and no marketability discount would be needed.

Generally, in a situation involving a controlling interest, any marketability discount is greatly reduced. This is the case because the owner of a controlling interest can market the company without any impediment—the only consideration is the cost of doing so. In addition, a controlling interest generally will be easier to market than a minority interest in a closely held stock.

Information on liquidity discounts can be found in *Valuing a Business: The Analysis and Appraisal of Closely Held Companies* (Pratt, Reilly, & Schweihs, 2000). According to this book, two comprehensive studies of liquidity discounts (conducted by Emory and Willamette Management Associates) covering 1975–1995 show liquidity discounts ranging to just above 40%. The median value for liquidity discounts allowed by the courts has been about 20%.

APPROACHES TO VALUING AN ASSET

The adjustments for controlling interest, marketability, and synergistic purchases discussed previously are made after a baseline valuation has been determined. The remainder of this chapter discusses various approaches to making the baseline valuation.

The many methods for valuing an asset, a business, or an interest or equity in a business may be categorized into the following three approaches. The **market approach** relies on prices that similar assets sell for in the marketplace. To account for differences across the assets being compared, such methods use financial ratios, such as price-to-ticket revenue, price-to-revenue, or price-to-earnings. Under the **income approach,** income or cash flow serves as the basis for the value of the business or asset. For the **cost** or **asset-based approach,** we determine what it would cost to recreate the business or asset.

Some businesses or assets lend themselves to certain valuation approaches more readily, whereas others can be valued with all three approaches. As we will see below, sport franchises are best valued under the market approach. On the other hand, a golf course can be valued with all three approaches. (What are other, similar golf courses selling for? What income is the golf course generating through greens fees, etc.? What would it cost to build a similar golf course?)

The valuation of sponsorships is an important and growing concern in sport. The methods most commonly used today are based on the market approach (what are similar sponsorships selling for?), but these are less than satisfying because the "similar" sponsorships may be under- or over-priced in terms of their true underlying value. Alternatively, some analyses measure the exposure (the number of people seeing the sponsor's ad or signage) and determine what it would cost to achieve the same exposure using some other form of media (sometimes called *media equivalency*). Ultimately, though, one wants to understand how a sponsorship leads to sales of the sponsoring company's products. Thus, the income approach would make the most sense. However, it is difficult to link a sponsorship directly to sales, because many other pieces of the marketing mix occur concurrently with the sponsorship, and because external factors (such as competitors' actions) and the economy in general affect sales as well. Regardless of whether you are valuing a golf course or a sponsorship, it is appropriate to review many possible methods for valuing the business, unless you are time- or budget-constrained.

Market Approach

Under one type of market approach, often called the *market transactions* approach, we determine the value of a company by reference to the value of comparable firms that have been sold within a reasonably recent period of time, with appropriate adjustments for the time value of money (see Chapter 4). The comparable firms may include closely held corporations, publicly traded firms, divisions or subsidiaries of larger firms, and so forth. Additionally, transactions involving some of the ownership or equity of the subject firm itself can provide excellent evidence as to its value. For instance, if the entire company was sold two years ago, this would provide some evidence for its value today. If one of the owners sold her 5% stake in the business nine months ago, that would also provide useful valuation information.

The choice of comparable firms is the first step in the process, and an important one. It may be necessary to make adjustments reflecting the differences between the comparable firms and the subject company. By comparing transaction price-to-revenue ratios or transaction price-to-earnings ratios (discussed later in this chapter), we can establish a basis for applying information about one firm to another. For valuation of sport franchises, it is also common to examine differences in attendance (price-to-ticket revenues) across comparables, the quality of the stadium and the terms of the team's lease, whether a new facility is in the works, and the status of future television and other media revenues.

Another type of market approach, similar to the market transactions approach, is often called the *market multiples* approach. This approach is based on the premise that the value of the business enterprise depends on what investors in a competitive market actually pay to own equity or shares of stock in similar companies. The first step is to select a sample of firms that are comparable to the subject firm. These are typically selected from companies that are traded on organized capital market exchanges (for example, the NYSE, American Stock Exchange, NASDAQ, and over-the-counter market). It is possible, however, to use closely held businesses and their information, assuming that the information is accessible and reliable. In the next step, we perform a financial analysis to select and apply appropriate multiples (for example, price-to-earnings ratio) to estimate the value of the subject company. The resulting estimate represents the fair market value of the subject company.

It is important to realize that market pricing multiples among comparable firms will vary depending on differences in expected growth rates, risk, and capital structure. These factors can vary across businesses in the same industry for many reasons. For instance, a firm with a new patent in place or a new line of products can expect higher growth rates than a firm without new products or patents. A firm with higher volatility in its quarterly earnings is a riskier business than one with stable earnings, and the price of a share of the riskier firm will likely be lower to reflect that risk. A firm's **capital structure** (amount of debt and equity) can affect its returns to shareholders and, in turn, its stock price and valuation.

Sometimes, a large sample of comparable firms is available, and we can employ statistical analyses to determine how observed market multiples correspond to fundamental attributes of the companies in the sample. For example, statistical analysis may reveal a relationship between price-to-sales ratio and gross margin. Then, we can use the statistical relationship to select the multiple for use in valuing the subject firm. The market multiples for a comparable firm may be unusually high or low due to transitory changes in the firm's operating performance. For example, if a comparable firm has temporarily low earnings or stock price, we must account for that in the analysis and choose the appropriate dates on which to compare the firms.

An important difference between the market transactions approach and the market multiples approach is that whereas the market multiples observed for publicly traded securities provide a value of the subject company's equity on a minority-interest basis (because the observed stock prices reflect transactions in minority interests), the market transactions approach provides an estimate of value to a control buyer. Observed prices in the market transactions approach will include premiums reflecting expected benefits to a buyer who seeks to benefit from synergies or better utilization of assets.

Let's put the market approach into practice and consider the various methods within this approach for measuring the value of a business: the price-to-ticket revenue ratio, price-to-revenue ratio, price-to-earnings ratio, and equity shares sold. For the purpose of this discussion, Major League Soccer will provide an example. If we wish to determine the value of MLS on June 30, 2006, we could use the market approach as a starting point. Recall that under this approach, we refer to the value of comparable firms or assets. To find a value for MLS, we could use the value of one team as a basis for valuing the other teams, and then we could determine how to value the activities of the league office itself and any other non-team assets.

In March 2006, Red Bull GmbH, a maker of energy drinks, purchased the operating interests of the MetroStars from Anschutz Entertainment Group (AEG) and renamed the team the New York Red Bulls. The transaction price of $25 million offers an important piece of information for valuing MLS. To value each of the teams in MLS we could use either of two financial ratios. These are the price-to-ticket revenue (P/TR) and price-to-revenue ratios. Because these ratios rely on market transactions and multiples of relevant ratios, such as price-to-revenue, they are considered applications of the market approach.

Price-to-ticket revenue ratio

Typically, an analyst would have access to the organization's financial information, including a team's total revenues and ticket revenues. Since we do not have access to this information, we will assume that the team's ticket revenues equal its annual attendance (241,230 for 2005) multiplied by the average ticket price ($14.50).* Our estimate of the Red Bulls' annual ticket revenues is $3.498 million, which we can compare to the team's total annual revenue of $8.5 million, as shown in Exhibit 10.3. The corresponding price-to-ticket revenue ratio is 7.1x. The "x" in 7.1x is a symbol that means 7.1 is a multiplier. In this case, the ratio is 7.1 times ticket revenue.

---

*The attendance figure was found at mlsnet.com, and ticket prices are from http://redbull. newyork.mlsnet.com/MLS/rbn/stadium/.

| **exhibit** | **10.3** | Preliminary calculations for valuation analysis of Major League Soccer as of June 30, 2006—similar transactions methodology. |

	DATE	TARGET	PRICE	TICKET REVENUE	TOTAL REVENUE	PRICE/TICKET REVENUE	PRICE/TOTAL REVENUE
Scenario 1	March 31, 2006	MetroStars/Red Bulls	$25,000	$3,498	$8,500	7.1x	2.9x
Scenario 2	June 2006	DC United	$33,000	$3,666	$11,000	9.0x	3.0x

$s in thousands

Note: Scenario 1 is based on the purchase price for the MetroStars. Scenario 2 represents a 2006 offer (including a term sheet and letter of intent) to purchase DC United for $33 million, and uses 2005 ticket revenue and attendance.

To estimate the value of MLS as a whole, we would apply this ratio—which accounts for differences in market size, attendance, and other factors that make each team unique, via ticket revenues—and apply it to the other teams in MLS. As shown in Exhibit 10.4, we multiply each team's ticket revenue by the price-to-revenue multiple. The third column shows the results for each MLS team using the Red Bulls price-to-ticket revenue multiple. We then add up the values for all

Valuation analysis of Major League Soccer as of June 30, 2006— similar transactions methodology. **exhibit** **10.4**

FRANCHISE	2005 TICKET REVENUE	TEAM VALUE USING P/TR RATIO[a] 7.1X	TEAM VALUE USING P/TR RATIO[b] 9.0X
Chicago Fire	$4,482	$32,034	$40,345
CD Chivas USA	6,263	44,762	56,375
Colorado Rapids	1,909	13,646	17,187
Columbus Crew	2,108	15,066	18,974
D.C. United	3,666	26,202	33,000
FC Dallas	2,014	14,395	18,129
Kansas City Wizards	1,415	10,113	12,737
Los Angeles Galaxy	9,802	70,061	88,238
MetroStars/Red Bulls	3,498	25,000	31,486
New England Revolution	2,572	18,381	23,150
Real Salt Lake	3,427	24,493	30,848
San Jose Earthquakes	3,129	22,363	28,165
Value		Ⓐ $317,000	$399,000
Ⓑ Plus: one new expansion team		$15,000	$15,000
Preliminary team value (end of 2005)		Ⓒ $332,000	$414,000
Adjustment to June 30, 2006		Ⓓ $343,000	$414,000
Adjustments for control		89%	89%
Implied value of MLS		Ⓔ $648,000	$782,000

$s in thousands

Notes:

[a]MetroStars price/ticket revenue multiple based on franchise transaction price of $25 million.

[b]DC United price/ticket revenue multiple based on 2006 franchise transaction price offer of $33 million.

Source: 2005 ticket revenue estimated from average ticket prices and attendance (mlsnet.com).

teams Ⓐ. Also reflected in Exhibit 10.4 is the fact that a new expansion team was added in Toronto in 2005 and began play during the 2007 season. We are assuming an expansion fee of $15 million Ⓑ, which must be added to the total value of the league (Halpin, 2005). Hence, the preliminary value for MLS is $332 million Ⓒ.

Before we accept this valuation, we must remember that we have been using ticket revenue figures and an expansion fee estimate from the year 2005. A very important aspect of valuation (discussed in Chapter 4) is to incorporate the concept of the time value of money. Hence, because we seek a valuation as of June 30, 2006, we must adjust for the time value of money.

Adjusting for the time value of money. For any valuation, we must select a specific date, the **valuation date.** Obviously, the value of a business can change from month to month or even day to day. An important principle of valuation is to consider only information that is reasonably known for the valuation date. In litigation, the parties must use an exact date so that they can work on the same issue (e.g., the value of company X on the date on which the contract stipulates that it will be sold). For a merger, the analyst might choose a current date, and if the merger is actually consummated six months later, then an adjustment might be made to reflect any change in value.

In our valuation of MLS, the valuation date is June 30, 2006, but the analysis utilizing ticket revenue is for 2005. In order to perform time value of money calculations, we need a specific beginning date, not just a year. How do we select a date? Revenue in MLS is generated and paid throughout the year, with most of it coming in during the season (April through November). Often, when an analyst does not have the exact details for the flow of revenue over the year, he or she may choose to use the **mid-year convention**—choosing a date halfway through the year (i.e., June 30), based on the notion that if half of the revenue came in before this date and half after this date, then it is a good approximation for valuation purposes to treat the revenue as if all of it came in on June 30. Alternatively, the analyst may choose to be "conservative" (as opposed to aggressive) and treat the revenue as if it became available to MLS on December 31, 2005. This approach is considered conservative because it accounts for the revenue later than it was actually generated and, therefore, based on the time value of money, this approach reduces the asset's value.

In Exhibit 10.4, the calculations for the Red Bull transaction show a value for MLS of $332 million, as of December 31, 2005. The next step is to adjust $332 million up to June 30, 2006. Presumably, MLS will have increased in value between December 31, 2005, and June 30, 2006. In fact, if the business grew at an annual rate of 6.5% prior to December 31, 2005, and nothing significant changed, then a fair estimate of its growth rate for the six months after December 31, 2005, would be based on 6.5%. Suppose for a moment that we were adjusting from December 31, 2005, to December 31, 2006. In this case, we would simply multiply $332 million by 6.5% and add the result to the $332 million. Since we are performing this calculation for one half year rather than one full year, we multiply $332 million by 6.5% *raised to the one-half power* ($0.065^{1/2}$), as shown in Chapter 4. (If the valuation date were July 30, 2006, then we would use the exponent 7/12.) Applying this calculation to MLS gives a value, as of June 30, 2006, of $343 million Ⓓ.

The rate at which a value is "grown" forward (6.5% in the MLS example) is called the **capitalization rate**. Essentially, the analyst is capitalizing the value to a different date. The choice of a capitalization rate is often controversial. One method for determining the rate is to use the rate of return from the bond market and adjust it upward to reflect the risk of the company. Another method is to refer to the P/E or P/R ratio of similar transactions and use the inverse ratio (Hall & Lazear, 2000, p. 304). For example, if a firm is sold at 16x for price-to-earnings, then the implied capitalization rate is 6.25% (the inverse of 16, which is 1/16).

Adjusting for the controlling interest premium. The final adjustment in Exhibit 10.4 is made to account for the controlling interest premium. The purchase of the MetroStar operations allows Red Bull to run the team. Red Bull now owns equity in MLS, but it does not *control* MLS. In fact, Red Bull is just one of 12 teams (13 when Toronto began play) in the league. Therefore, this transaction provides controlling interest in the team's operation (subject to the restrictions placed on it by MLS), but it does not provide control of MLS as a whole. In fact, if some party were to buy MLS outright, the new owner would be able to, among other things, choose the location of and the number of teams, the salary cap and revenue sharing rules (subject to any collective bargaining agreement with players that may be relevant), the types of players and coaches, the length of the season, and so forth. Given that the comparable transaction that we have used to value MLS (Red Bull) is not one that provides controlling interest in MLS, we must make an adjustment to account for control, in order to estimate the full value of MLS as a whole.

To estimate the control premium for MLS, we can use the control premiums discussed earlier (for the Celtics, Indians, NHL, and SIC 79), because these are comparable, in that they involve other sport teams and leagues. These premiums average 92% and have a median of 89%. (The actual figures are: Celtics, 154.80%; Indians, 127.04%; NHL, 89%; and SIC 79, 55.3%.) The *median* is the number that appears in the middle when the figures are listed in rank order. Typically, the median represents a list of numbers better than the average, because if the list includes one or a few numbers that are very high or very low, they will significantly skew the average but not the median. For example, the newspaper reports median home sale prices for a particular month and city, not average home sale prices. If one home sold for $5 million, but the rest were closer to $300,000, the one outlier would skew the results.

Applying the median control premium of 89% to $343 million gives a value for the control of MLS of $648 million Ⓔ ($343 million × 1.89 = $648 million).

As stated earlier, this control premium is much larger than is typical for other industries, reflecting the greater benefits of owning a sport league rather than, say, a mining company. The control premium, as used in this example, includes the ego or consumption value of owning a sport property. Other definitions of control premium include only the financial value of control; other aspects of the value of control (e.g., ego) are then accounted for with an additional premium.

Price-to-revenue ratio

In professional sport, a common starting point for franchise valuation is to examine the transaction price (or some other estimate of franchise value) divided by total annual revenues for the franchise. This is the **price-to-revenue ratio** (P/R ratio). For the popular franchise value estimates from *Forbes* magazine, analysts begin with price-to-revenue ratios based on actual transactions, apply them to all the teams in a league, and make adjustments for other factors, such as a new stadium under construction, a new local television contract about to begin, or a historical brand (Ozanian, 1999). In a recent interview, Randy Vataha (co-founder of Game Plan LLC, which recently offered to purchase the entire NHL) stated that only the price-to-revenue ratio has any real value in professional sports (Rascher, 2006). Additionally, in late 2001, Allan "Bud" Selig, Commissioner of MLB, in testimony before the U.S. Congress stated his estimates for each team's valuation and total revenues. The average price-to-revenue ratio was 1.96, with a very small variation across teams.* These estimates indicate that multiplying team revenue by 1.96 provides a very accurate starting point for team values in MLB in 2001. Academic research concurs. For instance, George Foster discusses the usefulness of market multiples in valuing sport teams, noting that financial statements (and the income estimates presented in them) offer a noisy basis for valuation (Foster, Greyser, & Walsh, 2005).

Returning to our MLS valuation example, in order to carry out a price-to-revenue analysis, we must calculate total revenues for MLS, not just team revenues, as in the previous methods. The price-to-revenue multiple comes from transactions involving other sport entities, such as the NHL, MLB, NBA, and NFL. Exhibit 10.5 lists league financial valuations from *Forbes* magazine for the NHL, NBA, MLB, and NHL, along with estimates of total revenues and attendance.[†] The table also gives multiples of league value to total revenue and to attendance for each league. Why attendance? For many industries, certain non-financial variables or ratios can provide insight into a firm's value. For instance, in media, TV ratings (the number of people watching) are helpful. In the cable business, the number of subscribers is an important metric. Similarly, the valuation of a dental practice relies on, among other things, the number of active patients. Ultimately, sports is about putting "butts in seats," so attendance is a good starting point. These non-financial variables are really proxies for financial variables that may not be publicly known, or can provide a potential purchaser with an idea of the base number of customers of a team or league, which the purchaser could, perhaps, increase the yield from.

Choosing a multiple. In choosing a multiple to apply to a variable such as total revenue, it is important to be able to compare the subject at hand to the comparable assets ("comps") being used. Key considerations in choosing a revenue multiple for the valuation of MLS include

- franchise value appreciation,
- stability of the league,
- cross-marketing and promotional opportunities,
- strategic/synergistic benefits with other business interests,
- image and public relations benefits,

---

*The standard deviation was 0.19, which is very small when compared with the mean. The P/R ratio for all but four teams was between 1.89 and 2.15.

[†]Sources for this type of information include annual issues of *Forbes* magazine where team values are reported, *Team Marketing Report,* ESPN.com, and Arthur Levitt's report on NHL financials.

Professional sport league valuations.   exhibit   10.5

League	Timing	Valuation from *Forbes*[a]	Total revenue[a]	Attendance[b]	Valuation estimates[c] Price/ revenue	Price/ Attendance
NFL	2004	$26,207	$6,029	17.271	4.35	1517.4
NBA	2003/04	$8,750	$2,932	19.981	2.98	437.9
MLB	2004	$9,960	$4,733	74.913	2.10	133.0
NHL	2003/04	$4,900	$2,238	19.855	2.19	246.8
				Multiples	2.60	342.4
MLS Scenario 1	2005	NA	143.4	2.900	705	884
MLS Scenario 2	2010	NA	179.4	3.500	881	1,066

In millions, except ticket prices and multiples

Notes:

[a]Source: NFL, NBA, MLB, and NHL 2002–03 and NHL 2003–04 from *Forbes'* annual issues on sports team values. These do not include controlling interest premiums.

[b]Total attendance from ESPN.com for Scenario 1 and estimate for Scenario 2.

[c]These have been adjusted for the controlling interest premium of 89%.

Scenario 1 is the sum of total MLS revenue for 2005 calculated as described in the text (backward-looking).

Scenario 2 is the sum of total MLS revenue for 2005 calculated as described in the text (forward-looking).

- personal/corporate prestige and recognition, and
- corporate/personal tax benefits.

In terms of these considerations, MLS compares satisfactorily to the other sport leagues. It has experienced franchise appreciation (the Red Bull transaction was for $25 million, up from an expansion fee of $5 million ten years earlier). The league is stable, having just surpassed its tenth season and on its way to having a full slate of soccer-specific stadia. The cross-marketing and promotional opportunities are strong—for example, the recent cross-promotional deal between Red Bull and the L.A. Kings of the NHL. The potential synergistic and tax benefits in MLS are the same as in other major sport leagues (perhaps even greater in MLS, with many team operators owning or managing their own stadia). Although the image and corporate prestige of MLS are not what they are in the NFL, MLS has certainly gained ground with its recent media deal and expanded coverage.

The median price-to-revenue multiple of MLB, the NHL, the NBA, and the NFL is 2.60 (see Exhibit 10.5). A review of other sport-related properties (see Exhibit 10.6) reveals somewhat similar ratios, although the variation is quite large

| exhibit | 10.6 | Price-to-revenue multiples of sport-related properties. |

SIC CODE		ANNUAL REVENUES	P/R RATIO	PRICE/ATTENDANCE RATIO
SIC 7941	Churchill Downs	$515	1.00	
	Magna Entertainment	$658	1.10	
	Global Entertainment (Central Hockey League)[a]	$14	2.60	
	Association of Volleyball Professionals, Inc.[a]	$13	0.80	
SIC 7948	Canterbury Park	$55	1.00	
	Dover Motorsports	$91	2.20	
	International Speedway	$740	3.70	
	Penn National Gaming	$1,165	3.00	
	Speedway Motor Sports	$481	3.50	
Other	Continental Basketball Association[a]	$10	1.00	
	Average NHL team[c]	$75	2.19	246.8
	NHL Bain final offer[a]	$2,238	2.15	
	Average MLB team[c]	$158	2.10	133.0
	Average NBA team	$98	2.98	437.9
	Average NFL team	$188	4.35	1,517.4
Average[b]		$433	2.25	583.8
Median			2.18	342.4
Average (based on the Rule of Ten; w/o Global Ent., AVP, Inc., CBA, and NHL Bain offer)			2.33	
Median (based on the Rule of Ten; w/o Global Ent., AVP, Inc., CBA, and NHL Bain offer)			2.60	

$s in thousands

Notes:

[a]May be outside of the ten-fold revenue rule.

[b]NHL is not double-counted in average.

[c]NHL and MLB have lost money in a recent year yet have maintained high price-to-revenue ratios.

for these other properties, from 0.80 to 3.70. Before choosing the appropriate multiplier for MLS, we must determine which of these properties are more comparable to MLS's business and why the ratios vary so much. One advantage for MLS over these other properties is that, as a single entity, it has complete control over player costs, which is the largest expense in most sports. (This is true notwithstanding competitive pressures from other soccer leagues abroad.) Recent financial problems in MLB and the NHL stem in part from the fact that both leagues pay a relatively high proportion of revenues to players in the form of salaries. Taking the median of the listed multiples (and excluding those that represent businesses that are either ten times smaller than MLS or ten times larger than MLS in terms of revenues) gives a price-to-revenue multiple of 2.60.* A full analysis of each of these companies in terms of profitability would be helpful. MLS reportedly is transitioning from being unprofitable to profitable, and its owners have invested millions of dollars to this end. If the league is less profitable than the comparables listed, then its P/R multiple should reflect this fact. However, the P/R multiples imputed from the Red Bull and DC United transactions are higher than 2.60.

Determining total revenue. The next step in valuing MLS is to determine MLS's total revenues. As with most closely held companies, MLS's financial information, such as revenues, is not publicly available. Depending on the circumstances, an appraiser may receive a great deal of relevant information from the subject company itself. For the purposes of explaining this method, we will create reasonable estimates. Publicly available information shows that MLS's national sponsorships, media, and licensing fees generate about $55 million per year (in mid-year 2006 dollars). Separately, let's assume that total team revenues are twice ticket revenues. Thus, looking back at Exhibit 10.5, Scenario 1, total revenue for MLS is estimated to be $143 million. It is important to note that this is a backward-looking estimate: it was actual *previous* attendance and ticket prices used to estimate team revenue, and actual media reports of MLS's intellectual property (IP; i.e., media, sponsorships, and licensing) revenue.

A forward-looking estimate is more relevant, because an investor cares about what will happen in the future, not the past—yet it is also more uncertain, because the future is unknown. In valuation, we try to look into the future by reviewing the past and use the best information about both. Exhibit 10.5, Scenario 2, focuses on the future view of MLS as a 16-team league in 2010, with all or most of the teams playing in soccer-specific stadia. The two strategic changes—adding more teams and more soccer-specific stadia—are part of MLS's near-term business plan. We estimate that team revenues would likely double in soccer-specific stadia. Again, the analyst would typically have access to historical financial information as well as business forecasts (e.g., what happens to a team that moves into a new soccer-specific stadium). In fact, most large businesses provide forecasts that can aid the appraiser in valuing the business. Of course, the validity of these forecasts must always be tested. Applying these assumptions regarding revenue (i.e., increasing from 12 to 16 teams, doubling team revenues in soccer-specific stadia, and increasing MLS's IP revenues by 5% per year through 2010) gives a revenue estimate for 2010 of $305 million.† Discounting this figure back to June 30, 2006, requires dividing revenue by one plus the discount rate raised to the power corresponding to the time difference.

---

*The exclusion of businesses that are too small or too large is based on the "Rule of 10" discussed by Curtiss, Lurie, & McMorrow (1999). A comparable business should be comparable in size (measured in revenues).

†Alternatively, one could add a team and its corresponding revenues each year until 16 are reached, then calculate the present value and take an average.

DC United of MLS

SIDEBAR

10.B

Comparing Multiple Valuations

To extend the example of MLS, during October of 2006, the league received an offer, including a term sheet and letter of intent, to purchase the DC United team for $33 million ("Prospective Grizzlies," 2006). The price-to-ticket revenue ratio based on this purchase price is approximately 9.0x ($33,000,000/$3,666,000; see Exhibit 10.4). A valuation of MLS based on 9.0x is $782 million, as shown in column 4 of Exhibit 10.4. The two valuations, $648,000 and $782,000, are different because of a number of factors that cannot be determined with certainty. This is one reason why analysts develop many estimates and then select a single final estimate or range.

One of the factors that affected the estimates is that the Red Bull transaction involved over $75 million in investments other than the team itself, some of which were paid directly to the seller, AEG. For instance, in addition to paying $25 million for team operating rights, Red Bull also paid $2.3 million per year for ten years of naming rights on the stadium (which will be owned by AEG). How we divide up the deal's total cash value between what is being paid for the team itself and the amounts paid for other assets is somewhat arbitrary. In fact, initial newspaper reports described the deal as a $30 million purchase (close to the amount predicted for the MetroStars/Red Bulls in Exhibit 10.4,

column 4). As discussed earlier, transfer pricing or related party transactions can be important considerations when we are valuing an asset.

A second factor affecting the estimates is that ticket revenue does not capture all of the revenue available to the buyer. In other words, DC United may have other revenue streams (e.g., concessions, merchandise, local media) that are significant compared to its ticket revenue.

Third, different approaches result in different estimates. Sometimes, these estimates vary quite a bit. For example, Exhibit 10.7 shows four recent actual team sale transactions in MLB. The price-to-revenue multiple is nearly twice as high for the Dodgers as for the Angels. The media reported that Disney had been trying to sell the Angels for some time, and that Arte Moreno, the buyer, used this to his advantage to negotiate a relatively low price for the team. Similarly, in the Dodgers deal, the buyer was reportedly most interested in obtaining the land, Chavez Ravine, on which the stadium sits. Again, it is important to understand the details of each transaction that is serving as a comp.

Finally, valuations based on ticket revenues may vary because listed ticket prices might vary across teams.

exhibit   10.7   Actual team sale transactions in MLB.

	DATE	TARGET	PRICE[a]	REVENUE[b]	PRICE/REVENUE
(1)	April 2003	Anaheim Angels	$185,000	$123,955	1.5x
(2)	January 2004	Los Angeles Dodgers	$430,000	$154,000	2.8x
(3)	May 2004	Tampa Bay Devil Rays	$180,000	$101,000	1.8x
(4)	March 2005	Oakland Athletics	$180,000	$116,000	1.6x
Average of all four scenarios:					1.9x
Standard deviation of all four scenarios:					0.6x

$s in thousands except price/revenue multiples

Sources:

[a]Various newspaper reports.

[b]*Forbes* magazine.

To find the discount rate, we reference Ibbotson's report on SIC 794 (Commercial Sports). Based on six companies in that industry, Ibbotson calculates that the median cost of equity capital is 12.48%. (MLS is an equity-financed business with little or no debt.) (See Chapter 7 for a discussion of the cost of equity, the cost of debt, and the weighted average cost of capital.) The time difference between end-of-year 2010 and mid-year 2006 is 4.5 years. Thus, we divide $305 million by $1.1248^{4.5}$ for a result of $179.4 million.

Future revenue in MLS is unknown; hence, the rate at which one needs to discount it to the present time is fairly high compared to the rate that we used in previous examples to bring historical numbers, which are known, up to the present time (6.5%).

We now apply these two revenue bases ($143 million and $179 million) to the median price-to-revenue multiple, 2.60, and add an 89% controlling interest premium, to find estimates for the value of MLS of $705 million and $881 million. If we base the value of MLS on the price-to-attendance multiple of $342 per attendee, the resulting figure ($884 million to $1.066 billion) is higher than that found using the price-to-revenue multiple. This is not surprising. The other four leagues have high team values, relative to attendance, because they earn a great deal of non-attendance-related revenue, especially media revenue. Therefore, their attendance multiples are correspondingly high, and applying them to MLS would imply that MLS also has very high media revenues, which it does not, compared with the other leagues. This is an example of the necessity of accounting for differences across the leagues. Also, this illustrates why total revenue captures all of these differences better than attendance or even ticket revenue.

To summarize, the rationale for the market transactions and market multiples methods is that we can estimate the value of a league by determining the value of each team, adding them, and applying an appropriate control premium. Now, if the league office also generates revenue, we must ask how to account for that. In MLS, the league office can make money, for example, by selling a player's contract to another league or by selling national sponsorships (e.g., adidas sponsors MLS to the tune of $10 million to $15 million per year). If cash from league operations flows to the owner of the Red Bulls (along with other owners in the league), then the purchase of that team's operations includes the right to a portion of these cash flows. Hence, the revenue generated by the league office would be reflected in the price that Red Bull paid for the team operations, but it is not reflected in the ticket revenues used in the creation of the ratio.

When valuing a business, it is always better to use a broader definition of revenue. As Exhibit 10.3 shows, the P/R ratios for the Red Bull and DC United transactions are closer than are the ticket ratios. Thus, the application of these ratios to each team's total revenue would yield closer valuations for MLS than the application of the ticket ratios.

SIDEBAR

The Value of Major League Baseball Teams: Take Annual Revenue and Double It!   10.C

In December of 2001, MLB Commissioner Allan "Bud" Selig was called before the House Judiciary Committee to discuss baseball's antitrust exemption and the possible contraction of a number of teams. As part of the proceedings, he released financial information about MLB and its franchises. Exhibit 10.8 summarizes the information and lists *Forbes'* estimates of franchise values.

Financial information for MLB and its franchises, including estimates of franchise values.

FRANCHISE	2001 REVENUES	SELIG VALUATION	*FORBES* VALUATION	SELIG MULTIPLE	*FORBES* MULTIPLE
Anaheim Angels	$91,731,000	$193,056,000	$195,000,000	2.10	2.13
Arizona Diamondbacks	$125,132,000	$243,832,000	$280,000,000	1.95	2.24
Atlanta Braves	$146,851,000	$283,055,000	$424,000,000	1.93	2.89
Baltimore Orioles	$128,302,000	$251,257,000	$319,000,000	1.96	2.49
Boston Red Sox	$176,982,000	$337,526,000	$426,000,000	1.91	2.41
Chicago Cubs	$129,774,000	$252,980,000	$287,000,000	1.95	2.21
Chicago White Sox	$111,682,000	$219,163,000	$223,000,000	1.96	2.00
Cincinnati Reds	$70,887,000	$155,178,000	$204,000,000	2.19	2.88
Cleveland Indians	$162,242,000	$311,230,000	$360,000,000	1.92	2.22
Colorado Rockies	$131,813,000	$257,597,000	$347,000,000	1.95	2.63
Detroit Tigers	$106,791,000	$218,709,000	$262,000,000	2.05	2.45
Florida Marlins	$60,547,000	$139,655,000	$137,000,000	2.31	2.26
Houston Astros	$124,629,000	$244,073,000	$337,000,000	1.96	2.70
Kansas City Royals	$63,696,000	$143,389,000	$152,000,000	2.25	2.39
Los Angeles Dodgers	$143,607,000	$278,107,000	$435,000,000	1.94	3.03
Milwaukee Brewers	$113,350,000	$228,444,000	$238,000,000	2.02	2.10
Minnesota Twins	$56,266,000	$131,621,000	$127,000,000	2.34	2.26
Montreal Expos	$34,171,000	$96,859,000	$108,000,000	2.83	3.16
New York Mets	$182,631,000	$349,593,000	$482,000,000	1.91	2.64
New York Yankees	$242,208,000	$457,876,000	$730,000,000	1.89	3.01
Oakland Athletics	$75,469,000	$161,458,000	$157,000,000	2.14	2.08
Philadelphia Phillies	$81,515,000	$174,782,000	$231,000,000	2.14	2.83
Pittsburgh Pirates	$108,706,000	$219,194,000	$242,000,000	2.02	2.23
San Diego Padres	$79,722,000	$168,112,200	$207,000,000	2.11	2.60
San Francisco Giants	$170,295,000	$334,282,000	$355,000,000	1.96	2.08
Seattle Mariners	$202,434,000	$386,077,000	$373,000,000	1.91	1.84
St. Louis Cardinals	$132,459,000	$256,689,000	$271,000,000	1.94	2.05
Tampa Bay Devil Rays	$80,595,000	$173,574,000	$142,000,000	2.15	1.76
Texas Rangers	$134,910,000	$261,076,000	$356,000,000	1.94	2.64
Toronto Blue Jays	$78,479,000	$166,788,000	$182,000,000	2.13	2.32
MEDIAN	$118,989,500	$236,138,000	$266,500,000	1.96	2.35
AVERAGE	$118,262,533	$236,507,740	$286,300,000	2.06	2.42
STANDARD DEVIATION	$47,435,620	$82,304,131	$131,980,184	0.19	0.36

Source: Forbes information from its issue of April 15, 2002, reprinted by permission of Forbes Media LLC ©2010.

Price-to-earnings ratio

Investors who are analyzing stocks commonly use a ratio called price-to-earnings (P/E): the cost of purchasing the stock relative to the earnings that it generates. The P/E ratio provides an estimate of how much money an investor will pay for each dollar of a company's earnings and allows for comparisons of the market values of companies of various sizes. Chapter 2 presents an example of the calculation of price-to-earnings for a sport retail organization, Under Armour. For sport teams, earnings are not reflective of value, because many owners are willing to tolerate low earnings or even lose money if it means winning more games, or just for the satisfaction of operating a team. Also, related-party transactions in sport make it difficult to assess actual earnings. Therefore, analysts do not use P/E ratios to value sport team properties and instead employ P/R ratios.

To summarize, under the market approach we look at similar transactions, compare them to the subject being valued, and make appropriate adjustments to determine the value of the subject business. Stock market investors often use P/E ratios to estimate enterprise or firm values, but for sport team valuations we use P/R ratios, because sport team owners do not always seek maximization of earnings. Also, because of related-party transactions, reported sport franchise earnings do not necessarily reflect a team's true value.

Selig claimed that each franchise was worth about twice its annual revenues. In fact, the standard deviation is so small that only three low-revenue teams (the Marlins, Twins, and Expos) appear above a 2.30x multiple, and only the Yankees fall below 1.89x. Yet, *Forbes* shows a P/R multiple of around 2.35x. Why would *Forbes* give a significantly higher multiple than Selig? One reason is that it is in MLB's interests to appear small and financially poor before Congress, rather than a highly profitable monopoly.

Similarly, Selig's information shows that MLB had total operating losses of $232 million for 2001, whereas *Forbes* shows an operating profit of about $74 million. Because of related-party transactions and transfer pricing, it is possible to report different amounts of revenues and expenses, depending how the revenues and expenses are assigned.

Equity shares of MLS sold

Within the market approach, another method for measuring the value of a business is to look at market transactions for known equity amounts in the subject business. For example, if an owner sold 1% of the business for $2 million, the implied value of the business (on a non-controlling basis) is $200 million. Exhibit 10.9 shows the adjustment for the time value of money from a purchase date of July 15, 2001, up to the valuation date of June 30, 2006. The capitalization rate used here is 6.5%. Based on this rate, $200 million on July 15, 2001, is equivalent to $273 million on June 30, 2006. Adding the controlling interest premium of 89% puts the value of MLS at $517 million. (We add the control premium because the 1% stake does not provide control of the league, whereas the value of the league in its entirety includes control.) Many things can change during a five-year period, so an analyst would probably have less confidence in this comp than in more recent comparables, such as the Red Bulls and DC United transactions.

exhibit   10.9   Adjustments in the valuation of MLS reflecting the time value of money.

	JULY 15, 2001	2001	2002	2003	2004	2005	2006
Interest purchased	1%						
Repurchase price	$2,000						
Implied league valuation on a minority basis[a]	$200,000	$205,860	$219,250	$233,510	$248,698	$264,873	$273,352
Required market return[b]	6.5%						
Adjustment for control	89%		89%	89%	89%	89%	89%
Implied league valuation on a control basis	$378,000		$414,382	$441,334	$470,039	$500,611	$516,634
Implied value of MLS	$517,000						

$s in thousands

Notes:

[a]The 2001 value is adjusted to the end of 2001 from July 15, 2001, the date of the transaction. The half-year convention is used for 2006, since the valuation date is June 30, 2006.

[b]This is the capitalization rate chosen for this analysis.

Income Approach

The income approach is based on the idea that the fair market value of an asset is equal to the present value of its expected future cash flows. An analysis of this type is often referred to as a **discounted cash flow** (DCF) analysis. We project cash flows for a number of years into the future and discount them back to the present (or the date of valuation), using a suitable discount rate. To calculate the fair market value of a business, we add the present value of expected future net cash flows to the residual value of the business and subtract outstanding debt. In other words, we discount each year's cash flow (whether positive or negative) and add them together. Separately, we estimate and discount the **residual value** of the business—what the business will be worth at the end of the period for which we have projected cash flows—whether it be liquidation or continued operations. Finally, we calculate the discounted value of remaining debt. The sum of all these amounts provides an estimate of the value of the business.

Steps in the income approach

Exhibit 10.10 provides an example of a DCF valuation analysis for NewFangled Sports Products, Inc. (NFSP, a fictitious sports product manufacturing company). Recall that the principle behind the DCF method is that the value of a business or asset is based on the cash that it is expected to generate, as opposed to what an investor would pay for a similar business (as in market approach) or what it would cost to recreate the business (as in the cost approach, discussed later).

Discounted cash flow valuation analysis.   **exhibit** 10.10

NEWFANGLED SPORTS PRODUCTS, INC.		PROJECTED				
	FYE current year	FYE CY+1	FYE CY+2	FYE CY+3	FYE CY+4	Terminal year
Revenue	$7,600	$8,000	$8,400	$8,900	$9,300	$9,800
Growth		5.3%	5.0%	6.0%	4.5%	5.4%
Cost of goods sold	3,700	3,895	4,089	4,333	4,528	4,771
Gross profit	3,900	4,105	4,311	4,567	4,772	5,029
SG&A	3,000	3,158	3,316	3,513	3,671	3,868
R&D	500	400	300	300	300	300
EBITDA	400	547	695	754	801	861
Depreciation & amortization	300	300	300	300	300	300
EBIT	100	247	395	454	501	561
Interest expense	5	6	7	8	9	10
EBT	95	241	388	446	492	551
Effective tax rate	40.0%	40.0%	40.0%	40.0%	40.0%	40.0%
Income tax expense	38	97	155	178	197	220
Net income	$57	$145	$233	$268	$295	$330
Debt-free net income	57	145	233	268	295	330
add: Depreciation/amortization	300	300	300	300	300	300
Gross cash flow	357	445	533	568	595	630
Capital expenditures	400	350	200	100	100	100
Change in net working capital	75	60	60	75	60	75
Net cash flow	($118)	$35	$273	$393	$435	$455
Discount period in years	0.50	1.50	2.50	3.50	4.50	
Discount factor[a]	0.9419	0.8354	0.7409	0.6571	0.5825	0.5825
Discount rate[b]	12.8%					
Perpetual growth rate[c]	3.0%					
Terminal value[d]						$4,665
Present value – cash flow/terminal value[e]	($111)	$29	$202	$258	$254	$2,717
Net present value	$3,349					

$s in thousands

Notes:

[a]Reflects mid-year discounting convention. Discount factor (the number that is multiplied by the net cash flow to make it discounted cash flow) is $(1/(1+d))$ for one year into the future, $(1/(1+d)^2)$ for two years into the future, and so on, where d is the discount rate.

[b]Based on the weighted average cost of capital as reported in Ibbotson's *Cost of Capital Yearbook* (data through June 2006) for SIC 3949.

[c]Based on estimated long-term cash flow growth rate of the economy in general.

[d]Terminal value = terminal year cash flow / (discount rate − perpetual growth rate)

[e]Present value to mid-current year.

Source: Fiscal year ending (FYE) CY−1 from audited financial statements and business forecasts.

How far out should the analyst project cash flows? The answer is for the lifetime of the business. Two important qualifications make the application of DCF manageable. First, it is seldom necessary to project cash flows beyond ten or 15 years, because a cash flow that far in the future is not worth a significant amount today, using typical discount rates (see Chapter 4). Second, once the business reaches a stable, mature growth period, we can calculate a "terminal" value. In fact, analysts typically assume that a company cannot continue to grow faster than the economy forever into the future, so its growth rate is constrained by the growth rate of the economy.

In Exhibit 10.10, we value NFSP from the current year (CY) to CY+4 at a higher than average growth rate. Then, we project that it will settle into a 3% annual growth rate in perpetuity (going forward forever). The revenues forecasted for a five-year period typically have the most impact on the final value: revenue growth drives income growth, which drives cash flow growth. To forecast revenue growth, we must consider

1. whether the industry in which the company operates is growing or shrinking, and at what rate,
2. how the company is doing in terms of market share compared with its competitors,
3. expectations for new product offerings,
4. expected price changes, and
5. any other factors that would affect demand for the company's product(s).

The revenue growth projected for NFSP is between 4.5% and 6.0%, based on business forecasts. We calculate net cash flow for CY by starting with revenue and then

1. subtracting variable costs, such as the cost of goods sold (COGS), to obtain gross profit,
2. subtracting other expenses such as selling, general, and administrative costs (SG&A) and research and development (R&D), to obtain earnings before interest taxes depreciation and amortization (EBITDA),
3. subtracting depreciation and amortization (D&A),
4. subtracting interest expenses to obtain earnings before taxes (EBT),
5. subtracting income taxes to obtain net income (a 40% corporate income tax rate is assumed),
6. adding back depreciation and amortization (D&A) to determine gross cash flow, and
7. subtracting capital expenditures and increases in net working capital to obtain net cash flow (NCF).

In Step 6, we add back depreciation and amortization after calculating income taxes to determine gross cash flow. This is because D&A expenses reduce the company's income tax liability, but they do not actually lower the real cash flow that is available to the company's owners—so we add them back after calculating income tax.

In Step 7, we subtract increases in net working capital and capital expenditures from gross cash flow to determine net cash flow. Net working capital refers to the cash needed to run the business on a daily basis (measured in annual dollars needed), which is not available to be given to the owners of the business because it is needed for operations. We calculate it simply by subtracting current liabilities from current assets. The change in working capital is its difference from year to year. We subtract increases in net working capital because that increase in net working capital is needed to run the business; therefore, that cash is not available as a cash flow to the owners of the company. In other words, if more working capital is required each year, more cash is needed for operations, and that cash is not available to the owners.

Valuation calculations in the income approach

Exhibit 10.10 shows that NCF for NFSP is negative during CY (even though net income is positive), but it becomes positive thereafter. Once we have estimated NCF, we discount it back to the middle of CY (June 30 of CY). For NFSP, at the end of CY, NCF is –$118,000, but when multiplied by the **discount factor** (DF, defined in note (a) in Exhibit 10.10) it becomes –$111,000 (noted as present value in Exhibit 10.10). We calculate the discount factor as follows:

$$DF = \frac{1}{(1 + i)^n}$$

where i is the discount rate and

n is the number of years in the period

For the current year, we are discounting the December CY value back to June CY, so $n = 0.5$. For CY+1, the estimate is for December of the year following CY, which is 1.5 years ahead of June CY, so $n = 1.5$, and so on for CY+2 through CY+4. We select a discount rate of 12.8%, which Ibbotson reports for SIC 3949 (Sporting and Athletic Goods, Not Elsewhere Classified). SIC 3949 includes K2, Inc. and Callaway Golf Co., among other smaller companies. We use the actual weighted average cost of capital (WACC) that NFSP faces. The rate of 12.8% is simply the median that Ibbotson reports for this industry, and we have selected it for illustrative purposes.*

The perpetual growth rate is the implied growth rate of NCF year after year beyond CY+4, and it therefore impacts the expected NCF only beyond the terminal year. To obtain the terminal year PV, we subtract the perpetual growth rate from the discount rate and divide the terminal year NCF, $455,000, by this

---

*As described in Chapter 4, if $100 in one year is worth $90 today (implying a discount rate of 11.1%), then an investor with $90 today would invest in a company only if that investment could grow from $90 to $100 in one year, or at a rate of 11.1%. Otherwise, the investor might go elsewhere to invest the $90. Thus, the discount rate comes from the opportunity cost that the investor faces when making an investment decision. If the investor requires a 11.1% return, then the cost of capital for the company (the price it must pay in order to return $100 to the investor at the end of one year) is 11.1%. For NFSP, if it can create $273 in cash flow for CY+2 and that is required by the investors of the company who put $202 in during mid-year CY, then, essentially, those investors are asking for a 12.8% return. Therefore, that is the discount rate needed to provide the investors' required return.

number.* The capitalized value of the company in year CY+5 and beyond is $4.6 million. To bring that back to mid-year CY, we multiply it by the discount factor (0.5825). The resulting present value of the terminal value of the company is $2.717 million. Finally, we add all present values to obtain the net present value (NPV) of expected future net cash flows, $3.349 million. In this example, there is no residual value, because the business is expected to continue operations indefinitely.† Assuming the present value of outstanding debt is $500,000, then a fair market value for NFSP is $2.85 million.

The income approach and sport franchises

The DCF method does not apply well to sport franchises because of the non-financial reasons for franchise ownership and related-party transactions. As further evidence that the DCF approach is not applicable to—or at a minimum understates the value of—sport franchises and leagues, *Forbes* estimates of team values for MLB for 2006 show that the three highest valued teams, the New York Yankees, the Boston Red Sox, and the New York Mets, are worth $1.206 billion, $617 million, and $604 million, respectively, yet they *lost* $50 million, $18.5 million, and $16.1 million, respectively (Ozanian & Badenhausen, 2006).

An accurate DCF analysis requires information about all of the net cash flows available to the team's owner, not just those that are accounted for on the team's financial statements. The analyst will need to know each team's net cash flow; each owner's salary, if any; the net cash flows from national sponsorships, licensing, and media; the net cash flow of the facility in which the team plays; and any revenues from other sources. For instance, a team owner might generate substantial net cash flow through local sponsorship, parking, and concessions but might "book" that information on a facility management company that he or she also owns. Without all of this information, DCF analysis of a sport team will likely show a value that is lower than the team's true value.

Cost Approach

Under the cost approach to determining the value of a business, the analyst discreetly determines the replacement costs of all of the firm's assets. This approach requires a discreet appraisal of current assets, tangible personal property, real property, and, occasionally, intangible assets. The sum of the asset values estimates the business's fair market value. This approach is appropriate for valuing assets for which substitutes could reasonably be bought or built.

The cost approach has never been an accepted approach for measuring sport franchise or league values. The cost approach can be an effective tool for measuring the value of certain assets, such as equipment or a training facility, but it is not

---

*See chapter Appendix 10.A for a proof that the discount factor's infinite geometric series converges such that NPV = NCF/(r–g), where r is the discount rate and g is the perpetual growth rate.

†If a business's sole income is a patent that is expected to run out in a certain number of years, then the analyst would determine the residual value of the assets (perhaps an office building, land, and cash), add that to the NPV of NCF, and subtract the NPV of any debt.

10.D

Most sport arenas are publicly owned or situated on public land and therefore are not subject to property taxes; they are not frequently bought and sold. Thus, it is rarely necessary to determine the value of a sport arena. However, in 2001, the Florida State Supreme Court determined that private organizations that lease space at public facilities are not necessarily exempt from paying property taxes (*Sebring Airport Authority v. McIntyre*). This judgment quickly became an important concern for the state's sport teams. Essentially, each team was going to be asked to pay property taxes for the sport arena in which it played.

A sport arena, such as the St. Pete Times Forum in Florida (formerly known as the Ice Palace), has a different value to a private buyer than to a public buyer. This is because the private buyer does not fully internalize the benefit of the arena to the community. Sport arenas often create positive externalities that overflow into the community. In the case of the Forum, these benefits include, but are not limited to, an increase in sales to nearby businesses (at least partially driven by spending from visitors to the community who attend arena events), an increase in value to nearby properties, a positive psychic impact on the community, additional tax revenues, and advertisement for the Tampa Bay region. The value of each of these aspects is difficult to measure. (See Chapter 12 on economic impact.)

The Forum, of course, also has a positive value to the owner of the Tampa Bay Lightning (an NHL team), which plays in the arena. The Forum, therefore, has a positive internality to the private buyer and a positive externality to the surrounding community and county (counties in Florida assess and collect property taxes). Whenever a particular entity has these characteristics, without public intervention the free market will produce an arena of less than the socially optimal size and quality. This is one of the reasons why the public often chooses to finance all or part of sport arena construction, notwithstanding whether the public actually receives the full value of the arena. The other reason for the public's willingness to finance arena construction is that the market for sport teams is competitive. If a team can credibly threaten to locate elsewhere, then it can extract more public financing for an arena than if there were plenty of alternative teams (see Chapter 9). As a result, when valuing the Forum, we must account for the private and public value.

The Forum originally cost $166 million to build, with the franchise (the Lightning's first ownership group) paying about $73 million of the costs. The day the Forum opened, it would not have been worth $166 million to a private buyer, because that buyer would not be able to capture the arena's full value, especially the overflow value that accrued to local businesses from arena attendees who spent money in local restaurants, hotels, and retail stores. Thus, from a private perspective, the arena is worth, say, $73 million (a reasonable figure because this is the price the franchise paid to gain access to the arena's cash flows). The public receives about $93 million in additional value from the arena ($163 million less $73 million). Under the cost approach to valuation, the arena is worth $166 million on opening day—the replacement cost. Under the income or market approach, the value is only about $73 million (as a rough estimate, not accounting for negotiating leverage, etc.)—what a private buyer would pay. So, which is it?

The appeals court in Florida sided with the Tampa Bay Lightning franchise, claiming that arena value is what a willing buyer would pay for the facility. The Lightning's second ownership group paid $25 million for the facility when it bought the team for $100 million ($25 million was allocated to the facility). Originally, the county assessed the building at $110 million, based on the construction cost (cost approach) and depreciation of approximately $50 million. The decrease from $100 million to $25 million reduces the franchise's property tax burden by 75%.

This example shows that even under an apparently simple approach, the cost approach, the valuation of an asset depends on the standard of value that is accepted. One could argue that the county is actually collecting property taxes that relate to the cost of the arena, because the arena's construction has raised property values for those restaurants and other businesses that benefit from it, thus increasing the property taxes of those businesses.

helpful for estimating the intangible assets that make up a substantial part of enterprise value in sport. Much of the value of a sport franchise, for instance, is in its ability to schedule games with other teams in the league as part of a championship season. This is not something that can be recreated in the marketplace. Consider, for example, the Kentucky Derby horse race. A competitor could host another race, but the value of the competing derby would not be as high as the Kentucky Derby, simply because the Derby has a brand and history that garner larger revenues.

As the sidebar illustrates, even the valuation of sport arenas is complex, due to the difference between the value of the arena to a private business owner and the value to the public in general.

CONCLUSION

Valuation is both a science and an art. For any valuation, the analyst should undertake to use all three approaches: market, income, and cost. If more than one approach may be used, the analyst's second task will be to integrate the findings into a single estimate of value. For some assets, it is possible to use all three approaches. A golf course, for example, could be valued based on the cash flow it generates from greens fees and the like (income approach), the price that buyers are paying for similar golf courses (market approach), and the cost of building a course from scratch (cost approach). Additionally, for the valuation of sponsorships in sport, analysts should employ the income approach along with the market and cost approach methods that are currently used. All three methods are valid, and their results should be compared when the analyst chooses the final estimate of value.

CONCEPT *check*

1. In Exhibit 10.8, why do the Expos have the highest price-to-revenue multiple?
2. Give examples of ways in which a sport team majority owner could violate fiduciary duties and financially harm the minority shareholders.
3. In a discounted cash flow analysis, what happens to the NPV, if, all else being equal, the discount rate goes up? What happens to NPV if the growth rate for the terminal value (perpetual growth rate) rises?
4. Give examples of how a sport franchise can use related-party transactions to reduce its net income. For each example, how does it reduce net income?
5. When an analyst is determining the value of a private company owned 100% by a single investor by analyzing the share prices of publicly traded companies, what adjustments must he or she make in order to determine a final value?

PRACTICE *problems*

1. If the minority price for a single share of stock of a company is $20, if there are 500 thousand shares of stock, and a person offers to buy the entire company for $14.5 million, what is the controlling interest premium being offered?
2. Using the same information, what is the minority or non-controlling interest discount for a company that has a control value of $14.5 million, 500 thousand shares, and a share price of $20?

CASE analysis

Net Present Value

Calculate the net present value of a sporting goods store, using this information:

- Valuation date of December 31 of the current year.
- Net cash flow for the current year of $200,000; next year estimated to be $225,000; the following year estimated to be $250,000; the year after that and terminal year, $275,000.
- NCF growth rate beyond the terminal year of 2.5% per year.
- Discount rate of 12%.
- What is the value if the discount rate is 15% and the NCF growth rate is 5.5%?

APPENDIX chapter 10

10.A   Proof of the Calculation of the NPV of the Terminal Value

Following is proof that the net present value of the terminal value is equal to the net cash flow divided by the difference between the discount rate and the growth rate of the business's NCF. Since $\infty - 1$ does not exist, but reduces to ∞, the last component of Eq. (1) has the same exponent in the numerator and denominator. Eq. (3) recognizes that the right-hand side of Eq. (2) is equal to NPV, as written in Eq. (1), plus $NCF/(1 + g)$.

$$NPV = \frac{NCF}{(1 + r)} + \frac{NCF(1 + g)^1}{(1 + r)^2} + \ldots + \frac{NCF(1 + g)^\infty}{(1 + r)^\infty} \tag{1}$$

$$\frac{(1 + r)}{(1 + g)} NPV = \frac{NCF}{(1 + g)} + \frac{NCF}{(1 + r)^1} + \frac{NCF(1 + g)}{(1 + r)^2} + \ldots + \frac{NCF(1 + g)^\infty}{(1 + r)^\infty} \tag{2}$$

$$\frac{(1 + r)}{(1 + g)} NPV = \frac{NCF}{(1 + g)} + NPV \tag{3}$$

$$NPV = \frac{NCF}{(r - g)} \tag{4}$$

references

Brunner, J. (April 5, 2006). Tax write-off may help ease owners' losses. *Seattle Times*.

Curtiss, R., Lurie, J., & McMorrow, S. (1999). The rule of 10: Size comparability and the market approach. *IBA News*.

Eichelberger, C. (January 11, 2006). Hockey teams gain investment luster as NHL refutes obituaries. *Bloomberg News*.

Fort, R. (2006). The value of Major League Baseball ownership. *International Journal of Sport Finance 1*(1), 9–20.

Foster, G., Greyser, S., & Walsh, B. (2005). *The business of sports: Text and cases on strategy and management*. Oklahoma City: South-Western.

Hall, R., & Lazear, V. (2000). Reference guide on estimation of economic losses in damages awards. In *Reference manual on scientific evidence* (2nd ed., 277–332). Washington, DC: Federal Judicial Center.

Halpin, J. (November 12, 2005). MLS closing in on Toronto Expansion. *MLSnet.com*.

Ibbotson & Associates. (2006). *Cost of Capital Yearbook*. Chicago: Morningstar.

Késenne, S. (2006). Competitive balance in team sports and the impact of revenue sharing. *Journal of Sport Management 20*(1), 39–51.

Ozanian, M. (September 20, 1999). What's your team worth? *Forbes.*

Ozanian, M., & Badenhausen, K. (April 20, 2006). The business of baseball. *Forbes.*

Pratt, S., Reilly, R., & Schweihs, R. (2000). *Valuing a business: The analysis and appraisal of closely held companies.* New York: McGraw-Hill.

Prospective Grizzlies Owner Davis Also Pursuing DC United. (October 11, 2006). *SportsBusiness Daily.* Retrieved December 1, 2006, from http://www.sportsbusinessdaily.com/index.cfm?fuseaction=sbd.main&storyID=SBD2006101116.

Rascher, D. (2006). Executive interview with Randy Vataha. *International Journal of Sport Finance 1*(2), 71–76.

Sebring Airport Authority v. McIntyre. 623 So. 2d 541 (Fla. 2d DCA 1993).

Shanahan, M. (December 28, 2004). Wyc Grousbeck would jump through hoops to make Celtics a winner again. *Boston Globe.*

Zimbalist, A. (October 18, 1998). Just another fish story. *New York Times.*

Zimbalist, A. (2003). *May the best team win: Baseball economics and public policy.* Washington DC: Brookings Institution Press.

11 Feasibility Studies

comparables analysis   cost-benefit analysis   market demand

competitive analysis   feasibility study   primary research

corporate depth   financing analysis   secondary research

KEY CONCEPTS

Introduction

When the construction of a new arena is under consideration, many questions must be answered: What would it cost to build? Where would it be located? How would it be paid for? Does it make sense for local government to help fund it? Would arena events generate enough revenue to justify building it? Feasibility studies help answer these questions.

FEASIBILITY STUDIES DEFINED

In general, a **feasibility study** is a study conducted to determine whether a project is likely to be practical and successful, considering such items as engineering, land use, financing, demand, and economic impact. Feasibility studies in sport are undertaken to determine the practicality and likely success of such projects as

- whether a city should build a community recreation center, a professional sport stadium or arena, or a public pool,
- whether a metropolitan area should lure a sport team to town, and how it could be done,
- whether a city should bid to host a major sporting event,
- whether an athletic director should build a new facility or renovate an existing one,
- whether a university should add a locker room to the campus recreation center,
- whether an entrepreneur should open a new health club, and
- whether a small town should build a new soccer field.

A feasibility study incorporates many **cost-benefit analyses**—analyses of the cost of a project in relation to its potential benefits. In terms of a sport facility, a cost-benefit analysis assesses whether there is likely to be enough demand for events at a new facility and enough corporate support for sponsorship of the facility. Together, these two assessments determine whether there is a *market* for the project. Additionally, a feasibility study analyzes how to fund a project, where it should be located, its cost, and its scale. It may also include information on the operation of the facility once it is in place or methods to secure a major tenant.

Phases of a Feasibility Study

Feasibility studies are often broken into two phases. The initial phase, or a Phase I feasibility study, tests whether a more in-depth analysis should be undertaken. It is typically based on secondary sources of information, including comparisons with other sport facilities and other similar cities or communities. Phase I is quicker to complete and is significantly less costly than a more in-depth study. The general purpose is to present the information that the parties need in order to proceed with project development discussions. If the project passes muster, then often a Phase II, or more in-depth, study is completed, based on primary data that are generated specifically for the study. A Phase II feasibility study for a sport facility lays out a specific financing plan (whereas a Phase I financing analysis will show a number of possible financing sources), actual site selection (not just possibilities), facility design details and renderings, a market demand analysis based on primary research about location (not just comparisons to other facilities and cities), and primary research on economic impact.

Parts of a Feasibility Study

A feasibility study typically consists of four main parts: analyses of

1. market demand;
2. location, construction cost, and engineering;
3. financing; and
4. economic and fiscal impact.

The findings in each of these sections will affect or be affected by the findings of the other sections. As Exhibit 11.1 illustrates, the analysis of market demand will help determine the suggested size of the facility, including the number of seats, luxury suites, premium food areas, and so forth (see arrow 1). The location, construction cost, and engineering analysis suggests a suitable location for the facility and determines the overall cost of construction, based on the size suggested by the market demand analysis. That cost will be an input into the **financing analysis**—an assessment of how much money will be needed to build the facility (arrow 2). The information about the cost and process of construction will help determine the economic and fiscal impact of the facility during the construction period (arrow 3).

The fiscal impact portion of the economic impact analysis provides information on how much government revenue the construction and operation of

The parts of a feasibility study.   **exhibit   11.1**

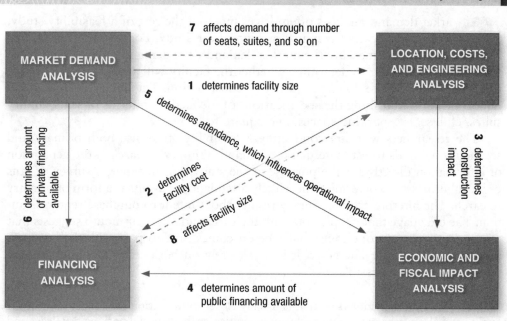

the facility will generate. That revenue will be considered in the evaluation of possible financing sources, and it will also be a factor in the determination of how much public money will be used to finance the construction (arrow 4). The market demand findings provide information on expected attendance for events at the facility. That information will factor into the analysis of the facility's economic and fiscal impact (arrow 5). Market demand findings will also help in the determination of how much net private revenue the facility and its events will generate. These private revenue sources and amounts (especially the possible naming rights sponsorship) will be listed as possible private financing sources (arrow 6).

Feedback loops in the process will cause readjustments in the original estimates. Once the location, costs, and engineering analysis determines the size of the facility and related costs, the facility size may change from the original estimate, which was based solely on market demand (arrow 7). The change in the number of seats and luxury suites will, for instance, affect the overall estimate of the number of customers. This estimate will then affect all of the other sections of the feasibility study. Another feedback loop links financing with the overall cost and size of the facility. The financing costs, largely determined by interest rates, will affect the overall cost of construction (arrow 8).

A detailed examination of market demand analysis follows, making up the bulk of this chapter. Because economic impact is an important and diverse topic, it has its own chapter (Chapter 12). Similarly, facility financing, briefly mentioned here, is discussed in detail in Chapter 9. A thorough examination of construction costs and engineering is beyond the scope of this text, but at the end of this chapter we summarize the elements of this part of a feasibility study.

MARKET DEMAND

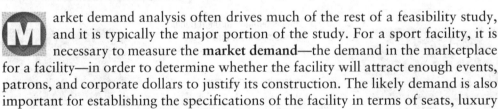arket demand analysis often drives much of the rest of a feasibility study, and it is typically the major portion of the study. For a sport facility, it is necessary to measure the **market demand**—the demand in the marketplace for a facility—in order to determine whether the facility will attract enough events, patrons, and corporate dollars to justify its construction. The likely demand is also important for establishing the specifications of the facility in terms of seats, luxury suites, club seats*, parking spaces, and square footage.

The researchers who are conducting a feasibility study use both primary and secondary methods to estimate market demand. **Primary research** is the generation of information directly for the purpose of the study. For instance, a survey of fans or local businesses to determine their likely attendance at events is a form of primary research. The interpretation of survey results about intent to purchase requires caution. The old adage that people vote with their feet and not their mouth suggests that respondents may say one thing, but when it comes time to part with their money, they may do another. Therefore, it is best to rely on both secondary and primary research, whenever possible.

---

*A club seat is an individual seat that is usually closer to the action than most seats in the facility and also often comes with exclusive amenities, such as special parking privileges and access to a club eatery. Typically, only season ticket holders may purchase club seats.

Secondary research typically involves the analysis of data that have already been generated for other purposes but might provide information for the question at hand. For instance, an analysis of attendance at other new sport facilities around the country, with adjustments for differences in the locations, might provide useful information on expected attendance at the facility that is the subject of the feasibility study. The use of information from comparable markets is similar to the use of comps for valuation, discussed in Chapter 10. This type of secondary research is known as **comparables analysis.** In the case of a sport facility feasibility study, it is based on the idea that if sport facilities are successful in comparable cities, then a facility will be successful in the city that is the subject of the study. The researchers of a feasibility study are trying to measure the expected value of various revenue streams (e.g., tickets) in order to predict the financial health of the proposed facility. An assessment of comparable markets and their facilities can provide insight about what to expect if a facility is built.

Market demand analysis for a sport facility feasibility study can be divided into the following subsections:

- individual ticket demand Ⓐ,
- corporate demand (club seats, luxury suites, and sponsorships) Ⓑ,
- event activity Ⓒ, and
- facility specifications and operating estimates Ⓓ.

Exhibit 11.2 shows how these subsections (labeled Ⓐ through Ⓓ) fit into the overall feasibility study.

The parts and subsections of a feasibility study.   **exhibit** **11.2**

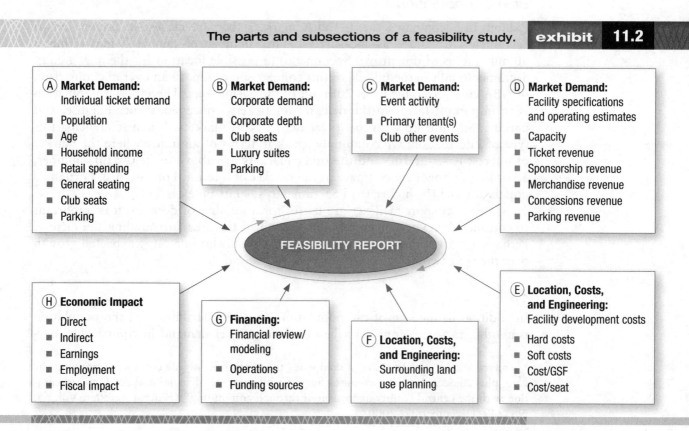

Individual Ticket Demand

To estimate ticket demand, we may use comparables analysis. Consider that a sport arena may host 150 events annually. These events will generate revenue from purchases of tickets, concessions, merchandise, and parking. Typically, we would look at the local population of likely attendees to see how it compares with other markets that have similar sport facilities with similar tenants.

To use the NBA's Sacramento Kings franchise as an example, a comparison of the population of Sacramento to other NBA markets would be an important first step in predicting the likely success of a new NBA arena in Sacramento. Throughout this chapter we will refer to a feasibility study completed in 2002 for a new NBA arena in downtown Sacramento, to provide a real-world example (Goal Group et al., 2001). In such a feasibility study, the researchers would study demographic and lifestyle information, such as the age, income, and purchasing habits of local residents or residents within 30 miles of the facility. The U.S. Census Bureau provides some of this information by city, county, or metropolitan statistical area.* Its American Factfinder program (http://factfinder.census.gov/home/saff/main.html?_lang=en) provides information about gender, age, education level, income, and so forth for a city or county name or ZIP code. Many private companies also provide market demographics, ethnographics, and lifestyle information down to the city block; examples are Claritas, Scarborough Research, and Insights Research Group. The researchers would also analyze the revenues of comparable sport arenas.

Size of population

Exhibit 11.3 compares the 14 NBA markets that are closest in population to Sacramento in 2000, as measured by the number of people living within a 30-mile radius of downtown Sacramento (a possible location for the new arena). Sacramento falls in the middle of this comparison group. In an overall comparison of NBA cities, Sacramento is 20th out of the 27 markets. Therefore, if population is an important factor in the demand for tickets, concessions, merchandise, and parking, Sacramento is in the lower tier of NBA markets. When referencing this type of information, we commonly speak in terms of an index where the market of interest is set at 100 and the other markets are above or below this number, according to how they compare to the market of interest. For instance, Portland's population is 11% higher than Sacramento's, so its index is 111.

Given that sport facilities are useful for a number of decades, it is important to consider the expected population growth of the area surrounding the facility. Perhaps a market that is currently relatively small shows a large expected growth over the next two decades (e.g., Las Vegas, Nevada).

Age

In addition to the size of the population, the age distribution of the population is another factor to consider when analyzing ticket demand in comparable mar-

---

*A metropolitan statistical area "comprises the central county or counties containing the core, plus adjacent outlying counties having a high degree of social and economic integration with the central county as measured through commuting" (*Federal Register*, Vol. 65, No. 249, December 27, 2000).

Comparison of NBA markets closest in population to Sacramento.   exhibit 11.3

Rank	Market	30-mile pop.[1]	30-mile pop. index	Age distribution 25–49[2]	Age distribution 25–49 index	Median household income[3]	Median household income index	% High household income[4]	% High household income index	Adjusted per capita spending[5]	Adjusted per capita spending index	Composite index[6]
1	Minneapolis	2,726,284	157	39%	104	$62,765	129	22%	156	$9,293	116	132
2	Seattle	2,782,434	160	40%	105	$61,923	128	24%	165	$7,943	99	131
3	Denver	2,418,237	139	40%	107	$60,146	124	22%	154	$9,080	113	127
4	Phoenix	3,136,149	181	37%	98	$48,822	101	15%	103	$8,820	110	119
5	Portland	1,916,612	111	38%	101	$52,416	108	16%	110	$10,135	126	111
6	Miami	3,459,806	200	24%	63	$37,152	77	9%	66	$10,514	131	107
7	Indianapolis	1,490,403	86	38%	100	$51,153	106	16%	110	$10,800	134	107
8	Charlotte	1,460,737	84	38%	101	$52,247	108	18%	123	$8,657	108	105
9	Cleveland	2,381,466	137	36%	95	$45,234	95	13%	93	$8,144	101	104
10	Orlando	1,705,416	98	38%	100	$45,674	94	12%	85	$11,172	139	103
11	Milwaukee	1,662,988	96	36%	97	$53,287	110	16%	112	$8,092	101	103
12	Sacramento	1,733,765	100	38%	100	$48,486	100	14%	100	$8,035	100	100
13	San Antonio	1,592,693	92	36%	96	$40,821	84	10%	72	$12,265	153	99
14	Salt Lake City	1,386,572	80	34%	92	$53,309	110	15%	105	$8,499	106	99
15	Memphis	1,147,825	66	37%	98	$45,180	93	14%	97	$10,001	124	96
	NBA small market composite, excluding Sacramento		121		97		105		111		119	110

Source indexes: Claritas and Dun & Bradstreet.

Notes:

[1] Population based on a 30-mile radius around each facility. Data from 2001.

   Index: Sacramento = 100 (i.e., Miami's population within 30 miles of facility is 100% greater than Sacramento's.)

[2] Age distribution based on percentage of individuals aged 25–49 within a 30-mile radius of each arena/site.

   Index: Sacramento = 100 (i.e., there are 7% more individuals in Denver with persons between the ages of 25 and 49 than in Sacramento.)

[3] Median household income for residents within 30-mile radius of each arena/site.

   Index: Sacramento = 100 (i.e., Minneapolis' ratio of median household incomes is 29% higher than Sacramento's.)

[4] Percentage household income over $100K for residents within 30-mile radius of each arena/site.

   Index: Sacramento = 100 (i.e., Denver's ratio of $100,000 households is 54% higher than Sacramento's.)

[5] Per capita spending of residents within 30-mile radius of each arena/site. Total retail sales are adjusted to the U.S. average.

   Index: 100 = U.S. average per capita spending. *Source:* Claritas, Places Rated Almanac.

[6] Ranked by total composite index, which is the straight average of the indexes for the five variables listed for each market.

   Index: Sacramento = 100 (i.e., Minneapolis' combined data across all categories is 32% more than Sacramento's.)

kets. The target market of many NBA teams is people between the ages of 25 and 49, because these are likely ticket buyers. Exhibit 11.3 lists the percentage of the population that falls within this age range, along with the index. Sacramento's population has a relatively high proportion of the target market.

Income

The income of the local population is an indicator of its ability to purchase tickets to facility events. In Exhibit 11.3, we see that Sacramento's median household income is below the 14-team composite average of 105. A more detailed analysis of income—specifically, the percentage of households whose annual income is greater than $100,000—shows a similar result. Households with larger incomes are more likely to purchase season tickets (as opposed to single-game tickets) or club seats.

Sport facilities offer tiered pricing and quality. At the bottom of the scale are the "cheap seats," which are often sold on an individual-event basis. Season ticket seats are closer to the playing surface, and even better seats—club seats—are very close to the action and provide other amenities. At the top of the pricing tier are luxury suites, which are small rooms that overlook the playing surface and provide tables, food, TVs, bathrooms, and more, in addition to seating. The fact that the percentage of households with income greater than $100,000 in Sacramento is below the NBA average suggests that it would be more difficult to sell season tickets and club seats in Sacramento than in the average market, all else being equal.

Spending by local residents

Another measure that may indicate the demand for sport facility event tickets is retail spending by local residents. Exhibit 11.3 lists the per capita retail spending of households within a 30-mile radius of the sport arena, adjusted for the cost of living. To derive this measure, we divide the total retail spending within 30 miles of the relevant arena by the population and then scale the result by a cost of living index. For instance, the total retail spending within 30 miles of the arena in Minneapolis is $30.524 billion. The cost-of-living index for Minneapolis (with the U.S. average = 100) is about 120.48, and the population within 30 miles of the arena is 2,726,284. Thus, the adjusted per capita spending is $9,293 ($30.524 billion divided by 1.2048 divided by 2,726,284), as shown in Exhibit 11.3.

$$\text{adjusted per capita spending} = \frac{\text{retail spending}}{\text{population}} \times \frac{100}{\text{cost of living}}$$

$$= \frac{\$30.524 \text{ billion}}{2.726 \text{ million}} \times \frac{100}{120.48} = \$9,293$$

This measure reflects the fact that although the median income in Sacramento ($48,486) is lower than that in Seattle ($61,923), it costs less to live in Sacramento than in Seattle. In markets with high retail spending relative to the cost of living, people are capable of purchasing tickets to sporting events by shifting some of their spending from general retail to sporting events. Thus, adjusted per capita spending is a factor used in the assessment of market demand. Other possible predictors of whether many fans would attend NBA games in a new arena might be the local television ratings of NBA games or the purchases of basketballs in the local market.

Annual revenues

Additional useful information in a ticket demand analysis is the annual revenues of the sport arenas in comparable markets. These revenues would suggest how successful these facilities are. If half of the facilities are struggling financially, this would indicate that if Sacramento were similar to those markets, we might expect its facility to struggle as well. Unfortunately, revenue information is generally not available. Additionally, each tenant has its own method of accounting for facility revenues, making comparisons difficult. See the discussion of transfer pricing in Chapter 10. Moreover, the winning prospects of the tenant(s) of a sport facility certainly affect ticket sales. However, reliance on a winning team over a few decades is not reasonable, given the tenuous and temporary nature of winning in team sports. Typically, an analyst assumes an average-quality team when conducting a feasibility study.

Information on competing sport franchises is useful in assessing ticket demand. For example, Cleveland and Milwaukee score close to Sacramento in the composite index in Exhibit 11.3, but both of these cities host MLB teams that account for millions of tickets sold each year, making those markets less comparable to Sacramento.

Using the data to calculate ticket demand

The analysis described above suggests which markets are most comparable to Sacramento—Memphis, San Antonio, Orlando, Salt Lake City, Indianapolis, and Charlotte—because they are closest to Sacramento's composite average and do not host MLB teams. Average attendance for NBA games in the comparable markets is about 18,000 per game, about 90% of capacity (based on data not included in this chapter). The Sacramento Kings averaged 17,317 in attendance from 1999 through 2001 (100% of capacity). In the end, a feasibility study must provide an estimate of sales of the various proposed products and services, not just comparisons across markets. This aspect of feasibility studies is discussed later in the chapter.

Corporate Demand

An important factor in sport facility market demand is corporate demand for season tickets, club seats, luxury suites, and sponsorships, which directly affects facility revenues. According to the NBA, over 50% of season ticket holders are corporations. Further, in smaller NBA markets, often over 90% of facility revenues comes from premium seating and sponsorships, which are mostly generated directly by corporations. Accordingly, assessment of corporate demand is an important component of the market demand analysis in a feasibility study. We will use a comparables analysis to estimate corporate demand for the Sacramento Kings.

Corporate depth analysis

Corporate depth, or the depth of a market's corporate base, provides information for predicting corporate-related revenues. One measure of corporate depth is the number of headquarters of Fortune 500 companies in the local area. We may also compile more detailed measures of the number of companies of certain sizes in an area. For instance, season tickets and club seats might be targeted to companies with at least $10 million in annual sales. Luxury suites and sponsorships might be targeted to companies with greater than $50 million in annual sales.

Exhibit 11.4 gives the number of companies with annual sales of $10 million to $50 million, and with $50 million or more in comparable markets. The Sacramento market does not include many large companies, even though it is a population center. Because it is the state capital of California, a very high proportion of Sacramento residents work for state government rather than corporations. This lack of corporate depth suggests that relying on corporate support for luxury suite and sponsorship revenue would be more difficult than in other markets of similar size.

exhibit 11.4   Corporate depth of markets comparable to Sacramento.

NUMBER OF BUSINESSES WITH 25 OR MORE EMPLOYEES

RANK[1]	MARKET[2]	ANNUAL SALES OF $10–50 MILLION	INDEX[3]	ANNUAL SALES OF $50+ MILLION	INDEX[3]	COMPOSITE INDEX[3]
1	Minneapolis	1,877	419	720	526	444
2	Seattle	1,212	271	449	328	284
3	Phoenix	1,150	257	405	296	266
4	Denver	1,065	238	421	307	254
5	Cleveland	1,094	244	386	282	253
6	Portland	893	199	339	247	211
7	Milwaukee	875	195	342	250	208
8	Miami	876	196	306	223	202
9	Indianapolis	687	153	301	220	169
10	Charlotte	674	150	282	206	163
11	Salt Lake City	569	127	215	157	134
12	Orlando	576	129	194	142	132
13	San Antonio	452	101	204	149	112
14	Memphis	447	100	176	128	106
15	Sacramento	448	100	137	100	100
NBA small market composite, excluding Sacramento		198		247		210

Source: Goal Group et al. (2001), Goal Group (2002), Dun & Bradstreet.

[1]Ranked by total composite index of number of businesses with at least 25 employees and at least $10 million in gross sales.
[2]Based on MSAs.
[3]Index: Sacramento = 100 (i.e., Charlotte has 50% more businesses with at least 25 employees and up to $50 million in sales than Sacramento.)

Suite and seat revenue potential

We can estimate the amount of revenue that can be generated by luxury suites by studying the results in comparable markets. Exhibits 11.5 and 11.6 show the wide range of suite revenue potential across NBA markets. Exhibit 11.5 provides the overall luxury suite capacity of each market, defined by multiplying the number of suites by the suite price for all sport facilities in the area, minus suite inventory (suites available in other sport facilities in the area). When we multiply the average suite revenue per large business across the markets ($17,522) by the number of similarly sized businesses in Sacramento (585) we obtain an estimate of $10.25 million in annual suite revenue, including event tickets. From this total, we must deduct the revenue from luxury suites in other facilities in the area to obtain a more realistic estimate of revenue for the proposed arena. In the Sacramento area, the local minor league ballpark, Raley Field, is the only facility with luxury suites. Raley Field's $1.225 million in luxury suites reduces the arena's suite revenue potential in the Sacramento marketplace to just over $9 million.

The analysis of club seat revenue potential is similar to that of luxury suites: we assess club seat inventory, price, and corporate depth across the comparable

Suite revenue potential analysis.   exhibit   **11.5**

RANK[1]	MARKET	AVAILABLE NBA SUITES	AVERAGE PRICE	OTHER SUITES[2]	AVERAGE PRICE	TOTAL SUITES	GROSS MARKET REVENUE	CORPORATE BASE[4]	AVERAGE REVENUE PER BUSINESS[5]	INDEX
1	Charlotte	12	$105,730	284	$119,832	296	$35,301,010	956	$36,926	340
2	Indianapolis	67	$152,238	280	$54,592	347	$27,565,696	988	$27,901	257
3	Memphis[3]	82	$119,146	82	$33,338	164	$12,503,722	623	$20,070	185
4	San Antonio	82	$119,146	14	$10,850	96	$9,921,872	656	$15,125	139
5	Sacramento	29	$177,000	35	$35,000	64	$6,358,000	585	$10,868	100
6	Salt Lake City	60	$81,088	62	$28,500	122	$6,632,280	784	$8,460	78
7	Orlando	26	$95,000	7	$10,850	33	$2,545,950	770	$3,306	30
Composite average		51	$121,335	109	$41,852	160	$14,404,076	766	$17,522	161

Source: Teams, Revenues From Sports Venues, Dun & Bradstreet, Kagan World Media, Inc.

[1] Ranked by total revenue per corporate business. Index: Sacramento = 100 (i.e., San Antonio's revenue per business is currently 39% greater than Sacramento's.)

[2] Other suites' prices are the weighted average of the NFL, motorsports, and minor league seat prices available in each market.

[3] Assumes the Memphis Grizzlies can achieve revenues similar to those of the San Antonio Spurs.

[4] Based on businesses with at least 25 employees and a minimum of $10 million in annual sales.

[5] Gross market revenue column divided by Corporate base column.

Primary Research on Corporate Demand

I n a Phase II feasibility study, rather than undertaking a comparables analysis, we may conduct primary research on corporate demand as an alternative method. Surveys of corporations to investigate their likelihood of buying premium seating and sponsorships would provide some direct evidence. Bear in mind that caution is necessary in interpreting survey results about intent to purchase. We recommend relying on both secondary and primary research whenever possible.

markets. As Exhibit 11.6 shows, the Sacramento market has relatively few club seats when compared to the other markets. This suggests that adding club seats to the marketplace via a new sport arena may be profitable. Exhibit 11.6 also provides the information necessary to estimate club seat revenues. Across the markets, the average club seat revenue generated per large business establishment in the community is $16,530. The number of large businesses in Sacramento is 585 (see Exhibit 11.5). Multiplying the two figures, we obtain a figure of $9.67 million for club seat revenue in the Sacramento marketplace. Raley Field's $1.83 million in club seat revenue reduces the estimate of club seat revenue from a new arena to about $7.85 million. This figure does not include event tickets, only the club seat premium.

exhibit   11.6   Club seat revenue potential analysis.

RANK[1]	MARKET	AVAILABLE NBA CLUB SEATS	AVERAGE PRICE	OTHER AVAILABLE CLUB SEATS[2]	AVERAGE PRICE	TOTAL AVAILABLE CLUB SEATS	GROSS MARKET REVENUE	BUSINESS PER AVAILABLE SEAT	INDEX	AVERAGE REVENUE PER BUSINESS	INDEX
1	Salt Lake City	668	$7,872	1,750	$1,350	2,418	$7,620,996	0.32	106	$9,721	176
2	Sacramento	352	$3,960	1,560	$1,172	1,912	$3,222,240	0.31	100	$5,508	100
3	San Antonio	2,403	$5,901	0	N/A	2,403	$14,180,103	0.27	89	$21,616	392
4	Indianapolis	2,500	$2,665	3,500	$1,250	6,000	$11,037,500	0.16	54	$11,172	203
5	Memphis[3]	2,403	$5,901	1,500	$875	3,903	$15,492,603	0.16	52	$24,868	451
6	Charlotte	0	N/A	11,358	$2,150	11,358	$24,419,700	0.08	28	$25,544	464
7	Orlando	0	N/A	0	N/A	0	N/A	N/A	N/A	N/A	N/A
	Composite average	1,388	$5,260	3,278	$1,359	4,666	$12,662,190	0.22	72	$16,530	300

Source: Dun & Bradstreet, Sacramento Kings, Sport Venues.

[1]Ranked by business per available seat. Index: Sacramento = 100 (i.e., Salt Lake City's business per available seat is currently 6% greater than Sacramento's.)

[2]Other suites prices are the weighted average of the NFL and minor league seat prices available in each market.

[3]Assumes the Memphis Grizzlies can achieve revenues similar to those of the San Antonio Spurs.

Naming rights and other sponsorship revenue

Naming rights are the largest single sponsorship revenue source for a sport facility. A simple analysis of the comparable market information in Exhibit 11.6 shows that a new sport arena would generate about $2 million annually in naming rights sponsorship revenue. We obtain this estimate by starting with the average naming rights revenue for the six comparable markets: $2.4 million (based on information not provided here). Sacramento's would likely be somewhat lower, about $2 million, because the other markets have more corporate depth. Additionally, based on similar comparisons, we expect that Sacramento could generate about $13 million per year in revenue from other sponsorship, signage, advertising, and print sales.

Event Activity

Another element in determining market demand or penetration for a feasibility study includes a competitive analysis of the supply of facilities and primary research on potential events. This is different from a comparables analysis, where we are trying to find similar situations from which to learn. In a **competitive analysis,** we directly investigate existing facilities (stadia, arenas, and amphitheaters) that might compete with the subject facility for hosting events. A sport facility essentially has two types of clients: attendees who show up for events and event property owners (or team owners) who decide where to hold their events or games. A particular market may have high incomes, a large population, and a lot of corporate depth, but it also may already have a lot of competition for shows or events, in the form of other arenas, stadia, or concert halls. For instance, a composite of markets with arenas similar in size to a proposed arena in Sacramento shows that those arenas typically host 47 NBA or NHL games, 37 other sport events, 19 concerts, 29 family shows, and 24 other events, for a total of 157 events annually.* ARCO Arena, current home of the Sacramento Kings, averages 176 events each year. Competition in Sacramento itself comes from a number of venues, although there are no other large arenas. For music shows, competition would be strongest with the Sacramento Valley Amphitheatre, because it seats 18,500, similar to the proposed sport arena. However, overall competition for hosting events is not particularly strong in Sacramento when compared to other markets.

Additionally, to estimate facility usage and number of expected events, we conduct primary research in the form of discussions with event owners, Clear Channel, AEG, IMG, and potential NBA, NHL, and indoor football tenants. These discussions should result in an estimate of the number and type of events that might be held at a new sport arena. Exhibit 11.8 gives an example for a new arena in Sacramento. This example is a conservative estimate. As with all feasibility analyses, it is important that the analysis be somewhat conservative, providing room for error without jeopardizing the facility's financial health.

---

*Analysis based on a two-year average of arenas in Indianapolis, Orlando, Salt Lake City, Columbus (Ohio), San Jose (California), and Nashville.

Kansas City . . . SIDEBAR

BBQ, Jazz, and Basketball?
A Statistical Approach to Feasibility

One limitation of the use of information like that given in Exhibits 11.3 through 11.6 is that we do not know the relative importance of each piece of information. The composite indices in these exhibits are straight averages of the data for each factor. This implies, for instance, that the age of a population is exactly equally important to the population number. What if the local market has a relatively high population but a relatively low income or age? Does that bode well for the market, or not? A recent research article tries to answer this question by analyzing markets for their visibility as hosts for an NBA team (Rascher & Rascher, 2004). By using regression analysis, the researchers created weights for some of the variables discussed thus far, along with many more. The measures of success used in the study were attendance, ticket revenues, and total team revenues. In other words, markets with high revenues were deemed to be successful, and the statistical analysis combined the variables into a single estimate of what attendance or revenues could be expected if a team were to move into a market that did not already have an NBA team.

Exhibit 11.7 shows the study's results. The cities are ranked by estimated gate receipts. Those cities in boldface did not have NBA teams during the period of the study, 1997–99.

This type of research is another method of measuring the feasibility of bringing a team to a particular city. It incorporates the information given in Exhibits 11.3 through 11.6 into a single financial estimate of team success. The researchers predicted that a team in Memphis would fare well in terms of gate receipts but only passable in terms of total revenues (as it has), and that a team in New Orleans would struggle financially—as it has. The estimate in attendance for Sacramento is 17,138, close to the Kings' historical average.

As another example of using this research to determine the feasibility of a facility project, consider the events in Kansas City surrounding the construction of the Sprint Center. In July 2004, the city was in the midst of a debate about the feasibility of building a new downtown sport arena. A referendum was placed on the ballot for a special election in August 2004. Without the benefit of results of a feasibility study, and without a major tenant in place, the public was being asked to vote to spend about $143 million in public money to build the arena. The hope seemed to be that "if you build it, they will come." However, we can conduct a quick assessment of the market by utilizing results from Rascher and Rascher (2004).

11.A

Kansas City is lower down the list than 11 other markets that do not have an NBA franchise. Expansions and relocations in the NBA are rare, but if an owner were to move or the league were to expand, there are many other markets that would likely be chosen instead of Kansas City.* Also, a simple measure of the inability of hosting a new team—population divided by the current number of major professional sport teams—puts Kansas City second to last, just ahead of Milwaukee, out of 48 cities. It already has an NFL and an MLB team—getting an NBA team would spread its population and corporate support thin. Support of the Kansas City Chiefs is slightly above the NFL average in terms of locally generated revenues (according to the most recent publicly available data, 1999–2000). Support of the Kansas City Royals is substantially below average for MLB. In fact, the Royals are estimated to be fourth from the bottom in terms of gate receipts and sixth from the bottom in terms of attendance.

When a city is trying to lure a team to town, projected facility costs rise, because the team has the leverage of competition among multiple cities. Moreover, if the team is not included in the construction design process, then once an owner does decide to move into the arena, millions of dollars' worth of upgrades and changes will have to be made and paid for by the public. For example, in 1990 the Suncoast Dome was opened in St. Petersburg at a cost of $138 million, with the hopes of luring an MLB team. In 1998 the Tampa Bay Devil Rays finally began play in the facility. The upgrades required cost $70 million, 50% of the arena's original cost. Not only were there significant public costs above and beyond the original construction costs, but also the public paid many years for a facility that did not have a major tenant. We can find similar recent examples in New Orleans and San Antonio, where the NBA owner required publicly financed upgrades of approximately 20% of the arena's original cost.

In summary, an assessment of Kansas City as a viable market for a third major sport franchise shows that the franchise would likely struggle.

---

*When the NBA's Grizzlies left Vancouver, British Columbia, for Memphis, the league shopped around and seriously considered moving the team to San Diego, Las Vegas, St. Louis, Louisville, Memphis, and New Orleans, but not Kansas City. When the Charlotte Hornets moved in 2002, Louisville, Norfolk, and New Orleans were considered before the league finally settled on New Orleans. When the NHL expanded in 1998–2000, the four expansion cities were chosen from a pared-down list of six cities. Oklahoma City and Houston were the final cities eliminated prior to the league's choosing Nashville, Atlanta, Minneapolis–St. Paul, and Columbus. Again, Kansas City was not even considered.

Results of study analyzing markets for hosting an NBA team.   exhibit   11.7

CITY/TEAM (RANKED BY GATE RECEIPTS)	FORECASTED ATTENDANCE	FORECASTED GATE RECEIPTS	FORECASTED TOTAL REVENUES
Chicago Bulls	20,108	$45,283,019	$103,944,723
New Jersey Nets	19,667	$44,609,289	$103,666,295
New York Knicks	18,717	$41,543,980	$96,906,295
Washington Wizards	19,704	$41,358,306	$83,281,956
Los Angeles Clippers	17,899	$38,422,655	$97,575,067
Los Angeles Lakers	17,899	$38,422,655	$97,575,067
Seattle SuperSonics	19,757	$38,312,641	$71,904,303
Detroit Pistons	18,249	$34,583,135	$77,497,291
Houston Rockets	18,325	$34,298,557	$69,692,269
Boston Celtics	18,218	$33,924,509	$68,763,022
Indiana Pacers	19,235	$32,993,512	$66,299,117
Philadelphia 76ers	17,729	$32,781,592	$75,895,337
Portland Trail Blazers	18,715	$32,330,039	$64,190,119
Memphis	18,796	$31,596,200	$59,847,117
Utah Jazz	18,622	$31,209,019	$62,109,120
Hartford	18,134	$30,943,166	$56,251,917
Phoenix Suns	18,286	$30,498,141	$72,479,118
Minnesota Timberwolves	17,526	$30,384,199	$67,701,633
Miami Heat	18,315	$29,977,964	$67,583,986
Baltimore	17,560	$29,429,689	$64,518,291
Louisville	18,311	$28,911,371	$59,396,878
San Diego	17,372	$28,460,087	$66,524,446
Las Vegas	17,545	$27,242,661	$59,699,671
Nashville	17,528	$26,882,101	$58,132,275
Milwaukee Bucks	16,978	$26,290,903	$58,624,142
Sacramento Kings	17,138	$26,101,881	$52,459,725
Golden State Warriors	15,762	$26,011,957	$63,966,882
Honolulu	16,467	$25,830,914	$50,552,504
San Antonio Spurs	17,354	$25,604,283	$54,161,323
Norfolk, Virginia Beach, Newport News	17,058	$24,720,174	$59,816,386
Dallas Mavericks	15,907	$24,685,943	$60,500,450
Charlotte Hornets	16,516	$23,644,230	$51,580,247
St. Louis	16,074	$23,606,227	$62,257,248
Atlanta Hawks	15,625	$23,464,312	$62,783,478
Orlando Magic	16,506	$23,263,533	$55,287,320
New Orleans	16,314	$22,026,250	$59,897,920
Jacksonville	16,085	$21,331,308	$54,111,519
Cincinnati	15,644	$20,361,607	$53,771,644
Cleveland Cavaliers	15,119	$20,272,483	$56,035,523
Austin–San Marcos	15,931	$19,766,609	$49,390,583
Denver Nuggets	14,939	$19,541,896	$51,326,220
Kansas City	15,280	$19,503,955	$54,329,534
Albuquerque	15,394	$17,362,572	$45,547,891
Columbus	13,879	$13,684,159	$45,976,470
Pittsburgh	13,357	$12,543,029	$48,788,601
Omaha	13,553	$12,345,181	$39,255,986
Buffalo–Niagara Falls	13,659	$11,974,656	$46,414,481
Oklahoma City	11,432	$11,114,854	$33,726,430
Tucson	11,071	$10,608,078	$31,618,100
El Paso	9,311	$10,178,875	$19,506,282

Note: Boldface cities are those without an NBA team in 1999.

Source: Rascher & Rascher, 2004, as appeared in *Journal of Sport Management*.

exhibit   11.8   Estimate of the number and type of events at a new sport arena for Sacramento.

Major Tenants	
NBA: pre-season	3
NBA: regular season	41
NBA: post-season	2
Total	46
Other Sports	
Hockey tenant (WCHL)	0
Hockey tenant (AHL)	0
Basketball tenant	0
Basketball tenant (WNBA)	18
Indoor soccer (MISL)	12
Indoor football (AFL)	0
Indoor lacrosse (NLL)	0
High school basketball	8
Other sports	16
Wrestling	2
Total	56
Family Shows	
Circus	8
Disney	8
SSL & other family	6
Ice and motor	10
Globetrotters	1
Other events	7
Total	40
Concerts	18
	160

Facility Specifications and Operating Estimates

The previous discussion focused on the analysis of market demand and likely attendance. Market demand analysis forms the basis for estimates of facility revenues. Exhibit 11.9 summarizes the facility-specific revenues that will be discussed. These do not include team revenues that come from the league office.

Facility revenues are typically split between the facility and the major tenant or tenants. (There may be more than one major tenant, especially in the case of a facility that hosts both an NHL and an NBA team or an NFL and MLB team.) An estimate of facility revenue is necessary to determine whether market demand is sufficient to generate revenues for the major tenant(s) and to pay facility financing

exhibit   **11.9**

Estimates of facility revenues resulting from the market demand analysis for Sacramento.

REVENUE SOURCE	AMOUNT	SEATING CAPACITY	AVERAGE PRICE
General tickets (Kings events only)	$21,320,000	10,400	$50 per game
Luxury suites (including event tickets and other events)	$9,000,000	1,224	$140,600 per suite
Club seat fees (all arena events)	$7,840,000	5,960	$1,315 for seat rights
Club seat tickets (all arena events)	$32,184,000	—	$5,400 for event tickets
Other arena events net tickets and rent	$3,800,000	—	—
Sponsorship (all arena events)	$13,000,000	—	—
Naming rights (all arena events)	$2,000,000	—	—
Merchandise (all arena events)	$1,125,000	—	$2.50 average per capita spending
Concessions (all arena events)	$6,075,000	—	$7.50 average per capita spending
Parking (all arena events)	$2,700,000	—	$9.00 average per auto spending
Total arena-related revenues	$99,044,000		

costs (both construction and operation costs). Negotiations for how the facility owner and major tenant will split revenues and construction/operation expenses often take place after the feasibility study is complete.

For instance, a basketball franchise might begin with information on market demand from a feasibility study and add its non-arena revenues (e.g., revenues from the league and from local TV and radio) to obtain total estimated franchise revenues, which it could compare to its estimated expenses. If the net profits are high enough, then the team could feasibly contribute to financing the facility construction. Similarly, if facility revenues are high enough, then the facility owner could contribute to the construction. Often, the total revenues generated by the facility do not appear to be adequate to cover the operating costs of the facility, the major tenant's portion of revenues, and construction costs. In these cases, the facility's proponents will argue that the facility will benefit the local community economically by attracting visitors and tourism to the region. If it can be shown that the extra spending in the community is sufficient to cover the facility's construction, then the local government may help to finance the construction.

The following sections present the steps in determining a feasible arena size, including the number of seats, club seats, and luxury suites and their respective prices and revenues. It also discusses the method for determining the expected ongoing revenues and expenses from the facility.

Arena size and ticket return

One method for estimating the optimal size of an arena is, once again, to look at comparable markets. As Exhibit 11.10 shows, we first divide the average population within 30 miles of the comparable markets (1,543,771) by the total number

| exhibit | 11.10 | Estimating the optimal size of an arena using comparable markets. |

Average 30-mile population of the comparable markets	1,543,771
Average capacity of the comparable markets for 41 home games	760,130
Ratio of population to capacity	2.03
Sacramento's 30-mile population	1,733,765
Sacramento's capacity based on the population-to-capacity ratio	853,680
Estimated capacity at 100% sold out (41 home games)	20,821
Estimated capacity at 90% sold out (41 home games)	18,739

of seats available in those comparable markets (760,130) to obtain the ratio of population to capacity (2.03). The number of seats is based on 41 home games at the average capacity of the comparable markets. Second, we divide Sacramento's population (1,733,765) by that ratio (2.03) and then by the number of home games (41). This results in a seating capacity of 20,821. This figure assumes 100% sellout. To be conservative, we use a 90% sellout rate, which gives a seating capacity of 18,739. This is closer to the feasible capacity of a new arena based on historical NBA averages.

Earlier in this chapter we found that about $7.85 million in club seat revenues can be generated. The estimates in Exhibit 11.9 suggest that 5,960 club seats should be built and should have an average price of $1,315, not including event tickets. Event tickets, based on comparables, would cost about $5,400 per year, generating over $32 million in club seat event ticket revenue. Luxury suite revenue was estimated at about $9 million per year, with prices, including event tickets, at approximately $140,600. This suggests that the arena should have about 64 luxury suites, with an average of 19 seats per luxury suite.

The ticket price for general seating is typically based on prices in comparable markets, which average around $50. To calculate the number of general seats, we subtract the number of club seats (5,960) and luxury suite seats (1,216) from total capacity (18,739). This works out to general seating of about 11,560. A sell rate of 90% would lead to 10,400 general seat tickets sold per game, netting over $21 million in general seating revenue. For other events in the arena, the facility owner will receive rent and/or a share of ticket revenues, depending on negotiations with the event owner. Based on comparables (not given here) the arena can be expected to receive approximately $3.8 million in rent and other event ticket revenue.

Other facility revenues

The primary revenue sources for a facility other than ticket revenues and rent are concessions, merchandise, and parking. We base an estimate of concessions revenue on average per capita concessions sales for events in comparable markets. Typically this figure is $7.50 per person. (Most of this information is not publicly available, because sport teams and arena operating companies are private businesses. Obtaining access to this type of information is one of the challenges of conducting a feasibility study.) If we assume that 1.8 million people attend arena events each year and that the facility earns a 45% gross profit (55% of retail price being cost of goods sold and staffing costs), we find concessions net revenue of approximately $6 million.

Merchandise net revenue is smaller, at about $1.125 million annually. We calculate this figure by assuming that a typical attendee spends $2.50, with 1.8 million attendees and a profit margin of 25%.

Parking revenue estimates are based on a long history of data on the number of cars per event attendee. Generally we expect that a parking space is utilized for every 4.5 attendees. This does not mean that each car contains 4.5 passengers on average, because some attendees will take other forms of transportation. Gross profit margins for parking are quite high, around 75%. Thus, the 1.8 million attendees will purchase about 400,000 parking spaces at approximately $9 per space, yielding about $2.7 million in parking net revenue.

Results of Market Demand Analyses

The end result of a market demand analysis is an estimate of expected quantities sold and prices for tickets, luxury suites, concessions, merchandise, sponsorships, and any other revenue streams, and the revenues generated from each one. This information will be used in the economic impact analysis, the analysis of financing, and the engineering analysis. For example, the calculation of economic impact depends partly on the number of people attending events at a facility. In the analysis of financing, concessions revenues and naming rights (a form of sponsorship) are often capitalized, and their value helps pay for the cost of construction (see Chapter 9). This affects the overall assessment of financing sources. The size of the facility is of course a significant factor in engineering and land use decisions. If a larger facility is built, not only might location be affected, but the overall cost will be higher and financing will be affected. The type and quality of the facility also affect demand, especially with respect to luxury suite sales and sponsorships. Higher-quality suites, which are more expensive to build, might elicit higher demand. Once again, the feasibility study is an iterative process, with many layers of adjustment and readjustment.

FINANCING

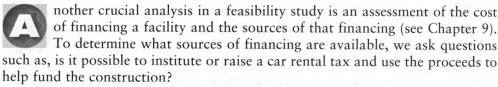 nother crucial analysis in a feasibility study is an assessment of the cost of financing a facility and the sources of that financing (see Chapter 9). To determine what sources of financing are available, we ask questions such as, is it possible to institute or raise a car rental tax and use the proceeds to help fund the construction?

This analysis is another iterative process (look back to Exhibit 11.1). The money that is available for construction affects the type of facility that can be built, and vice versa. The initial driver for money decisions is the number and types of expected events and the expected market demand. This basic information helps determine the appropriate number of seats and suites, which in turn allows us to calculate initial project cost estimates.

The economic and fiscal impact estimates provide information about the amount of incremental money that will flow into the local economy, including sales taxes (see Chapter 12). For instance, if the economic impact analysis shows that a facility will generate $2 million per year in incremental hotel taxes, then those $2 million might be earmarked to help finance the facility. Chapter 9 discusses sport facility financing in full detail.

LOCATION, CONSTRUCTION COSTS, AND ENGINEERING

A discussion of the location, construction costs, and engineering sections of a feasibility study is beyond the scope of this text. Briefly, these analyses focus on the hard costs (construction costs, improvements to the actual building) and soft costs (fees, engineering, consulting, moveable items such as furniture) of facility construction, architectural and engineering renderings, infrastructure issues (such as roadway or exit ramp construction, widening of streets, and traffic flow), environmental impacts, water and sewage needs, and so forth. This section provides a project cost estimate, which is needed to determine the economic and fiscal impacts of construction and is the most important input into the financing section.

CONCLUSION

The feasibility study is a very important component of any major facility construction project, because it specifies the size and cost of the facility, the expected revenues to be generated, the types and sources of financing, and the facility's likely economic impact. The feasibility study involves a complex analysis that includes surveying people and businesses, gathering data from other facility projects, and synthesizing the results into a report that decision makers can use to develop the facility. It requires the application of many of the sport finance tools described in this book.

CONCEPT *check*

1. What factor or variable is the most important in forecasting market demand for a new MLB stadium? Provide evidence for your answer.
2. What factor or variable is the most important in forecasting market demand for a new minor league baseball stadium? Provide evidence for your answer.
3. Is a comparables analysis a type of secondary research or primary research? Explain your answer.
4. Suppose a community is considering constructing a large pool facility for use by community residents. How might it go about conducting a feasibility study for the pool?
   a. Describe possible methods for determining annual usage at the pool.
   b. Describe possible methods for determining prices to be charged (if any) for entry, concessions, and any other services or items to be sold.

c. Describe possible methods for determining costs of construction, operations, and maintenance.

5. Why do analysts sometimes use retail spending as a factor in measuring market demand for a sport facility? What are the pros and cons of using it?

CASE analysis   *Preliminary Feasibility Questions*

As discussed in this chapter, a feasibility study for a sport stadium requires forecasting annual attendance and total revenues at the facility. Consider the following hypothetical situation. A small group of men and women in Ventura, California, are interested in building a minor league baseball stadium and moving an existing Single A franchise to the stadium. They plan to locate the stadium on the edge of Ventura's central business district. They would like you to answer a few key questions, given your expertise in sport management. For each response, give the reasons for your answer and the methods you used to arrive at it.

CASE QUESTIONS

1. Assuming a club that is average in terms of performance on the field, what would be the expected attendance per season during a typical year (once the "honeymoon effect" has worn away)?

2. What revenue would you expect to be generated from tickets, concessions, parking, and merchandise?

3. What revenues would you expect from naming rights and sponsorship?

references

Goal Group, LLC. (2002). *Analysis of a new sports and entertainment district in Sacramento.* A report for the City of Sacramento, the Sacramento Kings basketball franchise, and Union Pacific Railroad.

Goal Group, LLC, SportsEconomics, and Keyser Marston Associates, Inc. (December 18, 2001). *Analysis pertaining to a sports and entertainment district in Sacramento, California.*

Rascher, D.A., & Rascher, H.V. (2004). NBA expansion and relocation: A viability study of various cities. *Journal of Sport Management, 18*(3), 274–295.

12 Economic Impact Analysis

KEY CONCEPTS

- capture rate
- casual visitor
- construction impact
- direct impact
- displaced spending
- economic impact

- incremental spending
- incremental visitor
- indirect economic impact
- induced economic impact
- leakage

- multiplier
- multiplier effect
- operations impact
- reverse time-switcher
- time-switcher

Introduction

Economic impact is the net economic change in a host community resulting from spending attributed to an event or facility. An economic impact analysis is a type of cost-benefit analysis (an analysis or study of the cost of a project in relation to its potential benefits). It is based on the theory that a dollar flowing into a local economy from outside is a benefit to the locality. An economic impact analysis may be part of a feasibility study, or it may be a standalone source of information. Often, an economic impact analysis provides the public with important information regarding the return on an investment in a development project. Such an analysis makes it possible to compare a project to other possible public investment projects. An economic impact analysis may be performed for proposed events or projects (such as facility construction) or for events that have already occurred.

The most important principle in evaluating economic impact is to measure new economic benefits that accrue to the region *that would not occur, or have occurred,* without the project or event. This may sound simple, but once a facility has been constructed or a game has been played, the difficulty lies in measuring what would have happened in the region without the event having taken place.

Economic impact analyses are conducted for sporting events, teams, and sport facilities, among other things. An event, such as the Super Bowl, can have an impact on a community. A team may be thought of as a series of events (e.g., 41 regular season home games for NBA basketball teams); impacts may also result from the location of team headquarters in a local community. A sport facility can have an impact in the construction phase, during which millions of dollars change hands. It can also have an impact after it is opened, as hundreds of events may take place in the facility each year.

The financial return for residents in a community comes in the form of new jobs, new earnings or income, and new tax revenues.* Some of the new earnings go to local residents who work for the event, team, or facility. However, most of the earnings are generated for residents who are not directly associated with the sporting event, team, or facility, but who benefit from positive externalities. As stated previously, positive externalities, or overflow benefits, are those benefits that are produced by an event but that are not captured by the event owners or sport facility. For instance, when visitors go to San Antonio to attend the NCAA Final Four basketball tournament, they will probably spend money at local food establishments, gas stations, retail stores, and hotels. This spending benefits the owners and employees of those establishments, as a positive direct economic impact.

In this chapter, we first discuss setting the parameters for the analysis. The next section discusses the methodologies used in conducting an economic impact analysis. The extension of those techniques to team and facility impacts is next, followed by a discussion of common mistakes made in economic impact analyses.

---

*Additionally, local major sporting events enhance community and civic pride. This effect, known as psychic impact, is discussed later.

SETTING THE PARAMETERS

wo important parameters of events must be determined in the beginning stages of an analysis: the geographic area of impact and the type of spending.

Geographic Area of Impact

The geographic area of impact is an important characteristic of the analysis and should be determined early in the study. Generally, the geographic region selected is the region that is considering funding the event or facility. This definition of the impact region allows for a proper cost-benefit analysis. If a county government contributes funding for a sport facility, then the residents and businesses of that county are paying for the investment, and it is appropriate to determine the benefits that the county receives—not some other county or area—and compare the benefits to the costs. In reality, any major sporting event has an area of impact that is a continuous region, not divided by city or county boundaries, and the impacts decrease with distance from the event location.

Different definitions of the geographic area of impact will affect the amount of economic impact that is measured. For example, imagine a resident of Oakland, California, who would typically spend his entertainment dollars attending a movie near home, but who decides to attend a baseball game in San Francisco, 15 miles away. If he spends money at the event and in a restaurant next to the stadium, this spending may not be new spending in the San Francisco/Oakland/San Jose Consolidated Metropolitan Statistical Area (CMSA), because he would have spent the money in Oakland anyway. Instead, it is considered substituted, displaced, or redirected spending. In a conservative estimate, most local spending is considered to be **displaced spending**—spending by local residents on an event that would have been spent elsewhere in the local economy if the event had not occurred. For this reason it is not counted as part of economic impact. In general, it is improper to count this spending in the economic impact totals, because while more spending is occurring in San Francisco because of the baseball game, less spending is taking place in Oakland. If, however, the chosen geographic area of impact is just the city of San Francisco, then an Oakland resident who attends the game provides a positive direct economic impact on San Francisco. In contrast, a resident of Fresno, California (almost 200 miles away), who attends a baseball game in San Francisco would provide a positive economic impact regardless of whether the geographic area of impact was the entire CMSA or just the city of San Francisco.

Spending

Because spending by local residents typically should not be counted in an economic impact study, it is very important that the analyst differentiate between event attendees who are visitors (those who live outside the geographic impact area) and those who are local residents (those who live inside the area). We can also describe visitors as

- **Casual visitors**—visitors who were already in town for another reason and decided to attend the event.

- **Time-switchers**—visitors who would have come to town at another time, but opted to come to town during this time instead, in order to attend the event.
- **Incremental visitors**—visitors who came to town because of the event and would not have come to town otherwise. The direct spending of this group is fully counted in economic impact.

Exhibit 12.1 is a sample breakdown of attendees at an event. The spending of casual visitors and time-switchers should not be fully counted as new spending; only their **incremental spending**—the spending above and beyond what they would have spent—should be counted. For example, suppose a person on a business trip spends $200 per day on a hotel room, food, and transportation, and decides to attend the local NBA game, spending an additional $40 for a ticket. The incremental spending is $40, and only this amount should be counted toward the economic impact of the NBA team. The other $200 is economic impact coming from the business portion of the trip.

It is typically not practical to measure the incremental spending of time-switchers and casual visitors. It is difficult to know how much these individuals spent because of the event, beyond what they would have spent on their visit had the event not taken place. Since we usually cannot measure the incremental spending of casual visitors and time-switchers, we might use an estimate from some other source or simply state that this spending was not measured and the final estimate should be considered a lower bound for the economic impact.

A first step in measuring economic benefit is to analyze direct spending, which has two components. The first component is incremental visitor spending. As opposed to the spending of time-switchers and casual visitors, direct spending by incremental visitors is fully counted in economic impact. The goal is to measure the amount of spending in the geographic area of impact that goes to local businesses. For example, how much are people spending at sporting events? How much are incremental visitors spending on restaurants, retail, transportation, and so forth? Whether to count the

exhibit **12.1** Breakdown of attendees at an event.

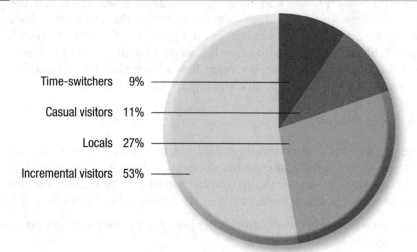

Time-switchers	9%
Casual visitors	11%
Locals	27%
Incremental visitors	53%

spending that takes place inside the sport facility is debatable. It is in the geographic area of impact, but how much of it goes to local businesses? To answer this question we might look at how much money from the event is spent locally, or we might find out what happens to the revenue spent inside the facility. Where does it go? Does the local government (often the owner of the facility) receive a percentage of it?

The second component of direct spending is organizational spending. How much do the event host committee, the event management company, corporate sponsors, and other related entities spend in the geographic area?

METHODOLOGIES FOR MEASURING EVENT ECONOMIC BENEFITS

 his discussion focuses on spending methodologies and fiscal or tax impact methodology.

Spending Methodologies

Economic impacts are often subdivided into direct, indirect, and induced impacts. Each of these is further subdivided into effects on total output, earnings or income, employment, and public finances. We use different methodologies for studying the spending at each of the stages.

Direct spending methodology

The analysis of **direct impact**—expenditures on a project or event that contribute to economic impact, also called direct spending—may involve secondary or primary research.

Secondary research. The market demand analysis discussed in Chapter 11 provides an estimate of the number of events that will take place at a facility and the expected attendance at those events. An economic impact study using secondary research begins with attendance estimates from the market demand analysis and adds other information about the expected patrons, such as what percentage are visitors and how much money they will spend. Often, this information is gathered from comparable events in other locations, as described in the previous chapter. For a feasibility study, secondary research methods are employed that are similar to the techniques for determining market demand. One method is to evaluate primary studies that have been conducted in other cities for similar projects, with adjustments to account for the differences in circumstances between the primary studies and the subject study.

Primary research: spectator surveys. To determine direct spending, we often create a survey instrument (a questionnaire) to guide interviews with event patrons in order to determine whether they are local residents or visitors, how much money they are spending because of the event, and other information that may be helpful. Exhibit 12.2 is a simple survey for measuring direct spending for an event. The data provide an estimate of the amount of spending per capita per day for incremental visitors for the different spending categories. It allows the researcher to identify casual visitors and time-switchers (see questions 9 and 10) and to account for the number of days a visitor is in town and for the size of groups.

exhibit	12.2	Example survey for measuring direct spending at an event.

2004 MAJOR LEAGUE BASEBALL ALL-STAR GAME
ECONOMIC IMPACT SURVEY

1. Are you attending the All-Star Game?   ☑ Yes   ☐ No

2. Your age: ☐ 18–24   ☑ 25–34   ☐ 35–44   ☐ 45–54   ☐ 55+

3. What is your gender?   ☐ Female   ☑ Male

4. Your annual household income: ☐ <$25,000   ☐ $25,000–$49,999   ☑ $50,000–$74,999   ☐ $75,000–$99,999   ☐ $100,000–$124,999   ☐ $125,000 +

5. What is your residential zip code?   _08055_

6. How long will you be visiting Houston?   _4_ day(s)   _3_ night(s)

7. While visiting Houston, **how many people in your party** will you be paying for, **including yourself**?   _3_

8. While in Houston during the All-Star Game, how much do you plan to spend **DAILY for the above group** on the following?

Lodging	$140
Transportation in Houston (rental car, gas, parking, taxi, bus, etc.)	$55
Event-related (tickets, concession, merchandise at All-Star Game)	$125
Food/beverage (not at All-Star Game)	$130
Entertainment (not at All-Star Game)	$75
Shopping (not at All-Star Game)	$120
Other (not at All-Star Game)	$20

9. Would you have visited Houston this weekend if the All-Star Game were not in town?   ☐ Yes   ☑ No

10. Does this visit to Houston replace any other past/future visit to this area?   ☐ Yes   ☑ No

When enough spectators are surveyed, one can estimate how much the typical visitor spends and how long he or she stays.* Given the percentage of survey respondents who are local residents versus visitors and an estimate of total attendance, we can estimate the total population of visitors at the event. Similarly, we can extrapolate the findings for the sample in terms of spending to represent the spending of the entire population of spectators. Exhibit 12.3 shows some intermediate calculations that were initial steps in measuring the economic impact of the 2004 MasterCard Alamo Bowl. The total number of spectators at the event (available from the facility manager) was multiplied by the percentage of survey respondents that were visitors, in this case approximately 60%,[†] to obtain the estimate of total visitors (39,350). An analysis of ticket sales and ZIP codes can

*Calculation of the necessary sample size is beyond the scope of this text. Consult a business research or marketing research methods text.

[†]Best efforts are made to survey a random sample of people attending the event.

also provide this type of information. Based on survey questions such as 9 and 10 in Exhibit 12.2, we can make similar adjustments to account for casual visitors and time-switchers, to obtain the number of "relevant" (incremental) visitors. In Exhibit 12.3, we first subtract people who are *only* time-switchers *or* casual visitors from the number of visitors and then subtract the visitors who are *both* casual visitors *and* time-switchers to calculate the number of incremental visitors.

In addition, the surveys can help us develop a typical visitor profile. In Exhibit 12.3, the typical visitor spent $169 per day outside the stadium and stayed 3.2 days, resulting in an average of $543 spent outside the stadium for the entire trip. Multiplying the number of incremental visitors by the amount that the typical incremental visitor spent provides an estimate of the spectator portion of direct spending.

Typically, direct spending by visitors attending an event occurs in several geographic categories simultaneously. As an example, consider the NCAA Men's Final Four basketball tournament, which has taken place in San Antonio, Texas, a number of times. Direct spending occurs in the city of San Antonio, in Bexar County, in the San Antonio MSA, and in the state of Texas. The area of impact defined for an economic impact study will depend on how the results are to be used. If the county

---

Visitor profile created from the results of a visitor survey.   exhibit   **12.3**

KEY FINDINGS FROM THE VISITOR SURVEY

CATEGORY	ESTIMATE
Total number of visitors participating in MasterCard Alamo Bowl activities	39,350
Number of time-switchers only	−2,069
Number of casual visitors only	−7,039
Number of visitors who are both casual visitors and time-switchers	−1,700
Number of incremental visitors: count toward economic impact[a]	**28,542**
Average expenditure estimates	
Average daily expenditure per incremental visitor outside Alamodome	$169
Average number of days stayed per incremental visitor	3.20
Average expenditure for entire trip per incremental visitor outside Alamodome	$543
Average expenditure for entire trip per incremental visitor inside Alamodome	$73
Total direct spending of incremental visitors outside Alamodome[b]	$15,487,693
Total direct spending of incremental visitors inside Alamodome[c]	$2,076,952

[a]Spending by time-switchers and casual visitors was not used in the impact analysis.

[b]Spending is only within the city of San Antonio.

[c]Spending includes tickets, concessions, and merchandise.

is investing in hosting the event, then county decision makers need to know the economic benefits and costs of the event. If the state is going to help fund the event, then state decision makers need to know the impact on the entire state. It is possible, but complicated, to measure the economic impact on more than one area. The direct spending measurement will be derived from the spending of visiting spectators and participants on entertainment, food and beverage, transportation, retail, lodging, and other miscellaneous spending, plus event-related spending by non-local businesses.

Primary research: corporate spending surveys. In addition to the visitor survey, the researcher may undertake a survey of the event management group, host committee, sponsors, and so forth to determine local corporate spending that is related to the event *that would not have occurred otherwise*. As with visitor spending, it is important to distinguish between corporate spending that would have taken place anyway and corporate spending that would *not* have occurred otherwise. A local restaurant chain may spend money to sponsor a local college football bowl game. It may also spend money with local advertising agencies and printers to promote or activate its sponsorship with a television commercial or billboard advertising. The money spent locally is counted toward the economic impact of the bowl game *if* the restaurant chain would not have made those purchases otherwise. If the bowl game were not taking place, and the restaurant chain would have advertised on television with a more typical restaurant ad, then the bowl game did not provide an economic impact to the local community in this case. It simply affected exactly how and why the money was being spent. The same amount would have been spent locally with or without the game; hence, there was no net economic impact. When a non-local business sponsors a bowl game, this is considered to be net new spending (unless the company would have spent the same money locally without the game). For practical reasons, and to develop a conservative estimate of economic impact, we do not consider spending by local companies to be new spending unless it can be specifically identified as new spending. Thus, spending by local companies is not typically counted toward economic impact. In other words, the researcher starts with the assumption that local spending is displaced spending and is not new incremental spending. If a company specifically states that its spending is new and would not have occurred otherwise, then that spending may be considered part of economic impact.

Indirect and induced spending methodology

The economic output that results from direct spending during an event subsequently affects many other industries and workers. For instance, when visitors attend the Men's Final Four, they may eat in a local restaurant before the event. With the money the visitors spend, the restaurant will pay employees, purchase food, pay for utilities, and so on. The food wholesaler will pay the farmer, who (if it is a small, local farm) will purchase clothing at the local retail store. These expenditures continue through successive rounds until the money ceases to circulate locally, when either it leaks out of the local economy or a resident or local company saves it for a significant period of time.

The spending described in the previous paragraph illustrates **indirect economic impacts:** impacts that occur in the area of impact that represent the circulation of initial visitor expenditures (direct impacts). The total of the successive rounds of spending constitutes the indirect impact estimate, which will be explained below.

The **induced economic impact** is the effect of direct and indirect economic impacts on earnings and employment. As the initial spending and subsequent spending occur, a portion goes to local residents and to the local government in the form of taxes. Increases in demand resulting from the economic impact lead to increases in employment, which will affect earnings. When we report these impacts, we describe employment impacts in terms of full-time equivalent (FTE) jobs and earnings impacts in terms of dollars of personal income. A more detailed discussion of induced economic impact occurs later in this chapter.

Multiplier effect to measure indirect and induced impacts. A **multiplier** is a number that helps researchers quantify indirect and induced economic impacts, by measuring the change in output for each and every industry as a result of the injection of one dollar of direct impact into any of those industries.

To derive a multiplier, we begin by categorizing the spending that represents indirect and induced economic impacts. The recipients of initial direct spending generally re-spend it in five ways:

1. With other private sector businesses in the same local economy—on inventory, maintenance, and so forth
2. With employees who reside in the same local economy—as wages, tips, and so on
3. With local government—as sales taxes or property taxes
4. With non-local governments—as sales taxes or taxes on profits
5. With employees, business, or organizations who reside outside the local economy

The first three types of spending recirculate money through the local economy. The last two categories of spending are considered **leakages**—the movement of money out of the geographic region. They reflect the degree to which a region is not economically isolated but engages in commerce with other regions. The larger and more diverse the geographic region, the less leakage, all else being equal, because a large region is usually relatively self-sufficient.

For the above five scenarios, we create input/output tables that disaggregate the economy into industries and quantify the flow of goods and services among them. We then mathematically derive multipliers that describe changes in output that result from changes in input. We apply a separate multiplier to each of the 528 industry groups (as defined by the U.S. Bureau of Economic Analysis).

Typically, the researcher does not actually create the multipliers for the 528 industry groups but instead purchases a regional multiplier model based on the USDA Forest Service IMPLAN (IMpact Analysis for PLANning) and data from the U.S. Bureau of Economic Analysis. Many vendors supply these multiplier tables, including the Minnesota IMPLAN Group and Regional Economic Models, Inc. The researcher either purchases the multiplier information for a county, city, MSA, or state from one of these vendors or, in some cases, gathers information from the U.S. BEA and derives the multipliers him- or herself.

For an example of the multiplier in action, consider a group of spectators from outside San Antonio who visit the city to attend the Men's Final Four and spend $1,000 total in the community. This initial direct expenditure stimulates economic activity and creates additional business spending, employment, household income, and government revenue in San Antonio. The initial spending (the direct impact) results in a ripple effect, termed the **multiplier effect.** The multiplier effect consists of indirect and induced impacts.

The local theaters, restaurants, retail stores, transportation providers, and others who receive portions of the initial $1,000 will spend the money in the five ways listed previously. The recipients of *those* expenditures will again spend the money in one of the five ways, and the chain of purchases continues. Exhibit 12.4 charts the direct and indirect effects of the original $1,000 of spending.

---

exhibit 12.4 Direct and indirect effects of initial spending.

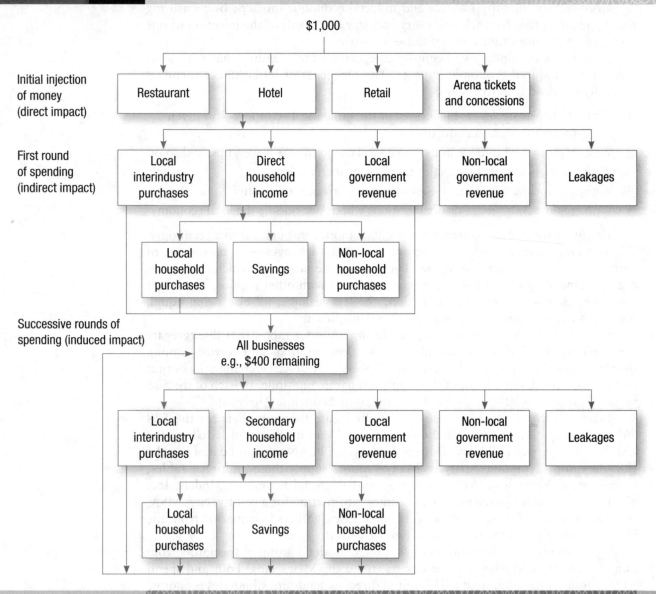

The manner in which the local economy is defined—especially its size—affects the values of the multipliers. In a smaller local geographic region, more game attendees will probably be visitors. This is an advantage to the local economy. However, smaller geographic areas suffer from a greater degree of leakage, because a small geographic region is less self-sufficient than a large region.

There are a number of different types of multipliers, and each has a specific purpose. The first type of multiplier is an output multiplier (also called a sales or transaction multiplier). It measures the indirect and induced effects of an extra unit of direct spending on *economic activity* within the local economy. This multiplier relates direct expenditures to the increase in economic activity that results from the spending and re-spending of the initial direct spending.

An income multiplier, the second type, measures the indirect and induced effects of an extra unit of spending on the level of *household income* in the local economy. It is the ratio of change in income to the initial change in expenditure. It is the clearest indicator of the effect of economic impact on the residents of the host community.

The third type of multiplier is an employment multiplier, which measures the direct, indirect, and induced effects of an extra unit of spending on *employment* in the local economy. It measures the number of full-time equivalent jobs supported in the local economy as a result of visitor expenditures.

Exhibit 12.5 is a multiplier table listing the output, earnings, and employment multipliers for industrial categories in the city of San Antonio.

Example of indirect and induced event spending analysis. To illustrate the analysis of indirect and induced spending, we refer to Exhibit 12.5. If a visitor to San Antonio spends $100 on lodging, this will create an extra $76 in indirect spending. Of that $100, $63 will be retained as income or earnings to residents of San Antonio. Given the employment multiplier for the lodging industry of 16.28, we can expect that for every $1 million spent in San Antonio on lodging, approximately 16 FTE jobs will be created. Another way to think about this is as follows: in order to

---

Example output, income, and employment multipliers.   **exhibit   12.5**

SAN ANTONIO MULTIPLIERS

	OUTPUT	INCOME	EMPLOYMENT[a]
Transportation	1.79	0.55	10.91
Retail	1.69	0.70	22.53
Lodging	1.76	0.63	16.28
Entertainment	1.87	0.52	27.46
Food and beverage	1.70	0.65	23.53
Miscellaneous	1.59	0.55	18.13

[a]The employment multiplier is measured on the basis of a $1 million change in output.

Source: Rascher, 2004; IMPLAN 2000.

create or support one job, the lodging industry has to take in a certain amount of money. We can calculate this amount by dividing the basis change in output by the employment multiplier:

$$\text{money necessary to support one job} = \frac{\text{basis change in output}}{\text{employment multiplier}}$$

$$= \frac{\$1,000,000}{16.28}$$

$$= \$61,425.06$$

This is the average total cost of employing a worker in the lodging industry, including benefits (e.g., health or retirement benefits), payroll costs (e.g., social security taxes), and assorted overhead.

To return to the example of the MasterCard Alamo Bowl, the results from the survey in Exhibit 12.2 allow us to calculate the total spending by category. The results, given in Exhibit 12.6, show that Lodging and Food & Beverage were the two categories with the highest spending for visiting spectators at the bowl game. The survey showed that the average incremental visitor spent about $123 on lodging. Given that there were 28,542 incremental visitors (see Exhibit 12.3), the direct economic impact for lodging is $3.5 million.

To calculate the total economic impact of the Alamo Bowl, we multiply each of the direct spending categories in Exhibit 12.6 by the appropriate multiplier given in Exhibit 12.5 and then total these eight amounts. In this example, spending inside the Alamodome is not included in the economic impact measurement. The measurement does include, under corporate spending, expenditures by the Alamo Bowl, the host committee, other corporate sponsors that hosted parties and bowl-related

| exhibit | 12.6 | Calculating total economic impact. |

CATEGORY	DIRECT SPENDING[a]	MULTIPLIER	TOTAL
Transportation	$1,685,852	1.79	$3,017,675
Retail	$2,613,793	1.69	$4,417,310
Lodging	$3,510,047	1.76	$6,177,682
Entertainment	$2,896,358	1.87	$5,416,189
Food & beverage	$2,933,265	1.70	$3,142,239
Miscellaneous	$1,848,376	1.59	$2,938,918
Inside Alamodome	—	—	—
Corporate/team/media	$4,450,128	—	$4,450,128
Total direct spending	**$19,937,821**	**Total economic impact**	**$33,574,109**

[a]Does not include spending within the Alamodome.

| Alamo Bowl example of induced economic impacts. | **exhibit** | **12.7** |

TYPE OF IMPACT

Earnings	$19,301,504
Employment	682

Note: Figures do not include spending within the Alamodome.

events, and the visiting team. We can easily calculate the indirect economic impact by subtracting the direct economic impact from the total economic impact.

total economic impact – direct economic impact = indirect economic impact
$$\$33,574,109 - \$19,937,821 = \$13,636,289$$

Exhibit 12.7 gives the induced impacts from the Alamo Bowl. These portions of direct spending are retained as income or earnings for local residents. The indirect spending resulting from the bowl game also contributes to increases in income. However, as discussed above, it is practically impossible to track indirect spending. For this reason, we use a general aggregate multiplier to estimate induced earnings impacts from indirect spending. This aggregate multiplier can be determined by calculating the weighted average multiplier for the city across all 528 industry categories. The employment impact from indirect spending is calculated in the same fashion.

Fiscal (or Tax) Impact Methodology

An analysis of the fiscal or tax implications of economic impact is often complex. First, the analyst must understand the tax code for the city, county, or state—a daunting requirement. Second, the task of separating tax revenue according to recipient, such as city, county, or state government, can be difficult. Third, accounting for tax-exempt spending by visitors and relevant local organizations can be time consuming, and it often results only in estimates of those exemptions. Fourth, accounting for the tax effects of indirect and induced impacts requires information that is not always readily available.

Continuing with San Antonio as an example, let's look at the fiscal impact of a sport event. During the event, sales and use, mixed beverage, hotel occupancy, and rental car taxes are collected from direct spending. In 2009, these taxes were:

- *Sales and use:* 1.125% to the City of San Antonio; 6.25% of the retail sale price of tangible personal property and selected services to the State of Texas; 0.5% to the Metropolitan Transit Authority; 0.25% to the Advanced Transportation District

- *Hotel occupancy:* 6% to the state; 1.75% to Bexar County; 9% to the City of San Antonio.

- *Alcoholic beverages:* Mixed beverages: 11.2% to the state; 1.4% to the county; 1.4% to the city. First sale taxes include a beer tax of $6 per barrel, an ale tax of 19.8¢ per gallon, a liquor tax of $2.40 per gallon, and a wine tax of 20.4¢ per gallon.

- *Rental car:* 10% to the state; 5% to the county.

We calculate direct fiscal impacts by multiplying the tax rates for each category by the direct spending for each category. (See Exhibit 12.8.) For example,

$$
\begin{aligned}
\text{fiscal impact for lodging} &= \text{lodging direct spending} \times \text{San Antonio} \\
&\qquad \text{hotel occupancy tax rate} \\
&= \$3{,}510{,}047 \times 9\% \\
&= \$315{,}904
\end{aligned}
$$

The calculation of fiscal impacts is complicated by tax exemptions. Not every item in a grocery store is subject to sales tax; in some states, sales taxes must be paid for food at a restaurant if you eat in, but not for takeout; and, often, cigarettes have a different tax rate than other grocery store items. To sort out these issues, we gather information from a variety of sources. For instance, the National Restaurant Association estimates that 10% of a typical restaurant bill is for alcohol. Thus, for San Antonio we can make an adjustment to account for sales taxes and alcohol taxes at restaurants.

We measure indirect impacts by applying recent historical aggregate average tax rates to the indirect spending estimate. Given that indirect spending is disbursed throughout many sectors of the local and state economies—some of those sectors being subject to certain taxes and others not—one way to estimate the fiscal impact of indirect spending is to analyze the total spending that takes place in a county relative to total taxes collected. In some states, the gross state product (GSP), an estimate of total spending in the state, is disaggregated by city and county. By combining that information with the total taxes collected in the city or county, we can obtain an estimate of the indirect spending tax rate. For instance, if total spending in a town during one year is $100 million, and the total of taxes collected in that town from all sources for that year is $5 million, then, on average, for every dollar spent, five cents is collected in local taxes. This type of calculation provides an estimate for the fiscal impact of indirect spending. Exhibit

exhibit   12.8   Calculation of fiscal impacts using Alamo Bowl example.

TAX CATEGORY	
Sales and use	$162,547
Alcoholic beverage	$4,107
Hotel occupancy	$315,904
Subtotal	$482,558
Indirect taxation	$331,961
Total fiscal impact	**$814,519**

Note: Figures do not include spending within the Alamodome.

12.6 shows indirect spending at the Alamo Bowl as $13.6 million. Using historical information, we know that the average tax collected in the city was about 2.4 cents per dollar (2.4344, to be exact). We can now calculate the fiscal impact of indirect spending pertaining to the Alamo Bowl.

$$\text{fiscal impact of indirect spending} = \text{indirect spending} \times \text{average tax rate}$$
$$= \$13,636,289 \times 2.4344\%$$
$$= \$331,962$$

MEASURING EVENT COSTS

We have explained techniques for measuring the economic benefits of an event. Now we turn to the costs of hosting the event. Many economic impact studies do not provide estimates of the costs of generating economic impacts. It can sometimes be difficult to determine the full costs of hosting an event and the entities responsible for paying those costs. For instance, if a host committee spent $4 million to bid for and host an event, and 75% of that money was spent locally, one may be tempted to count the $3 million as positive economic impact. However, if the source of the money is the local government, then the impact does not count. The money would likely have been spent in town even if the event had not taken place. If the source of funds was outside the community—perhaps the state government or non-local corporate sponsors, then the spending could be considered an economic benefit and counted as part of economic impact.

Although many economic impact studies do not address costs, a complete study does include an analysis of event costs. In addition to local government funding, these often include costs of security, ticket sales, printing, advertising, transportation, communication, travel, and lodging.

ECONOMIC IMPACT OF A LOCAL TEAM

Measuring the economic impact of an event is a formidable task, but measuring the economic impact of a team is even more complex. A team may be thought of as a series of events—for example, 81 home games for an MLB team. Typically, the analyst would gather data on one or two games and extrapolate the results to an entire season. Based on discussions with team officials, the researcher may choose to study a weekday game and a weekend game, because the mix of patrons probably varies the most across those two types of games. Additionally, we must measure the impact of the team as a local business, including organizational spending in the area and direct employment of the franchise. NFL teams often employ more than 200 people, including players.

Similarly, an NFL team may spend $150 million annually. The percentage that is spent locally is called the **capture rate**. Typically, a significant portion of organizational spending takes place outside the local city. In fact, a conservative estimate may be that only 10% is spent locally.* The largest single expense item is player salaries. For a proper estimate of organizational spending, the researcher

---

*A recent self-audit by a major professional sport team found a capture rate of 21% of the team's total budget.

SIDEBAR

The Games Trust Fund in Texas... Economic Impact in Action

12.A

In 1999, researchers conducted an economic impact study of the Pan Am Games in San Antonio, using secondary research, to see whether it would be worth the cost for San Antonio to try to win the bid for the 2007 Pan Am Games. San Antonio did not win the bid, but as a result of the study, the State of Texas passed a law (Texas Civil Statutes, Title 83, Article 5190.6) called the Games Trust Fund creating a pool of $10 million each year that local host committees in the state can tap to bring a major sporting event to town. (According to the law, eligible events include the Pan Am Games, Olympic Games, Super Bowl, NCAA Final Four, Bowl Championship Series Games, any of the major all-star games, World Cup soccer games, and the World University Games.) The amount of money that the host committee receives from the fund is based on the fiscal impact that the event would provide to the State of Texas outside the immediate region of the event (i.e., it does not include the local area impact, but the impact beyond that area still within the state), as determined through a secondary economic impact study. The funds are distributed prior to the event so that the host committee can provide a successful event with maximum economic impact. After the event, a follow-up analysis (primary research impact study) is performed to determine the accuracy of the original estimate.

In 2004, Texas hosted the NFL Super Bowl and MLB All-Star game in Houston and the NCAA Men's Final Four in San Antonio. The state comptroller required economic impact estimates for all three events in order to allocate funds according to the relative fiscal impacts of the three events. The economic impact study for the Final Four was so thorough, according to the comptroller, that the local host committee received just under $5 million, which was more than would have been the case had the study not been so thorough.* The law provided a rare opportunity to compare the results of a secondary research economic impact study (a forecast) and a primary research economic impact study (actual results). The forecast was approximately 10% lower than the figures found in the primary research economic impact estimate (post analysis).

*The original Pan Am Games study and the 2004 Final Four study were both conducted by Richard Irwin of Strategic Marketing Services and Daniel Rascher of SportsEconomics, LLC.

must account for where players reside, and the researcher may be even more conservative by assuming that players do not spend all their money but rather save a significant portion of it. To estimate the capture rates of franchise spending, we can audit the team's spending patterns. This is not often done, because of the high labor costs required to do so. Aside from organizational spending and employment, measuring the economic impact of a team is similar to measuring that of an event.

A feasibility study is often conducted prior to a team moving to town. In this case, the analysts employ secondary research methods similar to the techniques used in determining market demand. One method is to evaluate primary studies that have been conducted in other cities for similar projects, making adjustments to account for the differences in circumstances between the primary studies and the subject study. An assessment of common denominators, such as both cities having an NBA team, can also be helpful. For example, a feasibility study for San Antonio to host an NFL team might include the analysis of a primary economic impact study of the Indianapolis Colts. In adjusting the findings to fit San Antonio, the analyst might look at existing primary economic impact studies for the two relevant NBA teams, the Indiana Pacers and San Antonio Spurs.

ECONOMIC IMPACT OF A SPORT FACILITY

The measurement of a sport facility's economic impact can be controversial, because the results are often cited as evidence in debates over how much public funding the facility should receive (see Chapter 9 for more on this topic). A sport facility can provide economic impact both during the construction phase and during the operational phase, when it hosts hundreds of events. As already described, a facility will provide **operations impact** (impact generated through daily operation) from games and other events. A facility will also provide direct spending impacts, like those of a team. The methodology for measuring a facility's operational economic impacts is similar to that for events and teams.

The measurement of **construction impact**—the amount of money that comes into the community during the construction phase that would not otherwise have entered the community—has been perhaps the most controversial aspect of sport economic impact analysis. In general, if a city government spends money to construct a building, the net economic impact must be measured in terms of the forgone alternative uses of the same funding, i.e., the opportunity cost. Would other uses have had a greater or lesser economic impact? Typically, government spending is not considered to generate economic impact for a specific project, because that money could have been spent on another project. This is similar to the reason why spending by local residents is not generally considered to add to operational economic impact, as discussed previously. If a resident spends money at a football game, then he or she will not spend that money at the movies or for other local entertainment.

In terms of a facility, if a local government uses $20 million of its annual budget to build a sport arena instead of upgrading the facilities of the local school district, then the arena construction provides a construction impact only to the extent that it results in more private money being spent locally. If a team owner spends $30 million in conjunction with the local government to build a $50 million arena, then the $30 million in private funding would be a construction impact, but the $20 million in public funding would not.

SIDEBAR

Findings from the Sales Tax Method

12.B

Academic research conducted by economists to measure the economic impact of sport facilities often shows that these facilities have little or no economic impact on the community, primarily because of the high construction costs that the public usually pays. Certainly, the facilities do generate new revenues, because they draw people from out of town for events, but those incremental revenues do not cover the public's portion of the construction cost. Also, research into sales taxes collected in a county hosting a professional sport facility show that often the impact from the facility is too small to measure. Robert Baade, Victor Matheson, Brad Humphreys, and Dennis Coates, among others, have conducted numerous studies of this type (see Baade & Matheson, 2006, and Coates & Humphreys, 2003).

It may be difficult to discern the impact of a single business such as a sport facility on a county or metropolitan area over a period of time as long as a year or even a month, but the general belief is that events at these facilities crowd out regular visitors to a community, if the event is large, or cause visitors to substitute event attendance for another visit to the community, so the net effect is zero or small. However, the findings from surveys of visitors are contrary, in that even after accounting for time-switchers and casual visitors, these studies find there were incremental visitors who spent money in the community that they would not have spent otherwise. To reconcile these two opposed findings is fodder for future research.

COMMON MISTAKES IN ESTIMATING ECONOMIC IMPACT

As with all business research, economic impact analysis provides an *estimate* of the true impact. Analysts cannot avoid making assumptions, and they are well advised to minimize the number of assumptions and to test the validity of the assumptions. Controversy surrounds sport economic impact analyses, partly because many researchers do not, frankly, do a very good job of avoiding common mistakes. Such mistakes will cause the estimate to either over- or underestimate the true economic impact.

Causes of Underestimating

One of the main causes of estimates being too low is the fact that it is impossible to account for all local corporate spending that relates to an event. For instance, for events that are televised, expenditures by the media (e.g., ESPN) with local businesses to produce coverage of the event are not likely to be accounted for in the economic impact study. Most media organizations do not release the relevant information. Of course, we can make estimates.

Some events produce economic impact from visitors who come to town because of the event but do not attend the event itself. For the NCAA Men's Final Four basketball tournament held in San Antonio in 2004, approximately 7,000 visitors came to town for the event, but, for a variety of reasons, did not attend any of the games. Many studies will fail to measure impacts like this.

How the researchers treat blank survey responses can affect the final results. Counting a blank response as zero lowers the overall estimate of economic impact. Counting it as the average of other responses on the same question can result in a better estimate, unless the respondent meant for the answer to be zero but left it blank. Sometimes looking at the raw surveys will suggest the best way to treat the response. If the respondent answered some of the spending categories but left others blank, he or she probably intended the blank responses to mean zero.

As described above, to produce a conservative estimate, we do not count spending by local residents and by casual visitors and time-switchers toward economic impact, because we assumed that the spending would have occurred even if the event had not taken place. However, research shows that this may not always be the case. For example, after the MasterCard Alamo Bowl, local residents indicated that they spent, on average, just under $40 per person *more* in town than they would have if the event had not been held in San Antonio. Perhaps even more important is the notion of "vacationing at home," when a local resident stays in town because of an event instead of leaving town and spending money outside town (see Sidebar 12.C).

Often, fiscal impacts are not fully accounted for. This is especially true of business or personal income taxes collected on the earnings or income type of economic impact. User fees related to energy usage and airport taxes levied per person using the local airport are examples of other fiscal impacts that are often not accounted for.

Another shortcoming of standard economic impact analysis is that most measurements account only for current new spending, ignoring the possibility that an event might cause an increase in the number of future visitors to the community. For instance, the 2004 NCAA Men's Final Four basketball tournament economic impact analysis reported that approximately 20% of visitors said that after coming to San Antonio for the Final Four, they are likely to visit again. These future visits should be attributed at least partially to a particular event, yet they are often ignored. Media

SIDEBAR

Vacationing at Home

12.C

In a recent study, Steven Cobb and Douglas Olberding (2007) found that for a medium-sized marathon, approximately 20% of the local residents running in it should be considered in measuring economic impact, because the hometown marathon serves as a substitute for an out-of-town race. Thus, they are vacationing at home and spending their money at home rather than in some other town. Further research on the 2007 Valero Alamo Bowl found that 33% of the attendees who were Texas residents would have attended that bowl game had it been held outside Texas. Those residents' spending was kept within Texas instead of being spent outside the state.

We can gain further insight by looking at the results from the 2007 Dr Pepper Big 12 Championship, where 44% of attendees who were Texas residents would have attended that football game had it been held outside of Texas. A high fraction of those attendees indicated that they were fans of one of the two teams playing in the game, and they would have followed their team to whatever state hosted the championship game. These fans would have left town and spent their money away, but instead the money stayed within the state, thus adding to the economic activity in the state instead of leaking out to another state.

Psychic Impact   SIDEBAR

One role of government is to provide cultural, civic, and entertainment goods and services that residents enjoy but that no private firm is willing to provide. These goods whose consumption is non-excludable and non-rival are public goods, discussed in Chapter 9. In general, public goods are funded by governments in the appropriate jurisdiction (e.g., state parks, national defense), because private industry is not willing to offer them.

Major professional sport teams, entertainment districts, and sport and cultural events enhance the quality of life in a region, as do zoos, museums, aquariums, parks, the arts, and other public goods. Sporting events provide an entertainment option, especially for those who value attending or viewing spectator sports or attending related events, such as fan festivals. They also provide benefits that are public goods, including psychic impact.

Psychic impact is the emotional impact on a community that results when the community hosts prestigious events or major sport teams. Cultural events often are part of the fabric of a community, increasing civic pride and community spirit. Psychic impact includes emotional benefits received by members of a community who are not directly involved with managing an event but who still strongly identify with the event. Sport's psychic impact includes the pleasure and camaraderie that individuals feel when they attend or discuss games or teams. Most other industries do not provide the same degree of emotional impact.

12.D

For example, when Atlanta was awarded the 1996 Summer Olympics, local residents were moved by the announcement. Many people cried with joy. They felt that Atlanta had now proved itself as a "real" international city. Newspaper reports described the city as a sea of honking horns and cheers as people were swept up in jubilation. Is it possible to quantify in financial terms the collective emotional upswing of Atlantans? Another example comes from Minnesota, where a former governor, Arne Carlson, feels that "If you were to make a list of 10 or 15 of the most prized possessions of the state, [the Twins] would probably be one of them, and you never want to lose one of your prized possessions. Never" (Meryhew, 1997). Psychic impact techniques focus on measuring the value of psychic impact.* Event owners capture part of the value of psychic impact through ticket sales, merchandise sales, and so forth. However, much psychic impact is provided free to local residents through their sheer knowledge of the event. This is one of the reasons for the public/private partnerships that build sport venues. Proper decisions about the spending of public dollars require knowledge of both economic impact and psychic impact.

---

*Economist Bruce Johnson pioneered the application of research in psychic impact, also called psychic income or public consumption benefit, in sports. See Johnson & Whitehead (2000), Johnson, Groothuis, & Whitehead (2001), and Groothuis, Johnson, & Whitehead (2004).

---

coverage of an event can also inspire viewers to visit the host city in the future; this is termed the media impact. For example, 6 million spectators viewed the 2004 MasterCard Alamo Bowl on the ESPN national coverage of the game. During the game, the announcers often mentioned the name of the city, increasing viewers' awareness of it. Other media, such as newspapers, radio, and the Internet, provided free coverage of San Antonio during the game. It is extremely difficult to measure the way media coverage translates into actual new visitor expenditures. Notwithstanding, it is possible to calculate the expense that the local convention and visitors bureau would have to incur to obtain a similar amount of media coverage, based on standard advertising rates. Findings from studies suggest that San Antonio received nearly $1.8 million in media coverage from the telecast itself, not including other forms of media coverage. This area is ripe for future economic impact research.

Further, most economic impact analyses do not account for psychic impact, even though it could be an important factor in some cases.

Researchers have estimated that the Pittsburgh Penguins of the NHL are worth approximately $16 million per year to the residents of Pittsburgh solely in terms of emotional impact. This works out to an average of about $7.27 per person in the Pittsburgh MSA (Johnson, Groothuis, & Whitehead). The Indiana Pacers have an annual psychic impact on the Indianapolis community worth about $35 million per year (Alexander, Kern, & Neill, 2000). The Minnesota Vikings are worth approximately $10 per resident of the state in psychic impact (Fenn & Crooker, 2004).

How does one quantify happiness? The contingent valuation method (CVM) asks respondents how much they would be willing to pay for hypothetical projects. Researchers studying environmental impact often use CVM to measure the public's valuation of new parks, species preservation, pollution cleanup, and so forth. In sports, we might ask respondents to name the highest amount that they would be willing to pay, out of their own household budget, each year to make a new arena possible or host a major sport event in town. For example, if asked to contribute to a fund for a new arena or a major sport event, would you contribute $0, $5, $10, $15, $20, or greater than $20? How much would you pay to bring a professional sport team to your town or to help sponsor a national sport event?

The sport industry, more than most other industries, is about fanaticism, emotion, and community; to leave these impacts out of an analysis is to miss an important part of the picture. The reason the public funds museums, zoos, and orchestras are that these institutions enhance the community. Similarly, sport teams, events, and facilities are also public goods, enhancing the quality of life of the areas in which they locate. Analysts should measure these positive externalities in order to assess fully the impact that a sport team or facility brings to a locality. As Exhibit 12.9 illustrates, it may cost $100 million to build a local

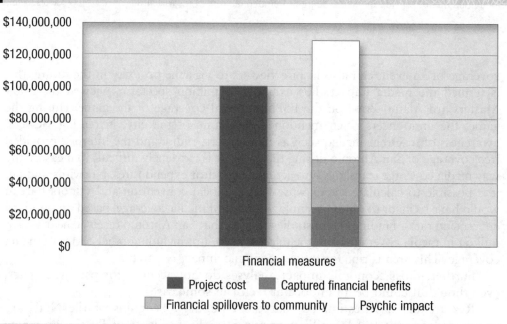

exhibit   12.9   Costs and impacts of a new sport facility.

baseball park, but the private financial gain by the facility operator or team might be approximately $22 million. In this situation, private investors will not build the facility. If businesses located around the facility, such as restaurants and retail stores, receive economic impact worth about $25 million, this still is not enough to justify expending private and public funds to build the facility. However, if the psychic impact is worth enough to push the total impact over $100 million, then construction financed through a public/private partnership may be worthwhile.

Causes of Overestimating

Overestimations of economic impact occur because most analyses do not account for **reverse time-switchers,** those local residents who leave town during the event period because of the event. Expenditures that reverse time-switchers would have spent in town are instead spent outside the local area. Only mega-events, when local residents expect traffic congestion or anticipate the possibility of renting their home out to visitors for a profit, typically have reverse time-switchers.

Economic impact analyses often neglect to account for important opportunity costs. For instance, if the Alamodome had to turn down a major event because of a time conflict with the MasterCard Alamo Bowl in 2004, then the net incremental gain from hosting the bowl must account for the lost economic impact of the other event.

Another potentially important opportunity cost is the impact from visitors who would have come to town under normal circumstances but were unable to because the event filled all of the hotels to capacity. If these would-be visitors came at some time anyway and lodged within the geographic area, then there is no loss in revenue. However, if any individuals did not come to town at all because of the event, then the economic impact analysis for the event should account for that loss.

In the parlance of economic impact analysis, what is often called economic impact is really gross economic benefit, because it includes all spending, even by local residents, and it does not account for the costs of hosting the event. When the analyst properly accounts for spending, costs, and other similar items, then economic benefit becomes economic impact, although it is sometimes called incremental economic impact. When we account for opportunity costs, such as capacity constraints at the sport facility or at local hotels, then we have what is often called the net incremental economic impact. A true economic impact analysis accounts for all of these adjustments; it nets out all effects to measure the true incremental impacts. When we read economic impact studies, we must know how these terms are being defined and used.

Perhaps the most egregious cause of overestimating economic impact is that the analyst has some incentive to find a very large impact. Often, these studies are paid for by advocates (such as franchise owners or politicians) for building the facility or bringing the event to town, especially if part of the funding will come from public sources. When we read these studies it may be difficult to follow the methodological details given (if any), but reverse-engineering the study shows that the analyst missed or misused steps discussed in this chapter.

For an unethical analyst, the easiest way to obtain a large economic impact estimate is to count all attendees at an event toward economic impact, not just

SIDEBAR

Economic Impact of the Dallas Cowboys . . . A Shootout between Dueling Studies

12.E

In 2004, while the Dallas Cowboys were campaigning for a local measure in the city of Arlington, Texas, that would provide $325 million toward financing a new football stadium for the Cowboys, two studies were conducted to measure the economic impact of the team and a new facility. The "Arlington" study estimated the impact of the team and a proposed new stadium to be built in the city of Arlington. The "Irving" study which was conducted after the Arlington study, measured the impact of the team and a proposed new stadium in the city of Irving (site of the team's current stadium at the time, Texas Stadium), and provided an assessment of the Arlington study. This is one of the rare cases where we have more than one economic impact study for a similar project, as well as a publicly available assessment of another study. The differences in the findings and methods are substantial (Turnkey Sports, 2004).

Both studies used approximately the same per capita out-of-stadium expenditure figure (about $46), but the operational economic impact of the Arlington study was $238 million per year, while the Irving study found an annual impact of $51 million.

The Arlington study used a capture rate of 75%, meaning that the study made the fundamental assumption that 75% of all out-of-stadium spending would occur within the city limits of Arlington. This figure was utilized even though the city of Arlington accounts for less than 6% of the Dallas-Fort Worth CMSA. By comparison, the Irving study assumed a capture rate for out-of-stadium spending of 18.7% for the city of Irving.

Also, the Arlington study did not account for displaced spending, meaning that it applied the 75% capture rate to 100% of the estimated 1.5 million attendees. Analysts for the Irving study determined that not all attendee spending can be counted toward economic impact, because a portion of the patrons (about 26%) are local residents, casual visitors, or time-switchers who would have spent this money within the city even if the stadium were not there. In short, the Arlington analysts applied the 75% capture rate to 100% of stadium attendees, whereas the Irving analysts applied their 18.7% capture rate to just 74% of attendees.

Additionally, the Arlington analysts included spending inside the stadium (comprising 82% of its direct impact measurement) in economic impact, meaning that they counted dollars coming in the door for ticket sales, parking revenues, concessions, catering, and novelty sales. The Irving analysts took the contrary position: that those revenue streams do not add one penny to economic impact. Rather, they counted only those monies that would flow out of the Cowboys' or stadium corporation's coffers and into the city of Irving. Under this approach, the budget expenditures by the Cowboys and stadium corporation entities are the only relevant source of dollars driving economic impact and, therefore, the only sources that were counted. In other words, the Irving study, right off the bat, disregarded 82% of the Arlington study's economic impact, and was correct to do so.

relevant or incremental visitors. Sometimes an analyst will even count a person who attends three days of an event as three individual people (simply adding up the stated attendance for each day of the three-day event, rather than determining the number of individual attendees). Another method is to count total spending by organizations, corporations, and local government related to the event as benefits rather than costs. Of course, all of these methods result in bogus estimates. If local government spends $1 million to help bring an event to town, that is a cost, not a benefit. If visitors attending a game spend $10 million buying tickets, merchandise, and concessions inside the game, and the owner spends $9 million of those revenues to produce it, the real economic impact would be $9 million (or $10 million, perhaps, if the owner's business is a local business)—not $19 million. When you read economic impact studies, consider the source and carefully review the methodology. See Exhibit 12.10 for guidelines for analyzing the methodology used in an economic impact study.

| Factors for analyzing the methodology used in an economic impact study. | exhibit | 12.10 |

CONSIDER WHETHER:

Local spending is not counted.

Only incremental spending by casual visitors and time-switchers is counted.

Incremental visitor spending is fully counted.

Spending within a facility is not counted.

Spending that comes out of the event, team, or facility is counted.

Only the organizational spending by the event host committee, event management company, and corporate sponsors in the geographic area of impact is counted.

Only corporate spending in the geographic area of impact that would not have occurred otherwise is counted.

Spending by organizations, corporations, and local governments related to bringing the event to town is counted as a cost rather than a benefit.

Leakages outside the geographic area of impact (sales and income taxes of non-local governments and spending with non-local employees, businesses, and organizations) are not counted.

Only the capture rate portion of franchise spending is counted.

Opportunity costs are accounted for.

CONCLUSION

Economic impact analysis is a widely used decision-making tool for private businesses and governments. Essentially, it is a form of cost-benefit analysis, where the analyst measures true costs and benefits to assess net effect or impact. The fundamental principle in economic impact is to measure the spending that resulted (or would have resulted) from the event, versus the spending that would have occurred otherwise. But for the event, what would spending in the community have been? This "but for" analysis is similar to economic damages calculations in litigation, where analysts try to determine what financial harm occurred, for example, from patent infringement or malfunctioning equipment, by estimating what would have happened without ("but for") the infringement or malfunction. Analysts conducting economic impact studies should continually ask themselves whether a specific set of spending measurements is truly new or incremental compared to what would have happened otherwise.

CONCEPT *check*

1. What is the difference between induced and indirect economic impact?
2. Can a person be both a casual visitor and a time-switcher for the same event?
3. Under what conditions should spending by local residents be counted in a calculation of economic impact?

4. In measuring the economic impact of a sport team, is it correct to count both the spending by fans inside the stadium and the spending by the team (in running its operations) in the community?

5. All else being equal, does increasing the size of the geographic area of impact raise, lower, or have no effect on the capture rate?

6. How would one determine the extent to which locals for a particular event are reverse time-switchers?

7. What are some of the causes of overestimating the economic impact of a sport event? Of underestimating?

CASE analysis   *Economic Impact Study Simulation*

Review the following description of an economic impact study and answer the questions that follow. When you have finished, you will have measured the economic impact of a large sport event.

You have been commissioned to analyze the economic impact on the city of Houston of the MLB All-Star Game recently played. Specifically, the community wants to know the direct spending impact, the indirect spending impact, and the fiscal/tax impact. Houston officials want to know whether it would be profitable to fund and bid for similar future events for the city. This event cost the City about $8 million to host.

You created a survey (Exhibit 12.2) and administered it to 342 people around Minute Maid Park during the game, making an effort to obtain a random sample. Only 325 of the surveys were usable because of various errors by the respondents. Imagine you entered the data into a spreadsheet and are now ready to analyze the economic impact. To allow you to do this analysis, your instructor will provide you with an Excel file containing two spreadsheets: Survey 1 and Key. Survey 1 is the spreadsheet in which the data has been entered while the Key spreadsheet descibes and explains each colum of data. Be sure to measure economic impact for all visitors, not just those who responded to the survey. (A survey is a sample of the target population.)

Based on discussions with the local organizing committee and Houston government officials, you determine that:

- Minute Maid Park seats 40,950.
- The game was sold out.
- The city sales tax is 7.75% and is collected on all goods and services except hotels.
- The city hotel occupancy tax is 15%.
- Hotel capacity in the city is 45,000 rooms. The typical occupancy rate is 83%.

- The average number of persons per room for large events such as this is 2.4.
- Total spending by the local organizing committee was $4.5 million, with 60% of that amount coming from organizations outside of the city. This is in addition to the amount the city itself spent. Minute Maid spent $1 million in town activating its sponsorship.
- The spending multiplier for the city of Houston is 1.6 (based on information from the Minnesota IMPLAN Group).
- Of spending inside Minute Maid Park (including tickets) for this event, 20% went to the city government (fiscal impact).

QUESTIONS

Note: A few data entry or survey respondent errors have been included in the spreadsheet.

1. How many people attended the All-Star Game in total?

2. How many visitors (people who are not local residents) attended the All-Star Game?

3. How many visitors who attended the game were time-switchers?

4. How many visitors who attended the game were casual visitors?

5. What number of visitors should be used in the calculation of the economic impact estimates?

6. What is the per-person spending per day by the incremental visitors for everything but lodging? (Use your result from Question 5.) What is that figure for lodging per night stayed?

7. What is the average length of stay for incremental visitors in terms of days and nights?

8. What is the per-person spending per stay by the incremental visitors?

9. What is the game's direct economic impact, not accounting for any hotel capacity constraints? (Be sure to account for the new/incremental spending by the event organizer and the costs of hosting the event.)

10. What is the total economic impact?

11. Based on hotel capacity information, how many typical visitors did the event visitors crowd out?

12. What is the direct and total economic impact, accounting for the crowding out?

13. What is the fiscal or tax impact of the event on the city?

references

Alexander, D.L., Kern, W., & Neill, J. (September 2000). Valuing the consumption benefits from professional sports franchises. *Journal of Urban Economics, 48*(2), 321–337.

Baade, R., & Matheson, V.A. (2006). Have public finance principles been shut out in financing new stadiums for the NFL? *Public Finance and Management, 6,* 284–320.

Coates, D., & Humphreys, B. (2003). The effect of professional sports on earnings and employment in the services and retail sectors in U.S. cities. *Regional Science and Urban Economics, 33,* 175–198.

Cobb, S., & Olberding, D. (2007). The importance of import substitution in marathon economic impact analysis." *International Journal of Sport Finance, 2,* 108–118.

Fenn, A., & Crooker, J.R. (2004). The willingness to pay for a new Vikings stadium under threat of relocation or sale. Unpublished document.

Groothuis, P.A., Johnson, B.K., & Whitehead, J.C. (Fall 2004). Public funding of professional sports stadiums:

Public choice or civic pride? *Eastern Economic Journal, 30*(4), 515–526.

Irwin, R.L., & Rascher, D.A. (February 4, 2005). *2004 Alamo Bowl: Economic and fiscal impact analysis.*

Johnson, B.K., & Whitehead, J.C. (January 2000). Value of public goods from sports stadiums: The CVM approach. *Contemporary Economic Policy, 18*(1), 48–58.

Johnson, B.K., Groothuis, P.A., & Whitehead, J.C. (February 2001). The value of public goods generated by a major league sports team: The CVM approach. *Journal of Sports Economics, 2*(1), 6–21.

Meryhew, R. (1997). How important are the Twins to Minneapolis? *Minneapolis Star Tribune.*

Rascher, D.A., & Irwin, R.L. (May 13, 2004). *2004 NCAA Men's Final Four: Economic and fiscal impact analysis.*

Turnkey Sports and SportsEconomics. (October 15, 2004). *Study of the economic and fiscal impacts for Texas Stadium and a new Cowboys stadium.*

P A R T   F O U R

Financial Attributes of Select Sport Industry Segments

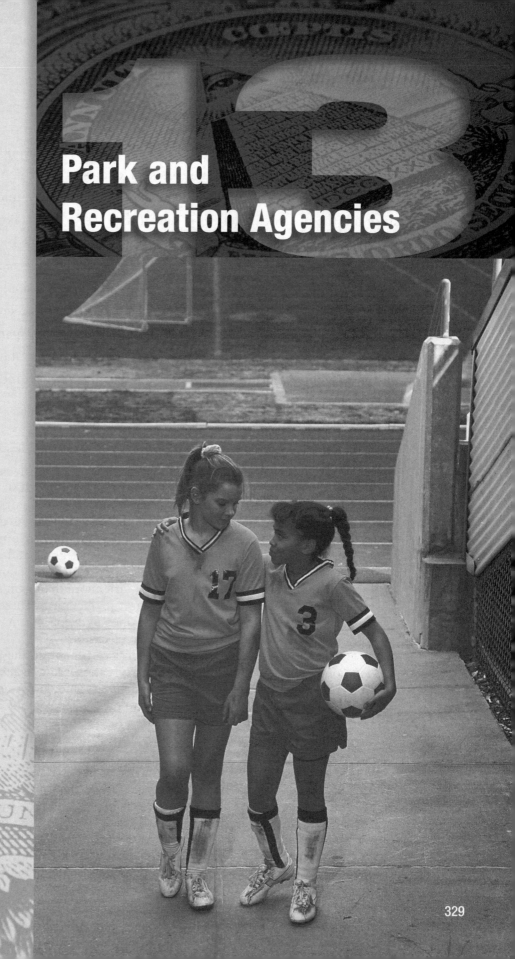

13

Park and Recreation Agencies

Introduction

When we think of the public sector in sport, our first thought is probably of state university athletic programs. However, in this chapter we focus on a less-often considered segment: park and recreation agencies. In general, these agencies provide sport that benefits the entire community. This sport meets the social needs of the community, and, because sport is being provided for all, these agencies generally have the power to levy taxes to fund their operations and facility construction. Because public funds are being used, managers in this sector are accountable to taxpayers, and they operate based on the perceived needs of the electorate (Brayley & McLean, 1999). The *Statistical Abstract of the United States: 2008* shows that a considerable number of taxpayer dollars are spent on parks and recreation. The U.S. Census Bureau report for 2007 indicated that state and local governments spent $30.5 billion in 2004, which was an increase of $5.4 billion from 2000. Hence, an understanding of this sector is important for a complete grasp of financial principles in the sport industry.

FINANCIAL MANAGEMENT TRENDS IN PARK AND RECREATION AGENCIES

Several trends over the past 30 years have affected the financial operation of park and recreation facilities (Bynum, 2002). Demand for recreation facilities and programs has increased significantly as residents have become increasingly aware of health and wellness. As demand has increased, the types of facilities and varieties of programming have increased as well, to meet consumer desire. Parks used to be fields of grass and woods; now they include interactive playgrounds, sporting courts, game fields, and advanced trail systems. Community centers, once offering little more than gym space and meeting rooms, have evolved into large multipurpose facilities. These venues frequently offer aquatics facilities, climbing walls, open gym space, running tracks, fitness centers, multipurpose rooms, and child care areas.

With a mandate to provide services benefiting the public health and welfare of the local community, park and recreation agencies have developed facilities and programs that appeal to a broad demographic. However, this approach results in controversies over pricing. For example, in one community an annual membership in the publicly owned and operated recreation center was $760. In addition to the annual fee, members were charged for fitness classes. A private health club in the same community required a $540 annual fee, which included fitness classes. The public recreation center's vast array of programming and amenities, designed to appeal to a broad population base, resulted in a pricing structure that was higher than that of the single-purpose private health club (Bynum, 2006). Some might find it improper that membership in a single-purpose private health club is more affordable than joining a recreation facility funded in part by taxpayer dollars.

Trends over the past 30 years have resulted in this pricing paradox. During the 1970s, discussions of pricing centered on keeping public recreation activities affordable for the broadest possible segment of the population. Activities and memberships were nominally priced, and some residents paid nothing at all. The philosophy was that every member of the community should be able to afford the programs and services offered. Since then, the size and scope of recreational complexes have grown and changed, while the demand for public dollars from other agencies for a variety of local purposes have increased. Meanwhile, communities were reducing state and local taxes. As a result, community sport and recreation departments are now expected to do two things: (1) provide a multitude of sport and recreation services to the community while keeping them affordable, and (2) provide programs and facilities that are financially self-sufficient or that generate enough revenue to offset any expenses not covered by an established subsidy. These conflicting expectations have led to the pricing situation discussed earlier.

Compounding the financial pressures that park and recreation agencies face when determining pricing, their revenue from user fees may have peaked (Bynum, 2006). Approximately one-third of the revenue that funds public recreation programs comes from user fees. If user fee income has indeed peaked, and local governments are also providing less financial support to mandated programs and services, the financial challenges facing managers of public sport and recreation programs and facilities will only increase.

John Crompton, one of the leading researchers on park and recreation finance, summarized the difficulties facing financial managers in this sector of the industry as follows. First, there is competition from non-profits such as YMCAs and Jewish Community Centers (JCCs). Non-profits often offer a similar variety of services and programs, closely competing with public recreation agencies in price as well. Second, the growth of similar facilities and services in the private sector, as mentioned above, increases competition. Crompton added that in the 1970s, there was no commercial sector in the park and recreation segment. Today, the commercial sector is able to "niche market" and compete directly with public recreation agencies. Third, over time the government has added to the services, programs, and responsibilities that its various agencies offer to communities across the country. As a consequence, less money is available for park and recreation agencies to offer programs and services (Bynum, 2006).

SOURCE OF FUNDS

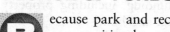ecause park and recreation agencies exist to meet the social needs of the communities they serve (Brayley & McLean), they receive funding from the public sector for both facility construction and facility/program operations. Their goal is to provide recreational sport facilities and programs that enhance quality of life for members of the community while serving the common good. To achieve this goal, the agencies' programs and services must be subsidized by tax revenues, because the fees charged do not fully cover operational costs. **Tax subsidies**—the use of tax receipts to fund a program or business—enable the agencies to offer programs for free or at a reduced cost.

Public sector sport is offered to serve societal need rather than profit potential (Brayley & McLean). Hence, the financial indicators of success are different from those discussed in the rest of this text. For the public sector, we measure success by comparing achievement to goals. Here, goals are not based solely on financial measures but on social outcomes, as well. We measure by comparing the social benefits derived from the programs to the expenses of achieving those outcomes.

With shrinking local and state revenues, public sector sport has increasingly had to turn to new sources of revenue to fund programming. Typically, municipalities have funded public sport facility construction through the sale of tax-supported municipal bonds, and local tax receipts have provided a majority of operational revenues. **Tax receipts** are tax revenues from all sources received by a municipality (Sherman, 1998). Municipal bonds and tax receipts are still used to fund construction costs and provide operational revenues today (Bynum, 2007a; LeBlanc, 2008), but public sport agencies have increasingly relied on other revenue sources, including revenues from advertising (Bynum, 2005) and corporate sponsorships (Bynum, 2003b).

Public Sources of Funds

In one of the most thorough studies on park and recreation center and program finance, Sherman (1998) detailed how these facilities were funded. Sherman found that 69% of construction funding came from taxes. For operations, 52% of funding came from tax revenues. Although these percentages are likely lower today, tax revenue and municipal bonds, as mentioned earlier, remain important sources of revenue. For example, in Cayce, South Carolina, a new tennis complex is being funded through tax-supported bonds. The Lexington County Recreation Commission (LCRC) and the City of Cayce are each paying for half of the $4.7 million project. The LCRC is using a portion of a $17 million tax-supported bond to pay its half of the costs. Residents of Cayce will see their taxes increase, as the city's half will be paid through general obligation bonds issued specifically for the tennis project (LeBlanc).

As another example, the operational budget of the Texas state parks system is partially funded by revenues from an excise tax on sporting goods sales. In 2007, $32 million of the system's $56 million budget came from this source. However, because several state parks have deteriorated as a result of insufficient funding, efforts have been made to dedicate all sales tax derived from the sale of sporting goods to the parks system. This would increase the amount provided to $105 million annually (Bynum, 2007a).

Below we discuss the major sources of public funding, including property taxes, sales taxes, excise taxes, pay-as-you-go financing, and bonds.

Property tax

The tax source most often used to fund the construction or operation of recreational sport facilities is the **property tax,** a government levy based on the value of property (Brayley & McLean; Sawyer, Hypes, & Hypes, 2004; Sherman). Property taxes generated 32% of all state and local tax revenue in 2004 (U.S. Census Bureau, 2007). Sherman (1998) reported that 73% of recreation construction and operation funding involved property taxes. Although this percentage is likely lower today, we can assume that property taxes still provide a majority of public sport funding.

In many states, two types of property are taxed: real property and personal property. *Real property* includes land and all structures built on or improvements made to the land. *Personal property* includes everything else that has value. Typically, automobiles, watercraft, motorcycles, trucks, and airplanes are taxed as personal property. Businesses often pay personal property taxes on furniture, fixtures, and equipment.

A wide variety of public entities establish a municipality's property tax rates. Returning to the example of Cayce, South Carolina, the city's residents live in one of three tax districts. These districts vary based on school district and whether they live within an established tax increment financing (TIF) district. As a result, residents pay three different property tax rates. In general, city or town councils, school boards, and special purpose districts such as parks and recreation departments determine their budgetary needs and the percentage of revenues needed from property tax sources. In essence, these public bodies determine the rate of tax, or **millage,** necessary to meet their budget. The specific **millage rate** for a particular resident in a tax district is the total of the levies by the city, county, school district, and any special districts in which that resident lives. One **mill** is equal to 1/1000 of a dollar (or 1/10 of a penny). Therefore, if a resident's tax rate is 315 mills, to determine the amount of tax owed, that resident would multiply the assessed value of his or her property by 0.315.

Assessing property value and tax due. The determination of the assessed value of a property is a complex operation usually undertaken by a city or county auditor or assessor. The taxes are then collected by city and county treasurers or tax collectors. The city or county auditor will prepare a list of the owners of all taxable real and personal property. The city or county assessor then appraises the value of this property and determines the property's **assessed value,** the product of its fair market value and its assessment ratio.

assessed value = fair market value × assessment ratio

The fair market value of a property is the value for which the property can reasonably be expected to sell on the open market with a willing buyer and a willing seller. The **assessment ratio** is the percentage of the property subject to taxation. Assessment ratios are set by elected officials. Exhibit 13.1 lists the assessment ratios for residents of Lexington County, South Carolina. Using Exhibit 13.1, we can determine the assessment value of an individual's primary residence by multiplying the assessment ratio for residential property by the value of the residence. If we assume the fair market value of a primary residence is $250,000, the assessed value would be

assessed value = fair market value × assessment ratio for primary residence
= $250,000 × 0.04
= $10,000

For this piece of property, $10,000 of its value would be subject to taxation. To find the amount of tax due, we multiply the assessed value by the millage rate.

property tax due = assessed value × millage rate

Again, the millage rate is the tax rate approved by the city councils, school boards, special purpose districts, and county council to meet the budgetary needs of each entity. In Lexington County, the total county operating millage in 2008 was 83.063

| exhibit | 13.1 | Assessment ratios by property type for Lexington County, South Carolina. |

Primary residence	4.0%
Second residence	6.0%
Other real property	6.0%
Commercial real property	6.0%
Agricultural real property—privately owned	4.0%
Agricultural real property—corporate owned	6.0%
Aircraft	10.5%
Business personal property	10.5%
Camper[a]	10.5%
Manufacturing, real and personal	10.5%
Motor home[a]	10.5%
Railroads, airlines, pipelines, real and personal	9.5%
Utility, real and personal	10.5%
Vehicle, personal	6.0%
Vehicle, personal[b]	10.5%
Watercraft/boat[a]	10.5%

[a]May qualify as primary or second residence.

[b]Vehicle, personal @ 10.5% if gross vehicle weight is in excess of 11,000 pounds and net vehicle weight is in excess of 9,000 pounds.

Source: http://www.lex-co.com/Departments/Auditor/proptaxinfo.html.

(County of Lexington). For a $250,000 property with an assessed value of $10,000, the property tax owed to Lexington County would be:

property tax due = assessed value × millage rate
= $10,000 × 0.083063
= $830.63

Calculating new property tax needs. As property tax revenue is one of the main sources of revenue for building and operating public recreation facilities, it is important to understand the impact of increased funding needs on the tax rate of those living in a community. Returning to Lexington County, South Carolina, let's assume that the board of the LCRC has proposed a new multipurpose recreational facility with a cost of $12.5 million and an annual operating budget of $1.8 million.

A municipal bond will be issued to pay for the construction cost. Because Lexington County has a credit rating from Moody's of Aa2 and Standard & Poor's of AA–, the LCRC can issue a $12.5 million, 30-year municipal bond at a rate of 5.30%. Assuming that the county will annually set aside the principal portion of the bond while making interest payments to bondholders, the county would need to budget 30 equal payments of $841,160.08.* Regarding the financing of operational costs, the LCRC assumes that 52% of the $1.8 million annual budget will be paid from an increase in the current millage rate for the district ($936,000 per year), with annual operating cost increases based on changes in the consumer price index. Therefore, the millage rate for those living within the LCRC district will increase to provide funds for the operating costs and the costs of construction.

To calculate the new millage required for the operating costs, we must know the **net assessed value** of property in the LCRC district, that is, the total assessed value of property in the district, less tax-exempt property. The net assessed value is calculated as follows:

net assessed value = total assessed value − tax-exempt property

Typically, property owned by non-profit and governmental entities is exempt from taxes. In 2008, the net assessed value of property in the LCRC district was $677,635,000, according to Lexington County records. Next, we divide the required tax by the net assessed value of property to obtain the tax rate.

$$\text{tax rate} = \frac{\text{required tax}}{\text{net assessed value}}$$

The required tax amount is the annual operating cost of $936,000. So,

$$\text{tax rate} = \frac{\$936,000}{\$667,635,000} = 0.001402$$

The tax rate of 0.001402 is the same as the millage rate; therefore, the millage rate must be increased by 1.402 mills.

To calculate the rate increase needed for the project's debt service, we will use the same process. However, the rate increase will be in effect only for the 30-year life of the project. With $841,160.08 needed annually to service the debt, the tax rate would be

$$\text{tax rate} = \frac{\text{required tax}}{\text{net assessed value}}$$

$$= \frac{\$841,160.08}{\$667,635,000}$$

$$= 0.001260$$

For the next 30 years, the millage rate must be increased by 1.260 mills.

The combined annual increase for the next 30 years is 2.662 mills. In 2008, the LCRC millage rate was 12.499. With the new project, the overall rate would increase to 15.161. This is a 21.3% increase over the current rate. The LCRC, now that it knows the overall millage required for the project, may need voter

---

*To calculate this payment, we use N = 30, PV = $12.5 million, FV = $0, I = 5.3%.

approval through a tax referendum to increase the millage rate. A property owner can calculate the impact of the proposed tax as follows. If the total assessed value of the property is $10,000,

property tax increase = assessed value of property × millage rate increase
= $10,000 × 0.002662
= $26.62

Sales tax

After property tax, the second most common tax source to fund the construction or operation of recreational sport facilities is the **sales tax** (Brayley & McLean; Sawyer, Hypes, & Hypes; Sherman), a tax on the sale of certain goods and services. Sales taxes generated 36% of all state and local tax revenues in 2004, according to the U.S. Census Bureau (2007). A majority of this revenue, however, funds services at the state level, not the local level. Sherman (1998) reported that only 26% of all recreational sport construction or operational funding involved sales taxes. This is quite low compared to the 73% funded through property taxes.

The rules and regulations regarding sales tax vary by state. These regulations can directly affect the sources of funds available at the local level for recreational programming and services. For example, South Carolina collects a 6% state sales and use tax. Nearly all retail sales are subject to the sales tax. A **use tax** is a levy imposed on certain goods and services that are purchased outside the state and brought into the state. A use tax may also be imposed on certain goods and services for which no sales tax is paid. Under South Carolina law, counties may collect an additional 1% local sales tax if the county's voters approve the tax. This tax may be used for county-defined purposes. Lexington County, South Carolina, collects an additional 1% school district sales tax that supplements K–12 funding within the county. Hence, sales tax revenue is not an option to fund recreational sport facilities or programs in the county. However, neighboring Richland County chose to impose a 1% local option sales tax. Local option sales taxes may be used for a wide variety of purposes. If a county chooses, funds generated through this tax could be used to fund recreation programs and facilities.

As an example of the differences between states, in Missouri, sales taxes are used at three levels of government to fund park and recreation programs and projects. A resident of Fenton, for example, will pay a sales tax of 6.825% for non-food sales, unless he or she is making a purchase in one of two transportation development districts (TDDs) located within the city limits. Within the TDDs, the general sales tax on purchases of non-food items is 7.825%. In either case, a portion of the sales tax supports parks and recreation. At the state level, 0.1% is designated for state parks and soil conservation. In St. Louis County, 0.1% is designated for the county's park and recreation programs. At the city level, 0.5% is designated for parks, recreation, and storm water removal. Overall, individuals making non-food purchases in Fenton pay 0.7% in state sales tax to fund state, county, and city parks and recreation services ("Welcome to Fenton," 2009).

The City of Fenton combines storm water removal and parks and recreation in one fund. For these services, total operating revenues in FY 2008 were expected to be $5.1 million (City of Fenton, 2008). Sales tax revenue was expected to contribute $3.1 million during 2008, or approximately 60% of overall revenue. In its proposal for FY 2009, sales tax revenue was to fund 60% of operations ($3.152 million). Additionally, 32% of revenue was to come from the operation of the city's recreation center, and 6% of revenue was to come from park and recreation programs (see Exhibit 13.2). The city will be using sales tax revenue to pay debt issued for the purchase of park property; to pay debt issued for the construction of the city's recreation center, RiverChase, and storm water improvements; and to meet a portion of the operational needs of the parks and storm water systems (see Exhibit 13.3). When the debt service obligations end in 2017, the city plans to use the monies previously dedicated to retiring the debt to help meet the operational needs of the services. Exhibit 13.4 provides an overview of the proposed 2009 budget for the city's storm water/parks fund.

Excise taxes

Whereas sales taxes are levied on certain goods and services by a state, **excise taxes** may be imposed on goods and services within a city, county, or state. Excise taxes may benefit park and recreation services and facilities. For example, Orange County, Florida, used an excise tax to fund a variety of sport, entertainment, and recreation venues (Brown, 2008). The county imposed a 6% hotel tax to generate revenue for a $1.1 billion project, including funding for renovation of the Citrus Bowl ($175 million), construction of a new performing arts center ($375 million), construction of a new sport and entertainment arena ($480 million) that will

Proposed FY 2009 revenues for the City of Fenton storm water/parks fund. exhibit 13.2

REVENUE SOURCE	
Sales tax	$3,152,000
RiverChase	1,630,000
Parks and recreation	308,000
All other revenues	79,000
Total revenues	$5,169,000

Source: http://www.fentonmo.org/docs/2009%20Approved%20Budget.pdf.

Storm water/parks fund sales tax use by the City of Fenton. exhibit 13.3

REVENUE USE	AMOUNT
Debt service	$2,173,000
Parks/RiverChase operations	979,000
Total	$3,152,000

Source: http://www.fentonmo.org/docs/2009%20Approved%20Budget.pdf.

exhibit   13.4   Budget for the Fenton storm water/parks fund, FY 2009.

Revenues

Operating revenues		
Parks operations	$ 308,000.00	5.3%
RiverChase operations	1,630,000.00	28.3%
Sales tax revenues	3,152,000.00	54.7%
Other operating revenues	69,000.00	1.2%
Subtotal – operating revenues	$5,159,000.00	89.5%
Capital grants	$604,400.00	10.5%
Total revenues	$5,763,400.00	100.0%

Expenditures

Operating expenditures		
Parks and recreation operations	$704,000.00	12.0%
RiverChase operations	2,022,000.00	34.4%
Building maintenance reserve	60,000.00	1.0%
Special events	79,000.00	1.3%
Storm water maintenance	47,000.00	0.8%
Subtotal – operating revenues	$2,912,000.00	49.5%
Debt service		
New park land	$620,000.00	10.5%
RiverChase construction	1,328,100.00	22.6%
Storm water improvements	224,900.00	3.8%
Subtotal – debt service	$2,173,000.00	37.0%
Capital expenditures	$792,000.00	13.5%
Total expenditures	$5,877,000.00	100.0%
Profit (loss)	$ (113,600.00)	

Source: City of Fenton (2008).

become the home of the Orlando Magic, and construction of five new recreation centers ($25 million) to be run by the county.

In Orlando the excise tax on hotel rooms was used to fund a wide array of projects, but excise taxes are often designed to impose the costs of specific services on those who actually use the services (Crompton, 1999). In Texas, for example, the excise tax on sporting goods sales is designed to tax those who use the state parks system (Bynum, 2007a). However, the amount of revenue the parks system could receive from this excise tax was capped at $32 million. As mentioned previously, if all the revenue from the tax were given to the parks system, the system would receive an estimated $105 million annually. Recognizing the problem, Texas Governor Rick Perry stated in his State of the State address, "Let's spend the sporting goods tax on what it was collected for: to create first-class parks that give our people open spaces and fresh air for needed recreation" (Bynum, 2007a, p. 2).

Pay-as-you-go financing

Rarely do municipalities adopt a pay-as-you-go approach when constructing new facilities (Crompton, 1999). One of the few examples is the City of San Antonio. For construction of the Alamodome, the city raised almost all of the $174 million needed through a voter-approved sales tax increase of 0.5 cents on every dollar spent for five years. It was estimated that if a long-term bond had been used to build the facility, the total cost of the debt service would have been $435 million, or $17 million per year for 25 years.

Municipalities typically choose not to use the pay-as-you-go approach for several reasons. For one, there is a delay between the decision to build a new facility and the collection of all the monies needed to construct that facility. In rapidly growing communities, this delay could lead to the overcrowding of existing facilities (see Sidebar 13.A). Another reason this approach is seldom used is that, from an equity perspective, the method is inequitable and inefficient (Crompton). Given the frequency with which people move in and out of communities, some residents may pay the full cost of a facility and never get to use it, because they have moved from the community. Others may benefit fully without making any financial contribution at all, if they move into the community after others have paid for the facility.

Bonds

Most public capital projects are funded through either short-term or long-term debt rather than a pay-as-you-go arrangement, because this debt places less of an immediate financial burden on taxpayers. Bonds are the traditional source of capital improvement revenue for governmental entities. As discussed in earlier chapters, simply stated, a bond is a promise by a borrower to pay back one or more lenders a certain amount of money plus interest over a certain period of time. Here, the borrower is the city, county, state, or recreation district. The lenders are the bondholders, the individuals and institutions that have purchased the bonds. Bonds are classified by their method of retirement. A **term bond** is paid in a single payment made at the end of the loan period. A **serial bond** requires regular payments on principal and interest over the life of the bond.

SIDEBAR

Pay-as-You-Go Financing for the Blythewood Baseball League Fields   13.A

In Blythewood, South Carolina, the 550 members of the Blythewood Baseball League currently use three baseball fields. The league has difficulty scheduling games and practices due to the demands of the large number of participants and teams. In many cases, games must be rescheduled because of rain, and in turn teams lose their practice times. T-ball teams must practice in nearby open spaces and can use the league's fields only for games on Saturdays between 11:00 a.m. and 1:00 p.m.

Further, the league is located in one of the fastest-growing communities in South Carolina. It is expected that the number of participants will increase to more than 600 in 2010. However, due to the poor credit market, the league was unable to arrange financing to build two new fields. As a result, the league has had to adopt a pay-as-you-go approach to building the fields and meanwhile limit the number of league participants to 550. The league is currently raising funds for construction of new fields and has also been working with the City of Blythewood to arrange financing for immediate construction.

In order to issue bonds, a municipality or district has to receive approval from either the voters or the appropriate legislative entity to borrow money. The process will vary in each jurisdiction depending on state and local laws. Once the borrower obtains legal authority to issue bonds, usually an underwriter issues the bonds on the municipality's behalf. The underwriter is typically a national or regional investment bank. The bank then sells the bonds on the municipality's behalf through either a competitive or negotiated sale (Bynum, 2003a).

Competitive versus negotiated issue. In a **competitive issue,** the municipality publishes a notice of sale, seeking bids from underwriters. The underwriter submitting the lowest bid, or lowest interest rate, will be selected to underwrite the bonds. For a **negotiated issue,** the municipality selects one underwriter, and the parties negotiate the terms of the sale. In either case, the parties will prepare the bond issue's official statement and obtain the bond's rating.

Typically, municipal bonds are negotiated issues (Bynum, 2003a), as this type of issue provides more flexible interest-rate schedules and is sold by the underwriter on the open market. Approximately 70% of all bond issues are negotiated sales. Once the underwriter issues and sells the bonds, revenue is available to the borrower. Exhibit 13.5 illustrates this process.

Revenue versus general obligation bonds. One of two types of municipal bonds will typically be issued to fund capital projects for community recreation programs (Bynum, 2003a): either revenue bonds or general obligation bonds. Recall that revenue bonds are secured by future revenues generated by the project being funded, whereas general obligation bonds are secured by tax revenues and the issuing entity's

---

exhibit   13.5   Negotiated issue of municipal bonds.

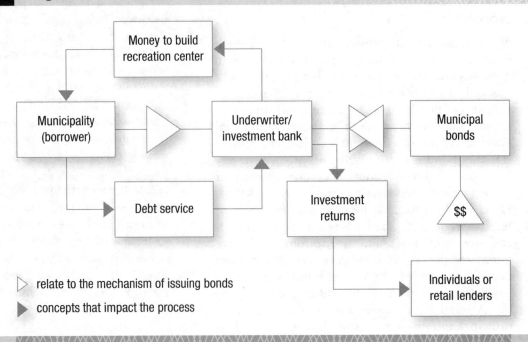

ability to impose new taxes. The latter must have voter approval prior to their issue.

To select the type of bond, the municipality or recreation agency must first determine whether the project will generate enough revenue to retire debt, operate the facility, and maintain the facility. If not, the municipality must determine whether supplemental revenue from an existing general fund or another recreation revenue source could pay for the project. If none of these revenue sources is available, a general obligation bond backed by a tax source will have to be used. In this case, the municipality must determine the tax source that will secure the bond. Frequently, this source is an increase in real property taxes. However, increases in sales tax are also common.

SIDEBAR

Bond Financing for the City of Fenton, Missouri   13.B

The City of Fenton, Missouri, used two types of bonds to finance two capital projects (see Exhibit 13.6 for debt service information by project). The first capital project, Fabick Property, consisted of land purchased for future park and recreation use. The total payment for the project in 2009 was $620,000. The second capital project was for the city's RiverChase recreation center. The debt service for the recreation center was combined with debt acquired for a citywide storm water project. For the recreation center alone, the projected payment in 2009 was $1.3 million.

Annual debt service for the Fenton storm water/parks fund by project.   **exhibit   13.6**

City of Fenton, Missouri	2009 Budget		November 24, 2008		

STORM WATER/PARKS FUND EXPENDITURES

Name	2005 Actual	2006 Actual	2007 Actual	2008 Amended	2009 Proposed	Percent
Debt Service Payments – Department 60190						
Contract services	$ —	$ 4,200	$ 9,600	$ 4,000	$ —	−100.00%
Fabick Property						
Bond principal	$ 380,000	$ 405,000	$ 430,000	$ 460,000	$ 470,000	2.17%
Bond interest	$ 184,207	$ 177,712	$ 169,122	$ 158,000	$ 144,600	−8.48%
Trustee fees	$ 5,215	$ 5,215	$ 5,215	$ 6,000	$ 5,400	−10.00%
Subtotal	$ 569,422	$ 587,927	$ 604,337	$ 624,000	$ 620,000	−0.64%
RiverChase Construction/Storm Water Improvements						
Note principal	$ 1,075,000	$ 1,005,000	$ 1,055,000	$ 1,100,000	$ 1,125,100	2.28%
Note interest	$ 469,994	$ 539,953	$ 495,148	$ 447,500	$ 419,500	−6.26%
Trustee fees	$ 6,870	$ 8,555	$ 5,195	$ 8,500	$ 8,400	−1.18%
Subtotal	$ 1,551,864	$ 1,553,508	$ 1,555,343	$ 1,556,000	$ 1,553,000	−0.19%
Total Expenditures	$ 2,121,286	$ 2,145,635	$ 2,169,280	$ 2,184,000	$ 2,173,000	−0.50%

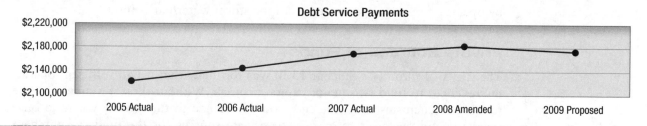

Debt Service Payments

For the purchase of the Fabick property, the city issued public facility authority (PFA) bonds. PFA bonds are similar to revenue bonds, discussed previously. The primary difference is that PFA bonds are issued by a public facility authority, a non-profit corporation established by the borrower according to Internal Revenue Service ruling 63-20. The PFA can hold title to a project, secure financing for the project, and later hand over the project to the city. For the Fabick property, the Fenton PFA issued bonds to finance the purchase of the land, holds title to the land, receives payment from the City of Fenton for use of the land through a long-term lease agreement, and will give the land to the city once the project's debt obligations have been discharged. The city pays for the project with the operating revenues of the storm water/parks fund (see Exhibit 13.4). Payments are made directly to the trustee of the Fenton PFA. In turn, the trustee makes the principal and interest payments on the bond.

PFAs are used to fund parks and recreation projects in Missouri because, under state statute, no public referendum is needed to issue bonds via a PFA. The PFA has no taxing authority, and the municipality is under no obligation to levy any form of tax to pay for the bonds. Exhibit 13.7 provides the debt service schedule for the Fabick Project PFA bonds.

For the RiverChase recreation center, the City of Fenton issued certificates of participation. The certificates of participation were issued by a lending institution to a trustee overseeing the recreation center. The city pays lease fees to the trustee, who then makes payments on the bond. As Crompton (1999) notes, the use of certificates of participation is growing. This is true especially in states that place strict limits on borrowing. For example, Missouri's Hancock Amendment sets tax and expenditure limitations in the state (Hembree, 2004). According to this amendment to the state's constitution, state and local budgets cannot grow faster than a resident's ability to pay for the growth. In essence, the amendment prevents state and local governments from increasing taxes for state and local revenues without voter approval. Twenty-three additional states have some form of tax and expenditure limitation similar to Missouri's Hancock Amendment.

As with Fenton's PFA bonds, the city formed a corporation to handle the financing of the RiverChase project. The corporation acts as a public trustee and issues certificates of participation to finance the project. Through the certificates of participation, a lending institution provides funds to the corporation/trustee for the project's construction. The trustee holds the title to the project for the benefit of the investors (certificate holders). The city then pays lease fees to the trustee, who in turn pays back to the financial institution the principal plus interest (Crompton). Exhibit 13.8 provides the debt service schedule for the certificates of participation.

Note that both the PFA bonds and the certificates of participation that the City of Fenton used to fund the Fabick Property and RiverChase projects were non-guaranteed. They were backed not by the full faith and credit of the city but by operating revenues generated from the storm water/parks fund.

Private Sources of Funds

The City of Fenton (see Sidebar 13.B) was fortunate that it had sufficient operating revenues to fund two major capital projects. Without those revenues and the funding mechanisms used, the city would have had to turn to the voters to raise taxes to fund the projects or turn to private sources for the funds to purchase

Debt service schedule for the Fabick Property. exhibit **13.7**

City of Fenton, Missouri   2009 Budget   November 24, 2008

PFA BONDS – SERIES 2003
FABICK PROPERTY PURCHASE PROJECT
DEBT SERVICE SCHEDULE

DATE	INTEREST RATE	PRINCIPAL	INTEREST	NET PAYMENT	ANNUAL DEBT SERVICE	O/S BONDS
						$5,985,000.00
1/1/2004	1.20%	$310,000.00	$82,670.25	$392,670.25		$5,675,000.00
7/1/2004			$93,528.75	$93,528.75	$486,199.00	$5,675,000.00
1/1/2005	1.50%	$380,000.00	$93,528.75	$473,528.75		$5,295,000.00
7/1/2005			$90,678.75	$90,678.75	$564,207.50	$5,295,000.00
1/1/2006	1.80%	$405,000.00	$90,678.75	$495,678.75		$4,890,000.00
7/1/2006			$87,033.75	$87,033.75	$582,712.50	$4,890,000.00
1/1/2007	2.30%	$430,000.00	$87,033.75	$517,033.75		$4,460,000.00
7/1/2007			$82,088.75	$82,088.75	$599,122.50	$4,460,000.00
1/1/2008	2.70%	$460,000.00	$82,088.75	$542,088.75		$4,000,000.00
7/1/2008			$75,878.75	$75,878.75	$617,967.50	$4,000,000.00
1/1/2009	3.05%	$470,000.00	$75,878.75	$545,878.75		$3,530,000.00
7/1/2009			$68,711.25	$68,711.25	$614,590.00	$3,530,000.00
1/1/2010	3.40%	$475,000.00	$68,711.25	$543,711.25		$3,055,000.00
7/1/2010			$60,636.25	$60,636.25	$604,347.50	$3,055,000.00
1/1/2011	3.60%	$485,000.00	$60,636.25	$545,636.25		$2,570,000.00
7/1/2011			$51,906.25	$51,906.25	$597,542.50	$2,570,000.00
1/1/2012	3.75%	$495,000.00	$51,906.25	$546,906.25		$2,075,000.00
7/1/2012			$42,625.00	$42,625.00	$589,531.25	$2,075,000.00
1/1/2013	3.90%	$520,000.00	$42,625.00	$562,625.00		$1,555,000.00
7/1/2013			$32,485.00	$32,485.00	$595,110.00	$1,555,000.00
1/1/2014	4.00%	$545,000.00	$32,485.00	$577,485.00		$1,010,000.00
7/1/2014			$21,585.00	$21,585.00	$599,070.00	$1,010,000.00
1/1/2015	4.20%	$510,000.00	$21,585.00	$531,585.00		$500,000.00
7/1/2015			$10,875.00	$10,875.00	$542,460.00	$500,000.00
1/1/2016	4.35%	$500,000.00	$10,875.00	$510,875.00	$510,875.00	—
		$5,985,000.00	$1,518,735.25	$7,503,735.25	$7,503,735.25	

exhibit   13.8   Debt service schedule for RiverChase and storm water project.

City of Fenton, Missouri   2009 Budget   November 24, 2008

CERTIFICATES OF PARTICIPATION – ALL SERIES
DEBT SERVICE SCHEDULE

Date	Interest Rate	Storm Water Portion Interest	Storm Water Portion Principal	RiverChase Portion Interest	RiverChase Portion Principal	Total Interest	Total Principal	Total Payment	O/S Bonds
12/29/2004									$15,845,000.00
3/1/2005		$25,770.29		$152,078.46		$177,848.75		$177,848.75	$15,845,000.00
9/1/2005	1.95%	$42,331.81	$155,767.50	$249,813.19	$919,232.50	$292,145.00	$1,075,000.00	$1,367,145.00	$14,770,000.00
3/1/2006		$39,119.56		$230,856.69		$269,976.25		$269,976.25	$14,770,000.00
9/1/2006	2.20%	$39,119.56	$145,624.50	$230,856.69	$859,375.50	$269,976.25	$1,005,000.00	$1,274,976.25	$13,765,000.00
3/1/2007		$35,873.44		$211,700.31		$247,573.75		$247,573.75	$13,765,000.00
9/1/2007	2.35%	$35,873.44	$152,869.50	$211,700.31	$902,130.50	$247,573.75	$1,055,000.00	$1,302,573.75	$12,710,000.00
3/1/2008		$32,417.57		$191,306.18		$223,723.75		$223,723.75	$12,710,000.00
9/1/2008	2.55%	$32,417.57	$159,390.00	$191,306.18	$940,610.00	$223,723.75	$1,100,000.00	$1,323,723.75	$11,610,000.00
3/1/2009		$30,385.35		$179,313.40		$209,698.75		$209,698.75	$11,610,000.00
9/1/2009	2.85%	$30,385.35	$163,012.50	$179,313.40	$961,987.50	$209,698.75	$1,125,000.00	$1,334,698.75	$10,485,000.00
3/1/2010		$28,062.42		$165,605.08		$193,667.50		$193,667.50	$10,485,000.00
9/1/2010	3.10%	$28,062.42	$168,084.00	$165,605.08	$991,916.00	$193,667.50	$1,160,000.00	$1,353,667.50	$9,325,000.00
3/1/2011		$25,457.12		$150,230.38		$175,687.50		$175,687.50	$9,325,000.00
9/1/2011	3.35%	$25,457.12	$173,155.50	$150,230.38	$1,021,844.50	$175,687.50	$1,195,000.00	$1,370,687.50	$8,130,000.00
3/1/2012		$22,556.76		$133,114.49		$155,671.25		$155,671.25	$8,130,000.00
9/1/2012	3.50%	$22,556.76	$178,951.50	$133,114.49	$1,056,048.50	$155,671.25	$1,235,000.00	$1,390,671.25	$6,895,000.00
3/1/2013		$19,425.11		$114,633.64		$134,058.75		$134,058.75	$6,895,000.00
9/1/2013	3.65%	$19,425.11	$185,472.00	$114,633.64	$1,094,528.00	$134,058.75	$1,280,000.00	$1,414,058.75	$5,615,000.00
3/1/2014		$16,040.25		$94,658.50		$110,698.75		$110,698.75	$5,615,000.00
9/1/2014	3.75%	$16,040.25	$191,992.50	$94,658.50	$1,133,007.50	$110,698.75	$1,325,000.00	$1,435,698.75	$4,290,000.00
3/1/2015		$12,440.39		$73,414.61		$85,855.00		$85,855.00	$4,290,000.00
9/1/2015	3.90%	$12,440.39	$199,237.50	$73,414.61	$1,175,762.50	$85,855.00	$1,375,000.00	$1,460,855.00	$2,915,000.00
3/1/2016		$8,555.26		$50,487.24		$59,042.50		$59,042.50	$2,915,000.00
9/1/2016	4.00%	$8,555.26	$207,207.00	$50,487.24	$1,222,793.00	$59,042.50	$1,430,000.00	$1,489,042.50	$1,485,000.00
3/1/2017		$4,411.12		$26,031.38		$30,442.50		$30,442.50	$1,485,000.00
9/1/2017	4.10%	$4,411.12	$215,176.50	$26,031.38	$1,269,823.50	$30,442.50	$1,485,000.00	$1,515,442.50	—
		$617,590.80	$2,295,940.50	$3,644,595.45	$13,549,059.50	$4,262,186.25	$15,845,000.00	$20,107,186.25	

park property and build the new recreation facility. A growing number of parks and recreation agencies do have to seek funding from private sources of revenue to meet budget shortfalls (Sherman). In fact, the City of Fenton expects to receive $604,400, or 10.5% of its storm water/parks fund revenues, from a private grant (City of Fenton). Other municipalities have turned to fundraising, advertising, and sponsorships to supplement their construction and operating revenues.

Fundraising and grants

Typically, facilities and programs rely on tax revenues and user fees to fund their operations (Sherman); less than 8% of operating revenues come from other sources. However, public construction projects rely more on funding from private sources. Approximately 30% of construction is funded through gifts (8%), grants (5%), and other sources (18%). For example, the $750,000 Shorewood Community Fitness Center in Wisconsin was built with funds generated in a decade-long fundraising campaign. In contrast, the Stacy Multi-Purpose Center in Princeton, Missouri, was funded through a single gift from Festus Stacy, a multimillionaire born in the community. The center includes a swimming pool, gym, weight room, and offices. Both the Shorewood Community Fitness Center and the Stacy Center are reserved for use by their respective local school districts during the school day and are open to the community after school hours and on non-school days.

These two facilities may be exceptions, according to Sherman (1998), because less than 5% of facilities—mostly those in smaller rural communities—rely on fundraising to generate revenue for construction. More likely, communities will seek grant revenue. In California, the City of Thousand Oaks' Sports Facilities Endowment Fund provides grants for the construction, expansion, or upgrading of area recreation facilities. The endowment, one of three held by the city, annually generates approximately $300,000 in interest from $6 million in investments (Cohen, 2008).

One of the most aggressive grant-seeking recreation departments is the Sapulpa Parks and Recreation Department in Oklahoma (National Recreation and Park Association, 2003). In 2003, the department received grant revenues from the Oklahoma Tourism and Recreation Department and the Fishing Access Development Grant. That same year, the department's total value of grants received since beginning its grant-seeking campaign in 1991 exceeded $1 million. In all, the Sapulpa department has received 51 grants from federal, state, and private funding sources to repair, renovate, and expand the city's recreation facilities and to construct new parks and recreation facilities.

Advertising and sponsorship

To fill gaps in appropriations from governmental entities, park and recreation departments have increasingly turned to advertising and sponsorship revenues. In fact, as mentioned previously, municipal recreation facilities nationwide are increasingly expected to be self-sufficient (Bynum, 2005). Revenue from sponsorships, for example, has helped the Buncombe County Parks and Recreation Department in North Carolina maintain operations and build new facilities. Facing a 15% budget reduction over a three-year period coupled with a 49% increase in facility usage, the department obtained sponsorship revenue from corporate partners such as Pepsi and McDonald's that supported the development and maintenance of a county sports park and the construction of two new swimming pools. The sponsorship revenues supplemented the department's annual budget and enabled the expansion of services to the county's residents (Bynum, 2003b).

The State of Michigan's Parks and Recreation Division (PRD) of the Department of Natural Resources is required under state law (Section 706 of 2007 PA 122) to report on its plan to generate sponsorship revenues to support state park and recreation operations. Its report to the state shows that the PRD has gone beyond pure sponsorship in an effort to obtain funds from private sources. It has received funds through a variety of funding methods, including gifts, grants, and donations. For example, the WK Kellogg Foundation provided $3 million in funding to construct universally accessible features in state parks and recreation areas. The Friends of the White Pine Trail donated $242,000 to match a Michigan Department of Transportation Grant to extend paving on that trail. The department also received donations to pay for two new playgrounds and sponsorship funding for new events held in the state's parks (Schafer, 2008).

The PRD also developed a naming rights policy and a sponsorship/partnership policy, each of which received approval from the state's National Resources Commission. The PRD also pursued the development of new events to be held in state parks (e.g., car shows), the development of a gift (donation) guide, and the redevelopment of the non-profit Michigan State Parks Foundation. Further, the PRD is working with the Citizens Committee for Michigan State Parks, whose charge includes studying options for long-term, sustainable funding (Schafer).

For the Pleasant Prairie Parks and Recreation Department in Wisconsin, advertising revenue is one of its main sources of non-membership revenue. Companies can advertise inside two facilities with signage, team sponsorships, and commercial time on the facilities' television monitors (Bynum, 2005). The department operates without tax proceeds and employs three staff members to operate the advertising program.

COLLABORATIVE FINANCING

Collaboration between organizations for the financing of new sport facilities has become an economic necessity. This is true for parks and recreation facilities as well. Whether the collaboration is a joint use agreement between two public entities, such as a recreation district and a school system, or a public/private partnership between, for example, a non-profit organization and a municipal recreation department, cooperation—usually in the form of joint use agreements and public/private partnerships—is becoming increasingly common.

Joint Use Agreements

We can find many examples of **joint use agreements**—formal agreements outlining how facilities will be shared—between public school districts and municipal park and recreation programs. In addition to field and/or facility usage, these agreements may cover the responsibility for construction costs, operational costs, maintenance, and management. For example, a joint use agreement allows a high school in San

Marcos, California to use a public park as a private facility. The 32-acre park includes a skate park, softball fields, and a soccer field. In Broomfield, Colorado, city revenues from new construction impact fees have been funneled from the city to the school district for construction of gymnasiums and athletic fields, which are shared by the school district and community members (Brown).

A joint use agreement must be clear in specifying

- who has access to each facility or field,
- who maintains each facility or field, and
- when each party will have access to facilities and fields.

The parties must ensure that the term of the joint use agreement is sufficient to offset the costs of the capital investments. The joint use agreement between county and school officials in Anne Arundel County, Maryland, provides an ideal example (Brown). The project involved the installation of three new synthetic turf fields each year at county high school stadia for four years, at a total cost of $10.7 million. Seventy-five percent of the funding for the new fields came from the county's recreation department. The department was able to secure a portion of this funding through a grant from Program Open Space, a Maryland Department of Natural Resources initiative. Program Open Space provides funds for the development of parks, conservation areas, and recreation areas. The county provided the funding to the schools because it would not have been able to construct new fields on its own. Through the partnership with the school district and a long-term use agreement, the recreation department was able develop new fields at less than $1 million per field.

The joint use agreement grants school programs exclusive use of the fields on weekdays until 7:00 pm (later on football Fridays) and until noon on Saturdays. The recreation department uses the fields for three to four hours during the week, ten hours on Saturday, and all day Sunday. This access alleviates overcrowding at existing recreation district facilities. In lacrosse alone, county recreation leagues fielded more than 400 teams. Field maintenance is the responsibility of the school district, as is operation of the concessions stands (Brown).

Public/Private Partnerships

Joint use agreements work well in some instances, and **public/private partnerships** work well in others. These partnerships are simply collaborations between the public and private sectors.

Altamonte Springs, Florida, has successfully used public/private partnerships over the past ten years (Bynum, 2007b). In 2007, the State of Florida reformed its property tax system, resulting in a tax freeze. The changes in tax law forced cities and counties to reduce their 2007 expenses by $2 billion. For fiscal year 2008, they were required to reduce expenses by another 3% to 9%. Park and recreation programs were targeted for cuts and had to develop alternative sources of revenue to save programs and facilities. Park departments have often entered into partnerships with private entities to manage publicly owned stadia, golf courses, and skating rinks, but Altamonte Springs was one of the first departments to outsource the operation of its recreation leagues and events, in an effort to cut expenses and generate additional revenue (Bynum, 2007a). Through a bid process, the Altamonte Springs leisure services department contracts with private companies for sport instruction and league and tournament play. The leisure services department provides facilities and marketing for recreation events and tournaments. For municipal sport programs, the city receives a percentage of registration fees. For events, the city receives 15% of registration fees and ticket sales. Sporting events are held on an average of 45 weekends each year, and the department bids for Amateur Athletic Union (AAU) tournaments, American Softball Association (ASA) regional and national tournaments, and the like. In addition to the previously mentioned revenue sources, the city may also receive a percentage of merchandise sold at events.

CONCLUSION

As in other sectors of the sport industry, the financial management of public sector sport is challenging. Though annual government spending on parks and recreation exceed $30.5 billion (U.S. Census Bureau), managers face many financial challenges. Crompton (1999) notes that competition from non-profits and the private sector creates pricing pressures for public recreation agencies charged with providing services across a diverse demographic. Further, these public agencies are seeing the erosion of their traditional tax-based sources of operating and construction revenue. As a result, the agencies are developing new revenue models to meet the demand for public recreation services.

Property and sales taxes still provide the majority of revenues for the construction and operation of parks and recreation facilities, but many states and municipalities restrict the use of tax revenue to fund new projects and programs. Therefore, public recreation agencies are now less likely to rely on general obligation bonds to finance new capital projects. Today, revenue bonds and certificates of participation are common means to circumvent the voter approval needed to finance a project through a general obligation bond. Further, park and recreation agencies are adopting some of the funding approaches that we associate with other sectors of the sport industry. Agency heads now focus on fundraising, grant seeking, sponsorships, and advertising as means to generate revenues. Park and recreation agencies are also increasingly entering into joint use agreements or public/private partnerships in their efforts to reduce expenses and generate revenue.

CONCEPT check

1. What factors will affect the type of bond that a city will choose to issue for construction of a new recreation facility?
2. In your hometown, how have local recreation facilities been financed?
3. What are the main sources of revenue for your hometown's recreation center?
4. What pricing paradox do the managers of public recreation centers face?
5. How should the manager of a public recreation center measure financial success?
6. Over the past 30 years, how has the funding of park and recreation agencies changed?

7. Explain the process of calculating the millage needed to fund a new recreation center.

8. The debt service schedules for Fenton, Missouri, are found in Exhibits 13.7 and 13.8. Why does the rate of interest that the city pays increase over time? Why does the city make two interest payments and one principal payment, in most years?

9. How does state tax law affect the financing of parks and recreation facilities and programs?

10. For the funding of projects, why are municipalities moving from the use of general obligation bonds to revenue bonds, PFA bonds, and certificates of participation?

11. How can an individual's experiences working in professional sport finance benefit a park and recreation agency?

12. What problems might arise in the negotiation of a joint use agreement?

PRACTICE *problems*

You are tasked with calculating the property tax needed to fund construction and operation of a $22.5 million complex. The facility's annual operating budget is forecast at $3.6 million, to be covered by revenues from programs offered at the facility. A 30-year general obligation bond with a rate of 5.5% will be issued to pay for the facility's construction costs. The net assessed value of property in the municipality is $725 million.

1. Calculate the amount that must be set aside each year to meet the bond's principal and interest obligations over 30 years.

2. Calculate the additional millage required to cover the project's debt service.

3. For an owner of property with a total assessed value of $15,000, by how much will property tax increase?

CASE *analysis*   *Billie Jean King National Tennis Center*

Perhaps one of the most successful public/private partnerships between a municipality and a private entity is the USTA Billie Jean King National Tennis Center. The National Tennis Center, located in Flushing Meadows, New York, is the world's largest public tennis facility. The partnership between New York City and the United States Tennis Association (USTA) is classified as a private-sector takeover. In a private-sector takeover, a private organization assumes responsibility for operation of a publicly owned facility. (See Chapter 9 for more information on public/private partnerships.)

The Problem

The partnership between the USTA and New York City began in the late 1970s (Specter, 1997). Prior to its move to the National

Tennis Center, the U.S. Open was played at the West Side Tennis Club. As its popularity increased, the tournament began to outgrow the site. At the same time, the relationship between the USTA and the West Side Tennis club was deteriorating. During negotiations for a lease extension in 1976, the USTA was presented with a take-it-or-leave-it option of paying $7 million for needed renovations at the club and ceding much of its control over the tournament and its revenues. The general attitude of the membership was that the tournament's success depended on the club. Then USTA president Slew Hester summed up their attitude thus: "The members of West Side do not need the U.S. Open as much as the U.S. Open needs the West Side Tennis Club" (p. 10).

The Plan

Faced with the club's unfavorable offer, Mr. Hester began to look for new sites in the New York area. While flying over New York City, he noticed the Singer Bowl, sitting vacant on the grounds of Flushing Meadows Park (the site of two World's Fairs). Thinking that the site would be perfect for the U.S. Open, he began to talk to city officials. Fortunately for the USTA, the city had been trying to sell the Singer Bowl for five years (Specter, 1997).

The Offer

In exchange for taking over the Singer Bowl and the land surrounding the stadium, the USTA offered to spend a minimum of $5 million to renovate the site and facility. The USTA sought a 15-year lease agreement giving them exclusive use of the facility for 60 days each year. Further, the USTA offered to maintain the site and operate it as a public municipal tennis facility. As rent, the USTA offered to pay the city 10% of court rental fees or an annual minimum of $125,000, whichever was higher. The city agreed, and the partnership between New York and the USTA began in 1977 (Specter).

The Results

The USTA spent $10 million renovating the Singer Bowl and developing the land into a world-class tennis facility. Out of the shell of the Singer Bowl, the USTA created Louis Armstrong Stadium and the Grandstand Court for tournament use. Outdoor courts were built for tournament and public use, as well as an indoor tennis complex with nine courts. Within ten months of renovations beginning, the first U.S. Open was played at the site. New York City had a new public tennis facility, and the USTA had created a facility to promote the game of tennis. The U.S. Open

soon was generating over $10 million per year for the USTA (Specter).

Today

The USTA and New York City have extended their initial 15-year agreement, as the partnership has been beneficial to both parties. In 1995, the USTA began a four-year, $285 million construction project to build Arthur Ashe Stadium and to renovate Louis Armstrong Stadium and the grounds of the National Tennis Center (United States Tennis Association, 2009). The USTA provided all funds for the renovations, which were completed with no costs to the city or its taxpayers. Today, the center remains completely public and is open for use 11 months of each year. The USTA also now pays over $1.5 million in rent per year.

The quality of the facility has improved since its opening. In addition to the stadium courts and grandstand court, 30 outdoor tennis courts are available for public use. The new Indoor Tennis Center has 12 courts, classroom space, fitness facilities, a pro shop, and a café. For the fans of the U.S. Open, Arthur Ashe Stadium seats more than 22,000; it is the largest tennis stadium in the world (United States Tennis Association, 2009). Revenues for the USTA have increased dramatically. According to the *SportsBusiness Journal,* the U.S. Open is the top standalone sporting event in the world, generating over $200 million in revenues and $100 million in profit (Kaplan, 2008).

CASE QUESTIONS

1. What benefits did the USTA receive when it entered the partnership with the city?
2. What benefits did the city receive?
3. Do the benefits to both parties seem equal? Why or why not?

references

Brayley, R.E., & McLean, D.D. (1999). *Managing financial resources in sport and leisure service organizations.* Champaign, IL: Sagamore Publishing.

Brown, N. (2008, January). Appearing act. *Athletic Business.* Retrieved August 11, 2008, from http://athletic business.com/articles/default.aspx?a=1692.

Bynum, M. (2002, October). Public enemies. *Athletic Business.* Retrieved January 27, 2008, from http://athleticbusiness.com/articles/default.aspx?a=1069.

Bynum, M. (2003a, August). Bonds. Municipal bonds. *Athletic Business.* 90–98.

Bynum, M. (2003b, August). Business class. *Athletic Business.* 42–46.

Bynum, M. (2005, December). Commercial success. *Athletic Business.* Retrieved August 11, 2008, from http://athleticbusiness.com/articles/default.aspx?a=1117.

Bynum, M. (2006, October). What price is right? *Athletic Business.* Retrieved January 27, 2008, from http://athleticbusiness.com/articles/default.aspx?a=1274.

Bynum, M. (2007a, April). A Texas u-turn. *Athletic Business.* Retrieved August 11, 2008, from http://athletic business.com/articles/default.aspx?a=1488.

Bynum, M. (2007b, September). Outside help. *Athletic Business*. Retrieved August 11, 2008, from http://athleticbusiness.com/articles/default.aspx?a=1627.

City of Fenton. (2008, November 24). *Approved budget*. Retrieved February 17, 2009, from http://www.fentonmo.org/docs/2009%20Approved%20Budget.pdf.

Cohen, A. (2008, November). Money for something. *Athletic Business, 32*(11), 89–91.

County of Lexington. (2009, April 14). *Annual budget overview*. Lexington, SC: Author.

Crompton, J.L. (1999). *Financing and acquiring park and recreation resources*. Champaign, IL: Human Kinetics.

Hembree, R. (2004, December). *The Hancock Amendment: Missouri's tax limitation measure*. Retrieved August 12, 2008, from http://www.truman.missouri.edu/uploads/Publications/MLA%2049-2004.pdf.

Kaplan, D. (2008, August 25). Putting on the show. *Sports Business Journal*. Retrieved August 28, 2008, from http://www.sportsbusinessjournal.com/article/59855.

LeBlanc, C. (2008, April 24). Cayce scores tennis complex. *The State*. Retrieved April 24, 2008, from http://thestate.com/local/v-print/story/384805.html.

National Recreation and Park Association. (2003). Oklahoma: Sapulpa puts parks dept. over $1 million mark. *Findarticles.com*. Retrieved March 19, 2008, from http://findarticles.com/p/articles/mi_m1145/is_11_38/ai_111403405/.

Sawyer, T.H., Hypes, M., & Hypes, J.A. (2004). *Financing the sport enterprise*. Champaign, IL: Sagamore Publishing.

Schafer, S.M. (2008, February 22). *Dear Senator McManus and Representative Lahti*. Retrieved January 24, 2009, from http://www.michigan.gov/documents/dnr/Parks corpsponsorshipmemo_226381_7.pdf.

Sherman, R.M. (1998, September). The numbers game. *Athletic Business*. 37–44.

Specter, D.K. (1997, February 20). A stadium is born. *Tennis Week*. 10–15.

U.S. Census Bureau. (2007). *Statistical abstract of the United States: 2008*. Retrieved February 12, 2008, from http://www.census.gov/statab/www/.

United States Tennis Association. (2009, January 27). History of the USTA Billie Jean King National Tennis Center. *USTA.com*. Retrieved March 11, 2009, from http://www.usta.com/USTA/Global/About_Us/USTA_Billie_Jean_King_National_Tennis_Center/Information/14189_History_of_the_USTA_Billie_Jean_King_National_Tennis_Center.aspx.

Welcome to Fenton. (2009). Retrieved February 17, 2009, from http://www.fentonmo.org/docs/TDD%20Sales%20Tax%20Letter-General.pdf.

College Athletics

Introduction

On June 24, 2008, Harvard beat Yale in the teams' annual regatta. Although this annual event goes unnoticed by most fans of college athletics, it is significant for its history. Yale and Harvard held their first crew competition in 1852. This regatta is generally considered to have been the first intercollegiate sporting event in the United States ("Harvard wins 20th," 2008). As an interesting side note, the first event was sponsored by the Boston, Concord & Montreal railroad company (Barr, 2008).

From this first race, college sport quickly grew. By 1905, the Intercollegiate Athletic Association of the United States (IAAUS) had been formed to govern college sport. In 1912, the IAAUS changed its name to the **National Collegiate Athletic Association.** Today, the NCAA, **National Association of Intercollegiate Athletics** (NAIA), and **National Junior College Athletic Association** (NJCAA) are the three main governing bodies overseeing college sport in the United States. As college sport grew, so did the business of college sport. From the sponsorship of the inaugural Harvard–Yale race, college sport has grown to a $40 billion+ business.

FINANCIAL STATUS OF INTERCOLLEGIATE ATHLETICS

Suggs (2002) provides an inside look at the financial operation of one of the most successful college athletic programs, The Ohio State University Buckeyes. When Suggs conducted this study, The Ohio State University athletic department had a $79 million budget,* 220 full-time employees, 37 teams, and 923 athletes. The department was one of a few self-sufficient athletic departments. For example, Ohio State's athletic department paid the university $12.5 million in overhead costs that year. This included $8 million for 400 scholarships. Further, the department paid $20 million annually in debt service for its on-campus facilities. Included in the debt service were the $200 million renovation of Ohio Stadium in 2001 and the construction of the $120 million Value City Arena. These new facilities helped the department to increase its revenues. Adopting revenue streams from professional sport, the new athletic venues generated revenue from luxury-box rentals, ticket surcharges, personal seat licenses, and club seating.

The University of Florida's athletic department is similarly sized. With a budget of approximately $85 million for the 2008–2009 academic year, the department has financial strength for the $28 million Heavener Football Complex to have been built without the use of state funds. Urban Meyer, the University of Florida's football coach, stated that the complex was needed to aid recruiting, because, he felt, the football facilities at Florida were in the bottom half of Southeastern Conference facilities. To Meyer, quality and up-to-date facilities are an important component of the recruiting process. Jamie Newberg, a national recruiting analyst

---

*For comparison, the average NCAA Division I – FBS budget was $23 million at the time (Suggs, 2002). Today, The Ohio State University athletic department has an annual budget of approximately $110 million, according to Ohio State's president, Gordon Gee. This currently is the largest athletic department budget in the United States (Fain, 2008).

at Rivals.com, agrees with Meyer's assessment. He stated that competing teams constantly pursue the latest and greatest facilities, which provide a recruiting edge. Florida's Heavener Football Complex houses the football program's staff offices and honors past Gator greats in its Gateway of Champions. Athletic director Jeremy Foley says the number one goal of the facility is to get people to walk in and say, "Wow" ("Gators add to," 2008).

The Florida athletic department is fortunate to have a strong development foundation, the University Athletic Association, Inc (UAA). In 2008, Gator boosters contributed $33 million to the UAA. For the football complex, which opened July 2008, the foundation received one $7 million donation and 16 additional donations of at least $1 million each. This enabled the foundation and the athletic department to avoid borrowing funds for the complex's completion; therefore, the department and foundation do not have to pay debt service on the facility ("Gators add to").

The Race to Build New Athletic Facilities

The construction of new athletic facilities at schools like The Ohio State University and the University of Florida has contributed to a phenomenon commonly referred to as the **arms race** in college athletics: the continuous building of bigger and better facilities for the sole purpose of landing key recruits. Ohio State is able to pay the debt service on its new facilities through funds set aside in its operating budget. As the athletic department is fully self-sufficient, meaning it receives no funds from the university's general budget or student fees, the department must generate the revenue to offset the cost of the building projects over the life of the financing for those projects. Florida was fortunate in that individual gifts generated enough revenue to cover the costs of building the new football complex, so no debt financing was needed. Both athletic departments are fortunate in being able to afford these facilities. Athletic departments that are not so financially sound face difficult decisions about the construction or upgrading of facilities in order to create their own "wow" moment on campus.

The construction of a new baseball stadium at the University of South Carolina illustrates the impact of the arms race on college athletic departments. Over the past ten years, the baseball team has made regular trips to the NCAA Super Regionals and three trips to the College World Series. To elevate the baseball program further and attract even better recruits, the head baseball coach and University's athletic director felt a new stadium was needed. The $40 million facility will house offices for coaches, indoor batting cages, chair-back seats for fans, and other modern amenities. Given average construction costs for Triple-A minor league baseball stadiums of $40 million to $50 million and for Double-A stadiums of $25 million to $35 million, the baseball stadium at the University of South Carolina will be equivalent to a high-end Double-A or low-end Triple-A facility. In fact, the new stadium is the most expensive baseball stadium ever built for a college team. For comparison, the new Louisiana State University baseball stadium, opening in 2011, will have a final cost of $34 million. Texas spent almost $28 million and the University of North Carolina is spending $17 million to completely rebuild their on-campus facilities. Even with new revenue-generating stadia, not all of these traditional baseball powers will turn profits (Morris, 2008).

Eric Hyman, athletic director at the University of South Carolina, stated in an interview that the $40 million baseball stadium makes little business sense (Morris). Hyman is responsible for finding the revenue needed to pay the stadium's debt service of $1.9 million per year for the next 30 years. Fans will have to pay higher ticket prices, will see increases in concessions prices, and will have to pay for seat licenses. Despite the additional revenue generated at the facility, the department may not earn enough new revenue to offset the expenses of the team and facility. For the 2008 season, the team had an operating budget of $1.2 million and revenues of $700,000—a deficit of $500,000. Hyman hopes that the new stadium will generate enough revenue to pay for the team's operating costs. Regardless, the athletic department must pay the stadium's annual $1.9 million debt obligation.

Kelderman (2008) reports that the arms race in NCAA Division I institutions has spread to Division III institutions, as well. Athletes competing at NCAA Division III institutions attend school without the benefit of athletic scholarships. In the Centennial Conference, made up of small liberal arts colleges, several schools have invested heavily in athletic facilities to recruit better athletes. Hence, even in an academic-focused league, competition for athletes is leading to heavy spending on college athletic facilities, resulting in increasing debt loads. For example, in 2008 Gettysburg College broke ground on a $25 million athletic facility, with construction completed in 2010. The facility has an eight-lane competition pool, a four-lane warm-up pool, and a modern hydrotherapy spa. Three years prior, Haverford College completed a $28 million athletic facility; in 2001, Ursinus College built a $13 million field house that includes two full-size batting cages, four basketball courts, three tennis courts, a volleyball court, and a six-lane, 200-meter track.

Funding sources for these new Division III facilities are similar to those used at the Division I level. The Gettysburg project was made possible by a $2 million gift from one alumnus, given because the donor felt that Gettysburg was at a competitive disadvantage without a new facility. By the time construction began, the college had raised $9 million from alumni donations. A student fee increase will be used to cover operating costs, expected to be $360,000 annually. Gettysburg's Board of Trustees will borrow to cover the remaining costs of the construction. Ursinus College also borrowed to complete construction of its new athletic facilities, issuing approximately $4 million in bonds (Kelderman).

From 2002 through 2007, colleges in the six major athletic conferences* in Division I raised close to $4 billion for new athletic facilities. These schools plan to raise $2.5 billion more between 2008 and 2012 for additional athletic facilities. Fourteen Division III schools built new athletic facilities during this time frame, as well, at an average cost of $20 million. As the president of Franklin & Marshall College stated, there is a "small arms race" going on at the Division III level (Kelderman).

---

*Often these conferences are referred to as BCS conferences. They include schools in the ACC, SEC, Big 10, Big XII, Big East, and Pac 10.

The Race to Change NCAA Divisions

The arms race affects more than facilities; it also affects an institution's choice of NCAA division. The transition to Division I from Division II is often difficult for a school; however, the lure of being a Division I institution is so great that the NCAA issued a four-year moratorium on new Division I applications at the beginning of 2007.

Presbyterian College is one example. The school has 1,200 students and has been classified by the Carnegie Foundation as one of the most selective liberal arts colleges in the United States. Athletics is an important part of student life at Presbyterian. The school fields 16 teams—eight men's and eight women's. Presbyterian recently decided to move from Division II to Division I, and the school was fortunate that its application was accepted prior to the NCAA's moratorium. One reason the school gives for the move up in classification was that similar-sized schools, such as Wofford College, Elon University, and Gardner-Webb University, had recently moved to Division I, and these moves had affected recruiting at Presbyterian. Potential recruits living within a one-hour drive of Presbyterian College were deciding to go to similar schools two or three hours away, solely because those schools were Division I. Presbyterian's head men's basketball coach felt that missing the chance to play in the NCAA Division I men's basketball tournament was too big a recruiting obstacle (Darcy, 2007).

Presbyterian was also fortunate that it was accepted into a conference, the Big South, two days after announcing its move to Division I. Beginning in the 2008/2009 academic year, the school's teams competed in the conference, although they would be ineligible for conference championships and NCAA post-season play until the 2011/2012 season (Darcy, 2007).

The financial impact of a move from Division II to Division I is staggering. Both revenues and expenses are altered dramatically. During the 2007/2008 season, Presbyterian had to play as an independent, meaning the school had no conference affiliation. Darcy (2007) chronicles the impact of the move on one of Presbyterian's programs, the men's basketball team. As a result of joining the Big South conference, in the 2008/2009 season, the men's basketball team played only five home games but 25 road games. On its longest road trip, the team was gone 11 nights, leaving in December on the day final exams ended. The team played in 12 states and traveled more than 13,000 miles by bus and plane. To generate revenue to pay for the trip, the team's road games, and the greater operating expenses needed at the Division I level, the coach scheduled games with four Atlantic Coast Conference (ACC) teams, three SEC teams, Ohio State, and Nebraska. Playing these major conference schools generated $650,000 in guaranteed money for Presbyterian. However, the school still did not have the funds to pay for administrative support, such as a coordinator of basketball operations (a position found in almost all Division I basketball programs). Instead, an assistant basketball coach had to take on those duties along with his regular coaching responsibilities. As of 2007, Presbyterian still needed to raise funds so that the school could offer additional scholarships and hire more coaches and administrative staff (Darcy).

Overall, the size and complexity of athletic department budgets have grown dramatically as the arms race continues into the 2010s. Whether it is construction of new athletic facilities or a move to a higher division, the impact on the athletic department's finances can be dramatic. But as Ohio State president Gordon Gee noted, his athletic department's budget, at $110 million per year, is nonetheless a fairly insignificant amount compared to the overall university budget of $4 billion (Fain).

FINANCIAL OPERATIONS

This section will focus on the financial operation of the NCAA—the national governing body most responsible for shaping and controlling intercollegiate athletics in the United States (Covell & Barr, 2010)—and its member conferences and schools. Discussions of financial issues in college sport focus primarily on **NCAA Division I** programs, usually those in the **Football Bowl Subdivision** (FBS). To gain a thorough understanding of the financial operations of college sport, we must undertake a broader examination. At the end of FY 2007, the NCAA had 1,033 active member schools and 34 provisional members (NCAA, 2007). Of its active membership, 119 were Division I – FBS members, 118 were **Division I – Football Championship Subdivision** (FCS) members, 92 were Division I – Other* members, 282 were Division II members, and 422 were Division III members. Athletic department revenue and expenses are smaller and less complicated the lower the school's classification.

National Collegiate Athletic Association

The NCAA has a net worth of $327 million (see Exhibit 14.1). Revenues for FY 2007[†] were $622 million (see Exhibit 14.1), an increase of 11.4% from 2006. The primary sources of revenue (approximately 82%) were television and marketing rights fees. Television revenue—specifically, the NCAA's contracts with CBS and ESPN—provides most of the $509 million in fees. The NCAA sold the television broadcast rights for the Division I Men's Basketball Championship, along with other championship and marketing rights, to CBS for $6.0 billion in 1999. The agreement has a term of 11 years, covering the 2003 through 2013 academic years. In 2007, the NCAA received $490 million from CBS. Exhibit 14.2 lists payments the NCAA will receive for the remaining years of the contract. Under the agreement, the NCAA has the option to renegotiate the contract in 2010 (NCAA, 2007).

Exhibit 14.2 also lists the payments the NCAA will receive from ESPN for television rights to the Division I Women's Basketball Championship and other NCAA championships that have not been granted to CBS. The agreement between the NCAA and ESPN, reached in 2001, guarantees the NCAA $163 million over 11 years, from 2003 to 2013 (NCAA, 2007).

The NCAA's expenses in 2007 were $575 million, an increase of 9% from 2006. The main expenses are the distribution of revenues to member institutions and costs associated with conducting championships (see Exhibit 14.1). The $332 million distribution to Division I members accounted for 58% of expenses in 2007 and represents an increase of $24 million, or 7.2%, from 2006. Revenue is distributed to Division I and Division II members annually.

---

*These are NCAA Division I institutions without a football program or with a non-scholarship football program.

[†]The NCAA fiscal year, September 1 to August 31, coincides with the academic year.

NCAA financial statements. **exhibit** **14.1**

NCAA BALANCE SHEET

Consolidated Statement of Financial Position
August 31, 2007

Assets	
Cash and cash equivalents	$7,209,112
Investments	321,970,021
Prepaid expenses	4,532,231
Receivables	70,733,813
NIT intangible assets, net	22,345,955
Properties, net	14,940,778
Other assets	2,036,103
Total assets	$443,768,013
Liabilities	
Accounts payable and accrued liabilities	$32,913,214
Distribution payable	12,575,595
Deferred revenue and deposits	5,648,634
Bonds payable, net	32,664,920
NIT payable, net	28,023,576
Accrued lease expense	4,927,691
Total liabilities	$116,753,630
Net assets	
Unrestricted	$276,312,342
Temporary restricted	50,554,007
Permanently restricted	148,034
Total net assets	$327,014,383
Total liabilities and net assets	$443,768,013

NCAA INCOME STATEMENT

Consolidated Statement of Activities
FY ended August 31, 2007

Revenues	
Television and marketing rights fees	$512,026,034
Championships and NIT tournaments	66,198,275
Investment income, net	32,981,412
Sales and services	7,612,372
Contributions – facilities, net	2,654,775
Contributions – other	318,939
Total revenues	$621,791,807
Expenses	
Distribution to Division I members	$331,925,602
Division I championships, programs, and NIT tournaments	58,305,606
Division II championships, distribution, and programs	26,639,186
Division III championships and programs	17,478,629
Association-wide programs	114,002,042
Management and general	26,431,656
Total expenses	$574,782,721
Change in net assets	$47,009,086
Net assets – beginning of year	$280,005,297
Net assets – end of year	$327,014,383

(continued)

exhibit   14.1   NCAA financial statements, continued.

NCAA STATEMENT OF CASH FLOWS

Consolidated Statement of Cash Flows
FY ended August 31, 2007

Cash flows from operating activities	
Change in net assets	$47,009,086
Adjustments to reconcile to net cash provided by operating activities:	
Depreciation and amortization	$3,524,228
Change in unrealized gain on investments	(10,192,756)
Realized gain on investments	(7,131,621)
Increase in accrued lease expense	496,442
Loss on disposal of properties	8,869
Changes in certain assets and liabilities:	
Receivables	(11,048,535)
Prepaid expenses	(1,208,625)
Other assets	193,008
Accounts payable and accrued liabilities	15,722,869
Distribution payable	(1,816,816)
Deferred revenue and deposits	(659,976)
NIT payable	(1,292,516)
Net cash provided by operating activities	$33,603,657
Cash flows from investing activities	
Capital expenditures	$(5,059,058)
Purchases of investments	(95,138,768)
Proceeds from sales of investments	71,490,755
NIT payable	(2,675,138)
Net cash used in investing activities	$(31,382,209)
Cash flows from financing activities	
Payment of bond payable	$(1,450,000)
Net cash provided by (used in) financing activities	$(1,450,000)
Net increase (decrease) in cash and cash equivalents	$771,448
Cash and cash equivalents	
Beginning of year	$6,437,664
End of year	$7,209,112

FISCAL YEAR ENDING	CBS	ESPN
2007	$490,000,000	$13,800,000
2008	$529,000,000	$14,800,000
2009	$571,000,000	$15,800,000
2010	$617,000,000	$16,800,000
2011	$657,000,000	$17,900,000
2012	$710,000,000	$18,800,000
2013	$764,000,000	$19,100,000
2007–2013 Total Payments	$4,338,000,000	$117,000,000

The amount of money that each school receives is determined from a formula created by the NCAA. For Division I members, funds are distributed based on seven criteria. The basketball fund distribution is based on a school's historical performance in the Division I Men's Basketball Championship. Schools also receive funds based on the number of sports they sponsor and scholarships they give. Funds are also granted to institutions for the academic enhancement of student-athletes and provision of student-athlete opportunities. The NCAA also provides conference grants and maintains a special assistance fund to assist student-athletes in emergency situations (Exhibit 14.3). Division II members receive a distribution based on the school's historic performance in the Division II Men's and Women's Basketball Championships and the number of sports sponsored, plus an equal amount given to all active members. The total of Division II distributions in 2007 was $4.8 million (NCAA, 2007).

The NCAA spent $78.4 million conducting championships during the 2007 fiscal year, an increase of 5.8% over 2006. Most was spent for Division I championships ($50.8 million). An almost equal amount was spent running Division II and Division III championships ($13.9 million and $13.6 million, respectively). Championship expenses are recorded in four categories: game expenses, championship committees, transportation, and per diem. For all championships, approximately 42% of expenditures in 2007 related to transportation, 32% to per diem, 23% to game expenses, and 3% to championship committees (NCAA, 2006).

Conferences

Revenue distributed to member schools flows from the NCAA to the conferences (see Exhibit 14.3). Each conference then sets policy determining the amount of revenue that an individual school receives (see Chapter Appendices 14.A and 14.B). The SEC, a conference affiliated with the Bowl Championship Series and considered to be one of six major college athletic conferences, has a much more complicated and detailed revenue sharing formula than the Mid-American Conference (MAC). The MAC, though a Division I – FBS conference, is considered to be a mid-major

exhibit   14.3   NCAA Division I revenue distribution plan.

FY 2007

Conference	Basketball fund	Academic enhancement	Conference grants	Special assistance	Sports sponsorship	Scholarship fund	Student-athlete opportunity fund	Total by conference
America East	$1,238,048	$547,200	$221,645	$297,787	$1,600,470	$1,515,617	$652,918	$6,073,685
Atlantic 10	4,775,328	851,200	221,645	447,543	2,149,887	2,017,207	873,008	11,335,818
Atlantic Coast	14,149,120	729,600	221,645	495,551	2,699,302	7,069,459	2,046,184	27,410,861
Atlantic Sun	1,238,048	486,400	221,645	196,321	812,181	901,648	241,320	4,097,563
Big 12	14,325,984	729,600	221,645	629,269	1,648,245	6,782,069	1,761,118	26,097,930
Big East	14,856,576	972,800	221,645	632,811	2,699,304	5,675,793	1,754,243	26,813,172
Big Sky	1,238,048	486,400	221,645	300,083	429,977	1,504,117	398,819	4,579,089
Big South	1,061,184	547,200	221,645	249,373	716,632	831,533	306,980	3,934,547
Big Ten	13,087,936	668,800	221,645	536,708	3,057,617	9,224,740	2,580,172	29,377,618
Big West	1,768,640	486,400	221,645	258,798	1,051,056	731,686	372,440	4,890,665
Colonial	2,122,368	729,600	221,645	338,978	1,743,797	2,549,092	895,850	8,601,330
Conference USA	7,782,016	729,600	221,645	515,125	1,146,608	5,387,936	1,345,363	17,128,293
Horizon League	2,299,232	547,200	221,645	253,920	788,291	749,279	348,927	5,208,494
Independents	—	243,200	—	275,844	167,214	28,063	8,919	723,240
Ivy Group	1,061,184	486,400	221,645	30,645	3,439,820	—	733,554	5,973,248
Metro Atlantic	1,238,048	608,000	221,645	260,024	1,266,046	257,511	322,805	4,174,079
Mid-American	1,945,504	729,600	221,645	510,065	1,481,033	5,765,317	1,511,864	12,165,028
Mid-Eastern	1,238,048	668,800	221,645	621,288	740,519	1,549,806	486,678	5,526,784
Missouri Valley	4,244,736	608,000	221,645	289,203	859,956	2,074,099	611,418	8,909,057
Mountain West	3,183,552	547,200	221,645	364,477	1,361,596	4,134,736	1,148,561	10,961,767
Northeast	1,061,184	668,800	221,645	382,793	1,863,235	766,820	554,651	5,519,128
Ohio Valley	1,061,184	668,800	221,645	412,766	931,619	1,969,519	601,995	5,867,528
Pacific 10	11,849,888	608,000	221,645	464,639	2,078,225	6,414,808	1,779,419	23,416,624
Southeastern	13,087,936	729,600	221,645	582,420	1,839,346	7,087,487	1,867,063	25,415,497
Southern	1,061,184	668,800	221,645	326,570	1,122,719	1,312,751	505,878	5,219,547
Southland	1,238,048	668,800	221,645	355,978	597,192	1,750,597	475,012	5,307,272
Southwestern	1,061,184	608,000	221,645	683,766	1,051,055	1,192,633	472,479	5,290,762
Sun Belt	1,061,184	790,400	221,645	514,198	907,731	3,551,795	1,065,615	8,112,568
The Patriot League	1,414,912	486,400	221,645	202,007	2,030,448	976,951	632,771	5,965,134
The Summit League	1,061,184	486,400	221,645	244,693	668,854	605,899	256,818	3,545,493
West Coast	2,829,824	486,400	221,645	160,024	525,529	300,968	173,886	4,698,276
Western	3,006,688	547,200	221,645	408,683	812,180	3,658,467	930,642	9,585,505
TOTAL	$132,648,000	$19,820,800	$6,870,995	$12,242,350	$44,287,684	$88,338,403	$27,717,370	$331,925,602

conference, as its football champion is not guaranteed a spot in one of the lucrative BCS-affiliated bowl games.* In fact, the MAC does not even discuss BCS revenue disbursement in its conference handbook (Mid-American Conference, 2007; see chapter Appendix 14.A).

Division I FBS, major conferences

Exhibit 14.3 illustrates the financial strength of the major conferences. On average, major conferences received $26.4 million in revenues from the NCAA, with a range of $23.4 million to $29.3 million. The five remaining Division I – FBS conferences received an average of $11.6 million, with a range of $8.1 million to $17.1 million. Non-FBS conferences received an average of $5.5 million in revenue, ranging from $3.5 million to $11.3 million. Revenues from post-season bowl games further strengthen the financial position of major conferences. For example, in 2006, bowl revenue was the third highest source of revenue in the SEC, after regular season football revenue and post season basketball revenue (Solomon & Perrin, 2008).

By reviewing conference tax filings (Form 990 – Return of Organization Exempt from Income Tax) we can further examine the differences among conference revenues in Division I. First, we must note the difficulty of making direct comparisons in collegiate sport between two similar organizations, as there is no standard for reporting financials. Exhibits 14.4 through 14.6 do, however, provide a basis for comparison. Exhibit 14.4 gives revenues and expenses for two major conferences, the SEC and Big XII. From the conferences' tax returns, we can see that the SEC reported its revenue in much greater detail than the Big XII. We can directly compare bowl game revenue and conference championship revenue. The Big XII earned $2.2 million more in bowl revenue than the SEC, and the SEC earned $5 million more from the conference championships listed on its filing. It is difficult to compare television revenues and basketball revenues, as the conferences report these revenues differently. The Big XII clearly lists the value of its television contracts, but the SEC combines its media money with other revenue earned for each sport (i.e., regular season football revenue, regular season basketball revenue). Clearly, the SEC was in the stronger financial position, as the conference's revenue was $23.9 million more than that of the Big XII.

In the SEC, schools on average received $10.2 million in revenue from the conference in 2007. This amount doubled since 1997. The growth of revenues in the SEC has mirrored growth in the popularity of college football. Football revenues accounted for 57% of SEC member institution revenues. In the Big 10, football revenues accounted for 49% of member institution revenues. Primarily because of the strength of football, the SEC and Big 10 were the two most lucrative conferences in 2007. From television revenues, marketing rights fees, and post-season football success, Big 10 schools averaged $70.4 million in revenue, while SEC schools averaged $66.8 million. In particular, television revenues tied to the broadcast of football games have been growing rapidly (Solomon & Perrin).

Prior to 1984, the NCAA controlled the television rights for college football. In that year, the University of Georgia and University of Oklahoma sued the NCAA, claiming that the NCAA's control over broadcasting violated the Sherman Act. The U.S. Supreme Court agreed that the NCAA's actions violated Section 1 of the Act

---

*The five Division I – FBS conferences not guaranteed a spot in the BCS are the MAC, Conference USA, Mountain West, Sun Belt, and Western Athletic Conference.

exhibit   14.4   Revenues and expenses of selected Division I – FBS major conferences.

SOUTHEASTERN CONFERENCE

Revenue

Regular season football games	$51,182,500
Postseason basketball games	26,952,015
Bowl games	22,955,410
SEC Football Championship	15,884,145
Regular season basketball games	13,067,500
NCAA Student-Athlete Assistance Fund	2,062,200
Sponsorship royalties	1,916,491
Championship fanfare and events	468,139
SEC Baseball Tournament	438,255
Prior years' events	334,605
NCAA grant	212,613
National Letter of Intent Program	87,575
Building allowance – BJCC	70,000
SEC Gymnastics Championship	37,937
Jefferson Pilot Internship	24,477
Jefferson Pilot Player of the Game	24,000
McWhorter Scholarship Endowment	10,000
SEC Soccer Tournament	425
Total revenue	**$135,728,287**

Expenses

Payments to members	
LSU	$10,714,082
South Carolina	10,431,122
Florida	10,327,492
Alabama	10,300,697
Tennessee	10,232,897
Georgia	10,216,567
Kentucky	10,191,107
Arkansas	10,146,562
Auburn	9,986,567
Mississippi	9,886,122
Vanderbilt	9,828,622
Mississippi State	9,766,122
Grants, scholarships, fellowships	2,401,154
Insurance, lighting, game guarantees	2,269,171
Salaries	2,122,519
SEC Football Championship	1,957,598
Post season Basketball Tournament	1,519,982
Bowl game insurance and other	1,082,023
Officiating	931,398
Sponsorship royalties	769,026
Medals, trophies, awards	520,938
Conferences, conventions, meetings	401,750
Travel	370,042
SEC Baseball Tournament	256,909
Occupancy	235,705
Legal fees	205,509
Football crossover fees	165,750
Non-revenue sports TV contract	90,000
National Letter of Intent Program	63,963
SEC Gymnastics Championship	34,380
SEC Soccer Tournament	4,015
Total expenses	**$137,429,791**

BIG XII

Revenue

TV contracts	$50,000,000
Bowl games	25,190,136
Men's Basketball Tournament	24,548,308
Conference championships	11,400,142
Office location incentive	208,000
NCAA basketball host	179,637
Royalties/licensing	175,990
Sponsors/corporate partners	143,000
Total revenue	**$111,845,213**

Expenses

Payment to members	
Texas	$9,679,299
Oklahoma	9,094,124
Texas A&M	8,226,241
Nebraska	7,809,622
Colorado	7,644,059
Iowa State	7,339,921
Kansas	7,277,446
Texas Tech	6,794,385
Baylor	6,632,243
Oklahoma State	6,623,634
Missouri	6,530,307
Kansas State	6,472,067
Member participation subsidy	12,234,802
Salaries	2,649,837
Other member reimbursements	811,450
Rental facility	700,219
Professional services	659,733
Miscellaneous	477,454
Promotions	456,132
Video reproduction	412,751
Contract labor	387,229
Lodging and meals	332,254
Hospitality	317,510
Officials	270,694
Member-administered expenses	221,292
Total expenses	**$110,054,705**

Note: Figures based on each conference's 2006 IRS Form 990.

(*NCAA v. Board of Regents*, 1984). After the ruling, most of the major football conferences and football independents (Penn State and Notre Dame) joined together as the College Football Association (CFA) to negotiate a collective television package for members. The Pac 10 and Big 10 negotiated their own television contracts. By 1991, Penn State and Notre Dame had left the CFA in order to negotiate on their own. The CFA was disbanded after the SEC left in 1995 to pursue an opportunity to increase its revenues through an exclusive contract with CBS. (CBS had just lost its NFL television package to Fox.) After the television contract was signed, total SEC disbursements to member schools increased from $45.5 million to $58.9 million. In 2008, with its television rights agreements with CBS, ESPN, and Lincoln Financial about to expire, the SEC considered following the Big 10 model with the launch of its own television network (Solomon & Perrin).

The Big 10 created its own network in 2007 with partner News Corp. The conference's 51% ownership stake in the network resulted in $66 million in new revenues during FY 2007. Over the lifetime of the agreement, the Big 10 could average $112 million annually, as the fees paid to the conference are expected to rise over the lifetime of the deal. At the same time the Big 10 was launching its network, it signed a ten-year, $1 billion national rights contract with ABC/ESPN. The Big 10 received $83 million during the first year of the agreement (2008), and the rights fees will rise over the life of the contract. Due to these television agreements, total Big 10 revenue increased 39.8% between 2006 and 2008, and distributions to member schools increased 30.9% (Broughton, 2008).

As the Big 10 illustrates, the earning power of a conference positively impacts its member schools. Most of a conference's revenue is distributed its member schools (see Exhibit 14.4). In the SEC, payments to member schools range from $9.8 million to $10.7 million. Mississippi State, the school receiving the least distributed income from the SEC, earned more than Texas, the Big XII school receiving the largest share of distributed income from the Big XII.

Division I FBS, minor conferences

Exhibit 14.5 highlights the revenue and expenses of two Division I – FBS minor conferences: the Western Athletic Conference (WAC) and Conference USA (C-USA). By comparing the revenues of conferences in Exhibits 14.4 and 14.5, we can see the importance of football in generating conference revenue. All four conferences play football at the same level, but not having a guaranteed place in the BCS hurts overall conference revenue, and member schools are affected, as well. Whereas the WAC received $8.8 million in bowl game revenue and C-USA received $3.4 million, the SEC received $23.0 million and the Big XII received $25.2 million. These figures make it clear that access to the major BCS bowl games is critical to conference revenue generation. Also, the WAC benefited from Boise State's appearance in a BCS game when Boise State received an automatic bid after finishing the football season with a 12–0 record.* This game alone was responsible for most of the $5.4 million difference in bowl revenue between the WAC and C-USA.

---

*The champion of C-USA, the MAC, the Mountain West Conference, the Sun Belt Conference, or the WAC earns an automatic bid to one of the BCS bowl games if it finishes either first or second in the final regular season BCS standings, is a conference champion ranked in the top 12 of the final BCS standings, or is ranked in the top 16 of the final BCS standings and its ranking is higher than a regular season champion of a major conference.

exhibit 14.5   Revenues and expenses of selected Division I – FBS Conferences, minor.

WESTERN ATHLETIC

Revenue

BCS and bowl game net revenue	$8,823,484
Membership dues/assessments	3,970,000
NCAA basketball tournaments	3,006,688
Television contract	900,000
Tournament revenue	56,301
Total revenue	**$16,756,473**

Expenses

Payment to members	$14,211,529
Student assistance/NCAA compliance	1,716,515
Athletic events/championships	1,673,692
Salaries	1,242,330
Occupancy	297,755
Professional services	285,947
Travel	234,528
Advertising	215,502
Conferences, conventions, meetings	176,634
Total expenses	**$20,054,432**

CONFERENCE USA

Revenue

NCAA Men's Basketball Tournament	$7,215,178
Television revenue	6,650,000
Scholarships	5,034,590
Expansion participation funds	2,576,004
Bowl revenue	2,358,219
C-USA Men's Basketball Tournament	1,254,355
Student-Athlete Opportunity Fund	1,066,407
BCS revenue	1,050,000
Sports sponsorships	1,012,810
C-USA Football Championship	982,405
NCAA enhancement fund	699,960
Total revenue	**$29,899,928**

Expenses

Payment to members	
Memphis	$3,077,833
Houston	2,646,804
Southern Mississippi	2,566,393
East Carolina	2,487,718
Alabama–Birmingham	2,448,158
Central Florida	2,347,558
Tulsa	2,246,794
Tulane	2,156,509
Texas–El Paso	2,087,298
Southern Methodist	1,770,082
Marshall	1,638,535
Rice	1,557,353
Payment to former members	
Cincinnati	406,542
DePaul	101,635
UNC–Charlotte	84,696
St. Louis	16,939
Championship expenses	2,961,186
Salaries	1,622,687
Support services	654,837
Marketing and promotions	494,686
Employee benefits	287,989
Championships	266,460
Conferences/meetings	203,785
Occupancy	158,958
Total expenses	**$34,291,435**

Note: Figures based on Western Athletic Conference's 2007 IRS Form 990 and Conference USA's 2006 form.

Exhibit 14.5 also illustrates the benefits of having 12 teams in a conference. With 12 teams, a conference is able to play a football conference championship game under NCAA rules. C-USA has 12 football-playing members, while the WAC does not. The difference meant an additional $982,405 in revenue for C-USA. Further, we can see the importance of quality basketball programs. Without a guaranteed annual participant in a BCS bowl game, conferences must rely on teams from schools like Memphis to generate revenues in the NCAA Men's Basketball Championship tournament. C-USA, being a stronger basketball conference, generated considerably more basketball revenue than the WAC ($4.2 million). The better basketball being played in C-USA, coupled with its 12 member institutions sponsoring football, significantly improves the conference's television revenue. C-USA received $6.7 million in television revenue, which dwarfs the $900,000 received by the WAC—although it is a small fraction of the $50.0 million the Big XII received.

Exhibit 14.5 reveals another impact of a conference having a championship football game. When the ACC expanded from nine member institutions to 12, a shift occurred across several Division I conferences, including C-USA. As a result of the shift, C-USA was making payments to four former conference members as well as current members (see Exhibit 14.5); however, it also received revenue from the new members of the conference. This revenue was recorded as the $2.6 million in expansion participation funds.

Exhibit 14.6 lists the revenues and expenses of the Atlantic 10 (A10) Conference. The schools of the A10 are Division I – FCS members, and the conference's main sources of revenue are related to basketball, as Exhibit 14.6 shows. The conference received $3.9 million from the NCAA for its men's basketball tournament appearances, slightly more than the WAC received ($3.0 million). The A10 basketball tournaments also generated an additional $1.52 million in revenue. Regarding football revenue, the conference received a Division I-AA grant for $225,000. (Division I-AA is the former designation for Division I – FCS schools.) Although a few members of the A10 play Division I – FCS football, the conference itself does not count football in its 21-sport league (e.g., the University of Massachusetts–Amherst is a member of the A10, but its football team plays in the Colonial Athletic Association [CAA]). As the A10 receives virtually no football revenues compared to schools in Division I – FBS conferences, distributions to A10 member schools are considerably less than the distributions to Division I – FBS member schools.

Schools

The revenues that member schools receive from conference distributions are important, but they are a small percentage of overall departmental revenues, according to Fulks (2008). On average, distributions from the NCAA and conferences account for only 14% to 17% of a Division I program's general revenues. For schools in major conferences, the largest portion of the athletic program's revenues comes from football (see Exhibit 14.7). At the high end, the average SEC school receives 57% of its revenues from football; at the low end, an average Big East school receives 36% of its revenues from football (Solomon & Perrin). However, even with large revenues coming from the NCAA and conferences, and football revenues supporting the overall athletic programs at major schools, it can still be difficult to earn a profit. For an example of the

exhibit   14.6   Revenues and expenses of a Division I Conference, non-FBS.

ATLANTIC 10

Revenue	
NCAA Tournament	$3,892,500
Atlantic 10 basketball tournaments	1,520,400
Television and advertising	981,600
Sponsorships	562,400
Member dues and assessments	360,000
I-AA grant	225,000
Dividend income	119,500
Total revenue	**$7,661,400**
Expenses	
Payments to members	
Xavier	$500,917
St. Joseph's	469,960
Temple	392,094
George Washington	290,210
Dayton	286,887
Richmond	215,840
LaSalle	203,114
Charlotte	194,221
Massachusetts	185,481
St. Bonaventure	184,425
Rhode Island	176,845
Duquesne	157,711
Fordham	145,042
St. Louis	67,161
Championship administration	1,647,900
Salaries	1,316,200
Television and advertising costs	1,067,400
NCAA student opportunity assistance	635,200
Meetings/conventions/travel	416,900
NCAA student special assistance	391,500
Sponsorship commissions/expenses	275,200
Officials	257,500
Rent and utilities	129,800
Banquets and awards	44,500
Total expenses	**$9,652,008**

Note: Figures based on the conference's 2006 IRS Form 990.

Michigan athletic department budget.   **exhibit**   **14.7**

FISCAL YEAR 2007 OPERATING BUDGET (in thousands)

REVENUES	BUDGETED AMOUNT	% OF TOTAL
Spectator admissions		
Football	$29,934	39%
Basketball	2,315	3%
Hockey	2,000	3%
Other	180	0%
Conference distributions		
Television (football and basketball)	6,287	8%
Football bowl games	1,726	2%
NCAA basketball	2,352	3%
Other	350	0%
Priority seating	9,425	12%
Gifts and scholarship fund	3,660	5%
Corporate sponsorship	5,041	7%
Licensing royalties	3,000	4%
Radio	1,875	2%
Facilities	1,850	2%
Concessions/parking	1,763	2%
Other	757	1%
Investment income	3,500	5%
Current revenues	**$76,015**	**100%**
EXPENSES		
Salaries	$24,391	35%
Student financial aid	13,725	20%
Team and game expense	12,066	18%
Facilities	5,888	9%
Deferred maintenance fund transfer	4,500	7%
Other operating and administrative expenses	6,118	9%
Debt service transfer to plant fund	2,156	3%
Current expenses	**$68,844**	**100%**
Net operating surplus	$7,171	
Transfers and capital expenditures		
Capital expenditures from current funds and transfers to plant fund	$(4,835)	
Transfers to endowment fund	(300)	
Net transfers and capital expenditures	$(5,135)	
Increase (decrease) in current fund balances	$2,036	

Source: University of Michigan (2006).

Financial Turnaround   SIDEBAR

When Eric Hyman was hired as the new athletic director at the University of South Carolina, he inherited a program that had lost $2.65 million in the previous year. In his first year as athletic director, the program lost another $2.46 million. Fortunately, the department had a reserve fund that covered some of the losses (Person, 2006a). However, the department eventually needed a $2.74 million subsidy from the university (Person, 2008). One reason for the department's poor financial shape was a recent change to the football coaching staff. The department owed buyouts to several members of Coach Lou Holtz' staff, and for a few months paid salaries to both Holtz' staff and new Coach Steve Spurrier's staff (Person, 2006a).

Upon arriving on campus, Hyman recognized the department's financial issues and set out to increase revenues and control costs. To increase revenues, Hyman turned to the department's strength. By raising ticket prices to football games by $10 per ticket, the program raised an additional $4.5 million (Person, 2006a). The department also began planning to overhaul its ticket distribution system for football games, in an effort to increase revenues from members of the Gamecock Club, the South Carolina athletic department's athletic support group. Under the existing system, to qualify for a season ticket package, an individual first had to make a donation to the Gamecock Club. Then, based on the amount of the person's giving and the number of years the individual had given, the department determined the person's season ticket package eligibility. Packages ranged from a full package (all seven home games) to a partial, four-game package (featuring the team's lesser opponents). Donors were rewarded for longevity, not the total amount they had given to the booster organization. To increase revenues, Hyman instituted a premium seating system.

South Carolina's premium seating system is referred to as yearly equitable seating (YES). The system was created in order to honor the loyalty of past donors while balancing donors' giving level and history of donations. To keep their seats for Gamecock football games during the 2009 season, members had to maintain their 2008 Gamecock Club membership status through annual giving to the club. The Gamecock Club members were also required to make a YES donation ranging from $50 to $395 per seat, based on seat location.

At Auburn University, a premium seating system was expected to generate an additional $3.5 million in revenues annually. To keep a seat located between the 30-yard lines and in the lower bowl, Auburn season ticket holders were required to make an additional donation of $400 per ticket. In other sections, season ticket holders were required to donate an additional $200 or $300 per seat (Person, 2006b).

The South Carolina athletic department's changes enabled the department to reverse its financial position. Exhibit 14.8 gives the department's 2007 budget. Revenues were forecast to increase 21% from 2006, with revenue from ticket sales increasing 38%, due primarily to the $10 per ticket price increase for football. Football ticket revenue alone was forecast to increase 44%. Overall, the department forecast a $1.0 million surplus at the end of the fiscal year (University of South Carolina, 2006).

Since 2006, the South Carolina athletic department has been able to replenish its reserve fund, as the department had surpluses in 2007 and 2008. In addition to increasing its football ticket revenues, the department signed a new nine-year, $50.5 million contract with ISP Sports under which the athletic department will receive an additional $2.4 million per year for multimedia rights (Person, 2008). The new football ticket distribution plan, announced late in 2008, was expected to improve the athletic department's financial position further.

---

financial difficulties that athletic departments face, please read Sidebar 14.A, which discusses the situation at the University of South Carolina.

The financial difficulties at the University of South Carolina described in Sidebar 14.A are not uncommon. Fitzpatrick (2007) notes that more than 90% of Division I athletic programs have expenses that exceed revenues on an annual basis. Fulks (2008), in his annual examination of NCAA revenues and expenses, added that only 19 NCAA Division I – FBS programs were self-supporting during FY 2006. He added that the median net revenue for the 19 schools was $4.3 million. For the 100 FBS schools that were not self-supporting, the median loss was $8.9 million. Compounding the financial difficulties for schools is the fact that although revenues

University of South Carolina athletic department budget.   exhibit   14.8

Revenues	FY 2007
Admissions	$18,104,044
Guarantees	284,700
Premium seating	2,760,000
Student fees	605,000
Gamecock Club revenues	13,000,000
SEC revenue	9,500,000
Other revenue	3,896,000
Total revenues from departmental operations	$48,149,744
Expenses	
Salaries	$14,417,131
Grants-in-aid	8,189,755
Team travel	3,012,541
General travel	618,665
Recruiting	907,419
Game services	2,004,725
Other services	1,074,069
Supplies and equipment	1,317,869
General and administrative	9,933,164
Guarantees	1,861,610
Total expenditures from department operations	$43,336,948
Operating revenue over expenditures before transfers	$4,812,796
Transfers	
Band/student government	$236,000
Capital transfer/other	250,000
R&R	2,200,000
Athletic debt service	1,250,000
University scholarships	250,000
Total transfers (net)	$4,186,000
Revenue over expenditures and transfers	$626,796
Arena budget summary	
Net arena revenue	$5,513,875
Net arena expenditures	4,706,070
Transfer for arena construction (suites)	500,000
Other transfers	175,000
Transfers from university	245,000
Net arena revenue over net arena expenses/transfers to debt service	$377,805
Increase (decrease) in athletic department fund balance	$1,004,601

Source: University of South Carolina (2006).

are growing each year, expenses are growing faster (Person, 2006a), due to increases in scholarship costs, escalating costs for football and men's basketball coaches, and the costs of building new or renovating old athletic facilities (Fitzpatrick).

Financial profitability

To examine an athletic department's profitability is a challenging task. As mentioned earlier, the reporting of financial data is not standardized (Fitzpatrick). One institution's method of recording revenues and expenses is likely different from another institution's. As a result, institutions often have difficulty comparing their financial performance to benchmarks published by the NCAA. Another source of difficulty is that individuals analyzing athletic department performance frequently treat revenues allocated to the department in varying ways. For example, for 2008 and 2009 the *Indianapolis Star* published on its website revenues and expenses of 164 Division I colleges and universities (http://www2.indystar.com/NCAA_financial_reports/).* The *Star* found that during FY 2005, 63 athletic departments either broke even or lost money. One hundred and one schools reported a profit. These results contrast with Fulks' (2008) statement that in FY 2005, only 22 Division I institutions (all FBS schools) were self-sustaining.

Exhibit 14.9 lists the revenues and expenditures for FY 2005 of Miami University (Ohio) and the University of Oregon, as reported by the *Indianapolis Star* (http://www2.indystar.com/NCAA_financial_reports/). Miami, a member of the MAC, had a net operating surplus of $502,720. Oregon, a member of the Pac 10, had a net operating deficit of $131,198. Before looking at the financial data, we would probably expect that a school affiliated with a major conference would be in better financial standing than one that is not. An examination of only the net operating surplus or net operating deficit (expense to revenue difference) would be superficial. To understand the financial strength of an athletic department, we must examine revenue closely.

When it reported that 63 schools either broke even or lost money in 2005, the *Indianapolis Star* was looking only at the expenses to revenue differences of each athletic department, while ignoring significant variations in the way departmental revenues were reported at many of the schools in the study. Revenues are reported to the NCAA in two categories (Fulks, 2008): **department-generated revenues** are those revenues generated independently by the athletic department and its programs; **allocated revenues** are revenues that the school transfers to the athletic department. These revenues are not generated by the athletic department but given to the department by the institution or a governmental entity. As Fitzpatrick notes, allocated revenues are bailouts by universities that enable their athletic departments to balance their books. When Fulks (2008) reported that 22 schools were self-sustaining in 2005, he meant that the revenues generated by the athletic department alone covered the department's operating expenses. These institutions did not need to allocate revenues to offset revenue shortfalls in their athletic departments.

---

*Data were obtained through freedom of information requests. The paper sent requests to the 215 public schools that participate at the Division I level. Requests were also sent to 112 private schools competing at the Division I level. Private institutions have no legal obligation to comply with such requests, and none have done so. Also, state law in Pennsylvania and Delaware exempts schools in those states from complying.

Revenues and expenses of selected Division I – FBS universities.   exhibit   14.9

FY 2005	MIAMI UNIVERSITY (OHIO)		UNIVERSITY OF OREGON	
	Amount	% of total	Amount	% of total
Revenues				
Department-generated revenues				
Total ticket sales	$882,338	4.3%	$12,151,382	30.4%
NCAA and conference distributions	1,191,328	5.8%	6,009,809	15.0%
Guarantees and options	546,214	2.7%	1,498,129	3.7%
Cash contributions from alumni and others	773,320	3.8%	11,651,406	29.1%
Third-party support	—		81,000	0.2%
Other				
Concessions/programs/novelties	127,833	0.6%	1,001,138	2.5%
Broadcast rights	36,000	0.2%	—	0.0%
Royalties/advertising/sponsorship	729,380	3.5%	2,154,291	5.4%
Sports camps	929,676	4.5%	888,084	2.2%
Endowment/investment income	408,156	2.0%	165,000	0.4%
Miscellaneous	471,946	2.3%	3,006,551	7.5%
Total generated revenues	$6,096,191	29.7%	$38,606,790	96.6%
Allocated revenues				
Direct institutional support	$3,384,300	16.5%	—	0.0%
Indirect institutional support	785,157	3.8%	—	0.0%
Student fees	10,291,120	50.1%	1,369,845	3.4%
Direct government support	1,519	0.0%	—	0.0%
Total allocated revenues	$14,462,096	70.3%	$1,369,845	3.4%
Total all revenues	$20,558,287	100.0%	$39,976,635	100.0%
Expenses				
Grants-in-aid	$5,858,446	29.2%	$5,519,836	13.8%
Guarantees and options	104,210	0.5%	1,718,525	4.3%
Salaries and benefits – university paid	6,238,346	31.1%	9,688,915	24.2%
Salaries and benefits – third party paid	—	0.0%	—	0.0%
Severance pay	—	0.0%	—	0.0%
Team travel	1,660,689	8.3%	2,397,397	6.0%
Recruiting	683,049	3.4%	832,184	2.1%
Equipment/uniforms/supplies	694,684	3.5%	296,035	0.7%
Promotion	248,721	1.2%	1,309,106	3.3%
Game expenses	401,031	2.0%	1,851,312	4.6%
Medical	108,674	0.5%	1,364,017	3.4%
Membership dues	163,368	0.8%	510,217	1.3%
Sports camps	683,051	3.4%	886,407	2.2%
Spirit groups	199,761	1.0%	340,614	0.8%
Facilities maintenance and rental	259,591	1.3%	6,675,536	16.6%
Indirect institutional support	785,157	3.9%	—	0.0%
Other	1,966,789	9.8%	6,717,732	16.7%
Total operating expenses	$20,055,567	100.0%	$40,107,833	100.0%
Expense to revenue difference	$502,720		$(131,198)	

Source: NCAA Financial Reports Database, available at http://www2.indystar.com/ncaa_financial_reports/.

The revenues and expenses of Miami and Oregon (see Exhibit 14.9) as reported by the *Indianapolis Star* show that 70.3% of Miami's revenues were allocated revenues, while only 3.4% of Oregon's revenues were allocated revenues. If we remove allocated revenues from the analysis,* Miami had $6.1 million of operating revenues and $19.3 million in operating expenses, for an operating expense to revenue difference of –$13.2 million. For Oregon, the expense to revenue difference is –$1.5 million. Hence, although the *Star*'s reports make it appear that the Miami athletic department was in the stronger financial position, in reality the athletic department at Oregon was much stronger, as it could nearly cover its operating expenses with its operating revenues, while Miami relied heavily on institutional support and student fees to operate its department.

Moreover, both the *Star*'s revenue and expense reports and Fulks' comments regarding self-sufficiency neglect a significant expense: debt service on athletic facilities. Both Miami and Oregon report only operating expenses and fail to include debt service and costs for replacement of facilities in expenses. The athletic department budgets given in Exhibits 14.7 and 14.8 show the impact of these expenditures on profitability. Michigan (Exhibit 14.7) had a net operating surplus of $7.2 million (operating expense to revenue difference), while South Carolina (Exhibit 14.8) had a net operating surplus of $4.8 million. After we remove non-operating expenses, the net increases in the fund balances were $2.0 million for Michigan and $1.0 million for South Carolina. Considering debt service reduces profit further and may turn a profit into a loss. Michigan had $4.8 million in debt service payments plus other non-operating expenditures, while South Carolina had $1.25 million in debt service plus other non-operating expenditures. Based on analysis of these two budgets, it is highly likely that the number of self-supporting Division I athletic departments is fewer than Fulks' estimate. In fact, Zimbalist (2007) estimated that fewer than ten truly generate a surplus.

Division I—School trends and performance

Exhibit 14.10 gives a breakdown of median revenues and expenses for Division I athletic departments by sub-classification. The median revenues are based on data collected for the *2004–2006 NCAA Revenues and Expenses of Division I Intercollegiate Athletics Programs Report* (Fulks, 2008). For FBS schools, the median revenue was $35.4 million, while the medians for FCS and non-football Division I programs (Other) were $9.6 million and $8.8 million, respectively. It is important to note that there was not much difference between the median values of total allocated revenues across all three subdivisions. The median was $7.2 million for FBS schools, $7.1 million for FCS schools, and $6.6 million for Other. The difference in total revenue results from revenues generated by the athletic department. The median was $26.4 million for FBS schools, $2.3 million for FCS schools, and $1.8 million for Other. Large differences in median values between subdivisions are found in ticket sales, NCAA and conference distributions, cash contributions, broadcast rights, and game day revenues (concessions/programs/novelties).

The median operating expense for an FBS school was $35.8 million; it was $9.5 million for FCS schools and $8.9 million for Other (see Exhibit 14.10). Likely,

---

*Indirect institutional support is recorded as both a revenue and an expense. When we remove it as an allocated revenue, we must also remove it from operating expenses.

Median operating revenues and expenses for Division I athletic departments by classification. exhibit 14.10

FY 2006	FBS	FCS	OTHER
Revenues			
Department-generated revenues			
Total ticket sales	$7,442,000	$278,000	$177,000
NCAA and conference distributions	4,863,000	395,000	232,000
Guarantees and options	738,000	234,000	90,000
Cash contributions from alumni and others	5,826,000	635,000	483,000
Third-party support	—	—	—
Other			
Concessions/programs/novelties	604,000	30,000	14,000
Broadcast rights	168,000	—	—
Royalties/advertising/sponsorship	1,334,000	150,000	172,000
Sports camps	77,000	23,000	30,000
Endowment/investment income	387,000	19,000	15,000
Miscellaneous	592,000	77,000	66,000
Total generated revenues	$26,432,000	$2,345,000	$1,828,000
Allocated revenues			
Direct institutional support	$2,118,000	$4,277,000	$4,602,000
Indirect institutional support	—	611,000	443,000
Student fees	1,418,000	872,000	511,000
Direct government support	—	—	—
Total allocated revenues	$7,202,000	$7,130,000	$6,592,000
Total all revenues	$35,400,000	$9,642,000	$8,771,000
Expenses			
Grants-in-aid	$5,798,000	$2,558,000	$2,516,000
Guarantees and options	940,000	36,000	17,000
Salaries and benefits – university paid	11,279,000	3,099,000	2,844,000
Salaries and benefits – third-party paid	—	—	—
Severance pay	—	—	—
Team travel	2,458,000	782,000	705,000
Recruiting	675,000	175,000	139,000
Equipment/uniforms/supplies	922,000	311,000	254,000
Fundraising	953,000	157,000	154,000
Game expenses	1,269,000	194,000	178,000
Medical	487,000	134,000	77,000
Membership dues	102,000	38,000	35,000
Sports camps	—	—	9,000
Spirit groups	115,000	15,000	17,000
Facilities maintenance and rental	2,569,000	134,000	132,000
Indirect institutional support	—	611,000	443,000
Other	2,869,000	544,000	414,000
Total operating expenses	$35,756,000	$9,485,000	$8,918,000

Note: Revenues and expenses were reported in median dollars. Median values cannot be added; therefore, the total amounts are the median totals for the data collected. They are not the summations of data presented in this table.

Source: Adapted from Fulks (2008).

the differences in expenses are tied to costs associated with running FBS football programs. For example, the varying costs for scholarship football players affected median values for scholarships across the three subdivisions. For the FBS, the median cost was $5.8 million; for FCS schools, $2.6 million; and for Other, $2.5 million.

Guarantees, a fixture of FBS programs with seven home football games per season, have a median of $940,000 for FBS programs, compared to $36,000 for FCS schools and $17,000 for Other. The cost of operating major programs, both football and basketball, is reflected in the median values of university-paid salaries and benefits; we see a large difference in median values between subdivisions: $11.3 million for FBS schools, $3.1 million for FCS schools, and $2.8 million for Other schools. The same can be said for major differences in median expenses between FBS schools and the rest of Division I schools for team travel, recruiting, game expenses, and facility maintenance and rental.

Fulks (2008) also analyzed trends during a three-year span (2004–2006). He noted that from 2004 to 2006, median revenues rose 16% for FBS schools, 13% for FCS schools, and 22% for Other schools. Expenses, however, grew at a higher rate during the same time frame, up 23% for both FBS and FCS schools and 24% for Other schools. As a result, median negative net generated revenue grew across all three subdivisions, as losses continued to grow for Division I athletic programs.

The major sources of revenue during each of the three years of the study were ticket sales and contributions from alumni and others. This was true across all three subdivisions. Similarly, two items were the major expenses across the three subdivisions: grants-in-aid (or scholarships) and salaries and benefits. The author noted that these two expenses make it difficult for athletic departments to control costs. As the cost of tuition increases nationwide, the cost for providing scholarships correspondingly increases for all schools. Market demand for top coaches drives the costs of salaries and benefits. For example, in 2006 the median FBS head football coaching salary was $855,500, a 47% increase over the 2004 median salary, $582,000. The median salary for FBS assistant football coaches increased 23% during the same time frame. For basketball, the median FBS head coaching salary increased 15% for coaches of men's teams and 20% for coaches of women's teams. The 2006 median salary was $611,900 for the men's coaches and $241,500 for the women's. Similar increases in median salaries were seen in the FCS and Other subcategories.

Fulks (2008) also discussed programmatic trends. One significant trend was the disparity in revenues and expenses of programs within Division I subdivisions. In the FBS, the second largest program-generated revenue was $105 million, while the median was approximately $26 million. For the FCS and Other subdivisions, the findings regarding revenue disparity were similar. For the FCS subdivision, the largest generated revenue was $15.2 million, and the median was $2.3 million. For the Other subdivision, the largest generated revenue was $12.5 million; the median was $1.8 million. Similar differences occurred in expenses as well. For the FBS subdivision, the figures for largest and median expense were $101.8 million and $35.7 million; for the FCS subdivision, $35.9 million and $9.5 million; and for the Other subdivision, $24.4 million and $8.9 million. Among FBS football and men's basketball programs, between 50% and 60% reported surpluses for 2004, 2005, and 2006. For FCS football, 4% of programs reported a surplus in 2006, and for FCS men's basketball the figure was 8%; 10% of Other men's basketball programs reported a surplus. Overall, the FBS departments have a greater ability to generate revenues compared to programs in the other two subdivisions. The FBS programs rely heavily on football revenues.

Division II—School trends and performance

Exhibit 14.11 gives revenues and expenses for the average Division II program. Division II programs are classified as either football and non-football. Unlike the Division I reports, the Division II reports provide information on average debt service and capital expenditures for programs in each classification. For Division II programs with football, the average generated revenues were $600,000, with allocated revenues adding $2.0 million. Non-football program-generated revenues averaged $316,000, with allocated revenues adding $1.3 million. We can see major generated-revenue differences between the two classifications in total ticket sales, cash contributions from alumni and others, and royalties/advertising/sponsorship. Under allocated revenues, a total of $474,000 more institutional support was provided for football programs than non-football programs.

As with revenues, expenses were greater for Division II programs with football. Although scholarship costs were only $114,000 higher for football programs, salaries were $443,000 higher for the programs. Debt service and capital expenditures added an average of $82,000 to expenditures for schools with football and $11,000 for schools without.

Fulks (2005a) discussed trends in Division II athletic department financial operations. The most recent benchmarks, published in 2005, cover the 2003 fiscal year. Though the report is a bit dated, it is still informative to examine the revenue and expense trends revealed in available data. Between 2001 and 2003, revenue increased 38% for programs with football and 42% for programs without, while expenses increased 19% and 25%, respectively. So, in 2003 it appears that, unlike today, revenues were increasing at a faster rate than expenses (similar results were found for Division I programs in 2003). However, the average operating loss for Division II schools grew during this time. Operating losses (with direct institutional support not included in revenues) increased $340,000 for programs with football and $170,000 for programs without. These results indicate that Division II institutions were increasing their institutional support at a greater rate than department-generated revenue was increasing. Therefore, the total rate of revenue growth was inflated in order to offset increases in departmental expenditures. The impact on revenue growth of increases in institutional support is evident, as 57% of revenue received by programs with football is direct institutional support, while the figure is 61% for programs without football. For Division II programs, student fees were the second-highest source of departmental revenues. As with Division I programs, the two largest expense categories were grants-in-aid and salaries.

Division III—School trends and performance

Exhibit 14.11 also provides revenues and expenses for Division III athletic departments, also classified as football or non-football. On the revenue side, the data are much less detailed than the data available for Division I and II programs. Only two categories were reported for department-generated revenues: cash contributions by alumni and others, and miscellaneous. Institutional support was also reported.

exhibit **14.11**   Average operating revenues and expenses for Division II and Division III athletic departments by classification.

FY 2003	DIVISION II		DIVISION III	
	FOOTBALL	NON-FOOTBALL	FOOTBALL	NON-FOOTBALL
Revenues				
Department-generated revenues				
Total ticket sales	$125,000	$30,000	$—	$—
Postseason compensation	8,000	16,000	—	—
NCAA and conference distributions	12,000	12,000	—	—
Guarantees and options	17,000	5,000	—	—
Cash contributions from alumni and others	209,000	82,000	198,600	169,200
Third-party support				
Other:				
Concessions/programs/novelties	17,000	11,000	—	—
Broadcast rights	3,000	2,000	—	—
Royalties/advertising/sponsorship	42,000	25,000	—	—
Sports camps	74,000	54,000	—	—
Miscellaneous	93,000	79,000	629,800	451,900
Total generated revenues	$600,000	$316,000	$828,400	$621,100
Allocated revenues				
Institutional support	$1,457,000	$983,000	$1,651,100	$993,200
Student fees	380,000	237,000	—	—
Direct government support	122,000	70,000	—	—
Total allocated revenues	$1,959,000	$1,290,000	$1,651,100	$993,200
Total all revenues	$2,559,000	$1,606,000	$2,479,500	$1,614,300
Expenses				
Grants-in-aid	$849,000	$735,000	—	—
Guarantees and options	12,000	7,000	11,200	4,900
Salaries and benefits	1,072,000	629,000	978,000	585,700
Team travel	260,000	179,000	236,900	144,700
Recruiting	43,000	18,000	46,400	19,200
Equipment/uniforms/supplies	155,000	94,000	147,500	85,000
Fundraising	29,000	18,000	72,000	58,900
Game officials	38,000	30,000	48,600	43,100
Contract services	51,000	36,000	62,600	38,100
Sports camps	43,000	33,000	96,700	337,900
Other	197,000	126,000	188,100	101,000
Total operating expenses	$2,749,000	$1,905,000	$1,888,000	$1,418,500
Debt service	$9,000	$5,000	$825,900	$70,300
Capital expenditures	73,000	6,000	345,500	114,600
Total expenditures	$2,831,000	$1,916,000	$3,059,400	$1,603,400

Source: Adapted from Fulks (2005a and 2005b).

Institutional support provides the majority of departmental revenues—67% for programs with football and 59% for programs without football. It is interesting to note that average institutional support for Division III programs with football is greater than that of Division II programs with football, even though Division III programs have no scholarship expenses.

Debt service and capital expenditure expenses were provided, as well as operating expenses. Division III programs with football had the largest average debt service and capital expenses among all Division II and III classifications. In fact, debt service was at least 11.5 times greater than the next highest average amount, while capital expenditures were three times greater than the next highest average. Debt service and capital expenditures were 38% of total expenditures for Division III programs with football and 12% for programs without football.

As with the benchmark data for Division II programs, the most recent publicly available Division III data cover the 2003 fiscal year (Fulks, 2005b). For programs with football, operating expenses had increased an average of 26% from 2001. The increase was 34% for programs without football. As Division III schools offer no grants-in-aid for athletes, major expenses were slightly different than for Division I and II programs. Still, salaries and benefits was one of the two major expenses. For programs with football, the second-largest expense was team travel, and for programs without football, camp expenses was the second-largest expense category.

ATHLETIC DEPARTMENT FUNDRAISING

Analysis of NCAA revenues and expenses shows that operating expenses are increasing faster than operating revenues. From 1995 to 2001, athletic department spending grew about 15% more than overall university spending grew. The desire of some university administrators and alumni to win, coupled with rising transportation and scholarship costs, has caused growth in athletic department spending to outpace overall university growth. As a result, schools have become increasingly reliant on allocated revenues, especially direct and indirect institutional support and student fees (Sylwester & Witosky, 2004).

However, with many public universities facing cuts in state appropriations, athletic departments are being pressured to reduce their reliance on allocated resources. Organizations such as the Drake Group and Coalition on Intercollegiate Athletics are examining ways to reform college sport, including finances. The financing of college athletics and the commercialization of many athletic programs are issues that unite university administrators, faculty, and students (Sylwester & Witosky, 2004).

On campuses where pressure is growing to reduce the athletic department's allocated resources, the development staff must find ways to generate greater amounts of revenue through giving. These development officers must raise increasing amounts of revenue not only for the operating budget but also to fund new athletic facilities on campus. Athletic fundraising, therefore, is crucial, as monies generated through the development office will offset the rising expenses of operating an athletic department and help to reduce the department's reliance on allocated revenues. According to *The Chronicle of Higher Education,* the largest athletic departments and their affiliated booster clubs raised $1.2 billion during FY 2007 (Wolverton, 2007). The majority of this money was raised through such initiatives as capital campaigns and annual giving programs.

The Capital Campaign

Much of the money that athletic departments raise goes to offset the costs of new facilities. From 2002 to 2007, the development efforts of athletic departments in a major affiliated conference generated a total of more than $3.9 billion in donations to pay for capital expenditures, with plans to raise an additional $2.5 billion for new buildings (Wolverton, 2007). Usually, when an athletic department needs to begin replacing its older facilities, the department will initiate a **capital campaign,** an intensive effort to raise funds in a defined time frame through gifts and pledges for a specific purpose. The Varsity Club at Indiana University began its For the Glory of Old IU capital campaign on July 1, 2006, and planned to continue it until June 30, 2010. The goal of the campaign is to raise $80 million, of which $30 million would go toward capital support, $25 million toward endowment support, and $25 million toward ongoing support (Indiana University Varsity Club, 2006). Another example is Clemson University's Tiger Pride campaign, a five-year, $30 million campaign to raise funds to improve athletic facilities. In 1995 the University of Washington began its $90 million Campaign for the Student Athlete, and the University of Maryland is currently conducting the Great Expectations campaign, intended to raise $133 million to improve athletic facilities on campus, fund scholarships, and endow coaching positions.

Making a case

One of the most important elements of a capital campaign is the **campaign case statement.** The case statement answers all the critical questions regarding the campaign and presents arguments for why an individual should support the campaign. The case statement also lets readers know how they can give to the campaign. According to Dove (2000), a typical case statement includes six sections:

1. institutional mission,
2. record of accomplishment,
3. directions for the future,
4. urgent and continuing development objectives,
5. plan of action to accomplish future objectives, and
6. the institution's sponsorship.

For a better understanding of each of these sections, examine the case statement presented in Exhibit 14.12 for the Indiana University athletic department campaign.

Major gifts planning

To reach a capital campaign goal, development departments need to receive major gifts from program supporters. Most development departments define a **major gift** as a donation worth $25,000 or more. The number, size, and types of major gifts needed to reach a campaign goal are determined through various mathematical formulae based on national giving patterns. From these formulae, we can develop a major gifts table. Dove (2000) notes that a major gifts table demonstrates the importance of major gifts to a campaign. Not only does the table provide an outline of the number and size of gifts needed to reach a campaign goal, it also serves as a reality test for the organization. After the table is developed, the organiza-

exhibit 14.12

Example case statement from *Are You Committed?*, the case statement for Indiana's For the Glory of Old IU campaign.

Institutional mission. According to Dove (2000), the case statement should outline the organization's role and philosophy. The IU athletic department's document contained the following statements regarding the department's mission:

- *Indiana University offers recruits the opportunity to get a top-notch education and compete on a national stage* (p. 3).
- *We can ensure that IU Athletics not only sustains, but excels academically and thrives athletically* (p. 3).
- *It's important never to lose sight of the primary mission of our athletic program. We're committed to making sure promising students receive the top-level educational opportunities that might not otherwise be available to them* (p. 13).

Record of accomplishment. In speaking of the department's record of accomplishment, the document contained the following:

- *We're proud of the 23 national team championships and 160 Big Ten championships our teams have earned* (p. 13).
- *As Hoosiers like softball player Michelle Venturella collect Olympic gold medals . . .* (p. 3).
- *A two-time (and counting) selection to the Academic All-Big Ten, president of the Student Athlete Advisory Council and an NWCA Scholar-Athlete, Max is proof that student athletes can compete successfully in a sport without missing out on any educational opportunities* (p. 7).

Future directions. The case statement should discuss the department's directions for the future. Indiana's case statement stated:

- *The North End Zone Facility is our way to give something back to the players who give so much to IU Athletics—the resources they need to succeed during and after college* (p. 5).
- *The proposed Academic Resource Center, built with help from Hoosier fans, will bring improved and expanded technology, dedicated study space, and access to academic advisors, tutors and mentors to all of our student athletes* (p. 7).

- *The Basketball Development Center will make a real difference for students like Whitney and Armon. With expanded and separate facilities for the men's and women's teams, including two practice courts, it will be easier for the coaching staff to accommodate class schedules, while giving players more opportunities to improve their skills* (p. 9).

Development objectives. Indiana's urgent and continuing development objectives, which include the campaign's priorities and costs as well as the master plan, are expressed in the following statements:

- *But, while every other school in the Big Ten Conference has recently completed or is in the process of finishing major new facilities to enhance athletic training and development, IU has only made modest improvements. As a result, we now face a significant recruiting disadvantage* (p. 3).
- *Our overall campaign goal is to raise $80 million in private support* (p. 3).
- *Five new important facilities: the North End Zone Facility, the Academic Resource Center, the Basketball Development Center, and new baseball and softball stadiums* (p. 3).

Plan of action. In outlining its plan of action, the Varsity Club stated:

- *To initiate these capital projects, IU Athletics will issue bonds guaranteed by future operating revenue. However, for this vision to become reality, we need to secure the necessary resources from loyal Hoosiers like you* (p. 3).
- *These goals will be achieved over the next few years through the generosity of loyal alumni, friends and fans who share a common bond— Hoosier pride. No student fees or state or university dollars will be used as funding sources* (p. 3).

Institution's sponsorship. Finally, the institution's sponsorship of the campaign is stated as follows:

- *In September 2006, the IU Board of Trustees approved and endorsed a facility enhancement plan . . .* (p. 3).

Source: Indiana University Varsity Club (2006). Reprinted with permission.

tion can determine whether it indeed has enough prospective donors to reach the campaign goal.

Gift table rules. There are three major mathematical ways to create a major gifts table (Dove). The first applies the **80/20 rule.** The rule states that based upon past giving patterns, 80% of the needed funds will come from 20% of the donors. So for Indiana, $64 million of the $80 million total would come from 20% of the campaign's donors. Trends in giving seem to be shifting, however. Therefore, some development officers rely on the **90/10 rule,** which states that 90% of the total money needed for the campaign will come from 10% of the campaign's donors. For the Indiana campaign, $72 million would come from 10% of those giving to the campaign.

The third model uses the **rule of thirds.** According to this rule, the top ten gifts to the campaign would account for 33% of the campaign's total goal; the next 100 gifts would account for an additional 33%, and the remaining gifts would account for the final third. For Indiana, $26.67 million would come from the top ten donors, $26.67 million would come from the next 100 donors, and the remaining funds would come from the rest of the campaign's donors.

Traditional gifts table. All of these rules will lead to the creation of similar major gifts tables. From these rules and tables, many campaigns develop a **traditional gifts table.**

For the $80 million For the Glory of Old IU campaign, we would develop a traditional gifts table as follows (see Exhibit 14.13). The lead gift, or the largest single campaign gift, is set at 10% of the campaign goal—$8 million. The amount of the next largest gift is set to half of the lead gift, or $4 million, and we double the number of donors needed—i.e., we double one to get two. The value of the next largest gift is half of the previous gift amount ($2 million) and the number of needed donors is double the last number (4). We continue this process until the campaign

exhibit 14.13 Traditional gifts table for $80 million campaign.

GIFT AMOUNT	PROSPECTS NEEDED	GIFTS NEEDED	CUMULATIVE TOTAL	% OF GOAL
$8,000,000	3	1	$8,000,000	10%
$4,000,000	6	2	$16,000,000	20%
$2,000,000	12	4	$24,000,000	30%
$1,000,000	24	8	$32,000,000	40%
$500,000	48	16	$40,000,000	50%
$250,000	96	32	$48,000,000	60%
$125,000	192	64	$56,000,000	70%
$62,500	384	128	$64,000,000	80%
$31,250	768	256	$72,000,000	90%
<$31,250	many	many	$80,000,000	100%

goal is reached. It must be noted that the table does not always work, especially as giving trends appear to be changing. In some instances, ten to 15 donors have given 50% to 70% of the campaign totals. In some campaigns, the lead gift is set at an amount less than 10% of the campaign goal because an analysis of potential donors reveals little potential for a large lead gift. If the lead gift is set at a level less than 10% of the goal amount, there is a good chance that the campaign goal will not be reached, as the mathematical standards that were developed based upon actual past giving to campaigns will not have been met (Dove).

When finalizing the gift table, we must factor all known information regarding major gift possibilities into its formulation. For example, if it is known that a donor plans to give a large portion of the campaign total at the launch of the campaign, this gift must be factored into the table. Also, the number of gifts that the program is seeking must be specified. Many athletic departments have conducted capital campaigns in part to endow athletic scholarships. If a goal of a campaign is to endow 20 scholarships, there must be 20 $300,000 spots on the gift table. (This assumes that an average scholarship costs an athletic department $15,000. Endowments generally pay at a 5% rate; therefore, $300,000 must be raised to endow each scholarship.)

Pre-campaign research. The goal of a campaign should be based on pre-campaign research to determine the level of giving that alumni and friends of the athletic program can provide. Once the potential for giving is determined, the campaign amount can be set and the gift table can be created. When setting a campaign goal and creating the gift table, it is important to remember that it takes many donors to reach each level of giving. Also, the gift table at each level of giving must match the donors' potential for giving at those levels.

Development officers have observed that three or four legitimate prospective donors are required per gift at each level of giving. For the Indiana campaign, three or four potential donors must have the ability to give at least $8 million, or it is unlikely that Indiana will receive its lead gift. Six to eight must have the potential to give $4 million, and so on. As we move down the chart, fewer prospects are required per gift. The table in Exhibit 14.13 is based on this fact. It assumes three prospects per gift, rather than making the more conservative assumption of four per gift. For example, if Indiana identified three potential donors to give at the $8 million level, one of those donors may decide to give. Suppose the donor decides to give $6 million rather than $8 million. This gift would be recorded at the $4 million level. Spillover from higher categories into lower giving categories occurs often, leaving fewer potential donors needed at lower levels of giving.

Identifying major donors and prospects

Dove (2000) states that in order to obtain major gifts, an organization must actively identify, cultivate, and solicit major donors. He adds that major donors have the following traits:

- They often desire to provide opportunities that they did not have, to help the less fortunate, to improve quality of life, and to help solve problems in society.
- They tend to be very religious, have a strong belief in free enterprise, and be basically conservative.

- They know someone in the athletic department or know something about the department, and they believe in someone working for the department or believe in something that the academic institution or athletic department represents.
- They view giving as an investment and will want to see, or at least understand, the return on their investment.
- They have the resources to make a major gift.

Knowing these characteristics of major donors, the athletic department can identify giving prospects. Dove (2000) defines a **prospect** as "any individual, foundation, corporation, or organization that has the potential to give and is likely to do so" (p. 95). When a donor has potential to give but little probability to give, the development office must cultivate the donor and move him or her toward becoming a probable giver. The first step is to identify and rate prospects. The research department will evaluate individuals affiliated with the athletic department and determine who is capable of making a commitment to the capital campaign. The researcher might begin with those who have previously given to the department. According to one development officer, among all donors who give above $25,000, 75% first gave a gift of $250 or less to an annual giving initiative. Further, 83% made annual fund donations for at least five years, and almost 60% have made annual fund donations for 11 years or more.

Dove summarizes the objectives and expected outcomes of the prospect research process. First, research must identify prospects and their relationships with other prospects and athletic department constituents. It must determine each prospect's association with the department, his or her previous levels of giving, and his or her interests in the department and also identify the prospect's wealth, ownership interests, control, and influence. Finally, the research staff must reduce the information into reports that pertain to the current capital campaign.

The development staff uses these reports to rate potential donors and implement a strategy for action for each—that is, a strategy for cultivating the prospect. The staff will determine which campaign items the prospect will probably support and decide which department member is best suited to cultivate the prospect. For example, suppose it is determined that a certain prospect is able and likely to give at the $2 million level. The prospect played tennis at the institution and currently holds basketball season tickets. Also, the prospect was an academic all-American. Based on preliminary research and information gathered through the cultivation process, the development staff will determine where the prospect is likely to give and target its solicitation of a gift based on that information. The staff might target this individual to give to a new academic enrichment center. A staff member overseeing academics would then be assigned to cultivate the prospect. The staff will determine a timeline for cultivating the prospect. According to one development officer, major gifts are usually closed after about nine meaningful contacts over a period of six months to two years.

Asking for donations

After the prospect has been identified, researched, rated, and cultivated, he or she must be asked to give the gift. Development officials hold varying opinions on when a prospect has been cultivated enough to be susceptible to responding positively to an "ask." A few officials feel it is best to ask for a gift right away, as the donor probably knows that you intend to do so at some time. Others feel that a predetermined number of contacts should be made prior to the request. Most state that you should ask when the time feels right.

Dove (2000) provides guidelines for asking for a major gift. First, the amount of money solicited must be sufficiently large. Often, development officers will ask for gifts two to four times larger than the prospect's giving rating. It is easier to move down to an amount that is acceptable for the prospect than to discover later that a prospect could have given more and try to obtain a higher commitment. Second, development officials should listen during conversations. Suppose that in conversations, the prospect described previously over and over mentions an affinity for basketball and asks questions relating to the basketball program's needs. That prospect would probably be more receptive to giving to basketball than to an academic center. The development officer must be flexible in presenting alternatives if the conversation indicates that the prospect may be more likely to give in an unexpected area.

Annual Giving Programs

Capital campaigns are important to the long-term plans of athletic programs, but annual giving programs are necessary to sustain operating revenues. For Division I institutions, contributions from alumni and others—the second-largest source of department revenue for the average FBS program and the largest for the other classifications (see Exhibit 14.9)—is the fastest growing source of athletic department revenues. In 1965, contributions from alumni and others accounted for 5% of the average Division I budget. This figure grew to 17% in the late 1990s and is now approximately 22%.

Athletic support groups

The athletic support group (ASG) or booster club is responsible for most athletic departments' annual giving programs. These groups are usually operated as non-profit organizations, which are tax-exempt, and they are separate legal entities from the college or university. They may also be operated as athletic department clubs. The Gamecock Club (http://gamecocksonline.cstv.com/sports/c-gamecock-club/index.html), for example, is the University of South Carolina's ASG. It is incorporated as a 501(c)(3) public charitable organization. According to the club's FY 2006 Form 990, the purpose of the Gamecock Club is "to support the University of South Carolina's Athletic Department by providing the necessary financial resources for scholarships and other educational services." Other successful ASGs, organized similarly, include North Carolina State's Wolfpack Club (www.wolfpackclub.com) and the University of North Carolina's Rams Club (www.ramsclub.com).

An individual's level of giving to an ASG results in his or her club membership classification. The level required for membership typically ranges from $100 to over $10,000. Members receive differing benefits based on their giving levels. For the most part, ASGs offer six to ten levels of membership, including student memberships. For the Wolfpack Club, current students can join for $30 and enjoy benefits including a club t-shirt, online access to *The Wolfpacker* magazine, the opportunity to purchase premium student seating at basketball and football games, meetings with coaches and athletes, a membership card, and a car decal. Non-students must pay a minimum of $120 to join at the base level, called the Teammate Club. The highest level of membership, the Lone Wolf level, requires a donation of at least $22,000. At this level, members receive a football and basketball preview magazine, a membership package and card, a car decal, season ticket applications for football and basketball, an option to purchase parking passes for athletic department events, and an invitation to an athletic director's dinner. In between are seven additional levels of membership, each with differing benefits. The benefits increase with the amount given in a year. Donations to the Wolfpack Club are 80% tax deductible.

The University of North Carolina's Rams Club is structured similarly. Students can join for $25. Non-students must pay $100 to become Tar Heel members of the club. The highest level is the Annual Scholarship level, which members must contribute at least $14,716. Again, benefits increase as giving increases. For Rams Club members, two additional categories are tied to endowed giving: the Half Scholarship and the Full Scholarship. Half Scholarship members agree to donate $100,000 over a five-year period, with an annual minimum of $10,000, and Full Scholarship members agree to donate $200,000 over a five-year period, with an annual minimum of $20,000. Rights earned by Half and Full Scholarship members include the ability to purchase season tickets to men's basketball (two and four tickets, respectively), which are at a premium in Chapel Hill.

Schools with smaller enrollments have succeeded in increasing departmental donations by focusing on the wealthiest donors. At Wake Forest University, the Moricle Society was created for donors who contribute at least $55,000 per year. These members of the Deacon Club, Wake Forest's ASG, receive free flights on team charters and may meet with coaches before games for private overviews of game strategy. The Moricle Society has obtained $1 million per year in additional revenue for the ASG.

Relation between annual giving and ticket sales

Most Division I – FBS athletic departments link the purchase of tickets to football and men's basketball events with annual giving. At North Carolina, the only way a donor can be sure to be able to purchase a season ticket to basketball is by giving at either the Full or Half Scholarship level. (Upon completing their five-year commitment, Half Scholarship members must remain at the Super Ram giving level or above [$2,500], and Full Scholarship members must remain at the Coaches Circle level or above [$5,000].) At the Annual Scholarship ($14,716) and Coaches Circle ($5,000) levels, a donor has the right to purchase season basketball tickets if they are available, but tickets are not guaranteed. The ability to purchase tickets for high-demand events and the location of tickets are based on a point system.

Point systems. Athletic departments have developed **point systems** to assign tickets to donors in an objective way. These systems vary slightly from institution to institution, but they generally award points based on the donor's amount of annual giving, the number of years or consecutive years the donor has given, and the number of years or consecutive years the donor has purchased season tickets. The more points earned, the higher priority the donor has to purchase tickets. The location of the donor's seat is also based on points earned.

The Wolfpack Club's website (www.wolfpackclub.com) provides an example calculation of a donor's points. A donor can earn points in four ways:

1. The donor receives one point for each consecutive year he or she has contributed to the club. For long-time donors, 1.2 points per year are earned for donations made in years 11 to 20, 1.4 points are earned each year for donations made in years 21 to 30, and so on.
2. The cumulative gift total—both annual giving and giving to capital campaigns—earns 0.008 point for each dollar of the cumulative gift total.
3. The donor receives 0.012 point for each dollar of current annual pledge.
4. Donors earn one point per year for ordering season tickets for football and one point per year for ordering season tickets for men's basketball.

Points are totaled, and the donor receives a ranking based on the total points. This ranking determines the donor's priority when ordering tickets and selecting seat location.

Suppose a member renews at the Lobo Club level and gives $600 for her annual membership. She has donated $6,000 in total, including payments toward one of the club's capital campaigns and her membership fees over the past five years. She has not ordered season tickets for football or men's basketball. The calculation for determining this club member's points is as follows:

- Five consecutive years of membership earns five points: $5 \times 1 = 5$ points
- With $6,000 of cumulative giving, she earns 48 points: $6,000 \times 0.008 = 48$ points
- The $600 donation this year earns 7.2 points: $600 \times 0.012 = 7.2$ points
- As she has not purchased season tickets to either men's basketball or football, no additional points are earned: $(0 \times 1) + (0 \times 1) = 0$ points
- Total points earned for this donor are 60.2: $5 + 48 + 7.2 + 0 = 60.2$ points.

Her rank, or priority, is based on the 60.2 points earned and where her points fall compared to the points of all other Wolfpack Club members.

For seven of ten athletic department donors, their only donation to the department is the fee to purchase football or men's basketball tickets (Wolverton, 2008). Wolverton observes that some universities now include donations to other school departments in the calculation of a donor's points. For example, the Tiger Athletic Foundation at Louisiana State University includes academic contributions in the calculation of points that earn premium seating rights and other athletic department–related benefits.

Seating policy restructuring. Because the ability to purchase tickets to high-demand games drives donations to ASGs, over time schools reassign seats and overhaul their point systems both to generate additional revenue and to make the system more equitable for long-time and newer donors alike. Some schools, such as the University of Maryland and The Ohio State University, reassign seats each season

SIDEBAR

Intra-University Development Issues

14.B

When donations go to an athletic department, many faculty members complain about the emphasis placed on athletics. At Oklahoma State University, T. Boone Pickens donated $165 million to the athletics department. At the time, the donation was the largest in the history of college athletics. The money was initially invested in a hedge fund managed by Pickens, and the amount of the donation is expected to grow to $343 million by the time it is spent. (Pickens waived all fees.) All of the money was to go toward athletic facilities. Football received $120 million for new offices, training rooms, and additional seating in the stadium, and $54 million went to a new multipurpose indoor practice facility. The tennis program received $15 million for a new, modern facility. A former chairman of Oklahoma State's Faculty Council was publicly critical of the gift and cited the donation as an example of the university's overemphasis on college athletics. Pickens countered that you give the money to the programs you choose (Wieberg, 2006).

Some are concerned that the increases in giving to athletics will impact the giving of gifts to the university as a whole. Zimbalist (2007) noted that at the University of Connecticut giving to athletics rose from $900,000 in 1989 to $4.29 million in 1993. Over that same period, all other university giving fell from $7.5 million to $4.29 million. The net result, therefore, was a $180,000 increase in giving to the university. Stinson and Howard (2007) note that for Division I FBS schools, athletic donations were 15% of an average university's total donations in 1998. By 2003, athletic donations accounted for 26% of the total. This trend has aroused fear on campus about the limited pool of money donors are willing to give. If more is given to athletics, less will be left for academic programs (Wolverton, 2007).

based on their point systems. Other institutions, such as Iowa State University and the University of Missouri, only reassign seats periodically based on their point systems.

As an example, Clemson University restructured its football seating policy after the 2007 season (Strelow, 2008). The restructured policy, according to Clemson officials, rewarded donors' loyalty as well as their giving. A reseating usually assigns seats to the donors who gave the most or who have earned the most priority points, but the Clemson policy gave current ticket holders the right to keep their premium seats (seating between the 30-yard lines) if they met the new monetary standards set for those seats. The resulting change affected membership in the highest categories of IPTAY, Clemson's ASG, as 70% of those in the newly designated premium seating area increased their giving level in order to retain their seats or to improve their seat location. For example, the Heisman level ($10,000) increased from 200 members to 316 members, and the McFadden level ($5,600) increased from 103 members to 459 members. In all, for the five highest membership categories ($2,100 plus), membership increased 54%. The increase in giving exceeded expectations, and demand for premium seats outpaced supply. Demand was so great that some donors who significantly increased their giving had to remain in their current seat location or even moved to slightly less desirable premium seats.

Seat licenses. In addition to complete restructuring of a seating policy, some schools have added a second layer of giving for premium seats (Emerson, 2008). These schools require a seat license, similar to the PSLs that have been sold in professional sport over the last two decades, on top of annual giving minimums for access to seating purchases. To purchase season tickets in the new baseball stadium, a fan at the University of South Carolina must be a member of the Gamecock Club and pay a seat license fee (see Exhibit 14.14). The club hopes that the seat licenses will raise an additional $570,000 per year for the baseball program. The seat license, refereed by the university as a seat donation, is tax deductible. The cost of each season ticket, then, is $210 plus the seat donation required to purchase the particular seat, plus the required donation to the Gamecock Club. (Annual

exhibit **14.14**

Seats and seat giving requirements for the University of South Carolina's new baseball stadium.

SEAT TYPE	NUMBER AVAILABLE	MINIMUM GAMECOCK CLUB MEMBERSHIP	SEAT LICENSE FEE
Black	1,746	Century/Classroom Club ($150)	$25
Garnet	1,807	Century/Classroom Club ($150)	$50
Gold	1,250	Century/Classroom Club ($150)	$75
Box	113	Full Scholarship ($1,350)	$115
Club	103	Silver Spur ($3,000)	$1,500
Suite	60	Garnet Spur ($7,000)	$35,000

Note: There are five suites, with 12 seats per suite. Fees are on a per-suite basis.

donations to the Gamecock Club bring privileges across sports. So, one donation made during the year can fulfill the season ticket requirements for both football and baseball.)

ENDOWMENT FUNDAMENTALS

Endowed giving has been mentioned already, but it merits a deeper discussion. Establishing and raising funds for endowments may be included in a capital campaign or an annual giving program. For an athletic department, an endowed fund is a fund made up of **endowed gifts.** These gifts, held by the department or its ASG in perpetuity, are invested, and only a portion of the fund's annual investment return is used for the fund's specific purposes. To protect against inflation, the remaining investment return is added to the fund's principal amount. The goal of the reinvestment is to maintain the value of the principal. Typically, athletic departments use endowed funds for scholarships, coaching salaries, or program-specific support. An endowment may be created through gifts of cash, publicly traded securities, stock in closely held corporations, real estate, or bequests. The donor may receive tax advantages including savings on income taxes, capital gains taxes, and transfer taxes, depending on the asset given and the gift arrangement.

CONCLUSION

Though it appears that college athletics is awash in money—from the NCAA's $490 million television contract with CBS to the profile of high-powered athletic programs—it is very difficult for an athletic department to generate more operating revenues than operating expenses, let alone be self-sustaining. This is especially true for Division I – FCS, Division I – Other, Division II, Division III, and non-NCAA schools. As allocated revenues are the foundation of many programs' revenues, financial pressures on campuses across the country are resulting in an increasing emphasis on athletic department development programs. At all levels, programs are implementing capital campaigns, creating detailed annual giving programs, and creating endowments to support the ongoing mission of athletics on campus in an effort to secure the financial future of intercollegiate college athletics.

CASE analysis   *Endowing Tobacco Road*

The University of North Carolina and Duke University have two of the more developed athletic department endowment programs in the NCAA. The main endowed fund at North Carolina is the Scholarship Endowment Trust, with $140 million in assets. From this principal, 5% ($7 million) is used to pay annual scholarship costs. The trust was built through endowed giving and the fund's investment returns. As mentioned previously, donors may endow scholarships in two ways: a full scholarship with a gift of $200,000, payable over a five-year period, or a half scholarship with a gift of $100,000, payable over the same period. The Scholarship Endowment Trust does not fully cover the costs of all of North Carolina's athletic scholarships. In 2007, the cost for 450 scholarships was approximately $8.5 million. North Carolina hopes to fund athletic scholarships fully through this endowment, but with the cost of education rising faster than inflation (North Carolina scholarship costs have doubled over the past 12 years)—and, more important, rising faster than the return rate of the endowment—North Carolina has had to continue to raise money for the fund.

In addition to raising funds to offset scholarship costs, North Carolina has begun to create endowments for each of its teams. The funds for the Sport Endowments are invested, providing an annual yield of 5%, which is the same yield provided by the Scholarship Endowment Trust. Sport Endowments provide supplemental income to each team's individual budgets, and the money may be used at the coach's discretion. Typically, this fund provides monies to enhance recruiting, team travel, and assistant coaches' salaries.

Duke University, through its ASG, the Iron Dukes (www.iron-dukes.net), has responded to North Carolina's endowment efforts with two major programs. First, Duke has created an endowment fund for scholarships. According to the Iron Duke website,

Many of our competitors in the athletics world compete without such reliance upon annual gifts to support schol-arships. Stanford and UNC, as examples, fund virtually 100% of their athletics grants-in-aid through endowment, freeing up annual funds to provide for facility and operating budget enhancements. The majority of our ACC counterparts provide more scholarships on an annual basis than we do, largely due to lower tuition costs. Stronger endowment support is critical for Duke to continue to offer competitive scholarship opportunities.

As Duke is a private institution, the cost of providing an athletic scholarship is considerably higher than the cost at North Carolina, a public institution. Only a partial scholarship at Duke can be endowed with a gift of $100,000, the amount North Carolina donors pay to endow a half scholarship. To endow a full scholarship at Duke requires a gift of $1 million. At North Carolina, the amount is $200,000.

Duke's second major endowment initiative is the Duke Basketball Legacy Fund, created in 2000 to fund Duke University men's basketball perpetually. The fund's yield is used for player scholarship costs, coaching salaries, operating income, facility improvements, and training needs. Since its inception, 30 donors have contributed at least $1 million each to the fund. Giving to the Legacy Fund has enabled the basketball program to fully endow eight basketball scholarships and a scholarship for the team's manager.

CASE QUESTIONS

1. How are development efforts used to fund athletics at your institution?

2. How do these development activities at your institution compare to North Carolina's and Duke's activities?

3. What risks are involved when relying on the interest earned from an endowment to fund an athletic department's program?

4. What are the benefits of using endowments?

CONCEPT *check*

1. How does money flow from the NCAA to its member institutions?

2. What differences in structure lead to financial differences among NCAA member institutions?

3. What financial role does college football play at NCAA Division I – FBS institutions? How does this compare to Division I – FCS institutions?

4. Why are athletic departments' development efforts so critical?

5. What problems may exist in the relationship between donations and ticketing at college athletic events?

PRACTICE *problems*

1. As director of development for Southern Ohio State University (SOSU), you have been charged with developing a plan to endow 12 men's basketball scholarships. The current cost of a scholarship athlete is $45,000. With tuition expenses expected to increase at a 5.5% rate annually and the endowment's return expected to average 7% over time, calculate the total amount that will have to be raised to fully endow the 12 scholarships.

2. Based on your work in Problem 1, develop a major gifts table for the capital campaign. Explain the method you used to construct the chart.

references

Barr, C.A. (2008). Collegiate sport. In L.P Masteralexis, C.A. Barr, & M.A. Hums (Eds.), *Principles and practice of sport management*, 3rd ed. (pp. 145–169). Gaithersburg, MD: Aspen.

Broughton, D. (2008, June 23). Big Ten posts record revenue. *SportsBusiness Journal, 11*(10), 35.

Covell, D. & Barr, C. A. (2010). *Managing intercollegiate athletics*. Scottsdale, AZ: Holcomb Hathaway.

Darcy, K. (2007, December 20). The schedule is from hell, but Presbyterian is loving life in DI. *ESPN.com*. Retrieved December 20, 2007, from http://sports.espn.go.com/espn/priont?id=3162742&type=story.

Dove, K.E. (2000). *Conducting a successful capital campaign*. San Francisco: Jossey-Bass.

Emerson, S. (2008, June 19). Season-ticket holders pitch in extra for seats. *The State*. Retrieved June 19, 2008, from http://www.thestate.com/gogamecocks/v-print/story/438056.html.

Fain, P. (2008, January 11). Buckeyes' leader believes presidents should help contain sports spending. *The Chronicle of Higher Education*. Retrieved June 18, 2008, from http://chronicle.com/weekley/v54/i18/18a02401.htm.

Fitzpatrick, F. (2007, May 17). Most Division I colleges have to subsidize sports, NCAA finds. *Philly.com*. Retrieved May 19, 2007, from http://www.philly.com/philly/sports/colleges/20070515.html.

Fulks, D.L. (2005a, February). *2002–03 NCAA revenues and expenses of Divisions I and II intercollegiate athletics programs report*. Indianapolis, IN: National Collegiate Athletic Association.

Fulks, D.L. (2005b, May). *2002–03 NCAA revenues and expenses of Division III intercollegiate athletics programs report*. Indianapolis, IN: National Collegiate Athletic Association.

Fulks, D.L. (2008, March). *2004–2006 NCAA revenues and expenses of Division I intercollegiate athletics programs report*. Indianapolis, IN: National Collegiate Athletic Association.

Gators add to football stadium. (2008, May 28). Ohio University Center for Sports Administration. Retrieved

June 7, 2008, from http://www.sportsad.ohio.edu/sports/news/spec-rel/052808.html.

Harvard wins 20th of last 23 Harvard–Yale regattas. (2008, June 14). *ESPN.com*. Retrieved June 21, 2008, from http://sports.espn.go.com/print?id=3443630.

Indiana University Varsity Club. (2006, July). *Are you committed?* Bloomington, IN: Author.

Kelderman, E. (2008, July 11). Small colleges sweat over sports facilities. *The Chronicle of Higher Education*. Retrieved July 7, 2008, from http://chronicle.com/weekley/v54/i44/44a00101.htm.

Mid-American Conference. (2007). *Mid-American Conference 2007–2008 Handbook*. Cleveland, OH: Author.

Morris, R. (2008, May 1). Fans will pay for elite aspirations. *TheState.com*. Retrieved May 1, 2008, from http://www.thestate.com/sports/v-print/story/391806.html.

NCAA. (2007, December). *2007 NCAA membership report*. Indianapolis, IN: Author.

NCAA. (2006, December). *2006 NCAA membership report*. Indianapolis, IN: Author.

NCAA v. Board of Regents, 468 U.S. 85 (1984).

Person, J. (2006a, May 14). In the red—$2,656,084. *TheState.com*. Retrieved May 15, 2006, from http://www.thestate.com/mld/thestate/sports/colleges/university_of_south_carolina.html.

Person, J. (2006b, May 14). Ticket distribution for football under scrutiny. *TheState.com*. Retrieved May 15, 2006, from http://www.thestate.com/mld/thestate/sports/colleges/university_of_south_carolina.html.

Person, J. (2008, June 19). Athletics firmly in the black. *TheState.com*. Retrieved June 19, 2008, from http://www.thestate.com/gogamecocks/v-print/story/438098.html.

Solomon, J., & Perrin, M. (2008, February 24). How the Southeastern Conference got rich. *The Birmingham News*. Retrieved March 17, 2008, from http://blog.al.com/bn/2002/02/how_the_sec_got_rich/print.html.

Southeastern Conference. (2007). *2007–2008 SEC Conference manual*. Birmingham, AL: Author.

Stinson, J.L., & Howard, D.R. (2007). Athletic success and private giving to athletic and academic programs at NCAA institutions. *Journal of Sport Management, 21,* 235–264.

Strelow, P. (2008, July 17). Clemson football tickets: Money can't solve everything. *The State*. Retrieved July 17, 2008, from http://www.thestate.com/sports/v-print/story/463115.html.

Suggs, W. (2002, November 29). How gears turn at a sports factory. *The Chronicle of Higher Education*. A32–A37.

Sylwester, M.J., & Witosky, T. (2004, February 18). Athletic spending grows as academic funds dry up. *USA Today*. Retrieved June 18, 2007, from http://www.usatoday.com/sports/college/2004-02-18-athletic-spending-cover_x.html.

University of Michigan. (2006, July). *Proposed fiscal year 2007 operating budget*. Ann Arbor, MI: Author.

University of South Carolina. (2006, June). *The University of South Carolina department of intercollegiate athletics proposed budget fiscal year 2006–2007*. Columbia, SC: Author.

Wieberg, S. (2006, August 16). Tycoon's $165m gift to Oklahoma State raises both hopes and questions. *USA Today*. Retrieved August 16, 2006, from http://www.usatoday.com/money/2006-08-15-pickens-oklahoma-state-donation_x.html.

Wolverton, B. (2007, October 5). Growth in sports gifts may mean fewer academic donations. *The Chronicle of Higher Education, 54*(6), A1.

Zimbalist, A. (2007, June 18). College athletic budgets are bulging but their profits are slim to none. *SportsBusiness Journal, 10*(10), 26.

APPENDIX *chapter 14*

14.A   Mid-American Conference Revenue Distribution Guidelines*

Distribution of Television Receipts

A. All funds received by a member institution for television rights to any game designated as part of the MAC television package or carried by a national network or cable company shall be forwarded to the conference office.

B. Total rights fees earned under the MAC national television contract for home regular-season football and all men's basketball appearances will be split between the participating institutions and the conference office. The conference will apply its portion of rights fees toward the production of regional telecasts of MAC football and basketball. Distribution of appearance fees to the institutions by the conference office will be made within 45 days following annual contract settlements (on or about August 15).

Division of Post-Season Basketball Tournament Revenue

- Revenue from the NCAA basketball tournament will be distributed equally 13 ways, with the conference office receiving one full share. Participating team(s) in the NIT basketball tournament receive all revenue from its participation in the first round games, and revenue from additional rounds will be distributed 30 percent to participating team(s) and 70 percent in equal shares to remaining institutions and the conference.

Football Bowl Reimbursement Policy

1. Motor City Bowl
   a. Institution retains all tickets sold (champion or runner-up).
   b. Institution returns first $60,000 in ticket revenues to MAC Office, institution then retains balance (at-large invitation).
2. GMAC Bowl
   a. Institution receives $300,000 reimbursement plus retains all tickets sold (champion or runner-up).
   b. Institution receives $240,000 reimbursement plus retains all tickets sold (at-large invitation).
3. International Bowl
   a. Institution receives $50,000 reimbursement plus retains all tickets sold (champion or runner-up).
   b. Institution returns first $10,000 in ticket revenues to MAC Office, retains balance (at-large invitation).

*From the Mid-American Conference 2007–2008 Handbook.

14.B   Southeastern Conference Revenue Distribution Guidelines*

The Southeastern Conference Executive Committee has issued the following policy statement relative to these revenues: All basketball and football revenues received by the member institutions which are to be sent to the Conference office for further distribution should be received in the Conference office within 40 days of receipt by the institution or by April 1 whichever is earlier. Any such revenue received after April 1 shall be remitted within 10 days after receipt by the institution.

31.20 Revenue Distribution – Basketball

31.20.1 Distribution of Revenue Generated by Basketball. The following basketball revenue received by the Conference office for distribution each year shall be divided into 13 equal shares with one share being retained by the Conference office and one share being distributed to each member institution.

a) Basketball Television – All revenue derived from national network and national cable basketball telecasts will be divided by the following formula:

   a. Appearance fees for non-Conference and Conference games shall be set by the SEC Executive Committee on an annual basis.

   b. All remaining revenue, including a Conference syndicated television package, shall be divided into 13 equal shares, with one share being distributed to each member institution and one share being distributed to the Conference.

b) NCAA Men's Championship Basketball Tournament – Each member institution shall receive $15 per mile one-way from its campus to the competition site for each round of the tournament in which they participate. In addition, each member institution shall receive $50,000 for appearing in the First and Second Round, an additional $50,000 for appearing in the Regional Round and an additional $100,000 for appearing in the Final Four. Funds from the participation pool of the Men's NCAA Basketball Tournament shall be used to provide these payments. All remaining revenue from the NCAA Basketball Tournament from the participation pool, sports sponsorship pool and the grant-aid-pool shall be divided into 13 equal shares with one share to each member institution and one share to the Conference office.

c) Southeastern Conference Men's Basketball Tournament. Revenues received by the Conference office each year for the Men's Basketball Tournament shall be divided as follows:

   a. Any revenue above full expenses of the participating teams as set forth in the Commissioner's Regulations shall be divided into 13 equal shares, with one share to each member institution and one share to the Conference.

d) Southeastern Conference Women's Basketball Tournament. Revenues received by the Conference office each year for Women's Basketball shall be divided as follows:

*From the 2007–2008 SEC Conference Manual, with permission.

a. Any revenue above full expenses of the participating teams as set forth in the Commissioner's Regulations shall be divided into 13 equal shares, with one share to each member institution and one share to the Conference.

31.21 Revenue Distribution – Football

31.21.1 Distribution of Bowl Game Receipts. Distribution of revenue (after allowable deductions) generated from member institutions participating in bowl games shall be as follows:

a) For bowl games providing receipts which result in a balance of less than $1,500,000, the participating institution shall retain $840,000 plus a travel allowance as determined by the SEC Executive Committee. The remainder shall be remitted to the Commissioner and shall be divided into 13 equal shares with one share to the Conference and one share to each member institution.

b) For bowl games providing receipts which result in a balance between $1,500,000 and $3,999,999, the participating institution shall retain $1,040,000, plus a travel allowance as determined by the SEC Executive Committee The remainder shall be remitted to the Commissioner and shall be divided into 13 equal shares, with one share to the Conference and one share to each member institution.

c) For bowl games providing receipts which result in a balance between $4,000,000 and $5,999,999, the participating institution shall retain $1,240,000, plus a travel allowance as determined by the SEC Executive Committee. The remainder shall be remitted to the Commissioner and shall be divided into 13 equal shares, with one share to the Conference and one share to each member institution.

d) For bowl games providing receipts which result in a balance of $6,000,000 or more, the participating institution shall receive $1,740,000 ($1,840,000 if the SEC team is a participant in the Bowl Championship Series game which determines the National Championship), plus a travel allowance as determined by the SEC Executive Committee. The remainder shall be remitted to the Commissioner and shall be divided into 13 equal shares, with one share to the Conference and one share to each member institution.

e) Bowl Revenue Protection Insurance and the cost of unused tickets up to 3,000 tickets, shall be deducted prior to Conference distribution.

31.21.2 Distribution of Football Television Receipts. Distribution of revenue generated from football television shall be as follows:

a) Network and National Cable Telecast:
   a. A member institution appearing in a non-conference game shall receive an appearance fee of $120,000;
   b. A member institution appearing in a conference game shall receive an appearance fee of $40,000;

c. A member institution appearing in a non-conference home game or a conference vs. conference game played on a non-traditional playing date to meet contractual commitments or to accommodate a request by the Conference office shall receive an appearance fee of $300,000 as the home team and $200,000 as the visiting team; and

d. All remaining revenue shall be divided into 13 equal shares with one share being distributed to each member institution and one share being distributed to the Conference.

b) Conference Syndicated Program. Revenue from a conference football program shall be divided into 13 equal shares with one share to each member institution and one share to the Conference office after home appearance fees and cross-over fees have been paid.

a. Home appearance fees shall be paid as follows:

1. First Home Appearance – No fee to host institution;

2. Second Home Appearance – $20,000 to host institution; and

3. Three or more Home Appearances – $40,000 to host institution for each appearance after second home appearance.

b. Any cross-over fees shall be set by the SEC Executive Committee.

31.21.3 Football Championship Game Revenue. All revenue remaining from the championship game after expenses of planning and conducting the event have been deducted shall be divided as follows:

a) Each participating institution shall be reimbursed for the actual cost of transporting an official party of 150 (including student-athletes, coaches, administrators, cheerleaders, bands, etc.) to the site (air or bus travel from campus to the site; local transportation is not included). This amount shall be approved in advance by the Conference office and must be supported by actual invoices. In addition, each participating institution shall receive $225,000 to cover all costs associated with institutional lodging, meals, local transportation and all other expenses related to the championship. Each participating institution will be financially responsible for payment for 150 rooms for two nights at the designated team headquarters hotel;

b) Each participating institution shall receive a band travel allowance of $50 per mile, one-way from its campus to the site (according to Rand-McNally Mileage Chart). Each institution shall be financially responsible for 100 rooms for two nights at its designated band hotel;

c) All remaining revenue shall be divided into 13 equal shares, with one share distributed to each member institution and one share to the Conference office; and

d) Institutions may petition to the Executive Committee prior to the game for an increase in the travel allowance only in the event actual expenses exceed the designated amount.

31.22 Revenue Distribution – Baseball

31.22.1 Distribution of Revenue Generated by Baseball. Revenues received by the Conference office each year for baseball shall be divided as follows:

a) SEC Baseball Tournament – All guaranteed revenues shall be divided as follows:
  a. Each participating institution will be provided a per diem of $75 per day for up to 30 individuals for each day the institution plays a game. The per diem revenue will be paid on a percentage basis of available funds;
  b. Each participating institution shall receive a travel allowance of $30 per mile one-way. The travel allowance will be paid on a percentage basis of available funds; and
  c. Any revenue above full expenses of the participating teams shall be divided into 13 equal shares, with one share to each member institution and one share to the Conference.

31.23 Revenue Distribution – All Other Sports

31.23.1 Distribution of Revenue Generated by Other Sports. Revenues received by the Conference office each year for all other sports shall be divided as follows:

SEC – Net Revenues from SEC championships (other than football, men's and women's basketball, and baseball) either bid, or held at a neutral or off-campus site, shall be divided as follows: one share to the Conference office, remaining revenue shall be divided evenly among institutions which sponsor teams in that particular sport.

31.24 Automatic Restriction Against Participation in Distribution of Conference Funds

31.24.1 Restriction Against Participating in Distribution of Conference Funds. Member institutions prohibited by the NCAA or the SEC from appearing on television programs and/or from participating in postseason football or basketball competition shall not be entitled to participate in the distribution of respective Conference funds derived from these sources during the period of such prohibition.

31.24.2 Escrow of Funds. All funds, except for the provisions of Bylaws 31.22.1 and 31.23.1 hereof, which would otherwise have been paid to the member institution involved shall be held in escrow by the SEC until the end of the five-year repeat violation provision of the NCAA. Thereupon, the institution involved will be restored an amount equal to 50% of the funds previously placed in escrow, provided the institution has not had a major violation within the past five years which has resulted in sanctions prohibiting the institution from sharing in the Conference's revenue distribution. Prior to such restoration, the Executive Committee may authorize the use of such portion of these funds as needed to compensate the other member institutions for any loss of revenue which results from contractual penalties that may be assessed against the Conference as a result of the involved member institution's inability to participate in Conference television or post-season events as a result of NCAA sanctions. The remaining 50% of the funds shall become the property of the SEC free and clear of all claims of the member institution involved and shall be distributed in equal shares to the remaining member institutions. An institution shall be permitted to defer the onset of revenue distribution withholding until the fiscal year following announcement of sanctions.

15
Professional Sport

Introduction

"NFL owners are fat-cat Republicans who act like socialists."

FORMER CLEVELAND BROWNS AND BALTIMORE RAVENS OWNER ART MODELL

Professional sport leagues operate differently from other businesses. Whereas most companies would like to dominate and even eliminate their competitors, individual franchises in professional sport leagues need other franchises to exist so that competitive games can be scheduled. Without competitors, a franchise is unlikely to attract many customers. Owners of professional sport teams must consider the impact of their financial decisions on the other owners in the league.

This is just one aspect of the fact that professional sport franchise owners often have different motivations in purchasing and operating a team than owners in non-sport industries. Certainly, one goal of every business is to generate revenues that exceed costs and expenses, and consistent generation of profits will maximize the value of the organization (Groppelli & Nikbakht, 2000). In most cases, shareholders will insist that management pursue the continual generation of profits. Although all professional sport owners certainly desire to generate profits, for some, **profit maximization**—the pursuit of the highest profits possible—is a secondary goal. In the early 1900s, the majority of professional sport owners operated their team as their primary income source, but most modern professional sport owners have already established highly successful organizations that have earned millions or billions of dollars in profits. To some of these owners, ownership of a professional sport franchise is primarily about competition, the opportunity to be a key figure within a community, and ego gratification (Rascher, Nagel, McEvoy, & Brown, 2004). These owners may be more interested in **win maximization**—the pursuit of winning as a primary goal.

Owners for whom profit maximization is not the primary goal typically focus their financial resources on their team's on-field success. The pursuit of winning may or may not increase the overall value of the firm. For example, in MLB, throughout the 2000s, the New York Yankees had the highest player payroll in the league. The Yankees' spending attracted numerous high-quality players who led the team to on-field success and higher profits. On the other hand,

in the early 2000s, the Arizona Diamondbacks, owned by Jerry Colangelo, spent lavishly in an attempt to sign players to win a championship. Though the Diamondbacks beat the Yankees in the 2001 World Series, Colangelo eventually experienced financial hardship, as the team did not generate enough additional revenues to offset expenses. The Diamondbacks had to decrease salaries, as well as other expenses, a few years after the World Series victory, and in 2004 Colangelo sold his interest in the franchise.

Within a league, the various team owners possess different financial resources that accrue from the team and other business ventures. The "excessive" pursuit of on-field excellence by one franchise or a small group of franchises could have an adverse financial impact on other owners. If an owner who has large financial resources elects to diminish or eliminate potential franchise profits in the pursuit of winning, other owners may not be able to compete in signing the best players. If many teams in a league do not appear to have an opportunity to acquire or retain top players, the league's **competitive balance** is disrupted. Competitive balance may be defined or measured by various specific metrics, but generally it is held that each franchise, if it executes a sound management strategy, should have a reasonable opportunity to compete for a playoff spot at least every couple of seasons. When competitive imbalance—or merely the perception of competitive imbalance—occurs, fans may lose interest not only in their local team but in the entire league.

Because of the unique financial nature of professional sports, where owners have divergent goals regarding win maximization versus profit maximization, league offices establish rules and regulations to ensure that individual teams, as well as the entire league, can succeed financially. Complicating this effort is the fact that each franchise operates in a **local market** that has distinct differences in population, economic activity, and passion for sport. League offices attempt to balance franchises' financial and competitive goals with the overall goal of increasing the financial viability of the league.

LEAGUE STRUCTURES

The most popular professional sport leagues in North America—MLB, the NBA, the NHL, and the NFL—began as regional enterprises with limited financial resources. During their early existence, financial survival was typically their most pressing concern. However, as these leagues became financially stable and began to expand, concern for the league structure and operating procedures became more important. Leagues that have been established more recently, such as Major League Soccer (MLS) and Major League Lacrosse (MLL), have been able to learn from the experiences of the "Big 4" professional leagues.

Franchisee/Franchisor Structure

North American professional sport leagues usually operate as quasi-socialist franchisee/franchisor cartels (Scully, 1995). Under the **franchise ownership model,** owners purchase individual franchises and then sign players, arrange for a facility in which to play games, conduct marketing activities, and control all other aspects of the team's operation. While operating their individual franchises, owners work with the owners of other franchises to set policies that affect the entire league.

Role of the commissioner

Typically, owners in a league hire a commissioner and establish a league office. The commissioner's office, in consultation with the owners, will negotiate national television contracts, establish relationships with vendors for league-wide licensed merchandise sales, hire and supervise game officials, and negotiate a collective bargaining agreement with the players' union. The commissioner is the "leader" of the league, but he or she remains the employee of the owners. Kennesaw Mountain Landis, former federal judge and the first MLB commissioner, worked under a "lifetime" contract, but today most commissioners do not enjoy such job security. Many fans believe that the commissioner's role is to do what is best for the sport, but in reality, it is to do what is best for the owners. Former MLB Commissioner Fay Vincent displeased the owners to such an extent that they gave him a vote of no confidence after he had served less than three years on the job. The vote effectively ended his commissionership, and he resigned on September 7, 1992.

SIDEBAR

Beyond the "Big 4"

15.A

In addition to the "Big 4," a number of additional North American professional sport leagues have been established or are emerging. Numerous minor league baseball leagues have operated for over 100 years, and many of their teams continue to set yearly attendance records. Sports such as lacrosse now have professional leagues that attract thousands of fans each year (Major League Lacrosse, National Lacrosse League). Leagues for individual sports such as golf (Ladies Professional Golf Association [LPGA]; Professional Golfers Association [PGA]), tennis (Association of Tennis Professionals [ATP]; Women's Tennis Association [WTA]), and bowling (Professional Bowlers Association [PBA]) have for many years operated popular events.

Every professional sport league or organization, regardless of its history or current operation, faces similar financial challenges. This chapter focuses primarily on the "Big 4" North American professional sport leagues, as well as the National Association for Stock Car Auto Racing (NASCAR) and Major League Soccer (MLS), because these leagues tend to have the highest revenues and the greatest diversity of revenue sources. In most cases, their considerable financial reserves ensure that they will remain in existence for many years into the future. Among the "emerging" leagues, the Arena Football League had one of the more stable financial foundations. Despite this, the league folded operations in 2009 with dwindling revenues and a stalling economy. Certainly, a variety of professional sport leagues are worthy of study and potential employment, and readers are encouraged to study the establishment, growth, and financial operations of other professional sport leagues.

15.B

The National Football League has been the dominant North American professional sport league for over 30 years. The NFL's tremendous financial success can in large part be directly attributed to Commissioner Pete Rozelle and his idea of *"league think."* When Rozelle became NFL commissioner in 1960, the 12-team league had low attendance figures for many of its games, and much of its television coverage occurred at the local level. Rozelle immediately began to lobby the NFL owners to think of the overall financial health of the league as their first priority and individual franchise profits as a secondary concern. His "league think" philosophy was intended to pull the disparate NFL owners together in their efforts. Although financially "stronger" franchises, such as the Cleveland Browns, New York Giants, and Washington Redskins, appeared to have power and financial status to lose in a "league first" environment, their willingness to pool television revenue was a critical factor in the rapid growth of the NFL's popularity in the 1960s. Without Rozelle's prodding and the willingness of NFL owners such as Wellington Mara to relinquish some of their short-term profits, the NFL likely would not be the most popular professional sport league in the United States today.

In addition to convincing the NFL owners that it would be in their best interests to collectivize some of their efforts, Rozelle also lobbied Congress for a special antitrust exemption for professional sport leagues. The pooling and selling of television rights by leagues was against the law until passage of the *Sports Broadcasting Act (SBA)* in 1961, which provided the exemption Rozelle sought. Once Rozelle had convinced the U.S. Congress that the SBA would not cause significant hardship to consumers, he negotiated a television contract with the Columbia Broadcasting System (CBS) that dramatically increased the revenues of every NFL owner. The NFL's television contracts continued to increase, in some cases dramatically, throughout Rozelle's tenure and after his retirement in 1989. Although every professional sport league has financially benefited from pooling television rights, the NFL has especially benefited, since it pools and sells every regular season and play-off game.

Rozelle's efforts to strengthen the league through collective action were not limited to television revenues. While owners in other leagues often voiced public disagreements over league operations, Rozelle kept the owners (except for Al Davis) primarily working toward the league's financial goals. The NFL's ability to maximize league revenues through shared ticketing and licensed merchandise revenues has enabled "small market" franchises, such as the Green Bay Packers and Pittsburgh Steelers, not only to exist but to prosper competitively and financially. NFL franchises are now by far the most valuable among the North American professional leagues, and much of that value is directly attributable to Rozelle's vision.

Role of the league owners

The commissioner's office will handle routine activities, but a major responsibility of league owners (or their representatives) is to meet regularly to vote on various league policies. Each league establishes rules and voting procedures for decision making. In some cases, a majority vote is all that is required, while in other cases a larger percentage, such as a two-thirds or three-fourths majority vote, is needed. League votes on certain issues can have a tremendous impact on the finances of the league and individual franchises. On occasion, individual owners, despite having agreed to operate under the league bylaws when they entered the league, have rejected league decisions and sought legal recourse.

The most famous example of an owner suing his own league took place in the 1980s and involved the NFL's Oakland Raiders. Despite sellout crowds in Oakland throughout the 1970s, by 1980 Raiders owner Al Davis desired to move his team to Los Angeles, where it could play in the Los Angeles Memorial Coliseum (which was much larger than the Oakland–Alameda County Coliseum). The move required yes votes from three-fourths of the owners—but instead they voted 22–0 (with some abstentions) against the move, partially because they felt it would send a bad message to every NFL fan if a team that had attracted sellout crowds simply abandoned its home marketplace (Harris, 1986; Shropshire, 1995). The Los Angeles Memorial Coliseum Commission (LAMCC) and the Raiders sued the NFL for restricting franchise movement. The LAMCC and the Raiders claimed that restricting movement was an unfair restraint of trade and a violation of antitrust law (*Los Angeles Memorial Coliseum Commission v. National Football League*, 1984, 1986). The Raiders and the LAMCC eventually won the case despite the negative public relations that the case created in the Bay Area and the efforts of the City of Oakland to retain the franchise (Harris). Numerous subsequent legal decisions established that professional sport leagues could require relocating teams to compensate the other league owners financially if the move had a negative effect on overall league revenue (Shropshire). The NFL's St. Louis Cardinals did provide compensation to the rest of the league's owners when they moved to Arizona in 1987, as did the Los Angeles Rams when they moved to St. Louis in 1995. Ironically, despite the extensive litigation the Raiders endured for their move to Los Angeles, Al Davis decided to move the franchise back to Oakland in 1995 due to the changing economic environment in the NFL (which placed greater emphasis on luxury suite revenues rather than general ticket sales) and promises of considerable upgrades to the Oakland–Alameda County Coliseum.

Single-Entity Structure

Despite occasional contentious battles with maverick owners, most North American professional sport leagues operate effectively with a franchisor/franchisee structure. However, recently some leagues have attempted to adopt a single-entity structure, in which owners purchase shares in the league rather than purchase an individual franchise. With a single-entity structure, the league office handles all player transactions, such as negotiating contracts and assigning players to teams. This structure is designed to disburse players throughout the league in a manner that encourages competitive balance, which should increase fans' interest. Under a single-entity structure, the league office will also negotiate sponsorship and media contracts for the entire league and will ensure that revenues are generated and utilized in a manner that maintains the league's financial solvency.

As discussed in Chapter 1, a single-entity structure will typically reduce league costs, as individual owners cannot sign players to salaries that do not conform to the overall goals of the league. In addition, the league office can ensure better cost containment for travel, equipment, and team staff. Although a single-entity structure provides some financial benefits, critics have argued that it reduces individual franchises' incentives to maximize their revenues (Mickle & Lefton, 2008). Most professional sport franchises generate a substantial portion of their revenues from local sources. Though the league office may be effective in negotiating national media contracts and sponsorship agreements, local sponsorships are difficult to identify and foster. In addition, if there is no incentive for individual teams to increase revenues, creative marketing activities that would attract additional customers are less likely to occur, which negatively affects the entire league. The Women's National Basketball Association initially operated under a single-entity structure but soon switched to a franchisee/franchisor model to encourage the maximization of local revenues. WNBA Commissioner Donna Orender noted,

SIDEBAR

American Needle to Alter North American Professional Sports?

15.C

Although the NFL operates under a franchisor/franchisee structure, it does conduct some of its operations as a single entity. In addition to packaging its television rights, it pools some of its other revenue sources, such as the sale of licensed merchandise. For many years American Needle, Inc. operated as one of the NFL's non-exclusive licensees for the design and manufacturing of headgear that bore the names and logos of the NFL and its franchises. However, in 2002, the NFL awarded an exclusive ten-year apparel contract to Reebok in an effort to better control merchandise output and to enhance overall NFL revenues (Yost, 2006). American Needle filed an antitrust suit against the NFL claiming that the exclusive contract with Reebok was an unfair restraint of trade (McCann, 2010). The NFL argued that for the purposes of selling licensed merchandise, it operated as a single entity and, therefore, could not be found guilty of conspiracy to unfairly restrain trade.

The NFL won its initial case and also prevailed upon appeal. However, American Needle and, in an unusual event, the NFL also appealed to have the case heard before the U.S. Supreme Court (McCann). The NBA and NHL filed supporting briefs to bolster the NFL's case. Each of these professional leagues (MLB already has a limited antitrust exemption) saw the case as an opportunity to prevent future antitrust scrutiny for various league-organized business practices that might otherwise be perceived as illegal restraint of trade. As of this writing, the Supreme Court had not ruled on this case. The Supreme Court's decision will likely be one of the most important legal cases in American professional sports history.

"While the launch model was successful, it became evident that owners wanted more control" (Mickle & Lefton, para. 10). However, as individual owners exert marketing and financial control in a franchisee/franchisor model, large revenue discrepancies can occur, which could hurt the league's overall competitive balance.

Major League Soccer began play as a single-entity league in 1996. Though the single-entity model enabled the league to build its fan base slowly and consistently, some of the players argued that the league structure unfairly and illegally held down player salaries. Because just two men, Lamar Hunt and Philip Anshuntz, were the league's primary investors and the "operators" of multiple franchises, the players felt that there was no incentive to compete for player services. In *Fraser v. Major League Soccer* (2000), a group of players filed an antitrust suit against the MLS claiming that the league's structure unfairly restrained trade, since players could not offer their services among the different MLS teams. The league countered that the single-entity structure instead prevented any unfair restraint of trade, because one individual entity cannot conspire with itself to hurt the marketplace ("Court accepts," 2000). In addition, the league argued that competition for player services had increased since the MLS was founded, because before 1996 there was no viable Division I professional soccer league in the United States. The court eventually ruled in favor of MLS, determining that its single-entity structure, though unusual in North American professional sport at the time, was legal under antitrust laws. The players lost the case, but the attention that the lawsuit drew led to negotiations between the league and the players that increased player benefits in the future. In addition, as the MLS became profitable, new investors were attracted, and the league began to incorporate elements of a franchisee/franchisor model (Wagman, 2008).

OWNERSHIP RULES AND POLICIES AND LEAGUE FINANCES

Every professional sport league has an interest in maintaining financially successful teams. Because a successful league depends on competent and well-financed owners, leagues establish ownership rules and policies to protect the solvency of every league member. If one or more of the league's franchises experience significant financial hardship, then the league itself might suffer.

NASCAR SIDEBAR

15.D

The National Association for Stock Car Auto Racing (NASCAR) has a unique ownership structure in North American professional sports. Founded by William France, Sr. in Daytona Beach, Florida, in 1948, NASCAR is a sanctioning body of automobile racing. NASCAR's early years were focused on organizing stock car races, primarily in the southern portion of the United States. Since the early 1980s, the popularity of NASCAR events has grown tremendously. NASCAR currently organizes multiple racing series, the Sprint Cup Series being the most popular. Each year, millions of fans attend NASCAR events, and millions more watch the races on television. Though William France, Sr. retired as chairman in 1972, NASCAR has remained largely a family-operated business, with William France, Jr. succeeding his father and grandson Brian France succeeding William Jr. in 2003.

Though NASCAR is certainly the dominant force in the North American automobile racing industry, it is "only" an organizer of events. The racing teams are owned and operated by other individuals. These racing teams hire drivers and all of the other employees necessary to prepare for competition. The racetracks are also owned by separate entities. However, the France family is the majority shareholder of International Speedway Corporation (ISC), an organization that currently owns and operates 12 racetracks that host NASCAR events. William France, Sr. founded ISC in 1953 as the organization that would build and operate the Daytona International Speedway. ISC experienced slow growth during its first 40 years of existence, until in 1999 it merged with Penske Motorsports, which gave it control of four additional tracks. Since the merger, ISC has continued to open new racetracks that have typically been awarded races in NASCAR's popular Sprint Cup Series.

The France family's "dual ownership" of NASCAR and selected racetracks has generated criticism of the family and legal challenges to NASCAR's structure. In 2005, Kentucky Speedway filed an antitrust lawsuit against NASCAR and ISC claiming that they had conspired to prevent eligible racetracks from submitting bids to host NASCAR events. Though Kentucky Speedway had hosted NASCAR Nationwide Series and Camping World Truck Series events, it had not been successful in its attempts to host a Sprint Cup Series event. A Sprint Cup Series event would have generated millions of dollars in additional revenue for the racetrack as well as the surrounding community. Kentucky Speedway argued that NASCAR could have made more money by running a Sprint Cup Series race at its venue than at some of the other venues that currently hosted Sprint Cup Series races. Kentucky Speedway felt that the France family had illegally conspired to keep the top NASCAR events out of Kentucky's newer and "superior" track in favor of other "less desirable" venues (some of which ISC controlled). The case generated considerable publicity in the sport business world, but it was thrown out of court in January 2008. Kentucky Speedway filed an appeal in July 2009, but in December 2009 it decided to drop litigation against NASCAR.

Each of the major North American professional sport leagues experienced numerous franchise problems during its early history. Some teams, such as the Akron Pros of the NFL, Louisville Grays of MLB, Pittsburgh Pirates of the NHL, and Toronto Huskies of the NBA, failed and no longer exist. Other teams, such as the NFL's Decatur Staleys (Bears) and the NBA's Fort Wayne Pistons, moved from their initial location shortly after being created in an effort to establish a viable fan base. Given these early franchise problems, it is no wonder that leagues sought to put rules and policies in place to protect the financial well-being of the league. This section will discuss league rules and policies regarding new ownership, debt, expansion, and territorial rights.

New Ownership

Each of the professional sport leagues has established rules regarding who may become an owner and join their "club." In many cases, the potential new owner must convince the current owners that he or she will work well within the estab-

SIDEBAR

Japanese Professional Baseball Problems Beginning to Change?

15.E

Professional baseball has been popular in Japan since its founding in 1936. Nippon Professional Baseball (NPB) operates with teams in two separate leagues (Central and Pacific) and utilizes rules similar to those of MLB, but it has a very different business model. Whereas most MLB owners are individuals who desire to achieve some combination of on-field and financial success, NPB franchises have traditionally been owned by corporations. In most cases, the owners of the NPB teams have not had direct profits as a primary motive. Instead, corporate owners have viewed their teams as marketing vehicles for enhancing the brand recognition and sales of the parent company (Whiting, 1989, 2004). Teams rarely considered implementing marketing initiatives to attract and retain customers or revenue-generating ideas that are commonplace in professional sport in the United States.

This financial and operating structure was adequate for many years, but it has recently created problems, as many prominent Japanese players have sought to leave Japan to play in MLB. With several of the top Japanese stars leaving—and access to MLB games in Japan growing because of new television distribution opportunities and the prevalence of the Internet—many baseball fans in Japan have decreased their consumption of NPB games and ancillary products. For years, the Japanese have taken great pride in developing some of the world's top baseball players through the country's unique baseball system. Unfortunately, the traditions and cultural expectations that have helped to develop top players have also hindered any change to NPB's business activities.

However, this may finally be changing. Former MLB managers, such as Bobby Valentine and Terry Collins, have taken jobs in Japan and attempted to incorporate revenue-generating ideas into the Japanese system. Changes have also come from younger Japanese baseball executives who were educated or employed in the United States. Although change has met considerable resistance in the past, the belief that the high-quality on-field Japanese baseball product may fade if changes to the business model are not implemented is slowly but steadily beginning to permeate some of the franchises and the league office (Nagel & Brown, 2009).

lished league structure. In 2009 Jim Balsillie attempted to purchase the NHL's financially struggling Phoenix Coyotes. Much of the resistance to Jim Balsillie's ownership was not related to his offered purchase price, financial reserves, or mental acumen, but rather to his earlier attempts to purchase NHL teams. In particular, other NHL owners were not happy with Balsillie when he attempted to purchase and relocate the Nashville Predators in 2007. Balsillie announced the purchase and move of the franchise before the league owners approved the sale, which caused consternation among the owners and in the commissioner's office. As another example, the NBA has fined Dallas Mavericks owner Mark Cuban over $1 million due to his actions and criticisms of the league since he purchased the team in 2000. There has been speculation that if the NBA owners had anticipated Cuban's behavior, they would have rejected his purchase. Although many owners may agree with some of Cuban's observations and opinions, the way he has voiced his displeasure regarding certain league activities has caused internal strife.

Potential personality conflicts are important considerations, but of greater importance is a potential owner's ability to operate a franchise without incurring significant financial losses. Each of the leagues requires that potential owners provide information regarding their finances. If a prospective owner does not have sufficient financial resources, the league is likely to reject the ownership bid in fear that a financial problem for an individual franchise could be detrimental to the entire league.

The NFL has the most strict ownership requirements of all the North American professional sport leagues, including a steep cash down payment requirement. Potential owners who cannot meet this requirement may find their bids rejected. In 2005, Reggie Fowler agreed to purchase the Minnesota Vikings from Red McCombs for $625 million (Casacchia, 2005). McCombs and Fowler announced the sale prior to the other NFL owners' granting final approval. The sale was to be historic, as Fowler would have been the first African American owner in the NFL and only the second African American owner in the "Big 4" leagues. However, the other owners rejected Fowler's bid because he was unable to meet the NFL's mandated 25% cash down payment (in this case over $150 million). Fowler's net worth was well over the purchase price, but his lack of liquidity forced the owners to reject his bid. The team was later sold to Zygmunt Wilf.

In addition to a cash down payment, the NFL also requires that an individual owner, rather than a corporation, operate the team. (The Green Bay Packers' current ownership is permitted because it was established prior to the current ownership rules.) It also requires that the individual majority shareholder have at least a 30% stake in the franchise (Clayton, 2008). In 2009, four of the five Rooney brothers who had inherited 80% of the Pittsburgh Steelers from their father, Art Rooney, Sr., sold some or all of their shares in order to meet the NFL's requirement (Prine, 2009). Prior to the sale that provided Dan Rooney with enough shares to meet the NFL's mandate, the five brothers each owned 16% of the team ("Art Rooney Jr.," 2008). In addition to the 30% requirement, the Steelers also had violated NFL rules against the ownership of gambling businesses, as some of the brothers had expanded their holdings in racetracks to include casinos.

Debt

Leagues also establish ownership rules regarding debt levels that a team may carry. For example, prior to 2005, MLB teams could carry debt equal to 40% of their franchise value (Kaplan, 2003). In 2005, MLB changed the debt limit to a maximum of ten times the team's earnings before interest, taxes, depreciation, and amortization. Up to 15 times was acceptable if the franchise had recently borrowed money to build a new stadium. In addition, MLB raised the required principal payments when teams paid back loans on the league's established credit lines. These rules are intended to protect franchise owners from reckless borrowing.

The MLB debt rules were applied in 2009 when Joseph Ricketts and his family purchased the Chicago Cubs out of bankruptcy. In perhaps the most complicated

SIDEBAR

Long-Term Family Ownership to End in Professional Sports?

15.F

With the recent rapid increase in the value of North American professional sport leagues, some concerns have been raised regarding the future ownership of franchises—particularly those in the NFL. The United States (as well as many individual states) applies an **inheritance** (or **death) tax** to wealthy estates when a person dies. In 2009, a 45% tax applied to any inheritances exceeding $3.5 million. If a person had an estate worth $5 million, the heirs would have had to pay $675,000 (45% of $1.5 million) in taxes. The inheritance tax is often altered by the President and the U.S. Congress—sometimes in an apparently haphazard manner—for political gain. In 2010, there was no scheduled federal inheritance tax, so a person's estate could pass directly to heirs without a federal tax consequence (though many individual states retained inheritance taxes). The 2011 laws scheduled a 55% inheritance tax on estates larger than $1 million—inspiring morbid jokes that it would be wise to pick 2010 to die rather than 2011 if a person was given the choice. The inheritance tax levels for 2012 and beyond will be established by the President and the U.S. Congress in 2011.

Inheritance taxes are a contentious political topic. Some believe that it is unfair to tax the assets of deceased individuals, as the money that person earned has already been taxed (in some cases multiple times). Others counter that considerable accrued wealth should not be permitted to be passed down from one generation to the next. Since many professional sport franchises are worth hundreds of millions of dollars, the potential cash needed to cover inheritance taxes may be overwhelming, and the heirs might be forced to seek loans or even sell the team. Former Cleveland Browns owner Art Modell sold the team partially due to concern regarding inheritance taxes. Jacksonville Jaguars owner Wayne Weaver has also contemplated selling his teams prior to death to avoid inheritance tax issues (Clayton, 2008).

sport franchise sale in history, the Tribune Company sold the Cubs, Wrigley Field, and other broadcast assets for $845 million (Sachdev, 2009). Once the Ricketts family established how they would fund and finance the purchase, MLB became concerned about their proposed debt levels. As a result, the Ricketts family had to agree to provide an additional $35 million in cash as an extra reserve in the event that projected cash flows did not meet expectations (Sachdev).

Leagues establish debt rules to prevent owners from experiencing significant financial problems, but in some cases a league must provide financial assistance when an owner does experience financial hardship. In rare cases, the rest of the owners in a league may elect to purchase the troubled team. Major League Baseball purchased the Montreal Expos in 2002 and owned the team until they moved the club to Washington D.C. and sold it to Theodore Lerner. When the Phoenix Coyotes declared bankruptcy in 2009, it was revealed that much of the team's recent activities had been funded and operated by the NHL (Sunnucks, 2009).

Professional sport leagues do not want to see any of their franchises experience bankruptcy. This has been a rare occurrence in the "Big 4" North American professional leagues since 1950, but teams such as MLB's Seattle Pilots (1969) and the NHL's Buffalo Sabres (2003) and Pittsburgh Penguins (1975 and 1998) have filed for bankruptcy. When a team enters bankruptcy, potential problems may arise for the league, as financial uncertainty exists—particularly if the team cannot adequately reorganize its debt or if a new owner is not immediately found to purchase the financially troubled franchise. The NHL worked to avoid the sale of the Phoenix Coyotes to Jim Balsillie once the team went into bankruptcy (Morris, 2009). Balsillie's plan to move the team to Hamilton, Ontario, Canada, might have generated increased revenues, but the NHL desired to keep the team in Arizona. Eventually the team was sold to Ice Edge Holdings, which agreed to keep the team in Phoenix (though it did plan to play a few games in Canada to increase potential revenue). Most of the recent bankruptcies in the "Big 4" have involved hockey franchises, but the Chicago Cubs, one of the most storied teams in all of sports, declared bankruptcy in 2009, indicating that even a rabid fan base and a strong media presence (the Cubs were owned by the Tribune Company) cannot shield a professional sport franchise from poor financial decisions and the impact of a slowing economy.

A league's purchase of a troubled team is a drastic move and one that happens rarely. However, leagues often will provide various types of financial support for franchises. One is **pooled debt.** When a lender evaluates a loan applicant, it will investigate the applicant's ability to repay the loan. Since the combined financial stature of an entire league is much stronger than that of an individual team, the league may apply for the loan. The NFL's now discontinued G-3 Fund (discussed in Chapter 7), established to assist teams building new stadia, is an example of a pooled debt instrument. The NBA recently utilized a pooled-debt instrument to assist financially struggling franchises. In 2009, the league borrowed $200 million to distribute to teams in need of cash. The loan was backed by the projected revenues of the entire league, resulting in a lower interest rate and a larger loan amount than teams could have secured individually. NBA Commissioner David Stern noted, "This was a show of strength in the creditworthiness of the NBA's teams" ("NBA lines up," 2009, para. 4). Some teams were criticized for utilizing the fund. The Orlando Magic and Utah Jazz were believed to be interested in tapping into the league's available credit due to cash-flow concerns. However, despite experiencing (apparent) financial difficulty, the teams signed players to high-priced contracts soon after the NBA announced the new financing. The Magic signed backup center Marcin Gortat to a five-year, $34 million contract, and the Utah Jazz signed backup power forward Paul Millsap to a four-year, $32 million contract. These contract signings suggested that the financial problems experienced by certain NBA franchises may have been due to their own decision making rather than a slumping economy.

Expansion

A critical element in any professional sport league's success is the ability to expand into new territories at appropriate times. When a league expands, current owners are likely to see their portion of shared revenue from media contracts and licensed merchandise decrease in the short term, as more teams are splitting the revenue. To compensate the current owners, the league typically charges new owners an **expansion fee,** which is distributed to the other owners. Prospective owners have typically been willing to pay expansion fees to join a league, as professional sport ownership is certainly an exclusive club. Though the initial financial return on an expansion team is often small or even negative, many wealthy individuals view sport franchise ownership as a new challenge that cannot be duplicated elsewhere. In addition, an expansion franchise presents an owner the opportunity to enhance his or her personal brand while providing a metropolitan area their first opportunity to have a "new" team—an exciting prospect, even if the team's on-field success in the first few years is limited. During the past 20 years, the expansion fees charged to new league owners have grown tremendously. Exhibit 15.1 lists expansion fees paid in the "Big 4" leagues from 1991 through 2010.

For most professional sport leagues, expansion is a critical component of their strategic plan. In the late 1950s, the NFL failed to recognize that it should expand to emerging metropolitan markets such as Denver, Boston, and Houston, which allowed the upstart American Football League to establish a presence in these areas. The leagues desire to expand at a rate that prevents rival upstart leagues from entering untapped metropolitan areas, but they typically will leave at least one or two viable cities unoccupied. This "failure" to meet potential demand is designed to preserve sufficient scarcity to motivate established markets to spend money to retain established teams. If the leagues allowed the supply of teams to equal or exceed the number of viable markets, teams would be less able to use the threat of relocating to force municipalities to build new stadia or remodel existing ones.

Territorial Rights

Ownership of a professional sport franchise confers a variety of benefits. One of the most important involves **territorial rights**—exclusive control of a predetermined area (typically a city's entire metropolitan area). In theory, the establishment of specific territories enables a professional sport team to market exclusively in that area without fear that another team in the same sport will enter the area and "steal" customers. Every professional sport franchise vehemently protects its ter-

exhibit 15.1 Expansion fees paid by the "Big 4" leagues, 1991–2010.

NHL

Year	Team	Fee
1991	San Jose Sharks	$50 million
1992	Ottawa Senators	$50 million
1992	Tampa Bay Lightning	$50 million
1993	Florida Panthers	$50 million
1993	Anaheim Mighty Ducks	$50 million
1998	Nashville Predators	$80 million
1999	Atlanta Thrashers	$80 million
2000	Minnesota Wild	$80 million
2000	Columbus Blue Jackets	$80 million

MLB

Year	Team	Fee
1993	Colorado Rockies	$95 million
1993	Florida Marlins	$95 million
1998	Arizona Diamondbacks	$130 million
1999	Tampa Bay Rays	$130 million

NFL

Year	Team	Fee
1995	Carolina Panthers	$140 million
1995	Jacksonville Jaguars	$140 million
1999	Cleveland Browns	$530 million
2002	Houston Texans	$700 million

NBA

Year	Team	Fee
1995	Vancouver Grizzlies	$125 million
1995	Toronto Raptors	$125 million
2006	Charlotte Bobcats	$300 million

ritory, as the limitation of direct competitors increases ticket prices and the value of media contracts. Since territorial rules reduce competition, fans of professional sport must pay a premium, especially in large cities. For instance, the New York City metropolitan market could likely support additional teams in the NFL, NBA, NHL, and MLB, but territorial restrictions limit entry to the market. Certainly, New York offers a higher population base and much greater potential corporate support for a third NFL or NBA team than exists in places such as Kansas City or Indianapolis.

Most professional sport owners purchased their teams with the expectation of control of an entire metropolitan territory, and they paid for that benefit. Therefore, territorial rules are likely to remain in force, particularly since North American professional sport leagues have successfully eliminated their direct competitors. In the past, teams such as the NHL's Anaheim Ducks and New Jersey Devils have provided compensation for "invading" another team's territory, after receiving permission from the league for the relocation.

Recently, Major League Baseball has experienced two significant territorial disputes. When MLB purchased the Montreal Expos and decided to move the team to Washington D.C., it infringed upon the Baltimore Orioles' territory. After extensive discussion and numerous legal threats from Baltimore Orioles owner Peter Angelos, MLB agreed to permit the Orioles to control a significant portion of the Washington Nationals' regional television rights and guaranteed Angelos $365 million if he ever decided to sell the team (Heath, 2005).

In the early 1990s, the San Francisco Giants, frustrated with antiquated Candlestick Park, requested access to unclaimed territories in Santa Clara and Monterey counties. After the Oakland A's and MLB voted to allow the team to move to either of the new territories, the Giants were unable to secure financing for a new facility in either of those counties. The Giants eventually built a new facility in San Francisco. Meanwhile, the A's have been enduring an untenable stadium situation since the city remodeled the Oakland–Alameda County Coliseum shortly after the Raiders returned in 1995. Although the A's supported the Giants' potential move to Santa Clara County, the Giants have countered any potential A's move to San Jose or any other Santa Clara County location. The Giants, despite failing to move from San Francisco, have steadfastly demanded that the territories they acquired when they considered moving should remain exclusively theirs. The A's, unable to pursue a Santa Clara County destination, have experienced recent financial hardship. Their dwindling fan base and lowered generated revenue may affect every other team in the Major League Baseball, but other franchise owners have been unwilling to rescind the Giants' rights to a portion of their territory (Nagel, Brown, Rascher, & McEvoy, 2007).

COMPETITIVE BALANCE

The numerous rules described previously are intended to establish a financially viable league, but more critical to a league's long-term success—and more likely to attract media and fan attention—are the league's efforts to maintain competitive balance, so that every team has a financial opportunity to field a competitive team. Determining the optimal level of competitive balance and then achieving that level is difficult, because each franchise operates in

Competing Leagues

SIDEBAR

15.G

The NFL, NBA, NHL, and MLB currently enjoy **monopolies** in their respective sports, as there are no viable competitors offering similar professional football, basketball, hockey, or baseball contests. However, each of these leagues has had to fight potential competitors. Major League Baseball has had the strongest monopoly among the four leagues. The last serious attempt to establish a viable competitor professional baseball league occurred when the Federal League formed in 1914. The Federal League was able to sign some established Major League players, but others were reluctant to sign for fear of being blackballed by their current MLB teams if the Federal League failed.

The Federal League experienced financial difficulty during the 1914 season, partially (the owners felt) due to the actions of MLB. During the off season, the owners filed an antitrust lawsuit against MLB arguing that MLB owners had established an illegal monopoly for the operation of professional baseball. In U.S. Federal Court, Judge Kennesaw Mountain Landis, who would later become Major League Baseball Commissioner, urged the parties to settle the dispute, so the case was not immediately deliberated. After the 1915 season, all of the remaining Federal League owners (the Kansas City franchise had declared bankruptcy and been taken over by the league) settled with the MLB owners, except for the Baltimore franchise, which elected to continue to pursue litigation. Eventually, the U.S. Supreme Court ruled that MLB was a legal monopoly immune from antitrust laws (*Federal Baseball Club v. National League,* 1922). No serious attempt has been made to compete with MLB since the Federal League. Perhaps the most noteworthy accomplishment of the Federal League, besides the antitrust ruling, was the construction of historic Wrigley Field, which was built for the Federal League's Chicago Whales.

MLB has experienced nearly 100 years of "peace" from potential direct competitors, but the other three major North

American professional sport leagues have faced much more competition. The NFL first encountered a viable competitor when the All-American Football Conference (AAFC) was formed in 1946. Though the NFL initially scoffed at the new rival, by 1949 the AAFC's Cleveland Browns, Baltimore Colts, and San Francisco 49ers had been admitted to the NFL through a merger agreement. The Browns were such a powerful team that they won the NFL title in the first year after the merger.

The NFL would later experience competition from the AFL. Multimillionaire Lamar Hunt had sought to purchase an NFL team in the late 1950s. When he was unable to procure a team, he solicited other wealthy people to start a rival league. The league was able to achieve success partially because of the commitment on the part of Hunt and other wealthy owners and partially because the NFL had sold coverage of its games exclusively to CBS. The American Broadcasting Company (ABC) and the National Broadcasting Company (NBC), being shut out of broadcasting NFL football, were eager to sign a deal with the upstart AFL. ABC signed an initial deal in 1960, and in 1964 NBC secured the AFL's television rights. The AFL experienced enough success that by 1969 it had merged with the NFL. Lamar Hunt not only helped build the AFL, but he also became one of the NFL's most influential owners.

The popularity of professional football prompted additional rival leagues to form. In 1974 the World Football League (WFL) was founded as a summertime and fall league. It signed a few established NFL stars but was largely unsuccessful. However, it did help to increase NFL salaries, which had been stagnant despite the growth in the NFL's popularity.

The United States Football League (USFL), which began play in 1983 as a springtime professional league, had some financially powerful owners and immediately signed television

a unique "local" market. Teams located in the largest metropolitan areas, such as New York, Los Angeles, and Chicago, have an inherent financial advantage, because these cities have more people to purchase tickets and other game-related products (such as parking and concessions), a greater number of corporations to lease luxury suites and buy expensive club seating, and many local media outlets bidding for the rights to broadcast the teams' games. Since many **stadium-related revenue sources,** such as the sale of luxury suites, are not shared with the rest of the league's teams, a perfectly fair revenue sharing system is an impossibility. However, leagues work to ensure that fans of each franchise can legitimately hope their team can be successful. The leagues have enacted a variety of "competition"

contracts with ABC and Entertainment and Sports Programming Network (ESPN). The league also signed some high-caliber NFL players and college stars, such as Herschel Walker, and promised to remain a viable enterprise. However, in addition to the typical problems that start-up leagues endure, numerous USFL owners, such as flamboyant Donald Trump of the New Jersey Generals, refused to adhere to the league's spending guidelines. With some owners signing players to exorbitant contracts and others unable to match that level of spending, the league began to unravel.

In 1986, the league made the critical decision to move to a fall schedule. The league had signed venue and media contracts to play football in the spring, but the NFL had already secured venues and television deals for Sundays in the fall. With the USFL in turmoil—primarily due to certain owners' desire to force a merger with the NFL rather than work to keep the league in operation—and no viable way to conduct a fall league, the owners elected to file an antitrust lawsuit against the NFL. The suit claimed that the NFL was a professional football monopoly that had illegally conspired to force the USFL out of business. The USFL named every NFL owner as a defendant, except for Oakland Raiders owner Al Davis, who testified on behalf of the USFL. The circuit court ruled in favor of the USFL but awarded the league only $1, which was trebled under antitrust laws to $3. When the case decision and awarded damages were affirmed under appeal (*USFL v. NFL,* 1988), the USFL became a footnote in the history of professional sports.

The NBA and NHL encountered rival leagues in the 1960s and 1970s. The American Basketball Association (ABA) was formed in 1967. To build excitement, the free-wheeling league utilized a red, white, and blue basketball, wide-open play, and a three-point shot. The league was able to sign many of the top amateur players, including Julius Erving, Moses Malone, Spencer Haywood, and David Thompson. Some of the league's teams were financially stable, but others experienced financial hardship. Far too often, teams had difficulty making their payroll, and numerous franchises relocated. At the conclusion of the 1976 season, the Indiana Pacers, San Antonio Spurs, New Jersey Nets, and Denver Nuggets were merged into the NBA.

In 1972 the World Hockey Association (WHA) was formed as a rival to the NHL. The WHA established some of its franchises in "open" hockey cities and, to attract players, attempted to pay higher salaries than those offered in the NHL. The WHA was involved in numerous legal battles with the NHL, most of which did not result in any financial advantage to the WHA. In 1979, four of the remaining six WHA teams were admitted to the NHL, but they each had to pay a $6 million franchise fee. The two WHA franchises that were not absorbed into the NHL were paid $1.5 million in compensation. Although the WHA was not tremendously successful, it was the first professional league in which superstars Wayne Gretzky and Mark Messier played.

Perhaps one of the more interesting side notes from the creation of the WFL, ABA, and WHA is that one man was involved in all three ventures. Attorney Gary Davidson founded or cofounded all three leagues. His tireless efforts to promote the leagues made him one of the most successful sport entrepreneurs of the 20th century. His leagues are estimated to have provided at least $500 million in direct economic impact—a considerable sum in the late 1960s and 1970s (Crowe, 2008). Although Davidson was approached on multiple occasions to begin other leagues, he left the fast-paced world of professional sports to remain close to his family in Southern California. He will be remembered as one of the more important figures in North American professional sport history.

rules and policies to create an environment that fosters competitive balance. This section discusses the financial implications of the rules and policies designed to ensure competitive balance, including those related to player drafts, salary slotting, free agency, player salary negotiations, luxury taxes, and revenue sharing.

Player Drafts

The **player draft** is the process by which the leagues assign incoming high school and/or college players to teams. Some leagues, such as MLB, also utilize other drafts to distribute current minor league players throughout the league. First conducted by the NFL in 1936 ("Pro football draft," n.d.) and later implemented by each of the other major North American professional sport leagues, player drafts "reward" poorly performing teams by awarding them higher draft picks. Typically, the worst performing team during the season will "earn" the first pick in every round of the upcoming draft, and the league champion will be awarded the last pick in each round. Every other team will draft in between the highest and lowest performing teams in inverse order of their success during the past season. Drafted players may negotiate only with the teams that selected them. In theory, this system allows the teams with the greatest "need" for an infusion of new players the best opportunity to acquire them. Although selected players have occasionally refused to sign, in the vast majority of cases drafted players begin their careers with the teams that selected them in the draft, as soon as possible after the draft. Of course, each team is responsible for determining the best players to pick, and there is no guarantee that they will make "correct" selections.

Salary Slotting

In an effort to control costs and assist franchises in salary negotiations, some professional sport leagues have established official or unofficial **salary slotting** (rules or recommendations regarding initial compensation provided to a player based on draft positioning) for selected players. The NBA has negotiated salary slots for first-round draft picks. Major League Baseball unofficially suggests salaries for each draft "slot"; however, many players and agents insist that their salaries be negotiated outside the Commissioner's suggestions. In 2009, overall number-one MLB selection Stephen Strasburg signed a four-year, $15.1 million contract, which eclipsed the previous record—a five-year, $10.5 million contract given to Mark Prior in 2001 ("Nats, Strasburg beat deadline," 2009).

The NFL owners have discussed including a salary slotting system in the next collective bargaining agreement with the NFL Players Association. NFL owners became particularly concerned when first-round picks JaMarcus Russell (2007) and Jake Long (2008) signed contracts that guaranteed them more than $25 million—more money than many established veterans would make over their entire career. Although the Players Association may not like the idea of "artificially" decreasing player compensation, the owners have hinted that a salary slotting system for incoming players would allow more money to be paid to established players. A salary slotting system would also minimize contract disputes, such as those that occurred in 2009 after the San Francisco 49ers selected Michael Crabtree with the tenth selection of the first round. Crabtree's agent argued that Crabtree was the best wide receiver in the draft and should have been paid more than Darrius Heyward-Bey, whom the Oakland Raiders selected with the seventh selection. Crabtree missed the first half of the season in the contract dispute.

Free Agency

For many years, players in each professional sport league had few rights regarding their conditions of employment. Leagues utilized **reserve clauses** that tied each player to his team in perpetuity. Fortunately for the players, starting in the 1960s, players associations began to exert more pressure on the owners through **collective**

NBA Draft Lottery

SIDEBAR

15.H

A basketball team has only five players on the court at one time, and the best players will usually play over three-quarters of every game. Hence, unlike the other major North American professional sport leagues, franchises in the National Basketball Association can be instantly and dramatically changed with the addition or subtraction of one superstar player. Some teams perceived that their best opportunity to achieve long-term success was to acquire the highest draft pick possible by losing games—so "unsuccessful" teams with poor records often decided to "tank" games by limiting their best players' minutes or by sitting "injured" players late in the season, once a playoff berth was not a possibility ("Why does tanking," 2007).

During the 1983/1984 NBA season, the Houston Rockets attracted attention from the NBA, the media, and fans as it made a series of questionable playing-time decisions during the second half of the season ("Coin flip," 2008). Many suspected that the Rockets worked to lose games in order to have a chance to pick University of Houston center Akeem Olajuwon with the draft's first selection. At the time, the NBA awarded the first pick in the draft to the winner of a coin flip between the teams with the worst record in the Western and Eastern Conferences. After the Rockets won the coin-flip and selected Olajuwon, the NBA announced that the 1985 draft order for the seven non-playoff teams would be determined by a **draft lottery,** a lottery used to determine the draft order of the non-playoff teams.

The 1985 lottery created considerable excitement, as the winner would likely select Georgetown University center Patrick Ewing. The team with the worst record in the league, the Golden State Warriors, "lost" the lottery and selected seventh in the 1985 draft. The New York Knicks, who had a better 1984/1985 record than the Warriors, won the lottery and eventually did select Ewing. The 1985 lottery aroused controversy, as some pundits continued to claim that the NBA had a vested interest in seeing its signature franchise in New York draft the best player (Simmons, 2007).

While denying any conspiracy, the NBA has made numerous changes to its lottery process. In 1987, the lottery identified only those teams selecting in the first three positions. The other teams would draft according to the inverse order of their record, starting with the fourth selection. In 1990, the lottery was altered to allow the 11 teams that did not make the playoffs to have a number of chances related to their record. The worst team received 11 chances, and the best non-playoff team received one chance. This format was changed in 1994 after the Orlando Magic won the lottery two years in a row—the second after having the best record of the non-playoff teams. The current system provides the team with the worst record a 25% chance to win and the team with the best non-playoff record a 0.5% chance to win. Despite these changes, the lottery format continues to be questioned.

bargaining—the process that occurs when workers in a company or industry agree to negotiate as one unit with management. In 1966, Marvin Miller became executive director of the Major League Baseball Players Association (MLBPA). By the time he retired in 1982, the MLBPA had become the most powerful sports union in North America. Miller's initial demands from the owners concerned "minor" issues involving working conditions, pension payments, and the right of players to profit from their likenesses. However, after achieving initial success, Miller took a series of actions that would lead to the greatest change in the salary structure of North American professional sport: the removal of the reserve clause. This created the right of players to become free agents.

Miller's first attempt to remove the MLB reserve clause involved Curt Flood, an outstanding outfielder for the St. Louis Cardinals in the 1960s (see Sidebar 15.I). Despite the failure of this attempt, Miller was convinced that the players were gaining momentum in their fight for greater rights.

The MLB owners had long contended that the reserve clause bound a player to his team for life, but the language in the MLB operating agreement noted that

SIDEBAR

15.1

Curt Flood versus MLB

Curt Flood was a key member of the 1964 and 1967 St. Louis Cardinals World Series Champion teams; he also appeared in three All-Star Games and won seven Gold Glove Awards. At the end of the 1969 season, the Cardinals traded Flood and other players to the Philadelphia Phillies. Flood refused to report to the Phillies, despite his $100,000 playing contract, and demanded that he be declared a free agent—in direct opposition to MLB's established reserve clause that bound a player to a team forever, even after his contract had been fulfilled. Baseball Commissioner Bowie Kuhn denied Flood's request, citing the provisions of the MLB standard playing contract.

MLBPA President Marvin Miller and the union supported Flood's refusal to report and provided financial assistance for Flood's lawsuit. The suit claimed that MLB's reserve rules were a violation of antitrust law, because they unfairly restricted the ability of players to bargain for their services (*Flood v. Kuhn,* 1972). Commissioner Kuhn and the owners fought the lawsuit all the way to the United States Supreme Court, where, in a 5–3 decision, the owners prevailed, as the court upheld the 1922 ruling declaring MLB immune from antitrust scrutiny (*Federal Baseball Club v. National League*).

Flood did return to play for the Washington Senators in 1971, but his one-year hiatus and the time devoted to the lawsuit had diminished his skills. After playing poorly in 1971, he retired. Although Flood was unsuccessful in his lawsuit, he has been remembered as an important figure in professional sports history. Flood's stance began to alter many fans' perceptions of baseball's employment rules. In 1998—one year after Flood died—the United States Congress passed the Curt Flood Act, which eliminated MLB's antitrust exemption with regard to labor issues.

teams controlled players only until they completed their contract and then played out their option (i.e., played another year without a contract). Players rarely played out their option, because they always signed contracts at the beginning of each year. However, in 1975, Andy Messersmith and Dave McNally played a season without signing a contract. Miller believed they had become free agents once the season concluded, and the dispute was submitted for arbitration. Arbitrator Peter Seitz encouraged the owners and players to settle the dispute rather than let him make the final determination, but he eventually ruled that Andy Messersmith and Dave McNally had indeed become free agents after playing a season without a contract (Miller, 1991).

The Seitz decision dramatically altered MLB. Other players began to play out their options and become free agents. Eventually, owners and players clarified free agent rules through the collective bargaining process. Other leagues have since enacted free agency rules. Players become eligible for free agency after achieving the required service time (typically four to six years in North American professional leagues). Before players become free agents, most earn salaries that are artificially depressed because they have little leverage (beyond retiring prematurely) in salary negotiations.

Player Salary Negotiations

When evaluating job opportunities, players are like anyone else in that they consider a variety of factors, such as location, work environment, and relationships with colleagues and supervisors. Potential salary is almost always a primary concern. In professional sports, salary is even more important, because the average playing career lasts only a few years. Since players' salaries are paid by individual franchises, the leagues must create an environment where each team has adequate financial resources to scout future players, re-sign their own players, and potentially bid for free agents. The leagues achieve this through two mechanisms: salary caps and, in MLB, salary arbitration.

Salary caps

A **salary cap** limits the compensation an employer may provide to its employees. In sports, a salary cap is designed to restrict salaries for teams across an entire league—

ideally, creating an economic environment where every team can be assured of cost containment as well as the opportunity to compete for player services. Professional sport team owners can no longer unilaterally implement a salary cap; they must negotiate with the players through the collective bargaining process. Each league has negotiated a variety of compensation systems.

NBA salary cap. Although unofficial and official salary caps existed in professional baseball before the 1930s, the first modern salary cap was implemented in 1983 by the NBA. Numerous NBA teams struggled financially in the late 1970s and early 1980s, and some were concerned that teams in larger markets would be able to outspend teams in smaller markets (such as Utah, Indiana, and Cleveland) to the point that smaller market teams would suffer considerably diminished on-court performances—which might, in turn, cause some franchises to declare bankruptcy and even cease operations. The NBA owners and players agreed to a salary cap to reduce the possibility that a small group of teams could sign all of the best players. Each year, the owners and players calculate the league salary cap based on overall league revenues. The cap has typically increased each year, but in 2009 the cap decreased due to a reduction of overall league revenues—partially related to the global economic recession (Abrams, 2009).

The NBA salary cap was designed to maintain a level salary field for every team in the league. However, given the nature of the sport of basketball, the loss of one or two players from a 15-player roster could radically alter the quality of a team's performance. For this reason, the NBA instituted a variety of rules as part of the initial agreement that allowed individual teams to circumvent the cap. The most prominent rule, the **Larry Bird exception**—so named because the Boston Celtics were concerned that the loss of Larry Bird to free agency would devastate their team—allows teams, in most cases, to re-sign their "own" potential free agents for salaries that would otherwise cause the team to exceed the designated yearly salary cap. This has created an environment where teams that have drafted quality players tend to have an advantage in free agency salary negotiations, as free agents can usually re-sign with their team for greater compensation than they could receive from other franchises.

More than ten years after the Larry Bird exception was instituted, the 1998/1999 NBA season was condensed due to a **lockout** (a decision by management to suspend operations while it negotiates with workers—in this case, players). One of the owners' concerns was the escalating salaries of the league's top players. For instance, during the 1997–1998 season, Michael Jordan's salary was $36 million, although the Chicago Bulls' team salary cap was $26.9 million. The lockout resulted in the NBA and the players agreeing to limit individual player salaries in addition to team salaries. For certain players whose current salaries exceeded the individual cap, the excessive salaries were grandfathered into the CBA.

As this discussion suggests, the complexity of the NBA's salary cap often causes confusion among journalists and fans. To mitigate this confusion, the NBA has released detailed salary cap information (Coon, 2009).

NFL salary cap. The NFL implemented a salary cap system in 1993 in an effort to maintain competitive balance among its franchises. Under the NFL cap system, similar to the NBA's, a maximum team salary is established each year based on overall league revenues. The NFL's system also sets a team salary floor (minimum amount paid in salaries per team), created to appease players' concerns regarding the unwillingness of some NFL owners to participate in the bidding for player services. Unlike the NBA salary system, which provides numerous loopholes for exceeding the cap, the NFL cap has a "hard" ceiling that must be maintained each year.

However, the NFL salary cap can be manipulated through the use of signing bonuses. If an NFL player signs a four-year, $4 million contract, each year his salary will count $1 million against the team's salary cap, and the player will receive $1 million during each season. Since NFL contracts are usually not guaranteed, the player risks not receiving all of the money if he is released (due to injury, ineffectiveness, etc.) before the full term of the contract is fulfilled. For this reason, players often negotiate bonuses that are paid immediately upon signing the contract. Although the player receives the total signing bonus in the first year, for the purpose of the salary cap the league allows the team to allocate the bonus over the years of the contract.

Suppose a player negotiates a $4 million signing bonus in addition to a $4 million four-year contract. The player receives $5 million in the first year of the contract, and the team has to allocate only $2 million each year to its salary cap total. If this player were to be cut after playing two years, he would only "lose" $2 million. Although the team will not have to pay the remaining years of salary on the contract, it will have to account for the remaining $2 million from the signing bonus on its salary cap. NFL teams have relied on the continuing escalation of the salary cap to provide additional space for "dead" salary cap money. Many long-term NFL contracts that provide large up-front signing bonuses are signed with both parties knowing that there is a small likelihood the contract will be completed. As long as revenues continue to escalate, the salary floor and ceiling will also escalate, enabling teams to continue to manipulate the salary cap limits.

The use of signing bonuses to circumvent the NFL cap in the short term is not without repercussions. In the 1990s, the Dallas Cowboys and other teams utilized signing bonuses to pay numerous players large salaries in the hopes of winning championships. The Cowboys were able to field successful teams in the short term, but as players retired, became injured, and so forth, the team was unable to sign other players under the cap, as they had used up their budget with past signing bonuses (Nagel, 2005).

NHL salary cap. For many years, the National Hockey League owners desired a salary cap, which the players resisted during collective bargaining negotiations. The 1994–1995 season was nearly cancelled when the owners locked out the players, but a partial season was played after the owners reluctantly agreed to forgo their demand for a salary cap. However, the 2004–2005 season was cancelled when the owners demanded a salary cap and the players refused to acquiesce. After the owners cancelled a complete season for the first time in major North American professional sport history, the players reluctantly agreed to return for the 2005–2006 season with a salary cap in place. In addition, the players allowed the value of every contract to be decreased by 24% (Fitzpatrick, 2005).

The NHL's salary cap is similar to the NFL's, as it has a floor and a ceiling that are based on league revenues. However, the NHL's cap does not allow the use of many "creative accounting" methods. Signing bonuses and other incentives are not as likely to be included in an NHL contract. Further, teams must be careful when signing long-term deals, as the NHL's CBA limits a team's ability to restructure an existing contract, and specific rules can penalize a team if an older player retires while under contract (Fitzpatrick, n.d.). In addition, the top NHL players cannot earn more than 20% of the team's salary.

MLB salary cap. Despite baseball's having been the first professional sport to institute salary caps, during the early part of MLB's history in the 19th century, the Major League Baseball Players Association has adamantly opposed any salary cap system. On August 12, 1994, the MLB players went on strike to protest a potential salary cap. The strike eventually resulted in the cancellation of the World Series for the first time since 1904. Although the players "won" the dispute— they avoided a salary cap—the cancellation of the World Series and the perceived greed of both the players and the owners caused outrage among fans. Major League Baseball players are adamant that they will continue to oppose the implementation of a salary cap (Bloom, 2009).

MLS salary cap. Major League Soccer, which operates as a single entity, with all player salaries paid from a league pool, approved a new salary structure in November 2006. Each team has a $2 million salary cap, but individual franchises can sign one player outside the cap limit. The first $400,000 of this "marquee" player's contract would be paid by the league, but the team would be responsible for the remainder. Each team can trade its marquee "slot" to another team, enabling that other team to sign up to two marquee players, whose salaries do not fully count against the team's cap. This rule is unofficially called the "Beckham Rule," because many anticipated that English star David Beckham might be attracted to the MLS if he could earn a salary comparable to what he was making in Europe ("MLS oks 'Beckham,'" 2006). It did not take Beckham long to fulfill the prediction: in 2007, he signed a multimillion-dollar deal with the Los Angeles Galaxy.

Salary arbitration

Unlike other professional sports, in Major League Baseball players have the right to **salary arbitration,** a process whereby an independent judge determines whether the team's submitted salary or the player's requested salary will be paid. The MLBPA initially negotiated the right to arbitration in 1973 and has consistently insisted that arbitration remain a key component of the MLB CBA (Haupert, 2007). Players with at least three years of MLB service time, as well as the top 17% of players (by service days in MLB) with two-plus years of experience, are eligible for salary arbitration if they are unable to reach a salary agreement with their team

---

SIDEBAR

MLB Collusion

15.J

The efforts of Marvin Miller and his successor, Donald Fehr, resulted in increased salaries for Major League Baseball players. With MLB's increased popularity during the early 1980s, the owners also saw their overall profits increase. However, many owners were not pleased that they could no longer artificially control players' salaries. In a series of acts that were eventually deemed illegal, the owners, under the direction of MLB Commissioner Peter Ueberroth, refused to offer contracts to other teams' free agents during the 1985 through 1987 off seasons. Prominent players were forced to return to their former MLB teams, as they received no viable contract offers.

In perhaps the most shocking example of the owners' conspiracy to artificially reduce salaries (collusion), Montreal Expo Andre Dawson essentially had to tell the Chicago Cubs to sign him for any price. While playing for the Cubs in 1987, Dawson won the National League Most Valuable Player Award while earning a salary well below market value. Eventually, the three years of owner collusion resulted in a court award to the MLBPA of $280 million in damages.

(Ray, 2008). Most players come to an agreement with their club before proceeding to arbitration, and the limited number of arbitration cases are closely monitored by both the players and the owners to detect any arbitration "trends."

Luxury Tax

In addition to individual player and team salary caps, in its efforts to promote competitive balance the NBA also imposes a **luxury tax** on high-spending teams to encourage teams to limit their player salaries. Whereas the salary cap is set at roughly 51% of the Association's basketball related income (BRI), the threshold for the luxury tax is set at roughly 61% of BRI (Coon, 2009). Teams that pay salaries in excess of the threshold must pay a dollar-for-dollar tax that is distributed evenly to all of the teams in conformance with the threshold. Teams that are close to or at the luxury tax level often avoid paying any additional salaries, since the dollar-for-dollar tax essentially means that a contract that causes the team to exceed the limit costs double the value of the contract. Further, teams that exceed the luxury tax limit cannot receive any luxury tax revenues. The luxury tax has helped to restrict some franchises' team salaries to a level that is above the salary cap and below the luxury tax limit, but a handful of teams continue to surpass the luxury tax in most years. The New York Knicks, for example, have consistently exceeded the luxury tax limit, paying taxes of $37.2 million in 2006, $45.1 million in 2007, $19.7 million in 2008, and $23.7 million in 2009 ("#1 New York Knicks," 2007; "Final 2007–2008 luxury," 2008; Garcia, 2009).

Although the Major League Baseball Players Association has adamantly opposed a salary cap, it has permitted the owners to implement a luxury tax. The luxury tax was first utilized in the 1997 through 1999 seasons, was phased out, and then was implemented once again, starting in 2003. The tax penalizes a first-time offender 22.5% of the amount that exceeds the tax limit. When a team exceeds the limit a second time, the penalty rate increases to 30%. For the third and any succeeding violation, the rate is 40% (Brown, 2007). Exhibit 15.2 lists MLB luxury tax limits and the penalties imposed upon violating teams. The New York Yankees are the only team that has violated the luxury tax limit in every season since 2003.

Revenue Sharing

Another important policy that professional sport leagues have implemented for competitive balance is revenue sharing. Whereas a salary cap is intended to balance teams' spending on players, revenue sharing is designed to narrow the gaps in the financial resources of the participating teams. Individual owners may earn revenues from various sources other than the teams they own, and the inequality of these non-league revenue sources can become a concern. Some owners may be able to accept a lower profit margin from the team or even take a yearly financial loss, while other owners may not be able to afford such losses. For instance, since Robert Sarver bought the Phoenix Suns in 2004, the team has sold two first-round draft picks to the Portland Trailblazers and has practically "given away" players such as Kurt Thomas and other first-round draft picks, in order to save money (Coro, 2007; Haller, 2007). Unlike Trailblazers owner Paul Allen, co-founder of Microsoft, Sarver operates his team with the financial bottom line as his primary

YEAR	THRESHOLD (IN MILLIONS)	VIOLATING TEAMS AND PAYMENTS
2003	$117.0	Yankees, $11,798,357
2004	$120.5	Yankees, $25,964,060
		Red Sox, $3,148,962
		Angels, $927,059
2005	$128.0	Yankees, $33,978,702
		Red Sox, $4,148,981
2006	$136.5	Yankees, 26,009,039
		Red Sox, $497,549
2007	$148.0	Yankees, $23,881,386
		Red Sox, $6,064,287
2008	$155.0	Yankees, $26,900,000
		Tigers, $1,300,000

Sources: Blum, 2008; Brown, 2007.

concern. This certainly can be frustrating for fans who want to see their team consistently strive to win championships (Simmons, 2008). Although it is difficult for leagues to maintain a financial environment of total equality, they pursue competitive balance by establishing rules and policies to govern revenue sharing and mitigate potential discrepancies.

Media revenue

North American professional sport leagues share revenues from "national" media contracts equally. The sharing of national television revenue permits every team to generate the same television revenue regardless of the number of their national television appearances. Every league shares national television revenues, but their sharing mechanisms have varying impacts. Each of the 16 games in the NFL's once-a-week schedule is broadcast under a national television contract, resulting in a much greater percentage of overall league revenues being shared than in other leagues. With the NBA and NHL's 82-game schedules and Major League Baseball's 162-game schedule, these leagues offer many games each week of the season. While some are broadcast under an equally shared national television agreement, the vast majority of these games are broadcast through an unshared "local" television agreement. Since the local television markets of the teams vary in size, the potential for generating revenue can vary considerably. For instance, the large population difference between the New York metropolitan area and the Minneapolis–St. Paul metropolitan area results in the potential of millions of additional media dollars for New York teams in MLB, the NBA, and the NHL.

Market-size differences have been exacerbated by the proliferation of regional sport networks (RSNs). These cable stations generate money through advertising and subscription fees, and, unlike traditional over-the-air television stations, typically elect to broadcast as many games as the local team will permit. Regional sport networks have provided large-market franchises with a tremendous financial advantage over their small-market competitors.

The recent growth of the Internet has provided North American professional sport leagues with the opportunity to share revenue streams from "emerging" media sources. However, the use of the Internet to generate revenues is still in its infancy. In 2000, MLB created Major League Baseball Advanced Media (MLBAM) to investigate and manage new media opportunities in areas such as online game streaming. MLBAM controls each of the teams' websites and generates revenues that benefit the entire league. Major League Baseball owners voted unanimously to create MLBAM, but the National Hockey League encountered resistance from the New York Rangers when it attempted to control every team's website. In 2007, the Rangers sued the NHL when the league threatened to fine the Rangers $100,000 a day for failure to relinquish control of the nyranger.com website. The Rangers eventually lost the case, and the NHL was able to recreate the Rangers' website to match the format of the other team sites ("Madison Square Garden sues," 2007).

Gate receipts

The NBA and NHL do not share revenues generated from gate receipts, while MLB teams in the National League share 5% and the American League share 20% with the visiting team (Dobson & Goddard, 2001; Zimbalist, 1992). NFL teams share 40% of their gate revenues with visiting teams, but the league allocates the revenues across the entire league, so the visiting team that may attract additional fans does not necessarily collect any additional revenue (Brown, Nagel, McEvoy, & Rascher, 2004). The Cowboys are heavily marketed and are one of the more popular teams, but owner Jerry Jones does not realize any added financial benefit when the Cowboys play a road game in front of capacity crowds. The 40% of the ticket sales for sold-out Cowboy games is redistributed throughout the league regardless of the Cowboys' opponents.

Merchandise sales

The four major North American sport leagues all share revenues from licensed merchandise sales equally among their teams (Grusd, 2004). The only money that teams retain is from sales of products in the team's facility or in local team stores. The NFL permits a franchise to opt out of the league-wide merchandising deal and keep more of their generated licensed merchandise revenues if the team agrees to pay a guaranteed amount back to the league. The Dallas Cowboys are the only NFL team to have opted out of the league-wide sharing agreement (Kaplan & Mullen, 2009).

Sponsorship agreements

Revenues from league sponsorship deals are also shared equally. League rules that are designed to increase the overall value of the league's brand also affect individual franchise's marketing arrangements. For example, in 1995, the Dallas

Cowboys violated the NFL's exclusive sponsorship agreement with Reebok when they signed an agreement with Nike ("Cowboys, Nike sign," 1995). Although the NFL sued the Cowboys and the Cowboys countersued, eventually the team was permitted to keep its agreements, as the parties settled out of court—possibly because the Nike deal (and others that violated NFL exclusivity arrangements) was signed with Texas Stadium (which Jones owned) and not directly with the team. Baltimore Ravens owner Art Modell noted the conflict that Jones' (and other owners') individual agreements could create for the NFL: "His marketing deals have been astonishing. . . . He just has to remember that this is a great league because we share our revenue. It's important that he not forget that in his quest to improve the Dallas Cowboys' balance sheet" (Eichelberger, 1999, para. 28).

Revenue sharing methods

Each league, regardless of its financial resources, must establish a revenue sharing percentage and develop a revenue sharing plan that fits the unique aspects of the league. Revenue sharing has become a critical aspect of recent collective bargaining agreements, and it will likely increase in importance in the future.

In the NHL, for example, the players and owners agreed to a complex revenue sharing plan that would augment the salary cap implemented after the lockout cancelled the 2004–2005 season. The bottom 15 revenue-producing clubs receive additional revenue sharing dollars beyond the equally shared sources, such as national television contracts (Bernstein, 2005). However, lower revenue-producing clubs in metropolitan markets that have at least 2.5 million households are ineligible to receive revenue sharing dollars. In addition, clubs must achieve predetermined attendance levels to be eligible to receive these revenue sharing dollars. NHL Deputy Commissioner Bill Daly noted, "You don't want a revenue-sharing program that doesn't incentivize performance" (Bernstein, para. 18). The NHL's complex revenue sharing formula has worked to stabilize the league, but some are concerned that too much money is being shared with teams in untenable positions. The majority of revenue sharing dollars have been directed to teams in the Southern portion of the United States (such as in the states of Florida, Tennessee, and Arizona), causing many Canadian owners to question why they are subsidizing teams in areas that have traditionally not been interested in hockey ("NHL owners growing wary," 2008). As previously mentioned, in 2009, the NHL had to take over financial control of the Phoenix Coyotes due to the team's mismanagement and failure to attract a sufficient fan base to generate revenues to cover costs, despite receiving revenue sharing dollars (Sunnucks).

Major League Baseball also recently implemented a new revenue sharing model. According to the established formula, the top 13 revenue-producing teams contribute to the bottom 17 revenue-producing teams, based on each team's distance from the revenue mean (Bloom, 2006). Teams are supposed to use revenue sharing and luxury tax dollars to improve their on-field product. Some are concerned that a few MLB clubs may simply be pocketing their revenue sharing dollars as profits. The Milwaukee Brewers, formerly owned by Commissioner Bud Selig and his family, received tens of millions of dollars in revenue sharing while fielding low-payroll teams in the early 2000s. This situation aroused speculation that Selig would not fine the team for pocketing revenue sharing dollars rather than spending them to improve the team ("HBO's Real Sports examines," 2004).

SIDEBAR

Fixing Free Riding with a Relegation System in European Soccer

15.K

Every professional sport league is concerned with the potential of free riding by its franchises, but many of the professional leagues outside North America do not have the same problems that the NFL or MLB may experience. Many European soccer leagues have a **relegation system,** in which, after each season, a certain number of the worst performing clubs will be sent down or relegated to a lower division, while a certain number of the top performing clubs from the lower division will be elevated to the higher division. Since the potential operating revenues are typically lower in a less desirable division, each year every franchise must attempt to maximize its on-field performance in order to remain in or earn a place in the higher division. The relegation system provides an effective incentive for clubs playing in a low or middle-level division to work to achieve success that will translate to a better division, higher revenues, and greater profits. Relegated teams will have decreased revenues, but most of the leagues provide some sort of phase-in or phase-out of shared revenues to minimize the immediate impact. In addition, some leagues may offer relegated teams a "parachute payment" if it appears that relegation could lead to bankruptcy. In England, Arsenal has not been relegated since 1919, and it is also one of seven teams not to be relegated since the Premier League was established as the country's top league in 1992.

Although establishment of a relegation system is occasionally discussed as a means to improve motivation and strategic management of certain North American professional teams, media and sponsorship contracts, as well as other logistical issues, make this highly unlikely in the near future, if ever. For instance, if a relegation system were to be implemented in MLB, national and regional television contracts may be devalued if larger-market teams are replaced by teams with much smaller markets. In addition, since the United States has a much larger geographic size than European countries, team substitutions could create scheduling difficulties and dramatically increase travel costs.

The Dallas Cowboys' dispute over its Nike deal and New York Rangers' dispute over control of its website created tremendous headlines and reinforced a common concern among owners of professional sport teams: that teams receiving revenue sharing dollars from the league may elect to **free ride**—to benefit at another's expense without expending usual cost or effort, in this case by electing to minimize their marketing efforts while receiving financial benefits from the "extra" efforts of more successful teams. Jerry Jones has been critical of other NFL owners who he feels have failed to maximize their revenue opportunities (Helyar, 2006). Whereas Jones invests heavily in marketing endeavors to advance the Dallas Cowboys brand, other owners appear content to maintain a smaller marketing staff and a lower advertising budget while they benefit from Jones' efforts. The Cowboys are certainly not the only large-market team in the major professional sport leagues to complain about the detriments of revenue sharing, but their complaints are certainly the loudest, since the NFL shares much more of its revenues than other leagues.

There is no perfect system to ensure competitive balance—particularly since every professional sport owner has a unique rationale for operating a franchise. "Perfect" competitive balance, in fact, is not necessarily a desirable situation, since it would mean every team finishes with the exact same number of wins as losses—something that would likely discourage a large portion of customers. Fans, whether casual or deeply committed, enjoy watching superior players from highly successful teams compete for championships. If the highly successful teams are always the same, problems arise. The key for each league is to develop a system whereby great players are not all playing for a small number of the league's teams.

EMERGING REVENUE SOURCES

Every professional sport league and individual franchise is constantly investigating and developing new revenue sources that address its unique financial issues. For example, over the past 15 years, the importance of a team's facility has grown. Most of the urban sport facilities built in the early part of the 20th century have been replaced, first by "cookie cutter" facilities that were primarily designed to offer large seating capacities and expansive parking areas in the 1960s and then, starting in the 1990s, by more "intimate" facilities. In the case of every new facility and those remaining historic facilities, such as Wrigley Field in Chicago and Fenway Park in Boston, the emphasis in construction and renovation has been revenue maximization.

An investigation and discussion of professional sport revenue sources could fill its own book. In the remainder of this chapter, we will describe some interesting revenue sources that are now influencing the financial management of professional sport organizations, including luxury seating, seat licenses, ticket reselling, variable ticket pricing, and securitization.

Luxury Seating

Franchises have always desired to sell a large number of season tickets, as these tickets provide revenue, facilitate game management, and earn interest, as the money is typically received prior to the season (and many of the season's expenses). Recently, luxury seating has become an important revenue source for many teams. In addition to "traditional" luxury suites and club seats, some facilities, such as the Palace at Auburn Hills, where the NBA's Detroit Pistons play, are offering luxury suites that do not have a direct view of the field of play. These luxury suites are part of a growing trend to attract higher end customers, who can afford to pay for exclusive access to certain areas of the facility. Whereas most teams 25 years ago worried primarily about the total number of attendees, now many teams pay significant attention to attracting a small number of affluent customers, whether they are individuals or businesses.

Seat Licenses

An indication of the trend toward high-priced seating is the use of **personal seat licenses** and **permanent seat licenses (PSLs)**. A PSL requires that a customer pay a one-time fee to reserve the right to purchase tickets for a specific seat. PSLs can generate a tremendous amount of money for a professional sport franchise, if they are designed and marketed properly. A permanent seat license typically is valid for the life of the facility, whereas a personal seat license may have a limited time frame. When the NFL's Carolina Panthers began construction of their new facility, they sold permanent seat licenses for most of the seats. All of the PSLs were sold, in most cases quickly. Conversely, when the Los Angeles Raiders returned to Oakland in 1995, many of the personal seat licenses that were sold to pay for upgrades to the Oakland–Alameda County Coliseum were valid for only ten years. This relatively short time frame, combined with owner Al Davis' less-than-stellar track record of keeping the team in one location for long periods of time, combined to leave many of the PSLs unsold.

The rights that are conferred to the PSL holder can vary. Often, a PSL holder will desire to bequeath, transfer, or even sell the PSL to another party. The specific language of the PSL determines whether a customer may confer ownership to another party and whether that transfer may be made in exchange for cash. In numerous instances, season ticket holders have believed that tickets are "theirs" to sell or transfer as they wish. In some cases, litigation has resulted (Reese, Nagel, & Southall, 2004). Teams now typically allow PSL holders to transfer their rights to another party, as long as they pay a handling fee to the team. Some teams have established websites where PSL holders can solicit bids for their ticket rights.

Ticket Reselling

Season tickets and individual game tickets are increasingly being bought and sold on the **secondary ticket market.** Ticket reselling or **scalping** has surely occurred since the first ticketed event in human history, but over the past ten years the prevailing view of reselling tickets has largely changed. No longer is ticket reselling done primarily by shadowy characters lurking on dark streets or in back alleys. Most municipalities have rescinded anti-scalping laws, and ticket reselling has become a multimillion-dollar enterprise. Teams and leagues have recently recognized the importance of acquiring this growing revenue source. In 2007, StubHub signed a contract to be Major League Baseball's exclusive secondary ticket provider (Branch, 2007), and other leagues have also formalized their secondary ticket resale operations.

Variable Ticket Pricing

The secondary ticket market is driven partially by the discrepancy between a ticket's initial price and its market price. For many years, teams set ticket prices without thoroughly researching the optimal price, often setting prices based on the previous year's prices, with some adjustment for the team's performance. Most teams did not consider individual games to have different potential demands, even though the airline and hotel industries had long since determined that the same seat or room can be priced differently based on, for example, the day of the week or month of the year. As research and technology in sports have improved, more franchises are employing **variable ticket pricing** (**VTP**) to capture added revenues by increasing initial ticket prices for highly demanded games and decreasing ticket prices for lower-demanded games, in an effort to attract customers who would not attend at the "typical" price. The complexity of VTP is likely to increase as teams continue to study their ticket prices and as more advanced computer software programs become available.

Securitization

It is obvious that the effort to increase revenues will remain critical for professional sport franchises in the future. As a means of leveraging their revenue streams, some sport organizations are investigating securitization—the use of contractually obligated future revenue as collateral for issued debt. For professional sport franchises or leagues, the contractually obligated income could be derived from media contracts, naming rights fees or other long-term sponsorship agreements, and luxury seating commitments.

Securitization works differently from a typical loan procured at a bank or other lending institution. The contractual ownership of the future revenues is sold to a trust that provides the bondholders primacy over claims of other debtors if the team or team owner should file for bankruptcy (Allen, 1998). Since the future revenues are contractually obligated, they are usually viewed as safer than other future revenue sources (such as ticket or concession sales) that may or may not materialize. Thus, bondholders will typically be more willing to purchase the bonds, and the bonds can be offered at a lower interest rate, decreasing the team's or league's cost of acquiring capital.

Although the bonds are safer, as we saw in the mortgage meltdown of 2008, contractually "guaranteed" future revenues may not materialize. The bond holder is secure from the initial bond issuer being unable to meet its financial obligations, but the entity actually paying to support the bond payments (such as a naming rights partner) may be unable to fulfill its obligation. (This was one of the major contributing factors in the 2008 financial crisis. Many bonds had been sold with future obligations guaranteed by mortgages on residential real estate. As the real estate market underwent a price correction, bond holders found that many of the homeowners at the other end of the securitization had stopped paying their mortgage notes.)

Major League Baseball and the NFL have established credit facilities by securitizing some of their future television revenue (Allen). The Staples Center in Los Angeles and the Pepsi Center in Denver were partially financed through securitization. In 2000, MLB's Detroit Tigers planned to refinance over $250 million through a new securitization proposal (Kaplan, 2000a). However, within a few weeks of announcing that the securitization plan would be implemented, the Tigers reported that they would have to seek loans through more traditional sources (Kaplan, 2000b). Upon closer investigation, the Tigers, who had just moved into the new Comerica Park, had experienced lower-than-expected revenues, and many of their anticipated contractually obligated revenue sources had not materialized, making the offering untenable in its current form. Although numerous other sport organizations have considered securitization, the Tigers' situation suggests that financial principles that have been implemented in other industries are not necessarily applicable in sport.

CONCLUSION

Every professional sport franchise and league will continue to develop financial tools to enhance its profitability. Leagues attempt to foster competitive balance among teams, but since each franchise owner has a unique rationale for owning and operating a franchise, achieving competitive balance among the teams will always be difficult, and "perfect" balance may not be desirable. Professional sport franchises share some of the characteristics of other businesses, but their financial management has unique aspects. As revenues, expenses, and potential profits continue to increase in the future, financial planning will become even more critical. No longer can a person expect to become a key member of a professional sport franchise without a thorough understanding of the numbers that drive the business.

CONCEPT check

1. What is the difference between win maximization and profit maximization? How can these different philosophies cause problems in professional sport leagues?
2. How does a commissioner interact with owners and players in a professional sport league? What are a commissioner's main responsibilities?
3. How do professional sport leagues such as the NBA, NHL, NFL, and MLB differ in structure from entities such as NASCAR, the PGA Tour, and the PBA Tour?
4. Why do professional leagues establish rules governing the financial operation of individual franchises?
5. Explain the concept of pooled debt instruments.
6. Why have so many rival professional sport leagues failed in the United States?
7. Explain the concept of competitive balance. How have leagues attempted to achieve competitive balance?
8. Discuss the differences between the salary caps in the NBA, NHL, NFL, and MLS.
9. List and describe the most important revenue sources for professional sport leagues. In what ways do you think these revenue sources will change in importance in the future?
10. Explain why a relegation system would be difficult to implement in North American professional sport leagues.

PRACTICE problems

1. If the federal inheritance tax is set at 45% of all assets above $3 million at the time of death, and a state's inheritance tax is set at 5% of all assets above $1 million at the time of death, what does an individual who dies owning a professional sport franchise that is worth $420 million owe in total tax liability? (Assume no other assets at time of death.)

2. If a 30-team league is contemplating expanding by two teams, how much money should it charge each new franchise to ensure that during the first year of the new 32-team league, each of the existing 30 owners will receive the same amount of revenue as they would have without the expansion? (Assume each owner makes $40 million per year from media contracts and $10 million per year from licensed merchandise sales, that the league will continue to share these revenues equally after the expansion, and that the media contracts are not scheduled to be renegotiated until a year after the expansion is completed.)

3. Last season, the top pick in a 30-team league's amateur draft signed a contract for $2 million per year. In the upcoming season, the league will implement a salary slotting system under which each pick will be compensated based upon his draft selection. If the compensation plan will be based on a 5% increase of the top selection's compensation from last year and a 1% decreasing scale for every pick after the first selection (second pick will earn 99% of what the first pick earns, and so forth), how much will the top selection in next year's draft earn? How much will the ninth pick earn?

CASE analysis

Structuring a League

You have been asked to consult for an entrepreneur who is assembling investors for a new professional sport league. A critical decision for the league will be whether to organize under a single-entity structure or a franchisor/franchisee model.

CASE QUESTIONS

1. Briefly describe how each structure works and explain the financial advantages and disadvantages of each structure.

2. How have these structures helped or hindered leagues in the past and present? Cite specific examples from existing leagues to support your answer.

references

#1 New York Knicks. (2007, December 6). *Forbes*. Retrieved July 29, 2009, from http://www.forbes.com/lists/2007/32/biz_07nba_New-York-Knicks_328815.html.

Abrams, J. (2009, July 8). N.B.A.'s shrinking salary cap could shake up 2010 free agency. *New York Times*. Retrieved July 12, 2009, from http://www.nytimes.com/2009/07/09/sports/basketball/09nba.html.

Allen, J.C. (1998, October 19). Using the future to pay for the present. *SportsBusiness Journal*. Retrieved August 30, 2009, from http://www.sportsbusinessjournal.com/article/19056.

Art Rooney Jr. could decide future of Steelers' ownership. (2008, July 10). *ESPN.com*. Retrieved August 28, 2009, from http://sports.espn.go.com/nfl/news/story?id=3482116.

Bernstein, A. (2005, August 1). Inside the complex NHL deal. *SportsBusiness Journal*. Retrieved April 29, 2009, from http://www.sportsbusinessjournal.com/index.cfm?fuseaction=article.main&articleId=46287&requestTimeout=900.

Bloom, H. (2006, October 27). Inside the latest MLB CBA. *SportsBusiness News*. Retrieved April 28, 2009, from http://sportsbiznews.blogspot.com/2006/10/inside-latest-mlb-cba.html.

Bloom, B.M. (2009, March 10). Fehr does not foresee a salary cap. *MLB.com*. Retrieved March 12, 2009, from http://mlb.mlb.com/news/article.jsp?ymd=20090310&content_id=3961482&vkey=news_mlb&fext=.jsp&c_id=mlb&partnerId=rss_mlb.

Blum, R. (2008, December 23). Yankees hit with $27 million luxury tax. *New York Post*. Retrieved May 3, 2009, from http://www.nypost.com/seven/12232008/sports/yankees/yankees_hit_with_27_million_luxury_tax_145590.htm.

Branch, A. (2007, August 2). StubHub! and MLB strike precedent-setting secondary ticketing deal. *TicketNews*. Retrieved August 30, 2009, from http://www.ticketnews.com/StubHub-and-MLB-Strike-Precedent-Setting-Secondary-Ticketing-Deal8227.

Brown, M. (2007, December 25). Breaking down MLB's luxury tax: 2003–2007. *The biz of baseball*. Retrieved May 3, 2009, from http://www.bizofbaseball.com/index.php?option=com_content&task=view&id=1805&Itemid=41.

Brown, M., Nagel, M.S., McEvoy, C.D., & Rascher, D.A. (2004). Revenue and wealth maximization in the NFL: The impact of stadia. *Sport Marketing Quarterly, 13*(4), 227–235.

Casacchia, C. (2005, May 26). Fowler's rile reduced in finalized Vikings sale. *Phoenix Business Journal*. Retrieved August 28, 2009, from http://phoenix.bizjournals.com/phoenix/stories/2005/05/23/daily38.html.

Clayton, J. (2008, July 15). NFL ownership growing increasingly complicated. *ESPN.com*. Retrieved August 28, 2009, from http://sports.espn.go.com/nfl/columns/story?columnist=clayton_john&id=3485962.

Coin flip to lottery: Did the Rockets tank to get Olajuwon? (2008, January 19). Retrieved July 4, 2009, from http://reclinergm.wordpress.com/2008/01/19/coin-flip-to-lottery-did-the-rockets-tank-to-get-olajuwon/.

Coon, L. (2009). NBA salary cap FAQ. Retrieved January 27, 2009, from http://members.cox.net/lmcoon/salary-cap.htm.

Coro, P. (2007, June 29). Suns sell pick, choose Tucker. *The Arizona Republic*. Retrieved April 29, 2009, from http://www.azcentral.com/arizonarepublic/sports/articles/0629suns0629.html.

Court accepts Major League Soccer's single entity defense in players' antitrust suit. (2000, Summer). Retrieved July 29, 2009, from http://law.marquette.edu/cgi-bin/site.pl?2130&pageID=494#5.

Cowboys, Nike sign 7-year deal. *The Washington Post*. September 5, 1995, http://www.encyclopedia.com/doc/1P2-847400.html.

Crowe, J. (2008, April 14). Start-ups or upstarts, Gary Davidson was there at creation. *Los Angeles Times.* Retrieved August 29, 2009, from http://articles.latimes.com/2008/apr/14/sports/sp-crowe14.

Dobson, S., & Goddard, J.A. (2001). *The economics of football.* Cambridge, UK: Cambridge University Press.

Eichelberger, C. (1999, August 12). Major gamble pays big rewards for Cowboys owner Jerry Jones. *The Journal Record.* Retrieved August 30, 2009, from http://findarticles.com/p/articles/mi_qn4182/is_19990812/ai_n10131411/.

Federal Baseball Club v. National League. (1922). 259 U.S. 200.

Final 2007–2008 luxury tax numbers. (2008, July 9). Retrieved July 29, 2009, from http://myespn.go.com/blogs/truehoop/0-33-31/Final-2007-2008-Luxury-Tax-Numbers.html.

Fitzpatrick, J. (n.d.). Retrieved December 27, 2008, from http://proicehockey.about.com/od/learnthegame/a/nhl_salary_cap.htm.

Fitzpatrick, J. (2005, July 13). NHL and players make a deal. Retrieved April 29, 2009, from http://proicehockey.about.com/od/thelatestonthelockout/a/cba_agreement.htm.

Flood v. Kuhn. (1972). 407 U.S. 258.

Fraser v. Major League Soccer. (D. Mass. April 19, 2000). 97 F.Supp.2d 130.

Garcia, A. (2009, July 8). Knicks and Mavericks hit hardest by luxury tax. Retrieved July 12, 2009, from http://www.nba.com/2009/news/features/art_garcia/07/08/salarycapinfo/index.html.

Groppelli, A.A., & Nikbakht, E. (2000). *Finance* (4th ed.). Hauppauge, NY: Barrons.

Grusd, B.L. (2004). The antitrust implications of professional sports' leaguewide licensing and merchandising arrangements. In S.R. Rosner and K.L. Shropshire (eds.). *The business of sports.* Boston, MA: Jones and Bartlett Publishers.

Haller, D. (2007, July 20). Kurt Thomas traded to Seattle. *The Arizona Republic.* Retrieved April 29, 2009, from http://www.azcentral.com/sports/suns/articles/0720kurttraded-CR.html.

Harris, D. (1986). *The league: The rise and decline of the NFL.* New York: Bantam.

Haupert, M.J. (2007, December 3). The economic history of Major League Baseball. EH.Net Encyclopedia. Retrieved July 10, 2009, from http://eh.net/encyclopedia/article/haupert.mlb.

HBO's Real Sports examines plight of the Brewers. (2004, February 25). *SportsBusiness Daily.* Retrieved October 15, 2008, from http://www.sportsbusinessdaily.com/article/83052.

Heath, T. (2005, April 1). O's get majority of TV deal. *The Washington Post.* Retrieved July 25, 2009, from http://www.washingtonpost.com/wp-dyn/articles/A15731-2005Mar31.html.

Helyar, J. (2006, March 6). Labor peace threatened by rift between owners. Retrieved March 18, 2006, from http://sports.espn.go.com/nfl/news/story?id=2354095.

Kaplan, D. (2000a, September 11). Tigers' finance plan uses a unique twist. *SportsBusiness Journal.* Retrieved August 30, 2009, from http://www.sportsbusinessjournal.com/article/10815.

Kaplan, D. (2000b, September 25). Tigers shelve $250M financing. *SportsBusiness Journal.* Retrieved August 30, 2009, from http://www.sportsbusinessjournal.com/article/10851.

Kaplan, D. (2003, November 3). MLB moves to tighten loan rules. *SportsBusiness Journal.* Retrieved August 29, 2009, from http://www.sportsbusinessjournal.com/article/34677.

Kaplan, D., & Mullen, L. (2009, June 8). Upshaw payout contributes to rare drop in NFLPA assets. *SportsBusiness Journal.* Retrieved March 18, 2010, from http://www.sportsbusinessjournal.com/article/62723.

Los Angeles Memorial Coliseum Commission v. National Football League. (1984). 726 F. 2d 138.

Los Angeles Memorial Coliseum Commission v. National Football League. (1986). 791 F. 2d. 1356.

Madison Square Garden sues NHL over promotion terms. (2007, September 28). *USA Today.* Retrieved April 28, 2009, from http://www.usatoday.com/sports/hockey/nhl/2007-09-28-msg-suit_N.htm.

McCann, M. (2010, January 12). Why American Needle-NFL is most important case in sports history. Retrieved March 18, 2010, from http://sportsillustrated.cnn.com/2010/writers/michael_mccann/01/12/americanneedlev.nfl/.

Mickle, T., & Lefton, T. (2008, August 4). Several leagues later, debate on single-entity model still lively. *SportsBusiness Journal.* Retrieved August 1, 2009, from http://www.sportsbusinessjournal.com/article/59720.

Miller, M. (1991). *A whole different ball game.* New York: Birch Lane Press.

MLS oks "Beckham Rule" to attract superstar players. (2006, November 11). Retrieved August 30, 2009, from http://soccernet.espn.go.com/news/story?id=391320&cc=5901.

Morris, J. (2009, August 20). Fight over ownership of Coyotes could have impact on other sport leagues. *Canadian Press.* Retrieved August 28, 2009, from http://www.sportingnews.com/nba/article/2009-08-20/fight-over-coyotes-ownership-could-impact-other-leagues.

Nagel, M.S. (2005). Salary caps. In *Encyclopedia of World Sport* (Vol. 3). Great Barrington, MA: Berkshire Publishing. pp. 1322–1323.

Nagel, M.S., & Brown, M.T. (Taipei, Taiwan, 2009). Exporting the business of baseball: Global impact of the American sports business model. *Proceedings of the Asian Association for Sport Management Conference.*

Nagel, M.S., Brown, M.T., Rascher, D.A., & McEvoy, C.D. (2007, Spring). Major League Baseball Anti-Trust immunity: Examining the legal and financial implications of relocation rules. *Entertainment and Sport Law Journal, 4*(3). Retrieved August 14, 2009, from http://www2.warwick.ac.uk/fac/soc/law/elj/eslj/issues/volume4/number3/nagel.

Nats, Strasburg beat deadline. (2009, August 18). Retrieved August 30, 2009, from http://sports.espn.go.com/mlb/news/story?id=4403920.

NBA lines up $200 million for teams. (2009, February 27). Retrieved August 29, 2009, from http://sports.espn.go.com/nba/news/story?id=3936991.

NHL owners growing wary of league's revenue sharing system. (2008, October 13). *SportsBusiness Daily.* Retrieved May 3, 2009, from http://www.sportsbusinessdaily.com/article/124637.

Prine, C. (2009, July 23). Four of five Rooney brothers sign off on deal to sell Steelers' shares. *Pittsburgh Tribune-Review.* Retrieved August 28, 2009, from http://www.pittsburghlive.com/x/pittsburghtrib/news/pittsburgh/s_634902.html.

Pro football draft history: 1936. (n.d.). Retrieved July 4, 2009, from http://www.profootballhof.com/history/general/draft/1936.aspx.

Rascher, D.A., Nagel, M.S., McEvoy, C.D., & Brown, M.T. (Melbourne, Australia, 2004). Is free riding a problem in sports leagues? Adverse incentives caused by revenue sharing. *Proceedings of the Sport Management Association of Australia and New Zealand Conference.*

Ray, J.L. (2008, February 23). How baseball arbitration works. Retrieved July 11, 2009, from http://baseball.suite101.com/article.cfm/how_baseball_arbitration_works.

Reese, J.T., Nagel, M.S., & Southall, R.M. (2004). National Football League ticket transfer policies: Legal and policy issues. *Journal of the Legal Aspects of Sport, 14*(2), 163–190.

Rovell, D. (2002, August 9). NHL franchise fees: Is price right? Retrieved August 29, 2009, from http://assets.espn.go.com/nhl/s/expansion4a.html.

Sachdev, A. (2009, August 27). Chicago Cubs sale: Ricketts family agrees to $35 million reserve fund. *Chicago Tribune.* Retrieved August 29, 2009, from http://www.chicagotribune.com/business/chi-thu-cubs-cushionaug27,0,399238.story.

Scully, G.W. (1995). *The market structure of sports.* Chicago: University of Chicago Press.

Shropshire, K.L. (1995). *The sports franchise game.* Philadelphia: University of Pennsylvania Press.

Simmons, B. (2007, April 19). Links while tossing around conspiracy theories. *ESPN.com.* Retrieved July 4, 2009, from http://insider.espn.go.com/espn/page2/blog/entry?id=2842986&searchName=simmons&campaign=rsssrch&source=bill_simmons.

Simmons, B. (2008, May 5). A requiem for the S.S.O.L. era in Phoenix. *ESPN.com.* Retrieved April 27, 2009, from http://sports.espn.go.com/espn/page2/story?page=simmons%2F080501.

Sunnucks, M. (2009, May 6). NHL takes over Coyotes web site. *Phoenix Business Journal.* Retrieved May 7, 2009, from http://phoenix.bizjournals.com/phoenix/stories/2009/05/04/daily46.html.

USFL v. NFL. 842 F.2d 1335 (2nd Cir. 1988).

Wagman, R. (2008, January 5). Garber's leadership has solidified MLS future. *SoccerTimes.* Retrieved July 29, 2009, from http://www.soccertimes.com/wagman/2008/jan05.

Whiting, R. (1989). *You gotta have wa.* New York: Vintage Books.

Whiting, R. (2004). *The meaning of Ichiro.* New York: Warner Books.

Why does tanking occur in the NBA but seemingly not in other leagues? (2007, April 9). *Sports Law Blog.* Retrieved July 4, 2009, from http://sports-law.blogspot.com/2007/04/why-does-tanking-occur-in-nba-but.html.

Yost, M. (2006). *Tailgaiting, sacks and salary caps.* Chicago: Kaplan Publishing.

Zimbalist, A. (1992). *Baseball and billions.* New York: Basic Books.

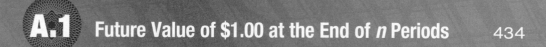

A P P E N D I X

Time Value of Money Tables

A.1 Future Value of $1.00 at the End of *n* Periods

$FVIF_{i,n} = (1 + i)^n$

PERIOD	1%	2%	3%	4%	5%	6%	7%	8%	9%	10%	11%	12%
1	1.0100	1.0200	1.0300	1.0400	1.0500	1.0600	1.0700	1.0800	1.0900	1.1000	1.1100	1.1200
2	1.0201	1.0404	1.0609	1.0816	1.1025	1.1236	1.1449	1.1664	1.1881	1.2100	1.2321	1.2544
3	1.0303	1.0612	1.0927	1.1249	1.1576	1.1910	1.2250	1.2597	1.2950	1.3310	1.3676	1.4049
4	1.0406	1.0824	1.1255	1.1699	1.2155	1.2625	1.3108	1.3605	1.4116	1.4641	1.5181	1.5735
5	1.0510	1.1041	1.1593	1.2167	1.2763	1.3382	1.4026	1.4693	1.5386	1.6105	1.6851	1.7623
6	1.0615	1.1262	1.1941	1.2653	1.3401	1.4185	1.5007	1.5869	1.6771	1.7716	1.8704	1.9738
7	1.0721	1.1487	1.2299	1.3159	1.4071	1.5036	1.6058	1.7138	1.8280	1.9487	2.0762	2.2107
8	1.0829	1.1717	1.2668	1.3686	1.4775	1.5938	1.7182	1.8509	1.9926	2.1436	2.3045	2.4760
9	1.0937	1.1951	1.3048	1.4233	1.5513	1.6895	1.8385	1.9990	2.1719	2.3579	2.5580	2.7731
10	1.1046	1.2190	1.3439	1.4802	1.6289	1.7908	1.9672	2.1589	2.3674	2.5937	2.8394	3.1058
11	1.1157	1.2434	1.3842	1.5395	1.7103	1.8983	2.1049	2.3316	2.5804	2.8531	3.1518	3.4785
12	1.1268	1.2682	1.4258	1.6010	1.7959	2.0122	2.2522	2.5182	2.8127	3.1384	3.4985	3.8960
13	1.1381	1.2936	1.4685	1.6651	1.8856	2.1329	2.4098	2.7196	3.0658	3.4523	3.8833	4.3635
14	1.1495	1.3195	1.5126	1.7317	1.9799	2.2609	2.5785	2.9372	3.3417	3.7975	4.3104	4.8871
15	1.1610	1.3459	1.5580	1.8009	2.0789	2.3966	2.7590	3.1722	3.6425	4.1772	4.7846	5.4736
16	1.1726	1.3728	1.6047	1.8730	2.1829	2.5404	2.9522	3.4259	3.9703	4.5950	5.3109	6.1304
17	1.1843	1.4002	1.6528	1.9479	2.2920	2.6928	3.1588	3.7000	4.3276	5.0545	5.8951	6.8660
18	1.1961	1.4282	1.7024	2.0258	2.4066	2.8543	3.3799	3.9960	4.7171	5.5599	6.5436	7.6900
19	1.2081	1.4568	1.7535	2.1068	2.5270	3.0256	3.6165	4.3157	5.1417	6.1159	7.2633	8.6128
20	1.2202	1.4859	1.8061	2.1911	2.6533	3.2071	3.8697	4.6610	5.6044	6.7275	8.0623	9.6463
25	1.2824	1.6406	2.0938	2.6658	3.3864	4.2919	5.4274	6.8485	8.6231	10.8347	13.5855	17.0001
30	1.3478	1.8114	2.4273	3.2434	4.3219	5.7435	7.6123	10.0627	13.2677	17.4494	22.8923	29.9599
35	1.4166	1.9999	2.8139	3.9461	5.5160	7.6861	10.6766	14.7853	20.4140	28.1024	38.5749	52.7996
40	1.4889	2.2080	3.2620	4.8010	7.0400	10.2857	14.9745	21.7245	31.4094	45.2593	65.0009	93.0510
50	1.6446	2.6916	4.3839	7.1067	11.4674	18.4202	29.4570	46.9016	74.3575	117.3909	184.5648	289.0022

13%	14%	15%	16%	17%	18%	19%	20%	25%	30%
1.1300	1.1400	1.1500	1.1600	1.1700	1.1800	1.1900	1.2000	1.2500	1.3000
1.2769	1.2996	1.3225	1.3456	1.3689	1.3924	1.4161	1.4400	1.5625	1.6900
1.4429	1.4815	1.5209	1.5609	1.6016	1.6430	1.6852	1.7280	1.9531	2.1970
1.6305	1.6890	1.7490	1.8106	1.8739	1.9388	2.0053	2.0736	2.4414	2.8561
1.8424	1.9254	2.0114	2.1003	2.1924	2.2878	2.3864	2.4883	3.0518	3.7129
2.0820	2.1950	2.3131	2.4364	2.5652	2.6996	2.8398	2.9860	3.8147	4.8268
2.3526	2.5023	2.6600	2.8262	3.0012	3.1855	3.3793	3.5832	4.7684	6.2749
2.6584	2.8526	3.0590	3.2784	3.5115	3.7589	4.0214	4.2998	5.9605	8.1573
3.0040	3.2519	3.5179	3.8030	4.1084	4.4355	4.7854	5.1598	7.4506	10.6045
3.3946	3.7072	4.0456	4.4114	4.8068	5.2338	5.6947	6.1917	9.3132	13.7858
3.8359	4.2262	4.6524	5.1173	5.6240	6.1759	6.7767	7.4301	11.6415	17.9216
4.3345	4.8179	5.3503	5.9360	6.5801	7.2876	8.0642	8.9161	14.5519	23.2981
4.8980	5.4924	6.1528	6.8858	7.6987	8.5994	9.5964	10.6993	18.1899	30.2875
5.5348	6.2613	7.0757	7.9875	9.0075	10.1472	11.4198	12.8392	22.7374	39.3738
6.2543	7.1379	8.1371	9.2655	10.5387	11.9737	13.5895	15.4070	28.4217	51.1859
7.0673	8.1372	9.3576	10.7480	12.3303	14.1290	16.1715	18.4884	35.5271	66.5417
7.9861	9.2765	10.7613	12.4677	14.4265	16.6722	19.2441	22.1861	44.4089	86.5042
9.0243	10.5752	12.3755	14.4625	16.8790	19.6733	22.9005	26.6233	55.5112	112.4554
10.1974	12.0557	14.2318	16.7765	19.7484	23.2144	27.2516	31.9480	69.3889	146.1920
11.5231	13.7435	16.3665	19.4608	23.1056	27.3930	32.4294	38.3376	86.7362	190.0496
21.2305	26.4619	32.9190	40.8742	50.6578	62.6686	77.3881	95.3962	264.6978	705.6410
39.1159	50.9502	66.2118	85.8499	111.0647	143.3706	184.6753	237.3763	807.7936	2,619.9956
72.0685	98.1002	133.1755	180.3141	243.5035	327.9973	440.7006	590.6682	2,465.1903	9,727.8604
132.7816	188.8835	267.8635	378.7212	533.8687	750.3783	1,051.6675	1,469.7716	7,523.1638	36,118.8648
450.7359	700.2330	1,083.6574	1,670.7038	2,566.2153	3,927.3569	5,988.9139	9,100.4382	70,064.9232	497,929.2230

A.2   Future Value of an Annuity of $1.00 per Period for *n* Periods

$$FVIFA_{i,n} = \frac{((1 + i)^n - 1)}{i}$$

PERIOD	1%	2%	3%	4%	5%	6%	7%	8%	9%	10%	11%	12%
1	1.0000	1.0000	1.0000	1.0000	1.0000	1.0000	1.0000	1.0000	1.0000	1.0000	1.0000	1.0000
2	2.0100	2.0200	2.0300	2.0400	2.0500	2.0600	2.0700	2.0800	2.0900	2.1000	2.1100	2.1200
3	3.0301	3.0604	3.0909	3.1216	3.1525	3.1836	3.2149	3.2464	3.2781	3.3100	3.3421	3.3744
4	4.0604	4.1216	4.1836	4.2465	4.3101	4.3746	4.4399	4.5061	4.5731	4.6410	4.7097	4.7793
5	5.1010	5.2040	5.3091	5.4163	5.5256	5.6371	5.7507	5.8666	5.9847	6.1051	6.2278	6.3528
6	6.1520	6.3081	6.4684	6.6330	6.8019	6.9753	7.1533	7.3359	7.5233	7.7156	7.9129	8.1152
7	7.2135	7.4343	7.6625	7.8983	8.1420	8.3938	8.6540	8.9228	9.2004	9.4872	9.7833	10.0890
8	8.2857	8.5830	8.8923	9.2142	9.5491	9.8975	10.2598	10.6366	11.0285	11.4359	11.8594	12.2997
9	9.3685	9.7546	10.1591	10.5828	11.0266	11.4913	11.9780	12.4876	13.0210	13.5795	14.1640	14.7757
10	10.4622	10.9497	11.4639	12.0061	12.5779	13.1808	13.8164	14.4866	15.1929	15.9374	16.7220	17.5487
11	11.5668	12.1687	12.8078	13.4864	14.2068	14.9716	15.7836	16.6455	17.5603	18.5312	19.5614	20.6546
12	12.6825	13.4121	14.1920	15.0258	15.9171	16.8699	17.8885	18.9771	20.1407	21.3843	22.7132	24.1331
13	13.8093	14.6803	15.6178	16.6268	17.7130	18.8821	20.1406	21.4953	22.9534	24.5227	26.2116	28.0291
14	14.9474	15.9739	17.0863	18.2919	19.5986	21.0151	22.5505	24.2149	26.0192	27.9750	30.0949	32.3926
15	16.0969	17.2934	18.5989	20.0236	21.5786	23.2760	25.1290	27.1521	29.3609	31.7725	34.4054	37.2797
16	17.2579	18.6393	20.1569	21.8245	23.6575	25.6725	27.8881	30.3243	33.0034	35.9497	39.1899	42.7533
17	18.4304	20.0121	21.7616	23.6975	25.8404	28.2129	30.8402	33.7502	36.9737	40.5447	44.5008	48.8837
18	19.6147	21.4123	23.4144	25.6454	28.1324	30.9057	33.9990	37.4502	41.3013	45.5992	50.3959	55.7497
19	20.8109	22.8406	25.1169	27.6712	30.5390	33.7600	37.3790	41.4463	46.0185	51.1591	56.9395	63.4397
20	22.0190	24.2974	26.8704	29.7781	33.0660	36.7856	40.9955	45.7620	51.1601	57.2750	64.2028	72.0524
25	28.2432	32.0303	36.4593	41.6459	47.7271	54.8645	63.2490	73.1059	84.7009	98.3471	114.4133	133.3339
30	34.7849	40.5681	47.5754	56.0849	66.4388	79.0582	94.4608	113.2832	136.3075	164.4940	199.0209	241.3327
35	41.6603	49.9945	60.4621	73.6522	90.3203	111.4348	138.2369	172.3168	215.7108	271.0244	341.5896	431.6635
40	48.8864	60.4020	75.4013	95.0255	120.7998	154.7620	199.6351	259.0565	337.8824	442.5926	581.8261	767.0914
50	64.4632	84.5794	112.7969	152.6671	209.3480	290.3359	406.5289	573.7702	815.0836	1,163.9085	1,668.7712	2,400.0182

13%	14%	15%	16%	17%	18%	19%	20%	25%	30%
1.0000	1.0000	1.0000	1.0000	1.0000	1.0000	1.0000	1.0000	1.0000	1.0000
2.1300	2.1400	2.1500	2.1600	2.1700	2.1800	2.1900	2.2000	2.2500	2.3000
3.4069	3.4396	3.4725	3.5056	3.5389	3.5724	3.6061	3.6400	3.8125	3.9900
4.8498	4.9211	4.9934	5.0665	5.1405	5.2154	5.2913	5.3680	5.7656	6.1870
6.4803	6.6101	6.7424	6.8771	7.0144	7.1542	7.2966	7.4416	8.2070	9.0431
8.3227	8.5355	8.7537	8.9775	9.2068	9.4420	9.6830	9.9299	11.2588	12.7560
10.4047	10.7305	11.0668	11.4139	11.7720	12.1415	12.5227	12.9159	15.0735	17.5828
12.7573	13.2328	13.7268	14.2401	14.7733	15.3270	15.9020	16.4991	19.8419	23.8577
15.4157	16.0853	16.7858	17.5185	18.2847	19.0859	19.9234	20.7989	25.8023	32.0150
18.4197	19.3373	20.3037	21.3215	22.3931	23.5213	24.7089	25.9587	33.2529	42.6195
21.8143	23.0445	24.3493	25.7329	27.1999	28.7551	30.4035	32.1504	42.5661	56.4053
25.6502	27.2707	29.0017	30.8502	32.8239	34.9311	37.1802	39.5805	54.2077	74.3270
29.9847	32.0887	34.3519	36.7862	39.4040	42.2187	45.2445	48.4966	68.7596	97.6250
34.8827	37.5811	40.5047	43.6720	47.1027	50.8180	54.8409	59.1959	86.9495	127.9125
40.4175	43.8424	47.5804	51.6595	56.1101	60.9653	66.2607	72.0351	109.6868	167.2863
46.6717	50.9804	55.7175	60.9250	66.6488	72.9390	79.8502	87.4421	138.1085	218.4722
53.7391	59.1176	65.0751	71.6730	78.9792	87.0680	96.0218	105.9306	173.6357	285.0139
61.7251	68.3941	75.8364	84.1407	93.4056	103.7403	115.2659	128.1167	218.0446	371.5180
70.7494	78.9692	88.2118	98.6032	110.2846	123.4135	138.1664	154.7400	273.5558	483.9734
80.9468	91.0249	102.4436	115.3797	130.0329	146.6280	165.4180	186.6880	342.9447	630.1655
155.6196	181.8708	212.7930	249.2140	292.1049	342.6035	402.0425	471.9811	1,054.7912	2,348.8033
293.1992	356.7868	434.7451	530.3117	647.4391	790.9480	966.7122	1,181.8816	3,227.1743	8,729.9855
546.6808	693.5727	881.1702	1,120.7130	1,426.4910	1,816.6516	2,314.2137	2,948.3411	9,856.7613	32,422.8681
1,013.7042	1,342.0251	1,779.0903	2,360.7572	3,134.5218	4,163.2130	5,529.8290	7,343.8578	30,088.6554	120,392.8827
3,459.5071	4,994.5213	7,217.7163	10,435.6488	15,089.5017	21,813.0937	31,515.3363	45,497.1908	280,255.6929	1,659,760.7433

A.3 Present Value of $1.00 Due at the End of *n* Periods

$$PVIF_{i,n} = \frac{1}{(1 + i)^n}$$

PERIOD	1%	2%	3%	4%	5%	6%	7%	8%	9%	10%	11%	12%
1	0.9901	0.9804	0.9709	0.9615	0.9524	0.9434	0.9346	0.9259	0.9174	0.9091	0.9009	0.8929
2	0.9803	0.9612	0.9426	0.9246	0.9070	0.8900	0.8734	0.8573	0.8417	0.8264	0.8116	0.7972
3	0.9706	0.9423	0.9151	0.8890	0.8638	0.8396	0.8163	0.7938	0.7722	0.7513	0.7312	0.7118
4	0.9610	0.9238	0.8885	0.8548	0.8227	0.7921	0.7629	0.7350	0.7084	0.6830	0.6587	0.6355
5	0.9515	0.9057	0.8626	0.8219	0.7835	0.7473	0.7130	0.6806	0.6499	0.6209	0.5935	0.5674
6	0.9420	0.8880	0.8375	0.7903	0.7462	0.7050	0.6663	0.6302	0.5963	0.5645	0.5346	0.5066
7	0.9327	0.8706	0.8131	0.7599	0.7107	0.6651	0.6227	0.5835	0.5470	0.5132	0.4817	0.4523
8	0.9235	0.8535	0.7894	0.7307	0.6768	0.6274	0.5820	0.5403	0.5019	0.4665	0.4339	0.4039
9	0.9143	0.8368	0.7664	0.7026	0.6446	0.5919	0.5439	0.5002	0.4604	0.4241	0.3909	0.3606
10	0.9053	0.8203	0.7441	0.6756	0.6139	0.5584	0.5083	0.4632	0.4224	0.3855	0.3522	0.3220
11	0.8963	0.8043	0.7224	0.6496	0.5847	0.5268	0.4751	0.4289	0.3875	0.3505	0.3173	0.2875
12	0.8874	0.7885	0.7014	0.6246	0.5568	0.4970	0.4440	0.3971	0.3555	0.3186	0.2858	0.2567
13	0.8787	0.7730	0.6810	0.6006	0.5303	0.4688	0.4150	0.3677	0.3262	0.2897	0.2575	0.2292
14	0.8700	0.7579	0.6611	0.5775	0.5051	0.4423	0.3878	0.3405	0.2992	0.2633	0.2320	0.2046
15	0.8613	0.7430	0.6419	0.5553	0.4810	0.4173	0.3624	0.3152	0.2745	0.2394	0.2090	0.1827
16	0.8528	0.7284	0.6232	0.5339	0.4581	0.3936	0.3387	0.2919	0.2519	0.2176	0.1883	0.1631
17	0.8444	0.7142	0.6050	0.5134	0.4363	0.3714	0.3166	0.2703	0.2311	0.1978	0.1696	0.1456
18	0.8360	0.7002	0.5874	0.4936	0.4155	0.3503	0.2959	0.2502	0.2120	0.1799	0.1528	0.1300
19	0.8277	0.6864	0.5703	0.4746	0.3957	0.3305	0.2765	0.2317	0.1945	0.1635	0.1377	0.1161
20	0.8195	0.6730	0.5537	0.4564	0.3769	0.3118	0.2584	0.2145	0.1784	0.1486	0.1240	0.1037
25	0.7798	0.6095	0.4776	0.3751	0.2953	0.2330	0.1842	0.1460	0.1160	0.0923	0.0736	0.0588
30	0.7419	0.5521	0.4120	0.3083	0.2314	0.1741	0.1314	0.0994	0.0754	0.0573	0.0437	0.0334
35	0.7059	0.5000	0.3554	0.2534	0.1813	0.1301	0.0937	0.0676	0.0490	0.0356	0.0259	0.0189
40	0.6717	0.4529	0.3066	0.2083	0.1420	0.0972	0.0668	0.0460	0.0318	0.0221	0.0154	0.0107
50	0.6080	0.3715	0.2281	0.1407	0.0872	0.0543	0.0339	0.0213	0.0134	0.0085	0.0054	0.0035

13%	14%	15%	16%	17%	18%	19%	20%	25%	30%
0.8850	0.8772	0.8696	0.8621	0.8547	0.8475	0.8403	0.8333	0.8000	0.7692
0.7831	0.7695	0.7561	0.7432	0.7305	0.7182	0.7062	0.6944	0.6400	0.5917
0.6931	0.6750	0.6575	0.6407	0.6244	0.6086	0.5934	0.5787	0.5120	0.4552
0.6133	0.5921	0.5718	0.5523	0.5337	0.5158	0.4987	0.4823	0.4096	0.3501
0.5428	0.5194	0.4972	0.4761	0.4561	0.4371	0.4190	0.4019	0.3277	0.2693
0.4803	0.4556	0.4323	0.4104	0.3898	0.3704	0.3521	0.3349	0.2621	0.2072
0.4251	0.3996	0.3759	0.3538	0.3332	0.3139	0.2959	0.2791	0.2097	0.1594
0.3762	0.3506	0.3269	0.3050	0.2848	0.2660	0.2487	0.2326	0.1678	0.1226
0.3329	0.3075	0.2843	0.2630	0.2434	0.2255	0.2090	0.1938	0.1342	0.0943
0.2946	0.2697	0.2472	0.2267	0.2080	0.1911	0.1756	0.1615	0.1074	0.0725
0.2607	0.2366	0.2149	0.1954	0.1778	0.1619	0.1476	0.1346	0.0859	0.0558
0.2307	0.2076	0.1869	0.1685	0.1520	0.1372	0.1240	0.1122	0.0687	0.0429
0.2042	0.1821	0.1625	0.1452	0.1299	0.1163	0.1042	0.0935	0.0550	0.0330
0.1807	0.1597	0.1413	0.1252	0.1110	0.0985	0.0876	0.0779	0.0440	0.0254
0.1599	0.1401	0.1229	0.1079	0.0949	0.0835	0.0736	0.0649	0.0352	0.0195
0.1415	0.1229	0.1069	0.0930	0.0811	0.0708	0.0618	0.0541	0.0281	0.0150
0.1252	0.1078	0.0929	0.0802	0.0693	0.0600	0.0520	0.0451	0.0225	0.0116
0.1108	0.0946	0.0808	0.0691	0.0592	0.0508	0.0437	0.0376	0.0180	0.0089
0.0981	0.0829	0.0703	0.0596	0.0506	0.0431	0.0367	0.0313	0.0144	0.0068
0.0868	0.0728	0.0611	0.0514	0.0433	0.0365	0.0308	0.0261	0.0115	0.0053
0.0471	0.0378	0.0304	0.0245	0.0197	0.0160	0.0129	0.0105	0.0038	0.0014
0.0256	0.0196	0.0151	0.0116	0.0090	0.0070	0.0054	0.0042	0.0012	0.0004
0.0139	0.0102	0.0075	0.0055	0.0041	0.0030	0.0023	0.0017	0.0004	0.0001
0.0075	0.0053	0.0037	0.0026	0.0019	0.0013	0.0010	0.0007	0.0001	—
0.0022	0.0014	0.0009	0.0006	0.0004	0.0003	0.0002	0.0001	—	—

A.4   Present Value of an Annuity of $1.00 per Period for *n* Periods

$$\text{PVIFA}_{i,n} = \frac{\dfrac{1}{i-1}}{i(1+i)^n}$$

PERIOD	1%	2%	3%	4%	5%	6%	7%	8%	9%	10%	11%	12%
1	0.9901	0.9804	0.9709	0.9615	0.9524	0.9434	0.9346	0.9259	0.9174	0.9091	0.9009	0.8929
2	1.9704	1.9416	1.9135	1.8861	1.8594	1.8334	1.8080	1.7833	1.7591	1.7355	1.7125	1.6901
3	2.9410	2.8839	2.8286	2.7751	2.7232	2.6730	2.6243	2.5771	2.5313	2.4869	2.4437	2.4018
4	3.9020	3.8077	3.7171	3.6299	3.5460	3.4651	3.3872	3.3121	3.2397	3.1699	3.1024	3.0373
5	4.8534	4.7135	4.5797	4.4518	4.3295	4.2124	4.1002	3.9927	3.8897	3.7908	3.6959	3.6048
6	5.7955	5.6014	5.4172	5.2421	5.0757	4.9173	4.7665	4.6229	4.4859	4.3553	4.2305	4.1114
7	6.7282	6.4720	6.2303	6.0021	5.7864	5.5824	5.3893	5.2064	5.0330	4.8684	4.7122	4.5638
8	7.6517	7.3255	7.0197	6.7327	6.4632	6.2098	5.9713	5.7466	5.5348	5.3349	5.1461	4.9676
9	8.5660	8.1622	7.7861	7.4353	7.1078	6.8017	6.5152	6.2469	5.9952	5.7590	5.5370	5.3282
10	9.4713	8.9826	8.5302	8.1109	7.7217	7.3601	7.0236	6.7101	6.4177	6.1446	5.8892	5.6502
11	10.3676	9.7868	9.2526	8.7605	8.3064	7.8869	7.4987	7.1390	6.8052	6.4951	6.2065	5.9377
12	11.2551	10.5753	9.9540	9.3851	8.8633	8.3838	7.9427	7.5361	7.1607	6.8137	6.4924	6.1944
13	12.1337	11.3484	10.6350	9.9856	9.3936	8.8527	8.3577	7.9038	7.4869	7.1034	6.7499	6.4235
14	13.0037	12.1062	11.2961	10.5631	9.8986	9.2950	8.7455	8.2442	7.7862	7.3667	6.9819	6.6282
15	13.8651	12.8493	11.9379	11.1184	10.3797	9.7122	9.1079	8.5595	8.0607	7.6061	7.1909	6.8109
16	14.7179	13.5777	12.5611	11.6523	10.8378	10.1059	9.4466	8.8514	8.3126	7.8237	7.3792	6.9740
17	15.5623	14.2919	13.1661	12.1657	11.2741	10.4773	9.7632	9.1216	8.5436	8.0216	7.5488	7.1196
18	16.3983	14.9920	13.7535	12.6593	11.6896	10.8276	10.0591	9.3719	8.7556	8.2014	7.7016	7.2497
19	17.2260	15.6785	14.3238	13.1339	12.0853	11.1581	10.3356	9.6036	8.9501	8.3649	7.8393	7.3658
20	18.0456	16.3514	14.8775	13.5903	12.4622	11.4699	10.5940	9.8181	9.1285	8.5136	7.9633	7.4694
25	22.0232	19.5235	17.4131	15.6221	14.0939	12.7834	11.6536	10.6748	9.8226	9.0770	8.4217	7.8431
30	25.8077	22.3965	19.6004	17.2920	15.3725	13.7648	12.4090	11.2578	10.2737	9.4269	8.6938	8.0552
35	29.4086	24.9986	21.4872	18.6646	16.3742	14.4982	12.9477	11.6546	10.5668	9.6442	8.8552	8.1755
40	32.8347	27.3555	23.1148	19.7928	17.1591	15.0463	13.3317	11.9246	10.7574	9.7791	8.9511	8.2438
50	39.1961	31.4236	25.7298	21.4822	18.2559	15.7619	13.8007	12.2335	10.9617	9.9148	9.0417	8.3045

13%	14%	15%	16%	17%	18%	19%	20%	25%	30%
0.8850	0.8772	0.8696	0.8621	0.8547	0.8475	0.8403	0.8333	0.8000	0.7692
1.6681	1.6467	1.6257	1.6052	1.5852	1.5656	1.5465	1.5278	1.4400	1.3609
2.3612	2.3216	2.2832	2.2459	2.2096	2.1743	2.1399	2.1065	1.9520	1.8161
2.9745	2.9137	2.8550	2.7982	2.7432	2.6901	2.6386	2.5887	2.3616	2.1662
3.5172	3.4331	3.3522	3.2743	3.1993	3.1272	3.0576	2.9906	2.6893	2.4356
3.9975	3.8887	3.7845	3.6847	3.5892	3.4976	3.4098	3.3255	2.9514	2.6427
4.4226	4.2883	4.1604	4.0386	3.9224	3.8115	3.7057	3.6046	3.1611	2.8021
4.7988	4.6389	4.4873	4.3436	4.2072	4.0776	3.9544	3.8372	3.3289	2.9247
5.1317	4.9464	4.7716	4.6065	4.4506	4.3030	4.1633	4.0310	3.4631	3.0190
5.4262	5.2161	5.0188	4.8332	4.6586	4.4941	4.3389	4.1925	3.5705	3.0915
5.6869	5.4527	5.2337	5.0286	4.8364	4.6560	4.4865	4.3271	3.6564	3.1473
5.9176	5.6603	5.4206	5.1971	4.9884	4.7932	4.6105	4.4392	3.7251	3.1903
6.1218	5.8424	5.5831	5.3423	5.1183	4.9095	4.7147	4.5327	3.7801	3.2233
6.3025	6.0021	5.7245	5.4675	5.2293	5.0081	4.8023	4.6106	3.8241	3.2487
6.4624	6.1422	5.8474	5.5755	5.3242	5.0916	4.8759	4.6755	3.8593	3.2682
6.6039	6.2651	5.9542	5.6685	5.4053	5.1624	4.9377	4.7296	3.8874	3.2832
6.7291	6.3729	6.0472	5.7487	5.4746	5.2223	4.9897	4.7746	3.9099	3.2948
6.8399	6.4674	6.1280	5.8178	5.5339	5.2732	5.0333	4.8122	3.9279	3.3037
6.9380	6.5504	6.1982	5.8775	5.5845	5.3162	5.0700	4.8435	3.9424	3.3105
7.0248	6.6231	6.2593	5.9288	5.6278	5.3527	5.1009	4.8696	3.9539	3.3158
7.3300	6.8729	6.4641	6.0971	5.7662	5.4669	5.1951	4.9476	3.9849	3.3286
7.4957	7.0027	6.5660	6.1772	5.8294	5.5168	5.2347	4.9789	3.9950	3.3321
7.5856	7.0700	6.6166	6.2153	5.8582	5.5386	5.2512	4.9915	3.9984	3.3330
7.6344	7.1050	6.6418	6.2335	5.8713	5.5482	5.2582	4.9966	3.9995	3.3332
7.6752	7.1327	6.6605	6.2463	5.8801	5.5541	5.2623	4.9995	3.9999	3.3333

Glossary

80/20 rule The expectation that 80% of needed funds to reach a capital campaign goal will come from 20% of the donors, based upon past giving patterns.

90/10 rule The expectation that 90% of needed funds to reach a capital campaign goal will come from 10% of the donors, based upon past giving patterns.

accounting profit Profit earned when revenues exceed costs and expenses over a particular period of time. Accounting profit does not necessarily accurately reflect the results of an individual's or organization's financial decisions.

accounts receivable Money owed by a company's customers.

acid-test ratio *See* quick ratio.

allocated revenues Revenues transferred by a school to its athletic department.

annual coupon interest payment A periodic return paid to the owner of a bond.

annuity A series of equal payments or receipts made at regular intervals.

antitrust exemption An exemption from the antitrust laws, which prohibit unfair restraints of trade and the creation of monopolies. Through Congressional or judicial action, some entities have been granted exemption from some or all antitrust laws. Major League Baseball enjoys a much stronger antitrust exemption than any of the other U.S. professional sport leagues.

arm's length Describes a buyer and seller who are not related to each other in any way, whether they are individuals, businesses, or estates; they have no familial relationship, neither company is a subsidiary of the other, neither company has an ownership interest in the other, and there is no financial relationship between the parties.

arms race The continuous building of bigger and better athletic facilities for the sole purpose of landing key recruits.

assessed value The product of the fair market value of a property and its assessment ratio (see **formula, p. 333**).

assessment ratio The percentage of a property that is subject to taxation.

asset-backed securities (ABS) Bonds guaranteed by a franchise's COI or expected revenue streams.

asset-based approach An approach to valuing an asset, a business, or an interest or equity in a business by determining what it would cost to recreate the business or asset. Also termed *cost-based approach*.

assets What a company owns, including items such as cash, inventory, and accounts receivable.

athletic support group (ASG) An organization responsible for an athletic department's annual giving programs, also known as a booster club.

auction-rate bond A form of long-term debt that acts like short-term debt, in which interest rates are reset through auctions typically held no more than 35 days apart.

balance sheet A picture or snapshot of the financial condition of an organization at a specific point in time.

bankruptcy The process of liquidation or reorganization of an insolvent firm.

base budget The expenditure level necessary to maintain last year's service level at next year's prices.

basis point A unit, representing one hundredth of a percent, used in measuring changes in financial rates.

benefit principle The idea that those who benefit from a particular project ought to be the ones taxed to pay for it.

beta coefficient (ß) A measurement of the volatility of a stock compared to market return, reflecting the degree to which the stock increases or decreases with an increase or decrease in the overall market.

board of directors An elected group whose job is to select the executives and management of the company.

bond A promise to pay back borrowed money plus interest to the investor who has purchased the bond; a financial mechanism for raising capital using debt as opposed to equity.

bond rating An estimation of the likelihood of a bond issuer's making payments in full.

budget A set of financial statements based on projections resulting from a particular scenario, generally the most likely or hoped-for scenario.

budget time horizon The shortest time period that can be predicted with a reasonable degree of certainty on the basis of past business decisions and commitments.

business planning horizon The period for which forecasts can be made with a reasonable degree of confidence, generally three to five years.

C corporation A business structure under which the company may seek investors and conduct business activities around the world. The corporation must hold annual meetings, elect a board of directors, and provide specific annual paperwork to the government and to shareholders. Often called C corp.

call premium A fee charged to a borrower for repaying the principal on a bond prior to the maturity date (**see formula, p. 173**).

call provision Provision allowing a borrower to repay a debt before the maturity date.

campaign case statement In fundraising, a pitch to donors that answers all critical questions regarding the campaign, suggests why an individual should support the campaign, and informs the reader how he or she can give to the campaign.

capital asset pricing model (CAPM) A method of analysis of the relationship between risk and rate of return, built on the notion that a stock's required rate of return is equal to the risk-free rate of return plus a risk premium, with the risk reflecting the portfolio's diversification.

capital budgeting The process of evaluating, comparing, and selecting capital projects to achieve the best return on investment over time.

capital campaign An intensive effort to raise funds in a given time frame through gifts and pledges for a specific purpose.

capital expenditure The funds used to acquire capital assets that will help the organization earn future revenues or reduce future costs.

capital expenditure budget A forecast of the expenses and income related to a capital investment.

capital gain The increase in a stock's price since purchase.

capital gains yield For a bond, the annualized percentage change in the price relative to the current price.

capital markets Markets for intermediate or long-term debt, as well as corporate stocks.

capital structure The amount of debt and equity that a firm has.

capitalist An economic system in which the majority of capital is privately owned.

capitalization rate Rate at which a value is "grown" forward; also, a rate applied to future income to determine its current value.

capture rate The portion of an organization's spending that is spent locally.

cash budget A forecast of how much cash an organization will have on hand in a specific time period and how much it will need to meet expenses during that time.

casual visitors Visitors attending a sporting event, who were already in town for a different reason.

central revenues Earnings that are paid directly to a league and then distributed to member organizations.

certificate of deposit (CD) An FDIC-insured debt instrument issued by banks and savings and loans with a fixed term and a specific interest rate. Certificate of deposits are intended to be held until maturity, and penalties are incurred if the depositor removes the money prior to the term's completion.

certificate of participation (COP) Financial instrument that a government agency or a non-profit corporation sets up to build a facility; often sold to one or more financial institutions to obtain the initial capital for construction. Then, the agency or non-profit leases the facility either directly to the tenant(s) or to a facility operator and uses the lease payments to pay off the COP.

closely held corporation An organization whose ownership shares are held by a family or a small group of investors.

coefficient of variation (CV) A measure of the stand-alone risk of an investment (**see formula, p. 68**).

collateral asset(s) pledged to a lender to be used as repayment of a loan in the event of default.

collective bargaining the process that occurs when workers in a company or league agree to negotiate as one unit with management to determine salaries and other working conditions.

collusion Secret agreement or cooperation for an illegal purpose.

common stock Shares of an organization held by its owners.

comparables analysis In a feasibility study for a sport facility, a comparison of similar cities to the one where the new facility is proposed, with the idea that if facilities are successful in those cities, they may be successful in the subject city.

competitive analysis In a feasibility study for a new sport facility, the investigation of existing facilities that might compete with the proposed facility.

competitive balance The condition under which every franchise, if it executes sound management strategy, has a reasonable opportunity to compete for a playoff spot at least every couple of seasons.

competitive issue A bond issue in which a municipality publishes a notice of sale, seeking bids from underwriters. The underwriter submitting the lowest bid, or lowest interest rate, will be selected to underwrite the bonds.

compound interest Interest that is calculated on both the principal investment and on the interest generated by that investment.

construction impact The amount of money that comes into a community during the construction phase of a building that would not otherwise have entered the community.

Consumer Price Index (CPI) The result of a calculation based on the prices of roughly 80,000 goods and services in more than 200 categories reflecting the current lifestyle of the typical American consumer to determine the overall change in real prices during a period.

contingent liabilities Debts that may or may not occur.

contractually obligated income (COI) A revenue stream that a team receives under multi-year contracts. These revenue sources may serve as collateral for loans.

controlling interest An ownership interest that effectively controls the business.

convertible bond A bond that offers some of the features of both equity and debt. The investor has the option to convert the bond into a fixed number of shares of stock in the company, at a stock price agreed upon at the issuance of the bond.

corporate depth The extent of a market's corporate base, including the number of headquarters of Fortune 500 companies in the local area.

corporate veil Legal separation between business owners and the organization, intended to eliminate personal liability.

correlation coefficient A measure of how closely the returns of an asset move relative to the returns of another asset held in a portfolio.

cost-based approach An approach to valuing an asset, a business, or an interest or equity in a business by determining what it would cost to recreate the business or asset. Also termed *asset-based approach*.

cost-benefit analysis An analysis or study of the cost of a project in relation to its potential benefits.

cost of goods sold (COGS) Those costs that are directly attributable to the production of goods or products, including raw materials and labor costs.

coupon rate The rate that a bond issuer pays for the use of money; equivalent to an interest rate.

covariance The degree to which two variables change together; in finance, it helps us find assets that move differently than those already held in a portfolio.

credit rating An estimate of an organization's ability to meet its financial obligations.

current expenditure A short-term expense that is completely written off during the same year as the expense is incurred.

current liabilities Liabilities due within one year.

current ratio A formula that measures a company's ability to meet its current liabilities with its current assets (**see formula, p. 44**).

current yield For a bond, the amount earned annually from an interest payment compared with the price, expressed as a percentage return (**see formula, p. 174**).

debt financing A method of raising capital in which an organization borrows money that must be repaid over a period of time, usually with interest.

debt ratio A measure of an organization's leverage, sometimes referred to as the debt-to-assets ratio (**see formula, p. 49**).

decision package A discrete addition to a reduced-level budget to maintain an existing program, serve an increased workload, or add a new program.

decision unit An individual or unit where budget decisions are made; responsible for creating decision packages in zero-based budgeting.

default The failure of an organization to fulfill its obligations toward a loan, often because it ceases operations or enters bankruptcy.

default risk The risk that a borrower will not pay back the principal of a debt plus interest.

default risk premium Premium added to the nominal interest rate to account for the risk that the borrower might default.

deferred compensation Salary whose payment is delayed under contractual terms; also known as deferred salary.

demand The quantity of a product or service desired by consumers.

department-generated revenues Funds generated independently by an athletic department and its programs.

depreciation The allocation of an item's loss of value over a period of time.

depreciation recapture Additional taxes that must be paid on an item that is found to have a higher salvage value than was initially estimated.

direct impact Expenditures on a project or event that contribute to economic impact.

discount A measure of risk or uncertainty of time influenced by the perception of future inflation, interest rates, and business activity.

discount factor *See* discount rate (1).

discount rate (1) A measure of risk or uncertainty used in present value calculations; also called capitalization rate. (2) The rate charged by the Federal Reserve on loans made to member banks. (3) The required rate of return to justify an investment.

discounted cash flow (DCF) analysis A valuation method based on the idea that the fair market value of an asset is equal to the present value of its expected future cash flows.

discounted payback period The number of years required to recover an initial capital investment, discounting the investment's cash flows at the investment's cost of capital.

displaced spending Money spent by a local resident on an event that is assumed would have been spent elsewhere in the local economy if the event would not have occurred.

distributed club ownership model A league structure in which each individual franchise has its own ownership group. League-wide revenues, such as those from national television contracts, are collected at the league level and distributed to each team to cover net costs. Team representatives select a commissioner to run the daily operations of the league. *See also* franchise ownership model.

diversifiable risk The portion of a stock's risk that can be removed through a well-diversified portfolio.

dividends Periodic payments made to shareholders of a company, as a way of distributing profits to the shareholders.

dollar return The return on an investment measured by subtracting the amount invested from the amount received (**see formula, p. 59**).

double-declining balance depreciation A variation of straight-line depreciation in which a much higher amount of depreciation is allocated to the early years of the depreciation schedule.

double-entry bookkeeping A method of recording financial transactions where each transaction made by an organization is entered or recorded twice, once on the debit side of the accounting records and once on the credit side.

draft lottery A lottery used in the NBA to determine the draft order of the non-playoff teams, in which a poorer record provides a greater chance to "win" the highest picks in the draft.

earnings before interest and taxes (EBIT) A useful measure of income or profit (**see formula, p. 50**).

economic impact The net economic change in a host community resulting from spending attributed to an event or facility.

economic profit Profit determined after including opportunity costs.

economics "The study of how people choose to allocate their scarce resources" (Wessel, 2000 [Ch. 5 References]).

efficiency principle The notion that a tax should be easy to understand, simple for government to collect, low in compliance costs, and difficult to evade.

endowed gifts Funds donated to a department in perpetuity that are invested, with only a portion of the fund's annual investment return used for the fund's specific purposes.

entrepreneur A person who establishes a business venture and assumes the financial risk for it.

equity A measure of ownership.

equity financing Financing in which the sport organization exchanges a share or portion of ownership of the organization for money.

excise tax Tax on goods and services that may be imposed within a city, county, or state.

expansion fee A fee changed to the owners of the newly established franchise when a professional sport league expands, to compensate current league owners for the short-term decrease in shared revenue from media contracts and licensed merchandise.

expected rate of return The sum of each possible outcome (return) multiplied by its probability.

expected return on a portfolio The weighted average of the expected returns of a set of assets (**see formula, p. 69**).

expense budget A list of a business unit's primary activities, with a dollar amount allocated to each.

expenses Funds flowing out of an organization as costs of doing business.

express partnership A general partnership created by a contract between the parties.

fair market value The net price for an asset that would result in a transaction between a willing buyer and a willing seller, neither of whom is under compulsion to buy or sell, both having reasonable knowledge of the relevant facts, and the two parties being at arms' length.

fair tax A national sales tax proposal that would repeal all current federal taxes and replace them with a tax on retail products and services.

feasibility study A study conducted to determine whether a project is likely to be successful, considering such items as engineering, land use, financing, demand, and economic impact.

federal funds rate The interest rate on overnight loans between banks.

Federal Reserve The central bank of the United States. It is the primary organizing body that attempts to maintain the overall economic health of the United States.

fiduciary duty The responsibility of a company's management to act in the best interests of all shareholders.

finance The science of fund management, applying concepts from accounting, economics, and statistics.

financial management A sector within firms that is concerned with the acquisition and use of funds to meet the goal of wealth maximization.

financing analysis An assessment of how much money will be needed to build a facility.

fiscal policy The use of government revenue collection and spending to influence the economy.

fiscal year A 12-month period over which a company budgets its money.

fixed costs Expenses that do not vary with volume of sales.

flat tax A federal levy that would require every American to pay the same income tax rate, rather than rates based on each taxpayer's yearly income.

forecast A prediction of future events and their quantification for the purpose of budgeting.

franchise The right of an owner to operate a team within a certain territory.

franchise free agency The ability of a team to relocate to another city when it is not obligated to a facility through a lease or a municipality through an agreement.

franchise ownership model A league structure under which individual owners, rather than the league office, own and control teams. *See also* distributed club ownership model.

free ride To benefit at another's expense without making a usual cost or effort.

Freedom of Information request Request filed by a citizen under the Freedom of Information Act to discover where and how a government agency is spending its money.

fundraising The generation of revenue through the solicitation of money or pledges.

future value (FV) The worth of an asset at a certain date in the future, determined by calculating the change in value of money when an interest rate is applied over the intervening period of time.

general obligation bonds (GOBs) Bonds that last about 20 years, secured by tax revenues and the issuing entity's ability to impose new taxes, with interest paid each year directly out of the general funds of a local government.

general partnership The joining of two or more individuals with the intent to own and operate a business.

generally accepted accounting principles (GAAP) A standard set of guidelines and procedures for financial reporting.

gift financing Charitable donations, either cash or in-kind, made to an organization.

globalization The integration of economies into one "world economy."

going concern An organization that we assume, for budgeting purposes, will operate indefinitely.

government financing Funding provided by federal, state, or municipal sources, including land use, tax abatements, direct stadium financing, state and municipal appropriations, and infrastructure improvements.

grant Monetary aid that does not have to be repaid.

Great Society A set of initiatives, including Medicare and Medicaid, intended to combat poverty, passed in the 1960s during President Lyndon B. Johnson's administration.

gross domestic product (GDP) The market value of all final goods and services produced within the borders of a county, state, country, or other region in a year.

gross domestic sports product (GDSP) The market value of a nation's output of sport-related goods and services in a given year. This includes the value added to the economy by the sport industry, as well as the gross product originating from the sport industry.

horizontal equity The idea that those with similar incomes should pay similar amounts of a tax.

implied partnership A general partnership that is not established by a contract but created by the parties' merely acting as partners.

income approach An approach to valuing an asset, a business, or an interest or equity in a business, under which income or cash flow serves as the basis for the value of the business or asset.

income statement A statement of a company's income over a specified period of time, typically issued on an annual or quarterly basis. Also called a statement of earnings or profit and loss statement.

incremental budgeting A form of line-item budgeting in which next year's budget is arrived at by either decreasing or increasing last year's budget, based on projected changes in operations and conditions.

incremental cash flow Cash flow created through the implementation of a new project.

incremental spending Spending above and beyond what a person would have spent had an event not taken place.

incremental visitors Visitors who came to town because of an event and would not have come to town otherwise.

indirect economic impact Economic impact that represents the circulation of initial expenditures (direct impacts) in an economy.

induced economic impact The effect of direct and indirect economic impacts on earnings and employment.

inflation The devaluation of money over time.

inflation premium The portion of an investment's return that compensates the investor for loss of purchasing power over time, calculated by determining the expected average inflation rate over the life of the security.

inheritance (death) tax A levy upon an estate applied when the owner dies.

initial cost The actual cost of starting a project, adjusted for any installation, delivery, or packing costs; discounts to the initial price; the sale of existing equipment or machinery; and taxes.

initial public offering (IPO) The offering of shares of a company to the public in order to generate cash for the business, when no shares had previously been available.

interest coverage ratio A measure of a firm's ability to pay the interest on its debt. Sometimes called the times interest earned ratio (see formula, p. 50).

interest rate risk The risk of a decrease in the value of a security due to an increase in interest rates.

internal rate of return The discount rate at which the present value of estimated cash flows is equal to the initial cost of the investment.

inventory turnover ratio A measure of how often a company sells and replaces its inventory over a specified period of time, typically a year.

investment risk A measure of the likelihood of low or negative future returns.

investments Security choices made by individual and institutional investors as they build portfolios.

jock taxes Special taxes that apply to professional athletes' income earned in a particular city, county, or state.

joint use agreement A formal agreement for the sharing of a facility between two or more parties.

junk bond A bond with a significant chance of default and a much higher coupon rate, receiving a bond rating below BBB.

laissez-faire Describes an economic policy in which the government has little involvement in the business environment beyond setting and enforcing rudimentary laws.

large-cap company A publicly traded company that has a market capitalization of at least $5 billion.

Larry Bird exception A provision that allows NBA teams to re-sign their "own" potential free agents for salaries that would otherwise cause the team to exceed the designated yearly salary cap; so named because the Boston Celtics were concerned that the loss of Larry Bird to free agency would devastate the team.

league think The philosophy, initially advocated by NFL Commissioner Pete Rozelle, that team owners should think of the overall financial health of the league as their first priority and individual franchise profits as a secondary concern.

leakage The movement of money out of a geographic region.

lease revenue bonds A version of revenue bond in which the revenue stream backing the payment of the bonds is a lease.

level of risk A comparative evaluation of risk. Some firms or assets have a lower degree of risk and some have a higher degree of risk.

leverage How a company chooses to finance its operation with debt versus equity. A company that relies extensively on borrowing money is considered to be heavily leveraged. Such a company faces greater risk of financial problems than one not so reliant on debt.

liabilities The financial obligations or debts owed by an organization to others.

limited liability corporation/limited liability partnership (LLC/LLP) A business structure under which shareholders' distributions are taxed as ordinary income and shareholders are shielded from personal liability.

limited partner A partner who is liable only for his or her direct financial contribution and is not permitted to participate formally in the company's operation.

line-item budgeting Approach in which line items, also known as objects of expenditure, are the main focus of analysis, authorization, and control.

liquidation The sale of an organization's assets piece by piece, effectively removing the firm from existence.

liquidity The ease and speed with which an asset can be converted to cash.

liquidity premium A premium added to the interest rate of a security that cannot be converted to cash in a short amount of time at a reasonable price. Also called the marketability premium.

liquidity spread The difference between a long-term interest rate and a short-term interest rate.

loan A sum of money borrowed from a financial intermediary, such as a bank or insurance company, that must be paid back over a specific period of time and with interest, the fee for borrowing the money.

loan pool A league-financed fund from which franchises can borrow at relatively low cost.

local market The area in which a franchise operates, with distinct differences in population, economic activity, and passion for sport.

local option sales tax A special-purpose tax levied at the municipal level.

local revenues Team earnings from home ticket sales, local television and radio, advertising, and sponsorship, that are shared within the league.

lockout A decision by management to suspend production while it negotiates with labor.

London Interbank Offered Rate (LIBOR) A benchmark interest rate based on the average interest rate that banks in the London interbank market pay to borrow unsecured funds from each other.

long-term liabilities Liabilities due after one year.

luxury tax A fee imposed on franchises that exceed a salary threshold.

M1 A measure of liquid assets in the form of cash and checking accounts in the total money supply.

M2 A measure of liquid assets in the form of cash and checking accounts (*see* M1) plus all money in savings accounts and certificates of deposit in the total money supply.

M3 A measure of liquid assets in the form of cash and checking accounts (*see* M1) plus all money in savings accounts and certificates of deposit (*see* M2) plus the assets and liabilities, including long-term deposits, of financial institutions.

macroeconomics The study of forces that affect numerous or even all sectors of the overall economy.

major gift A donation worth $25,000 or more.

market approach A method of valuing an asset, a business, or an interest or equity in a business that relies on prices that similar assets sell for in the marketplace.

market capitalization The market price of a company, computed by multiplying the number of outstanding shares by the price per share.

market demand The demand within a marketplace for a facility.

market risk The portion of a stock's risk that cannot be eliminated through a diversified portfolio; it is measured by the degree to which the stock moves with the market.

market value An estimate of the value of a company according to the stock market (see **formula, p. 52**).

marketability A measure of the readiness with which an asset may be sold or liquidated.

maturity The time when a liability or debt is due to be paid, or the number of years from issuance until that date.

maturity risk premium A premium added to the interest rate of a security that accounts for interest rate risk.

microeconomics The study of issues, such as supply, demand, and pricing, that occur at the firm level.

mid-year convention The practice of using June 30 as the accounting date for a cash flow when an analyst does not have the exact details of the cash flow over the year.

mill A measure of tax rates equal to 1/1000 of a dollar, or 1/10 of a penny.

millage/millage rate The tax rate approved by a public body such as a state or local government, city council, school board, special purpose district, or county council to meet the budgetary needs of each entity; the total of the levies by the city, county, school district, and any special districts in which a particular resident lives.

minority discount Discount applied to the purchase price of stock when the purchaser has no controlling interest.

minority partner An owner who holds less than a 50% stake in a jointly owned business.

mixed costs Expenses that include both fixed and variable elements.

modified internal rate of return The discount rate at which the present value of a project's cost is equal to the present value of the project's terminal value.

modified zero-based budgeting (MZBB) A budgeting concept that starts at a base higher than zero and matches spending levels with services to be performed.

monetary policy Policy the government sets to control the supply, availability, and cost of money.

money markets Markets for highly liquid, short-term securities.

monopoly The status of an individual or organization that has no viable competition and, hence, complete control of the distribution of a product or service.

multiple owners/private investment syndicate model An ownership model in which a group of individuals pool their resources to purchase a franchise and incorporate as a partnership, LLC, or the like. The most common model of team ownership.

multiple owners/publicly traded corporation model An ownership model in which a franchise is governed by a board of directors who are elected by shareholder vote. The board of directors appoints the team's senior management. With the exception of the Green Bay Packers, this model is not currently used in the United States.

multiplier A variable that helps researchers quantify indirect and induced economic impacts, by measuring the change in output for each and every industry as a result of the injection of one dollar of direct impact into any of those industries.

multiplier effect The ripple effects of initial spending (direct impacts), consisting of indirect and induced impacts.

naming rights The right to place a firm's name on a facility; a form of sponsorship.

National Association of Intercollegiate Athletics (NAIA) One of three main governing bodies overseeing college sports in the United States.

National Collegiate Athletic Association (NCAA) The largest of the three main governing bodies overseeing college sport in the United States, and the primary governing body; formerly the Intercollegiate Athletic Association of the United States.

National Junior College Athletic Association (NJCAA) One of the three main governing bodies overseeing college sport in the United States, with membership made up of junior and community colleges.

NCAA Division I One of three classifications of NCAA university membership. Division I includes the subclassifications (a) Football Bowl Subdivision (FBS), requiring the institution to sponsor a minimum of 14 sports—these schools sponsor fairly elaborate football programs and must meet minimum football attendance requirements; and (b) Football Championship Subdivision (FCS), also requiring a minimum of 14 sports—these schools sponsor football programs but have no minimum football attendance requirements.

NCAA Division II One of three classifications of NCAA university membership, requiring the institution to sponsor a minimum of ten sports.

NCAA Division III One of three classifications of NCAA university membership, requiring the institution to sponsor a minimum of ten sports. Athletes cannot receive financial aid related to their athletic ability in this division.

negotiated issue A bond issue for which a municipality selects one underwriter and the municipality and underwriter negotiate the terms of the sale.

net assessed value Taxable worth of property, the difference between total assessed value and tax-exempt property.

net present value A capital budgeting method in which the present value of a project's future cash flows is compared to the project's initial cost.

net profit margin ratio A measure of the effectiveness and efficiency of a company's operations (see **formula, p. 51**).

nominal interest rate The interest rate actually charged for a given marketable security, consisting of the real risk-free rate of interest plus multiple risk premiums. These include risk premiums based on the risk of time and the level of risk, which reflect the riskiness of the security itself, and premiums reflecting inflation and liquidity (the marketability of the security). Also called the quoted interest rate (see **formula, p. 63**).

nominal risk-free rate The real risk-free rate of interest plus an inflation premium (see **formula, p. 63**).

nominal value The face value of money.

non-excludable Describes a good that a team cannot prevent someone from consuming or from enjoying.

non-profit organization An organization not conducted for the profit of owners. Typically, a non-profit organization's activities are devoted to charitable activities, such as education. Revenues generated by non-profit organizations are treated differently for tax purposes than those of for-profit entities.

non-rival Describes a good that can be consumed by one person without preventing another person from consuming it.

North American Industrial Classification System (NAICS) Classification system used by the U.S. Census Bureau to measure and track economic activity in the United States. The sport industry is not classified as a distinct industry and is scattered across at least 12 different NAICS-defined industries.

operations impact The economic impact of a facility generated through its daily operation.

opportunity costs The cost of a financial decision in terms of forgone alternatives. For example, often part of the public's financing for a stadium involves giving away the land or leasing it for a below-market rate. The public's total cost is not just what it directly spends to support building the facility, but also what is "lost" (taxes, etc.) by not utilizing it in another manner.

output budgeting Budgeting in which specific goals and objectives form the framework for a strategic process.

owners' equity An estimate of the ownership value of a company. Also called shareholders' equity or stockholders' equity.

pay-as-you-go A financing method where projects are paid for with current assets rather than borrowed funds.

payback period The number of years required to recover an initial capital investment.

payments in lieu of taxes (PILOT) Payments that are made to a local government instead of paying franchise, property, or sales taxes.

periodic expenses Expenses that do not occur regularly throughout the year but must be budgeted for during the year, such as new vehicles, retirement bonuses, and other one-time events.

permanent seat license (PSL) The right to purchase tickets for a specific seat location, for the life of the facility, with fewer restrictions on exchange or sale than those for personal seat licenses.

perpetual growth rate An expected annual growth rate in a dividend payment, in perpetuity.

perpetuity An annuity that has no scheduled ending.

personal seat license (PSL) The right to purchase tickets for a specific seat location, sometimes limited to a period of time that may not match the expected lifespan of the facility.

planning The establishment of objectives and the formulation, evaluation, and selection of the policies, strategies, tactics, and actions required to achieve those objectives.

player draft The process by which leagues assign incoming players throughout the league.

point system System in which donors earn points based on their giving characteristics, which qualify them to purchase tickets for high-demand events or tickets in a desired location.

pooled debt Debt instruments that have the backing of an entire league rather than an individual team, usually providing a more favorable interest rate than the individual franchise could obtain.

portfolio A combination of financial assets held by an investor.

positive externalities Benefits produced by an event that are not captured by the event owners or sport facility being used; also termed overflow benefits.

present value The current value of a payment that will be received or paid in the future, computed by applying a discount rate measuring risk and uncertainty.

price What one party (the buyer) must give to obtain what is offered by another party (the seller).

price elasticity of demand The percentage decrease in the number of units sold compared to the percentage increase in the unit price.

price/earnings (P/E) ratio An estimate of how much money investors will pay for each dollar of the company's earnings, used widely to measure corporate performance and value (see **formula, p. 53**).

price-to-revenue (P/R) ratio Transaction price divided by total annual revenues; a common starting point for franchise valuation.

primary research The generation of information directly for the purpose of a study.

prime rate The rate banks charge their "best" customers, usually those that are the largest and most stable or have been with the bank the longest.

private financing Financing that does not use public dollars.

probability distribution A list of all possible outcomes of an investment in terms of expected rates of return, with a probability assigned to each outcome.

production opportunities The reason a company needs capital and the possibility that the money can be turned into more money or benefits.

profit maximization The pursuit of the highest profits possible as an organization's primary goal.

program budget A budget in which expenditures are based primarily on programs of work and secondarily on character and object.

program planning budgeting system (PPBS) An approach to developing a program budget that falls between the line-item budget and the performance budget.

property tax A government levy based on the value of property, including real property (land and structures built upon the land or improvements made to the land) and personal property (everything else that has value, such as automobiles, trucks, furniture, and equipment).

prospect Any individual, foundation, corporation, or organization that has the potential and likelihood to give to an organization.

psychic impact The emotional impact on a community of having a local sport team or hosting national or international events.

public facility authority (PFA) bond A type of municipal bond used for the construction, renovation, or improvement of public facilities.

public finance The use of public funds to finance a project. For the construction of an arena or facility, tax revenues are typically used to retire debt service.

public good A good that is non-rival and non-excludable.

public sector sport Sport programs offered to serve societal need rather than profit potential.

public/private partnership A collaboration between the public and private sectors.

quick ratio A measure of a company's ability to meet its current liabilities with its current assets, not including inventory (see **formula, p. 46**).

rate of return The gain or loss of an investment over a period of time (see **formula, p. 59**).

real risk-free rate The rate of interest on a riskless security if inflation were not expected; the rate of interest on a short-term U.S. Treasury bill in an inflation-free environment.

real value The value of money after taking inflation into account; often referred to as purchasing power.

recession Two consecutive quarters or more of negative growth in a nation's gross domestic product.

reduced-level budget The percentage below the base budget that a budget is required to be reduced.

reinvestment rate risk Risk related to declining interest rates, primarily affecting short-term bills; the risk measures loss of income that would occur if the interest rate on a bond is lower at the time the funds are reinvested.

related-party transaction A transaction between two businesses that have some form of pre-existing relationship.

relegation system System under which, after each season, a certain number of the "worst performing" clubs will be "sent down" or relegated to a lower division, while a certain number of the "top performing" clubs in the lower division will be elevated to the higher division, to incentivize every franchise to maximize its on-field performance.

relevant risk The contribution of a single stock to the riskiness of a diversified portfolio.

required rate of return The profit that an investor would require from a particular investment, whether in stocks or bonds, in order to consider it worth purchasing, given the riskiness of the investment.

reserve clause An agreement among owners that ties a player to a team in perpetuity.

residual value What a business or asset will be worth at the end of the period for which cash flows are projected.

retained earnings A portion of earnings that a firm saves in order to finance operations or acquire assets.

return on equity capital The combination of dividend payments and capital gains on an investment.

return on equity ratio A measure of the rate of return a company's owners or shareholders are receiving on their investment (see **formula, p. 51**).

revenue bond A form of public finance that is paid off solely from specific, well-defined sources, such as hotel taxes, ticket taxes, or other sources of public funding. Also, bonds that are secured by the revenues to be generated by the project being funded. If the source of funding does not meet expectations, the bonds will not be paid off in full.

revenue budget A forecast of revenues based on projections of the organization's sales.

revenue sharing The sharing of revenues among teams in a league to support weaker franchises and increase the competitive balance within the league.

revenues Income generated from business activities, such as the sale of goods or services.

reverse time-switcher Local residents who leave town during an event period because of the event.

risk A measure of the uncertainty of returns or uncertainty about future conditions that may affect the value of money.

risk averse A quality that investors tend to display: when presented with two alternatives for investment with the same expected rate of return, most investors will select the investment with the lower risk.

risk of time The fact that risk increases as the length of time funds are invested increases.

risk premium The difference between the rate of return for a risky investment and the risk-free rate.

risk-free rate The interest paid on risk-free investments that pay a guaranteed return, such as U.S. Treasury bills.

rule of thirds The expectation that the top ten gifts to a campaign will account for 33% of the campaign's total goal, based upon past giving patterns.

salary arbitration A process whereby an independent judge determines whether the salary that a team submits for a player or the salary that the player requests will be paid.

salary cap A limit on the compensation an employer may provide to employees; in sport, a salary cap restricts salaries for teams across an entire league.

salary slotting League-established rules or recommendations regarding initial compensation provided to a player based on draft positioning.

sales tax A tax on the sale of certain goods and services.

scalping Pejorative term for the resale of tickets.

scarcity Availability of a resource does not meet current demand.

secondary research The analysis of data that have already been generated for other purposes but might provide information for a study.

secondary ticket market The market for the reselling of tickets.

secured claim A debt for which the borrower provided collateral; an asset that the creditor has the right to seize if the debt is not paid.

securitization The use of contractually obligated future revenue as collateral for issued debt.

security market line (SML) A formula for evaluating the risk and return merits of an investment (see **formula, p. 72**).

sensitivity analysis The process of developing several forecasts under different scenarios and assigning probabilities to each scenario to arrive at an acceptable forecast.

serial bond A bond requiring regular payments on principal and interest over the life of the bond.

Sherman Antitrust Act An 1890 law that forbids contracts or other actions among businesses that would restrict competition.

simple interest Interest that is calculated only on principal.

sin taxes Taxes on alcohol and tobacco.

single entity structure A league structure in which owners purchase shares in the league rather than in an individual franchise.

single owner/private investor model An ownership model in which one individual owns the firm.

small-cap stock The stock of a publicly traded company with a market capitalization between $250 million and $1 billion.

socialistic Describes an economic system where the government takes an active role in owning and administering a means of production.

sole proprietorship A business that is legally owned and operated by a single individual.

sponsorship A form of advertising in which a firm pays for exposure that supports the firm's marketing objectives.

Sports Broadcasting Act (SBA) A 1961 law providing an antitrust exemption that permitted professional sport leagues to sell their television rights as a league package.

stadium-related revenue source A non-shared source of revenue from sales related to the venue where a team plays, such as the sale of luxury suites.

stand-alone risk An investor's risk if only one asset were held.

standard deviation (SD) A measure of variability in a distribution of numbers, denoted σ.

statement of cash flows A report that tracks cash in and cash out of an organization and provides data as to whether a company has sufficient cash on hand to meet its debts and obligations.

step costs Expenses that are constant within ranges of use but differ between ranges.

stock A share of ownership in a company.

stock exchange/stock market An organization that provides a place and means for brokers to trade stocks and other securities.

stock market index A measure of a section or sections of a stock market.

stock option A contract that allows a party to purchase a specified number of shares of stock for a certain price.

straight-line depreciation A depreciation method in which the total cost of the item, less its estimated salvage value, is divided by its useful life to determine its yearly depreciation allowance.

strategic planning horizon The far future, planning for which is concerned with the long-term aspirations of the organization and management.

subchapter S corporation A business structure under which shareholders' distributions are taxed as ordinary income and shareholders are shielded from personal liability. Often called an S corp.

sum of years' digits depreciation A method of depreciation that takes the non-linear loss of value into account.

sustainability Meeting today's needs without compromising the future generations' ability to meet their own needs.

synergistic premium An additional amount that a buyer would be willing to pay for an asset or business because ownership would provide benefits beyond those of owning the asset or business as a standalone investment.

synthetic fixed-rate bond A bond that has elements of both a fixed-rate bond and a variable-rate bond.

tax abatement A government's forgoing of collection of taxes.

tax increment financing The use of only additional or new taxes generated from a certain source, such as property taxes, to help finance a sport facility. Once the facility is built, any increases in tax revenues resulting from the improvement of the area are used to pay off the tax increment bond.

tax receipts Tax revenues from all sources received by a municipality.

tax subsidy The use of tax receipts to fund a program or business.

term bond A bond paid in a single payment made at the end of the loan period.

terminal value The future value of a project's cash inflows compounded at the project's cost of capital.

territorial rights The exclusive control of a predetermined area (typically an entire metropolitan area), which enables a professional sport team to market exclusively in that area without fear of the presence of another franchise.

time value of money The yearly, monthly, or daily changes in the purchasing power of money.

time-switchers Visitors who would have come to town at another time, but opted to come to town during this time instead, in order to attend the event.

total asset turnover ratio A measure of how efficiently a company is utilizing its assets to make money (see formula, p. 47).

total expected return The rate of return expected on an asset or a portfolio of assets when all terms of gain are combined.

tourism tax Tax on hotel stays or rental cars; may also include food and beverage taxes in certain districts.

trade credit An agreement between a manufacturer and a retailer that after the manufacturer ships its product to the retailer for sale, the retailer may delay payment for a period of time depending on the terms.

transfer pricing The pricing of assets transferred within an organization.

units of production depreciation Deprecation calculated by dividing the total number of items produced during a given year by the total number of items the asset will produce during its useful life.

unsecured claim A debt for which the investor has no right to seize any assets from the company or person who borrowed the money.

unsecured debt Debt not secured by an underlying asset or collateral.

use tax A levy imposed on certain goods and services that are purchased outside the state and brought into the state.

valuation date The specific date selected for the valuation of a business or asset.

value added tax (VAT) A consumption tax levied on any value that is added to a product.

variable costs Expenses that change with volume of sales.

variable ticket pricing (VTP) A method of placing various values on entry to games, with higher initial prices for highly demanded games and lower prices for lower-demanded games.

vertical equity The idea that a tax should not cause poorer persons to bear a disproportionate share.

volatility The amount of fluctuation that occurs in a series of similar investment returns and the degree to which the returns deviate from the average. More volatility translates into greater risk.

wealth maximization Maximizing the overall value of the firm. This is the goal or outcome of financial management for most organizations.

win maximization The pursuit of winning as a primary goal.

yield curve The graphic depiction of interest rates against time to maturity for bonds with equal credit quality, including government bonds.

yield to maturity (YTM) The percentage rate of return on a bond if an investor holds the bond until its maturity date; often used to denote the total annualized return from owning a specific bond. It is the same as the total expected return.

zero-based budgeting (ZBB) A budgeting approach and financial management strategy that requires building a budget from a zero base rather than the previous year's budget.

Index